COMPARATIVE ECONOMIC DEVELOPMENT

COMPARATIVE
ECONOMIC DEVELOPMENT

Ralph H. Blodgett

PROFESSOR OF ECONOMICS
UNIVERSITY OF FLORIDA

Donald L. Kemmerer

PROFESSOR OF ECONOMICS
UNIVERSITY OF ILLINOIS

McGRAW-HILL BOOK COMPANY, INC.

New York   Toronto   London

1956

COMPARATIVE ECONOMIC DEVELOPMENT

Library of Congress Catalog Card Number 55–12094

THE MAPLE PRESS COMPANY, YORK, PA.

PREFACE

During the past generation the people of the world have been brought closer together by far-reaching improvements in transportation and communication. In the last century man learned how to communicate effectively with his fellows faster than he himself can travel. Airplanes have brought all parts of the world within a couple of days' travel of all other parts. This means that educated citizens must know more about their fellow men—their traditions, their way of life, and their ethical values—than they ever have before. Most assuredly, as voters and probably as individuals, we are going to have to deal increasingly with people of other lands. The fact that the United States has largely dropped its isolationist attitude since World War I and is today the world's leader is evidence of a widespread recognition of these changes.

The background of economic history which freshmen and sophomores receive in college, however, still consists chiefly of American economic history. That is good as far as it goes, but, as already indicated, we need to know more than our own history. A child's horizon widens as he matures, expanding from his neighborhood to his town to his region and to his country. Similarly, the educated American should further widen his horizon to the Western world, and then to the whole world. It is the purpose of this book to help with that widening process. Since the human mind can absorb just so much information at one time without becoming confused, we have confined our attention to four nations only. These are the United States, Great Britain, Russia, and Germany. They are the major Western powers of modern times, and they also give us insight into four different types of economy.

This book is not intended to be a text in economic history, nor is it intended to be a text in comparative economic systems. It is a combination of the two, designed for use as an orientation type of economics course. The authors feel that there is latent demand for a course of this kind, but it has been slow to materialize because of the lack of a textbook. Our publishers shared this feeling and so did other publishers. The book thus represents some academic pioneering.

Since the book is intended for use chiefly among first- and second-year students, the approach is more factual and historical than it is economic. We endeavor to show how the geography, the resources, the history, and the economic problems faced by each of four nations determined to some degree the type of economy that it eventually developed. The organization used in economic history texts has been employed in arranging the story of each nation. In dealing with each nation the student begins with an examination of its resources, the background of its people, and the processes of government. He then moves on to the nation's agricultural development and to the improvements in transportation and communication which made possible the wider markets that gave rise to industrial progress. Industry, of course, had to be financed and provided with a labor supply, and chapters on these topics logically come next. Then the goods must be sold at home or abroad, and this is the essence of commerce. Finally, we must sum up the accomplishments of the nation's economy over the centuries, especially since the Industrial Revolution began, and indicate some of the current problems of the nations, how they are meeting them, and perhaps why they have chosen to do so in that particular manner. Some of the problems discussed are common to all four economies, and some are different. Increased government regulation appears to be a common characteristic of our industrial age. But the manner of regulating and the persons whom the regulation is intended to help most will vary from nation to nation. Totalitarian economies impose regulations to keep the populace under control so that the lot of those in authority will be easier. Democratic economies impose regulation more for the purpose of obliging the players in the game of making a living to play fair. As the last chapter shows, it is not so easy as one might suppose to compare the success of the four economies, for some have hardly been tried—a generation is too short a period to judge by—and also the aims of the economies are by no means the same. Demonstrating all these facts to the student should help to make him more understanding of the rest of the world, more patient and willing to let time rather than the heavy hand of force resolve national differences, and thus improve to some slight degree the chances for peace.

It is accepted practice in a preface to give credit to those who helped put the book together and yet did not achieve recognition as authors. Frequently, the authors owe to them that last degree of polish that makes the difference between an ordinary chapter and a good one or even an excellent one. In certain parts of this book such improvements are most assuredly attributable to friends who have been generous with their helpful criticism. First of all, in this connection, we want to acknowledge our indebtedness to Mr. Howard Shuman, formerly instructor in English economic history at the University of Illinois and now legislative assistant to Senator Paul Douglas. He originally wrote the three chapters on British manufacturing, British labor, and British transportation and gave many helpful suggestions on the other British chapters, especially the concluding one. We have, however, recast to a considerable degree what he did, so that if these chapters have minor or major faults, it should be assumed that they are our responsibility. Other colleagues to whom we are especially indebted are Professor William Woodruff of the University of Illinois for suggestions for improving the chapter on British population and resources, and Professor Paul D. Converse whose criticisms gave the chapter on American commerce the virtues it may have. Finally, Mrs. Barbara Shoho, who typed the American and British chapters two or three times, did no ordinary job but always had a sharp eye for arithmetical errors, grammatical slips, and editorial inconsistencies.

RALPH H. BLODGETT
DONALD L. KEMMERER

CONTENTS

PART FOUR. GERMANY—FASCISM AND THE RETURN
TO CAPITALISM

PART FIVE. CONCLUSION

Part One

THE UNITED STATES—CAPITALISM

CHAPTER 1

POPULATION AND RESOURCES

For more than a century, Europeans, and other peoples too, have looked upon the United States as a land of promise. The Germans call it "the land of unlimited possibility." Hundreds of millions have dreamed of coming to this New World and starting life over, or at least of giving their children that opportunity, and tens of millions have actually done so during the past century. Today, the United States is the hope of the civilized world. The responsibilities this nation carries are heavy. How well can it meet them and live up to the high standard of performance expected of it? To give a sensible answer, we must first take inventory of the nation's human and natural resources. That will be the aim of this chapter. Then we shall examine the history and functioning of the various segments of the economy. That larger task will be attempted in the chapters to follow.

AREA AND POPULATION

The 48 states that make up the United States cover 3 million square miles (in round numbers). Outlying territories and possessions, the chief of which is Alaska, add half a million more. Such figures have little meaning unless they are translated into comparisons. The United States and its various holdings constitute 6 per cent of the land area of the world. They are equal to 80 Pennsylvanias. They are approximately twenty times the area of Germany before World War II; they are forty times the area of the United Kingdom and one-quarter the area of the British Commonwealth; and they are almost half the area of present-day Soviet Russia. Other countries approximately the same size as the United States are China, Canada, Brazil, and Australia. All the rest are noticeably smaller.

The estimated population of the United States in 1956 was 165 million. The world's population is at least 2,600 million; therefore, this country has 6 per cent of the world's population as well as 6 per cent of its land. Our population in 1940 was approximately twice that of Germany and

1

three times that of the United Kingdom, but it was only three-quarters that of Russia and but one-quarter that of the British Commonwealth. If we leave out India, however, the British Commonwealth was not markedly more populous than this country.

THE WESTWARD MOVEMENT

It was more than a century after John Cabot discovered North America (1497) for the King of England before the first successful English colonies were established at Jamestown, Plymouth, and Salem. For another century the settlements hugged the eastern seaboard. Half of our history, at least in terms of years, had taken place when we declared our independence in 1776. At that time we consisted of 13 states lying between the Appalachian Mountains and the Atlantic Ocean. Thanks to the enterprise of George Rogers Clark and a few hundred pioneer soldiers, most of the English outposts in Illinois and Indiana were captured during the Revolution. When the peace treaty was signed, we held all the land east of the Mississippi River, south of Canada, and north of Florida. This more than doubled the size of the new United States. Two decades later (1803) the famous Louisiana Purchase carried our boundaries to the crest of the Rocky Mountains, and again the size of the nation was more than doubled. Between the Rockies and the Pacific Ocean lay another 1,000 miles. Florida, Texas, and Canada were also in foreign hands. The attempt of the Western war hawks to "liberate" Canada in 1812 was unsuccessful. But by 1819 all of Florida had been acquired; in 1845 Texas joined the Union; and in 1846 England ceded us the Oregon Territory south of the 49th parallel. In 1848 we acquired the present regions of California, Arizona, New Mexico, Nevada, and parts of Wyoming and Colorado from Mexico, which had had the poor judgment to dispute our accepting Texas as a state. Finally, in 1853, Mexico sold us a strip of arid territory called the Gadsden Purchase, whose chief merit was a low-altitude pass into California for a proposed transcontinental railroad. Thus the present continental boundaries of the United States were achieved a century ago when the country had only 25 million people. All we had to do was fill in and develop this vast and rich domain.

The Federal government held over a billion acres of land, which it was anxious to sell cheaply, or trade on advantageous terms, or even give away. The Homestead Act of 1862 provided that individuals might have 160 acres free if they would live on the tract for five years. Railroad companies received huge grants to encourage them to build. Most of the land, however, was bought cheaply by speculators. By 1890 the frontier was said to be closed; that meant that there were no important areas left with less than two residents per square mile. But the government continued to give away land under the Homestead Act until 1935. By 1912, however, the last mainland state, Arizona, had been admitted to the Union.

After the Gadsden Purchase territorial acquisitions were made at a much slower pace. The major nations of the world began enlarging their overseas empires in Africa and Asia toward the end of the century, but we were too busy at home and too feeble in a naval or military way to join vigorously in this imperialistic race. Consequently, we got only some of the less accessible or less attractive areas. The largest of these was Alaska, hastily purchased from Russia in 1867 for $7 million. It was known as "Seward's Ice Box," which indicates how little enthusiasm many had for this action of the Secretary of State. It was, however, to prove to be an excellent investment. A few years later Congress honorably rejected an opportunity to acquire Santo Domingo under shady circumstances. And in the 1890s we were equally scrupulous about annexing Hawaii, a group of semitropical islands about the area of Connecticut and Rhode Island. The war with Spain in 1898 added Puerto Rico, Guam, the Philippines, and control of Cuba for a few years. The Philippines, twice the area of Illinois and more populous too, was the largest acquisition but was given independence in 1946. We still have Puerto Rico, which may someday become a state, and Guam, which serves as a naval station. Other territories that we acquired were part of Samoa in 1899 and the Virgin Islands in 1917, both useful chiefly as coaling stations, and the 10-mile-wide Panama Canal Zone leased in 1904. We took no land following World War I, but we do hold some former Japanese naval-base islands as a result of World War II. All this suggests that the United States lost interest in acquiring territories about a century ago. That is partly true.

On the other hand, we found, almost unconsciously, more subtle ways of making our influence felt. During all this period the nations bordering the Caribbean Sea sold more than half their exports to, and bought more than half their imports from, the United States. To the north Canada became our best customer and we hers. This economic interdependence has fostered political interdependence too, with the United States generally assuming leadership. Also, since 1823 we have warned European countries not to colonize in Latin America or interfere with Latin American governments. That is the Monroe Doctrine. The occasional presence of American marines in such nations as Nicaragua, Haiti, and Cuba a generation or more ago kept their governments on good behavior and protected American investments. More recently we extended our influence part way across Europe by the military and financial aid we gave under the Marshall Plan and other forms of assistance. Similarly, we have endeavored through the United Nations to protect Asiatic countries such as Korea, Japan, Pakistan, and Indo-China from being overrun by Communist neighbors.

POPULATION GROWTH

For over two centuries, from 1650 to 1900, the population of the United States doubled about every twenty-five years. Thus, if you will remember that the nation had a population of five million in 1800, you can estimate with reasonable accuracy backward and forward from that date what the population of the country was at any particular time. For example, it was 2½ million during the Revolution; it was about 20 million in 1850. But since the 1870s the population has been growing at a progressively slower rate. There is no easy rule-of-thumb method of estimating it now for any extended period. Yet, it may help to remember that in the present century the population has taken fifty years to double.

The population growth of the United States since the latter part of the seventeenth century—by which time most of the Colonies had been planted—has been the result primarily of natural increase. For about a century, from 1820 to 1925, this natural increase was generously supplemented by immigration. In that hundred years approximately 30 million immigrants came to this country and remained. In no decade, however, did the number of arrivals exceed population growth through natural increase. The number of immigrants was larger relative to the population in the 1850s than at any other time, including the 1900s, when over a million sometimes arrived in one year. It is not because of their numbers, large as they were, however, that the immigrants influenced the country's development, but for other reasons.

POPULATION GROUPS

Most Americans, until about a century ago, were Anglo-Saxon or Teutonic in origin and Protestant in religion. The Protestant German and Presbyterian Scotch-Irish immigrants of the eighteenth century, and even the Catholic Irish and Catholic South Germans who came in the mid-nineteenth century, were not far removed in their cultural background from the basic English population with whom they amalgamated. These more easily assimilable immigrants of Northern and Western Europe are sometimes referred to as the "old" immigration to distinguish them from the "new" immigration who began to arrive in ever larger numbers after 1882. The "new" immigrants were largely Latin, Slavic, or Jewish in origin, and they came from Italy, Austria-Hungary, Russia, and other countries in Southern and Eastern Europe. At the same time, immigration from Northern and Western Europe fell off sharply. Americans began to worry over the change in the character of the immigration as well as over the fact that a million persons arrived in several of these years. After World War I several immigration laws were enacted. From then on the flow of immigrants thinned and in the depression-ridden 1930s dried to a mere trickle. The alien groups that caused so much worry at the time of World War I have now been largely assimilated.

The major problem recently has been that of assimilating Negroes. For the the past century, Negroes have constituted about 10 to 15 per cent of the population, a proportion that has, however, been steadily declining. Although three-quarters of the Negroes in the United States still live in the South, there has been a heavy migration to Northern cities, such as New York, Chicago, and Detroit. This is the new migration problem, and it is an internal one.

The sizable flow of immigration, the rapid increase in population, and the backwardness of medical science tended, until recently, to give the country an energetic and youthful population. Over two-thirds of the immigrants were male and also over two-thirds of them were between the ages of sixteen and forty-four years. Thus they came in the most productive years of their lives and helped build the nation's great network of railroads and do the heavy work in the mills and factories that were everywhere springing up. Many of the women who came were of child-bearing age. The opportunities of the New World encouraged people to have large families at an early age.

The United States has been a nation of young people during most of its history. Admittedly, life expectancy was shorter in the nineteenth century. Nevertheless, the energy and exuberance of youth led men and women to undertake tasks which older and wiser heads might have avoided. Some of these attempts met with failure but many succeeded. The opening of most of the continent in one century is the best demonstration of their success. The last two generations have seen a definite aging in the population, as Table 1-1 shows. Notice in particular the rise

Table 1-1. Age Groups in Percentages, 1870, 1900, 1950, 1975

Age group	1870	1900	1950	1975 (Est.)
Under 20..........	49	44	34	28
20–44.............	36	38	38	36
45–64.............	12	14	20	25
65 and over........	3	4	8	11
Total...........	100	100	100	100
Median age........	20.2	22.9	30.2	35.0

SOURCE: *Statistical Abstract of the United States, 1954*, p. 33; U.S. Department of Commerce, *Historical Statistics of the United States, 1789–1945*, p. 28.

in the median or average age, and also the rise in the proportion of
people of forty-five and over. This trend is expected to continue for at
least another generation. While better health at upper middle age may
well accompany the trend, nevertheless the number of dependents will
increase. More of these will be old instead of young. It is alleged that
all this may make us a less venturesome and less energetic people.

If age and experience bring wisdom, the nation's better judgment may
offset its reduced enthusiasms. Wisdom also comes through learning by
the experience of others, that is, through education. In 1953 there were
about 23.2 million children in our elementary schools, 7.3 million in our
high schools, and over 2.4 million in our colleges. As a people we devote
a tremendous amount of time to education, more per capita probably
than any other nation in the world. From the days of Thomas Jefferson it
has been recognized that only an educated and informed people can
make a success of democracy. With every generation since then, the
country's youth has received more and better schooling. In colonial and
pioneer times children received little formal education because the business of making a living in the wilderness took most of their time. Pressure
for free public schooling came from early trade unions in the 1830s. High
schools became more common after the War between the States, and
land-grant colleges began to appear as a result of the Morrill Act of 1862.
The percentage of children aged five to seventeen enrolled in public
schools grew from 57 in 1870 to 82 in 1950, and the quality of the education improved immensely. Especially great advances have been made
in the last generation, as evidenced by the fact that 7 out of every 10
World War II white draftees had at least some high school education, in
contrast with only 2 out of 10 World War I white draftees. These advances in education should improve the judgment of the people.

LAND AREAS

The United States may be divided into five regions, namely, the Northeast, the Middle West, the South, the Plains and Rocky Mountains, and
the West Coast (see Figure 1). Let us look at these briefly, examining the
topography, climate, soil, and vegetation of each.

The Northeast is the oldest and smallest of the five regions. It contains
the eight states north and east of Pennsylvania and Pennsylvania itself.
Most of it is rolling country and the northern parts are littered with rocks
from the last ice age. It is also cut up by several minor mountain ranges.
Except for the Hudson River the streams are either short or shallow and
hence not important commercially. The climate ranges from 20 degrees
below zero on some winter days to 90 and more above on some summer
days. Moreover, the temperature varies sharply from day to day. This

kind of climate is believed to stimulate men's energies more than any other. There are 30 to 60 inches of rainfall a year, which is a desirable amount. The soil varies; it is either thin or worn out in New England, but it is moderately good in the three Middle Atlantic states. Because of the nature of the soil and the proximity of large seaports and manufacturing cities, dairy farming and truck farming predominate in settled areas, and subsistence farming in the remoter sections. Lumbering was a major industry in the Northeast a century ago; today it is a minor one.

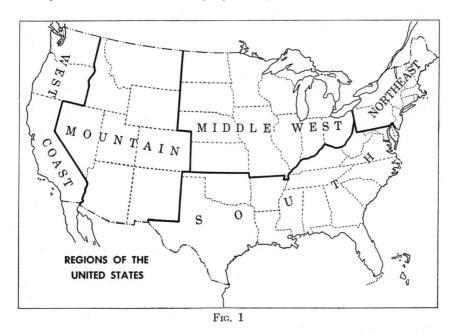

Fig. 1

The Middle West has been variously defined, but for our puposes it is the upper part of the Mississippi valley, that is, the dozen states embraced by the two great arms of the Mississippi River, the Ohio extending to the east and the Missouri to the west. Although parts of this vast area are hilly, there are no real mountains in it and most of the land is monotonously flat. There are glaciated sections in the north. The region contains not only the three large rivers already mentioned but also four of the five Great Lakes. These inland seas are a fine natural waterway. Then there are secondary rivers such as the Miami, Wabash, and Illinois, and the Red River of the North. Rainfall, except on the western and southern fringes, varies between 20 and 40 inches a year. The climate is invigorating and resembles that of the Northeast, except that the extremes of temperature are more pronounced. In many parts of this area the soil is extremely rich, especially in such states as Illinois and Iowa. Accordingly, this is the "breadbasket of the nation." Its dozen states contain half of the nation's farm land, whether measured in terms of acreage or of value. Within this area lie the wheat belt, the corn belt, and the majority of livestock farms and dairy farms. It is one of the richest and most productive agricultural regions of the world. Half a century ago Wisconsin and Michigan were also leading lumber-producing centers, especially of hardwoods, but lumbering has now ceased to be a major industry. Also, the Middle West, with the Northeast, is the industrial heart of the nation; the other areas are predominantly agricultural.

The South is almost definable as the former slaveholding region, the area south of the Mason-Dixon line[1] and of the Ohio and Missouri Rivers. It extends from the Atlantic Coast on the east to about the 100th meridian on the west. Most of the land is gently rolling or flat, but there are some modest mountain ranges in the east running from Maryland south to northern Georgia. The region is plentifully supplied with long, gently flowing rivers rising in the interior and emptying in the Atlantic Ocean or the Gulf of Mexico. Some of the more important of these are the Potomac, Savannah, Tennessee, Cumberland, Mobile, and of course, the Mississippi, the Father of Waters, with its two great southern tributaries, the Arkansas and the Red. Rainfall varies from 20 to 80 inches, being lightest in the west. The climate is semitropical; there is almost no snow and the summers are sultry. Temperatures may go below freezing in the winter and above 100 degrees in the summer. Spring comes early. The quality of the soil varies greatly; it is extremely rich in parts of the lower South but thin and poor in some upland areas of Tennessee, Kentucky, and Arkansas and in the pine barrens in the middle part of the Atlantic seaboard states. Erosion has been a serious problem over the past century because the rains have fallen on plowed ground in winter as in summer. The vegetation in this warm region is generally luxurious. Cash crops are cotton, tobacco, wheat, sugar, and rice. Corn is grown everywhere. The South was the leading timber-producing area of the country a generation ago and still ranks second. Industrial centers are found in interior North Carolina and Georgia, northern Alabama near Birmingham, and in eastern Texas.

The arid Plains and Rocky Mountains together make up the largest and least productive region. Although consisting of eight large states, only one of them—Colorado—has a population of over a million. Two great north-south mountain ranges, the Rockies on the east and the Sierra Nevadas on the west, enclose most of this region and bar the entrance of rain clouds. "The skies are not cloudy all day," and almost everywhere rainfall is below the agricultural minimum of 20 inches a year. Irrigation is necessary for farming. The upper waters of the Colum-

---

[1] Pennsylvania's southern border.

bia in the north and of the Colorado River in the south are valued chiefly for irrigation. They are not navigable. As for Great Salt Lake in Utah, it is the highly concentrated dregs of a former ocean. In the north of this region the climate varies from well below zero to 80 degrees above, and in the south it ranges from below freezing to over 100 degrees in sheltered valleys. Yet the soil lacks only water to be very productive, as can be seen in sections where irrigation has been developed. Without water the land grows only grass, cactus, sagebrush, and the like, and consequently is good only for cattle and sheep grazing. The mountainous areas produce some timber, largely softwoods. Except in the vicinity of Denver and Salt Lake City, there are no major industries.

The West Coast region, made up of the three large states of California, Oregon, and Washington, is the fastest growing and least homogeneous of the five areas. Its population still more than doubles every 25 years. About a tenth of our people live there. Facing the Pacific Ocean in a world where commerce and civilization have moved steadily westward for several thousand years, this region undoubtedly has a great future. There is only one great river in it, the Columbia in Oregon. Consequently, there are only a few seaports, Seattle on Puget Sound, Portland 100 miles up the Columbia at the junction of the Willamette, San Francisco with its magnificent bay, Los Angeles, a man-made port, and San Diego, famed as a naval base. Rainfall is heavy in the north, where the skies are overcast much of the year, and it is light in southern California, whose hillsides are baked brown each summer. The climate of the north resembles that of England and Germany, wet and with few extremes of temperature. Southern California has a Mediterranean type of climate, dry, mild, and sunny. Most of the farming is carried on in a few celebrated fertile valleys. These are the Imperial in the extreme south, the great San Joaquin, which runs for 400 miles down the center of California, the Willamette, which is similarly located in Oregon, the Columbia River valley running east and west in Oregon, and the lowlands around Puget Sound. All this farm land added together is equal to the farm land in two average Middle Western states. Some of the valley land has to be irrigated despite its fertility. Away from these valleys, much of the land is just as arid and useless as the worst to be found in the Rocky Mountain region. The favored crops in the southern valleys are citrus fruits, cotton, grains, and vegetables; those in the north are fruits, grains, and vegetables. In addition, the two northern states have for the past generation been the leading timber-producing area of the country. The seaport cities are industrial centers of mounting importance.

RESOURCES

A good rough measure of any nation's economic strength is its developed power resources. Most of the strong nations today are manufacturing nations. Vast amounts of power are needed to run industrial machinery. It is these machines and this power that make the United States a wonderland of productivity. Aladdinlike, the average American worker has almost a hundred energy slaves to do his bidding. Four major power resources have provided this energy in the last half century. They are coal, oil, natural gas, and water, and they are important in that order. Coal has declined relatively, whereas oil and, to a lesser extent, natural gas, have gained in importance. All, however, have grown in absolute terms. Let us look more closely at these resources and at the nation's supply of them.

Coal, the leading source of power, is abundant in this country. A tenth of the nation is underlaid by it. We possess about 42 per cent of the world's known coal reserves and have enough coal, at present rates of consumption, to last for well over a thousand years. We have only begun to use our coal supply. A century ago wood was our chief fuel; as late as 1880 wood still met half of our fuel needs. Then coal became tremendously important in a few years, providing 89 per cent of our power energy in 1900. By the late 1920s coal provided 65 per cent of our power. Today it provides only about a third. The chief users of coal now are the coke manufacturers (for making steel), other manufacturing plants, public utilities, and, together, railroads and retail dealers of coal for home use. Each of these groups uses close to one-fourth of the total production.

For our purpose of broad analysis there are four types of coal. Only two of them are to any degree scarce. The four are anthracite, semibituminous, bituminous, and inferior grades, chiefly lignite. The anthracite is used chiefly for heating homes, and we have used up a fifth of our supply of this coal. What remains should last almost 200 years. A more serious scarcity is that of semibituminous or coking coal, so necessary for making steel. Ordinary bituminous coal, however, which is what most factories and power plants need, is quite abundant. And there are vast supplies of inferior grades of coal, almost none of which has yet been mined. This last is the type that Nazi Germany relied on heavily for both coal and oil in World War II.

American coal resources are advantageously located, on the whole. Only New England has no adequate supplies and so has developed no heavy industries. The major anthracite field is in eastern Pennsylvania not far from the largest Atlantic Coast cities. The best coking coal is found at Connellsville in western Pennsylvania about 40 miles from Pittsburgh. One reason that the area in and around Pittsburgh is a manufacturing center is that the tristate area of Pennsylvania, Ohio, and West Virginia produces most of the country's coal. Iron ore is brought here to be made into steel. Next in importance to the tristate area is Illinois, which is near the Chicago and St. Louis industrial markets. In the South the chief coal deposit is located near the steel-making city of Birmingham, Alabama. There are other coal areas in Kentucky, Indiana, Kansas, and Colorado. In general, the Rocky Mountain region has low-grade coals in enormous quantities but has not developed them to any marked degree. There is virtually no coal at all on the Pacific Coast. That lack has handicapped the industrial development of this region and may continue to do so. The West Coast is well supplied with other fuels, however.

About a third of our power today comes from oil. We produce and we consume approximately 60 per cent of the world's oil. We own the majority of the world's automobiles and tractors. Unlike our coal resources, our oil supplies are limited. For a generation now the conservationists have been warning that at current rates of consumption the known oil supplies will last only fifteen to thirty years. We continue to increase our consumption of oil only by finding new supplies, often at deeper levels. Indeed, we have been increasing the use of scarce oil faster than the use of abundant coal. The automobile is largely responsible. This cannot go on indefinitely. We may some day have to get most of our oil from shale in the Far West or from coal, as the Germans did in the last war. Oil production has been moving west in the past century. The first successful well was drilled at Titusville in northwest Pennsylvania in 1859. Fields were then opened in Ohio and Indiana, but oil production remained east of the Mississippi until almost the end of the nineteenth century. Most of this oil was used in kerosene lamps. Another important use was as lubricants. With the coming of the twentieth century, most oil was manufactured into gasoline. New sources of supply had to be found, and most of them were discovered beyond the Mississippi River. The California field was opened shortly before 1900, the Gulf Coast field about 1901, and the greatest field of all, the Mid-continent in Kansas, Oklahoma, and inner Texas, about 1904. The Mid-Continent has been the leading producer for over a generation. Because most of these oil regions are far from their major markets, some 130,000 miles of pipelines have been built. The underground form of transportation carries 75 per cent of all oil shipped. Two of the largest of these, the Big Inch and the Little Inch, were built during World War II and are over 1,000 miles long, extending from Texas to near New York City.

Natural gas is produced along with petroleum in many fields. It provides the country with a quarter of its fuel and power. It is one of the

finest fuels in existence, for it may be piped without any processing to
the factory or to the kitchen stove where it is to be used. Moreover,
natural gas yields almost twice as much heat as the same amount of gas
manufactured from coal. Yet vast amounts of this fine resource have been
thrown away because it must be tapped to get the oil, and it cannot be
stored or shipped without the installation of expensive equipment. Only
in recent years have the necessary pipelines been put into operation, so
that distant cities, like Chicago, for example, may enjoy the benefits of
this low-cost, clean fuel.

Water power, sometimes called "white coal," has been the hope of
many during the past half century but it has not lived up to expectations.
It satisfies only 4 per cent of our power needs. One difficulty, loss of
power in transmitting electricity long distances, has been partly overcome. The problem of expensive installations, which take years to pay
for themselves, remains. Further, the fact that we are today using a
fifth of the available water power indicates that it can only supplement
other fuels. It is a major source of power in only a few localities, such
as Buffalo near Niagara Falls, the Tennessee valley, and the vicinities of
the large government dams at Grand Coulee in the far Northwest or
Boulder in the far Southwest.

Atomic power is still an industrial energy of the future. It is easy to
expect too much of it. Although tremendous energies may be released at
relatively low cost, they must be used on the spot for the foreseeable
future. That is because four-fifths of an electricity bill goes to pay the
costs of transmitting the power.

METALS

The United States is, on the whole, well supplied with primary metals.
These are iron, copper, aluminum, zinc, and lead. Table 1-2 shows how
important we are as producers and consumers, and how long the known
reserves of these and a few other metals will last at recent rates of consumption. Of the important metals on that list only tin is in short supply,
although recently bauxite, from which aluminum is made, and lead have
threatened to become problems.

Chief among the metals is iron, so important to a modern industrial
nation. It constitutes about 85 per cent, by weight, of all the metals we
mine. Since World War II the United States has produced annually almost as much steel as all the rest of the world combined. Three states, in
1951, produced practically all the iron ore mined in this country.[2] They
were Minnesota, Michigan, and Alabama. Minnesota supplied two-thirds
of the total from its three iron ranges, the Mesabi, Cuyuna, and Ver-

[2] U.S. Bureau of Mines, *Minerals Yearbook,* 1951, p. 671.

Table 1-2. Production, Consumption, and Reserves of Chief Metals in the
United States

Metal	Percentage of value of all metals mined in U.S., 1951	Percentage of the world's production, 1951 (mine basis)	Percentage of U.S. produc-tion to U.S. consumption, 1937	Years known reserves will last at rate of consumption, 1939–1944
Iron................	38	40	98.4	76
Copper..............	17	32	121.0	19
Aluminum (bauxite)...	1	18	59.6	23
Zinc................	15	27	97.1	20
Lead..........	8	21	103.9	10
Tin....	..	..	0.2	0
Molybdenum.........	3	87	249.8	157
Tungsten............	2	12	41.0	2
Gold...............	4	6		
Silver..............	2	20		

SOURCE: *Statistical Abstract of the United States, 1948*, p. 748; National Resources Planning Board, *Industrial Location and Natural Resources*, December, 1942, p. 152; W. N. Peach and W. Krause, *Basic Data of the American Economy* (Homewood, Ill.: Richard D. Irwin, Inc., 1949), p. 88; U.S. Bureau of Mines, *Minerals Yearbook*, 1951, pp. 29, 37.

milion, of which the Mesabi is the largest and most famous. It is a tre-mendous open pit in which giant shovels dig heavy reddish earth in several-ton scoops. This soft ore is about half iron. As a result of the de-mands of the last war, this deposit is showing signs of exhaustion. Michi-gan's upper peninsula also boasts three iron ranges, the Marquette, Meno-minee, and Gogebic. They produced almost a tenth of the country's iron in 1951. Most of the ore from these six iron ranges is shipped from some Lake Superior port in specially constructed ships to some steel-producing center on or near the southern shores of the Great Lakes, such as Gary, Indiana, Cleveland and Youngstown, Ohio, and Pittsburgh, Pennsylvania. These cities are close to supplies of coking coal, limestone, and scrap iron and are near the major markets for steel products. The third iron- and steel-producing area of note is at Birmingham in northern Alabama, where coal, iron ore, and limestone lie in abundance close together. If its market were larger, this would be one of the most favorably situated places in the country for iron and steel production. Almost a tenth of our iron ore came from there in 1951. East Coast mills import their ore from Cuba, southern Chile, and Venezuela. Rich ore discovered recently north of Quebec province promises to be an important future source of iron. Even if all these rich ranges should some day give out, there are still abundant low-grade ores that could be mined. It should also be remembered that an iron or steel product, when worn out, is still scrap and is raw material for a new product. Some day the scrap-iron holdings of our junk dealers may be our richest iron mines.

Of the industrial nonferrous metals copper is most abundant in the United States. It is the best low-priced conductor of electricity, which makes it a vitally important metal in an electrical age. Half of our domestically mined copper comes from Arizona, a sixth from Utah, and most of the rest from other arid and remote Western states such as Montana, New Mexico, and Nevada. It, too, is dug from open-pit mines. Because only a low percentage of the ore is copper (1 to 3 per cent) and because the mines are far from the market, the ore must be partially refined on the spot. This is done by the flotation process. The discovery of this process a few years ago made possible the use of lower-grade ores than were commercially practical before and increased considerably the nation's effective reserves of copper. This manner of increasing reserves is just as important in a progressive nation as are discoveries of new mines.

Aluminum ranks next in importance in terms of the value of the finished metal. This light and yet strong metal, so expressive of the streamlined twentieth century, was classed as "precious" a few generations ago, but it may some day be cheaper and more widely used than iron, for it is one of the most abundant metals in the earth's crust. It abounds in every clay bank and in the earth underfoot. Unfortunately, the cost of separating aluminum from clay and earth is prohibitive; terrifically high temperatures must be generated. Perhaps such heat at low cost will become available in an atomic age. But meanwhile aluminum must be got from bauxite, which will give up the metal at less cost. The principal deposits of bauxite are in Arkansas, but they have to be supplemented by imports from Dutch Guiana. Even bauxite requires considerable power for its reduction, and so aluminum manufacturing depends on abundant deposits of coal in southern Illinois and on cheap electric power in Tennessee and in upstate New York.

Zinc and lead, the twin dull metals, rank next in importance. Oklahoma provides the zinc and Missouri the lead. New mines of both in Idaho make that state rank second. Zinc's chief use is as a cheap protection for iron against rust through galvanizing. Zinc is also mixed with copper to make brass. Lead is used in storage batteries, for cable coverings, and in paints, and it serves as a protection to persons working with radioactive metals. Like copper ore, lead and zinc ores are low grade and must be partially refined by the flotation process before they are started toward their market. The country is poor in high-grade deposits of these metals but has large low-grade reserves.

Of the other metals listed in Table 1-2, tin is almost nonexistent in this country. We import it from Malaya and Bolivia. A tin can, however, is mostly steel; only the inner coating is tin and there are substitutes for that. The country is rather poorly supplied with alloy metals. The greatest alloy asset is the mountain of molybdenum in Colorado. That alloy intensifies the effect of other alloys. The second most plentiful alloy metal is tungsten, found in Nevada. It gives steel a sharp cutting edge. We also have some vanadium, which imparts heat-resistant qualities to steel, and a small amount of manganese, which makes steel tough and nonmagnetic. Canada has vast supplies of nickel, although we have virtually none. Chrome and other alloys have to be imported from afar. As for the precious metals, platinum is scarce, and gold and especially silver are obtained as by-products of copper, lead, and zinc mining. This country is the world's third largest producer of gold and has $21 billion of it stored away in places like Fort Knox. That $21 billion is over half the world's monetary supply of gold. The world's supply of gold has tripled since 1900, largely as a result of improved methods of mining and refining.

Among our industrial minerals are limestone, used as a flux in iron and steel manufacture; sulfur, which is employed in making paper, plastics, dyes, and explosives; sodium salts, used for bleaching and soaps; fluorspar; and various abrasives. The three basic fertilizer minerals, nitrogen, potassium, and phosphorus, exist in virtually unlimited quantities.

In summary, the United States is fortunate in its mineral supplies. Power resources are ample, especially coal; iron is abundant; and there are almost no serious scarcities of other metals. The greatest shortages are tin, chrome, ferromanganese, platinum, nickel, and asbestos. True, the nation would like to have more oil, coking coal, copper, lead, zinc, and tungsten, but these shortages are not critical. Our most basic metal, iron, moreover, is favorably located on the shores of Lake Superior, whence it can be hauled cheaply to centers where coal is abundant.

OTHER RESOURCES

Because we live in an industrial age, it is easy to forget some of the resources upon which we depended so heavily a century ago, resources like lumber, fisheries, and water, which are still of more vital concern than many of us realize.

Some mention has already been made of forests, which provided the basic construction material in the age of wood that preceded the age of steel. Even today four out of five homes are built of wood. Originally, almost half of the nation was in forests. For a long time trees were as much a nuisance as they were a help, for pioneers had to clear them from the land before they could begin to farm. Accordingly, until the present century little effort was made to preserve this resource, except in the older areas of settlement. Even today we are cutting trees faster than we are replacing them, and every generation has to find its timber in more remote areas. For example, in 1889 Wisconsin was the chief timber-producing state; in 1909 the South produced more timber than any other region; and since 1929 the Far Northwest has supplied most of the timber we need. The chief market for timber has long been the populous region east of the Mississippi and north of the Ohio. In 1890 the average haul to market was 200 to 300 miles; in 1940 it was 800 miles. No wonder the price of mill lumber tripled in that half century. Per capita consumption of lumber fell from almost 400 cubic feet to about 200 from 1890 to 1940, but even at the lower figure it was much larger than the average German consumption of 25 feet.[3] Despite the disturbing fact that we cut more timber than we replace, we still have vast timber resources and we are improving our methods. We are using more substitutes, such as concrete; we are learning to use wood more economically—plywood has been one answer; and the government now owns one third of our standing saw-timber supply and leases it for cutting only under strict conditions concerning methods of operation and replacement of trees.

Fisheries fall into two main categories, salt water and fresh water. In 1953 the value of the commercial catch of all fish was about $325 million. Only a very small part of this catch was obtained in fresh water, chiefly the Great Lakes. For centuries the coast of New England was the chief source of supply of this low-priced and healthful food. In recent years more fish have been caught off the Pacific Coast. Cod, haddock, and mackerel have long been famous in New England; salmon and tuna are the leading products of the Pacific Coast grounds. Whales were once an important product of the sea; they supplied the oil to light lamps in our homes, but they are no longer of importance.

Another resource, water, is often overlooked because it has usually been so plentiful and cheap. Recently, a water shortage in New York City has called the public's attention to water's importance. In the 1930s lack of rain in the Dust Bowl of Kansas and Oklahoma led to tremendous wind erosion. The skies were yellow for days, and the nation learned that certain types of farming are impractical where water is scarce. Lack of water hampers industrial development too. In states like Wyoming which have great coal resources, industrialization is retarded partly for lack of water. It takes 60 tons of water to manufacture one ton of steel, and nearly all industrial processes use considerable quantities of water. For-

[3] Per capita consumption did not change materially between 1940 and 1952, but total consumption rose about 20 per cent along with the population. *1954 Commodity Yearbook*, p. 226.

tunately all but the arid Rocky Mountain and Plains states and parts of California are generously supplied with water.

OUR POLITICAL ECONOMY

An intelligent and energetic people, an abundance of natural resources, and an invigorating climate go far toward building a great nation. But they are not enough. China has all these characteristics, albeit too many people, and has progressed slowly in recent centuries. One of her handicaps has been a weak central government. Since the adoption of our Constitution in 1789, this country has enjoyed a strong government. Politically it is based on democratic principles; economically it is based on capitalistic principles. We are interested chiefly in its capitalistic features.

A capitalistic economy rests on four institutions. The word "institution" here means an accepted or customary way of doing or viewing things. The four institutions are acceptance of the profit motive, respect for private property, the freedom of the individual to select his own enterprise or occupation, and the right to compete with anyone, which includes the right to set prices without interference from private monopoly or government. The theory is that if a person is encouraged to work for his own profit, he will work harder than if another reaps the profit. If the property in which he invests his earnings is protected, he will save more and thus accumulate more capital. It is capital, that is, tools and equipment, that makes workers especially productive. If he may select his own occupation, he will tend to choose what he likes best, or at least he will like it better and be more inclined to work hard at it. And if all may compete freely, the most efficient producer will tend to triumph, which should increase the general standard of living.

The thoughtful reader has by this time said to himself, "That certainly is an oversimplified and idealized picture of the economy in which I live." It is. Admittedly, the profit motive stimulates laziness and selfishness as well as industriousness. Enjoyment of private property is impaired by taxation and the government's right of eminent domain. A person is not free to become a doctor unless he can pass the medical examination, and another is not free to become a steel magnate unless he has a private fortune with which to buy a steel plant. Finally, the far-flung influence of large established industries prevents newcomers from entering the field or from setting prices freely if they do break in. And government regulations set public-utility rates, and sometimes building rentals and other prices. In reality, the idealized system is subject to many qualifications. What must not be lost sight of, however, is that our economy probably comes closer to that ideal than any other one does.

We should ask ourselves why we chose this type of economy or at least why we drifted into it. Also, why has it apparently been very successful, judging by our material progress in the last 150 years? Are we not moving away from our professed ideal rather than toward it? If so, why are we moving away from it? These questions cannot be answered offhand. The reader must first know more about the major segments of our economy and about the major trends in them in recent years. The next six chapters will deal with developments in these fields, namely, agriculture, transportation, industry, finance, labor, and commerce. Then in the eighth chapter we shall generalize on our findings and attempt to answer those questions. In the sections of this book dealing with other economies a somewhat similar method of analysis will be followed.

QUESTIONS FOR STUDY

1. Describe how the United States acquired various territories and grew to its present size between 1783 and 1853. What outlying possessions have been acquired since then?

2. How many people lived in the United States in 1800? In 1850? In 1900? What is a quick way of estimating the population of the nation at any time down to about 1900?

3. What is the difference between the "old" immigration and the "new" immigration? What have immigrants contributed to the growth of the American economy?

4. Characterize each of the five major regions of the United States as to climate, geography, major products, and population density.

5. Discuss the rise and decline of coal as a natural resource. What other resources have been taking its place and why?

6. Describe the location of our major iron-ore deposits and show the importance of iron in our economy. What other major metals do we have in abundance? Which are scarce?

7. What is meant by a "capitalistic economy"? On what economic "institutions" is capitalism based?

CHAPTER 2

AGRICULTURE

George Washington was elected to the Presidency by the farmers of America. In those days 95 per cent of the new nation's population was rural, and most people made their living by farming. After the War between the States, industry supplanted agriculture as the chief source of income in the nation. Since World War I more than half the population has lived in cities. Today about one person out of six is a farmer or farm laborer or of a farm family. Farmers still have a lot to say about who is to be elected President, as anyone who takes an interest in politics knows.

Most of the farmers of Washington's time were engaged in what is known as subsistence farming—they farmed chiefly to feed their families. Occasionally, they sold a few surplus products to people in the towns, but since most other people were farmers, the market for farm products was limited. The great exception to this rule was the South, where quite a number of people were engaged in another kind of farming, commercial farming. The staples or cash crops that these farmers at first produced were tobacco and rice, but in the 1790s cotton and sugar were added, and cotton shortly became the chief commercial crop.

Today, most of the nation's farm income is derived from commercial farming, yet approximately half of the nation's farmers are still subsistence farmers or close to it. The majority of these live in the South. It is estimated that in 1944 half the farms of the country produced only 10 per cent of the farm products, and conversely, 10 per cent of the farms produce half of the farm products.[1] On the one hand, therefore, half the farmers could be eliminated and the supply of farm goods would not be greatly diminished. On the other hand, the best farms are as efficient and productive as fine industrial plants, and many of them are highly specialized in what they produce, whether it be citrus fruits in California, corn and soy beans in Illinois, or cotton in Mississippi.

In Washington's time, the average farmer could put just about all his farm equipment over his shoulder, including the plow, and carry it to

[1] W. N. Peach and W. Krause, *Basic Data of the American Economy* (Homewood, Ill.: Richard D. Irwin, Inc., 1949), p. 221.

the field. Tools were simple then—an ax, a hoe, a spade, a sickle, and the like. Today, Middle Western farms require such costly equipment as combines, tractors, seeders, cultivators, corn pickers, and trucks. Since 1880 the value of farm implements and machinery on the average farm has risen from $100 to $1,100. In central Illinois the average farm needs $10,000 of equipment. The increasing use of machinery explains why we are able to produce more food for more people and yet devote a smaller part of our total effort to farming. If farmers still used the primitive implements of 1800, we should nearly all have to engage in agriculture to survive.

Concurrently with the increasing use of equipment the average size of the farm has grown. There were 5½ million farms in the country in 1952 as compared with 4 million in 1880. Twice as much land was under cultivation. The size of the average farm had increased from 134 acres in 1880 to 215 acres in 1950, an increase of 60 per cent. The sections where farms had grown most were the Rocky Mountains and California. In the East they had changed but little. Even in the grain-growing Middle West the change had been slight. The amount of improved land, however, had about doubled, on the average, for the nation as a whole.

During the past century and more the agricultural regions of the United States have become increasingly specialized. The lower Southern states, from the Carolinas in the East to Texas in the West, are famous for the short-staple cotton that they produce. At the time of the War between the States this cotton constituted 60 per cent of our exports, and cotton is still a major export today. Other specialized regions in the South are Louisiana for sugar cane and rice, and Virginia, Maryland, North Carolina, Kentucky, and Missouri for tobacco. On the Pacific Coast, California is famous for her citrus fruits, as, of course, Florida is in the East. California also ranks high today as a producer of cotton. In the North the Great Plains states, two tiers deep, south of the Canadian border, produce spring wheat. (It is too cold there for wheat to survive in the ground over the winter.) Between the spring-wheat states to the north and the cotton states to the south are the winter-wheat states, stretching from the Appalachians to the Rockies. These great wheat belts also produce vast quantities of corn. Corn is by far the most valuable of all the grains we produce, but it does not loom as important commercially because most corn is fed on the farms to the cattle, hogs, and chickens. Other specialized areas are Wisconsin and New York for cheese, and New England and the Middle Atlantic states for apples and truck-gardening crops. The Western Plains states and Illinois produce great herds of cattle and hogs, and the Rocky Mountain states specialize in sheep. The cash income derived from crops and from livestock in 1952 is itemized in order of size in Table 2-1. Obviously a great change has taken place in farming in 150 years. How did it happen and what have been its consequences?

Table 2-1. Cash Farm Income, 1952
(In billions of dollars)

Crop	Cash income	Livestock	Cash income
Food grains*.............	$ 2.5	Cattle and calves........	$ 6.2
Feed grains, hay..........	2.0	Dairy products..........	4.6
Cotton and cotton seed.....	3.0	Hogs...................	3.5
Vegetables...............	2.0	Poultry and eggs........	3.4
Tobacco.................	1.1	Sheep and lambs........	0.4
Oil crops†...............	1.0	Other..................	0.3
Fruits and tree nuts.......	1.1		
Others...................	1.3	Subtotal..............	$18.4
Subtotal...............	$14.0	Grand Total........	$32.4

* Wheat, rye, rice, buckwheat.

† Chiefly peanuts, soybeans.

SOURCE: *Statistical Abstract of the United States, 1954*, p. 651.

THE AGRICULTURAL REVOLUTION

In the nineteenth century the United States changed from a nation of subsistence farming to one of commercial farming and industrial greatness. Such a change is revolutionary, and this one is called the Agricultural Revolution. It was closely related to the other economic revolutions that we shall examine, namely, the Industrial Revolution and the Transportation Revolution. The Agricultural Revolution was characterized not only by a basic change in the farmer's attitude toward the purpose of his profession but also by changes in his method of farming. Several of these changes are especially noteworthy—those in crop specialization, those in equipment and stockbreeding, those in farm size, and those involving investment and marketing procedures. We have space here to examine in detail only two of the changes in method.

Crop Specialization. One might suppose that the area that had been most specialized in colonial times, the South, would be the first to use laborsaving equipment. It was not. Tobacco requires frequent and careful handling. Even today there are very few machines for handling tobacco. For similar reasons it has taken 150 years to develop a satisfactory cotton-picking machine. The only notable machine to serve the South's commercial agriculture was the cotton gin for cleaning cotton, which was invented by a New Englander, Eli Whitney. That invention had the effect of making it worthwhile to raise short-staple cotton all over the lower South and therefore of fastening Negro slavery on the South for two generations. Had it not been for the cotton gin, slavery might have died a natural death soon after 1800 and the South might have become more industrialized and its agriculture more mechanized. But Negro slaves were trained to handle only the crudest equipment—shovel plows and heavy hoes—and the Negroes were given little incentive to improve their skills. Slaveowners devoted surplus capital to adding more land to their plantations, or to adding more slaves, or both. There was little improvement in farm equipment in the South before the War between the States.

In the North, on the other hand, among the principal crops were wheat and other small grains, such as oats, rye, barley, and buckwheat. These were widely demanded and lent themselves to standardized treatment. The principal mechanical advances were achieved in their production. According to H. W. Quaintance, it required only 5 per cent as many man-hours in 1895 to produce a bushel of wheat or cultivate an acre of land in wheat as it did in 1829.[2] Improvements in equipment which made this sort of thing possible under ideal conditions included the self-scouring steel plow drawn by a horse in place of a light wooden plow hauled by a slow-moving ox. They also included a metal harrow whose teeth could be set at any pitch instead of a homemade wooden frame with wooden teeth, a grain drill instead of hand sowing, a horse-drawn cultivator instead of hand hoeing, a harvesting machine instead of a sickle, or occasionally a combine instead of a sickle and hand flail. Mere mention of these improvements gives us some idea of the arduous labor that farmers once performed to obtain a bushel of wheat. It also suggests the tremendous saving in effort brought about by the newer methods.

The Harvesting Process. A good idea of the time and effort saved by mechanization can be got by examining the evolution of the harvesting process. Let us start with the hand sickle. With it a farmer could reap three-quarters of an acre in a day. The sickle was replaced by the scythe and then by the cradle. The advantage of the scythe was that the farmer could work standing up; the virtue of the cradle was that it laid the cut grain in a neat pile ready to be picked up, bound, and stacked for curing. A farmer with a cradle scythe could cut 2 to 3 acres of wheat in a day. Two helpers were needed to shock and gather up what the cradler cut.

The next big advance was Cyrus McCormick's reaper, which McCormick patented in 1831 but did not market until the 1840s. It was a horse-drawn vehicle with a platform projecting from one side and with cutters on its front edge. The first model simply caused the cut grain to fall on

[2] H. W. Quaintance, *The Influence of Farm Machinery on Production and Labor.* (New York: The Macmillan Company, 1904), p. 21. Leo Rogin later pointed out that conditions had to be ideal for this much saving to take place. See *Introduction of Farm Machinery* (Berkeley, Calif.: University of California Press, 1931), pp. 213–229, 241–243.

the platform. Every few yards some one walking beside the machine had to shove the pile of grain off the back of the platform with a rake. A reaper could harvest 10 acres in a day, but five followers were required to gather and shock the grain. The next improvement was a revolving rake attached to one wheel of the harvester, which automatically cleared the platform every quarter revolution. That saved the effort of one man and speeded things up, but other laborers still had to follow to gather and shock the sheaves. Shortly before the War between the States the reaper was further improved by enlarging the platform so that the grain fell on an endless canvas belt that carried the grain up to a counter where two men gathered and bound it before tossing it off to be stacked in the field. This machine grew in popularity during the War between the States, when labor was scarce. Such a machine could harvest 10 acres in a day and dispense with at least ten followers. It was succeeded by the wire self-binder, which was never fully accepted because of the danger of bits of wire getting into the shelled grain. The very successful Appleby twine binder followed the wire binder in the late 1870s. The small model was pulled by two horses and cut a 5-foot swath. It could be operated by one man and harvested almost 8 acres per day. The larger model was pulled by four horses and cut an 8-foot swath. It harvested 18 acres a day. The twine binder was one of the really great improvements of the century (see Table 2-2). The next advance, the steam combine, was used almost exclusively in California in the nineteenth century. One of the larger of these cut 24 acres a day and also threshed the grain. It required a crew of four men and the efforts of 24 horses to pull it.

Table 2-2. Acres of Wheat Harvested per Man per Day

Implement	Decades	Cutting	Binding	Total
Sickle.................................	1790–1800	¾	¾	⅜
Cradle.................................	1800–1850	2	1	⅔
Reaper.................................	1840–1850	10	2	1⅔*
Self-rake..............................	1850–1860	15	3	2½
Harvester.............................	1860–1880	10	5	3⅓
Twine binder (5 ft, 2 horses)..........	1880–1900	....	...	7¾
Twine binder (8 ft, 4 horses)..........	1890–1910	....	...	18
Combine..............................	1890–1920	....	...	6†
Modern combine (6-ft swath)..........	1940–1950	....	...	15†
Self-propelled combine (10-ft swath)....	1950–	....	...	30†

* The arithmetic may not be apparent here. One man could cut 10 acres; it took five others to bind what he cut, thus six men could cut and bind 10 acres in one day. This is 1⅔ acres per man day.

† Combines also thresh the wheat.

SOURCE: From data in Leo Rogin, *Introduction of Farm Machinery* (Berkeley, Calif.: University of California Press, 1931), *passim.*

Within the past generation the old harvesters and combines have been supplanted by a newer, more efficient type of combine, which not only cuts and threshes the grain but bags it too and so saves even more hours. A modern combine cutting a 6-foot swath will harvest 15 acres of wheat in a working day. Incidentally, the working day is not as long as it used to be. The larger self-propelled model can take care of 30 acres in a day.

Notice that throughout this evolutionary process each new implement not only enabled the farmer to harvest more acres but also included more and more of the processes beyond the mere cutting of the grain, which was all that the farmer with a sickle could do at the start. The gains are made clear by Table 2-2. Where once a farmer needed a large family or several helpers to farm 100 acres, now one man can farm 400 acres of grain by himself if he has the proper equipment. We should not assume from this, however, that all farming has made as great strides as has grain farming, for that is not true. New implements for the mass production of other crops are constantly being developed, however.

It is marketing surplus crops that distinguishes commercial farming from the older subsistence farming. And it was the profit from marketing that stimulated farmers to improve their implements, rotate their crops, fertilize the soil, and improve their animals. Until they saw the savings in these procedures and the greater profits to be had, farmers showed little interest in changing their methods. But emphasis on marketing brought not only new farming techniques; it also brought new problems.

THE OVERPRODUCTION PROBLEM

The War between the States drew hundreds of thousands of young men into the Northern armies. Most of them came from farms. To harvest the crops and feed millions of people, who had to be fed regardless of war, the older men, boys, and women left on the farms made more use of machinery. For example, in 1861 the McCormick company was making only 1 self-raking reaper for every 500 hand-raking machines, but by 1865 the ratio was 2 self-rakers to every hand raker.[3] After the War between the States westward migration was stimulated by the promise of free or cheap land under the Homestead Act and the Preemption Act, by the sale of land by railroads, by the existence of railroads themselves, and by the growing market for farm products in the industrial East. In the 1860s production was attuned to demand. But in the 1870s, a decade of agricultural progress and industrial depression, the two got badly out of step. This was, in fact, an era of agricultural "overproduction."

The term "agricultural overproduction" means that certain farm products, such as corn and wheat, were being produced in greater amounts

[3] Rogin, *op. cit.*, p. 100.

than could be sold on the market at prices that would cover costs. They could be sold, but only at a loss. This raises the question of why farmers did not leave the farm and do something more rewarding. Thousands of farmers' sons did; that is why our cities grew so fast then. But the older men and women and those who preferred country life clung to farming. It is not easy to change the routine of one's life and learn a new skill, to decide to leave the variety of farming and become a factory operative, at a monotonous job. Many had investments in their farms that would have been hard to liquidate. They might have to farm at a loss for several years, but the loss was concealed in land that was not adequately fertilized, or in an unrepaired barn, or in long hours of work at what proved to be a very low rate of pay when the crop was sold. Farmers kept hoping that the next year would be better, as it often is in farming, and sometimes was then. Meanwhile, to keep up their income and their standard of living, they planted more rather than less. This only worsened the farmers' situation in general.

The question arises, what else could they have done? What are the cures for overproduction in agriculture? In theory there are five, or perhaps six. They can best be understood by analyzing our definition of overproduction, that is, the production of more than can be sold at a price that will cover costs. The cures are (1) doing nothing, letting competition weed out the inefficient; (2) increasing demand; (3) decreasing supply; (4) subsidizing the farmer; (5) cutting costs; and (6) raising the price level with the hope that farm prices will rise faster than other prices. Those are the possible cures. Some are better than others; some can be carried out quickly; some take time to effect; and some ran counter to the accepted government practices of that period. Let us see which remedies were simply out of the question and which were used.

When a section of the population demands that something be done to relieve their distress, doing nothing is not a satisfactory answer. Besides, this remedy works very slowly with farmers, who can subsist on their farms seemingly indefinitely. Generally, they are reluctant to give up a "way of life" that they are accustomed to.

As for increasing the demand for grain, that was next to impossible. Grain production in this country was rising faster than the population was growing. Efficient new devices like the harvester were responsible. Also, Eastern Europe was offering stiff competition to our grain exports in the European market. Increasing the demand is an ideal remedy in theory, but it was difficult to achieve in practice, especially in a short time. Besides, who was to take the responsibility for achieving it? As yet the Department of Agriculture, founded in 1862, did not even have Cabinet status.

Decreasing the supply was out of the question at this time. It was futile for the individual farmer to reduce his output, for he could not hope to affect the price appreciably, and even if he did, others would quickly step in and fill the shortage. To succeed along this line, all the farmers would have had to have been organized and made to agree to cut their output. That is a farm monopoly. No private person or farm group could have hoped to organize millions of individualistic farmers. The government's doing that, as it did in the 1930s, was impossible then. This was an era of extreme *laissez faire,* and no administration would have considered such a plan.

Subsidizing the farmer was also contrary to the laissez-faire philosophy of this time. True, industries enjoyed tariff protection. Tariffs take extra dollars from people by preventing them from buying cheaper foreign goods. That is a concealed payment. To have taxed people openly to pay farmers because they were in economic distress would not have been tolerated.

One of the best ways to solve the overproduction problem is to cut costs. There were many ways of doing this. One was to use more labor-saving machinery. That of course helped some farmers at the expense of others less quick to adopt this method. Another way was to cut transportation costs. The farmers devoted a large amount of time to this. The Granger movement of the 1870s is best remembered for its organized effort to obtain minimum and undiscriminating railroad rates by action of state legislatures. Railroads were new then, and much had been expected of them when they were first built, perhaps too much. But the railroads were having their problems too. Although some of them had been extravagantly built and had yielded lush profits at times, their good days came to an end about 1873. The depression of 1873–1878 saw more business failures each year than the year before. That was bound to affect the freight business. Railroads are industries with high overhead costs, which means that when business slacks off rates should theoretically be raised for the road to break even. If raising rates is not possible, at least they should not be lowered, as the farmers were demanding. Accordingly, although the Grangers got the principle of rate regulation accepted, they did not effect a material reduction in rates. Still another way of cutting costs was to buy farm machines on a cooperative basis and to sell grain through a cooperatively run grain elevator. The farmers in the 1870s, despite some disappointments, probably accomplished more by cutting costs than by anything else.

The sixth method of handling overproduction is to bring about a rise in the price level. The farmers of the 1870s were especially tempted by this method. Between 1865 and 1880, for example, wholesale prices of farm products, roughly what the farmer got for his crops, fell 45 per cent, but the cost of living, or what the farmer paid for what he bought, declined only 20 per cent. Because farmers sell wholesale and buy retail, and because it is difficult to vary the supply of their crop once it is planted, farmers generally prosper in a period of rising prices and suffer in a period of falling prices. Obviously they would want to change the falling trend of prices into a rising trend.

At first the farmers supported what was known as the Greenback movement. They contemplated the issuance of more paper money, payment of war bonds in greenbacks instead of in gold, and some capital loans in greenbacks to farmers.

Another inflationary program was the Free Silver movement. Its sponsors proposed a restoration of the "free coinage" of silver, abandoned in 1873. The program would have put the nation ostensibly on a bimetallic standard again, but actually on a silver standard. Since most of the leading nations were abandoning silver as a monetary standard, and since vast quantities of the metal were being mined in our West, the price of silver was falling steadily. To tie our money to it would have tended to give us a rising price level. Although many farmers wanted this, the majority of the country had experienced enough inflation during the War between the States and preferred a gold standard. The country adopted the gold standard in 1879. True, that decision gave us a steadily falling price level, which became so painful that in 1896 the whole matter was reexamined. It was the main issue in the Bryan-McKinley campaign of that year. Again the decision was in favor of gold. The fault with the Greenback and Free Silver programs was that they were palliatives rather than cures.

In the late nineteenth century the overproduction problem was solved chiefly by cutting costs, a good method, and by an attempt to promote inflation, an understandable wish of the farmers but a poor method.

Prosperity Again. The years between 1900 and 1930 were, on the whole, pleasant ones of progress and prosperity for the farmer. Since the period contained few problems, it is historically less important than the decades before and after, and so we shall pass over it briefly. It did, of course, provide the background for the 1930s, and the prosperity of this preceding era made the hard times of the 1930s more difficult to endure.

After 1896 the general price level began a long rise, which lasted until 1920. This was in contrast to the downward price trend of the generation after the War between the States. For example, in December, 1886, the price of a bushel of wheat was $2.06; in December, 1896, it was $0.72, and in December, 1919, it was $2.13. With prices rising, farmers' incomes bought more city-made goods, and farmers were better able to pay their debts.

The era also brought marked improvements in farm machinery. Accordingly, farmers put more land into crop production. This might have been expected to bring on a condition of overproduction once more, but it did not. There were a number of reasons for that. The portion of the population living in cities was growing rapidly. Railroad transportation was improving and rates were tending downward. In the latter part of the period hard roads and trucks made their appearance (it costs only a third as much to carry a ton of produce over a macadam road as it does over a dirt road), and better methods of marketing farm products were put into practice. Thus demand was increasing and costs were declining. In fact, the ratio of farm to city prices in the happy years of 1910–1914 was selected in the 1930s by the Department of Agriculture as the "norm" or "parity." "Ideal" would have been a more accurate term.

The period of World War I and immediately after, 1914–1920, was one of booming prosperity. Europeans were busy fighting, and the United States became the "breadbasket" of the world. In these years wheat prices doubled and the price of top-grade farm lands in Iowa and Illinois reached $400 per acre. That destructive invention of World War I, the tank, had a productive twin brother, the gasoline farm tractor, equipped with treads in its infant days. Better equipment, higher prices, and year after year of prosperity led many persons to put land under the plow that previously had not been worth cultivating. It led others to mortgage their farms to buy more land at high prices. If the prices of farm crops had remained high, the farmers' speculation, for this was what it was, would have turned out satisfactorily. But prices fell.

As soon as the Armistice was signed in November, 1918, and the armies were demobilized, reconstruction of war-torn areas began. Much progress was made in 1919, and by 1920 Europe was feeding itself fairly normally. That cut the demand for American crops and knocked down our farm prices. Net farm income was almost halved between 1920 and 1922. Many farmers who had mortgaged their farms and paid high prices for Iowa and Illinois or other lands in anticipation of continued $2 wheat were unable to meet their mortgage payments. Distress was widespread. The Presidential campaign of 1924 saw a sizable third party dedicated to the relief of distressed farmers.

Throughout the latter 1920s the farmers continued to complain, although this was a golden era for the industrial and commercial segments of the economy. Bills were drawn up in Congress to help farmers market their surplus crops abroad at government expense. First Calvin Coolidge and later Herbert Hoover vetoed them. Had the farmers been able to see what lay ahead in the 1930s, they would have been less unhappy over the 1920s, which, after the initial 1920–1922 adjustment, were not as bad as they seemed. The price level and the net income to farmers remained remarkably stable from 1923 to 1929. The 1920s merely suffered in contrast with the prosperity of 1910–1920.

Overproduction Again—in the 1930s. The Wall Street panic of 1929 threw the nation into the worst depression of its history. Not until World War II did the farmers fare well again. The farmers were among the first to feel the depression and they suffered severely. An Illinois farmer with a net income of $6,741 in 1929 was doing better than average if he got above $2,285 in 1932. That is quite a cut in income and something hard to adjust to. Many a man tried to grow more crops to compensate for the fall in prices. For the individual farmer, this was a partial solution; for farmers as a whole, it just made the situation worse.

Once again the farmers were faced with the old problem of overproduction. But the political and economic atmosphere had changed considerably since the 1870s. Our economic system was more complex. More people lived in cities and were employed in factories. When factories laid them off, they were without a means of subsisting. The millions of unemployed—the number increased every year, 1930, 1931, 1932—demanded that something be done to end the hard times, thus increasing the pressure on the government to take action. In 1932 industrial workers, farmers, merchants, and many others cast a laissez-faire Republican administration out of office and put in a Democratic administration committed to action. One of the first segments of the economy to receive attention was the farmers. All they had got until then was the Federal Farm Board to stabilize prices, and that had not been effective.

There were still the same six remedies for agricultural overproduction. Congress, after three years' delay, was under pressure to get results quickly. A speedy solution was more important than a lasting one. There was little that Congress could do either to increase demand or to cut costs quickly. But Congress could curtail supply and could subsidize the farmer. Such actions, moreover, were no longer taboo, for the age of *laissez faire* had passed. Accordingly, Congress resorted to first one and then the other of these methods. Also, Congress took steps to increase the price level to stop the deflation, which was ruining farm incomes and driving farmers more deeply into debt. Thus Congress did three things. Let us look at each in some detail and see how successful they were.

In May, 1933, Congress passed the first Agricultural Adjustment Act (the AAA). It was based on the principle of reducing the crop supply to raise the crop price. Basically, this is the principle followed by a monopolist. How can one make a monopoly out of several million farmers? Only by organizing them to act in unison in obedience to certain government orders. In its first year the Agricultural Adjustment Administration endeavored to limit the output of six crops—wheat, cotton, corn, milk, tobacco, and rice—and the number of hogs. Since the act was not passed until May, the orders were to plow up every third row of cotton. In subsequent years the AAA reduced the acreage planted be-

low the "normal" amount previously planted. To obtain funds with which
to compensate the farmer for the reduced acreage, Congress imposed a
tax on the processor of his corn, cotton, and so forth. It was expected that
this tax would be included in the price the consumer ultimately paid.
The economic consequences of the AAA were many. We have time to
look at only a few of the more important ones. For example, what use
should the Southern cotton farmers make of their unused cotton land?
Some planted peanuts. Soon there was a surplus of peanuts, and that
crop had to be added to the crop-control list, which grew longer every
year.

If the price of cotton was raised by the government-sponsored cotton
monopoly, what was to prevent the English, who normally bought some
40 per cent of our cotton, from seeking cheaper sources of supply in
India, Egypt, and Brazil? As cotton prices crept higher, they did just
that, and the share of our cotton crop brought by the English declined.

Farmers were induced to cultivate their crop lands more intensively.
By using the hybrid corn then coming into vogue, some farmers got almost as many bushels from their restricted acreage as they had from
the larger acreage they tilled before the AAA.

Many people thought it strange economics to take out of production
a third of the good land on a fertile farm and a third of the poor land
on a poor farm. Less effort would produce the same results on less land
if all the fertile land were cultivated and all the poor land were abandoned. That objection was never answered.

There seemed to be something fundamentally wrong in a program designed to make farmers richer by paying them to produce less.

Finally, how was the program designed to bring about a permanent
solution to overproduction? It simply was not. Actually, it worked the
other way. If people are paid more for a crop, they will try to produce
more of it. True, it was a handicap to have to do so on less land, but
many ingenious farmers found ways. This made the overproduction problem more acute instead of solving it.

The Supreme Court declared the original AAA unconstitutional in
1936. Congress then passed a revised version requiring that the land
taken out of production be subjected to soil-conservation treatment. That
act is still in force.

Ways were also found to subsidize the farmer. For example, loans
were made to growers on stored wheat, corn, cotton, tobacco, and so
forth. The government paid storage costs and loaned the farmers sometimes as much as the full value of the crop. If the price fell, the farmer
simply failed to pay back the loan and let the government keep the collateral, namely, the stored crop. This amounted to subsidizing the farmer
when he overproduced.

The farmer also gained from government manipulation of the monetary system. The original AAA carried an amendment, called the Thomas amendment, which was designed to raise the price level to a 1926 base. The 1920s now looked better to the farmers. The Thomas amendment gave the President power to take any or all of the following actions. He might order the issuance of $3 billion in greenbacks. He might put the nation on a bimetallic standard. He might order the Federal Reserve to buy $3 billion of government bonds in "open-market operations." This would enable banks to lend more money to customers. He might devalue the dollar as much as 50 per cent. All these powers were calculated to increase the money supply and raise the price level.

Fortunately, President Franklin D. Roosevelt exercised only one of these powers. In 1933–1934 he cut the value of the dollar 41 per cent. That was expected to raise the price level by 69 per cent (100/59 is 169), or back to the 1926 level. The concept behind the Thomas amendment was little different from the Greenback and Free Silver programs of the 1870–1896 period; in contrast, however, part of the cheap money program of the amendment was put into effect. To have expected immediate results would have been naïve. In the long run, prices might be expected to rise, but the degree of rise depended on many unforeseeable factors. In the next few years farm prices rose 26 per cent, but how much of this was owing to drought, how much to normal recovery from the depression, and how much to devaluation it would be hard to say.

In summary, the problem of overproduction in the 1930s was met by reducing the supply, subsidizing the farmers, and trying to raise the price level. All were methods that could be instituted quickly by the Federal government. None of them solved the basic difficulties—insufficient demand and high costs. Indeed, if anything, they postponed indefinitely the solution of the farmers' problem.

Today's Impasse. Since about 1940 the American farmer has enjoyed greater prosperity than he ever knew before. Cash farm income to farmers in 1947–1949 consumer dollars rose from $3.6 billion in 1940 to $9.4 billion in 1952.[4] The income is given in comparable dollars because prices rose 90 per cent in those twelve years. There would appear to be little reason for further government aid for farmers.

The reasons for continuing the floors, parities, loans, and subsidies are largely political. By 1954 the situation was becoming ridiculous. It was estimated that government storage costs alone were $30,000 a day. And butter, which enjoyed price supports, was selling for three times as much as oleomargarine, but the government was the chief buyer at that price and had accumulated vast amounts. After much debate the parity figure was cut from 90 per cent to 82.5 per cent. Some farm prices began to fall

[4] Derived from *Statistical Abstract of the United States, 1954*, pp. 329, 652.

and it was feared this might lose farm votes for the party in office. Yet if these aids are continued even in times of lush prosperity and inflation, there is less incentive to cut costs and to diversify crops. The farm segment of the economy is subsidized at the expense of other segments. The Federal government seemingly has a bear by the tail and dares not let go. That is frequently the case after a subsidy program has been in operation for a while.

CONCLUSIONS

In 1935 an English economist, J. W. F. Rowe, wrote of the world's experience with commodity-control schemes. He made two particularly cogent observations. First, a generation earlier such schemes, he said, would have been regarded as examples of unsound economics. Second, devices to limit the supply, like the AAA program, would work temporarily, experience showed, if the industry was not a declining one. If it was, such devices were unlikely to succeed at all.[5] Let us examine these two comments.

Economic theory differs from time to time, for it is an outgrowth of economic conditions. The world's famous economists—Adam Smith, Thomas Malthus, David Ricardo, J. M. Keynes—developed theories to deal with current situations. Smith sought to discredit excessive government regulation, Keynes to remedy a great depression. So it is in the economics of agriculture too. Around 1900 there were more small business units, including farms, per capita, more of a laissez-faire atmosphere prevailed, and competition was more looked to as a solution for our economic ills than it is today. Now business units are larger, there are fewer of them per capita, the investment is greater, and men look to government regulation rather than to themselves for the solution of economic ills. Which generation was right? Which economic theory was right? The answer must not be abstract but must be in keeping with the economic conditions prevailing. At the same time, we must keep in mind that whether we deal with human beings in small business units or in large ones, we are still dealing with human beings, in the final analysis.

What of Mr. Rowe's second comment? American agriculture is not a declining industry, but neither is it growing as rapidly as some other branches of the economy, such as manufacturing or transportation or commerce. It is time that we asked ourselves what problems crop restrictions, parity formulas, and generous loans have solved after more than twenty years. Have they not satisfied chiefly the farmers' demands for greater economic security? More security is, after all, a common and an understandable human goal.

[5] J. W. F. Rowe, *Markets and Men* (New York: The Macmillan Company, 1936), pp. 2, 195.

This is perhaps an appropriate time to philosophize. If farmers are to have more economic security, why should not everyone else? The trend seems to be toward security. But security costs money and someone must pay for it. We can pay only by being more efficient and more progressive, that is, by being willing to make changes. Yet change is almost the opposite of security. People seek security against the pains, inconveniences, and other costs of change. If more and more of us are to enjoy security, will not that make our economy more inflexible and costly, so that it may collapse in some major economic and political tornado? Such inflexibility seems to have been a major reason for the downfall of civilizations in the past. Arnold Toynbee has pointed out that nations, in order to survive, must be able to meet and adjust to the challenge of new situations. And there is an old saying that the one thing that is certain in this world is change. How high a price, then, will we pay for greater security?

QUESTIONS FOR STUDY

1. What is meant by the Agricultural Revolution? When did it take place in this country? Why then?

2. What regions are most famous for the following products: cotton, winter wheat, spring wheat, tobacco, cattle, hogs, sheep, citrus fruits, dairy products, truck-garden crops? Which grain crop has the greatest value?

3. In the handling of what crop was the greatest progress in mechanization made during the nineteenth century? Why in that crop? Describe the progress made.

4. What is meant by "overproduction"? What are the theoretical remedies for it when it occurs in agriculture?

5. How was agricultural "overproduction" handled in the generation after the War between the States? Why were these and not other remedies used?

6. How was agricultural "overproduction" handled in the 1930s? Why were these and not other remedies used? What have been some of the problems created by the remedies that were used?

7. Why do you suppose the AAA program was sometimes referred to as the "farmers' monopoly"? Is it possible to justify the farmers' having a monopoly? Should not the people of every occupation, then, be assured of having their monopoly too?

CHAPTER 3

TRANSPORTATION AND COMMUNICATION

Low-cost transportation makes it possible for different and distant parts of the country to exchange products that each has in abundance, Florida oranges say, for Maine potatoes, or Detroit automobiles for Hollywood movies. Cheap transportation and communication are essential for a high standard of living. It is no accident that our rising standard in the last century has been accompanied by a growing network of transportation and communication facilities. Today there is hardly a village not served by at least one form of modern transportation. In 1940 the nation had some $62 billion invested in various forms of commercial transportation and perhaps $10 billion more in communication. With present values the figure is probably close to $150 billion. Virtually all the investment is privately owned, although the government regulates most of it. Table 3-1 gives some idea of the relative importance in 1952

Table 3-1. Commercial Transportation, 1952
(In billions)

Form of transportation	Ton-miles	Percentage	Passenger-miles	Percentage
Railroads...............	623.5	54.9%	34.7	7.2%
Inland waterways.........	170.0	15.0	1.4	0.3
Pipe lines................	157.5	13.9		
Motor carriers of property..	184.1	16.2		
Private automobiles.......	.....	....	410.3	85.5
Busses......	.....	....	21.1	4.4
Airlines	0.4	....	12.6	2.6
Total................	1,135.5	100.0%	480.1	100.0

SOURCE: Interstate Commerce Commission, *67th Annual Report*, 1953, p. 29. For investment, see *National Traffic Pattern*, 79th Cong., 1st Sess., S. Doc. 83, pp. 9–10.

of the various forms of transportation in our economy. Let us look back and see how transportation reached this stage of development, what significance attaches to the changes made, and what major problems we still face.

In the development of the various forms of transportation and communication, the same basic pattern keeps repeating itself, with minor variations. The pattern consists of growing investment, increasing pressure on the owners to make that investment pay, cutthroat competition, victory by one company in a region or, more likely, a decision by the major contestants to divide the business or fix common rates, and finally the discouraging of new competitors, of whom there are few anyway because of the mounting cost of the equipment. Complete monopoly is not the last stage, however, for various forms of transportation compete with one another.

WATER TRANSPORTATION

When the first settlers came to America, they had to rely on nature's highways, namely, navigable rivers and the ocean at the front door of every colony. For the first century there were almost no settlements farther up those rivers than the first falls or rapids. Water transportation remained of primary importance until just before the War between the States. Some states built canals, such as the famous Erie Canal. Water transportation dictated the location of our major cities; even today our 20 largest cities are situated on the ocean, the Great Lakes, or a major river. Because of their preoccupation with water transportation to the Old World and to fishing grounds, Americans early improved ship design and construction. The schooner, a trim, easily managed vessel, was invented in the eighteenth century, the steamboat early in the nineteenth century, and the clipper ship forty years later.

Rivers. Within the nation the undeveloped Middle West was isolated from more advanced regions by mountains on the east and by inability to navigate easily against the strong currents of the Mississippi and Ohio Rivers. Henry Shreve and others solved this problem about 1816 by inventing a steamboat that would provide cheap upstream transportation on Western rivers. In the next generation steamboats increased in speed, size, cost, and number. Steamboats lasted, however, only about three years, on the average, because of the hazards of river navigation. To make them profitable within their life expectancy, they were built as economically as possible and driven hard. Captains and owners were under temptation to establish speed records to obtain publicity and attract patronage. Boiler explosions sometimes resulted. Steamboat travel was dangerous, but little was done in this laissez-faire age to regulate the abuses of this form of competition. Steamboats lost their importance after the War between the States and are of no significance today.

Canals. A people who have long depended on rivers, lakes, and oceans for transportation and who seek to improve their transportation methods

are likely to think first of new forms of water travel. Canals around falls
or around rapids in rivers, or short canals connecting two bodies of water
are a natural next step. Most of the first American canals were of this
character. The canal era really began, however, with the Erie Canal
project in 1817. This canal was to run 350 miles across upstate New
York from Albany on the Hudson in the east to Buffalo on Lake Erie.
The canal ran through the Mohawk valley and served a thriving grain-
producing region. When completed in 1825, it was already a proven
success. Other states to the south and west and bordering on the Great
Lakes hastened to build their imitations of it. Pennsylvania produced a
rival system of canals and primitive railroads across difficult terrain at
great cost. It was ingenious but not commercially practical. Ohio, Indiana, and Illinois built canals connecting the Ohio River in the south,
and the Illinois River in the west, with the Great Lakes and through
them with the Erie Canal itself. Most of these projects were unsuccessful too. Except for the Erie Canal, the only canals that were financially
successful were some built in the vicinity of New York and Philadelphia
to haul coal to those growing cities. The canals were financed largely by
state bond issues. They were bigger projects than a corporation could
hope at this time to undertake.

In the twentieth century interest in canals revived again. As before,
some canals, like the enlarged Sault Ste. Marie Canal, the Panama Canal
(opened in 1914), and the Galveston ship canal, were successful and
worth their cost. Others, like the New York State barge canal, a modern
version of the Erie Canal, have been costly failures or, like the projected
St. Lawrence Waterway, are open to serious question. All of them are
government-financed projects. In general, railroads provide cheaper
transportation than artificial waterways. Such waterways are most clearly
justified when they are short and connect bodies of water that carry a
large amount of traffic. The Sault canal, the Panama Canal, and Africa's
Suez Canal fit this description. Except for slow, heavy, cheap freight, all
but natural waterways are an increasingly outmoded avenue of transportation. The impracticality of most of our 27,000 miles of artificial
waterways, and especially of the long ones, would be more obvious to
everyone if the shipper and the carrier had to pay all the costs of building and maintaining their "roadbed" (the canal), as railroads do. Instead, the taxpayer is saddled with them. Taxes pay the interest on most
of the $3 billion that have been spent on these waterways. In 1948 the
General Accounting Office told Congress that, in some cases, "the
benefits are not sufficient to cover the cost of out-of-pocket expenses."[1]

[1] John Beckley, "All the Railroads Want is a Fair Deal," *Reader's Digest*, July,
1950.

HIGHWAYS

At the end of the seventeenth century a New Jersey boy, Lewis Morris, who would someday be governor, ran away from home and made his way to Virginia. What was deemed remarkable at the time was that he went by land instead of by sea. Most roads were local and were poorly kept at that.

A generation later stagecoach and freight-wagon lines began operations between the larger eastern seaports. Not until just before the Revolution did Daniel Boone lead settlers through the Cumberland Gap in the southern Appalachian Mountains. Thereafter until the end of the century his route, known as the Wilderness Road, was the chief trail to the Appalachian west. Two others were Braddock's Road, hacked out by army engineers for the ill-fated expedition against Fort Duquesne (1755), and Forbes's Road, also of military origin (1758), through southern Pennsylvania. These trails were generally used by mule pack trains rather than by wagons. Turnpikes did not come into prominence until the last decade of the eighteenth century. The best known of these, the Lancaster Turnpike, opened in 1797, ran 60 miles from Philadelphia, a leading seaport, to Lancaster, in the heart of a fine agricultural region. That area, incidentally, was already famous for its sturdy Conestoga horses and for the covered wagons that were later known as prairie schooners—the trucks of that bygone period. The trading possibilities between agricultural Lancaster and commercial Philadelphia are obvious. The success of the Lancaster Turnpike encouraged the building of many other toll roads.

Since building turnpikes required considerable capital, and since the returns were uncertain and perhaps slow, these undertakings were financed through a new form of business organization known as the corporation. The corporation was more flexible than the partnership, for associates could be added or dropped without necessitating a reorganization of the company each time. It also gave the investor more protection against creditors if the road failed, and thus it attracted more capital. Out of some 335 business corporations chartered in the decade of the 1790s, two-thirds were turnpike companies. State and Federal governments also built turnpikes. In 1802 the Federal government laid plans for a national road to the West, but little progress was made before the War of 1812. Serious military losses in Western fighting, resulting from lack of supplies, demonstrated the urgent need for such a road. After the war, that lesson, together with the demands of Baltimore merchants and of Western pioneers, led to the completion in 1817 of the road from Cumberland, Maryland (the high point of navigation on the

Potomac River), to Wheeling, on the Ohio River. Eventually, the road was continued to Zanesville, Columbus, Indianapolis, and finally to Vandalia, Illinois. During the next twenty years turnpikes were built between major towns in many parts of the country. Manufacturing leaders and seaboard merchants were enthusiastic supporters of these devices to widen the markets for their products. But turnpike building declined following the severe panic of 1837. Although surfaced-road mileage doubled by the end of the century, there was not another era famous for road building until the coming of the motorcar.

The invention of the first internal-combustion gas engine by George Selden in 1877 marked the beginning of a new era in private transportation. Before 1910 the automobile was largely a rich man's toy. Roads were few and poorly maintained. This was the period of veils, dusters, and derisive shouts of "Get a horse." About 1908 Henry Ford began making low-priced cars for the common man, and by 1914 he had produced his millionth car. Activity in road building quickened. The transcontinental Lincoln Highway was created in 1914, at least in blueprint form, although it took one tourist two months to cross on it, a trip that yielded enough adventures for a book. World War I gave further impetus to automobile and truck transportation, as Table 3-2 shows. By

Table 3-2. Surfaced Highways, Automobiles, Trucks, 1794–1952

Date	Miles of surfaced roads*	Auto registration	Truck registration
1794	31		
1800	1,200		
1837	58,327		
1900	128,500	8,000	
1910	203,839	458,377	10,123
1915	275,930	2,332,426	158,506
1920	369,122	8,131,522	1,107,639
1925	521,000	17,439,701	2,483,415
1930	694,000	22,972,745	3,518,747
1940	1,367,000	27,372,397	4,590,386
1945	1,527,000	25,691,434	4,834,742
1952	1,782,475	43,653,545	8,962,367†

* Road figures are estimates before 1910, surveys thereafter.

† Includes bus registration. This has never been large. There were 17,808 busses in 1925; there were 112,253 in 1945.

SOURCE: U.S. Department of Commerce, *Historical Statistics of the United States, 1789–1945*, pp. 220, 223; *1954 Statistical Abstract of the United States*, pp. 555, 564.

the end of the decade 1910–1920, motor-vehicle registration had tripled and surfaced-road mileage had doubled. By 1930 the figures had doubled again, and the automobile industry, which had gone unnoticed in the

1899 census, was now the nation's largest. Ford was a billionaire. The 1920s, moreover, saw the building of tens of thousands of miles of concrete roads and the installation of the highway numbering system.

During the depression of the 1930s the state governments built more roads. To finance this construction a few of them revived the turnpike or toll-road system. The most famous of the new turnpikes was the Pennsylvania Turnpike, now extending 350 miles from Philadelphia to the Ohio line and tunneling through seven mountain ranges, which automobiles formerly had to climb over. Since World War II there has been another burst of turnpike construction; there is hardly a Northeastern or Middle Western state that does not have one built or projected.

Although automobile manufacturing fell off in the 1930s, the number of registrations still increased. Then during World War II the production of private cars ceased altogether so that the automobile plants might make planes, tanks, and military vehicles. One result was that by 1945 the age of the average car was nine years instead of five as before the war. Another was that the years following the war brought new peaks in automobile production. The American people today own almost 80 per cent of the world's automobiles, enough so that everyone may ride at once. That sometimes seems to happen on Sunday afternoons.

Automobiles, trucks, and hard roads have wrought great changes in American social and economic life. The automobile has ceased to be a luxury and has become a necessity. The social life of nearly everyone, and particularly that of people in rural areas, has been widened. Village markets have declined in importance and urban markets have increased. This has probably freed people from the grip of local monopolies, but it has strengthened the power of national ones. The automobile has brought traffic problems and laws to ease them, government responsibility to provide and maintain more roads, new taxes, and problems arising out of competition with other forms of transportation. The automobile industry itself has become so important that major disturbances in it affect the economic life of the whole nation.

RAILROADS

The Baltimore and Ohio was the first railroad operated in this country. For the first twenty years of their existence, down to about 1850, railroads were merely short links in existing chains of transportation whose main parts were rivers, canals, and stagecoach lines. The railroads' chief business was carrying passengers, not freight. The trains were light and slow and they operated chiefly in the daytime. Wrecks were few and not serious. Because of their sad experience with canal building, the states would have little to do with railroads after 1837. Thus, like the turnpikes, railroads had to be financed by corporations. The state-owned canals were sometimes hostile to the railroads. The state of New York, owner of the Erie Canal, once forbade any railroads paralleling the canal to carry freight except when the canal was frozen. Around 1850 the first railroad lines were completed through the Appalachian Mountains, and henceforth railroads were a major, and an increasingly important, form of transportation, as Table 3-3 shows. Middle Western products that had formerly gone down the Mississippi to market were now diverted to other markets in the East by the new railroads. Direct trade between the East and the Middle West grew.

Table 3-3. Railroad Mileage, 1830–1952

Date	Miles*
1830	73
1840	2,818
1850	9,021
1860	30,626
1880	92,147
1900	193,346
1920	252,845
1940	233,670
1953	225,242

* Does not include second, third, etc., tracks.

SOURCE: Through 1880; U.S. Department of Commerce, *Historical Statistics of the United States, 1789–1945*, p. 200; since 1880, *Statistical Abstract of the United States, 1948*, p. 519; *1955*, p. 567.

One result of the War between the States was the building of transcontinental lines across the middle of the country, the first running from Omaha, Nebraska, to Sacramento, California. It was completed in 1869 with much fanfare, including the driving of a gold spike. Its anticipated success led to other transcontinental projects. Three more were completed in the early 1880s. These first four were generously assisted by land grants from the government and by government loans. Yet despite this public aid, all these roads went through receivers' hands in subsequent years. Four other transcontinental roads were built in this country and in Canada. But far greater mileage was laid down in the eastern half of the United States, where many local roads connected thousands of towns and villages that previously had had no rail outlets. Table 3-3 shows that the period of the 1880s was the decade of greatest growth; total mileage reached its peak in 1916. About this time railroads were by far the most important form of transportation. They had replaced water transportation and were not yet being plagued with automobile, truck, and airplane competition. Railroads, however, competed vigorously among themselves. That is a significant story in itself.

As railroads became longer, and as their equipment became heavier and more complex, the investment in railroads mounted. Their overhead costs rose. By overhead costs is meant costs that must be met regardless of whether the road is doing much business. Overhead costs include taxes, interest on bonds sold to build the road, depreciation caused by weather, and wages and salaries of employees who cannot be laid off. The interest on bonds is especially important. It is this matter of overhead that makes railroads a "natural monopoly." If too many lines were built between, say, New York and Cleveland, what would be the result? We do not have to guess, for the Pennsylvania, New York Central, and Erie railroads did just that about the time of the War between the States. Any freight that will tend to pay operating costs (fuel, some wages, wear-and-tear depreciation) and leave something over to apply against overhead costs is worth seeking when competition is keen. Of course, all costs must be met over a long period, but for a while a railroad can survive by covering operating costs and some overhead costs.

The Pennsylvania, New York Central, and Erie railroads were especially anxious to obtain the business of big shippers who would assure them of sizable and regular shipments. John D. Rockefeller's Standard Oil refineries, the largest in Cleveland, got especially low rates for a while by promising each of the three roads a certain amount of oil business each month. Such a situation may have a variety of consequences, most of them undesirable. It gives the big shipper, Rockefeller in this case, an unfair advantage over his competitors. He eventually forced them all to sell out to him. If the railroads agree to divide the business, as they did in this instance, they become a railroad monopoly, and some of the gains of competition are lost to the public. To make up for the low rates that they grant large shippers, the railroads must charge smaller shippers, or shippers at noncompeting points, higher rates. In the Mississippi valley in the 1870s and 1880s rates on grain shipments were sometimes twice as high between producing areas and markets served by one railroad as they were between places served by two or more railroads. Still another outcome of this competition between railroads may be that there is not enough business for two roads, and so the weaker one goes bankrupt and is bought by the stronger. Again the result is a monopoly. But now the region must pay rates high enough to support the equipment and roadbed of two lines, although one would be enough. Once laid down, railroads are unlikely to be abandoned or torn up. These are some of the reasons that railroads are called natural monopolies.

By the 1870s it was apparent that railroad rates would have to be regulated to prevent rate competition that would end in undesirable monopolies. At first, the states regulated the railroads, largely at the instigation of the farmers; later, in 1887, the Federal government began to regulate the rates of railroads engaging in interstate commerce. For several years government regulation of railroad rates met with strong opposition, but after the passage of the Hepburn Act in 1906, during Theodore Roosevelt's administration, the power of the Interstate Commerce Commission (ICC) over railroads and other forms of interstate transportation increased steadily. The Commission gained jurisdiction over pipelines, express companies, and sleeping-car companies in 1906, and over telephone and telegraph lines in 1910, and it regulated interstate trucking and commercial aviation for a while. The Valuation Act passed in 1913 required that a commission determine the value of all railroad lines so that the ICC might estimate the proper return on properties in different parts of the country and establish rates that would yield such a return.

The Transportation Act of 1920 virtually acknowledged that railroads were natural monopolies and indicated that a 6 per cent return on carrier properties was appropriate. Yet from 1921 to 1952 steam railroads have earned 6 per cent, as a whole, in only two years and over 5 per cent in only six years. This may suggest that the Commission has been unduly strict in its regulation of railroads. More detailed study would reveal that some railroads have done very well, especially some coal roads and Western roads, that some roads would not economize unless forced to do so, and that some never should have been built. Yet railroads cannot be expected to modernize their equipment rapidly if they have only limited earnings with which to make large expenditures.

In the spring of 1955 it was proposed in Washington that Congress reduce the powers exercised by the ICC over the railroads. The argument in favor of this was that the controls were put on the railroads over half a century ago when the railroads were virtually a transportation monopoly. They then carried some 90 per cent of all passengers and freight. But in 1953 they carried only 6 per cent of the passengers and half of the freight. They must now compete with automobiles, trucks, busses, pipelines, airplanes, and river and lake shipping. Most of these other means of transportation were developed in the past half century, and most of them enjoy Federal or local subsidies. It is urged that if the railroads are to meet this competition they must be freed of the trammels that were placed upon them when they were monopolies. The suggestion made but slight headway. To take powers from a government bureau or commission is always difficult.

AIRPLANES

Aviation began with Orville Wright's flight of 100 feet, lasting twelve seconds, at Kittyhawk, North Carolina, in 1903. Commercial aviation began in 1918 and for years consisted almost exclusively of the transportation of government mail. Charles Lindbergh's sensational trans-Atlantic flight in 1927 gave tremendous stimulus to aviation. In the next three years the number of companies more than doubled. Competition was keen and mail concessions were necessary for continued success, although they too were in an experimental stage. For a while mail subsidies were paid on a poundage basis. Any company could make a profit by shipping heavy articles back and forth by air mail over its route. When this was realized, the basis of payment was changed to space available.

About 1930 Postmaster Walter F. Brown divided the country into several major areas and allocated these to five major companies, three of them transcontinental lines. Essentially the same division of territories exists today, with the Transcontinental and Western Airline serving the north, the United Airlines serving the center, and the American Airlines the south. About 1934 scandals over the allocation of mail contracts, which had not been given out on a competitive-bid basis, resulted in regulation of the air companies by the ICC for four years. Then in 1938 authority over the airlines was transferred to the newly created Civil Aeronautics Board. Functioning in much the same way as the Interstate Commerce Commission functions for railroads, it has regulated commercial aviation since that time.

Tremendous progress has been achieved in commercial aviation in recent years, as Table 3-4 shows. The number of revenue passengers carried has doubled every two or three years. Also, the freight business, minuscule as it is, has been growing at about the same rate. The number of companies and the number of planes that they operate have been relatively stable, but that is because the planes are becoming larger and

Table 3-4. Civil-aviation Statistics

Item	1934	1940	1945	1954
Number of operators, domestic......	24	19	20	32
Route-miles operated, thousands.....	29	43	49	78
Airplanes in service................	423	369	421	1,336
Average available seats.............	9	17	20	50
Passengers by air vs. by Pullman, per cent..........................	3	14	13	51 (1948)
Passenger fatalities per million revenue-miles, domestic..............	0.7	0.4	0.4	0.04
Revenue passengers, millions........	0.5	2.8	6.6	32.0
Municipal airports.................	980	1,031	1,220	2,272 (1950)
Commercial airports...............	872	860	1,509	2,329 (1950)

SOURCE: *Statistical Handbook of Civil Aviation,* 1949, pp. 6, 61, 71, 79, 85, 89, 99; *Statistical Abstract of the United States, 1955,* p. 581.

more expensive all the time and may continue to do so. The lifting power of the average plane doubled every seven years until 1949. Average seating capacity quadrupled between 1934 and 1952. Thus the companies continually have to increase their investment in planes and equipment.

The expensive task of building airports was at first left in the hands of municipalities. In some instances cities constructed them in the hope of stimulating local commerce. Yet on the whole progress was slow, and this held back aviation just as a shortage of roads would handicap the automobile industry. In 1946 the Federal government agreed to allocate $500 million over seven years for airport construction, to be matched by local or private grants. Since then the number of airports has increased more rapidly.

Despite the startling progress just described, the aviation business was in some ways a sick one after World War II. The aircraft-manufacturing companies, overexpanded because of the war, found military and commercial airplane orders insufficient to support them in the manner to which they had been accustomed. Orders for private planes have been disappointing—the initial cost is too high, airports are still too few, and navigating difficulties are great. As for commercial airlines, they must emphasize economy and speed on the one hand and safety on the other. Safety is vital—a serious accident hurts the business of all lines—but safety requires constant vigilance, repairs, and replacements, and all these are expensive. Yet the airlines must attract business away from railroads, which are safer and more reliable. It is a tribute to their enterprise that airplane traffic since 1948 has surpassed Pullman traffic. Airplane traffic measured in passenger-miles in 1954 exceeded that of train coaches (commuter traffic excluded, however). For airplanes to compete successfully with trains, rates must be kept low, and a steady flow of traffic must be maintained. The companies still need the help of mail subsidies. Their profits have been meager, yet they must be used for investment in new equipment. Thus air transportation is an industry whose profits are uncertain and whose greatest promise still lies in the future. Such a business must depend heavily on the government for support, and the government watches it closely.

METHODS OF COMMUNICATION

Communication is as important as transportation although the investment in it is not so great. Ideas, after all, can be carried more cheaply than goods. Most products have to be advertised, ordered, and the terms of financing and delivery arranged before they are transported. Thus cheap communication is just as important to a widening of markets as is low-cost transportation. Improved communication has come simultaneously with improved transportation. Carrying messages has been among the first business of new forms of transportation; stagecoach lines and post roads first carried mail, and so did commercial airlines.

Five methods of quick communication stand out today. They are the postal service, the telegraph, the telephone, the newspaper, and radio and television. The first three are used chiefly for person-to-person communication; the last two, newspapers and radio and television, are methods of reaching masses of people. The mass method is, on the whole, the more modern development. Let us look at the evolution in this country of two person-to-person methods of communication and of one mass method.

POSTAL SERVICE

The British government began a postal service in the Colonies in 1707. In 1753 Benjamin Franklin, as deputy postmaster, established weekly deliveries of mail the year round. By the Revolution there were 76 post offices, most of them along 2,400 miles of post roads. It is estimated that these offices handled 250,000 letters a year. The first contract for transporting mail by rail was negotiated in 1835. About this time express companies began to compete with the government post offices, whose rates were so high as to discourage communication. Popular sympathy was with the private express companies and against the government's "odious monopoly." Only a cheap postage law passed in 1845 saved the government service. Thereafter, low postal rates greatly stimulated use of the government's service. Postal treaties with other nations extended the range of mail deliveries to many parts of the world. Many specialized services were offered by the Post Office Department as its business steadily expanded every decade. There were the money-order system (1864), special delivery (1885), rural free delivery (1896), parcel post

Table 3-5. Postal Statistics, 1850–1953
(Dollar figures in millions)

Year	Pieces of mail handled (000,000,000 omitted)	Annual profit or loss*	No. of post offices	Gross expenditure
1850	0.1†	+$.3	18,417	$5.2
1900	7.1	−5.4	76,688	107.7
1912	17.6	−1.8	58,729	248.5
1927	26.7	−31.5	50,266	714.6
1953	50.9	−650.4	40,609	2,742.0

* 95 out of 110 years recorded losses since 1845.
† For 1847.
SOURCE: *Statistical Abstract of the United States, 1954,* p. 535.

(1913), and air mail (1918). By 1944 the Post Office Department was doing more than $1 billion of business every year, generally at a loss (see Table 3-5). This was because of the low rates charged for delivering periodicals, not to mention free services to Congress and various other branches of the government.

TELEGRAPH

The earliest of the modern electrical forms of communications was the telegraph, invented by Samuel F. B. Morse in 1837. He persuaded Congress to appropriate $30,000 and strung wire from Washington to Baltimore in 1844. News of the nomination of Henry Clay by the Whigs was one of the first messages transmitted over this line. After three years Congress decided against making the telegraph a government agency like the post office. This was a disappointment to Morse, who firmly believed that it should be a government monopoly.

In the 1840s private companies were organized throughout the country, some of them leasing Morse's patent, some relying on other patents. Most of these lines were put up rapidly, the construction in many instances was poor, and messages sent from one part of the country to another, through the hands of several companies, were frequently garbled or even lost. It was difficult to undo the damage or assess the blame. Such unreliability hampered the growth of the telegraph. Yet despite these difficulties and the amazing reluctance of various businesses to use the new device, it developed steadily. Railroads were among the first customers; in fact, many early telegraph lines were built beside railroads. By the end of the 1840s newspapers also were making increasing use of the telegraph. By the latter 1850s the nation was covered with a network of telegraph lines. Six large companies, each covering a region of its own, provided the service and managed to preserve an armed truce among themselves. Out of this group two companies, the Western Union and the American, emerged as the strongest, the "finalists," so to speak. The War between the States stimulated further technical progress. A third hastily constructed line appeared briefly but was absorbed by the Western Union. The Western Union was now overcapitalized and weaker than its rival. Rather than engage in a business war, Western Union offered American advantageous terms to merge, and American accepted. Western Union was a natural monopoly, like the railroads, but it achieved national scope even before they did.

As a result of absorbing two other big companies in a short period, the capitalization of Western Union grew from about $400,000 in 1858 to $40 million in 1867. Its stock was badly "watered," and since it was under pressure to pay dividends to its many stockholders, it had to keep its rates up. Its situation was soon made worse by the activities of a predatory financier named Jay Gould, who developed rival lines on two occasions to force Western Union to buy them. Eventually Gould gained control of Western Union itself. Gould was notorious as an exploiter of the properties that he owned, but fortunately he acquired Western Union in his declining years. For two generations now Western Union has not had any sizable rivals except Postal Telegraph, which it acquired a few years ago. The telegraph has working agreements with the transoceanic cable companies, which appeared with the laying of first successful transatlantic cable in 1866. Telegraph lines have been subject to regulation by the ICC since 1910. The Commission keeps the rates of these monopolies within reason. At present the telegraph and cable companies do about $250 million of business a year, Western Union's share of this being close to 90 per cent.

RADIO

The first scheduled radio broadcast was from Pittsburgh in late 1920. By 1922–23 radio was becoming a nationwide fad. People sat up nights trying to get distant stations—Chicago, New York, Puerto Rico, or if one were very lucky, London. The number of broadcasting stations grew rapidly, and the number of receiving sets mushroomed from an estimated 400,000 in 1922 to 5,700,000 in 1926. Competition was keen between stations, but most of them were able to serve only a limited area; thus they could not advertise effectively, and consequently they could not afford good programs. To remedy this, several networks were formed in 1924. A longer step was taken in 1926 when the Radio Corporation of America, originally founded in 1919 at the government's instigation, in turn established the National Broadcasting Company and gathered into it a large network of stations and a host of business talent in radio. This looked like an unbeatable monopoly. Yet the following year a rival network, the Columbia Broadcasting System, rising fast from modest beginnings, made itself known. And a few years later a third, the Mutual Broadcasting Company, appeared. Although newspapers began to own and operate their own stations, most of the radio business was done by the three radio networks.

Congress took steps to regulate this new and rapidly growing form of communication by enacting the Radio Act of 1927, which provided for the Federal Radio Commission. In 1934 this commission was replaced by the Federal Communications Commission, which was given authority over telephone, telegraph, and cable communication as well as radio. The new commission was empowered to license broadcasting stations for half-year periods. Radio prospered in the depression decade.

The fireside talks of President Franklin D. Roosevelt in the 1930s stimulated great interest, although it would be a mistake to assume that the radio dealt primarily in news; talks and news together in 1938 took up only 20 per cent of radio time. Music and entertainment absorbed the remainder; they were what the public wanted. Since the radio was supported by private advertising, the people were given what the majority wanted to listen to. That and the commercials constitute the price that must be paid for privately operated radio. By 1950, 96 per cent of all American families had radio sets. We owned some 115 million, over half those existing in the world. It is alleged that three-quarters of these are turned on at some time during the day.

SIGNIFICANCE OF THE CHANGES

We are apt to complain that this is an age of monopoly. In a very loose sense this is true, for in one service or industry after another *a few* big companies do the lion's share of the business. That is what economists call "oligopoly," strictly speaking, or control of the market by a few. Oligopoly is the next thing to monopoly, in numbers if not in economic evolution. It should be clearly understood, however, that neither monopoly nor oligopoly is new in this world. Far from it. Gristmills, general stores, stagecoach lines, and many other services were local monopolies for centuries, and we still have local monopolies in every town and village today. It is not monopoly and oligopoly that are new; it is the scale of them that is new. Many powerful regional and national monopolies and oligopolies have developed in the last generation. As will be shown in a later chapter, these national monopolies and oligopolies have been made possible by the tremendous advancement in transportation and communication just described. The lowered cost of their services has widened the markets of many industries from local to regional and even national scope.

The first regional and national monopolies sold something which transportation and communication agencies could handle easily in large amounts—the services of these agencies themselves. The telegraph was one of the first national monopolies, and railroads like the New York Central were among the first regional monopolies. For reasons already discussed, companies in these high-overhead public-service industries waged economic battle with one another. Either one emerged victorious, or several formed working agreements or pools among themselves to share the market, or they combined. The result was in many cases national or regional monopoly or at least oligopoly.

This trend toward concentration in telegraph and railroad lines foreshadowed a similar trend in industrial production in the decades that followed. Improvement in transportation—the average freight rate fell two-thirds between 1865 and 1916—was a major factor in bringing this about. Cheaper transportation meant wider markets, and wider markets meant more competition at first, which necessitated new methods of cutting costs. More specialization helped cut costs, for with specialization less-skilled labor could be employed to do some jobs, and machines could be installed to do others. Machines are costly and so is the power equipment to run them. Investment in these raised overhead costs, and that, in turn, led to further cutthroat competition, the weeding out of the weak, the formation of pools, and the rise of monopolies and oligopolies. Thus cheaper transportation was a major factor in the trend toward concentration in industry.

Cheaper transportation and communication also led to more regional specialization. The Middle West became a grain- and meat-producing area first; later it became, like the Middle Atlantic states, an industrial region. New England concentrated on light industries, fishing, truck farming and dairying. The South specialized in cotton, sugar, tobacco, and rice. The Plains and Rocky Mountain states became famous for their cattle and sheep, the Northwest for its lumber and salmon canneries, and California for citrus fruits. Within these areas cheaper transportation and communication made it possible for individual towns and cities to gain prominence in the production of certain goods; for example, Pittsburgh in steel, Chicago in meat packing, Akron in rubber products, Waterbury in watches, Lowell in textiles, Hollywood in movies, and Milwaukee in beer. No longer did each region have to be self-sufficient, thanks to better transportation and communication. This increased efficiency and improved the national standard of living, but it also created some new problems.

Still another significant consequence was the more rapid spread of ideas, whether a more effective way of raising wheat, the latest dress style or hat for milady, the most recent good story from Broadway, a new economic theory, or a new recipe. The new means of communication carried the idea out and the orders back; the new low-cost transportation delivered the goods. As a consequence, the people, although more specialized in their occupations, became increasingly alike in their customs, beliefs, and purchases. This made the country more homogeneous and to some degree stronger.

QUESTIONS FOR STUDY

1. What is the most important form of freight transportation today? Of passenger transportation? How does this compare with the situation about 1900?

2. Why was water transportation so important in this country until about a century ago? Why did state governments build canals at a time when railroads had already been invented? How successful were the canals?

3. There were two great periods of highway building in our history. When were they? What has been the importance of each to our economic development?

4. Describe the chief accomplishments of railroads in the nineteenth century, telling where the first ones were built, when they crossed the Appalachian Mountains, when the first "transcontinental" was completed, and which was the decade of greatest railroad building.

5. Why are railroads sometimes called "natural monopolies"? When were railroad rates first regulated? How successful was regulation at first? When did the Federal government recognize the railroad's "natural-monopoly" character? Are railroads as much monopolies now as formerly?

6. Discuss the landmarks of progress in commercial aviation. What is the justification for granting regional monopolies to major airlines and for paying them generous subsidies for carrying mail?

7. What are the major methods of personal and of mass communication? Compare the government's attitudes toward three of them. Why has it varied so much?

CHAPTER 4

MANUFACTURING AND TRUSTS

About 150 years ago the trend toward mechanized manufacturing was well under way in England, but it was barely starting in this country. Samuel Slater became the manager of the nation's first successful factory in 1790. Formerly a foreman in an English cotton-textile mill in Lancashire, he memorized the plans of the best English spinning machinery, slipped out of England for America, and made arrangements to produce thread in Pawtucket, Rhode Island, for two Quaker merchants to sell. Children supplied much of the labor, and a husky Negro provided the power to run the wheels of this first factory. At about the same time Alexander Hamilton, Secretary of the Treasury, was urging the government to encourage manufacturing.

THE INDUSTRIAL REVOLUTION

The time was ripe for our industrial age to begin. The country was rich in such natural resources as lumber, coal, iron, lead, and water power. There were enough people (five million in 1800) to provide an adequate supply of labor, and the population was growing. There were enough city markets to absorb the products of the first small factories. Transportation in the form of turnpikes, canals, and steamboats would shortly increase the number of these markets. The government was strong enough to provide a stable currency, a banking system that was good for that era, and a feeling of confidence among men of wealth that their property would be protected. This last factor was important, for it encouraged people to save and to use their savings in productive ways.

Two other conditions for an American Industrial Revolution had been lacking but were now supplied. One was a desire by capitalists to invest their savings in manufacturing instead of in commerce. Trade with Europe at war was very lucrative. The other was some protection from lower-cost but superior English goods. The years 1806–1815 supplied these two necessary conditions. Various barriers to trade appeared in the form of British orders in council, French decrees, American embargoes and nonintercourse acts, and finally the War of 1812 itself. The significance of these trade barriers was that, if manufactured goods were to be had in this country, we had to make them. The virtual exclusion of English goods from the American market for eight years acted like a high protective tariff for our few infant industries. It encouraged some merchants to switch their capital from commerce to manufacturing. The American Industrial Revolution really got under way, and from this time on our manufacturing activity grew rapidly. Some of the more important early industries were textile manufacturing (cotton and wool), iron making, flour milling, meat packing, and shoemaking. Most of these products could be produced in large amounts in standard sizes or forms and could stand the cost of shipment some distance to markets. Most factories, however, were small and served local areas.

The wealth of the United States grew from $500 million in 1790 to $16 billion in 1860. After allowance has been made for population increase, the average person living in 1860 had $3\frac{1}{2}$ times as much as his ancestor in 1790. Some of the 1860 wealth was represented by factories, railroads, and other industrial requisites that were virtually unknown at the earlier date. The value of manufactured products was close to $1 billion, having increased about tenfold between 1810 and 1860. By 1860 about 4 per cent of the population was employed in manufacturing. (Today's figure is about 10 per cent.)

From 1860 to 1900. The second half of the century was a period of tremendous industrial expansion. It was a period of growing specialization, which separated the worker from his boss, ended his ownership of his tools, and diminished his interest in the quality of the product. It was a period of growing cities, of chimneys belching forth black smoke, of slums, and of immense profits for a few, sometimes gained by dint of efficiency and sometimes won by questionable business practices. The country grew up and became a great nation. New major industries were coal mining, oil production, and steel manufacturing. We surpassed England in the 1890s in annual pig-iron production. The value of manufactured products increased more than tenfold in half a century. One reason for this rapid advance was that investment in manufacturing equipment was now greater. The average wage earner had four times as much mechanical help as before.

Since 1900. In the most recent half century further improvements have been made. Some of the worst industrial abuses, such as smoke nuisances, unprotected machines, thoughtless and harsh treatment of workers, and dubious business ethics, have been largely eliminated. The automobile industry, unmentioned in the 1899 census, became the nation's *leading industry* a generation later. It introduced the assembly line, which was imitated by numerous other industries. Additions of improved tools, equipment, and power, always representing the investment of dollars saved by industry or by individuals, gave the average worker about $6,000 of equipment in 1929 compared with about $2,000 in 1899. Since then the investment has continued to increase, and the quality of the equipment has improved. As a result the productivity of the wage earner in manufacturing almost quintupled between 1899 and 1955. The gain has been at the rate of 3 per cent a year in the last generation. Because of the equipment they use, present-day American workers turn out twice as much per hour as our closest industrial competitors do. Table 4-1 shows the increase in the number of manufacturing establishments and the increase in the number of wage earners, the amount paid in wages, and the value added by manufacture between 1899 and 1952.

Table 4-1. All Manufacturing Industries in the United States, 1899–1952

Year	No. of establishments	Average no. of wage earners	Wages	Value added by manufacture
1899	205,000	4,850,000	$2,260,000	$4,650,000
1952	267,000 (est.)	15,900,000	$43,400,000	$108,500,000

SOURCE: U.S. Bureau of the Census, *Annual Survey of Manufactures*, 1952, p. 13.

Industrial Concentration. While our output was growing and investment per industry was mounting, the average size of the firm was increasing. This means that the number of companies or establishments in many industries was declining. A few companies were becoming the chief producers. By 1879 the Standard Oil Company refined 90 per cent of the nation's oil; in 1899 the United States Shoe Machinery Company held patents on some 90 per cent of all shoe machines; and in 1901 the billion-and-a-half-dollar United States Steel Company controlled over 60 per cent of all plants making steel. There were other such monopolies, or "trusts" as they were called.

In industries in which no one company gained control of production, it was generally true that two, three, or four companies did. For example, today the three great automobile companies, General Motors, Chrysler, and Ford, and two lesser ones, American Motors, and Studebaker-Packard, dominate the automobile industry, which once was in the hands of dozens of manufacturers. Meanwhile, cars with names formerly well-known have disappeared from the highways. Stars, Franklins, Jordans, Stanleys, Wintons, Maxwells, Hupmobiles, and many others are today to be found only in automobile graveyards, if there. The companies that made them were absorbed by the larger companies or were liquidated or failed. This development has occurred especially in industries in which the product is largely machine-made and in which the machinery requires a sizable investment of capital.

We have seen the general picture of industrial change and the trend toward industrial concentration in the last 150 years. Let us now look more closely at changes in two specific industries, one making a consumers' good, that is, something that we use personally, and one making a capital good, that is, something that is more useful to us indirectly. The two choices are shoes and steel.

The Shoe Industry. The story of the rise of the shoe industry in the United States is typical of the Industrial Revolution in many industries both here and abroad. In colonial times or on the frontier a pioneer generally made his own shoes out of leather he tanned himself. He had a few simple tools, such as a knife, a needle, an awl, a hammer, and lasts. The shoes were crude and they fitted only approximately; there were not even lefts and rights. In time, someone in the area who was especially skillful with leather made shoes for his neighbors in exchange for services they could render him, or perhaps for surplus flour or salt or cloth. If he liked that way of making a living, he began to travel to neighboring communities. He became an itinerant shoemaker. Usually he stayed at his customer's house, used the customer's leather, and took his pay in surplus products.

As communities grew into villages, or as the shoemaker became better known, or perhaps as he tired of the wandering life, he settled down and let his customers, now more numerous, come to him. He supplied the leather now; he made the shoes on order; and perhaps he took his pay in cash. When business was dull, he made up extra shoes of common sizes. If he accumulated too many of these, he took them to a neighboring town and traded them at the general store. The storekeeper tossed the shoes in a barrel and let customers paw among them and pick out a pair that fitted.

Storekeepers found that the shoe barrel, like the cracker barrel, attracted customers, and they asked the shoemaker to keep them supplied. With this business to keep him occupied, the shoemaker sometimes taught other members of his family to do the simpler operations of shoemaking, or perhaps he took on an apprentice. There was a good living in shoemaking. The apprentice learned the trade and went into business for himself, in time competing with his former employer. Another general store sought to attract business by selling shoes at a lower price.

About this time a person whom we may call a merchant capitalist appeared. Perhaps he was a former shoemaker, perhaps a storekeeper, perhaps just an enterprising apprentice whose head was keener than his hands were skillful. He undertook to supply leather to a group of partially trained people who would make parts of shoes in the winter, when they had plenty of time. He would come by, pick up these parts, and deliver them to another group who knew how to make still another part of the shoe, and so on until the shoe was completed. All this required much traveling, but the merchant capitalist paid his semiskilled workers less than he would have had to pay skilled shoemakers. He also packed the shoes in cases and shipped them to distant markets, in the West Indies, the South, and later in California.

This "putting out" of parts of the shoes developed certain disadvantages. Some workers did better work than others; some did their assignments on time, and some were generally late. Thus orders to distant places were not always ready when ships sailed, and business was lost. Some shoemakers wasted leather atrociously. Sewing machines were appearing, but the capitalist could not afford to equip his scattered part-time workers with such expensive equipment. He therefore concentrated more operations at his assembling point, or "central shop." Before long, the machinery, the workers, the leather, and the shoemaking operations were all located in this one building. Thus the shoe factory was born.[1]

Notice that the steps in the development of the shoe factory follow each other in simple and logical sequence. No step seems revolutionary. Yet the transition, in two generations or less, from shoes made in the home by the father to shoes bought from the factory was revolutionary. What happened in shoes happened in other products, although every step mentioned above was not always present in the sequence. Also, it is still going on. There are industries still in the home stage (some cooking), or in the shop stage (custom tailoring), or in the "putting-out" stage (dressmaking in sweatshops). In different parts of this country, and in different parts of the world, industries are in varying degrees of advancement toward the factory. Even the factory process may be simple, making shoes in a dozen operations, or complex, making shoes on costly machinery in about three hundred operations.

Iron and Steel. In contrast with shoes, iron and steel were almost never made in the home, even at the outset. They are the basic materials for tools and weapons, and they began their existence at the workshop or mill stage. Most tools and equipment used to be made of tough woods, such as hickory or oak, or of cast iron (hard but brittle), or of wrought iron (malleable but soft). Few tools were made of steel (hard and malleable) because steel was so difficult and expensive to produce. For centuries only experts in a few places knew how to make good steel, and they handed their secret down from father to son. Thus it was that the steel swords of Damascus or of Toledo were so highly valued. Only

---

[1] Blanche Hazard, "Organization of the Boot and Shoe Industry in Massachusetts Before 1875," *Quarterly Journal of Economics*, February, 1913.

a rich man could afford steel armor in the Middle Ages. Cheap steel was not invented until the Industrial Revolution was well started.

By the early nineteenth century it was essential that a hard, durable, malleable, and cheap metal be produced for making the equipment and machines that the new machine age seemed to require. In the 1850s two men, almost simultaneously, found a cheap way to produce steel. Henry Bessemer in England and William Kelly in America observed that if a blast of air was blown through molten iron, the impurities, chiefly carbon, would burn out. Then a known amount of carbon could be added and diffused throughout the molten metal, and steel would be obtained quickly and cheaply. It was a discovery of tremendous importance for the modern industrial age. A lawsuit delayed the use of the process in this country for another ten years, but cheap steel came rapidly into prominence after the War between the States. Steel rails outlast wrought-iron rails by many years, so the railroads were the biggest market for steel, But steel had many other industrial uses.

Unfortunately, Bessemer steel sometimes developed flaws in cold weather, with occasional disastrous consequences to railroads and expensive machines. About 1868 a more reliable method of making cheap steel was found. It was called the "open hearth process." The open-hearth process had other advantages: it was more suited than the Bessemer process to the iron ores found in this country; and it made use of scrap iron, which was a source of growing importance. By 1908 the open-hearth method was used more than the Bessemer process. Most steel is made in open hearths today. The crucible process (a second cooking) and the electric furnace (which provides very even temperatures) are used for the finest grades of steel. These grades are quite costly.

How important iron and steel are in the present age may be gauged from the facts that they make up 85 per cent of all metals by weight, that one out of every four industrial employees works with them, that the average house contains 4 tons of them, and that no nation can be a first- or even second-class power without adequate iron resources.

UNDERLYING CAUSES OF CHANGES IN INDUSTRY

The sort of changes taking place in the shoe industry and in the steel industry during the last century were occurring in many other industries. Three additional reasons for the quickening pace at which industry was growing deserve mention. They are improved power, the patent system, and the corporation.

Improved Power. Greater output depended upon cheaper methods of providing power. Slater's cotton mill was first run by the muscles of a sturdy Negro. Horses on treadmills also provided power for early factories. Windmills long were favorites for grinding flour. Water mills were the chief source of industrial power until the middle of the nineteenth century. At first simple varieties were used, but later more powerful mills were substituted, for which expensive dams had to be built. Next the engineers learned how to harness the larger and swifter streams.

Steam power succeeded water power in the 1840s as coal came into use. This shifted the center of our industrial activity toward Pennsylvania, which had a large coal supply but not adequate water power. Steam was more reliable, for it did not depend on streams that froze in winter and dried up sometimes in the summer. But steam also had its disadvantages. It required a large plant and great quantities of coal, which had to be hauled, and it could not be applied smoothly.

After about 1900 electric power replaced steam power in more and more plants. One electric-power plant could supply several industries, and households as well, with as little or as much power as they wanted. True, a large investment and great quantities of coal were still needed, but there was less duplication of equipment. Electric power could be applied smoothly and could be turned on and off easily. The development of small electric motors in recent years has further simplified the power problem.

The invention of the internal-combustion engine made it possible to provide small amounts of power at low cost in widely scattered places. Today, nations that are industrializing for the first time may use these engines and spare themselves such primitive methods as windmills, water mills, and treadmills, and such cumbersome methods as steam power.

All in all, ample power cheaply delivered in large or small amounts has been a major factor in increasing industrial production. Nations' standards of living may be fairly accurately gauged by their per capita amount of horsepower, and in that regard the United States leads the world. By 1940 every American worker had four times as many energy slaves at his beck and call as his English counterpart, and six times as many as the German worker.[2]

The Patent System. Americans were stimulated to experiment and constantly to seek better mechanical methods not only because labor was scarce but also because our patent system offered hope of a handsome reward to an inventor. The owner of a patent is assured a monopoly of the production and sale of his invention for seventeen years. This system has been in operation since 1790. By 1860–1870, 2,500 patents per year were being granted, and in recent years the figure has been close to 45,000. Not always does the inventor get the full benefit of his patent. Eli

[2] Whereas in 1850 men and horses provided 94 per cent of the power and machines 6 per cent, by 1950 machines provided 92 per cent. J. F. Dewhurst, *America's Needs and Resources* (New York: The Twentieth Century Fund, Inc., 1947), p. 682.

Whitney was unable to protect the cotton gin, and Elias Howe had to fight an expensive lawsuit to make good the patent on his sewing machine. But the patent system stimulated these and millions of other inventions. Fulton, McCormick, Morse, Bell, Edison, Steinmetz, and many others benefited from the patent system. Perhaps Eli Whitney's greatest contribution was not his famous cotton gin but the idea of interchangeable parts, which he applied to firearms about 1798. Interchangeable parts made possible colossal savings in repairing broken equipment and replacing lost parts.

All too often we allot the credit to the first person to invent something that is commercially practical, and we forget the hundreds who subsequently added improvements. For example, the combine which farmers use today is vastly superior to McCormick's reaper, but it is a rare person who can name even a few of those who have contributed the later improvements. Yet the patent system encouraged these improvements, which have increased production and substantially raised our standard of living.

The Corporation. Individual proprietorships and partnerships were not suitable for large business units. Big companies needed lots of money. Individuals or partners did not always have adequate funds for business expansion, and even when they did, they did not want to risk it. Putting their money into expansion meant risking not only those funds but perhaps additional money if competition should become keen and losses had to be incurred for a while to protect the first investment. And if the venture should turn out badly, the individuals or partners would lose still more, perhaps even their homes and personal property. Thus the owners of business concerns came to favor the new corporate business form.

The business corporation first made its appearance in this country in the 1790s and was used primarily by turnpike companies and to a lesser degree by bridge companies, water companies and banks. All were more or less public utilities. Later it was adopted by textile mills and railroads, and then by many other concerns. The corporation was essentially an artificial person set up to own a business. The corporation, or artificial person, did not die. Ownership of it could change easily through the sale of shares of stock. It could sue or be sued. Most important of all, if it ran out of funds, it was bankrupt; those who owned it were not obliged to give it any more funds. This limited-liability feature probably constituted its greatest appeal. Anyone investing money in stock in a corporation might lose all his investment, if the corporation proved a failure, but there his losses ended. Thus the corporate device encouraged more persons to invest, and it also encouraged the concerns themselves to take somewhat greater risks. This, of course, had its bad as well as its good features, but it is significant that the use of the corporate device grew.

With it also grew the importance of investment bankers, whose business it was to market corporation bonds and stocks, and also the importance of stock exchanges, where these securities could be quickly bought and sold. Without the corporation and its attendant institutions, it would have been much more difficult, if not impossible, to mobilize the funds needed by the growing business units of the Industrial Revolution.

The corporation had another great advantage: it was easy to direct. A corporation works like an army under the command of a general and his staff, whereas a large partnership works more like a town meeting. Prompt and secret decisions are important in business and are vital to the survival of a big business.

Summary. At least three developments were important in speeding up the Industrial Revolution over the last hundred years, in making industry bigger, and in making industrialists more powerful. They were improvements in power, which enlarged and quickened production, the patent system, which promoted invention, and the rise of the corporation, which attracted investors and simplified the job of management. These factors operated in addition to those mentioned earlier in the chapter as prerequisites for an industrial revolution and also to revolutionary changes in other segments of the economy, such as transportation, agriculture, and finance.

MANAGEMENT'S RESPONSIBILITY FOR CAPITAL

The large investment in the new factories, and sometimes it was tremendous, also brought changes in its wake. In many plants the investment per worker amounts to $10,000 or even more. In the last half century alone the value added by manufacture in the average establishment has increased fifteenfold. Those who are responsible for managing such valuable properties must have a keen interest in their success. If these men are owners, wholly or partly, it is their own fortunes that they are watching over; if they are hired managers, they have a sizable salary and a professional reputation at stake.

Success depends on making a handsome profit in good times and on protecting the investment at all times. If the overhead costs are large and if competition is keen, success may be difficult to achieve. Businessmen may defeat their competitors by using better methods or by temporarily lowering prices. If these methods do not succeed, they may follow the advice of the adage, "If you can't beat them, join them," and make agreements fixing prices or dividing the market. Such agreements, called "pools," were easier to achieve half a century ago than they are today, for pools are now forbidden, and the government is more vigilant. The important fact, however, is that the men responsible for a large investment have strong inducement to use ingenious methods to protect it.

Modern factories are capable of large output when operating at full capacity. Under the stress of World War II our industries virtually doubled their output. Capacity production, moreover, is generally low-cost production, because the overhead cost is divided among a large number of units. The inducement to operate at or near capacity is great. If advertisements are clever or if installment buying is encouraged to keep customers coming, an industry may work itself into a difficult position. It may expand its plants to a point where it can no longer maintain high output. This is especially true if the product takes a long while to wear out, like a refrigerator or an automobile. If the demand for the product falls off, unit costs go up, because the overhead cost remains about as large as before. A condition of overproduction may result.

One of the problems growing out of the Industrial Revolution is that of unwanted surpluses. This problem appeared because more producers were now producing for the general market instead of chiefly in response to specific orders. Some of our worst economic problems of the last century have been problems of plenty. This is in contrast with the famines that beset more primitive civilizations. Setting up a monopoly is increasingly the modern solution to this problem of surplus, or overproduction.

Overproduction, we have seen, means producing more of a product than can be sold at prices that will cover costs. There are four ways for a manufacturer to combat overproduction. One is to increase demand. Despite the wonders of advertising, it is not easy to do that quickly. Obtaining a tariff that shuts out the products of foreign competitors may help, however. A second way is to cut costs, but that is also difficult to do quickly. A third is to obtain a government subsidy, but only a few defense industries are likely to get favors of this kind. The fourth, and usually the quickest, is to achieve a monopoly by buying up the chief competitors, or by defeating them in a business war, or by making an agreement with them to sell fewer products at higher prices. Just as all roads once led to Rome, so all quick solutions seemed to lead to monopoly or at least to oligopoly.[3]

THE TRUST PROBLEM

A strong trend toward monopoly appeared in certain industries around 1900, in the steel industry, for example. By examining further developments in that now-familiar industry we can understand better why some industries were, and still are, especially susceptible to monopoly.

---

[3] "Monopoly" means one seller or a group acting in collusion as one seller. "Oligopoly" means few sellers. The term monopoly is used loosely throughout the chapter to indicate partial price control by one or even by a few acting somewhat in unison over a national market or an important regional market.

The Steel Trust. The steel industry had a tendency toward monopoly for the same reasons that railroads did. The manufacture of steel requires very costly equipment. The blast furnaces that make pig iron, the open-hearth furnaces, crucible furnaces, and electric furnaces that make steel, the rolling mills that shape the ingots, and the by-product ovens that manufacture the coke essential for making steel are all costly. Even a small mill requires several million dollars' worth of equipment. This has been a high-fixed-cost industry since the latter part of the nineteenth century. The men whose money was invested in such large undertakings were aware of the losses they would suffer if their costly equipment was not kept busy. It was so expensive to shut down and reopen a blast furnace that they did so only in extreme cases.

The steelmakers early tried to obtain as steady a market as possible for their products. At first they engaged in cutthroat competition to obtain the essential customers. Next, the producers of wire, tubing, plate, and other steel products began forming wire monopolies, tubing monopolies, and the like. This was in the early 1890s. These manufacturers of secondary steel bought their raw material chiefly from three primary manufacturers, Federal Steel, National Steel, and Carnegie Steel. The strongest of these was the last, then under the control of Andrew Carnegie. In time, the secondary manufacturers decided that they could produce steel ingots more cheaply than they could buy them, and they began to erect a plant for that purpose. Carnegie's answer was to begin the construction of plants to make wire, tubing, plate, and pipe. If all the new plants begun by both groups had been completed, the nation would have had far more steel-producing capacity than it needed. To market their products the contestants would have had to engage in costly cutthroat competition. Carnegie was likely to win such a war because he had more savings, hence greater staying power. The secondary producers knew this and decided to buy out Carnegie.

Carnegie was not unwilling to sell but he knew his strategic advantage. He asked a fabulous price and he got it. Then other major primary and secondary manufacturers essential to the new combination were also able to demand generous prices for their plants. The investment-banking house of J. P. Morgan conducted negotiations and earned a generous reward for its efforts. The final result was a holding company, the United States Steel Company, capitalized at about $1.4 billion, one-third in bonds and two-thirds in stock. Because of the inflated prices paid for Carnegie's plants, and for the others too, most of the stock was "water"; in other words, its nominal value was based on anticipated earnings and not on actual value of the equipment.

Generous earnings were anticipated because the new steel trust controlled 60 per cent of the steelmaking capacity of the nation. Rather than oppose this behemoth the various "independent" steel companies that controlled the other 40 per cent made working agreements with it, known as pools, fixing the price of steel or assigning markets. The price of steel rails, which under competition had varied widely (sometimes selling for as little as $17 a ton), now remained unchanged for over ten years at $28 a ton.[4] When government pressure made the continuation of pools and other obvious price-fixing arrangements impossible, the trust substituted a more subtle device.

The new device was the setting of prices by the "Pittsburgh plus" system. Pittsburgh was the center of the steel industry and the home of the United States Steel Company. Under this system each steel product had the same price and was sold at this price plus transportation from Pittsburgh. That applied to steel products made in all plants, whether they belonged to the United States Steel Company or to independents, and in all parts of the country. Thus an independent plant in Chicago might sell girders to a construction company in Chicago at the "base" price for girders plus transportation from Pittsburgh even though the girders were actually transported only a short distance across Chicago. The "phantom freight" that was collected was extra profit for the independent plant.

The system had several advantages. It kept most companies from invading each others' markets, and it especially kept independents out of United States Steel's home market in Pittsburgh. It really amounted to a monopoly involving the entire steel industry. The system deceived the Supreme Court, which in 1920 said that the United States Steel Company was not a monopoly, overlooking the fact that the whole steel industry was a monopoly. Pittsburgh plus was changed in 1923 from a single to a multiple basing-point system, and it continued that way until the Supreme Court outlawed the basing-point system in 1948. There has been more competition in the industry since the beginning of the 1930s, however.

Despite methods that were monopolistic, the steel industry made great progress in this period. By-product coke ovens replaced the wasteful beehive type; the open-hearth process of making steel continued to supplant the Bessemer process almost everywhere; improved rolling mills were invented and installed; all kinds of steel alloys were discovered for making steels for special purposes; light steels came into prominence; and by the middle 1940s this country was manufacturing about half the world's steel. Thus monopoly did not prevent progress, although it may have delayed it.

Antitrust Action. The public early came to resent the economic power of monopolized industries such as the steel trust, the oil trust, the tobacco

[4] Eliot Jones, *The Trust Problem in the United States* (New York: The Macmillan Company, 1924), chap. 9, especially pp. 206, 229–230.

trust, the sugar trust, and the shoe-machinery trust. Some state legislatures took action to protect the public against the trusts, but state laws did not suffice. Then in 1890 Congress passed the Sherman Antitrust Act, which made illegal monopolies in restraint of interstate trade. But the government lost an early suit against the sugar trust, the E. C. Knight case of 1894, and the Sherman Act had little effect for several years. Finally, in 1904, the government invoked the law successfully against a transcontinental railroad monopoly. This was the Northern Securities case of 1904, and it marked the start of President Theodore Roosevelt's fame as a trust buster. He used the law against numerous other big monopolies, chiefly industries, and his successor, President William Taft, continued that work.

The numerous court cases against trusts under Roosevelt and Taft revealed certain unfair methods that had been especially effective in building monopolies. One of these was the tying clause; for example, a tobacco company might insist that a retail store handle all its products if it wanted to carry the company's most popular or desirable brand. Another unfair method was the security holding company, and still another was the interlocking directorate. Congress passed the Clayton Antitrust Act in 1914 to outlaw, in large part, these aids to monopoly. In the same year, by another law, the Federal Trade Commission Act, Congress set up a commission to study unfair trade practices and take administrative action against them. This was the high point in Congress's move against trusts.

Monopoly Trends, 1914–1948. The feeling against trusts died out as a result of World War I. The war showed that inflation as well as trusts might make prices go up. It also revealed that substantial gains were to be had when big companies pooled their secrets and cooperated. And after a war against a powerful enemy, when life itself had been at stake, people were unable to revive their interest in a mere war against trusts. Then in 1920 the Supreme Court ruled that the United States Steel Company was not a monopoly. If United States Steel was not a trust, it was clear to big business that almost any combination was legal. Businessmen began to act on that assumption as soon as business conditions again made combinations desirable. Just as 1898–1903 produced a swarm of trusts, so did the boom years of 1927–1929.

Then came the Great Depression. To survive it many companies had to resort to cutthroat competition and to the most questionable of practices to get orders. This distressed both the government and the big established companies. Partly to restore prosperity and partly to make business police itself, Congress passed a new law in 1933. This was the National Industrial Recovery Act (NIRA), which suspended all antitrust laws and invited businesses to draw up codes of fair business practice. Some 677 of these codes were drawn up, largely by the big companies in the various lines of business. Most of the codes limited production in some way and discouraged newcomers from entering business and small concerns from expanding. This was perhaps the high point in the new legislative and judicial trend favoring trusts. In 1935, however, the Supreme Court declared the NIRA unconstitutional, thus ending this phase.

In 1936 Congress, in the Robinson-Patman Act, legislated against chain stores and in favor of small independent companies. The Justice Department was encouraged to prosecute trusts, and it began to do so on a fairly extensive scale. During World War II the antitrust laws were ineffective, as they had been during World War I. Since then the government has again taken action against trusts. The nation's most famous trust used to be the Aluminum Company of America. During the war the government had to set up additional aluminum plants of its own, and afterward the government insisted on selling these plants to new companies to give the old monopoly some competition. Another important move against trusts was the outlawing of basing-point systems in 1948 by court decision. The modern attitude of the Justice Department comes close to identifying guilt with large size in a monopoly case.

Security and Power: Opposite Sides of the Same Coin. The pressure is strong, it must be obvious by now, for industries with high overhead to move in the direction of monopoly. Whatever the form of the combination or agreement, the purpose is to alleviate uncertainty. A virtual monopoly can establish a regular pace of production, and it has some assurance that it can dispose of its goods in anticipated amounts and at a certain price. This greater security not only takes much of the worry out of business but it adds to profits. It has generally been assumed that the great tycoons of industry sought monopoly to gain great profits, for the successful ones like Rockefeller and Carnegie became immensely wealthy. But perhaps their search for security has been underestimated. Security is a universal human goal.

Security and power are closely related. The person who enjoys absolute security in life is the master of his own destiny, and, since our lives cross those of others every day, such a person is going to be master of the destiny of others as well to a considerable degree. When a manufacturer gains greater security, it is at the expense of others—maybe his workers, maybe his customers, maybe his competitors, maybe the persons from whom he gets his raw materials, maybe the farmers and others from whom he buys the necessities of life, and maybe all of them. These others are not going to take a diminution of their own security without protest. As soon as they realize what is happening, they fight back. That is just what happened toward the end of the last century.

Transportation agencies like railroads, and important heavy industries like oil refineries, sugar refineries, and steel mills were the first regional and national monopolies. The men who worked for them, the farmers who used the railroads, the customers who bought kerosene and sugar, all of them felt the force of these new powers and sought to restore the balance. To deal with national industrial monopolies, the workers sought to establish national unions, and eventually they succeeded. Likewise the farmers, with the aid of the government, eventually set up monopolies in various farm products. The agency arranging this, the Agricultural Adjustment Administration, was discussed in a previous chapter. The farmers and the customers also tried to restore the balance in political ways. The monopolist's power over his own property was reduced. Railroad rates were fixed, big industries' rights to buy out competitors were questioned and later denied, and in time, heavy taxes were imposed on excessive profits. Workers, farmers, and consumers, acting through the government, tried to counterbalance the rising power of the railroad and industrial magnates. How successful were their efforts to control monopoly?

Fundamental Solutions to the Trust Problem. The government has used six fundamental methods in dealing with monopoly. At first the government ignored it. In its local manifestations the government still ignores it. That is *laissez faire*. The original theory was that no business would exploit its advantage unduly, for this would stir up enmities and competition that would injure the exploiter in the long run. This rationalization proved too optimistic. Big monopolies exploited their advantages to reap immediate profits despite the public's attitude.

In dealing with public utilities, such as the telegraph, or with the railroads, the government used rate regulation. This was discussed in the chapter on transportation. It is moderately effective, although there is a tendency to set railroad rates unduly low (but utilities rates sometimes too high). Also, there is no provision for "decontrolling" when new forms of competition appear.

During the 1930s a new way of dealing with utilities came to the fore. This was the "yardstick" method. The government set up a power plant of its own, ran it economically (in theory at least), and told private power companies that their costs should not exceed government costs and their rates should not exceed the rates of the government's plant. In the Tennessee valley government plants also made munitions, controlled floods, and manufactured fertilizer. There was sharp difference of opinion about whether enough costs had been allocated to the electric-power part of this joint project, and even about whether some costs, for example, taxes, had been adequately counted.

Under the antitrust laws, the government has prosecuted trusts, and the courts have on occasion ordered the dissolution of big companies. But the cases have been long-drawn-out, expensive, and not always successful. Also, orders to dissolve trusts, even when they seemed to have been carried out, have not broken up the monopolies. The Standard Oil Company was not effectively dissolved until many years after 1911 when it was supposedly dissolved into 34 parts.

A fifth way of handling monopolies is for the government to take them over and run them. Some European governments have operated railroads from the beginning, and we have run the post office for over two centuries. England has nationalized coal production. The United States has thus far nationalized few services and no industries. It may be significant that England, which has nationalized more than has the United States, never had any antitrust laws. When control was needed, it took that more drastic form.

The sixth and last way of dealing with monopolies is merely a combination of the other five. That is the policy we have actually followed, and it may be the best, for different monopolies may best be regulated in different ways.

QUESTIONS FOR STUDY

1. What are some of the conditions that must exist in a country before an industrial revolution is likely to take place? When did the Industrial Revolution begin in this country? Why then?

2. Describe the evolution of shoemaking from home to factory. What was the chief characteristic of the "domestic stage"? What was the advantage of the "puttting-out" system when it began? Why did it die out? Did the evolution of other industries follow this same pattern?

3. What have been some of the high points in the development of the iron and steel industry? What was the significance of the discovery of the Bessemer process? Of the open-hearth process?

4. What are some of the major underlying causes of the great growth that characterized American industry in the nineteenth century? Could this growth have taken place without the appearance of the modern corporation?

5. Why has the problem of "overproduction" appeared in industry so often in the last century? What are the ways of solving it?

6. What is a "trust"? Why did trusts appear towards the end of the nineteenth century? How was the steel trust formed and how did it maintain its control?

7. What did the government do to regulate trusts? Why did it feel that regulating the trusts was necessary? How effective was the attempt to regulate trusts?

CHAPTER 5

FINANCE

The financial structure of the American economy may at first glance appear complex and confusing. But if we break it down into its chief parts, we can understand it fairly easily. These parts are money, long-term capital, investment banking, short-term capital, commercial banking, and central banking.

THE MONETARY SYSTEM

In colonial times money in the form of gold and silver coins was scarce. If the colonists brought much over with them, they soon sent it back for equipment, supplies, clothing, and other necessities. Capital was scarce and the frontier absorbed it as a sponge does water. Fortunately, the colonists lived a more self-sufficient life than we do today and needed less money. Even so, they had to find some satisfactory substitutes for specie. Usually, the substitutes were the cash crops of the colony, such as furs in New York, tobacco in Virginia, rice in South Carolina, and wampum (Indian beads) on the frontier. But commodity money was cumbersome.

In the eighteenth century most of the Colonies experimented with paper money. This began in Massachusetts in 1691 when the legislature, lacking funds to pay off a returning army, issued bills of credit, which circulated as money until they were redeemed. Other legislatures, unwilling to endure the pains of taxation, followed Massachusetts' example. Some of the Colonies, such as Massachusetts and Rhode Island, issued these bills of credit in great quantity. Paper money made gold and silver coins scarcer than ever. Gresham's law operated: cheap money drives good money out of circulation.

The nation had its worst experience with paper money during the Revolutionary War. There are three basic ways of financing any war; namely, by taxation, by borrowing, and by issuing money. Since the major controversy was about taxation by a distant authority, the states refused to give their Continental Congress power to tax them. They themselves raised little by taxes. Borrowing was equally unproductive, for few "patriots" were wealthy, few persons wanted to lend to a rebel colony fighting a great nation, and we had no experience in floating bonds. That left only the third way, issuing money. There was plenty of experience in that. The war was financed in large part by paper money, most of it issued by the Continental Congress, but some by the states as well. The Continental dollar became so nearly valueless that it gave rise to the phrase "not worth a Continental." It was some time after the Revolution before the nation again got a respected monetary unit.

Among the motives for drafting and adopting the Constitution were the desires of propertied people for a stronger central government possessing the power to tax, for a money based on gold and silver instead of on promises, and for a government that would not impair contracts and would respect private property. On the subject of money the new Constitution said: "The Congress shall have power . . . To coin Money, regulate the Value thereof, and of foreign Coin, . . . "; and also, "No State shall . . . coin Money; emit Bills of Credit; make any Thing but gold and silver Coin a Tender in Payment of Debt . . . ."[1] With Alexander Hamilton as Secretary of the Treasury, these purposes of the Constitution were enacted into law. Later, with John Marshall as Chief Justice, the laws were strengthened by Supreme Court decisions upholding property rights.

The new nation made the dollar the unit of value because the Spanish silver dollar had been the best-known coin for over a century. The American dollar was slightly smaller than the Spanish one. But our specie supply included many foreign coins for another two generations, since coins were then difficult to manufacture. The dollar contained either 371.25 grains of pure silver or 24.75 grains of pure gold.[2] The United States was on a bimetallic standard. This meant that gold and silver coins were full legal tender (good for payment of all debts), that all specie was redeemable in gold or silver, that there was free coinage of gold and silver, and that owners were free to melt or export their coins. When the owner of silver bullion brought it to the mint to be struck into coin, he was following the same course of action as a farmer bringing his wheat to the mill to be made into flour. Both wanted their raw materials to be processed into something they could use. Both had as much ownership in the processed product, coin or flour, as in the raw material and might do with it what they pleased. That meant either using it in the country or sending it out of the country.

[1] Art. I, Secs. 8 and 10 of the Constitution.
[2] There was a small coinage fee for gold at first. Also, each coin is made up of nine parts precious metal plus one part alloy to give it hardness.

It is a mistake to assume that most of the money in circulation before the War between the States was specie; it was bank notes. None of these notes were legal tender, although the notes of the First Bank of the United States (1791–1811) and of the Second Bank of the United States (1816–1836) were acceptable in payment of Federal taxes, which was about as good as being legal tender. In 1830 the ratio of bank notes to specie was 2 to 1, and in 1860 it was 2½ to 1. By the middle 1850s checking accounts were larger than bank-note circulation. There had to be enough specie to serve as reserve for them also.

At the outbreak of the War between the States there were some 1,600 banks in the country, each with eight to ten denominations of bank notes. Many of these notes had been counterfeited, and the notes of banks in some parts of the West and South especially were circulating at a discount. To protect bankers and others against such hazards two types of publication existed. One was a booklet called *Bank-Note Detector,* revised about once a year, and the other was a weekly periodical called a *Bank-Note Reporter.* The *Bank-Note Detector* was to help people identify counterfeited and raised notes. The *Bank-Note Reporter* gave the rates of discount at which notes of little-known or weak banks were acceptable. This was a shameful state of affairs and one fraught with risk for the average small businessman. It meant also added expense for the customer. In practice, merchants hesitated to refuse most bank notes at par lest they alienate a customer. They had to take a loss on worthless or discounted ones, and to make up for this business risk they had to have a more generous markup in pricing their goods. It had been realized for some time that a way must be found to correct this money situation.

Lincoln's Secretary of the Treasury, Salmon P. Chase, was determined to solve the bank-note problem. He was also eager to find new markets for government bonds. A solution suggested itself which was more obvious then than it may seem now. About a dozen states had been operating under what was then called the "free-banking" system. That system first appeared in Michigan and New York in 1837–1838 and spread later to various Western states. In order to start a bank all that a group of persons had to do was to obtain, say, $25,000 of state-approved bonds and deposit them with the state official in charge of regulating banks, receiving in exchange an equal amount of bank notes. They were then ready to start their banking business. If their loans were wise, they got double interest, interest on the notes they loaned and interest on their bonds in the state official's safekeeping. If their loans were unwise, and many customers failed to pay, the bank failed. Innocent holders of bank notes would then be compensated by selling the securities in the state officials' hands. If this system worked on a state level, why not on a national level? It would provide a national currency redeemable at par everywhere, and it would also provide a market, it was hoped, for millions of government bonds. Out of this reasoning came the National Currency Act of 1863, later amended many times and better known as the National Banking Act.

While it was doing a reform job Congress tried to remedy some other glaring faults of banking. It did such a good job, however, that few banks thought it profitable to join the National Banking System. Most banks preferred to keep their more lenient state charters. To force the reforms on the bankers, Congress passed a law in 1865 providing for a 10 per cent annual tax on the notes of all state banks after July 1, 1866. Thereafter, most banks took out national charters, and for the next quarter century there were more national banks than state banks.

Forcing the banks to obtain national charters had, however, another important consequence—the more widespread use of checking accounts. The use of checks had been growing in the more settled Eastern areas because of its convenience. It was now worth while for the banks to encourage it. Banks could make only double interest by loaning bank notes; if they persuaded a customer to take his loan in the form of a checking account, the interest profit might be increased several times. Legal reserve requirements (net) against deposits varied from 6 to 25 per cent. By the turn of the century, between 80 and 90 per cent of all business, measured in dollars, was consummated by check payments. Demand deposits were by far the most important "money," although most people overlooked the fact that their checking accounts were money.

During the War between the States, the North faced a choice among the usual three methods of financing war. Believing that the insurrection would be put down shortly, the government at first called out a mere 75,000 troops for three months only and did little to increase taxes. The government exhausted its credit at the banks quite early and issued some $50 million of Treasury bills somewhat similar to the colonial bills of credit. Meanwhile the Union forces were defeated at the First Battle of Bull Run and elsewhere. By the end of 1861 the banks had to suspend specie payments, and they remained suspended for seventeen years. A penniless Treasury soon had to issue a new paper money, greenbacks. A total of $431 million was out at the peak of circulation. At first the war was paid for by paper money, although eventually it was financed chiefly by borrowing and secondarily by taxes, which became more burdensome from 1863 on.

One of the questions of the day was whether Congress was permitted by the Constitution to issue legal-tender paper money. Up to this time that had been regarded as forbidden. The pressure of necessity led the Supreme Court to hand down a series of favorable decisions the chief of which was *Juilliard v. Greenman* (1884). Henceforth, legal-tender paper money was constitutional.

A second question was how soon the country would resume specie payments. Prices in greenbacks were higher than prices quoted in gold. For example, in 1864 it took over two greenbacks to buy a gold dollar; in 1865, 1.6; in 1869, 1.3; in 1875, 1.15; and finally at the end of 1878 the premium disappeared. All this did not happen easily, however. Prices in greenbacks had almost doubled during the War between the States, and for a paper dollar and a gold dollar to be interchangeable, prices had to be reduced. The reduction came about chiefly because production increased more rapidly than the money supply. Falling prices are economically painful to the farmer and the debtor. Despite strenuous objections by farm groups and others, resumption of specie payments was scheduled for January 2, 1879, and it took place according to plan. Thereafter, greenbacks were redeemable dollar for dollar in gold coin.

After the War between the States prices declined until 1896. Wholesale prices fell from 132 in 1865 to 46.5 in 1896, and retail prices fell from 191 to 69—a decline of two-thirds in both cases.[3] To ease the pain of falling prices, farmers and others agitated, after the 1870s, for free coinage of silver. Silver was now cheaper than it had been, owing to new discoveries, improved mining methods, and declining demand for it on the part of European nations. To put this country on a bimetallic standard, as the agrarians were demanding, would have relieved the farmers' distress. Although they deserved relief, it might have set off another period of rising prices, and people had too recently experienced inflation during the war to want to see inflation happen again. The controversy was not settled until the election of 1896, in which the advocates of bimetallism, led by William Jennings Bryan, were defeated. Then, in 1897, prices started to rise, thus eliminating the chief reason for bimetallism.

In 1900 Congress specifically declared the nation to be on the gold standard and took steps to ensure its staying on should another emergency threaten, as had happened in 1893. Businessmen had for some time protected themselves against departure from the gold standard by writing into contracts what was known as the gold clause. This clause stated that the debt would be repaid in gold dollars of the same weight and fineness as those loaned. The nation was off the gold standard for over two years, 1917 to 1919, during and just after World War I, but the gold standard and gold clauses were not an issue again until 1933–1934.

From 1922 to 1929 the country was prosperous, indeed business was booming, and speculation in securities caused the price level of common

[3] U.S. Department of Commerce, *Historical Statistics of the United States, 1789–1945*, pp. 233–236.

stocks to double in four years and many of them rose tenfold or more. When the boom collapsed in October, 1929, a depression began which reached its low point in 1932–1933, by which time the level of common stocks was about a quarter of what it had been in 1929.[4] The general price level dropped about 25 per cent, and there were an estimated 12 million persons unemployed. Economic distress was world-wide. Nation after nation devalued its currency and abandoned the gold standard.

The Franklin Roosevelt administration, elected in 1932, took office in the midst of a nationwide banking crisis and soon afterward abandoned the gold standard. In the hope of raising prices to the level prevailing in the supposedly normal year 1926, Congress devalued the dollar 41 per cent in January, 1934, at which time we returned part way to the gold standard. The purpose of devaluation was to raise prices by 69 per cent and thus relieve the distress of the farmers and debtors. A gold dollar now contained 13.71 grains of pure gold instead of 23.22 grains, as it had previously. Out of each old gold dollar 1.69 new ones could be made ($23.22 \div 13.71 = 1.69$). But this tinkering with the dollar had little immediate effect on the price level. By 1940 retail prices had gone up only 8 per cent.

The Federal government was now controlling the money supply, the monetary standard, and the price level more than it had ever done before. The new monetary standard did not permit the citizen to have gold coin. Coining gold was no longer like milling flour. If the size of the dollar might have to be reduced, it was to the interest of the government to hold on to all gold coins so that it, and not some fortunate citizens, would reap the profit. The Supreme Court, with some reluctance, said that the gold clauses, which had been devised for occasions just like this, were unenforceable. The government's economists argued that a panicky, or at least unreasoning, people should not be permitted to draw out gold reserves, thereby making it more difficult for banks to make loans and thus accentuating depressions, as had been done several times in the past, most notably in 1933. Abandoning the practice of making all dollars redeemable in gold may have protected the government from the people, but it henceforth put the people at the mercy of their government. No longer could the citizen who feared inflation protect himself and at the same time bring pressure on his government to straighten out its finances by demanding gold coin. Specie payments were suspended somewhat as in the days of the War between the States.[5] The price level doubled in the next twenty years, partly as a result of devaluation in 1934, partly as a result of World War II, and partly as a result of unhampered peacetime

---

[4] *Ibid.*, p. 281.

[5] Foreign treasuries and central banks can still demand gold from our government. That was not the case in the period of the War between the States.

deficit financing. At this writing the government has balanced its budget only three times in twenty-five years.

CAPITAL GROWTH

Business capital may be classified in many ways, but grouping it into long-term capital and working capital is the most useful classification for understanding its function. Investment in plant and equipment is long-term capital; investment in inventory, fuel, wage outlays, and credit extension to customers is working capital. As the Industrial Revolution, with its expensive mechanization, has progressed, long-term capital has grown in importance. Let us look at the institutions which have helped provide these capital funds. Many of them are banks of various kinds.

We should first understand, however, that the businesses themselves provided the bulk of their own capital. For example, during his lifetime Samuel Slater (1768–1835), who began with an expert knowledge of textile machinery but no physical assets, built up a fortune of some $690,000 by plowing back most of his earnings and acquiring shares in new textile plants. The capital of literally thousands of businesses, small, medium, and large, in manufacturing, commerce, and agriculture, has been built up in this way since America was first settled. During the nineteenth century the rule of thumb of many companies, when it came time to distribute profits, was "a dollar for dividends and a dollar for improvements." It still is essentially that. The classic example of the company that grew and grew by ploughing back its earnings is the Ford Motor Company. It was established in 1903 with a capitalization of $100,000, about $28,000 of it in cash and the rest in plant and equipment. By 1923 its worth was estimated at $1 billion. In other words, a share worth $100 in 1903 would have been valued at $1 million twenty years later.

Capital was still a scarce factor of production a century and a half ago. Census estimates place capital invested in manufactures at $50 million in 1820 and at $1 billion in 1860.[6] The capital per manufacturing worker increased from $550 in 1850 to $11,000, a century later.[7] And in 1850, according to the Twentieth Century Fund, 94 per cent of the goods manufactured per hour were manufactured by the power of humans and horses and only 6 per cent by machines, but by 1940 machines provided about 92 per cent of the power.[8] These improvements required

[6] Victor Clark, *History of Manufactures in the United States, 1607–1680* (New York: McGraw-Hill Book Company, Inc., 1929), vol. I, p. 369.
[7] E. A. J. Johnson and H. Krooss, *The Origins and Development of the American Economy* (New York: Prentice-Hall, Inc., 1953), p. 174.
[8] J. F. Dewhurst, *America's Needs and Resources* (New York: The Twentieth Century Fund, 1947), p. 682 and appendix 32.

heavy investments of capital. To provide this capital the American people and their business firms have saved and invested from their incomes about 20 per cent a year since 1869, except in the depressed 1930s.[9]

Corporations. Since most people spend almost all that they earn and many spend more than they earn, much of the saving for investment had to be done by the wealthy and by corporations. The business corporation was a development of the nineteenth century. Its characteristics of divisible shares, unlimited life, and legal entity made it more flexible than the partnership. Limited liability guaranteed investors against loss beyond what they had invested and so attracted capital. By 1939 half of all manufacturing concerns were incorporated and did over 90 per cent of the business. For investment to be profitable, it must be used; output must be maintained at or near capacity. This requirement means that markets must be steadily expanded, especially in industries producing durable goods. These circumstances generated keen competition, caused failures, and also led to many consolidations and even to monopolies. For example, there have been over 1,500 automobile concerns in the past half century; only 6 remain. Without the corporate device capital could not have been so readily mobilized.

Investment Banks. The investment-banking houses which sold the securities of these corporations were frequently disturbed by all this competition and by the loss of profits and the failures it engendered. After all, if the New York Central Railroad built a line parallel to the main line of the Pennsylvania, and the Pennsylvania retaliated by acquiring one parallel to the main line of the New York Central, it was clear that, whoever won this war, the stockholders of one or both companies would suffer reductions in dividends and perhaps worse. This was bound to reflect on the investment house that had sold the securities here and abroad, perhaps with glowing promises of high earnings. And so, when just this situation arose in 1885, J. P. Morgan called the presidents of the two railroads together on his yacht, *Corsair,* and persuaded them to end their war.[10] This sort of thing happened repeatedly during the career of the elder Morgan.

Sometimes Morgan effected a peaceful settlement; sometimes he promoted the formation of a giant holding company, as in the case of United States Steel in 1901, the nation's first billion-dollar corporation; and sometimes he bought out rising companies or persuaded them to limit the scene of their operations. Morgan and his associates spoke much of the "community of interest." What they meant was that companies in the

[9] Simon Kuznets, *National Product Since 1869* (New York: The National Bureau of Economic Research, 1946), p. 119. This is a gross figure and includes construction.

[10] F. L. Allen, *The Great Pierpont Morgan* (New York: Harper & Brothers, 1949), pp. 47–53.

same field had a common interest in keeping peace, for there was enough business for all if some did not become too greedy. Morgan encouraged informal understandings and even formal monopolies. Because of his power to provide or withhold investment funds and his influence over commercial bankers, investment bankers, and many large companies, he and his associates were finally accused of controlling a "money trust." In a congressional investigation in 1911–1912 Morgan stoutly denied his power, but the investigating committee reported that there actually was such a trust.[11] Little was done, however, to curb the power of Morgan and his associates at this time. Then Morgan died in 1913, and World War I soon diverted the public's attention.

In the 1920s commercial banks like the Chase National and National City conducted an investment-banking business on a large scale. The once-powerful firm of J. P. Morgan and Company did less than 15 per cent of the investment-banking business in 1929.

Many of these newer houses became more interested in the quantity of issues they sold than in their quality. Salesmen were encouraged to sell bonds and stocks much as they might a gadget being vended from door to door. Even worse, some houses speculated in certain securities, and banks used their investment affiliates to dispose of issues which they did not want to keep.[12] The panic of 1929, a nationwide epidemic of bank failures, and congressional investigations revealed these practices.

Reform bills were enacted to prevent the recurrence of dubious practices. The Banking Act of 1933 forbade commercial banks to have affiliates that sold securities. The Securities Act of 1933 and the Securities Exchange Act of 1934 set up a Federal commission to watch over the activities of investment banks and stock exchanges. In marketing securities, investment bankers were now obliged to supply a prospectus with full information about each company whose issues they were handling. If an issue eventually proved bad and a buyer could show that essential information had been omitted from the prospectus, which might have deterred him from buying the security, he might sue the investment house. The ancient rule had been changed from "Let the buyer beware" to "Let the seller beware." The memory of the 1929 panic, the low interest rates prevailing since, and the costs and risks of marketing securities, have all hurt the investment-banking business in recent years.

Commercial Banks and Long-term Loans. Commercial banks are supposed to limit themselves largely to short-term loans because they must pay most of their depositors on demand. Walter Bagehot once remarked that the first thing a banker should learn is the difference between a

[11] Pujo Subcommittee on Money Trust Investigation, *Report of the Committee,* p. 129.
[12] F. Pecora, *Wall Street under Oath* (New York: Simon and Schuster, Inc., 1939), pp. 93–95.

promissory note and a mortgage, for his business should be only with the former. Yet from the beginning, under pressure from the government and from the people of the community, commercial banks have made many long-term loans. Also, when not enough short-term loans have been available to use the deposits in a bank, bankers have been tempted to make longer-term loans, and they have usually yielded. Besides, many apparently short-term loans have actually been long-term ones because they were regularly renewed.

The nation's first bank, the Bank of North America, was set up in 1781 to make loans to our Revolutionary government. During the period before the War between the States, long-term loans on real estate were common to the point of abuses; because of the land speculation they encouraged, they led to panics in 1819 and 1837. When the National Banking System was set up, one of its reform provisions was that national banks might not lend on real estate collateral. State banks, being under no such limitations, continued to lend on real estate, however. Since the founding of the Federal Reserve System in 1913, this prohibition on national banks has been moderated. After the War between the States, bank investments in government bonds and other forms of long-term indebtedness amounted to about half of all the loans and discounts of banks, and since 1935 investments have exceeded loans.

When investments were increasing during the 1920s, banks were criticized for becoming less "liquid," that is, they were less able to pay their depositors in cash on short notice. They excused themselves by saying that the securities were "shiftable" and could be liquidated easily on the securities markets. This illusion lasted until late in 1929 when nearly everyone tried to shift or liquidate at once, and few could do so except at a heavy loss. The Banking Act of 1935 instructed the Federal Reserve System to watch the quality of bank loans and keep a watchful eye for speculation. Since World War II big banks in large cities have made many so-called "term" loans to their corporate customers. These run for as long as five or more years but are generally repayable on an installment basis.

The decline of the House of Morgan and the impact of the Great Depression reduced the long-term investment business, but not as much as it appeared to. What banks and investment houses were reluctant to touch, the government now often financed. This was in keeping with the new economic philosophy that investment was the key to prosperity. Many government agencies have been created since 1932 to finance or guarantee loans that private institutions were reluctant to touch. Perhaps the outstanding one is the Reconstruction Finance Corporation (RFC), originally founded in 1932 to save some big banks, railroads, and insurance companies in need of cash. An energetic Texas businessman, Jesse

Jones, was put in charge of it and soon was lending tens and hundreds of millions of dollars. Because of the vast sums he controlled, this important government official was known as the J. P. Morgan of the 1930s. The RFC had made loans totaling close to $50 billion by 1945 and had made a profit for the government in doing so.

Working Capital. Working capital, made up generally of short-term funds, has come from somewhat the same sources as long-term capital; namely, a business's own resources, the companies it buys from, commercial banks, agricultural banks, and the short-term securities markets.

At first a business had to provide its own working capital or rely on those from whom it bought or perhaps to whom it sold. In colonial times customers who had charge accounts generally paid only once a year. This practice would have tied up the merchant's or manufacturer's capital rather tightly except that he often bought his goods on equally long terms. Generally the credit trail led back to England. English buyers customarily paid American sellers promptly. Thus before there were commercial banks, the supplier served as a banker. But it is primarily with commercial banks that we shall deal here.

BANKING

There were no commercial banks until near the end of the Revolutionary War when Robert Morris set up the Bank of North America in Philadelphia (1781). Soon Boston, New York, and Baltimore had to have banks too. In 1791 the First Bank of the United States was founded through the efforts of Secretary of the Treasury Alexander Hamilton. In 1811, when the First Bank lost its twenty-year charter, there were 88 commercial banks. The attitudes of some of these banks may have had considerable influence in the defeat in Congress of the bill to recharter the First Bank.

The bankers had their reasons for opposing the First Bank. A commercial bank not only accepts money on deposit for safekeeping and loans money; it also creates and loans its own credit. This last needs clarification. Few individuals would be able to circulate their own IOUs for money, but banks were once able to do so. The IOUs that passed as money were known as bank notes. A bank note is the bank's promise to pay on demand in the coin of the country, usually specie. Nowadays only the Federal Reserve Banks have the power to issue bank notes. Commercial banks, however, still create their own credit in another way and loan it. The present way is for a bank to write so much on its books to the borrower's account and let him draw checks against it. The bank owes the customer all his deposits and must pay him when he asks for them. But in the beginning banks loaned mostly with bank notes.

A very early question was how many bank notes was it safe for a bank to create and loan—two, three, five, ten, twenty times its cash reserve? Bankers had to experiment to find out. If the banker loaned too little, he was not making the most of his opportunities. Also, his customers were probably critical of him for not helping them build up their businesses and develop the community. If he loaned generously, he earned lots of interest and made handsome profits and was regarded, for a while at least, as a benefactor of his community. It was easier to follow this second course of action. But bankers also found that it was easier to loan than to collect. If banks tried to force collection, they were soon looked upon as harsh and unreasonable. Then the bankers needed someone to blame.

For half a century the First Bank of the United States and later the Second Bank of the United States took the blame. By charter these huge banks were fiscal agents of the Treasury, which meant that they received Federal money and paid it out. Bank notes which they received for the government account or any other account were only other banks' IOUs. The responsible thing for the First Bank to do was to present them for redemption. The First Bank did that for much the same reason that you should promptly cash a check. But in presenting these notes, the First Bank was drawing out other banks' reserves and sharply reducing the amount of loans that it was safe for those banks to make. That reduced their income, made them stricter about collecting loans that had run for some time, and antagonized their customers. The bankers put the blame on the First Bank, which was already suspected of being unconstitutional, was feared for its great size, and was envied for its special privileges. Yet the unpopular First Bank was performing the very valuable service of limiting the supply of bank notes and preventing speculative booms and inflation.

When the First Bank lost its charter, the number of commercial banks quickly increased from 88 in 1811 to 246 in 1816, and their note circulation quadrupled in five years. The banks were loaning too freely. Prices rose. After 1814 banks had to suspend specie payments, except in New England. Although the suspension was partly attributable to the War of 1812, a more important cause was the absence of the First Bank, which would have served as a policeman. People soon realized that, and in 1816 Congress established the Second Bank of the United States. It was poorly run in its early years and got into political difficulties in its later years, so that it too was not rechartered.

Next there grew up a patchwork of substitutes for the Second Bank. New England had its Suffolk Banking System, with the Suffolk Bank serving as a regional First or Second Bank. After 1846 the Federal government set up the Independent Treasury System and required all money paid to it and by it to be in specie. Certain states, such as New York,

Louisiana, Ohio, and Indiana, had good banking systems. In many parts of the country, however, the banks were loosely run, and their notes circulated at a discount. Something had to be done to correct the situation, and in 1863 the National Banking System was founded to do it.

The National Banking System. The new National Banking System gave the country as a whole an immeasurably better banking system than it had had previously. The minimum capitalization for a national bank was set at $50,000 in towns of not over 6,000 population, and more for larger places. Half of this had to be paid in immediately and the other half within six months. The stockholders were subject to double liability. Branches were virtually forbidden. The bank might not make an unsecured loan of more than 10 per cent of its capital and surplus. Loans against real estate collateral were forbidden. Bank notes were backed more than 100 per cent by government bonds. All national banks had to redeem national bank notes at par. The law corrected many of the worst abuses of the previous eighty years.

The new system soon developed serious faults. The supply of bank notes did not increase or decrease with the needs of business. Instead, the supply depended on the amount of government bonds the national banks held, and this, in turn, depended often on factors other than business needs. The supply of bank notes sometimes fell off when it should have increased, and vice versa.

A second fault was that the national banks put some of their deposits and part of their reserves in the big New York City banks, which loaned them to brokers to finance stock-market speculations. If anything went wrong in this sensitive market, or if the banks in the interior needed their funds quickly, it might precipitate a stock-market panic and a series of bank runs. This happened on four occasions—in 1873, 1884, 1893, and 1907.

A third fault was that when there was a run on the national banks there was no central bank to whom they could turn for assistance. The National Banking System lacked a head: it was a system without a central bank.

Establishment of the Federal Reserve System. In the panic of 1907, which was felt most in New York City, the bankers had turned to J. P. Morgan for aid. Funds were raised to assist as many distressed banks and brokerage houses as possible, and Morgan was given the final say concerning who was to receive assistance. He was, so to speak, a one-man Reconstruction Finance Corporation and central bank. He kept the panic from getting worse, but in doing so he demonstrated his great financial power for all to see.

Congress took steps to prevent, if possible, another such panic. Machinery was set up, under the Aldrich-Vreeland Act of 1908, for creating additional cash if another emergency should arise. The National Monetary Commission was established to study the central banks of other nations and recommend a suitable kind for us. The most dominant person on this commission was Senator Nelson Aldrich. He personified conservatism in his day. Aldrich prepared a plan similar to the subsequent Federal Reserve System, except that the control of the single central bank was vested in directors chosen directly or indirectly by the big New York banks. Since these banks were under the influence of Morgan, whose "money trust" was to be investigated in 1912, Aldrich's plan was severely criticized.

When the Democrats won the Presidential election of 1912, Aldrich's plan was revised. Now there were to be 12 regional banks, called Federal Reserve Banks. The Federal Reserve Board, at the top of the System, was to be appointed by the President of the United States. The Federal Reserve System was a system of bankers' banks superimposed upon the National Banking System. All national banks had to join; other banks might if they met certain requirements. After 1917 member banks kept all their legal reserves in the regional Federal Reserve Bank. The Federal Reserve Banks issued their own bank notes, which were backed by gold and by customers' promissory notes and drafts. Within limits, the supply of money now rose and fell with the needs of business. Member banks might borrow from Federal Reserve Banks. The Federal Reserve influenced the quantity of credit available and tried to prevent booms and to ease depressions by its rediscount-rate policies, and later by other credit control devices. The new system was a great improvement over the old.

Booms and Depressions in the 1920s. The Federal Reserve System was extremely helpful in financing World War I but was not successful in controlling the large postwar booms. To control a speculative boom, the System should set the banks an example of high interest rates. But to oblige the Treasury in 1919, it kept its interest rates low. That encouraged borrowing and fed the first boom. The boom collapsed in June, 1920, and a short but serious depression ensued in which the wholesale-price level fell 40 per cent within a year.

In 1922 the Federal Reserve authorities, almost by accident, discovered a device that would enable the System to control booms and ease depressions much more effectively. This was the "open-market operation" by which the Federal Reserve is able indirectly to increase or decrease member-bank reserves and thus encourage or discourage their loaning. For the next few years the Federal Reserve authorities were under the happy illusion that they had a device which would end the possibility of another depression. It worked quite well in small recessions, but it was applied too late to stop the boom of 1927–1929.

Credit control devices are like the brakes on a car starting down a long hill. If applied gently, before there is much momentum, they will stop the car, but if not applied until there is great momentum, they may do little good. In 1928 almost no one could foresee a panic and great depression. Anyway, few persons in positions of authority wanted to take the responsibility for spoiling the existing prosperity and being thoroughly disliked for their trouble.

After the depression was well under way, and several thousand banks had failed, the Federal Reserve was of course criticized for not having prevented it. There were many congressional investigations of the stock market, foreign securities, and so forth, and various reform measures were proposed and enacted. The Securities and Exchange Commission, mentioned earlier, was set up. The Federal Reserve Board was given greater powers over bank personnel and was granted authority to raise reserve requirements to as much as double what they had been. National banks lost the power to issue bank notes (1935). The Federal Deposit Insurance Corporation (FDIC) was founded to guarantee bank deposits and restore the people's faith in banks. Most banks joined the FDIC, which insured the deposits of every depositor up to $5,000 (now $10,000).

NEW FISCAL POLICIES

More important than the specific reforms enacted was the new philosophy of government which came into vogue. The administration virtually resolved that it would not permit another great depression if it could possibly be avoided. To prevent a depression one must have a theory about the cause. The most widely accepted theory was that of an English economist, John Maynard Keynes, and of his various followers. They said that continued expansion of private investment was the key to prosperity, but that this investment had fallen off in the United States because the country now had a "mature economy" and was no longer growing. To restore prosperity, government must invest when and where private individuals no longer dared to do so. To provide the needed funds, the government itself might have to operate at a deficit. Restoration of prosperity also required the cooperation of the Federal Reserve System in keeping interest rates low to encourage private investment and in helping the government manage its growing public debt. Although the Federal Reserve cooperated, another depression occurred in 1937–1938, and as late as January, 1940, there were still over 10 million persons unemployed. Not until World War II did the nation pull out of this economic slough.

The Federal Reserve became even more the creature of the administration during World War II and after. The dependence was traceable to the theory that interest rates must be kept low to keep down the cost of the war. The administration also ordered that the prices of government securities must be kept at par or above so as not to frighten the investor in government securities. This also called for low interest rates. The results of that policy were disastrous. In order to keep security prices up, the Federal Reserve had to buy securities at par when no one else would. This had the effect of increasing commercial-bank reserves, which in turn caused banks to lend generously. Low interest rates were already stimulating others to borrow. The results were a tripling of demand deposits between 1939 and 1952 and a 90 per cent rise in the cost of living.

It might be asked why the government permitted inflation to continue. On the one hand, the causes were so involved and the inflation so gradual that the public did not protest vigorously. On the other hand, the Treasury wanted to keep down the cost of servicing the debt. Those fearful of a new depression insisted on low interest rates. Also, banks and other institutions feared that if the Federal Reserve no longer supported the government-securities market, their bond holdings—close to half of the banks' earning assets—would drop sharply in value and threaten them with insolvency.

It is just as difficult politically to let interest rates and government securities find their natural level in the market as it is to take away tariffs from a protected industry, or subsidies from farmers, or rent controls from tenants. Yet as long as low interest rates and supported securities prices continued, the Federal Reserve was unable to stave off a speculative boom, and prices continued to rise. In March, 1951, the Federal Reserve stopped supporting government securities, at least regularly. Since then it has been trying, with moderate success, to regain its former powers. In a democracy it is easier to grant a subsidy than it is to withdraw it.

SIGNIFICANCE OF THE CHANGE

Over the past 150 to 200 years the United States has accumulated a vast amount of capital. Our reliance on machines to do almost everything in the factory, field, office, and home is one of the things that impresses foreigners. There has been a significant and continuous change in the relation of the economic factors of production—land, labor, and capital. Where once capital was perhaps the scarcest of the three, now it has become the most plentiful. A generation ago people of wealth had spacious homes, large estates, and many servants. Today the trend is toward smaller homes and toward mechanization such as the thermostat to tend the furnace, the electric dishwasher, the electric washing machine and the dryer, the home freezer, the vacuum cleaner, and the power lawn mower. It is simply too hard to get and to keep the personnel to maintain a large establishment. Labor is almost fully employed, and the cost of labor is high. Interest rates, which reflect the price of the use of capital, are lower in this country than anywhere else in the world. If capital continues to increase, the nation's standard of living should continue to rise as we add more mechanical servants to our retinues.

Prosperity, and with it a high standard of living, depends on continued savings, wise investment, and capital growth. Both the Keynesian and the classical economists agree on that. And as long as the memory of the Great Depression of the 1930s lingers, it is probable that the Washington administration, whether Democratic or Republican, will see to it that any lag in private investment which might lead to a depression (and political defeat) is supplemented by generous expenditures for public works. As long as Russia threatens, large military expenditures should suffice.

QUESTIONS FOR STUDY

1. Why was there a shortage of gold and silver money in early America? What did the colonists use as money in its place? What was the attitude towards paper money by the time the Constitution was adopted?

2. What was the bimetallic standard? The gold standard? When did we have these standards? Why did we prize them? Why did we sometimes abandon them, as in 1861 and 1933?

3. What are the three basic ways of financing a modern war? Which way is economically the soundest? Why is that way not the only way used? Why do we use the least sound way at all?

4. How has American business obtained the bulk of the long-term capital that it has used? What is the function of corporations in providing capital? Of investment banks? What harmful policies have investment banks sometimes been guilty of?

5. What is a commercial bank? Why should commercial banks concentrate on short-term loans? Why have they not always done so? What have been the consequences?

6. What is a central bank? What useful central-bank service did the First Bank of the United States perform? Was the National Banking System a central-bank system? The Federal Reserve System? How successful has the Federal Reserve System been?

7. What did J. M. Keynes and his followers think was the matter with the American economy in the 1930s? What was their solution? What was the great danger in Federal Reserve support of the price of government bonds after World War II? When did this policy stop?

CHAPTER 6

LABOR

The nation's total labor supply is not much less than its total population. True, infants, young children, invalids, the aged, and a few very wealthy persons do not work, but out of a population of over 165 million only about a sixth fall into those categories. A third of the total population are wage earners, another third keep house, and the remainder are employers, farmers, professional men, and students. The combined efforts of most of these 165 million people contribute to the material and intellectual advancement of the nation. Compare this situation with that of three centuries ago, when a few tens of thousands of settlers, scattered along the fringes of the eastern seaboard, used primitive tools and methods to make a living from the resources of the New World. It was two centuries before they effected very noticeable changes. Changes became evident as the population became larger, more diffused over the continent, more concentrated at key points, and more mature in years.

For over 250 years before 1900 the population doubled approximately every twenty-five years. Since then population growth has slowed, except in the Far West, so that it required some fifty years for the 75 million of 1900 to double to 150 million.

The people also spread out over the continent; by 1850 the population center was near Parkersburg, West Virginia (just Virginia then), by 1900 it had moved to Indiana, and by 1950 to Illinois. Even now almost half of the people are crowded into the fertile farming land and the industrial centers north of the Ohio River and the Mason-Dixon line and east of the Mississippi River, which is only about a seventh of the area of the country.

People were also moving from the country into the towns and cities. In 1790 there were only a dozen towns with 5,000 people or more, whereas by 1950 there were almost 2,500, and 60 per cent of the people lived in towns or cities. City workers tend to be specialized, often to the point of being only semiskilled or even unskilled, but they are very productive. And the cities are focal points for producing, assembling, and marketing goods. Some cities are famous for only one or a few products,

84

such as Bethlehem for steel and Akron for rubber, and draw to themselves workers with skills in those lines.

The United States has been a new country in the youth of its population as well as in recency of settlement. The heavy beards worn by many of our nineteenth-century ancestors deceive us into thinking they were older than they were. Indeed many never became old at all. The average life expectancy at birth in 1799 was thirty-five, compared with almost twice that age today. The average white person in the United States was only sixteen in 1800, compared with twenty in 1860 and thirty today. In 1800 only a tenth of the white population were over forty-five, whereas today almost a tenth are over sixty-five. Before the War between the States many a woman was haggard from overwork and the bearing of many children and near the end of her life span by the age of forty. Today we say that "life begins at forty."

CHANGED OUTLOOK OF WORKERS

A century and a half ago most free men, perhaps 80 per cent of them, were self-employed. The vast majority were small farmers. The hired man or employee was the exception. Most young men expected to own their own farms or small businesses soon after they grew up. Nowadays the situation is quite different. Approximately two out of every three men from fourteen to sixty-four are employed by someone else. This change has had profound consequences. A majority of men now look on the business of making a living from an employee's viewpoint rather than from an employer's viewpoint. This observation is not intended to deprecate either viewpoint.

The employer is interested primarily in getting the most for his money; he wants his employee to work as long and to produce as much as possible at the least cost. The employee, on the other hand, wants to be well paid for a minimum amount of work during a short workday under pleasant working conditions. In addition, he would like financial safeguards against such security hazards as accidents, unemployment, and old age. In a democracy in which employers or self-employed people outnumber employees, the employer attitude is more likely to prevail, and in a democracy in which employees are more numerous, the opposite is true. The employees look to their unions or to the government to protect them from their employers.

The employee attitude is likely to become more pronounced as the Industrial Revolution progresses because, as factories become larger, production is broken up into more operations. There are some 300 steps in making shoes today. Operations that once required a skilled craftsman can now be done by several semiskilled or unskilled operatives, many of them using machines to perform their tasks. A few years ago I watched a young woman working at the end of an assembly line in a soap-flakes factory. Her sole responsibility was to drop the guarantee slip in the open box, after which a machine automatically sealed the box. Eight hours a day she labored at this monotonous job. How much pride was she likely to take in the finished product? How could she estimate the value of her services to the company? What, in all probability, was her chief concern as she did this work? Admittedly, this is an extreme case of a worker specialized to the point of no skill. A machine would soon take over her job. Is it any wonder that these human automatons have little interest in the quality of their work, the welfare of the company, or the virtues of free enterprise, and think chiefly of their pay check? The wonder is that companies keep them as interested as they do. What loyalty they have is more often directed to their union. One-quarter of the 63 million employed are today organized into unions, chiefly under the American Federation of Labor and Congress of Industrial Organizations.

RISE OF UNIONS

From the point of view of capital, the Industrial Revolution meant the coming of factories; from the point of view of labor, it meant the growing importance of unions. As capital formed into larger units and capitalists hired more men, the men, to increase wages and improve working conditions, had to combine into groups in self-defense and choose a spokesman to represent them.

Unions appeared in the latter stages of the evolution toward the factory. The first unions were of journeymen (skilled workers hired by the day) in such occupations as cobbling, printing, carpentry, baking, hat making, and the like.

The developments in shoemaking demonstrated why unions appeared at this juncture. In Massachusetts shoemaking had reached the domestic stage by the early nineteenth century. That means that the shoemakers and their journeymen were making shoes for sale to merchant capitalists who bought them to sell in city markets or even in California or the West Indies. When the merchant capitalists competed in city markets, they used price cutting as the chief device to make a sale. This was before the days of brands, and it was early in the history of advertising. A cut in price, when the chief cost item was labor, had to be offset by some cut in the cost of labor. There were at first two possibilities. The capitalist could pay the master shoemaker less per pair of shoes, and the shoemaker, in turn, would have to cut the pay of his journeymen. The alternative was for the shoemaker to hire more apprentices, to whom he had to pay little or no wages. Both these solutions were opposed by journeymen because sooner or later they would lower journeymen's income and living standards. They organized temporarily, and from the start their chief weapon of protest was the strike. Yet the men were still close enough to their employers that they could say, as one group did in 1835, "We would not be too severe on our employers; they are slaves to the capitalists as we are to them."[1]

The first continuous organization of wage earners was the union of Philadelphia shoemakers, established in 1792. By 1901 a million persons were members of unions, about 1 out of every 27 employed. Today there are 16 million union members, or about 1 out of every 4 employed.

Let us examine four major stages in the growth of unions to their present position.

Pre-Civil War Unions. Before the War between the States unions were few and largely confined to crafts. The organizations were local; that is, there was little effort to correlate the aims and activities of unions in different cities. That was partly because it was not yet important—markets were still largely local—and partly because unions were considered illegal. They were sometimes attacked as conspiracies to raise established wage rates or as combinations in restraint of trade. For this reason unions often disbanded after accomplishing their immediate goals. Not until 1842 did a state court, in Massachusetts, uphold the legality of a union. And even those unions that did endeavor to maintain a continuous organization were unable to survive such depressions as that of 1837. The cause of the laboring man was, however, promoted by two other groups.

The first political labor organizations were local. The best-known one, the Mechanics Union of Trade Associations, began in Philadelphia in 1827. It was not until the 1820s that the laboring classes gained the right to vote—property qualifications had excluded them—and they soon announced several political goals. Among these were free public schools, abolition of imprisonment for debt, democratization of compulsory militia laws, the ten-hour day, and the passage of mechanics' liens laws. A mechanic's lien law gave the laborer first claim on any article he was making in case his employer went bankrupt and could not pay him. Some of the local leaders also expounded the doctrine that it is the laborer who gives value to goods, thus implying that other people were parasites. These local labor parties never became national and could point to little in the way of definite accomplishment, although many reforms that they agitated for were eventually obtained.

Intellectuals also espoused the cause of the laboring man, especially in the decade of the 1840s, sometimes called the "hot-air" period of Amer-

[1] S. Perlman, *History of Trade Unionism in the United States* (New York: The Macmillan Company, 1929), p. 23.

ican labor. For example, Albert Brisbane popularized Fourier's phalanxes. This was a plan to increase worker efficiency by making the work more interesting (through job rotation) and more rewarding (through profit sharing). The Brook Farm experiment is the most famous example of this idea. Essentially, it was a plan to turn back the clock by eliminating the wage system; yet at the same time it was a device to keep the obvious advantages of new large-scale production. Another intellectual plan was agrarianism, whose aim was to give every man a chance to have a farm of his own and thus raise the wage level. The advocates of this plan helped to gain the Homestead Act of 1862 but were otherwise unsuccessful. A third plan was represented by the communistic settlement of the English manufacturer-reformer, Robert Owen, and his son, Robert Dale Owen, but this, too, broke down. A fourth plan was embodied in cooperative producing organizations, some of which were successful. On the whole, the workingman paid less heed to his intellectual well-wishers than they did to him.

Up to the time of the War between the States, then, unions were still few, local, and short-lived, but they had attracted attention to their causes and gained some acceptance in the new industrial world.

The Knights of Labor. The War between the States, like any modern war, brought tremendous orders at generous prices for standardized products—shoes, uniforms, processed foods, weapons, ammunition, and so forth. This is precisely the condition that encourages the growth of the factory system. Operations may be broken down into simple, easily learned steps, unskilled laborers can be hired at lower wages, and machines may be devised to perform some of the operations. Industrial progress continued to be great after the War between the States. This trend led to attempts to organize unskilled workers. The attempts were unsuccessful for a number of reasons, although the effort advanced the cause of labor.

It was in 1869 that Uriah Stephens, a Philadelphia garment worker, founded the Knights of Labor as a secret organization. The new union grew slowly, but it survived the long depression of 1873–1878 and eventually had a membership in 1886, at its peak, of 700,000. Membership was on a broad base: it included employers and employees, skilled and unskilled workers, men and women—all might join. Only such alleged social parasites or undesirables as bartenders, bankers, and stockbrokers were excluded. The union was organized on a geographical rather than on a craft basis. Locals were made up of a dozen or so members, sometimes of the same craft, sometimes of different crafts. Locals were then joined into district assemblies, in which crafts were mixed. At the top was the General Assembly. When it was not in session, power resided in an executive committee presided over by the Grand Master. After 1878 the Grand Master was Terence Powderly, who was famous for the great power he wielded over labor. He was not always careful or wise in exercising this power. Locals had very little autonomy in the Knights of Labor.

The Knights hoped to better the condition of workingmen in many ways. Their most basic and least-understood aim was to do away with the wage system. Wages are so much a part of our present-day economy that it is hard to conceive of a union seriously advocating the abolition of the wage system. Yet the Knights did advocate that, just as Brisbane had in the 1840s. They were closer to an age in which most men worked for themselves, not for others, and they yearned for the independence and dignity of a system in which employer and employee were more nearly equal. To achieve this aim, the Knights proposed to set up producers' cooperatives. The funds to establish them were to come from union dues.

The Knights of Labor collapsed rapidly in the later 1880s for a number of reasons, but only three of them need concern us. (1) The cooperatives established by the Knights were not successful, for they lacked the capital and the managerial talent to compete with private business. Workers disliked seeing their hard-earned dues wasted on these unsuccessful projects. (2) The efforts of the Knights to aid unskilled labor broke down. When strikes were successful, the skilled workers felt, and rightly so, that their participation had been largely responsible, and they disliked sharing the gains with the unskilled workers. And when strikes failed, the skilled were inclined to blame the unskilled for the waste of time and loss of pay. The skilled workers gradually began to drop out and join the craft unions, which enfeebled the organization. (3) Finally, the centering of power at the top in Powderly's hands resulted in the calling of several unnecessary sympathetic strikes, in inability to prevent violence in certain areas, and in general loss of understanding between the leaders and the led.

Yet it would be a grave mistake to assume that the Knights had lived in vain. They could point to many accomplishments. They were the first national union to survive a major depression. They were the first large union to do much for the unskilled. They stiffened our immigration laws, being largely responsible for outlawing contract labor (1885). They did much to publicize the cause of organized labor. And they taught their successor, the American Federation of Labor, the mistakes it should avoid.

The American Federation of Labor. Samuel Gompers, a cigar maker by profession and of Dutch-Jewish parentage and English birth, knew about unions from childhood. In the depressed 1870s he learned that strikes called on the spur of the moment were likely to fail, that strikes against laborsaving machinery were futile, and that unless workers paid dues to a union and could expect some benefits in bad times, many would drop out. He and his friend Adolph Strasser organized the cigar makers on these principles, and they were so successful that other unions copied their policies. In 1881 Gompers and Strasser set up a loosely organized federation of unions, and in 1886 they founded the more closely knit American Federation of Labor. Gompers was its president every year but one until he died in 1924.

The American Federation of Labor avoided some of the mistakes made by the Knights. In its early years the AFL excluded unskilled workers, women, and Negroes because they were hard to organize well. The AFL was a federation of national trade unions. Each national trade union was made up of all the individual unions of that trade in the towns and cities across the nation. The members of each union had a common bond of interest. There was to be no "dual unionism," that is, the AFL recognized only one national union in each trade. This avoided jealousies and prevented an employer from playing one union against another. Authority to call strikes rested largely in the hands of local unions, not at the top, as in the Knights. The AFL also differed from the Knights in resolving not to support any political party. Perhaps the biggest difference between the two unions lay in their fundamental philosophies. The AFL was a "business union": it was strictly opportunistic. If the time seemed ripe for a union to demand higher wages, shorter hours, or better working conditions, it felt free to strike for them. The AFL had no dreams of abolishing the wage system and no intention of wasting its income on setting up cooperatives.

The AFL grew slowly in the 1890s and more rapidly after the turn of the century. Gompers and a few others were for years the chief organizers, and much of their time was devoted to this work. Management was often hostile to unions. Gompers saw his organizations prosecuted under the antitrust laws. Yet the AFL was gradually accepted. Compared with the noisy and violent, although small, Industrial Workers of the World (IWW), which flourished shortly before World War I, it seemed very respectable.

After the United States entered World War I, Gompers was appointed to the War Labor Board, and labor got representation on various other wartime boards. This was the first time organized labor had ever had such recognition during a war. The government soon agreed to accept union standards of pay, hours, and working conditions in war contracts. In return, the unions gave a no-strike pledge for the duration of the war. Since many contracts were on a cost plus 10 per cent basis, employers objected less than they might otherwise have to union standards or even to granting wage increases under the pressure of war-induced inflation.

AFL membership grew from two million to four million between 1914 and 1920.

Soon after the war ended, the government contracts, with their cost plus 10 per cent feature, also came to an end. Many companies had to think again of making ends meet in a competitive consumers' market rather than in a market in which the government took all their output at a price above costs. Trouble was in store for unions and laboring men. There were many major strikes in the next few years and the unions lost most of them. A two-year depression began in June, 1920, and made matters worse for the time being. AFL membership fell off about a quarter. But the picture was not all bad. The sharp decline in prices that came with the depression was not accompanied by a corresponding fall in wages. There resulted, therefore, a substantial increase in real wages, so that with a return of prosperity in 1922 labor's economic position was good.

Up to this time union membership had grown in times of prosperity and declined in periods of depression. This is what should be expected, for more men are employed in prosperity, it is easier for them to pay dues, and the benefits of union membership are more obvious. But this general rule seemed almost to operate in reverse in the prosperous 1920s and during much of the depressed 1930s.

AFL membership remained stationary in the prosperous period 1923–1929, when the nation's working force was increasing 10 per cent. There were two basic reasons for this. Workers were probably treated better, and strenuous efforts were made to keep employees from joining unions. To be more specific, on the one hand, many plants adopted all kinds of welfare measures, such as company athletic teams, hospital care, pension plans, and the like—all calculated to make workers loyal and appreciative of the company's concern for them. On the other hand, to keep unions from getting a hold on the company, such devices were used as black lists, labor spies, injunctions, and "yellow-dog" contracts. Under a yellow-dog contract, a worker agreed not to join a union and so might be discharged if he broke his promise.

Where unionization seemed inevitable, company unions, alias employee-representation plans, were resorted to. The weaknesses of most company unions are that they collect little in dues and hence have no effective strike fund, their leaders are fellow employees instead of men hired by the union and so may be fired, and the company unions do not have national affiliations. It is significant that the majority of strikes in this decade were not over wages or hours, but over "recognition." In other words, many employers had not yet accepted collective bargaining, and so the first job of any new union was to obtain recognition as the employees' bargaining agent.

Another important development after about 1900 was increasing specialization and mechanization of industry. That caused the AFL to relax more and more its restrictions on admitting unskilled laborers. A few amalgamated unions were admitted and even some industrial unions, although the AFL still considered itself a skilled workers' union. An amalgamated union consists of locals of various associated crafts in a certain industry, which belong directly to the national union. For example, an amalgamated textile union in a New England factory might consist of a local union of weavers, one of spinners, and one of loom fixers. An industrial union is open to all workers in an industry. For example, everyone from floor sweeper to crane operator in a steel plant may belong to the local of the United Steel Workers of America in a Youngstown plant. In other words, a growing proportion of workers was now semiskilled and unskilled, but little was being done to organize them. What was being done took place within a framework that was becoming increasingly archaic. Organizing steelworkers on a craft-union basis was like stuffing the proverbial square peg into a round hole. The need for modern organizing methods was evident.

The Congress of Industrial Organizations. Shortly after the inauguration of President Franklin Roosevelt in March, 1933, the National Industrial Recovery Act was passed. It was an omnibus affair. Its chief provision for labor was clause 7a, which guaranteed labor the right to collective bargaining. Alert union organizers set to work organizing new unions, and union membership, which had been declining between 1930 to 1933, began to rise again. It was soon evident, however, that membership in industrial unions was growing about ten times as fast as that in craft unions. There were at least three basic reasons for this.

First, industrial unions were not hampered by jurisdictional disputes and related problems. For example, should a semiskilled worker in an automobile factory who worked on automobile floor boards be assigned to the carpenters' union or to the sheet metalworkers' union or to the body workers' union? In organizing any large factory, the number of such problems was legion, jealousies were sometimes intense, and the progress of organization had to be slow if the factory workers were to be channeled into craft unions.

Second, the craftsmen in some of these unions were reluctant to accept as, say, carpenters, men who could perform only a few specialized tasks. Also, the union leaders feared that if their unions were overrun by such newcomers a different set of policies would prevail and a new set of leaders might replace them.

Third, there was the dim memory, or at least the tradition from the 1880s, that the skilled workers had little to gain from mixing with the unskilled. It was not widely enough recognized that the structure of industry itself had changed greatly in the intervening half century.

At the 1934 annual meeting of the American Federation of Labor in San Francisco the advocates of industrial unions urged that industrial unionism be encouraged in mass-production industries to make the most of the opportunities presented by clause 7a. The convention adopted a cleverly phrased resolution which each side interpreted as a victory. At the 1935 convention in Atlantic City it became evident that the craft-union advocates intended to slow down the swing to industrial unions. A vote was taken on the issue, and the industrial-union advocates were defeated 2 to 1. Still they persisted. A fist fight broke out between William L. Hutcheson, of the carpenters' union, and John L. Lewis, of the United Mine Workers. The AFL was split in two. Lewis resigned as vice-president of the AFL and took his United Mine Workers with him.

In November, 1935, the CIO, called the Committee for Industrial Organization at this time but later called the Congress of Industrial Organizations, set up its headquarters in Washington. In addition to the United Mine Workers there were six other mass-production industry unions, chiefly in the textile and garment industries. The membership totaled about a million workers. These unions were suspended from the AFL. They were bitterly denounced as guilty of dual unionism, and when they refused to recant and return, they were expelled. Within two years CIO membership increased to over three million and included 32 unions. Some of the mass-production industries organized by the CIO were steel, cement, oil, rubber, and automobiles.

Organization of the automobile industry was particularly eventful. The chief organizer, Homer Martin, a former preacher, made haste with more zeal than good sense. He had a major strike on his hands before either his Automobile Workers' Union or the CIO was ready for it. To win that strike, the men occupied the plants instead of walking out of them. This dramatic "sit-down" strike was successful because Governor Frank Murphy of Michigan, fearing bloodshed, refused to have the trespassers ejected from the buildings. This kind of strike was declared illegal in the Fansteel case in 1938, but it worked in this important crisis in the early days of the CIO. The significance of the episode is that it demonstrated the imagination, vigor, and violence of the new industrial union.

In the years that followed, occasional attempts were made to bring the AFL and the CIO together again, but without success. Nevertheless, the two organizations became more and more similar in structure. The AFL relented and took in many industrial unions, and the CIO saw the need for craftsmen and took in trade unions. The two giants became almost as much alike as Tweedledee and Tweedledum, except that the AFL was larger than the CIO. In 1955 they finally agreed to unite again.

GAINS OF LABOR

Employees have been interested in improving their wages, hours, and working conditions and in winning recognition of their union as their bargaining agent. This last aim was especially important until it was assured by law in the 1930's. Let us see what, in a broad way, labor has gained in a century and a half.

The length of the working day is important. Men working for themselves 150 years ago worked from sunrise to sunset. Many an employer and professional man still works similar long hours. In the early shops, mills, and factories, the employees worked the same number of hours as the master worked, often twelve to fourteen a day. Long hours were a natural carry-over from farm life. But employees soon sought to fix a limit to their workday. By the 1830s workers were demanding a ten-hour day, although twelve hours was still the average in manufacturing. The workday was cut to eleven hours by 1860, to ten by 1890, to nine by 1914, and to less than eight today. Some occupations, such as the highly unionized building trades, have always led the way in the matter of shorter working days; others, such as the steel industries, which had a twelve-hour day as late as 1923, have lagged far behind. The steelworkers lacked a strong union until the late 1930s.

Real wages are what the laboring man's money wages will buy. Real wages thus depend not only on wages but on prices. If wages remain unchanged but prices fall, as happens in a depression, real wages rise for those who keep their jobs. Contrariwise, if prices rise but wages lag behind, as happens during a wartime inflation, real wages fall. In general, the real wages of unionized workers have risen more than those of nonunionized workers, although exceptions to this generalization may be found. For example, during World War II the real wages of nonunionized farm workers rose because farm workers were scarce.

Real wages rose about 20 per cent between 1840 and 1860, according to the Aldrich report, although for certain industries undergoing mechanization they fell. From 1860 to 1890, according to Alvin Hansen, real wages rose 68 per cent, largely because of falling prices during the generation after the War between the States. From 1890 to 1913 prices were rising again and real wages remained about the same. Since 1914 real wages of manufacturing workers have risen greatly. By 1923 weekly wages were 30 per cent above those of 1914, according to the Bureau of Labor Statistics, but by 1932 they were down 10 per cent. World War II helped them immensely, and by 1946 manufacturing workers were twice as well off as they had been in 1923. Since 1946 their real wages have risen about 19 per cent. In summary, the average manufacturing worker gets six times as much real income as his forefathers in 1840 did.

Along with improvements in wages and hours have come equally important changes in working conditions. During the century and three-quarters of this nation's existence, industrial accidents have been responsible for many times as many injuries and deaths as all the wars we have fought. Even during World War I, for example, when 130,000 American servicemen died, more men were killed at home in industrial accidents. In the early days of factories and mines, deaths were caused by uncaged machines, explosions, falling rocks, and unmarked hazards like open shafts. The financial as well as the physical cost of injuries was generally borne by the worker and his family. The courts were inclined to judge the victim or his fellow worker to be at fault, or they took the position that the victim had known beforehand that he was entering a hazardous occupation. Since about 1908, and especially since 1933 when Congress and the courts began to take a different attitude, more of the burden has been shifted to the employer, with the expectation that he would pass it on to the consumer. In short, part of the cost of the product is injuries, and the consumer must pay for them. This method stimulates the employer to protect the worker better, so as to hold accidents to a minimum and thus maximize his business profits. Some idea of the better conditions that have resulted may be gleaned from the accident records in anthracite coal mining, which go back rather far. In 1870, 13.5 persons were killed for every million tons of coal mined, in 1900, 7.2 persons, and in 1951, 2.4 persons.

Improvements in working conditions suggest a change in popular attitude and therefore in the government's attitude toward labor. In the nineteenth century the emphasis was on property rights, and much was heard about the due-process clauses of the Fifth and Fourteenth Amendments to the Constitution. In the last two generations the emphasis has shifted to human rights. Samuel Gompers feared from the start that the Sherman Antitrust Law of 1890 would be used against unions and asked that unions be specifically exempted from its provisions. Subsequent events proved that his fears were justified. For example, the United Hatters of North America organized a secondary boycott against a Danbury hat company, and the company prosecuted them for combining in restraint of trade and won heavy damages. Many workers had their homes sold from over their heads to compensate the corporation. It is very doubtful whether such an occurrence would be tolerated by public opinion today, whatever the legal merits. Gompers' emotional statement had great appeal then and still has. He said, "The labor of a human being is not a commodity or article of commerce. . . . You cannot weigh a human soul on the same scales on which you weigh a piece of pork. You cannot weigh the heart and soul of a child with the same scales on which you weigh any commodity."[2] The legal logic of this is weak but its political force in influencing legislation is strong.

After 1933 the government was increasingly concerned with the one-third of the population that was "ill-fed, ill-clothed and ill-housed" and was willing to tax corporations heavily to remedy the situation. And in 1946 a full-employment act was passed whose stated purpose was to achieve "maximum employment, production and purchasing power." The Federal government assumed responsibility for achieving these goals. This change in attitude and this growing emphasis on human rights have provided an atmosphere more favorable for the attainment of union goals.

SIGNIFICANCE OF THE CHANGES

The power of unionized workers has become tremendous in the last half century. At present a quarter of all employed people are unionized and the proportion in factories is about 70 per cent. A union is a labor monopoly. It may be benevolent or arrogant, easygoing or exacting, honest or corrupt, but it is a labor monopoly. Its leaders will be tempted to get as much as possible for members for much the same reason that corporation managers try to get as much as possible for stockholders. An extreme case is the United Mine Workers of America, headed by John L. Lewis, who is reported to have said on one occasion to the representatives of the coal operators: "You need men and I have all the men and they are in the palm of my hand; and now I ask, 'What am I bid?' "[3]

At first, workers could choose whether or not to join a union. But years ago the joiners began to deride those who stayed out as "free riders," that is, men who let others strike and take risks and yet expected to share the benefits. All kinds of pressures, from ostracism to physical violence, were applied to those reluctant to join unions. And once in, further pressures were exerted to make men retain their membership and to collect dues from them. During World War II, for example, the "checkoff" was imposed on many employers. That meant that a worker's union dues were deducted before he got his pay and were turned over to the union by the company. And there is the "union-shop plan," under which a man does not have to belong to a union to get a job, but must join within a stipulated time to keep the job.

The workers themselves have come more and more to rely upon unions. One worker rarely has much bargaining strength unless he is quite

[2] S. Gompers, *Seventy Years of Life and Labor* (New York: E. P. Dutton & Co., Inc., 1925), vol. II, pp. 285, 296.
[3] A. H. Raskin, "John L. Lewis: God of Coal," *American Mercury*, May, 1948, p. 523.

skilled. With growing specialization, and that means the breakdown of skills, the men must depend on organized action (unions) for their gains.

Industrial workers who unionize get wage increases. Often their achievement is publicized through strike victories. The relatively high standard of living of printers, carpenters, miners, railroad engineers, firemen, conductors, and brakemen is well known and suggests to others the advantage of belonging to a well-established union. Is the standard of living of the workingman higher as a result of the growth of unions? Opinions on this differ sharply. Some economists believe that in the long run most wage gains of one group of employees are made at the expense of other groups. The proportion of the national income going to wages and salaries increased from 55 per cent to 60 per cent between 1929 and 1950; during this time the proportion of unionized employees tripled. This suggests that sooner or later most workers may come to believe that they must unionize or perish. And that points to further growth of unionization.

Today when a big union like the United Automobile Workers goes on a strike against, say, General Motors, it is truly a battle of giants. It has been a long, long time since workers were willing to rely on the original idea of the strike; namely, making the employer realize how much he needed them and thus persuading him to acquiesce in their demands. Now we have a barrage of propaganda from both sides, political pressures behind the scenes, costly lawsuits, threatening picket lines, and too often some violence.

Worse than a big company strike is an industry-wide strike, such as the United Mine Workers frequently call in the coal industry or such as the United Steelworkers called early in 1952.[4] An industry-wide strike more or less ties up a basic industry, and the effects are soon felt across the economy in every industry using substantial amounts of the struck product, say coal or steel. If the strike were carried on long enough, the whole economy would virtually grind to a stop.

The question is bound to arise on the occasion of such strikes whether this is the proper way to settle wage and other industrial disputes, for it causes serious inconveniences, loss of income, and hardship to innocent and helpless people in countless other industries. The public has turned to the Federal government for protection in such instances. During World War II sheer self-preservation caused the government several times to "nationalize" the coal mines temporarily to keep production going. Later that was done with railroads and in 1952 with the steel industry. Such ownership by the government generally continues until the two sides reach an agreement. Since the workers keep their jobs but the

[4] The only thing worse than an industry-wide strike would be a general strike. This nation has never had one. One was tried in England in 1926.

owners no longer have real control of their plants, the pressure is heavier
on the owners, and they generally have to meet most of the union demands to get their plants back. Thus if the union can force the government to take over the industry, it has in reality won the strike. To achieve
that goal, all it needs to do in the first place is to make unreasonable demands and hold to them.

Out of these developments in recent years there emerges a definite
trend. This is a trend toward greater power in the hands of labor, especially organized labor, in our democratic government. Given a democratic nation composed mostly of employees, that is probably to be
expected.

QUESTIONS FOR STUDY

1. How and why has the attitude of American workers changed in the last
century?

2. Account for the rise of unions in the early part of the nineteenth century.
Why did unions precede factories? Describe the characteristics of unions
before the War between the States.

3. What was the significance of the Knights of Labor? Why did they want
to "abolish the wage system"? Account for the breakdown of the Knights of
Labor.

4. How did the American Federation of Labor differ from the Knights in its
organization and aims? How did it profit from observing the mistakes of the
Knights?

5. Account for the fact that organized labor made virtually no progress
during the prosperous 1920s and yet made great advances during the depression-ridden 1930s.

6. Account for the rise of the Congress of Industrial Organizations in the
1930s. The CIO followed some of the same policies that caused the Knights
to fail; why did it not fail also?

7. What have been some of the gains in working hours, real wages, and social
security obtained by laboring people during the last century? What are some
of the abuses of which organized labor is sometimes guilty?

Chapter 7

FOREIGN AND DOMESTIC COMMERCE

The United States with its great area, its variety of climates, and its abundance of natural resources is one of the most self-sufficient nations of the world. Even so, we depend upon other nations for many goods that we use every day. The coffee you drink in the morning may come from Brazil, the sugar you may use in it from Cuba, the china cup from which you drink it from England, the silver spoon with which you stir it perhaps from Mexico, the pulp in the newspaper you read from Canada, the wool in your winter suit from Australia, and some of the rubber in the tires you ride on from Malaya.

As transportation and communication across the world improve, we draw an increasing number of things from foreign lands. And they buy our cotton, sewing machines, automobiles, motion pictures and many other articles. As the standard of living rises here and abroad, what were once luxuries come to be regarded as necessities, and the amount of foreign trade increases. This country now has the largest foreign trade of any country in the world.

Yet great as is our foreign trade, it is but a relatively small fraction of the total commerce of the nation. Most of that is domestic commerce. In 1846 foreign commerce was one-eighth of total commerce; in 1908 foreign commerce was one-tenth of the total; and in 1951 it was one-eleventh. It grew from $43 million in 1790 to $235 million in 1846, $3,400 million in 1908, and $28,300 million in 1953.

FOREIGN COMMERCE

Thus far, foreign commerce has been spoken of as synonymous with merchandise exports and imports. We have, however, other business transactions with the peoples and governments of foreign lands. What these are and their relative importance may be seen by examining the balance of international payments (see Table 7-1).

Since neither we nor other peoples normally give away goods or services—and even when we do, they are carefully recorded—international

Table 7-1. Balance of International Payments, 1953
(In millions of dollars)

Exports of goods and services:

Merchandise	$16,437
Transportation	1,287
Travel	545
Misc. services, private and gov't	1,168
Income on investments, private and gov't	1,900
Total	$21,337

Imports of goods and services:

Merchandise	$11,904
Transportation	1,117
Travel	908
Misc. services, private and gov't	2,251
Income on investments, private and gov't	448
Subtotal	$16,628

Export balance of goods and services:

Unilateral transfers (mostly foreign aid)	$6,684
Gold imports	−1,163
Private loans, long and short	369
Government loans, long and short	221
Foreign capital movements	−1,133
Miscellany and errors	− 269
Subtotal	4,709
Total	$21,337

SOURCE: *Statistical Abstract of the United States, 1954*, p. 895.

payments always balance. If there is an excess of exports, it must be offset by loans abroad, imports of gold, services to tourists, or, in unusual circumstances as in 1953, by gifts to foreign governments.

The leading items in our balance of international payments are merchandise exports and imports. These are one-half to three-quarters of the total. In recent years the United States has tended to import raw materials and to export manufactured and semimanufactured goods. The other items, except gold shipments, are sometimes known as "invisible" imports and exports. People are frequently confused about whether a certain item, say a loan or a shipping service, is an invisible export or an invisible import. The test is a simple one: if Americans are paying for it, it is an import on our balance sheet, but if foreigners are paying, it is an export. The most important invisible item usually is capital movements or loans. It is foreign aid in Table 7-1. Also significant are the purchase and sale of shipping services and the purchase of various services by American tourists.

There would be more foreign commerce if the nations of the world did not erect trade barriers against one another. This country is guilty along with many others, although it does not use as many different devices as some other nations. We rely almost exclusively on tariffs, that is, duties on goods being imported.

DOMESTIC COMMERCE

The figures for domestic commerce are at best approximations; they are the sum of all wholesale and all retail trade. In 1948 domestic commerce totaled about $320 billion, roughly two-fifths of it being retail trade and three-fifths wholesale.[1] The Department of Commerce divides retail stores into those selling durable goods and those selling nondurable goods. The American people spend more money on food and automobiles, that is, on eating and running (on wheels), than on anything else. Next in importance are homes and clothing.

There were in 1948 almost 1,750,000 retail stores. Almost half were food stores or eating and drinking places. There were also about 200,000 gasoline service stations and 100,000 each of apparel, lumber and building materials, and hardware stores. Of these many stores the big ones did the lion's share of the business. Those with annual sales of over $100,-000 did two-thirds of the total business, although they numbered only 6.6 per cent of all retail stores. Contrariwise, the two-thirds of the stores with sales under $30,000 a year accounted for only 6.8 per cent of the total sales. This domination by the large organizations is repeatedly encountered in our economy, in industry, banking, transportation, and even agriculture.

A large part of the total retail business—24 per cent in 1948—is done by chain-store organizations. The most important chain stores are those selling groceries—the Great Atlantic and Pacific Tea Company, Safeway, Kroger, National Tea, American Stores, and others. They do almost a fifth of all chain-store business. Next in volume of business is the kind of department store that is also part of a chain organization: Macy's, Sears, Penney, May's, Allied, Best's and others that have 11 or more outlets. Other important chain types are apparel chain stores and variety stores like Woolworth's or Kresge's. Still other chain lines are drugs, automobile parts, building materials, gasoline, and eating and drinking places.

In rural areas a few old-fashioned general stores are still found because there are not enough customers to warrant establishing specialized stores, or not more than a few. A good idea of what rural areas and small towns were like a few generations ago may be got from observing these stores. At the other extreme is the highly specialized type of store found in large cities, like stores that sell only to tall girls or to large men, cheese stores, record shops, and perfume stores. Only in a metropolitan area is there enough business, day in and day out, to support businesses like these.

[1] *Statistical Abstract of the United States, 1954,* pp. 872, 880.

Wholesaling. Retailers may obtain their merchandise in a variety of ways, such as directly from the manufacturer, or from a broker, a commission agent, a jobber, or a wholesaler. It sometimes happens that merchandise passes through the hands of virtually all of these. When a general storekeeper buys a small lot of, say, cosmetics, they pass through the hands of several middlemen before they reach him. On the other hand, when the Pennsylvania Railroad buys some freight cars, the purchase is a direct one from the factory. The higher the price of the merchandise and the closer it is to being a piece of capital equipment, the fewer the middlemen. Also, big stores, chain stores, mail-order houses, and large department stores generally buy directly from the factory or just through brokers.

The Department of Commerce lumps most of these middlemen into one group which it calls "wholesale trade" although it includes wholesalers, manufacturers' sales branches, petroleum bulk stations, agents and brokers, and assemblers of farm products. In 1948 there were 243,000 such establishments, altogether doing $189 billion of business. Almost a third of the business was in the three Middle Atlantic states of New York, New Jersey, and Pennsylvania, which contain two great cities, New York and Philadelphia, and several other large ones, such as Pittsburgh, Newark, and Buffalo. Of all these establishments, 60 per cent were true wholesale houses but they did less than one-third ($50 billion) of the business in 1948.

Produce Exchanges. Over 40 different kinds of raw materials are sold in the first instance in commodity or produce exchanges, usually by commission agents to wholesalers or to processors and manufacturers. Among the best-known exchanges are the Chicago Board of Trade and the New York Cotton Exchange. There must be an ample supply of a raw material in order to warrant the machinery of a commodity exchange, and the material must be subject to standardization so that it may be sold by sample or contract. There are exchanges in dozens of large American cities. The products that are sold through them include wheat, cotton, hides, raw silk, wool, various nonferrous metals, lard, peanuts, and soybeans, to name just a few. The buying and selling of "futures" in these commodities is a chief business at the larger exchanges. A future is the right to demand delivery at an agreed-upon price at a specified future date. Although actual delivery is generally not demanded, the future contract serves a useful purpose. It enables processors to "hedge" on their purchases. Hedging is protecting yourself against price changes you do not want to happen by betting that they will happen. Thus processors shift some of the risk in their occupations to persons who make it their business to take these risks. Although there is gambling on the produce exchanges, the services of distributing the goods and of evening prices from one season to another do a great deal of good.

Somewhat similar to the commodities exchanges are the stockyards of Chicago, Kansas City, Fort Worth, St. Joseph, and other cities, where hogs, sheep, and cattle are bought and sold. The differences are that sale is not by sample and there is no futures market.

All these exchanges and the securities exchanges of New York, Chicago, and other cities are subject to regulation by Federal and sometimes state commissions, which lay down the rules of trading and see that they are enforced.

Distribution Costs. The cost of distributing goods is in the aggregate about equal to the cost of producing them. Among distribution costs are the costs of transportation, financing, advertising, and selling.

The cost of transportation is part of the cost of any article, whether it moves by rail, truck, inland waterways, pipeline or airplane. The cheaper the transportation, the wider the market is likely to be, and therefore the greater the economies of large-scale production. American transportation equipment is probably the best in the world.

Advertising is probably blamed more than any other operation for increasing the prices of goods "unnecessarily." The total outlay in 1951 for newspaper, magazine, television and radio, direct-mail, and outdoor advertising was about $6.5 billion. This is equal to 4 per cent of the total costs of all the goods sold through retail stores. That does not seem excessive. Of course, certain items like cigarettes carry a sizable advertising cost, about 11 per cent in a recent year, according to the Federal Trade Commission, compared with 5 per cent for other cigarette-selling expenses. In return for the price he pays for advertising, the consumer receives radio and television programs, and he is informed of improvements (some real and some largely imagined) and of new products. On the other hand, he is sometimes paying a price to enable one company, with cleverer advertising writers, to draw him away from another. But that is part of the cost of having a somewhat competitive economy which promotes efficiency and progress. It may be worth paying a higher price some of the time.

Finally, there is the selling cost, that is, the wages of salesmen, the cost of displays, of packing, assembling and "dividing," storing, grading, gathering market information, recording sales; the cost of the risks of spoilage, of not selling, or of bad debts; and the profit of the middleman. Merely to mention some of the things that must be done to goods as they travel from the hands of the producer to those of the consumer is to explain why the cost of distribution is as large as that of production and must probably remain so. The wonder is that it is not greater.

At least we may be grateful that within the nation there are no important tariff barriers, as there are between nations. The United States is one of the largest free trade areas in the world. Permitting consumers to buy their goods where they find the most desired quality for the lowest price encourages efficiency in production. It works toward a lowering of cost or an improvement of quality or both.

COURSE OF THE CHANGE

This vast and intricate machinery for buying and selling countless goods, the endless variety of the goods themselves, and numerous regulations governing their merchandising are the result of centuries of evolutionary change.

Evolution of Foreign Trade. The one thing that was plentiful in early America was land, with the natural resources upon it and under it and in the sea. Since labor and capital were scarce, only those resources which could be skimmed off with the least effort and were also in demand in England and Europe were developed for trade. An important reason for founding the first Colonies was to develop a source of supply of ship masts and timbers and naval stores. These were among the first products shipped home to England from Virginia. They were as vital to a naval power like England in that age of wooden sailing ships as steel and oil are in our modern age. Other crops and resources that the Southern Colonies developed were tobacco—Europeans early acquired the pipe-smoking and snuff-taking habits—and later rice and indigo. Grain stuffs and pig iron were chief exports from the Middle or "bread" Colonies, and fish and whale oil from New England. Since the English had little use for the fish and breadstuffs of the New England and the Middle Colonies, these had to be sold elsewhere in Europe or in the West Indies.

The colonists spent most of the funds they got in England, however. They liked England's superior manufactured goods—her textiles, ironware, farm tools, china, cabinetwork, and pewter—and they drew heavily on their credit in England, often going deeply into debt.

England had various laws such as the Navigation Acts of 1651, 1660, and 1663 and others such as the Wool Act, the Hat Act, the Iron Act, and the Molasses Act which obliged the Colonies to ship their basic raw materials to England, import manufactured goods largely from or through England, and not to manufacture goods that would compete with those of England. There was much profit to be had in selling manufactured goods at the start of the industrial age, and English merchants wanted it for themselves. This collection of laws and regulations, which we now call "mercantilism," was one of the causes of the American Revolution.

After the Revolution, American merchants were able to import more freely from Europe when they had the cash, but they could not export as freely as Americans had hoped, for this country was now outside the English mercantile system. Also, it was still outside the mercantile systems of France, Spain, Holland, and other countries. The United States continued to import largely from England because the English had the goods which Americans wanted most and, more important, English merchants were willing to sell on longer and better credit terms.

About the turn of the nineteenth century the United States developed a crop which the British imported in vast quantities, namely, cotton, the raw material for England's rapidly growing textile industry. By 1860, 60 per cent of all American exports consisted of cotton, most of it going to England. Tobacco, naval stores, and wheat were other major exports. Manufactures constituted only 11 per cent of the total but were increasing relatively. Continental Europe, South America, and China were becoming markets for American goods and sources of imports too.

After the War between the States industrialization of the nation went on at a more rapid pace, and exports and imports reflected this change. By 1914 exports of finished manufactures had risen to 31 per cent and by 1953 to 70 per cent of total exports. Meanwhile, imports of finished manufactures had declined from 70 per cent of total imports in 1850 to 20 per cent in 1953. At the same time England and other parts of Europe lost ground continually to Canada and Latin America as the sources of American purchases and as chief markets of this country. That was inevitable, for other American nations were raw-material producers and their economies dovetailed with that of the United States, whereas England's industries competed with ours.

Foreign Investments. The United States remained in a debtor position because of extensive investments by foreigners here until World War I but had an excess of merchandise exports from 1874 on. That was because the interest and principal payments growing out of foreigners' investments here had grown large. Since about 1916, however, the United States has been a creditor nation. It made large loans to its allies in World War I. Later, it invested heavily all over the world, at the rate of half a billion dollars a year in the 1920s. Canada, Latin America, and, for a while, Germany were favorite investing areas. When many of these investments turned out poorly in the depressed 1930s, and especially the securities investments, the American appetite for foreign investments was dulled for a while.

By 1953 our private investments abroad had reached $24 billion. In addition, the United States government has loans to various foreign nations of another $16 billion. Merchandise exports had been exceeding imports year after year after World War I, and some economists were saying that the only way the United States could maintain its pace in exports was to lend and give away a large amount each year. Others saw as the solution a policy of lower tariffs and of "trade not aid."

Tariffs. It has been difficult to reverse a tariff policy which allegedly encouraged American industrial growth. In the early decades of the nation's history some revulsion against English mercantile regulations kept duties low. In the 1790s Alexander Hamilton vainly urged a policy of mild protection for infant industries until they could grow up and fend for themselves. A mildly protective tariff was imposed in 1816 to protect the new industries from the competition of England's older and more efficient ones. In 1824 rates became more protective and in 1828 even higher. The South protested, for the planters sold most of their cotton abroad and either had to pay high duties on goods they imported or else pay higher prices for protected goods manufactured in the North. From 1828 until the War between the States, except in 1842, the tariff came down because the Democratic party, controlled by the South, won most of the elections.

With the secession of eleven Southern states and the outbreak of the War between the States, the Republicans imposed higher duties to raise the revenue needed to put down the rebellion. These duties were only partially removed after the war. This pleased the protected industries, which supported the Republican party. Until World War I, Republicans were victorious at almost every election, and so rates kept rising until a peak was reached with the Dingley Tariff of 1897 whose average rate was 57 per cent. The election in 1912 of a Democratic president, Woodrow Wilson, brought a sharp reduction in duties in 1913, but the outbreak of World War I in 1914 ended any opportunity to test the low-tariff policy.

Wars stimulate nationalism and demonstrate the need for home manufacture of products needed for defense and self-sufficiency. When the Republicans returned to office in the 1920s, three more tariff laws were enacted culminating in the Smoot-Hawley Act of 1930. That was another high-water mark and played a part in deepening the depression of the 1930s. In any event, it was becoming increasingly clear that this nation, now in a creditor position, would have to choose between lowering its tariffs to collect on past loans, as England had done for a century, or making bigger and bigger loans and experiencing periodic defaults. The United States has tended to make the second choice. That choice pleased the manufacturers of goods which had to face foreign competition, and it helped investment bankers.

The return of the Democrats to power in 1933 ushered in another trial of lower tariffs. The average duty at this time was 45 per cent. The Reciprocal Trade Agreements Act was passed in 1934. This law, which has come before Congress for extension every one, two, or three years, gives the President, through his Tariff Commission, the power to lower or raise duty by up to 50 per cent of the original duty. In 1945 Congress granted the President authority to do the same to any then-existing duty, that is, to start over again with the 1945 situation as a new base. Thus if a duty on chinaware had been reduced from an original level of 80 per cent to 40 per cent, it could be reduced again to 20 per cent. In 1955 the President was authorized to reduce duties an additional 15 per cent. Thus he could cut a duty on chinaware, just mentioned, from 20 per cent to 17 per cent.

It has been hard to shake the protectionist traditions; it is said that most businessmen are instinctively protectionist. Besides, they are politically well organized, whereas the consumer, who is hurt by tariffs, is generally ignorant of what is going on or indifferent, and is unorganized. Nevertheless, there appears to be a growing belief that a lower tariff is a more enlightened policy.

Evolution of Domestic Trade. There was relatively little domestic trade in colonial times partly because most necessities that were bought were imported from Europe and partly because the settlers were largely self-sufficient. True, as the colonial settlements grew and developed, and their numbers increased, some coastwise trade sprang up. But most stores were general stores; specialty stores were limited to towns and there were few towns.

The Brown brothers of Providence, Rhode Island, were typical high-class merchants of the period just before and during the Revolution. They started with a retail business, importing many of their goods, and in time developed some manufacturing and wholesale sidelines as well. To get funds to pay for English imports they had to trade with the West Indies, and they built up a candlemaking business, which brought them considerable cash as well as enhanced their reputation. They soon had to turn over part of their cash to the whalemen of Nantucket, who had a virtual monopoly on the spermaceti from which the best candles were made. Since cash was invariably scarce, it took planning and even questionable tactics to keep everyone reasonably content and the business going.

The evolution of store merchandising during the nineteenth century parallels in many ways the evolution of the factory system, which is traced in Chapter 4, on manufacturing, with shoemaking as the example. Pioneers bought little, lived simply, and themselves made most of what they used, or perhaps exchanged skills with a neighbor. Manufacturing and merchandising were identical at this initial point. Occasionally the little community would be visited by a peddler who had various useful knickknacks such as tinware, baskets, spices, thread, and perhaps clocks to offer, who told many stories and brought news of the outside world, and who was a smart trader. The similarity between the traveling man who offered services, like the itinerant cobbler, and the one who offered goods, like the peddler, is obvious. Both sought out the customer in his home. The customers were so scattered that the businessman had to do this to keep busy.

In time, the community became sufficiently settled so that there was enough business to support a general store. Quite possibly the store-keeper was a former peddler who had tired of the wandering life. The storekeeper traveled to New York or some other large city once or twice a year to stock up on goods. As the village grew larger, specialty stores began to appear, such as hardware stores, dry-goods stores, and saloons. Those who first set up specialty stores sometimes profited greatly, for they were able to buy more skillfully and in larger quanti-ties than a general-store merchant, and they could give better service to their customers. Specialty stores became common before the War between the States.

As the business grew, keeping adequate supplies on hand took more time, and the owner had to turn over some of his selling responsibilities to clerks. More important, he came to depend on traveling salesmen and specialists to supply him with attractive goods and to do some of his advertising for him. For example, soon after storekeepers from the country began going to New York, they were met at their hotels by agents of importing houses or of factories or warehouses, who would "drum up" trade with them. It was not long before the "drummers" were visiting the country stores and taking orders, thus saving the store-keeper some of his expensive trips. Wholesale depots were set up at strategic points in the interior to speed up the time of delivery, for the man who could give quick delivery when shelves needed restocking could win more storekeeper customers. Jobbers too appeared, who made it a business to buy and assemble "lots" of hardware, drugs, dry goods, and so forth, for storekeepers.

The period after the War between the States saw the rise to popu-larity of three new types of stores: the department store, the chain store, including the variety store; and the mail-order house. All repre-sented an integration of wholesaling and retailing and to some extent of manufacturing. Stores of these kinds claimed to be eliminating some of the profit of the middleman.

The first of these new types of stores was the department store. Among the earliest were John Wanamaker's in Philadelphia; A. T. Stewart's, Lord and Taylor's, and Macy's in New York; Jordan Marsh's in Boston; and Marshall Field's in Chicago. Many of them had started as dry-goods stores. They all appeared in large cities. They succeeded because they combined the virtues of the newer specialty store—skillful, large-scale, low-cost buying—and of the older general store—single overhead and the opportunity for the customer to do all her shopping in one place. Later, many of them added various services such as delivery of goods, credit, restaurants, and hairdressers. They went in extensively for advertising, and they operated on a fixed-price basis —the custom of higgling over every transaction had died out.

The Great Atlantic and Pacific Tea Company was one of the very first chain stores. It was started about 1859 and had four outlets in New York by 1865. Cash-and-carry grocery stores, however, did not appear until about 1908, and the A & P's economy stores began to appear in 1913. There were 3,100 A & P economy stores by 1917 and over 15,000 in 1930. About 1916 Clarence Sanders, of Memphis, opened one of the first self-service stores, called the Piggly-Wiggly, and in the 1930s the cash-and-carry and self-service ideas were combined on a large scale and the supermarket was born. All these types of grocery chain stores, and other chains as well, with their low prices, extensive advertising, and out-of-town ownership and control, antagonized many local merchants.

The variety store, or five and ten cent store, was a particular type of chain store. Frank Woolworth's first successful one was opened in Lancaster, Pennsylvania, in 1879. He featured tinware at the outset, but gradually added a variety of goods such as candy, celluloid dolls, Christmas decorations, chinaware, jackknives, and so forth. As long as Woolworth lived (he died in 1919), nothing in his stores sold for more than ten cents. To get the cost down to where he could sell for ten cents or less, Woolworth bargained closely and sometimes bought in very large lots. One of his unfulfilled ambitions was to offer a practical pocket watch for ten cents. By 1900 he had 60 stores, and in 1913 he built the famous Woolworth Building, a skyscraper office building in New York, out of his profits. Woolworth paid his clerks little, for he believed in making his goods sell themselves. As a young man he had been a poor salesman but a good display man. The Five and Ten offered to the economy-minded buyers of the cities and towns the sort of article that the peddler had once carried around the countryside.

To the farmer who complained so bitterly in the 1870s and 1880s and 1890s of the profits of the middleman, the mail-order house had strong appeal. Montgomery Ward exploited this market, starting in 1872, and Sears Roebuck, which started as a watch-selling and watch-repairing business, followed in 1886. Selling by catalogue and giving money-back guarantees were economical and successful methods. In time, these houses came to manufacture some of the articles they sold. They also opened department stores in many shopping centers.

Consumer Credit. Along with the rise of new types of stores came revolutionary changes in credit terms. In colonial times customers who bought on credit paid once a year, or even every other year. Storekeepers took into account in bargaining with a customer whether he was likely to pay his bills soon or after a long time. Most stores had to extend credit to their customers, for many customers were farmers who sold about once a year whatever cash crop they raised. By the time of the War between the States people tended to pay their bills about every six months, for stores made an additional charge if payment was not made by then. With the coming of more factories and the rise of the city, working people were paid more frequently. City stores now expected payment every month or two.

Another credit device developed in the 1870s. Stores and traveling salesmen began to sell goods on the installment plan with regular weekly or monthly payments. Articles such as furniture, stoves, musical instruments, sets of books, and sewing machines were sold this way, at first only to people of quite good credit. Then the policy was extended to working people of limited means. In the twentieth century automobiles, all kinds of electrical household appliances, and even homes have come to be sold on this basis. By the 1920s installment buying had become so important that it is sometimes cited as a factor leading to the depression of the 1930s. Since 1929 total consumer credit, of which installment credit is most important, and charge accounts next, has averaged around 10 per cent of national income, except during World War II when the Federal Reserve put limitations on its use.

Although more business is done on credit in this nation than in any other in the world, it is dangerous to grant credit freely. Institutions have arisen, however, whose function it is to reduce that risk. In the 1820s and 1830s a firm of silk merchants, Arthur Tappan and Company, kept minute notes on the credit standing of their customers and even of potential customers. Lewis Tappan, a younger brother, kept the records. Other merchants sometimes drew on this specialized knowledge. In 1841 Lewis Tappan founded his Mercantile Agency and sold his laboriously accumulated information on the credit standing of firms and individuals all over the nation. Ten years later the company had branches in several large cities. Eventually the firm acquired the name of Dun and Bradstreet, the firm whose credit-rating service is so widely known today.

Advertising. Newspaper advertising began in the *Boston News-Letter* in 1704 but was strictly of the informative or lost-and-found kind during the rest of the eighteenth century. Newspapers were expensive, for the type was hand set. Then in 1820 the introduction of the Foundrinnier system of printing made possible larger newspapers at less cost. Penny papers appeared in the 1830s. Advertisements were still small although they occupied the front page. When the War between the States began, war news took over the front page.

After the War between the States, national advertising developed along with national monopolies (trusts), almost nationwide railroad networks, and national labor unions. In fact, each of these influenced the rise of the others. Among the first products to be nationally advertised were patent medicines like Dr. J. C. Ayer's Sarsaparilla, and later Castoria and Lydia Pinkham's compound. Soaps were publicized in the 1870s, bicycles in the 1880s, and breakfast cereals in the 1890s. About the turn of the century Eastman Kodaks, Gillette razor blades, and Wrigley chewing gum owed much of their growth in popularity to national advertising. Newspapers spread knowledge of these products, their trade-marks, slogans, and brand names, much more rapidly than word of mouth. Toward the close of the century magazines, too, carried more advertising. In 1899 Cyrus H. K. Curtis took over the little-read *Saturday Evening Post* and made it one of the most effective advertising media of the nation. One consequence of all this national advertising was that people demanded products with familiar names, storekeepers insisted on them, and the wholesalers had to supply them even though the profit they got on them was less. Advertising was taking over an important function of the middleman, namely, the wholesaler's task of creating and widening markets.

Legislation against Unfair Competition. The development of advertising and the keen competition that it engendered, and the rise of new institutions like the chain store and installment credit posed new problems and led to the passage of regulatory legislation. One of the biggest problems was dishonest advertising. Better-business bureaus, chambers of commerce, and self-improvement in business ethics especially in large companies, have made advertising more honest over the decades. The Pure Food and Drug Act of 1906 prohibited the use of poisonous ingredients, required manufacturers of proprietary medicines to indicate the percentage of narcotics the medicines contained, and subjected manufacturers and distributors to Federal prosecution for misleading statements. The Wheeler-Lea Act of 1938 (the Food, Drug and Cosmetics Act) somewhat extended the force of such legislation. The Federal Trade Commission is authorized to prosecute manufacturers and distributors guilty of false advertising in interstate commerce.

Because the prices of certain articles that were nationally advertised were well known, stores sometimes sold these items at a discount to demonstrate that they were offering a bargain. The stores made up the loss on other articles. Competing stores resented it, customers demanded explanations, and the brand-name companies tried to stop the practice. They succeeded in 43 states and then in 1937 secured passage of the Miller-Tydings Act, which sought to enforce resale-price maintenance on nationally adverised articles everywhere. The law was fairly well enforced during the war and postwar periods when many goods were scarce and retailers courted the good will of manufacturers. But in the mid-1950s an inventory glut developed and competition was keen. "Discount houses" offered nationally advertised brands of toasters, electric mixers, radios, washing machines, and the like, at "cut" prices. It became apparent that many discount houses got their products with the connivance of the manufacturers. Retail stores were badly hurt by this unfair competition. Discount houses had small overhead, sold only popular items, and offered no repair services. Finally, the Federal Trade Commission ruled that it was up to the manufacturer to sell only to those who maintained prices. If he would not do this, then the retail stores were not bound to maintain prices on his nationally advertised brands. This has seriously impaired the effectiveness of laws to maintain resale prices.[2]

The animosity of local stores against department stores, mail-order houses, and chain stores has already been mentioned. It was widely believed, and even so stated by the Federal Trade Commission, that the growth of chain stores was "based largely upon special price concessions from manufacturers." The chain stores said they got discounts in buying, say, canned peaches, because they bought them in carload lots. The independent stores contended that the discount the chains got was greater than was justified by large-scale buying. The Robinson-Patman Act of 1936 limited the amount of discount a buyer might receive. But the law is complicated and has been hard to administer.

Installment selling likewise developed abuses which were eventually curbed by state laws and by self-improvement. But the problem of the possible effects of mounting indebtedness on the economy during World War II was handled by the Federal government. To prevent credit expansion in the form of installment buying at a time when inflation was feared, Congress permitted the Federal Reserve Board to make the terms of credit more severe. In general, every customer was required to make a down payment of one-third of the value of the article and to pay his debt within one year. Charge accounts might not go unpaid more than two months. This was known as Regulation W and was in force during most of the 1940s. This regulation was not aimed at stopping any unethical practice. Rather it was intended to benefit the majority of the people by limiting the supply of bank-created money, and hence restraining inflation. It antagonized industries that sold on installments, finance companies, and the people of limited means who bought on the installment plan. These groups contended that the regulation bore too heavily on certain classes and did not control credit well anyway. Congress later took away from the Federal Reserve Board the power to impose Regulation W.

[2] *Wall Street Journal*, Feb. 21, 1955.

REASONS FOR THE CHANGE

Over the course of two centuries there were many changes in the organization and methods of foreign and domestic commerce. And with these changes came considerable legislation. Let us see some of the underlying reasons for these fundamental changes.

Trade was very simple as long as markets were small, but with improvements in communication and transportation that began with the turnpikes, canals, and steamboats and continued with railroads, automobiles and trucks, and airplanes, a whole series of changes in methods began to occur. Take the case of the Erie Canal whose completion in 1825 reduced the cost of shipping a ton of goods from Buffalo to Albany from $100 to $10. Markets which had been out of reach because of high transportation rates now were open for exploitation. Eastern farmers had to meet the competition of the low-cost lands farther west; Western pioneer industries had to compete with more efficient ones to the east. Thenceforth, each region specialized more in what it could do better. Each increased its output in order to serve more distant markets. Wholesale merchants handled larger quantities and set up warehouses near distant markets or dealt with other wholesalers there. Also, there was growing specialization in the kinds of products they handled. A clothing merchant, instead of dealing in all kinds of apparel, would handle only men's suits, or men's shoes, or collars.

The warehouses, the larger inventories, the crews of salesmen, and the increased advertising all added up to a greater investment. And what was true of wholesale establishments was true of retail stores. Inventories were larger, the building, the location, and the furniture and fixtures were more costly, there were more employees, and there was more advertising. A little country store in the 1830s could get along with a stock of $3,000 of goods for the year and with the owner and his family doing all the work. Today, the retail stores that do an average amount of business do $300,000 in a year.

So much investment involves considerable risk and responsibility for the owner and manager. The temptation is strong to eliminate as much of the risk as possible. That may mean handling only well-advertised brands, or it may mean resorting to questionable advertising occasionally, or organizing local opinion against chain stores, or following the adage, "If you can't beat them, join them," and becoming part of a voluntary chain. Or it may mean cutting prices, even on branded products, to attract customers or to stay in business. A store with a sizable investment may lose money for some time by living off depreciation reserve accounts and bank credit before it goes into bankruptcy. That the pressure on retail merchants must be tremendous is apparent from the fact that about half of all new retail businesses last only two years. All these pressures and practices necessitate legislation to ensure that the game of business is being played fairly.

SIGNIFICANCE OF THE CHANGE

Increasing specialization may take one or both of two basic forms. It may be geographical: Florida, California, and Texas produce and market most of the citrus fruits. Or it may be specialization in the handling of products: one store sells only women's dresses, another men's shoes. Both types of specialization result in greater output, lower prices, and better quality and contribute toward raising the standard of living. But specialization makes us all more dependent on one another and on the smooth functioning of a complex economic system. City dwellers, and they constitute over half the population, depend on the marketing mechanism for their vegetables, meats, and dairy products. If farmers cannot dispose of their crops readily, or if retail grocers cannot obtain fresh fruits, eggs, and vegetables promptly, there are inconveniences and business losses all along the line. Strikes, transportation interruptions, bankruptcies, and crop gluts or failures occasionally demonstrate this interdependence.

Similarly, when some ambitious merchant overstocks an item that has gone well in the past, perhaps radios, and the market for them decreases, or when Cuban sugar producers raise too much of their product, there is the familiar problem of "overproduction." It may cause failures among merchants, as well as among the producers, if the merchants are specialists and already have large inventories. The solution favored by businessmen for cutthroat competition or overproduction is control of the supply, alias monopoly. Rarely nowadays does this mean "cornering" the market.[3] It does mean assuring a merchant that he is the sole outlet in a certain town or area for, say, Oldsmobile cars, or Monarch peaches, or Shell gasoline. This moderates the problem for the merchant but cannot eliminate it. After all, customers may shift to other brands, and if goods move slowly, "price wars" will develop sooner or later. When big investments are at stake, the wars may be severe and the losses heavy. Foreseeing this, the contestants may be tempted to make agreements to fix prices or even to oppose the entry of new firms into their business. Then the Federal Trade Commission or the Antitrust Division of the Justice Department must step in and attempt to restore fair competition.

Overproduction in one or more large products, like automobiles or major crops, may lead to depression, and then the interdependence of all

---

[3] We are not considering the government-sponsored commodity-control programs. These are for the producers, not the marketers.

merchandising specialists spreads the effects of overproduction as rats spread the plague. Inability of cotton dealers to market cotton profitably or of automobile dealers to dispose of cars leads to layoffs in the field or the factory. The unemployed workers, in turn, postpone buying new cars or clothes, economize at the grocery store, and cut down on entertainment, which affects the profits of these areas of production and of the merchants who sell the goods. In short, the calculations of a big merchant as well as of a leading manufacturer as to his future market, and the ability of the merchant to market his goods, determine whether an important segment of the economy runs smoothly and prosperously or does not. And when many merchants overestimate their needs at one time, as they did in 1919–1920, right after World War I, a major depression may result, as happened in 1920–1922. The same sort of situation developed again in 1953–1954, but fortunately it was on a smaller scale and was less serious.

QUESTIONS FOR STUDY

1. How much larger is our domestic commerce than our foreign commerce? Has this been true for a long time? What is the significance of it? How is domestic commerce defined?

2. Which is larger, wholesale trade or retail trade? How important is the role of chain stores in retail trade? Has the trend in recent years been toward eliminating the middleman or increasing his importance?

3. How much of the cost of the average product is cost of distribution? Why is distribution cost such a large proportion of total cost?

4. What have been some of the major trends in our foreign trade in the last 150 years as regards the character of imports and of exports? As regards our chief customers and sources of supply? Foreign investments? Tariffs?

5. Show how the evolution of retailing from peddlers to department stores parallels in many respects the evolution of shoemaking from itinerant cobblers to shoe factories.

6. Describe the advances made in consumer credit in the last 150 years. In advertising. Why has government regulation of these become increasingly necessary?

7. Why is it so vital to the health of the economy that merchants not build up too great inventories and that they make a reasonable profit in their business?

CHAPTER 8

THE AMERICAN ECONOMY

What would a farmer of George Washington's time have thought of the America of today? He would of course be impressed by the automobiles and airplanes, tall buildings, telephones, radio and television sets, canned food, and ready-made clothes. Yet he would soon become used to these. It would take him more time to adjust to the subtle changes in points of view, in basic assumptions, in economic conditions, which are not as obvious as a radio or even as an electric wave. These changes in attitudes make earning a living very different today from what it was then. As the physical improvements have appeared, they have altered our economy and our attitudes. They explain why people today accept ways of doing things that our forefathers would not have tolerated and why, contrariwise, we will no longer accept methods that our ancestors took for granted. Yet not everyone goes along with the changes and new attitudes; some do not understand the reasons for them and are reluctant to accept them.

COURSE OF THE CHANGE

The changes in our environment and in our attitudes mentioned above and in the previous chapters took place in a number of ways. The adoption of the Constitution and the establishment of a strong Federal government encouraged saving and investment and had a stimulating effect on business. The Transportation Revolution, which featured first turnpikes, then canals, steamboats, railroads, and steamships, and later automobiles, pipelines, and airplanes, widened markets. More farmers produced crops for sale as well as for subsistence. They employed farm laborers, compared their cash outlay and cash income, and tried to widen the profit margin. They adopted more efficient methods that previously had not seemed worth trying. This was the Agricultural Revolution. These crops, raised by better methods and transported over better roads, went to seaports and to factory towns where the workers were so busy in new mills that they had to buy their food instead of raising it.

116

New mills were turning out thread and cloth, carpets and clocks, fire-arms and plows, ironware and brassware in increasing quantities to ship over the turnpikes, canals, and railroads to farmers and others through-out the expanding young nation. This was the Industrial Revolution. New methods of financing these myriad activities and of organizing busi-ness companies might be called the Financial Revolution, just as new methods of marketing and of using mercantile credit might be called the Commercial Revolution. Finally, the wage system, labor organizations, time and motion studies, and protective legislation for workers con-stituted a Labor Revolution. All in all, the nineteenth century saw more economic changes in the Western world than almost any century since man has recorded his history. The consequences of these changes were bound to be far-reaching.

The population has increased tremendously as a result of the dis-coveries of the new scientific age. That age brought great improvements in medicine. The average life expectancy of a human being at birth has increased and population has risen sharply, despite the fact that people now have smaller families to maintain a higher standard of living. The population doubled every quarter century almost to 1900 and doubled again in the next half century. Most people today live in or near urban communities. Over half the population live in less than half of 1 per cent of the area of the country. The average age of people increased from sixteen to thirty in the last 150 years and is still increasing. Finally, the average size of the family today is less than four persons, whereas a century ago it was close to six.

The average size of factory, store, trade union, bank, farm, railroad—almost any type of business that might be named—has increased. For ex-ample, between 1880 and 1900 the number of railroads was reduced from 1,500 to 80 by consolidations. Not only do each of these larger business units do more business than before, but the amount they have invested in plant and equipment has similarly increased. Along with larger plants and more equipment came still another change. Production became more "indirect." The pioneers picked wild fruit directly from the forest, and the equipment that they used to gather their food and meet other needs was simple, such as nets, hoes and sickles, and guns. It was Eli Whitney, father of the idea of interchangeable parts in America, who first made dies and forms for manufacturing guns for the government. This idea spread to the making of plows, clocks, and other articles. And then came the machine-tool industry, which produces accurate measur-ing devices like micrometer calipers and machines like turret lathes, planers, and borers with which to make machines with which to turn out goods. When the Ford Company gave up making Model T cars in 1927, it had to cease production for several months to tool up for production of the new Model A. Likewise, it took an investment of some $2 billion in research and plant to produce the first atom bomb. A man of the eighteenth century brought back to this twentieth-century world and shown all the intricate steps involved in the roundabout way we go at producing anything in quantity would think the modern world was full of Rube Goldbergs. Yet for prolonged large-scale production, this round-about approach is the least costly.

All these important changes, and others as well, have been going on for over a century and a half. As a result, the economic pressures of to-day are different from those of Washington's day, the rules of making a living have been modified, and the attitude of the people has altered. Yet the tradition of 150 years ago, the freedom of the frontier, and the guarantees of the Constitution have prevented our way of life from alter-ing radically at any one time.

REASONS FOR THE CHANGE

The reasons for some of the changes are fairly obvious. For example, an increasing population, over half of whom live close together in towns and cities, requires more rules to keep peace and order. No one par-ticularly cared or interfered if the frontier family of Daniel Boone's day carried firearms without a license, hunted all year, dumped garbage and sewage in the rivers, slaughtered a hog where they pleased, did not send their children to school, and helped themselves to timber from govern-ment land. None of these acts, which a good citizen would not commit today, did noticeable harm to his fellow citizens. They were included in the frontiersman's "freedom," for freedom is the right to do anything that does not harm a fellow man or diminish his freedom unreasonably. As the frontier became more settled, rules were made to protect the timber on government land, to stop pollution of the rivers, to limit the use of firearms, to zone certain areas to keep out, say, slaughterhouses, and to require a minimum of schooling for children. More laws require a larger police force, more records, more courts, and a more intricate and more costly government. Today, earning the money to protect his freedom against all kinds of potential menaces takes more of a man's earning power than is needed to feed him.

Another consequence of a growing population is that the influence of the individual diminishes, since he is now one among many thousands in his community or among millions in his state and country. The only way that he can counteract this tendency is to become a member of one or more pressure groups, whether trade union, chamber of commerce, trade association, tariff league, farm lobby, or association of women voters. If he becomes an influential member of such an organization and it gains influence with local, state, or national governing bodies, his power is increased by a "leverage" process. Often, a spokesman for such an organization says he represents thousands of people, although most of them do not even know he is there. If his organization is well disciplined, like a union, he may have considerable influence. And even if a member is not a leader, he may gain a certain vicarious pleasure from just being a member of an influential organization. Is it any wonder that we are known as a nation of "joiners"? To an increasing degree, laws are made through the influence of the people who head organizations rather than through the opinions of prominent individuals who have no organization backing.

As the business unit grew in size and the number of customers increased, the investment in plant and inventory also increased. To obtain capital for larger operations, more and more companies resorted to the corporate form of business. Again the result was a diminution of the democratic process within the company. Partnerships are usually democratic. Corporations are oligarchic: most shareholders in a corporation of any size have no voice in making business decisions. Of course, changes in management may take place in the long run, if the company is poorly run, if profits are small, and if the value of the stock declines.

The larger the investment that a manager or president is in charge of, the more responsibility he feels, and if he is successful, the more pay he may expect. On the other hand, if he fails, he may expect to be severely criticized and to feel the pressure of others looking for his job. It is no wonder that he seeks to eliminate risks and to stabilize the flow of business. For example, if he is in the oil-hauling business, as three railroads serving Cleveland were about 1871, he may be willing to divide the business with his competitors. Or if he is in the candy business, he may be willing to sell a large amount at a seemingly sacrifice price to get and keep the custom of a large and steady buyer like Woolworth's Five and Ten. Some efforts to stabilize the flow of business are sensible and ethical; others are questionable; and still others have been illegal under the common law for centuries. For the manager, a reasonable profit coupled with steady growth spell security, just as an annual wage, social security, and a strong union spell security to the factory worker, or a permanent job and a pension do for a college professor. Security is something that people in all walks of life seek.

Some types of business make enough sales in a year to pay several times for the capital invested. Grocery stores, variety stores, and meatpacking establishments have a rapid turnover but make only a small profit on each item sold. Businesses with such a rapid turnover are often easy to enter, are generally very competitive, and have a high rate of failure. An opposite type of business makes only enough sales in a year to pay for a fraction of the capital invested; the cost of the equipment is expected to be spread over a period of ten to fifty years. Public utilities, steamship lines, railroads, steel mills, automobile companies, mines, and timber preserves are examples of this second type. Such businesses are hard to establish because of the tremendous investment needed; witness the failure of Henry J. Kaiser in setting up an automobile company. They are monopolistic or at least oligopolistic (only a few big companies), and it takes a long time for one to fail. There are also many businesses in an intermediate category.

It is the public-utility type of business that interests us here. As the economy matures, as markets widen and investments accumulate, as the nation acquires more heavy industries, a larger portion of industries fall into this large-investment or heavy fixed-cost category. To protect the investment, near monopolies are formed. They may be the result of agreements between competitors or the result of business wars. When this first took place in the latter part of the nineteenth century, the railroad, industrial, or other monopolies charged extortionate prices. This led to the enactment of antitrust laws and the Interstate Commerce Act and to the establishment of public-utility regulatory commissions either to break up the monopoly or to regulate the rates that these companies might charge for services. Again, the more such laws or commissions that are necessary, the more complex and expensive the government becomes. Yet if the commissions are not created, the consumer must pay an unreasonably high price, and the opportunities for independents to exist or for new companies to start are more limited. The practices of the Standard Oil Company of New Jersey and of the Southern Pacific Railroad Company in the 1890s are evidence of this tendency. The Southern Pacific insisted on seeing the books of California lemon growers and charged a rate which barely left them in business. When a tariff was put on lemons, the railroad company adjusted its rates so as to reap all the benefits.[1]

EXAMPLES OF THE CHANGE

To illustrate the changes in legislation in the course of a century or two, let us review some of the high points in each of seven areas.

Once the frontier was open to settlers and squatting was encouraged by the Preemption Act and the Homestead Act; now both these laws have been repealed and the frontier has been closed since 1935. In 1952 the Federal government was leasing five times as many acres of land for mineral and other uses (excluding timber) as it had in 1942.[2] The cheap-land frontier has ended.

[1] O. Lewis, *The Big Four* (New York: Alfred A. Knopf, Inc., 1938), pp. 368–369.
[2] *Statistical Abstract of the United States, 1943*, p. 922; *1953*, p. 175.

Less than a century ago, although farming was the leading occupation, there was virtually no legislation to assist farmers. The Department of Agriculture was founded only in 1862. Today, we have parity formulas, support programs for major crops, and free or low-cost advice to farmers from state and Federal governments. For 1956 the Federal government budgeted $2 billion to help American farmers.

Although state governments made capital investments in canals, turnpikes, and even railroads before 1837, the Federal government pursued a policy of avoiding them, as was evidenced by President Andrew Jackson's veto of a bill for Federal investment in an intrastate turnpike in Kentucky (Maysville veto). Likewise, the Federal government was unwilling to acquire the telegraph as a national monopoly and hesitated a long time before taking full control of the post office. But in 1887 Congress began regulating interstate commerce by passing the Interstate Commerce Act, which affected railroads. The government did not, however, really begin to enforce the act until about 1906. And in 1934 Congress set up the Federal Communications Commission (FCC) to regulate wire and radio communication (which the Federal Radio Commission and the Interstate Commerce Commission had previously handled). A few years ago, the FCC had enough power to delay the broadcasting of color television, a government right which the businessman of a century ago would have found it difficult to understand.

In the area of manufacturing, trade practices of a century ago were subject to few rules, although the common law forbade combinations in restraint of trade. But many a manufacturer found it easy to evade those rules, and profitable as well. Today, the Federal Trade Commission, set up in 1914, scrutinizes any new, and many old, trade practices and has been helpful in reducing misbranding, false advertising, commercial bribery, and other evil forms of competition. The Sherman Antitrust Act of 1890 and the Clayton Antitrust Act of 1914 have checked the unbridled growth of nationwide monopolies.

For a long time immigrants were encouraged to come to this land of opportunity. In the 1850s the proportion of foreign-born to American-born was at its maximum. The Oriental Exclusion Act was passed in 1882, and contract labor was forbidden in 1885 to please the Knights of Labor. Since then the laws limiting immigration have come thick and fast, especially after World War I. Today, no more than 150,000 immigrants may enter in a normal year from outside the Western Hemisphere.

The laws governing trade unions have also altered. The laws against combinations and conspiracies of a century ago made it illegal until about 1842 for a worker to belong to a union. For another ninety years custom and the power of the employer made it dangerous, in many occupations, to be a union member. Gradually the worker and the union gained their freedom. They then abolished some of the rules like the injunction and the yellow-dog contract which had kept them under control for so long. During the 1930s and early 1940s organized labor acquired so much power that the employer dared not state his side of the case to his workers when a strike was pending, lest he appear to be bringing undue pressure on them. Industry-wide strikes slowed the productive pace of the whole economy. Congress passed the Taft-Hartley Act in 1947 with the aim of protecting both the public and the labor unions' membership from abuse of power by labor leaders. It forbade closed shops, limited campaign contributions by unions, outlawed excessive dues, permitted temporary Federal injunctions in national emergency cases, and forbade featherbedding. The significant fact is that the Federal government has set up all kinds of rules about the operation of labor unions and the conduct of strikes.

Although the hand of government was felt quite early in the area of finance, it was not heavy a century and a half ago compared with its weight today. Banks then created money freely. True, the First and Second Banks of the United States regulated bank-note issues somewhat, but this very power was an important excuse for not rechartering them. In general, states in the older sections of the country had better banking laws or banking systems. Nationwide reforms were achieved with the passage of the National Banking Act in 1863, although the new system lacked a central bank. National banks, which were privately owned institutions, retained the right of note issue. Not until the War between the States did the government regain power to issue legal tender paper money. In 1913 Congress added a central bank, which has since taken over the issuing of bank notes. National banks lost that privilege altogether in 1935. Also, after World War I and especially after the Great Depression, the central banking system became a device for preventing speculative booms and alleviating suffering from panics. It has been used to protect citizens against nationwide economic disaster just as the air force is a weapon to protect them against military disaster.

Meanwhile Federal taxes, which had taken less than 1 per cent of the citizen's income in Washington's time, now take a quarter of it. The Federal government concerns itself not merely with military protection, foreign affairs, and courts of justice, but with myriad other matters that affect the citizen's welfare.

In the realm of commerce the hand of the Federal government was once felt only in the form of a few import duties. Now those duties are heavier, more numerous, and more complicated. As for domestic commerce, which formerly was almost completely unfettered, now there are rules governing advertising, branding and labeling, the discounts manufacturers may offer to chain stores, and the bargains on branded products retailers may offer to customers. The sale of securities, which once operated under the rule, "Let the buyer beware," now operates under an opposite rule, "Let the seller beware."

In almost every area of economic activity the Federal government, and state and local governments too, have stepped in to give greater protection to the citizen and at the same time to increase their own authority.

PROBLEMS, SOLUTIONS, AND TRENDS

The chief problems that the people of the United States face are how to remain politically and economically strong so as to ward off the barbarian hordes without who are mouthing "Communism" to justify their envy, and how to maintain a sane middle course internally between depression and inflation. A depression is a tragic and painful economic illness that comes when an economy gets out of balance, but it may serve to purge the economy of the weaklings and the extremists whose influence and decisions have caused the depression. The trouble is that in an economy as immense and rich as the American one, a depression that does much purging lasts a long time. That hurts many millions of innocent people, exhausts their patience, and raises in their minds serious questions about the practicality of capitalism. This plays into the hands of those advocating Communism. To avoid a serious depression, financial palliatives may be applied, such as public-works programs, central-bank operations to create additional credit, subsidies and loans to sick industries that have enough political power to get them, and even a lightening of the tax burden. The fact is lost sight of that all this may later cause creeping inflation, prolong the influence of the weaklings and extremists, or postpone the depression and thus worsen its severity.

Man lives only a few decades, and his mature and influential life is even shorter. He wants his mature years to be happy and prosperous. For a nation to survive external perils and internal temptations requires courage on the part of its leaders. It also calls for enough people with self-discipline to keep those leaders in office and with courage themselves to follow sensible policies. In the end, the welfare of the nation depends on the people rather than on the leaders. The leaders must remain in power in order to lead. If what they do displeases the voters, even though it is good for the nation, those leaders will be removed from power and others will be elected in their stead.

When corruption appears in this democratic nation, when inefficiency and mistakes become too obvious, or when a depression takes place, the remedy has always been to change administrations. In bygone times each administration let automatic danger signals work and observed certain traditions that were strong in the public's mind. There was the gold standard; if the people demanded gold in large amounts and panic threatened, a change in adminstration became imminent. If the budget went unbalanced for long, it was a sign that the political house needed cleaning. If there was a depression, a change in administration soon followed. In more recent times the gold standard has been abandoned, the tradition of a balanced budget is almost outmoded, and administrations sniff a depression in every tainted breeze and pursue inflationary fiscal policies to avoid it. Harry Hopkins remarked that the Democrats' policy was "to spend and spend and elect and elect." This policy shocked many people. But the Republican administration has promised to take any needed steps to avoid a depression and has been willing to delay balancing the budget and to relax credit controls should the economy show signs of sluggishness. In other words, both administrations pursue a "spend and elect" policy; they differ slightly in degree and more in candor. This is inevitable in a democracy.

The trends toward more regulation, more government expenditures, and even government ownership in areas like electric power in the South or timber preserves leads the nation away from capitalism. Yet despite these trends, the tradition of individual enterprise and competition has remained strong in the nation because we are still close to the nineteenth century with its many opportunities to exploit land, resources, and new forms of business under a minimum of restriction. There are still more opportunities, and more freedom to exploit them, in this country than in most parts of the world.

QUESTIONS FOR STUDY

1. What have been some of the major changes in economic and social attitudes since the time of George Washington?

2. What are the main reasons for these changes in attitudes?

3. Why are so many industries tending toward oligopoly or monopoly?

4. Give examples of the need for regulation in the various segments of the economy, such as agriculture, manufacturing, labor, finance, commerce, and transportation.

5. We are inclined to blame "politicians" when there is corruption, or when the government is run badly, or when the economy does not operate smoothly. Who is really to blame and why?

6. Why is more government regulation necessary today than was the case a century ago?

7. Is our economy still primarily capitalistic?

Part Two

GREAT BRITAIN—THE WELFARE STATE

CHAPTER 9

POPULATION AND RESOURCES

The British have a confident saying, "There'll always be an England." There has been an England for over a thousand years now, and it has not been successfully invaded since the landing of the Normans in 1066, despite threats from Spain, France, and Germany. Britain's political boundaries have changed less than those of any other European power. For a people to remain independent so long requires intelligence, steadfastness, courage, and some flexibility as well. The reward of these qualities is much the same in the community of nations as it is in a community of individuals. Over most of that time Britain has grown in strength, wealth, and world influence.

During the nineteenth century, through her scientific and industrial progress, her colonial empire, and her policy of maintaining a balance of power on the continent, she became the leading nation of the world. Thanks to Britain, the nineteenth century was a relatively peaceful century, and that contributed heavily to the prosperity and progress that were achieved. To understand how a nation as small as Britain could gain such tremendous influence, we shall examine first her human and physical resources, and then the development of various segments of her economy, such as agriculture, transportation, manufacturing, finance, labor, and commerce.

AREA AND POPULATION

The United Kingdom consists of England, Wales, Scotland, and "the six counties" in northern Ireland that are not a part of the Irish Free State and have a parliament of their own.[1] The United Kingdom took its present form in four steps. Wales was joined to England by an act of union in 1536. A second act of union brought Scotland into the group in 1707. The nation now took the name of Great Britain. Ireland joined them by a third act of union in 1801. The official name became the United

[1] Their parliament is like a state legislature. Northern Ireland also sends representatives to the British Parliament.

Kingdom of Great Britain and Ireland. When the Irish Free State formally got its independence on April 18, 1949 (actually in 1922, however), the official name became the United Kingdom of Great Britain and Northern Ireland. The term "England" is often used loosely, sometimes meaning England proper, sometimes England and Wales, and sometimes the present United Kingdom, although this last usage is becoming outmoded.

The United Kingdom today contains 94,279 square miles. It is slightly larger than New York and Pennsylvania combined, half the size of pre-Hitler Germany, $\frac{1}{30}$ the size of the United States, $\frac{1}{90}$ the size of the U.S.S.R., and $\frac{1}{150}$ of her own Commonwealth, as the British Empire is now called.

Growth of the Empire and Commonwealth. The territorial expansion of England proper may be dated from about the time of Queen Elizabeth I, the last third of the sixteenth century. England's merchants traded with the far corners of the world, her seamen challenged the control of the New World by Spain and explored its islands and coasts, and a few settlers attempted, without success, to plant colonies in North America. England's claim to territory in the New World rested on John Cabot's discovery of North America in 1497.

Beginning in 1606, English settlers planted colony after colony along the eastern seaboard of North America and in the West Indies. A century later there were about a dozen mainland colonies and several island ones, with roughly a third of a million persons. England also secured a firmer grip on Ireland. Meanwhile, she gained foothold conquests in the East Indies, in India, and in Africa. England made progress at the expense of Spain in the sixteenth century and at the expense of Holland in the seventeenth century. France became her chief rival in the eighteenth century. As a result of the so-called Second Hundred Years' War, really six separate wars between 1689 and 1815, with England and France always on opposite sides, Great Britain added to her colonial empire. She acquired Newfoundland, Nova Scotia, additional parts of India, important West Indian sugar islands, and Canada. She got Florida from Spain for a time. But she lost the United States, and France helped bring that about. Captain Cook's voyages to the South Pacific led to the colonization of Australia and New Zealand toward the end of the eighteenth century.

There was little British territorial expansion during the first two-thirds of the nineteenth century, but during the last third Britain got a chain of dependencies in Africa stretching from Cape Town to Cairo and many coastal colonies as well. She consolidated her hold on India and acquired islands for coaling stations in far-flung parts of the world. By the closing years of Queen Victoria's reign Great Britain was at the height of her power. She issued a postage stamp with a world map on it showing her holdings marked in red. Truly it could be said that the "sun never sets on the British Empire." World War I was a tremendous economic strain on Great Britain. Nevertheless, she added several former German colonies in Africa and the Pacific to her Empire.

But even as Great Britain grew stronger, there were signs of decline. After the American Colonies rebelled successfully, Parliament allowed more self-government to Canada, and later to Australia and New Zealand, South Africa, and even to Ireland. Ireland finally got complete independence in 1949. After World War II India and Pakistan split off into virtually autonomous nations, and Burma left altogether. Today the British Commonwealth contains 12 million square miles of territory and over 600 million people. Belonging to it are the United Kingdom, numerous Crown Colonies, self-governing Colonies like Rhodesia, and autonomous Dominions like Australia, New Zealand, Canada, South Africa, Pakistan, and Ceylon. All of these pay allegiance to the Crown. India is still a member of the family in a general way although she is not a Dominion and pays no allegiance to the Crown. This rather vague organization is a typically British solution to a difficult problem. The important thing is that it does hold the British family of peoples together. From the viewpoint of both population and territory, the British Commonwealth is the largest political body the world has ever known. But no one should expect the members of it to react promptly to the will of a central authority.

Present Population. The United Kingdom consists of less than 0.2 per cent of the world's land. On it in 1953 were 50.8 million people. That was about twice the population of New York and Pennsylvania, three-quarters that of pre-Hitler Germany, one-third that of the United States, one-quarter that of Russia, and one-twelfth that of the British Commonwealth. In other words, the United Kingdom is one of the more densely populated countries in the Western world. The most densely populated part of all is England and Wales, which have a density of 753 per square mile. In Europe only Holland exceeds it (764), although Belgium comes close (750). In the United States, lower New England[2] (539) or New Jersey (645) are most comparable. In Asia only Java has a greater density. It is small wonder that Englishmen jokingly complain that their half of the island is "paved."

In the United Kingdom 79 per cent of the population was urban in 1953, whereas only 60 per cent was urban in the United States in 1950. Almost a quarter of Britain's population live in London and its administrative environs. The city of London (8,300,000) is somewhat larger than New York City. Glasgow and Birmingham also exceed the million mark,

[2] Massachusetts, Connecticut, and Rhode Island.

and Liverpool, Manchester, Sheffield, and Leeds top half a million. Altogether, 60 cities exceed 100,000, and about 90 others have over 50,000. The most populous sections of the United Kingdom are London, the Midlands, the Newcastle region in northeast England, the Bristol and southern Wales area, and the Scottish Midlands. The least densely settled sections are northern Scotland, parts of southern Scotland, mountainous central Wales, and the Lake Country in northern England, all with less than five persons per square mile, and thus comparable to our Rocky Mountain states.

There are several other population conditions worth noting. The United Kingdom has about 6 per cent more women than men. Women have outnumbered men for over a century, so this situation is not solely the result of two world wars. In 1953 two-thirds of the population were in the "working" age range of fifteen to sixty-four. Of the remainder, about 11 per cent were older and 22 per cent were children. The trend is toward a greater proportion of older people and a smaller proportion of children, but the proportion of working age is expected to remain about the same. The average age in 1950 was thirty-five, compared with thirty in the United States. The average life expectancy of an English man was sixty-six in 1950–1952. This compares with forty-two in European Russia in 1926–1927, fifty-eight in Western Germany in 1949–1951, and sixty-seven in the United States in 1950. In all these nations a woman's life is four years or more longer than a man's.[3]

Great Britain has virtually no race problem. There are few Negroes or Orientals and only half a million Jews.

Educationally, culturally, and politically the English are one of the most advanced peoples on earth. Probably less than 1 per cent of the population over fourteen are illiterate, compared with 2.5 per cent over fourteen in 1952 in the United States.[4] The government provides state-supported education for everyone through primary and secondary schools, and education is compulsory between the ages of five and fifteen. The British Education Act also requires all boys and girls between fifteen and eighteen to attend county colleges at least part time. Colleges do not give degrees, as they do in the United States. Only universities grant degrees and there are but 14 universities. University education is on a very selective basis, and those who have university degrees frequently hold important government or other positions.

Growth of Population. It is only in comparatively recent times that the population of Great Britain has become large. As long as the nation remained predominantly agricultural and commercial, it could support

[3] *Statistical Abstract of the United States, 1954,* pp. 956–957.
[4] The United Kingdom gives out no illiteracy figures. The last ones were 0.8 per cent for women and 1 per cent for men in 1914.

only a few million. In 1570 the British Islands are estimated to have had 4.2 million persons; in 1750, 6.5 million. Population growth had been slow. After 1750 the population increased rapidly to 16.3 million in 1801, 27.5 million in 1850, and 41.6 million in 1901. A comparable figure for today would be 53.5 million, with 3 million from the Irish Free State included. As early as 1851, half the population lived in cities.

The population has grown in the last two centuries, first because medical progress has been able to reduce the death rate, and second because technological progress in providing food and other health needs has prolonged life expectancy at every age. After the 1850s Britain used the earnings from industrial exports to import more and more of her food. In 1860, 25 per cent came from abroad, in 1880 about 60 per cent. In recent decades British population growth has again slowed down. Whereas in mid-Victorian times the average family had 5.5 children, the present average is about 2. Couples married in 1925–1929 had an average of 2.2 children, and it was the manual laborers with 40 per cent larger families than the others who kept the average this high. These changes have increased the average age, which in turn, has led to a more conservative outlook, fewer hasty judgments politically, and a growing desire for economic security.

REGIONAL CHARACTERISTICS

The United Kingdom has little land space, and yet half of it is used for grazing cattle. Only a fifth of the land is in crops. Large amounts are put to no use at all.

This island nation may be divided into two major parts, highlands and lowlands. If a diagonal line were drawn from the mouth of the Exe River in Devonshire (southwest England) to near the mouth of the Tees in Durham (northeast England), with few exceptions the land would be low on the eastern, or European, side, and high on the western, or American, side. The lowlands extend to the west coast only around Liverpool. The lowlands are heavily populated, and the highlands are lightly settled. The lowlands contain the arable lands. On the borders between highlands and lowlands are most of the coal and other mineral deposits, such as tin and copper. These borders are in Wales, in the Pennine Chain, stretching north and south in upper England, and in Cornwall.

The United Kingdom may be subdivided into about eight reasonably distinctive geographic regions (see Figure 2). All Scotland, like all Gaul, is divided in three parts, but all are highland to a greater or lesser degree. These are the Highlands of Scotland, in the north, the Midland valley of Scotland, and the Lowlands of southern Scotland. England also is sometimes divided in three parts, namely, northern England, the Midlands, and southern England. In addition, there are Wales on the west, and northern Ireland across the Irish Sea. Let us look at the physical and economic characteristics of these eight regions, starting in the far north.

The Scottish Highlands should include the Hebrides Islands to the west and the Orkneys and Shetlands to the north. The Highlands are perhaps

FIG. 2.

the most picturesque part of the United Kingdom but also one of the most barren regions. It is a country of plateaus 2,000 to 3,000 feet high, and it is generally grassy. The highest peak in the British Isles, Ben Nevis, rising 4,400 feet, is in the Highlands. The soil is poor and rocky except in the east and in the Orkneys. The sky is overcast and rainfall is heavy. There are some forests around Aberdeen in the east. The chief occupations are fishing, by people living near the coast, and cattle grazing. The rougher grazing land is used for sheep, but great tracts have no economic use at all. Life is hard in the Scottish Highlands; one has to economize to survive, and the "closest" of Scots are found here, by tradition in Aberdeen.

Scotland has a wasplike waist with a bay on either side, the Firth of Forth on the east and the Firth of Clyde on the west. In the waist are situated the two large cities in Scotland: Edinburgh, the capital and the smaller is in the east, and Glasgow is in the west. Scotland's coal fields are found chiefly around Edinburgh and the Firth of Forth. This is the industrialized area of Scotland.

The Lowlands of southern Scotland are moorlands. The land graduates down to rolling pastoral plains in the west and sometimes to well-wooded country in the east near the Tweed River, the eastern boundary between Scotland and England. Many sheep graze in the Lowlands, the black-faced ones being found on the higher and poorer lands. Oats, potatoes, and turnips are raised on the farms. In the west, Ayrshire dairy cattle are kept, and the countryside resembles that of Ireland. Ayrshire also has Scotland's second largest coal deposit.

Northern England includes all those counties south of the border and north of a line cutting across England from the north coast of Wales to the north coast of the bulge on the eastern side, called East Anglia. In the northwest is the Lake Country, picturesque and unproductive like northern Scotland. Sheep abound in the highlands. To the east are Northumberland, Durham, and York. Farming is good along the east coast. Durham is famous for its Durham, or Shorthorn, cattle, and York produces wheat. Market gardening is profitable near cities like Sheffield, Leeds, York, Newcastle, and Hull. And there are two great coal fields, one in Durham and one near Sheffield. South of the Lake Country and west of York is Lancashire, bordering the Irish sea. Its cities—Liverpool, Manchester, Oldham, and Blackpool—are so famous for their industries that they have kept people from realizing that this is a fairly rich agricultural area too.

The Midlands, a rectangular region, is the center of England and her heart industrially. The base rests on a line running east and west approximately 50 miles north of London. The sides extend through the middle of the country as far north as the southern boundaries of Yorkshire and Lancashire. The Wales bulge is to the west and the East Anglia bulge to the east. Birmingham, Nottingham, and Stoke are the leading cities. Here are carried on the great textile, steel, pottery, automobile, brewing, shoe, and lead industries of the United Kingdom. The nation's chief coal mines are located here. Farming is poor in the Midlands, but the land is admirable for cattle grazing.

Wales, west of the Midlands, is about the size of the state of New

Jersey. It is a region of rugged mountains whose ranges run in a southwest direction, the valleys opening into England. Important coal fields are found in southern Wales. Central Wales is high, rough pasture land on which sheep may graze only part of the year. Around the fringes of Wales are lower, better pasture lands for sheep and some cattle. The only really good farming region is the Plain of Hereford, near the southeast border. Except in this one area, the rainfall is too heavy for satisfactory farming.

The rest of England, rather arbitrarily lumped together under the designation of southern England, is a hodgepodge. The southeastern bulge is East Anglia, consisting mostly of Norfolk and Suffolk counties. It was once extremely isolated. Marshlands, called the Fens, on the west made it accessible only from the south. Like Wales, it is something of a country within a country, but unlike Wales, it is flat, lacks mineral resources, and is noted chiefly for farming.

Across England on the west is the region around Bristol, which is on the Severn estuary. The countryside is flat but wet and only moderately suited for agriculture. Many dairy cattle are raised here. Bristol was long famous for its chocolate and candy industry. Zinc, brass, tinplate, and automobiles are produced in this secondary industrial region. Bristol is no longer the leading seaport it once was.

The London area, which includes the countryside for 50 miles or so north and west and shorter distances south and east, is a very important industrial area. Light industries predominate here, such as clothing, boots and shoes, woodworking, paper, paints, food processing, and leather. There is also some metal manufacturing and making of electrical apparatus.

The southern tier of counties along the English Channel has much of England's remaining timber, in the east, and a major port, Portsmouth, in the center. Industrially it is unimportant and it lacks mineral resources, but it produces market-garden crops, cattle, and sheep.

The peninsula of Devon and Cornwall is beautiful rolling country with some high moorlands. Being so near the sea, the climate is mild and sunny. Dairy cattle are found in quantity, and oats are the chief grain crop. Devonshire cream and Cornish butter are famous. In the past this region produced large amounts of copper, lead, and tin.

To complete the picture of the United Kingdom we must look briefly at "the six counties" in Northern Ireland with Belfast as their capital. This region is about the size of Connecticut. The whole island of Ireland is like a saucer; it consists of a central plain surrounded by a rim of hills. On the north the rim of hills is broad and takes up most of the six counties. These uplands are similar to the uplands of southern Scotland. Rainfall is heavy and the pastures are very green. Dairy cattle, hogs, and sheep are raised, and potatoes, oats, and some barley and wheat are cultivated. The chief industries around Belfast are linen manufacturing, shipbuilding, ropemaking, distilling, and the manufacturing of machinery.

On the whole, the climate of the United Kingdom is too wet. The westerly winds blowing over the warm Gulf Stream become laden with moisture, strike the cooler land mass that is the British Isles, and drop their rain. The western shores of the islands are consistently wetter and warmer than the eastern shores. The western shores get too much rain for good agriculture, the eastern ones about the right amount. It rarely snows in the British Isles: a winter temperature of below freezing is considered cold. Yet because the English heat their homes less than do Americans, visiting Americans generally complain of the cold in Britain. The British look upon a summer temperature of over 85 degrees as very hot.

RESOURCES

The stage of development of a nation's industries depends a lot on the accessibility, as well as the extent, of a nation's resources, on how readily they can be extracted or harvested, processed or smelted, and transported.

Industrial power is a nation's muscles, the slave gangs of modern man. How much industrial power does the United Kingdom have? Britain produces no natural gas and virtually no oil. She must import virtually all the oil that she uses. Also, her hydroelectric power resources are not large. Although the rainfall is heavy, the mountains are not high enough to develop a good head of water. Scotland has developed more water power than England and Wales. Most of the industrial power which Britain uses comes from coal.

Coal. The United Kingdom has been very fortunate in its coal resources. "Known coal-fields extend under 12 per cent of the surface of England and Wales and under 5 per cent of that of Scotland."[5] Every part of the main island has coal under it or not more than 50 miles distant. Originally, the coal was not deep and the seams were easy to work. This fact helps to explain England's early industrialization. Long before England's forests gave out, her industries were using coal. Coal has been used since the late Middle Ages in small industries and homes. Yet despite the abundance and accessibility of coal in former times, the best mines today are deep and increasingly costly to work. An English miner gets only a fifth as much coal in a day as an American.

The country is also fortunate in having all kinds of coal, such as anthracite (a fifth of Welsh coal is anthracite), coking coal, steam coal, gas

[5] A. Demangeon, *The British Isles* (London: William Heinemann, Ltd., 1939), p. 254.

coal, and coal well located for loading on ships in the vicinities of New-castle and of Swansea. Britain has very little brown coal. Peat exists in quantity in Scotland, in a few parts of England, and in Wales, but most of it is gathered by individuals for their own use.

The leading coal fields in 1953 were found in and near the Midlands. They produced over half the coal; the fields around Newcastle yielded 19 per cent; those of Scotland, 11 per cent; and of South Wales, 12 per cent. The total production was 224 million tons, a trifle less than before World War II. There is still enough coal in the United Kingdom to last another six hundred years at the current rate of consumption if one counts all the known coal of more than 1-foot thickness within 4,000 feet or less of the surface. If this calculation seems unrealistic, we should re-member that new discoveries are still being made. An important one was made in Kent several years ago.

No other mineral resource is as important to the United Kingdom as coal, whose value makes up almost 90 per cent of everything mined. And it is coal, of course, that provides practically all the gas that is burned and that runs virtually all the generators that make electricity. The nation's railroads and ships use coal rather than the more expensive oil. Formerly, Britain exported a quarter of its coal, and coal ranked high among exports. In 1953 it ranked thirteenth, although this was the best year for coal in a long time. Because of the extreme importance of coal to the British economy, the economic welfare of the nation depends to a marked degree upon its abundant supply, cheap production, and effi-cient marketing, as the economist Stanley Jevons long ago indicated.

Metals. Iron constitutes less than 2 per cent of the value of English minerals. A century ago England produced half of the world's iron, but today she imports over half of the ore her industries use. Nor is the domestic ore high in metallic content. Most of it is mined around the southeastern part of the Midlands in Lincolnshire, Leicestershire, and Northampton. A secondary source is in the vicinity of Newcastle. Only one other place matters and that is Furness, north of Liverpool in Cum-berland. Scotland no longer has an appreciable supply and Belfast im-ports hers.

Other metals for which England was once famous are tin, lead, zinc, and copper. None of these is now a resource of much consequence. Tin was mined in Cornwall as early as the fifth century before Christ. The Cornish mines were worked early because they were near the surface. In recent centuries they were important in the manufacture of pewter. They reached their peak of production about 1870. Today, most of the tin ore that Britain processes comes from Malaya; less than 5 per cent is produced at home.

The mining of lead also dates from Roman times. It became quite important in the Middle Ages for roofing and piping in cathedrals. Its peak also was reached about a century ago. North Wales, Durham in northern England, and Derbyshire were the centers of production. Today, Britain imports about 90 per cent of the lead that her industries use.

Zinc, which makes brass when combined with copper, was of importance in the sixteenth and seventeenth centuries for cannon, brass being easier to work for this purpose than iron. It reached its peak about 1880. Domestic zinc mines supply only about 10 per cent of the zinc smelted in England today. Most of these mines are near the mouth of the Severn in southwest England.

Copper was developed along with zinc for making brass in the sixteenth century. Strenuous efforts at that time to discover new deposits met with some success. The chief mines were in Cornwall, near Bristol, and in Staffordshire. Also, the island of Anglesy, off north Wales, once had a hill of copper. A century ago half the copper of the world was produced in the British Isles, but today domestic production is of no consequence. All the ore is imported from the richer and more easily worked deposits of Chile, the United States, and elsewhere.

Other Minerals. The decline in importance of iron and the nonferrous metals and even of coal should not blind us to the fact that the United Kingdom has other mineral resources. Exceptionally fine china clay is obtained in Devon and Cornwall for one of the major industries of the Midlands. Feldspar, flint, gray clay, and other raw materials for the pottery industry are available close by. Fluorspar, an industrial flux and a raw material in glassmaking, comes from Derbyshire in central England and so do barites for making the best paper. The highest grade of salt is obtained from a large salt field in Durham. Salt is useful in chemistry as well as in the kitchen, and Britain has a large chemical industry.

Forests. Before minerals of all kinds were as important as they are today, the British people made much use of wood. The islands have an ideal climate for forests and were once covered with oak, beech, and ash. The oak was, and perhaps still is, the characteristic British tree, but the forests have largely disappeared. Before World War II, among 26 European nations Great Britain stood last in forest resources on a per capita basis. In 1947–1949 only 6.5 per cent of the nation's land surface was forested (with trees over 3 inches in diameter). This amounted to 3,600,-000 acres, more than half of them in England and over a third in Scotland. The most densely forested sections are northeast Scotland, southeast England, and south Wales. The majority of these forests are relatively young, so that little timbering can be done currently.

The quality of the forests is also declining, although the percentage of hardwoods is still high (60 per cent). But when oak trees are cut, the less valuable birches frequently succeed them, and recently planted trees are generally some form of pine, because these mature faster. Four-fifths of the nation's forests are privately owned, which makes supervision of them difficult.

Efforts are being made to improve the forestry situation. The Forestry Commission was established at the end of World War I. Since then the government has acquired forestable lands, established national forest parks, and laid down strict rules for the cutting of timber. There are large land areas in Britain that are little used and yet suitable for forestation. The clayey soils of parts of England could again produce the fine oaks that the charcoal burners of past centuries used up. The wet and cool climate farther north is admirably suited to growing conifer forests, as in Scandinavia and the American Northwest.

Fisheries. Britain's fisheries are still significant, although they are only a tenth as important as mining or agriculture. In 1953 they supplied $130 million of fish and employed about 40,000 persons. Britain exports about a third of these fish, chiefly to the Catholic nations of Southern Europe.

The United Kingdom is well situated for fishing. The surrounding waters, including most of the North Sea, are relatively shallow. There are also plateaus, or banks, like the Dogger Bank (7,000 square miles) in the center of the North Sea. The warm currents of the Gulf Stream supply ample plankton for the fish to feed upon. Most of the fish caught are cod brought in by trawlers which haul an open net along the ocean floor. The chief fishing ports are on the east coast of England and Scotland. The leaders are Hull, Grimsby, and Yarmouth in England, and Aberdeen in Scotland.

Other Resources. Heirlooms are still another resource of the British— castles, cathedrals, Roman ruins, quaint villages, art collections, museums, and other historical and literary landmarks. The cultural resources of a people who have resisted invasion for almost nine hundred years are bound to be tremendous. Not the least of them are British traditions of pomp and ceremony, such as the changing of the guard, military tatoos, introductions to the King and Queen, and the coronation of a new monarch. In 1953 the United Kingdom was visited by over 800,000 persons who spent about $200 million.

Perhaps the greatest resource of all is the character of the British people. Other nations have greater natural resources and have done far less with them. The British people have stamina, intelligence, a strong sense of duty and patriotism, a veritable worship of "fair play," and an ability to rise to the occasion in an emergency, as witness countless heroic episodes in their history, such as the defeat of the Spanish Armada or the turning back of the Nazi air invasion in September, 1940. This "will" not only to survive but to be a credit to themselves and their nation is what has made the United Kingdom a great nation for most of the last thousand years. It has been the country's greatest resource. It goes far to explain why the British have been able in recent times to accomplish so much with so little.

EVALUATION OF RESOURCES

The resources of the United Kingdom may be evaluated by a number of criteria. Are they well located within the nation for the most convenient use of most of the people? Are they well located for trade with other parts of Europe and of the world? Is the quality of these resources high, so that they may be developed with profit to their owners and to the British nation? Are the methods of industrial and agricultural production sufficiently advanced for the best exploitation of these resources? And are the major resources being worked off sufficiently to obtain the maximum output from the physical assets of the country?

Location of Resources. Probably a major reason why the British Isles developed industries so early is their geographical and climatic location. They are as close as 20 miles to the coast of France, which is advantageous for trade with Europe. Yet for almost a thousand years the English Channel has acted like the moat of a medieval castle, aiding the British to repel invaders. The Isles are warmed on the west by the waters of the Gulf Stream; if they were not they would be as cold as southern Alaska or the Straits of Magellan. They are cooled by the cyclonic winds of the northern temperate zone, which have a stimulating effect on the inhabitants. Where these winds and their temperate, yet changeable, weather are found, according to Ellsworth Huntingdon, also are found the great industrial regions of the world. The British Isles have a head start in any race to the markets of the American continent to the west.

The British Isles are surrounded by the Atlantic Ocean, including the North Sea, and have a score of deep-water ports. Many of the rivers are navigable some distance inland by small vessels. Fairly large vessels go up the Thames to London, up the Mersey to Liverpool, the Clyde to Glasgow, the Humber to Hull and Grimsby, the Tyne to Newcastle, the Tees to Middleborough, and the Severn to Bristol. In the eighteenth century, when vessels had a shallower draft and the rivers were less choked with silt (perhaps because there were more forests then), there was virtually no place more than 15 miles from the ocean or a river navigable to the ocean. This must be reckoned as a major reason for the nation's early mercantile and industrial development. Such waterways are a free roadbed provided by nature. Thus in the United Kingdom most raw materials, processing centers, and home markets have been fairly accessible to one another.

It has already been pointed out that Great Britain was once heavily forested with fine hardwoods, many of which provided charcoal for the early industries. Also, coal is found fairly near the surface in most parts of the kingdom. These fuel resources meant that iron, tin, copper, lead, and zinc ores could be smelted near the mines. The nation's industries developed early because facilities for water transportation held down transportation costs in an age when the difference in cost between water and land transportation favored water transportation more than it does today.

Quality of Resources. A distinction should be made between the quality of the nation's resources in the seventeenth and eighteenth centuries and their quality today. For the most part, either the best have been used up or higher-grade competing resources have been found in other parts of the world. The forests have largely been depleted, especially the stands of oak. The best veins of coal near the surface have been worked out, so that today British coal mines are being worked much more deeply than are American mines, and this reduces the amount mined in a day. There never has been much hydroelectric power. As for other mineral resources, a country which once produced half the world's copper and iron now produces only a fraction of its own needs. The fisheries have lost in relative importance. The wet climate and large amount of clayey soil make the United Kingdom only a fair agricultural region, especially on the western side. Meanwhile the population has reached 51 million. Although that means a larger working force, it also means more mouths to feed. Altogether, more people must make a livelihood from fewer resources. That puts a greater burden on the energy, intelligence, and organizing capacity of the British people.

Production. A good picture of the production of natural resources in the United Kingdom can be had by examining Table 9-1. It shows that

Table 9-1. Production Per Capita in United Kingdom and United States, 1953

Item	United Kingdom	United States
Personal income	$747	$1,778
Coal mined, tons	4.4	3.2
Wheat harvested, bushels	1.7	7.9
Yield per acre, bushels	38	17.3
Cattle held	0.2	0.4
Sheep held	0.4	0.2
Timber cut, cubic feet	0.16	19.4
Fish landed, pounds	26	28
Iron mined, pounds	620	1,220*

* For 1952.

SOURCE: *Statistical Abstract of the United States, 1954; Annual Abstract of Statistics,* 1954 (London: HMSO). Conversions by D. L. Kemmerer.

the United Kingdom produces more coal per capita than the United States (but needs five times as many miners to produce each ton), raises twice as much wheat per acre, keeps twice as many sheep per capita, and lands about as much fish per capita. On the other hand, the United Kingdom suffers woefully in comparison in the production of wheat, timber, and iron. The basic fact stands out that the islands are over-populated and the resources partly used up.

THE BRITISH POLITICAL ECONOMY

Although democracy dates back to ancient Greece, its greatest development in recent centuries has been in England. The influence of democratic England has been felt throughout the world, through her former Colonies, like the United States, through her Dominions, her present Colonies, and even her Continental neighbors. Both men and women over twenty-one are entitled to vote in Britain, and in recent national elections about four-fifths of them regularly exercised that right. They take their politics seriously.

Although the British Empire has a Queen, she exercises little power and is chiefly a symbolic figure to whom most parts of the Commonwealth pay allegiance. The United Kingdom has a "responsible" government, in contrast with our American "representative" government. The party with the majority of the 625 members of Parliament chooses the Prime Minister and other ministers from among its members. It governs until it loses the majority or loses an election, which must be held every five years anyway. There is also an upper house, the House of Lords, but it has not had much power since 1911. There is no written constitution; the so-called constitution is a collection of legal precedents accumulated over the centuries. Any of these precedents may be changed at any time by simple act of Parliament. The English government has been one of the most stable in the history of Western civilization.

As in the United States, capitalism in England developed along with democracy. Capitalism, it will be recalled, rests on four basic institutions: the profit motive, respect for private property, freedom of enterprise, and competition. Competition includes the right to set prices. The development of capitalism has had its ups and downs. It started as a reaction against the rigidities of the feudal system, which broke down about the time of the great bubonic plagues of the fourteenth and fifteenth centuries and of the rise of nationalism. Some of capitalism's institutions were still not fully developed in the eighteenth century. Many prices and wages were fixed by custom, so there was not yet full freedom to set prices. Nor was there full freedom of enterprise, especially if an Englishman did not live in the mother country—American colonists were forbidden to manufacture woolen goods, beaver hats, and certain iron goods, for example. Such restrictions on commerce are generally called "mercantilism."

With the development of new markets abroad and of improved methods of manufacturing at home, mercantilism broke down and was replaced by *laissez faire,* a policy of freeing business from interference by government. Under this hands-off policy Britain prospered tremendously, both commercially and industrially. It was capitalism in perhaps its purest form, but a capitalism characterized by many abuses—exploitation of the labor of women and children, dangerous factory conditions, low wages, long hours. It was not long before reforms began to be made.

The modern English economy has developed out of the reaction to the many abuses of *laissez faire.* Other factors have had their influence too, such as growing population, dwindling resources, exhausting wars, and the burdens of a vast empire. The Labor party took full control of the government at the end of World War II. One of its aims was to better the condition of the common man, who felt that he had not shared sufficiently in the past in the prosperity of the Empire. He also felt that the wealthy should share in any "austerity" which must be borne if the nation was to regain its place in the world despite dwindling resources. Between 1945 and 1950 Britain put several of her major industries, including coal, utilities, steel, railroads, and Bank of England, under government ownership. In recent years others, although still privately owned, have become subject to numerous restrictions—one cannot issue new securities, import goods from abroad, or cut timber without government permission, for example. Meats, citrus fruits, and many other foods were on ration lists for over a decade. There is not a major area of economic activity—agriculture, manufacturing, transportation, labor, finance, commerce—that is not subject to many regulations.

Britain's economy is often called the "welfare state." It is an economy of decadent capitalism. To understand how the nation reached this stage of development it will be helpful to examine briefly the happenings in each of the above-mentioned six areas of economic activity. This will be done in the chapters that follow.

QUESTIONS FOR STUDY

1. How did the four parts of Great Britain evolve into one country? How did the British Empire develop? The Commonwealth? What is the relation of Canada to the Commonwealth? Of India to the Commonwealth?

2. What are the chief characteristics of England's population? How does England compare with other nations of the world in density of population? What is the significance of this situation?

3. Characterize each of the major regions of Britain as to climate, geography, major products, and population density.

4. What has been the significance of coal as a British resource? Have there been any power resources to rival coal in Britain?

5. What metals have been important in the past in Britain's economic development? Are any of them important today?

6. What other important resources does Britain have? How does Britain compare with the United States in the matter of natural resources and agricultural commodities on a per capita basis?

7. How does Britain's "responsible" government differ from our own "representative" government? How does Britain's constitution differ from ours? How does Britain's capitalism differ from ours?

CHAPTER 10

AGRICULTURE

English agriculture has changed tremendously since the Middle Ages, although the countryside still shows traces of medieval ways of farming. Some seven hundred years ago England had a population of less than two million, compared with twenty times as many persons today. Most of them were farmers, and they raised almost all that they ate and wore. The country imported little, and to most persons "sugar and spice and other things nice" were unknown. Most people just existed in thatched cottages or wattled hovels, often sharing the comforts of home with their beasts. Even salt was scarce, and spoiled meat helped spread the dreaded leprosy. Today, most of England's farms sell some goods in the markets, and only 5 per cent of the working population is engaged in agriculture. The nation imports a third of its food. This occurs despite enormous improvements in agricultural methods.

AGRICULTURE BEFORE 1750

The methods and customs of agriculture of the past still make their influence felt in the present. Early English agricultural progress falls into four major periods: the manorial system in feudal times, the breakdown of the manorial system after the Black Death, the first enclosures of the fifteenth and sixteenth centuries, and the second enclosures of the seventeenth to the nineteenth centuries.

Farmers did not live alone and far apart in medieval England; rather, they lived together in a village and went out to their fields to work. The village lay around the home of a nobleman or of a churchman, and he gave the people protection and directed their activities. The manor house was sometimes a castle but usually was less pretentious. The fields just outside the village were laid out in long strips, and each villager had a strip in several fields, perhaps 20 or 30 strips in all. About half of all the strips belonged to the lord of the manor and were known as the "demesne." The villagers also had the right to pasture their cattle on what was called the "common" and to cut wood in the woodland.

142

The system of scattered strips was originally set up to divide the land fairly but it was inconvenient in the long run and required a great deal of cooperation. The people, whether cotters or villeins, literally belonged to the lord and might not leave the manor, even to marry or enter the service of the church, without his permission. The villein generally devoted half his workweek to cultivating the lord's demesne, half to his own strips. The system rested heavily on custom, and there was little in it to yield anyone a profit or stimulate the use of better methods. The crop yields were poor, the cattle were scrawny, and life was day-after-day drudgery.

A change was gradually taking place, however. The population of England was increasing, and the greater demand for food led the more enterprising villeins to sell some of their surplus. Now they might pay the lord in cash instead of in labor for the use of the land. The lord liked this because the laborers whom he hired gave their time and effort more willingly than the villeins whose obligation rested on custom. Thus the manorial system was already beginning to crumble when the Black Death accelerated the process.

The Black Death started in Constantinople in 1347 and spread throughout all Europe, killing half of the population. The disease was carried by rat fleas. When the plague passed, the lord of the manor found his holdings enlarged through the death of tenants, crops unharvested, food prices at famine heights, and a shortage of villeins to work on the land. All kinds of economic adjustments had to be made. The lord could find no tenants to replace the victims of the plague, and when he hired laborers, he had to pay them higher wages.

Within a few years after the Black Death, commutation of payment in labor to payment in money became common. Workers began to realize how they had been exploited under the old system. Peasant revolts, such as the Great Rebellion of 1381, flared, and Levellers (fourteenth-century subversives), such as Wat Tyler and John Ball, demanded more democracy. Lords continually had to make concessions to obtain labor, and villeins obtained their freedom in one way or another and became "copyholders." A copyholder held his land from year to year, his title being evidenced by a copy of an entry on the manor roll, and he paid his rent in cash.

In the fifteenth century another important change took place; there was a sharp rise in the price of wool. This led to the first enclosure movement. The growth of the woolen industry in the Low Countries as well as in England stepped up the demand for wool. Increasing their flocks of sheep appealed to many big landowners who were victims of a new kind of plague, the fever to get rich. There was only one difficulty and that was arranging a large enough piece of enclosable pasture land. The lord could turn his demesne into pasture if he could disentangle it from his tenants' holdings. Usually this was not difficult. But when he began to enclose the common pasture lands, there was trouble; the tenants needed that for their animals. Still, an energetic lord could overawe them with threats of eviction or of costly law suits. Lands were consolidated, the amount of pasture land increased, and more sheep were raised. Many tenants were deprived of their means of livelihood, and some of them, unable to find jobs in the towns, became "sturdy beggars" or highwaymen. By about 1600 the first enclosure movement had run its course.

In the seventeenth century there was a second enclosure movement, this time for the purposes of providing wealthy merchants with landed estates and of employing improved methods of agriculture. The newly enriched merchants of this period copied the manner of living of the landed nobility. They had always admired the landed gentry; now they had enough money to acquire estates and servants and be like them. But they remained merchants in spirit, a characteristic that led them to improve their lands. A primitive form of scientific crop rotation began to supplant the ancient three-field system,[1] the growing of turnips was advocated, and some drainage was put in. Finally, the lawyers found ways to enforce the feudal custom of entail and thus keep the consolidated estates undivided in the hands of one family. As the Agricultural Revolution got well under way in the eighteenth century, the number of consolidations increased sharply. In the early nineteenth century there were even more.

THE AGRICULTURAL REVOLUTION

For centuries the "magnificent inertia" of farmers had kept them from trying new methods. What had been good enough for grandfather was good enough for father, and then for son. Thomas Coke of Norfolk (1752–1842) sowed his grain by drilling for sixteen years, and with marked success, before a neighbor began to copy him. Methods and tools improved little until about the eighteenth century.

There were several causes for the changes that now took place. One was the second enclosure movement. This movement was given continued impetus by the developments in other segments of the economy. In the eighteenth century the English population began to increase more rapidly. That meant more mouths to feed and better markets for agricultural products. Markets were further widened by the industrialization of the textile, iron, and other industries, whose workers became increasingly dependent on farmers to feed them. Both the Agricultural and

---

[1] The three-field system consisted of planting one field in wheat, one in oats or rye, and letting one "lie fallow," or rest, each year. Since weeds grew in the fallow field, this form of rotation was rather ineffective.

Industrial Revolutions were facilitated by improvements in transportation, canals and turnpikes at first, and railroads in the nineteenth century. Without low-cost transportation—Britain was favored by nature in this respect anyway—specialization in agriculture and industry would have been slower.

The Agricultural Revolution was a transition from primitive to scientific agricultural methods and from predominantly subsistence farming to a more commercial type of farming. Among the important changes were the introduction of better methods of crop rotation and better farm equipment, the appearance of farm machinery, improvements in livestock breeding, the rise of agricultural societies, and legislation by Parliament affecting the conduct of agriculture. Let us look at a few examples of these developments.

Improvement of the Land. One of the reasons for the first enclosure movement had been that the land was wearing out and was more productive as pasture land. An important innovation in the seventeenth century prepared the way for a reversal of this process. Sir Richard Weston introduced clover from Holland. Clover, like other legumes, has nitrogen-fixing nodules on its roots and thus fertilizes the soil instead of exhausting it. British farmers began planting clover instead of letting their land lie fallow each third year. Also, the clover was easy to harvest and was a valuable forage for cattle. As was to be expected, adoption of this improvement was slow; the planting of clover did not become widespread until the eighteenth century.

Weston also tried to popularize the planting of turnips, but it remained for another to succeed in this. This was Charles, Lord Townshend, who became famous in the 1730s as "Turnip" Townshend. Turnips yield more animal feed per acre than almost any other crop and provide food for man too. They also fit well into a crop-rotation system that emphasizes grains like wheat and oats. By providing stock feed they increase the size of herds and thus the amount of manure and so improve the soil.

Almost simultaneously with the introduction of clover and turnips, Jethro Tull invented the drill and cultivator. This made it possible to plant turnips and grain in rows instead of sowing broadcast, to eradicate weeds by easier cultivation, and to increase crop yields noticeably.

More progress in restoring the soil, through better crop rotation, drainage, and manuring, would probably have been made if tenants had been surer that they could keep their land or that they would be recompensed for their improvements. With few exceptions most farmers were tenants at will and had almost no assurance of compensation.

Other Improvements. Robert Bakewell, of Leicestershire, made important contributions to livestock breeding around 1760. Previously, the theory had been that cattle were improved by mixing breeds. They were allowed to run together in the common pasture. Bakewell boldly began to inbreed to develop animals with desired characteristics, and he also segregated his stock. Bakewell's first experiments were with sheep—the average weight of a sheep's carcass was 28 pounds in 1700 and 80 pounds in 1800. Later, he turned his attention to cattle, and the average weight of a carcass rose from 370 to 800 pounds in the eighteenth century.

To spread the knowledge of better agricultural methods these pioneers of more scientific farming wrote books, established museums, and published articles in newspapers. Jethro Tull, who invented the drill, was roundly abused at first and did not live to see his new ideas exclusively adopted, but Robert Bakewell got quite a following of foreign and English nobility, who came to see his museum and listen to the "master." In 1787 the Highland Society in Scotland was founded to propagandize better agricultural methods, and in 1793 the Board of Agriculture was set up in England, with Arthur Young as its first secretary. It was highly successful for about thirty years, thanks to the enthusiasm and prolific pen of Young. There was not in England, however, any everyday farmers' society similar to Elkanah Watson's Berkshire Society, which gave America the county fair.

As farmers became more cost conscious, they began to give some attention to farm machinery. Growing cost consciousness reflected the growing market for farm products as more workers were attracted into the towns to work in mills and factories and as more farms were put on a part-time commercial basis. Tull's drill and cultivator were not widely adopted. An experimental threshing mill was invented in 1743, but there was not an effective one until Andrew Meikle invented his in 1798. Its use spread gradually, to nearby Lancashire by 1800, to North Wales by 1813, and to Kent in southeast England by 1830. A practical haytedder appeared in 1814. In 1812 John Common, of Northumberland, was awarded a gold medal for a reaping machine, but it was greeted with such lack of enthusiasm that he ceased working on it. The horse rake came in 1841, steam plows about the middle of the century, and harvesting machines from America a generation later.

Improved methods of crop rotation, better breeds of stock and their segregation, and the purchase and care of farm machinery, all called for the use of more capital than farmers had previously used. It must be remembered that the vast majority of farmers in Britain were still tenants. Therefore "high farming," or much capital investment, spread slowly and was limited chiefly to those who, through business or by inheritance, could risk the funds.

The Agricultural Revolution would not have been possible without the savings that British merchants accumulated over generations of trading. And the Industrial Revolution would not have been possible without these savings, without the surplus food made possible by the Agricultural Revolution, and without the labor supply released by more efficient farming. Equally true, the farmers could not have sold their surplus if markets had not sprung up in new industrial cities. The whole process was one of action and interaction. Occasionally, some segment of the economy fell behind in the march of progress and sought to obtain, or to reactivate, special legislation for itself from Parliament.

The Corn Laws. The big landowners, many of whom were grain farmers, got the help of Parliament in protecting their production of corn. In Britain the word "corn" is synonymous with our word "grain." American corn (usually called "maize") is almost unknown in England; it is not liked; and it does not thrive. Therefore, the Corn Laws were laws protecting the home production of grain, especially wheat. Being an island, England had been conscious for a long time of the need to be self-sufficient in grain. The Tory landlords made the most of this when they could. Corn Laws of a sort may be traced back to Norman times, but the first modern Corn Law was passed by Parliament in 1436. In the next three and a half centuries the Corn Laws were sometimes enforced and sometimes not.

In the early nineteenth century the demand for Corn Laws was revived. Inflation and other economic disturbances of the period of the French Revolution and Napoleonic Wars had increased the demand for wheat. Lands were made into wheat fields which could only be profitable as long as wheat remained very scarce. Rather than back out of this uneconomic situation, the landed interests got Parliament to grant bounties on the export of grain, to keep high the minimum price at which grain might be imported, and to impose stiff duties when imports were allowed.

The significance of the Corn Laws is that, like the American AAA program of the 1930s, they kept the price of grain higher than it would have been in a free market and encouraged some farmers to grow grain who otherwise would not have done so. They did all this at the expense of the nonfarming population, who had to pay a higher price for their bread and other grain products. Making a living by getting a subsidy, instead of by improving farming methods, may have discouraged some farmers from turning to scientific farming as soon as they otherwise would have done.

When more Britons got the vote in 1832, they decided to do something about this undemocratic subsidy. The country was becoming increasingly industrial, and in another twenty years half the population would be living in urban areas. Also, many industrialists believed they could pay lower wages if the Corn Laws were repealed. The Anti-Corn Law

League was formed, and its activities, together with the catastrophe of the Irish potato famine, finally brought about repeal of the Corn Laws in 1846.

Two other pieces of legislation, passed in the first half of the nineteenth century, also stimulated self-improvement in agriculture. One was a revision of the Poor Laws in 1834, which reduced the burden on the taxpayers to support the poor. The other was the Tithe Commutation Act of 1836, which had the effect of fixing the payment a farmer must make. Now he could improve his land and his buildings without exposing himself to higher taxes and tithes. The writings of Sir Humphrey Davy on the use of guano, manure, and other fertilizers encouraged many farmers to make these improvements. Farmers were also improving drainage. At last, some everyday farmers were paying attention to the agricultural societies and the agricultural scientists.

A CENTURY OF BRITISH AGRICULTURE

There are four fairly distinct phases in the history of British agriculture in the century from 1846 to 1939. The period from the repeal of the Corn Laws in 1846 to about 1870 was one of prosperity, a golden era. In contrast, the remainder of the century brought falling prices and great hardship. The nation did better again before, during, and right after World War I until the onset of the Great Depression. After 1931 Britain, like the United States, witnessed the application of economic controls and panaceas to make the country more self-sufficient. The trend of the period as a whole is unmistakable, a shift from free trade and self-reliance to great dependence on the government.

A Golden Era of Agriculture. Contrary to dire prophecies by many landowners, repeal of the Corn Laws was followed by prosperity rather than distress. True, people ate less home-grown wheat, and the price of wheat declined, but the population was growing—it grew from 20 million to 27 million between 1841 and 1871—and the prices and production of oats and barley were rising. With improved methods of farming, costs were falling, and better transportation was cutting the cost of getting the produce to market. In addition, the Crimean War (1854–1856) and the American War between the States (1861–1865) helped keep up the prices of most of the crops that the British farmer raised.

There were a number of significant improvements in this period, although some came with amazing slowness. Also, some primitive methods persisted right down to modern times. Yet farms tended to become larger, 51 per cent of farms were 50 to 500 acres in size in 1851, 72 per cent in 1885. Drilling grain replaced sowing broadcast; better plows were used, even steam plows; steam threshing took the place of the flail; and the Royal Agricultural Society offered prizes for improved machines and encouraged the use of farm machinery.

A Generation of Agricultural Discontent. The last third of the nineteenth century was a dismal period for the farmers of Britain, just as it was for the farmers of the United States, and for somewhat the same reasons. The causes may be summed up in a few words: falling prices the result, in considerable part, of greater production, which, in turn, was the result of more efficient methods of cultivation, better transportation, and more foreign competition. Britain, particularly, felt the competition of the United States and Canada in grain, of Australia in wool, and Argentina in beef. The cost of shipping wheat from Chicago to Liverpool was cut in half between 1868 and 1885 and was again halved by 1902. Germany and other Continental nations met this competition with higher tariffs, but the British, remembering their long struggle to get rid of the Corn Laws, stuck to a free trade policy. The British farmers suffered the consequences. Some gave up farming; arable land declined one-fifth from 1871–1875 to 1906–1910. Some parried the blow by shifting to more perishable commodities, such as milk, fruit, garden produce, and fresh meat, or to cheap bulky items, such as potatoes or hay, that could not stand long-distance transportation. Most of them had to stay and bear it, hoping each year that the next year would bring an upturn in prices. But wheat prices kept sinking, from 56½ shillings a quarter (8 bushels) in 1877, for example, to 22½ shillings in 1894. Landlords felt obliged to help their tenants by reducing rents, but eventually the tenants recognized that as much relief as could be expected had been received from the landlords. Many farmers abandoned improvements like drainage and fertilization in the struggle to survive, and the land deteriorated.

What, it may be asked, did the government do to help the farmer? Two Royal Commissions were appointed to investigate in 1879 and 1893, but nothing of consequence came of their findings. The Board of Agriculture was established in 1889 to collect and disseminate information. Steps were taken to reduce taxes on farm lands. The most important development was a series of three laws, each more effective than its predecessor, in 1875, 1883, and 1906, obliging landlords to compensate their tenants for unexhausted improvements at the end of their tenancy. Finally, a beginning was made toward a system of agricultural education for young people desiring to become farmers. None of these developments, however, resulted from the demands of any farmers' organization that might be compared with the Grange in America.

There were further improvements in scientific farming and in farm machinery. For example, grain harvesters, developed in the United States, were imported in the 1870s and 1880s; the hay tedder, invented earlier in the century, at last came into widespread use; and the milk separator was invented in 1879. There was also steady progress in stock-breeding and in animal medicine; many animal diseases were virtually stamped out, the last epidemic of pleuropneumonia among cattle occurring in 1898. Generally the investment of more capital in equipment is accompanied by a growth in the size of farms, but because the British were forced by foreign competition to devote more attention to specialized activities such as fruit farming, poultry raising, dairying, and stock-breeding, the size of farms showed a tendency to decline.

This bleak era for farmers ended about the turn of the century. Prices turned up in 1896 in Britain as in America. Renegotiation of rents, better agricultural methods, adjustments to the kinds of farming to which Britain was suited in a smaller world, and elimination of some inefficient farmers were all factors in bringing about the revival.

Agriculture before, during, and after World War I. British agricultural prosperity before World War I depended on the farmers' acceptance of the realities of their competitive position. In the five years prior to 1914 Britain imported 80 per cent of her wheat, 40 per cent of her meat, and much of the fodder for her home-grown meat. The majority of the population now lived in urban areas, and the amount of land under cultivation was declining. This was all right for an advanced industrial nation existing in a peaceful world in which international trade was relatively untrammeled. But survival itself was at stake if those conditions ceased, as they did after 1914.

Britain and Germany each tried to blockade and starve the other. Germany used the submarine, a new weapon whose sneak attacks seemed particularly barbaric to a world not used to them. Submarines sank millions of tons of shipping. Although Britain was handicapped, and food and other supplies were abnormally scarce, the flow of goods was not cut off. Submarines caused great anxiety, especially around 1916. Accordingly, Britain revised her agricultural policies to deal with the situation.

An ambitious food-production policy was put into operation in December, 1916. Committees were assigned in each county to be the agents of the Board of Agriculture and to direct activities at this local level. These committees had generous powers. They might instruct farmers what crops to grow, require them to plow up grassland, take over uncultivated or poorly cultivated lands and assign them to persons who would cultivate them, and determine whether certain lands should be fertilized. The Food Production Department of the Board of Agriculture was established. Besides setting quotas for regions and crops, it also served as a source of supply when there was special need for labor, machines, seed, or fertilizers.

This "plough policy" was undertaken too late to be successful in 1917 but it was highly so by 1918. Some 2½ million additional acres of land were cultivated in 1918. Production of wheat, oats, and potatoes were all 50 per cent greater than the prewar average. Although this was accomplished, in part, at the cost of reduced production of milk and meat, Britain was producing 24 per cent more calories than she had before the war. There were other adjustments too. The cattle farmers could not be expected to plough up their pastures unless they were assured that their crops would be profitable. Therefore, the Corn Production Act of 1917 guaranteed minimum prices on various grain crops in the years ahead. Market prices were actually above these minima. Landlords were forbidden to raise rents and thus take the gains from guaranteed minimum prices. Even agricultural laborers were guaranteed minimum wages.

When the war suddenly ended in the autumn of 1918, Britain was hardly in a position or in a mood to scrap all this legislation and let farmers drift back to their old way of life. Not only had much land been put under cultivation at considerable cost, but more important, the British had been given an object lesson in their need for self-sufficiency in food in the event of war. For a while elaborate steps were taken to put increased production of home-grown crops on a permanent basis. Under the Agriculture Act of 1920 guaranteed minimum prices were set for wheat and oats, although a commission was to revise these minimum prices each year. Farmers cultivating their land in an unsatisfactory manner could be turned out; minimum wages for farm laborers were continued; and a landlord who turned out a tenant for any reason except bad farming was required to pay him a generous compensation.

These plans for a brave new agricultural world were much too ambitious. Depression struck Britain in mid-1920 and sent food and raw materials prices plummeting. Within two years wheat and oats prices were halved. The government abandoned its scheme for rehabilitating British agriculture on a grandiose scale. The Corn Production Act of 1921 repealed the Agriculture Act of 1920, and British agriculture went part way back to *laissez faire.*

But English agriculture did not go all the way back even though the falling farm prices of the 1920s were reminiscent of that bleak era at the end of the previous century. New traditions had been taking hold, almost imperceptibly at first, and they could not be forgotten. Farmers, whether landowners or tenants, had tasted the sweet security of supported prices on key commodities like grains. Now sugar became the favored child. From 1924 on, subsidies were paid to growers of sugar beets—the British could not forget the scarcity of sugar during the war and were ensuring that this would not happen again. Sugar-beet acreage increased eighteenfold in the next ten years. Tenants now expected more considerate treatment; they had got voluntary rent reductions from landlords in the

1890s, and the government had held rents down during the war. Tenants were also assured of compensation for their unexhausted improvements and plenty of notice if they were to be ousted. Laborers had enjoyed the experience of minimum-wage protection. The public itself had come to expect farmers to submit to government regulation, to raise specified foods, and to cultivate their land well or get off it in times of emergency or even of anticipated emergency.

The investment in farming continued to increase. It took the form of gasoline tractors—an invention of World War I—trucks, an occasional combine, some milking machines, the beginning of electrification, improved dairy cattle (the average cow gave 12 per cent more milk in 1931 than in 1925), and greater use of crop strains that were disease resistant. Mechanization was increasing at a good pace.

Unlike the situation in the United States, growing investment in British agriculture was accompanied by a trend away from farm tenancy. In Britain, tenancy was almost the rule at the outset. In 1913, only 11 per cent of the land in England and Wales was farmed by its owners; in 1927, 36 per cent. A similar change took place in Scotland.

A familiar consequence of growing investment was that it made farmers more conscious of marketing problems, of farm prices, costs, and profits. Farming became more a business and less a way of life. To make profits more likely and losses less so, some farmers were willing to trade independence for government aid. At least they did not object as vigorously as they once would have when it was pressed upon them.

Growing Regulation of Agriculture. In Britain as in the United States the suffering caused by the Great Depression led to increased government activity on behalf of the afflicted segments of the economy. The old policy of *laissez faire* in agriculture was abandoned in 1931 beyond further doubt, and state intervention became permanent. State intervention resulted in more food being produced in Britain, although the total food supply, counting imports, was less plentiful.

The motives for the change were economic and political. The government sought to make farm life more remunerative and thus check the urbanization of the British Isles. Also it sought to make Britain more self-sufficient in the event of war. While food imports would still be necessary, these were to be obtained to a greater extent from within the Empire so as to tie the Dominions closer to the Crown.

The new policy was carried out largely through a series of laws known as the Agricultural Marketing Acts, the first of which was passed in 1931 and the most important in 1933. Under these two acts, marketing boards were established, elected by the producers and exercising such extensive powers as buying, selling, processing, regulating the amount of production, fixing prices and other terms of sale, and making rules covering grading, packing, and transporting. Any commodity might be regulated in this fashion provided the operators of two-thirds of the productive capacity agreed. Only producers of hops agreed at first, because the first act failed to grant authority to regulate imports. As soon as this oversight was taken care of in 1933, additional commodity schemes were set up. Among the chief products covered were hops, milk, pigs, bacon, potatoes, and wheat. How well these schemes worked and how completely they changed the ways of British agriculture can best be seen by looking at two examples.

Wheat accounted for under 2 per cent of the agricultural output of England and Wales in 1931. Wheat prices had been dropping sharply, partly because of the world-wide depression and partly because of foreign competition. The government dared not revive the Corn Laws and tax wheat imports, so it chose the alternative of a subsidy on wheat. The subsidy was based on the difference between the average sale price of the year and the price of wheat in a given standard year, provided that no more than 27 million hundredweight were produced. If production exceeded that figure, the subsidy was to be reduced in proportion. Thus farmers were encouraged to increase their output. British farmers increased their wheat acreage almost 50 per cent between 1931 and 1937, mostly at the expense of oats and barley. In 1937 and 1939 oats and barley were brought into a similar scheme. The funds for the subsidy on wheat came from a tax on flour, which was passed on to consumers in the form of a higher price for flour or bread. It was the same device that was being used in the American AAA program.

The most debated of the commodity schemes was that dealing with milk. From 1922 to 1933 milk was sold privately but under an arrangement between farmers and dairymen negotiated through the National Milk Council. Milk was sold in two markets, called the liquid (drinking) and the manufacturing (cheese, and so forth) markets, at two prices. When the depression brought a fall in prices in the manufacturing market because of foreign competition, many farmers tried to shift to the liquid market. A marketing act for milk had to be passed. A way was found to sell all milk at a pooled price whatever market it was destined for. For a while that seemed to solve the problem, but it solved it too profitably. Farmers produced more milk, driving prices down, and the government had to guarantee a minimum price. Under this subsidy plan, however, the government saw to it that milk was sold under cost in schools and in certain distressed areas.

The results of these various marketing programs are that more of certain farm products are produced in Britain than would be produced under *laissez faire*, the consumer pays higher prices, and the government provides a subsidy to the producers. In the course of less than a century

Britain completed the cycle from protected agriculture through *laissez faire* to protected agriculture again. But now, in contrast with protection under the Corn Laws, more than the grains are protected; the protection takes the form of subsidies instead of tariffs; and protection is accompanied by complex producing and marketing rules.

RECENT DEVELOPMENTS IN BRITISH AGRICULTURE

Recent developments fall into two phases, the period of World War II, when once again the beleagured isle had to increase its agricultural self-sufficiency, and the postwar period under a Labor Government, when shortage of foreign exchange necessitated the continuance of agricultural self-sufficiency.

British Agriculture in World War II. In 1939 Britain was still importing two-thirds of her food and had only 13 million acres of land under the plough, despite the marketing programs described above and the efforts to make the nation more self-sufficient. Without these programs she would have been worse off in 1939 than in 1914; as it was she was about as well off. Once again the menace of Germany's submarines and a Europe under German domination compelled Britain to raise more food. Also, she needed her money to buy vital war materials, and her ships to carry them. It seemed best to produce the bulky products in Britain and thus get the best use of shipping space.

The need was clear and the British rose to the occasion, reaching the peak of their effort in 1943. After that, American supplies and the changing tide of war relieved some of the pressure, and the totals for certain commodities declined, although they were still higher than in 1939 (see Table 10-1). At the 1943 peak Britain was growing two-thirds of her food and importing one-third, just reversing the prewar proportions.

The legislative machinery that had been set up in the 1930s to increase agricultural output was used to stimulate wartime production. Some threats and inducements were added to patriotic exhortations. For example, the state threatened to seize a man's land if he did not employ it properly; and, starting in May, 1939, just before the outbreak of war (the 1938 crisis over Czechoslovakia was in peoples' minds), a bonus of 2 pounds sterling per acre was given to farmers for bringing into use land that had been in grass for seven or more years. Considerable amounts of land, such as fen lands in East Anglia, hill lands in Wales, common lands in Devon, and abandoned farm lands in many regions, were reclaimed. By 1943 arable acreage was as great as in 1918, and subsequently even greater.

There were 62 county committees, each appointed by the Minister of

Table 10-1. United Kingdom Agriculture, 1938–1953

Item	1938	1943	1945	1953
Arable land, million acres	13.0	18.7	19.2	18.1
Crop area in wheat, million acres	1.9	3.5	2.3	2.2
Yield per acre, wheat, cwt	20.4	19.9	19.1	24.0
Wheat harvested, million tons	2.0	3.4	2.2	2.7
Barley harvested, million tons	0.9	1.6	2.1	2.5
Oats harvested, million tons	2.0	3.1	3.2	2.8
Potatoes harvested, million tons	5.1	9.8	9.8	8.3
Vegetables, million tons	2.1	2.8	3.1	2.8
Sugar beets, million tons	2.2	3.8	3.9	5.3
Total cattle, millions	8.8	9.3	9.6	10.4
Total sheep, millions	26.8	20.4	20.2	22.5
Total pigs, millions	4.4	1.8	2.2	5.2
Total poultry, millions	74.2	50.7	62.1	92.1

SOURCE: *Annual Abstract of Statistics,* 1952 (London: HMSO), pp. 185–188; 1954, pp. 166–168.

Agriculture. Each committee had a subcommittee whose job it was to make recommendations about the ploughing up of grassland. If a farmer lacked the capital to undertake recommended ploughing, the committee made arrangements to take over the land. The farmer was usually willing, for ploughing would increase the land's value, and he expected to get it back at some future time. A committee could force a reluctant farmer to plough, but desiring the farmer's cooperation, it rarely used this power. The committees also concerned themselves with the growing of needed crops, with the use of fertilizers, with drainage, and even with the amount of livestock farmers kept. And they disseminated information on new farming methods.

Where labor was lacking and was badly needed, the Ministry of Agriculture attempted to supply it. The number of agricultural workers was increased by using prisoners of war, organizing the Women's Land Army, using school children, and even calling on the regular army. In addition, large numbers of agricultural machines, such as are used in America, were built or imported. The number of tractors in use tripled in three years.

As a result of all these efforts, agricultural production increased some 70 per cent over 1939 in the last three years of the war. One price of this greater production was greater government control over the way the farmer used his land and over what he raised.

British Agriculture since World War II. The postwar trend has been to consolidate the wartime gains in food production and to refine and extend government controls.

When the war was over, farmers, like other Englishmen, hoped for an end of restrictions, a return to more pasture farming, as in prewar days, and a restoration of normal conditions. They were disappointed. Dollars were scarce. Britain could not afford to import more food or more livestock feed. Milk production had to be kept at a high level. The emphasis continued to be on raising grain crops and other foods for human consumption. The plowing-up policy continued, for urban developments, strip mining, road building, and forestry projects were constantly making inroads on the supply of arable land. In 1950 there were 2 acres of permanent grassland for each 3 in 1939.

Britain was more successful than almost any other European nation in keeping her level of food production from falling much below war levels. Some of this success is attributable to greater use of farm machinery (see Table 10-2). The rest may be explained by a determination

Table 10-2. Farm Machinery, 1942–1954
(In thousands)

Machinery	May, 1942	January, 1946	January, 1954
Total tractors..	117	203	439
Tractor-drawn plows	112	179	334
Combines	1	3	22
Milking machines	30	48	102

SOURCE: *Annual Abstract of Statistics*, 1942 (London: HMSO), p. 188; 1954, p. 169.

to keep food production at a high level. To achieve this, wartime legislation was recodified, modified, and somewhat extended. The Hill Farming Act of 1946 paid farmers half the cost of work done on approved projects, and the Livestock Rearing Act of 1951 did the same for suitable lands in upland areas.

The outstanding piece of farm legislation was the Agricultural Act of 1947. It was based on the "twin pillars" of stability and efficiency. To achieve stability, the government sought to guarantee prices and assure markets for 12 major crops. To achieve efficiency, these crops were to be produced at minimum prices consistent with "proper remuneration and living conditions for farmers and workers in agriculture and an adequate return on capital invested in industry."[2] But farmers were not guaranteed against losses. The county committees were made permanent and might still dispossess an inefficient farmer, and there was opportunity for reviewing guaranteed prices. Just the same, the prices were fairly generous. A policy of expending £40 million in government loans a year for new investment appeared to some critics as sheer

[2] Preface of the 1947 act.

featherbedding. The new system has achieved more stability than efficiency, since the penalties for poor farming are not severe. Nevertheless, home-produced food in 1949–1950 contributed 39 per cent of the calories consumed, as against 30 per cent in 1939, when there were three million fewer people.

CONCLUSIONS

British agriculture has changed greatly in the last thousand years, and even in the last 150 years. Britain's population has increased greatly, and only a minority of the people are now farmers. Methods of farming have improved tremendously. Britain now imports more than half her food instead of producing it at home, and for economic and military reasons the government would like to reduce the proportion of food imported.

A glance back over Britain's agricultural history suggests the following conclusions. Improvements in methods were generally made at times when landowners, or recently the government, consolidated landholdings, as after the Black Death, during the first and second enclosure movements, during World War I, and before, during, and after World War II. Appreciable advances in methods and increased production in this century were probably the results of the government's generous assistance in the form of instruction and subsidies. Left to its own devices, British agriculture would very likely have declined more than it has.

QUESTIONS FOR STUDY

1. What were the four main periods of agricultural development in Britain through the eighteenth century? Explain the importance of the Black Death. Distinguish between the two enclosure movements.

2. What was the nature of the Agricultural Revolution in Britain? Why did it take place when it did?

3. What were the Corn Laws? Why did Britain have them? Why did she repeal them? What changes in policy necessarily accompanied their repeal?

4. What were the four periods of British agriculture following the repeal of the Corn Laws? Briefly describe each one. Do these periods parallel the ups and downs of agriculture in the United States?

5. What did Britain do to increase her agricultural output during World War I? Did she try to maintain the pace after World War I? Did all this tend to introduce more regulation into the British economy?

6. What agricultural policies did Britain introduce in the 1930s that resemble the American AAA program? How successful were these policies?

7. What did Britain do to increase her agricultural output during World War II? Did she try to maintain the pace after World War II? Why? How successful has she been?

CHAPTER 11

TRANSPORTATION AND COMMUNICATION

A "revolution" in transportation and communication is necessary before a nation can proceed from an agrarian economy to a modern industrial economy. Such a revolution is required before farmers can shift from self-sufficiency to growing crops for market and before industries can specialize and sell in distant places. Such a revolution is essential, too, before the people of a country can be united politically. The easier movement of goods and people which characterizes industrial countries began at an earlier date in Britain than anywhere else. Britain is favored by an abundance of natural waterways; she has the ocean and seas around her and innumerable navigable rivers. Nature's gift of waterways, however helpful to start with, was insufficient for a modern industrial society.

THE TRANSPORTATION REVOLUTION

The first improvements in transportation were made in road building. The eighteenth century was an Age of Bad Roads, roads which were little more than bridle paths or earthen tracks. Road signs were virtually unknown, and travelers of the period constantly reported losing their way. Inland commerce was carried on by peddlers or by traveling merchants with gangs of pack horses. In the south of England some improvement had been made in main roads; travel from London to Bristol or Bath was comparatively easy. The north-south roads, however, from London to Lancashire or Yorkshire were intolerable. The long, straight roads, which were a legacy of the Romans, had seen 14 centuries of unrepaired use. Wheeled vehicles had left huge ruts, and even the improved roads were often banked so steeply as to cause accidents like that which befell George II and his Queen when their coach turned over at Parson's Green in 1730.

Growing awareness of these conditions, along with other events, combined to bring needed changes. Arthur Young propagandized for better roads through numerous editions of the *Annals of Agriculture*. Suppressing the Rebellion of 1745 demonstrated the sad condition of the roads, and of north-south roads in particular. The beginnings of industry, the expansion of internal trade, and the necessity for better methods of getting coal from mine to consumer also showed the need for improvements.

The upkeep of roads had long been the responsibility of the parishes. The Highway Act of 1555 required each parish to appoint an unpaid surveyor of the highways. At first four days and later six days of labor per year were demanded of each parishioner. The act was unsuccessful. It was difficult to enforce, and even where enforced, the work was given grudgingly and was of poor quality. The act was finally repealed in 1835.

Meanwhile, Parliament established a new principle of payment for road upkeep. In 1663 it set up the first turnpike trust on a portion of the Great North Road. This marks the beginning of the turnpike era. Private companies provided for the upkeep of portions of main roads and charged travelers for the convenience. At first, turnpikes were unpopular and there were occasional riots, of which those near Bristol are best known. The destruction of toll bars was made a felony in 1738. Between 1750 and 1775 over 450 turnpike acts were passed and by 1820 over 1,000. After mid-century many turnpikes went bankrupt because of railway and canal competition; some were amalgamated; and others were abandoned. In 1864 the turnpike system was discontinued, and by 1894 the last of the turnpikes had disappeared. In 1888 the entire cost of main roads became the responsibility of the counties.

The turnpikes were of great benefit, but their usefulness can be exaggerated. There was no uniformity in tolls or the condition of the roads. Some pike owners were interested in making quick profits but no repairs. As late as 1820 less than one-sixth of the 125,000 miles of roads were turnpikes. Yet many improvements in road transportation had come about. The famous coaching age began in 1784 when John Palmer established the first mail coaches to Bristol from London.

This was also the period when the ideas on road improvement of three famous roadbuilders gained acceptance. John Metcalfe (1717–1810), known as "Blind Jack of Knaresborough," was the first modern road engineer. He was famous for his skill in grading and surveying roads. Thomas Telford (1757–1834) devised solid foundations, drained roads, and built bridges. He built roads with curved, firm surfaces and avoided steep grades. The road from Glasgow to Carlisle (1814), that from Shrewsbury to Holyhead (1815), and over 900 miles of roads and 1,200 bridges in Scotland were his heritage. The best remembered of the three roadbuilders was John Macadam (1756–1836), a poor Scots boy whose name has entered the English language. He devised a method of roadbuilding based on the principle that loose, sharply pointed, small stones would, when packed, provide a strong, yet elastic, foundation. Macadam's public controversy with Telford helped to popularize modern methods of roadbuilding. In 1827 he became the Surveyor General of Highways in England. The reforms of Metcalfe, Telford, and Macadam were accepted after about 1810, and improvements in travel resulted. The work of these men, together with the later use of concrete, provided the United Kingdom with her modern network of highways.

Canals. In many respects the history of English canals parallels the history of English roads and turnpikes. The canal era began in the 1760s, although the English had already improved some of their rivers by dredging, deepening, and widening. The Fens[1] had been drained by canals, too, and the first lock had been built on a canal at Exeter as early as the sixteenth century. Like the turnpikes, canals were built by private individuals who got charters from Parliament. There was no uniformity in their size, quality, or rates, nor in their profitability. The acts granting the charters were, incidentally, an important step in the development of the joint-stock company and the modern corporation.

The first important canal was the Duke of Bridgewater's canal from Worsley to Manchester, completed in 1761. Before the days of railroads, canals did much to cheapen transportation, open up new markets, help feed the cities, provide fuel for the new blast furnaces, and stimulate the growth of port cities. The canals not only connected the four greatest ports of the country by internal waterways but provided a market for their goods and returned products from the hinterland for consumption and export.

The Bridgewater Canal was the product of a partnership of the Duke of Bridgewater and James Brindley, an illiterate engineering genius. The Duke's canal halved the price of coal in Manchester, and its success prompted Bridgewater and Brindley to build another canal from Manchester to Liverpool. Its completion made it possible to deliver raw cotton to Manchester factories without following the difficult course of the Mersey River. Other canals soon opened up the interior of England to trade and transport. The Staffordshire and Worcestershire was opened in 1772, and the Grand Trunk Canal was completed in 1777; these connected the Mersey, Trent, and Severn Rivers. The Birmingham and Coventry and the Oxford canals, completed in 1790, connected London by way of the Thames to the Midlands and the north of England. The Grand Junction Canal, authorized in 1793, improved the network of waterways between the ports of London, Liverpool, Bristol, and Hull.

Farm products, coal, tin, salt, building stone, and other building materials were among the most important products carried by the new canals. Josiah Wedgwood brought clay from Cornwall to his Stafford-

---

[1] See above, p. 132.

shire pottery works by way of the new network. The shipment of his finished pottery along the smooth water routes was perhaps the most striking example of the growth of an industry because of the canals.

So successful was the north-south network that it brought on a canal-building mania in the years 1791–1794. Parliament granted over 80 charters in three years. Many of the canals were never completed. Nevertheless, by 1830 a system of canals and improved waterways comprising over 4,000 miles in England and Wales had been developed. Despite an increase in the absolute amount of traffic after 1830, the period to 1914 was one of relative decline, for canals failed to keep pace with other forms of transportation.

Canals were vital to the development of the Industrial Revolution even though few existed in the far north of England, in Wales, or south of a line drawn from London to Bristol. They cut shipping costs by one-half to two-thirds, especially on bulky items like coal. They especially benefited factory towns, port cities, and various commercial groups.

The canals had serious shortcomings, however. The old adage that a chain is no stronger than its weakest link was especially applicable. A small lock or narrow section could nullify the benefits of many miles of improved sections. Owing to poorly designed sections, canal barges were limited to 7 feet in width and to a loaded draft of less than 4 feet if they were to be towed any distance in the country. There was little incentive for one company to improve its locks if a bottleneck farther on prevented exploitation of the improved area. Thus, owing to the laissez-faire nature of the construction and ownership, the full potential of the system was never realized. The government, after losing money on one of the few canals it subsidized, did not consider a national plan for their development until 1909. After 1830 the railways bought many of the canals to avoid competition. This they were permitted to do despite the argument of that day that canal competition would keep the railways from charging high rates. After 1844 the railways were forbidden to buy canals, but they had already bought a third of them. Parliament passed a law in 1850 requiring the railways to maintain the canals in their existing condition. Meanwhile, the Board of Trade was starting to regulate rates, although effective regulation had to wait until the Railway and Canal Act of 1888.

From 1906 to 1909 a British Royal Commission studied the problem of how more efficient use could be made of English canals. It recommended the enlargement of four different groups of waterways, subsequently known as "The Cross," but the recommendations were not carried out. In World War II, however, the canals were useful to the British government as a supplement to railway traffic. They were placed under the Ministry of War Transport and supervised by a central committee and six regional committees. In 1948 they were nationalized, along with other major forms of transportation, under the Docks and Inland Water-ways Executive.

Railways. After 1830 the operation and control of canals was closely linked with railways. (Railroads are always called "railways" in England.) Railways, like canals, owe their origin to the need for a cheap means of transporting coal. The first railways were found in coal mines. Wooden rails were laid to get coal carts from the coal face to the pit heads. Such mining wagonways were used in Nottinghamshire as early as 1597. After the first third of the eighteenth century, iron plates were commonly placed on top of the wooden rails. Similar methods were soon used to transport coal from the pit head to wharfs along nearby streams. These "plateways" soon gave way to iron rails on wooden ties, or "sleepers," which were covered with earth to form a firm footing for the horse-drawn carts. Further changes included flanged rails and then flanged wheels to keep the carts on the tracks.

These early railways were only for the use of private companies. The first public railway in England, the Surrey Iron Railway, was chartered in 1801 and opened in 1803 between Croydon and the Thames River at Wandsworth near London. As with canals and turnpikes, tolls were charged for its use. The means of locomotion included not only horse power but also human power, sails, and stationary steam engines placed alongside the railways.

In 1821 Parliament sanctioned the building of a railway from Darlington to Stockton on the Tees River in the coal-mining county of Durham in the north of England. Completed in 1825, it carried passengers as well as coal. George Stephenson was the engineer. At first, private coaching companies used the line. The Stockton and Darlington was not the immediate success that the Duke of Bridgewater's first canal had been, but it was successful enough for Stephenson to be asked to build the Liverpool and Manchester Railway, which was opened in 1830 despite great opposition from the canal and turnpike companies, farmers, and religious groups. The opening celebration was marred by the accidental death of William Huskisson, then president of the Board of Trade, one of the leading political figures of his day. He was knocked down and killed by the train.

The canal companies had a monopoly in many areas by the 1820s. Much of the incentive for railway building came as a result of their highhanded methods, excessive rates, slow operations, and general disregard for the public interest. An often-cited example is that it took longer for cotton to be shipped from Liverpool to Manchester by canal than from the United States to Liverpool by ocean vessel, because of the inefficiency of the canal monopoly.

The success of these first two railways led to other construction. Lines from Liverpool and London were joined at Birmingham in 1837, so that through travel was possible from London to the north. The Great Western Railway to Bristol, Wales, and the west of England was opened in 1838. In fact, there was a mild boom in 1837, and still another in the years 1844–1847. Many of the major lines in the country were built or at least planned in this latter period. By 1850 about 6,000 miles of lines were open and that many more chartered. The capital investment in the period 1825–1850 totaled £350 million. Yet average length of line was estimated at only 15 miles! There were far too many companies.

Early railway building was not without its problems. Unlike railroad lines in the United States, France, and Germany at later periods, the British lines rarely had government support; indeed, the government usually was hostile to them. It cost the Liverpool and Manchester £70,000 to get its charter from Parliament. The railways were developed in areas heavily populated. The rights of way and station sites were more expensive than they were in western United States, where the railroads preceded the people. Preliminary expenses alone, for legal and other costs, amounted to £4,000 per mile, and land, which was given freely by the United States government to many of its railroads, cost the railways from £4,000 to £8,000 per mile in England. The north of England, Wales, and other sections are rolling and semimountainous, unlike the prairies of the Middle West or the North European plain, which also added to the cost of construction.

Because the English were the first to build railways, there were heavy costs owing to their experimental nature. At least six widths for gauges were tried. The most common were the 7-foot gauge of Brunel and the Stephenson gauge of 4 feet, 8½ inches. In the Battle of the Gauges the Stephenson gauge triumphed. Roads like the Great Western, which used Brunel's gauge, did not complete the change-over until near the end of the century. That eventually meant extra expenses in rebuilding track. Parliament early laid down safety conditions, which further increased costs. To guard against criticism, railways in England were built more substantially than in the United States or Germany. L. C. A. Knowles estimates that English railways cost £54,000 per mile (£64,000 if Wales is included), compared with £13,000 in the United States and £21,000 in Prussia.[2] Thus English railways were saddled with enormous overhead costs from the beginning.

The railways might have done better if they could have counted on a growing economy. But the British economy grew slowly, especially after World War I. British railways carry only about 60 per cent of the ton-miles of freight today that they carried in 1908. The competition of other

[2] L. C. A. Knowles, *Industrial and Commercial Revolutions* (New York: E. P. Dutton & Co., Inc., 1930), p. 257.

forms of transportation, especially of trucks in the last ten years, has been felt.[3] Vigorous economies and finally nationalization of the railways have resulted.

The setting of freight rates has posed thorny problems too. At first, railways were established on the principle of supplying only a roadbed for private carriers. Many private companies owned their own railway cars, just as others owned barges for use on canals. As late as 1913 one-half of the freight cars were privately owned. Because of this, rates might be charged for half a dozen different services, or for just a couple. If a private company provided its own cars and loaded and unloaded them, the public carrier's charges were limited to those for hauling and for the use of stations and other property. The problem of short hauls was a hard one too. No place is more than 90 miles from a major port, and the coastal shipping often competed with the railways for long hauls. Because of this complex situation, it was extremely difficult to compare rates and to determine what charges were fair and equitable.

The railways were eager for as much business as possible, in order that their fixed costs, which do not vary, could be spread over as many units as possible. This early led to cutthroat competition. Rebates, discriminatory rates among persons, higher rates for short hauls than for long ones, the use of "fighting lines" against opponents, and reclassification of goods in lower rate brackets were among the many abuses which the railway companies found it necessary to indulge in if they were to stay in business.

The railways attempted to solve their problems by consolidating and establishing monopolies. They also set up the Railway Clearing House in 1842 to regulate and supervise themselves. The government refused to recognize that, owing to their high fixed costs, the railways were natural monopolies. Instead, the government attempted to enforce competition, the very thing the railways were trying to avoid because in the long run competition increased costs and yet did no good. At the same time, successive governments refused to regulate the roads effectively because public interference was anathema to the laissez-faire governments of the day. It was only in the last quarter of the nineteenth century that public policy shifted from enforcing competition to accepting monopoly and attempting to regulate it.

Various commissions and tribunals were established from the earliest days of the railways. We have seen that the railways were enjoined from buying canals and required to keep those they owned in their existing state of efficiency. How much better it might have been if the government had allowed railways to own and consolidate the canals into a

[3] Trucks (called "goods vehicles") tripled in number between 1944 and 1953. *Annual Abstract of Statistics,* 1954, p. 197.

national system of feeders for the railways! In 1846 Parliament established a railway commission under the Board of Trade, the British equivalent of the American Department of Commerce. It was temporary, however; it lacked enforcement powers and refused to face up to basic problems. Parliament established another commission under Cardwell's Act in 1854, but it too was ineffective. Railway regulation finally came into its own in 1888 when Parliament passed the Railway and Canal Act establishing a permanent tribunal. This act required companies to present details of their rates to the Board of Trade, and a commission of three experts had power to establish maximum rates. Most railways promptly raised their rates to the maximum. After 1893 railways were allowed to raise existing rates to the maximum only after justifying their charges before the commission. One bad effect of this legislation was that railways failed to lower rates even when it would have been justified by economies and efficiencies. They feared that they would fail to get increases at a future date if they were needed. In the meantime, consolidation continued, and various regulatory bodies broadened the scope of their control beyond rates and profits, even to include working conditions among the "navvies," the English name given to the laborers who built the canals and railways.

During World War I the British railways were run by the government under the Regulation of the Forces Act of 1871. Their efficiency was greatly improved by the establishment of a national network. It was impossible to unscramble almost 120 railways, which had been consolidated under government operation during the war. In 1919 the Ministry of Transport was formed. By the Railways Act of 1921 they were amalgamated into four large groups: (1) the Great Western, (2) the London, Midland, and Scottish, (3) the London and North Eastern, and (4) the Southern Railways. Rates were to be established to yield them incomes comparable with what they had received in 1913. The Great Depression, however, prevented any such earnings. Even in a relatively good year like 1938, net revenue was only half that anticipated by the Railways Act of 1921.

In 1933 there was a further amalgamation. The London transport system, including busses, coaches, trams, and the underground railways, was placed under a public corporation called the London Passenger Transport Board (LPTB). Transport facilities in an area of 2,000 square miles thus came under public ownership. In 1939, as during World War I, the four main railways and the LPTB were placed under government control. Finally, on January 1, 1948, Parliament nationalized the railways, which had over 20,000 miles of lines, along with canals, long-distance road haulage, docks, long-distance busses, and the LPTB. All were placed under the British Transport Commission, which acquired all their assets. In addition, the Transport Act provided for "public authorities known as Executives to assist the Commission in the discharge of their functions." The Conservatives replaced the Labor Government in 1951, and Parliament in the summer of 1953 denationalized the road-haulage facilities acquired under the Transport Act of 1947. Provisions were also made for preparing and publishing a decentralization scheme for the railways. The terms of the act were liberalized with regard to rate increases and other restrictions on the railways.

In the history of British railways one may see almost every conceivable policy of railroad operation—*laissez faire,* government-enforced competition, government regulation, and finally, government ownership. The final step had many causes. Some are indigenous to all forms of large-scale transportation. Transportation companies are high-fixed-cost institutions which become natural monopolies either by way of cutthroat competition with the winner taking all, or by consolidation for mutual benefit before cutthroat methods settle the struggle. As railways have a public responsibility, their trend toward monopoly has not gone unregulated in any modern country, and in most, government ownership has been the eventual result.

In Britain there were special causes why railways could not be profitable without abusing their obligation to the public. First, there was their extraordinarily high cost of construction. This meant higher rates than is usual for public transportation bodies. Second, many companies felt impelled to use unfair methods to stay in business. A third factor was the reluctance of the government throughout most of the nineteenth century to come to grips with the problems that turnpikes, canals, roads, and railways presented. Fourth, because of the smallness of the country British railways were never able to gain the advantages from long hauls and large-scale enterprise which businesses with high overhead costs find necessary. An example of this is the number of people employed on British railways. With only one-tenth the number of railway-miles as in the United States, British railways, in 1945, employed almost 50 per cent as many people. Short hauls and small or express-type shipments made this necessary. Finally, as the twentieth century progressed, with its two major wars and its catastrophic depression of the 1930s, public ownership seemed the only feasible course if British transportation was to serve the public.

The British transportation system under private enterprise and government regulation faced a paradox. If it acted in its own interest to gain profit, it inevitably operated against the public interest. Conversely, if it acted in the public interest, it operated against the interests of itself and those investors who depended on its profits to sustain their investments. In such circumstances, public ownership appeared to be the only alternative. It is yet to be established, although it has not been disproven, whether this policy will provide the country with a transportation system able to keep pace with the expansion of Britain's economy.

OCEAN SHIPPING

Modern ships are products of the nineteenth century. In the preceding two hundred years there had been little advancement in design or size except for a few large ships of the East India trade which exceeded 1,000 tons. From the end of the Napoleonic Wars in 1815, when the British and American fleets emerged supreme, until the American War between the States in 1861–1865, the story of shipping has two main themes. The first is the American superiority in building and operating wooden sailing vessels, a superiority which American shippers exploited to the full. Packet lines, first inaugurated by a New York firm, ran regularly scheduled Atlantic sailings after 1818, and the beautiful clipper ships developed in the 1840s secured and held the American position of preeminence. The day of the sailing vessel was limited, however.

While the Americans were basking in their superiority, the British developed and exploited the iron steamship. The development of the iron steamship by the British, then, is the second theme. They made major improvements in hulls, engines, and methods of propulsion. The first wooden paddle-wheel steamer was the *Charlotte Dundas*, which plied the Clyde River at Glasgow, Scotland, as early as 1802. In 1838 four vessels made the distance between New York and England by steam alone, although the *Royal William* had plied the shorter route from Nova Scotia as early as 1833. The Cunard Line was formed in 1839 with four paddle steamers and a mail contract which served as a government subsidy. These early ocean steamships had many shortcomings to overcome. Isambard Brunel combined steam engines and iron hulls when he built the *Great Britain* in 1845. John Ericsson invented the single-screw propeller, and then the double-screw propeller, to replace side paddles.

Most improvements added to the cost of the shipping business. By mid-century one man or a few persons could no longer buy a ship for, say, £4,000. The value of a ship was rising fast. Yet increasing the number of partners in order to obtain additional capital had its drawbacks. People were reluctant to venture their savings with others if their own liability was unlimited. Also, the more numerous the partners, the more difficult it was to manage the enterprise. In 1854 Parliament passed the Merchant Shipping Act stating that ownership of a ship might not be subdivided beyond a sixty-fourth. Then in 1862, with new ships costing £100,000, Parliament passed the British Companies Act, which permitted seven or more persons to set up a joint-stock company with limited liability. This greatly stimulated the flow of capital into shipping.

These, then, were some of the changes that made it possible for the British to regain world leadership in shipping and shipbuilding. In the years preceding World War I the British were building over half the world's tonnage of ships. Apart from some subsidies in the form of mail contracts and minor building subsidies, the policy of *laissez faire* prevailed. The Navigation Acts and the Corn Laws had been repealed by 1850. Their repeal ushered in over half a century of free trade. Ships spend most of their time away from the country of their origin, so rate regulation was long regarded by the British government as impracticable. This attitude did not change until after World War I.

The absence of regulation did not mean that the shipping industry remained competitive. It faced the same type of problem that had plagued canals and railways. Competition in shipping also leads to cutthroat methods and then to monopoly. Shipping pools appeared and they used such devices as mergers, agreements, and combination to obtain their monopoly. "Fighting ships," which were run at a loss if necessary, were used by powerful "rings" to ruin smaller competitors. By 1877 a system of deferred rebates was established. Shipping rings rebated a portion of their charges to customers but only after a minimum period following their services had elapsed. This guaranteed that the customer would continue to use their lines.

In the three years following World War I the British share of world merchant shipbuilding dropped from 50 to about 30 per cent. Although it increased again before the depression of the 1930s, the annual output in Britain and elsewhere exceeded the world's needs by several million gross tons. This excess capacity made a "sick" industry of shipping, as it had already done to coal, engineering, steel, and textiles. Britain changed from a policy of *laissez faire* to one of regulation and rationing excess capacity in the period between the two world wars. The instrument of this policy was the National Shipbuilder's Security, Ltd. It bought redundant yards, closed down the least efficient builders, and gained a cushion for the industry in the form of government subsidies and benefits. The price of ships was reduced by about 6 per cent. After 1934 the volume of output rose again. Thus shipping and shipbuilding, like so many other of Britain's old industries, succumbed to regulation and state control because of its high-fixed-cost nature and the inability of competition to make it efficient. Another reason that the government had to do this was to offset the policies of foreign governments who aided and subsidized their own shipping on grounds of national defense and economic expediency.

During World War II British production of merchant vessels dropped to less than 15 per cent of the world total although the tonnage built was double that of the 1933–1938 period. The United Kingdom concentrated on building naval vessels, while the United States produced merchant ships. Owing to war needs, the absolute amount of world shipbuilding capacity increased by about four times. Thus the drop in Britain's share of the world total in the war period does not indicate inefficiency in production. World War II sinkings reduced the British merchant fleet to 14 million gross tons by 1945, but production since then has increased it to over 18 million gross tons (1953). This is somewhat higher than the prewar tonnage and comprises over half the active world merchant fleet.

COMMERCIAL AVIATION

The British have been in the forefront in promoting commercial air transportation. They initiated a London to Paris cross-channel service in 1919. Competition among private companies soon became so severe that in 1921 the government chose to subsidize two companies. The cost of the subsidies and the need to expand services led to the appointment of the Hambling Committee in 1923. It recommended that existing companies be amalgamated and be given a monopoly and a subsidy. In March, 1924, Imperial Airways, Ltd., was formed to operate and develop overseas services in the Empire. Like the governments of most other countries, the British selected one airline as a "chosen instrument."

Meanwhile, a number of private independent companies were developing a European service, unsubsidized by the British government. In 1935 the Fisher Committee recommended that the government support a number of them by subsidies and delineate the routes for each. British Airways was established in 1935 as the "chosen instrument" to provide European service.

The development of Empire routes progressed very quickly. The first, from Cairo to Baghdad, began as a mail service carried by the air force. Imperial Airways took it over in 1926 and extended lines to Karachi, India (1929), Brisbane, Australia (1936), and Singapore and Hongkong (1937). An African service began in 1931 which eventually connected Egypt with Capetown.

Dissatisfaction with Imperial Airways policies led to the appointment of the Cadman Committee in 1937. As a result, all the "chosen instruments" were merged into the British Overseas Airways Corporation. The public corporation, known as BOAC, was formed in 1940. The Civil Aviation Act of 1946 provided for three companies, the BOAC, the British European Airways (BEA), and the British South American Airways (BSAA). BSAA was merged with BOAC in 1949, at which time there were some 83,000 miles of British routes.

At the end of World War II British commercial aviation was in a different position, for the British had concentrated on the manufacture of fighter planes while America made bombing and transport planes. The facilities for the latter were quite easily converted to making commercial transports. The British had to do something new or unusual to get back into the race. Sir Frank Whittle had been the designer of the first practical turbojet, which was flown in 1941. The British, therefore, concentrated their energies on the design and manufacture of turboprop and turbojet airplanes. The development of the Comet in 1949 put them clearly in the lead in this new phase of commercial aviation. Then a series of Comet air disasters in 1954 temporarily threatened that leadership. It appears, however, that jet airlines are a practical development and will be increasingly used for long-distance commercial flights.

In ownership and operation, British airlines have gone through the same stages as other forms of commercial transportation, except at an accelerated pace. Private enterprise conducted the early stages of development. Soon, problems of competition, especially with foreign lines, brought the government into the picture, first to regulate and subsidize by the "chosen instrument" policy, and then to own. Government ownership was brought about by governments of various ideological views. BOAC was nationalized by the Conservatives in 1940, and BEA by a Labor Government in 1946.

COMMUNICATION

The British have been leaders in the development of the telegraph, telephone, and radio. All began as private operations and within a generation were government controlled. Only the radio will be discussed, however.

The Marconi Company Works at Chelmsford broadcast the first musical program in Britain in 1920. There was regular service, of a kind, the next year and in 1922 Marconi operated out of London. The British Broadcasting Company was formed in 1922 and was controlled by a privately owned radio-manufacturing industry. Broadcasting became a government-sponsored monopoly in 1927 under the Board of Governors of the British Broadcasting Corporation (BBC). The BBC is supported by a yearly license fee paid by the owners of radio and television sets, much as automobile owners buy a license for their cars. The amount has been supplemented by Parliamentary appropriation, but the BBC has been singularly free from political interference on matters of programing or anything affecting freedom of expression. The British system is famous for the quality of its programs. This is largely because the BBC can select good programs which they believe the viewing public should have instead of having to broadcast ones which will attract many prospective buyers of, say, soap or deodorants. Lately, however, the BBC has been experimenting with some commercial programs.

There are, essentially, four methods of supporting broadcasting: the wholly commercial system in the United States; the old British method of government monopoly supported by licenses and subsidies; the mixed Canadian system, which combines the British and American methods; and the systems completely dominated by totalitarian governments.

CONCLUSION

Apart from automobile travel and newspapers, almost every modern means of transportation and communication in Great Britain is now government owned or regulated. Those which were developed first, like the canals and railways, passed through the stages of *laissez faire*, government-enforced competition, government-regulated monopoly, to government ownership. Those developed in the middle of the nineteenth century, like the telephone and telegraph, were placed under a Post Office monopoly after a few years of private ownership. The twentieth-century industries, like the radio and airplane, have seen government control, regulation, and ownership almost from the first stage of development. Most forms of transportation and communication have been plagued by heavy overhead costs and yet "affected with a public interest." Successive governments have approached the question of their regulation, and later of their ownership, as a practical rather than as an ideological problem.

QUESTIONS FOR STUDY

1. How has Britain's geography and location given her great transportation advantages for the last five hundred years?
2. What did the Transportation Revolution consist of in Britain? When did it take place and why then? Who were some of the chief figures in carrying it out? What did they do?
3. The canals were built during a period of *laissez faire*. It made them less effective than they otherwise might have been. Show how this was so.
4. How do English railways differ from American ones? Why was building them so much more expensive? How were they operated during World War I? What effect did this have on their subsequent organization? When were they nationalized?
5. The British merchant marine was in some respects falling behind the American one until about the middle of the nineteenth century. What happened that gave Britain a great advantage again? Why has Britain been more willing to subsidize her merchant marine than we have ours?
6. How does the history of commercial aviation repeat the trends and experiences of earlier forms of transportation?
7. How has the British operation of the radio differed from our own? What are the advantages and disadvantages of the British system? Are there any other systems of operation besides these two?

CHAPTER 12

MANUFACTURING

Historically, Britain was the cradle of the Industrial Revolution and, later, the "workshop of the world." She provided many of the basic inventions and innovations which characterize modern industrial society. Her industry is still advancing, for her postwar production exceeds her prewar production by a considerable margin.

On the other hand, the demands on Britain's industries, just to meet the needs of an expanding population and to pay her way in the world, are greater than her production capacity, despite her postwar recovery. Because they have been losing ground relatively, although their absolute accomplishments have been great, Britain's industries are the object of considerable controversy. To some critics, Britain is bankrupt, inefficient, unproductive, and fettered by state intervention and government ownership of industry. To others, her planned economy is a landmark in human history; her industrial efficiency has never been higher, the standard of living exceeds any she has achieved before, poverty has been virtually abolished, the rate of capital investment is high, and the export of manufactured products surpasses previous records.

To get perspective on modern Britain's industrial achievements, let us look at the history of British industry from 1750 to 1914. We shall then describe her existing industrial situation and judge it against that historical background.

THE INDUSTRIAL REVOLUTION TO 1914

The Industrial Revolution was characterized by a shift from production in the home to production in the factory. Regular hours of work and payment of wages on an hourly basis took the place of work "at will" in the home and payment for the amount accomplished. Other major characteristics of the "revolution" were the application of steam power to machines and its substitution for human, animal, and water power, and a shift of the population from rural to urban dwellings.

The early period of the Industrial Revolution in England runs from about 1750 to 1850, although its effects on society were felt more after 1815 than before. The dates are arbitrary, and the movement was more a slow "evolution" than a quick and radical change, which the term "revolution" denotes. It began with a series of inventions in the textile industry, the development of iron and steel for making machines and other industrial products, and the use of James Watt's double-acting steam engine to provide power.

The Industrial Revolution began in England because of several favorable circumstances. First, specialization in manufacturing is dependent on the demand for products, which in turn rests on the extent of the market. England was particularly favored by her proximity to the sea and by an abundance of navigable rivers. The products of new industries could therefore reach distant markets during the canal period, even before railways. In most countries the extensive building of roads, canals, and railways has been necessary before industrialization could get far.

Second, England had gained commerical supremacy before 1750. Trading companies like the East India Company and the Hudson Bay Company accumulated vast sums. These funds supplied the capital for the Industrial Revolution, while Britain's colonial empire provided raw materials and, in turn, was a market for her goods.

Third, the Industrial Revolution was accompanied by a shift from subsistence to commercial farming. That shift provided the food for the growing cities. The growth of the cities was partly a result of the break up of the old feudal system of rural living, with the concomitant land enclosures, and partly a result of the tremendous increase in population in the eighteenth century because of the rising standard of living and improvements in health and hygiene. It is estimated that between 1750 and 1800 the population increased by 50 per cent.

Finally, the political and economic climate of the late eighteenth and early nineteenth centuries contributed to the rise of industry. The Glorious Revolution of 1688 had wrested power from the monarchy and diffused it among the landed aristocracy. The landed gentry were more willing to compromise with the new industrialists and the rising middle classes than was the aristocracy in countries like France and Prussia. Successful businessmen did not find the English caste system difficult to penetrate. They soon owned land and acquired power and position in the country.

On the economic front, the writings of Adam Smith, who published his *Wealth of Nations* in 1776, of David Ricardo, John Stuart Mill, and Thomas Robert Malthus provided an intellectual justification for the highly individualistic economic system called *laissez faire*. They denounced the previous system of mercantilism, under which economic control had been centralized, and advocated free trade. They favored letting prices and wages be set by market forces and leaving business unhampered by government.

This then is the setting in which the Industrial Revolution took place. The first inventions were in textiles. A disparity in production between spinning and weaving existed. One weaver, operating at home under the putting-out system, needed several spinners to supply the yarn that he wove into cloth. John Kay's invention of the flying shuttle (an improved weaving machine) in 1733 aggravated this situation. Methods to improve the spinning process were in great demand. James Hargreaves' spinning jenny in 1764 and Richard Arkwright's water frame in 1770 equalized the two processes of spinning and weaving. Then another bottleneck developed. Samuel Crompton's spinning mule in 1779 and Edmund Cartwright's power loom in 1785 made textile manufacturing so efficient that it consumed raw cotton faster than it could be supplied. Eli Whitney's invention of the cotton gin in America in 1793 solved this problem. By now, production of textiles in factories was replacing the old putting-out system centered in the home.

Rapid advances were also taking place in iron production. Iron was needed to replace wood in making machines. John Roebuck built the Carron Ironworks in Scotland in 1760 and the Darby family established large ironworks at Coalbrookdale in Shropshire. John Wilkinson did much to popularize iron. He built the first iron bridge in 1779 and the first iron boat in 1787. He never wrote a letter without using the word "iron," and he was buried in an iron coffin. Matthew Boulton was also important in the development of the iron industry. He succeeded Roebuck as the partner of Watt. The famous firm of Boulton and Watt built iron steam engines. Two important developments enabled iron products to undergo a period of rapid improvements. When the supply of English timber neared exhaustion, the Darbys substituted coal and coke for charcoal in manufacturing iron. The iron industry could now rely on the one raw material which England had in abundance. Henry Cort's puddling process (1784) was an improved method of producing wrought iron, the material used in most finished iron products.

James Watt greatly improved Thomas Newcomen's steam engine, whose chief use was to pump water out of mines. In 1782 Watt developed a double-acting engine which would turn a wheel and thus provide power to operate the new machines of the Industrial Revolution.

By 1850 the early period of the Industrial Revolution was over. The last vestiges of mercantilism were removed when the Corn Laws were repealed in 1846 and the Navigation Acts were revoked in 1850. Free trade, advocated so enthusiastically by the new "classical" economists, became law through the political efforts of William Gladstone, Robert Peel, Richard Cobden, and John Bright. British industry, based on textiles, iron and steel, steam power, and coal, became preeminent in world trade.

But even before 1914 these "old" industries were destined to face growing competition from those of new industrial nations. The American steel industry surpassed British iron and steel production by 1890 and so did the German steel industry by 1900. Fortunately, by the time the old industries were suffering a relative eclipse, a new age of chemical, oil, electrical, rubber, and aluminum industries had begun. Automobiles and the new light consumer industries also took up the slack. British industry was still in "rude good health" on the eve of World War I. The story from that time on has been one of relative decline. Not least among the causes were the two world wars.

PRESENT-DAY BRITISH MANUFACTURING

Types of Ownership. One way of classifying the industries of a country is according to type of ownership. There are three basic types in Britain. First come the so-called nationalized industries or public corporations. They are owned by the government. These industries provide about 20 per cent of the goods and services. Although their number is small, they employ between 10 and 15 per cent of the 22 million people in civilian occupations. The only one that actually manufactured goods was the Iron and Steel Corporation, and that is now denationalized. Virtually all the others provide services, such as the railways and air lines, or they are in the nature of a public utility, such as suppliers of electricity and gas. The National Coal Board is in a special position, but mining coal is obviously different from, say, manufacturing chemicals, vehicles, textiles, clothing, food, drink, and tobacco.

Second, there are approximately 12,000 public joint-stock companies whose shares are listed on the stock exchange and whose ownership is thus freely transferable. As in American corporations, the shareholder-owners actually have little power; authority rests with management. The nationalized industries and the joint-stock companies together provide over half the employment of the country and supply about 90 per cent of the manufactured products.

Third, there are approximately 230,000 small organizations—partnerships, small companies, and individual employers like farmers and professional people. They provide jobs for 40 to 50 per cent of Britain's workers and constitute 95 per cent of the operating units, but they produce only a small proportion of the manufactured goods.

The 9 million people employed in manufacturing constitute about 40 per cent of the working population of Great Britain. In terms of numbers of employees the most important manufacturing industries are engineering, shipbuilding, and metalworking with almost 2 million people; the motor-vehicle industry with over 1 million employees; the textile industry with roughly 900,000; and the food, drink, tobacco, and related industries with an almost equal number. The clothing, paper, printing, and chemical industries follow in importance if measured by the number of persons employed.

Some of the manufacturing industries are much more essential and efficient than others. Over one-third of the net output of manufacturing is provided by the metal industries—engineering, vehicles, and metal manufacturing. These industries accounted for over 40 per cent of Britain's export earnings from 1945 to 1950, and in 1952 they provided over 50 per cent of the exports. The relative importance of this segment of manufacturing has grown and so has the average size of the concerns. On the other hand, the textile, clothing, and paper industries have contracted. It is fortunate that the greatest expansion has taken place in the metal and engineering industries, for Britain's survival depends on their exports. Relative changes in output and employment in the various segments of manufacturing in 1935 and 1948 are given in Table 12-1.

Table 12-1. Relative Changes in Industrial Output and Employment, 1935–1948
(In per cent)

Industry	Value of net output			Average persons employed		
	1935	1948	Change	1935	1948	Change
Engineering, electrical, etc......	11.8	16.7	+4.9	11.9	17.4	+5.5
Textiles........................	9.4	8.6	−0.8	13.8	9.1	−4.7
Building and contracting........	9.2	10.3	+1.1	11.4	13.9	+2.5
Mining and quarrying..........	8.4	8.3	−0.1	11.8	9.1	−2.7
Vehicles.......................	6.0	7.3	+1.3	6.2	7.8	+1.6
Chemicals......................	5.5	5.2	−0.3	2.8	3.7	+0.9
Metal manufacture.............	5.4	6.3	+0.9	5.0	5.6	+0.6
Clothing.......................	4.8	3.9	−0.9	7.2	5.2	−2.0
Other industries...............	39.5	33.4	−6.1	29.9	28.2	−1.7
	100.0	100.0		100.0	100.0	

SOURCE: Rearranged from a table in British Information Service, *Labour and Industry in Britain,* vol. 10, no. 2, p. 63, June, 1952.

Production and Productivity. Let us next compare postwar production, that is from 1946 to 1952, with prewar production. The record of British industry is good. British industry recovered more quickly from the war and achieved greater production than that of any other European nation physically damaged by the war. This statement may seem unusual, for the world tends to think of the postwar British economy in terms of crisis, austerity, sacrifice, rationing, devaluation, and bankruptcy. The figures for increased output and productivity in industry tell a more favorable story. Whether the prewar year of 1938 or the postwar year of 1946 is used as 100, by 1951 the index for the physical volume of output in manufacturing was at 150.

The figures showing increased productivity, or output per person, are more important, in some respects, than those showing total output. The productivity index for manufacturing was at 127 in 1951. This represents an increase of about 5 or 6 per cent a year per employee since the end of the war. It is approximately 10 per cent per year for those who actually work on the production lines. The production figures for certain industries are especially impressive. Steel production rose from 10.4 to 15.6 million long tons between 1938 and 1951. Production of vehicles has shown unusual increases—40 per cent in automobiles, 148 per cent in trucks, and an increase from 10,029 to 140,210 in tractors. Britain's agriculture is now one of the most mechanized in the world. Metal manufacturing and the light electrical trades are also highly productive.

On the other hand, coal mining has shown no gain (225 million long tons in 1952 compared with 227 million in 1938), although the industry has recovered from its wartime slump. By 1951 cotton-cloth production had dropped one-third since 1937 and woolen fabrics had fallen 13 per cent below 1938. The decline of coal and textiles, which have been in the past vital to the British economy, is a serious national problem.

Problems of Postwar British Industry. Why, despite a good over-all increase in production, does British industry face serious difficulties? Much of the answer lies in the magnitude of postwar needs. The example of passenger-car production may help make the problem clear. Passenger-car production and exports for the years 1938 and 1951 are given in Table 12-2.

Table 12-2

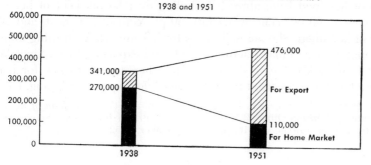

PASSENGER CAR PRODUCTION IN GREAT BRITAIN
1938 and 1951

In 1938, 270,000 of the 341,000 cars produced were sold at home to domestic consumers. In 1951, only about 110,000 of the 476,000 cars produced were for the home market. Thus, in 1951, exports of cars took all the increased production and 60 per cent of the prewar production. Consumers, after the war, waited two, three, and even four years for a new car. The British people appeared less well off than before the war notwithstanding the tremendous postwar production efforts.

Why must British industry do even better than it has thus far for the country to survive and pay its way in the world? First of all, there are the effects of the war. One-third of her 12 million houses were destroyed or damaged between 1939 and 1945; one-half of her merchant marine was sunk. Britain lost a total of $18 billion of capital assets. Bombs were responsible for $10 billion damage to buildings, equipment, machinery, and shipping, according to the report of the Economic Cooperation Administration (ECA) Mission to the United Kingdom.

Another loss was "disinvestment," or the inability to replace, maintain, and repair the physical assets of the country during the war. There was a disinvestment of about $18 billion, and production in 1946 was about the same as the 1935–1938 average. Early estimates were that it would take seven years to make up for the wartime loss at the prewar investment rate. Yet the job was done in four to five years, by 1950. The United States and Britain had opposite experiences during the war years. America increased her investment by over $16 billion during the war, and her production was 75 per cent higher in 1946 than the 1935–1938 average. Since the war, the ratio of increased production has been about the same in both countries. The wartime period of disinvestment, together with differences in resources and density of population, account for much of the differences between the health of the British and American economies.[1]

Britain's problem of recovery is enhanced by the traditional need to import and export. Britain must import huge supplies of food, raw materials, and manufactured goods in order to feed, clothe, and supply her home population of 51 million people. Before the war she bought 75 per cent of her food from abroad, including over 80 per cent of her wheat and cheese, 90 per cent of her fats, 50 per cent of her meat, and 70 per cent of her sugar. She normally pays for her imports by turning imported raw materials into manufactured goods and exporting them. Since World War I she has not earned enough from her exports to pay for her imports. The funds received from the "invisible" exports—shipping, banking,

[1] T. Balogh, "Investment in Britain and the United States," *Bulletin of the Oxford Institute of Statistics*, June, 1952, pp. 183–887; British Information Service, *Labour and Industry in Britain*, vol. 10, p. 136, September, 1952.

insurance, interest on overseas investments, and the tourist trade—helped to make up the difference, so that her economy appeared fairly healthy in this respect. In the early stages of World War II, before American lend-lease, she was obliged to sell most of her foreign investments to get money to buy arms and munitions to fight Hitler. She also lost much of her merchant marine. During the time when she was unable to pay for food and raw-material imports she accumulated vast debts. These became known as "sterling balances" and were owed for goods received from such countries as India, Pakistan, Palestine, Argentina, and Egypt. Since the war she has been paying off these debts by way of "unrequited exports"; these countries have been receiving machines and goods from Britain by drawing on their sterling balances.

Another major problem is that the "terms of trade" have been going against Britain. The world prices of the food and raw materials she must import have been rising much faster than the prices she receives for the manufactured goods she exports. The trade deficits after the war, which accounted for the repeated crisis atmosphere, were largely attributable to price increases of food and raw-material imports. She had to draw heavily on her dollar reserves to pay for these. Price increases were especially severe after the Korean War began. The result is that Britain must export an ever-larger amount of manufactured goods to pay for the same amount of imports.

Britain has attacked these problems in three ways. She has cut her imports, especially from the United States and other dollar areas. She has increased her exports and has made a special effort to sell goods to the dollar areas. She has limited the volume of personal consumption, things like food, refrigerators, and automobiles, to about 12 per cent more than before the war. Whereas before Britain bought 75 per cent of her food abroad, now she buys 60 per cent. The production of all industry has increased by over 40 per cent, but exports have grown by over 75 per cent. This is the result of considerable planning. It was thought at the end of the war that, if Britain could do this well, she could survive without repeated crisis. It was believed that she would be able to pay interest on her war debts, repay the sterling balances, make up for the loss of her foreign investments, and still import a little more than before the war. By a determined effort she accomplished her production and export goals, and then she found that they were not enough. That is why people differ so sharply on how successful Britain's recovery and postwar economy have been. In the words of Charles Dickens, "It has been the best of times and the worst of times."

MONOPOLY, DEPRESSED INDUSTRIES, AND THE
PREWAR ECONOMY

Not all the problems of British industry can be explained in terms of external influences. Some have internal causes, such as inefficiency. One reason for inefficiency is the growth of monopoly in the interwar years. Britain had no antitrust legislation to deal with it; in fact to a considerable degree the government encouraged monopoly.

British industry has used all the known devices of monopoly. The most common form is the price association. While keeping their names and nominal independence, firms form an association to restrict prices and limit output. According to W. Arthur Lewis, a well-known British economist, about 30 per cent of British manufacturing was under private monopoly control at the end of World War II. It was "principally concentrated in four groups of trades, iron and steel, engineering, nonferrous metals and chemicals." The price-association type of monopoly encourages inefficiency. Its very purpose is to protect the weak producers by setting prices at levels which protect them. Efficient firms are not allowed to undersell.

The other type of monopoly found in Britain is "combines" (the British term for trusts). They suffer from inefficiencies too. They often buy firms at inflated prices to gain control of an industry and to get it into the hands of a few men. Most combines are formed to eliminate price competition and not to root out inefficiencies, or to promote technological improvements, or to save on marketing, advertising, or raw-material costs. The proof of this is that many combines allow the individual firms to keep their old names, sales forces, and executive organizations.

Moral questions also arise. Monopolies are usually undemocratic; they can hardly be otherwise. It may be questioned whether a democracy can afford to leave in the hands of a few private individuals great power over wages, employment, and a country's economic activity.

The reasons why Britain has had no antitrust legislation may be made clear only by reviewing the history of British industry in recent times. Until World War I British industry, in general, was virile and highly competitive. Britain followed free trade policies and the country was known for its industrial efficiency. In this "citadel of capitalism" there was little need for antitrust legislation.

The country was at war from 1914 to 1918. The government encouraged production. Materials were allocated and industry operated at capacity. This was no time to "bust" trusts or to attack business firms on which the government relied for war production. In fact, monopoly was promoted.

Part of the time between wars Britain suffered from severe depression. The government pursued a policy of protecting business, not dismantling it. Overproduction appeared in some of the high-fixed-cost industries. By that it is meant that more goods were produced than could be sold at the costs of production, not that there were too many goods and services for the consumers in the country. Widespread unemployment ensued. Large sections of the country were known as "depressed areas." Iron and steel, coal mining, engineering, shipbuilding, and the textile industries—the backbone of the British economy—declined and became known as "depressed industries." The government wished to protect them, to limit the bad effects of their excess capacity, and to promote their reorganization into groups so as to lessen cutthroat competition and to stimulate employment.

To attain these goals, the government promoted monopoly through price associations, mergers, and combines. In 1931 Britain also turned away from free trade and toward tariff protection and the promotion of cartels. For example, in 1935 the British iron and steel industry joined the infamous Continental Steel Cartel. It had been formed in 1925 when the governments of France, Germany, Belgium, and Luxembourg promoted it to limit output, distribute production, and control markets. To deal with this cartel, the British government had promoted a British iron and steel monopoly by way of a tariff. When this failed to revive Britain's steel industry, British iron and steel joined the Continental Cartel. It was a case of "if you can't beat them, join them."

Coal is another example. Coal production after World War I scarcely equaled that of 1913. Strikes and unrest in the industry accounted for the majority of man-days lost in the country. The miners were also the focal point for the General Strike of 1926. The coal industry was "sick." Repeated efforts to increase production failed, and other countries captured Britain's overseas coal markets. Finally, the British government promoted district coal cartels to regulate prices and output according to a national plan. Much the same story may be found in the shipbuilding industry, which closed down 30 per cent of its capacity. The textile industry lost half of its overseas markets and 90 per cent of its Far Eastern markets, mainly to Japan.

The "old" industries were in grave difficulties. What of the "new" mass-production industries like automobiles, electricity, chemicals, synthetics, and aluminum? The automobile industry remained competitive, but both private and public monopolies were promoted in electricity and chemicals. The British General Electric Company became a member of the electric-lamp cartel involving German, Holland, and Swiss firms. Cable manufacturing was cartelized. At home, the 1926 Electricity Supply Act put generating plants under a form of public control. The Imperial

Chemical Industries, Ltd. (ICI), was erected by a merger of four other chemical groups in 1926.

Thus between wars the old industries became monopolized, either privately or by government policy, to prevent greater disaster. In addition, some of the major new industries joined cartels or formed monopolies. Antitrust legislation would have contradicted, flatly, the policies which were being carried out.

During World War II the same circumstances existed as during World War I. Rationing, allocation of scarce raw materials, and shortage of supplies ruled out any major attempt to curb monopoly. In the postwar period, the British government has taken belated action through the Monopolies Commission to restore a modicum of competition in some sectors of manufacturing. As yet, few, if any, results have accrued. Nationalization, or the creation of super-government-owned monopolies, has remained the major answer to the problem of industrial monopoly. A brief description of this program follows.

THE NATIONALIZATION OF BASIC INDUSTRIES

Much has been written of the nationalization of basic industries in Great Britain. What is meant by nationalization? What industries have been nationalized? These are more difficult questions to answer than it would seem.

Some people assume that a nationalized industry is one which produces a commodity, is owned by the government, and is national in scope. This is an inadequate definition. Some nationalized industries are not national in scope, such as the London Passenger Transport Board. In this case, a part of the industry in one section of the country was made a government monopoly. Other so-called nationalized industries, such as the British Broadcasting Corporation or the Bank of England, are scarcely industries at all. Still others, such as the Admiralty Dockyards and the Royal Ordnance Factories, are industries because they actually produce goods. Yet they have long been owned by the government and they produce only for the government. The Iron and Steel Corporation (now denationalized) was never wholly government-owned. Only sections of this industry were purchased by the government. Finally, the Post Office, which in Britain owns the telephone and telegraph, is a service which people rarely think of as a nationalized industry.

All these nationalized industries have only two principal characteristics in common. Each provides some kind of good or service for the public or for the government. The government either owns the industry outright or owns enough of it to control and regulate its operations.

Historically, the nationalized industries can be divided into two groups.

There are the industries which were nationalized one by one, by a variety of Governments, and over a long period of time preceding 1945. Then there are the new "nationalized" industries, which the Labor Government put under government ownership in the period 1945 to 1951.

The old group contains the Post Office, including the telegraph (1870) and telephone (1880), the Royal Ordnance Factories, the Admiralty Dockyards, the British Broadcasting Corporation (BBC) (1927), the London Passenger Transport Board (LPTB) (1934), the Central Electricity Board (1926), and the British Overseas Airways Corporation (BOAC) (1940).

Except for the BOAC and the BBC, these industries have a distinctive form of organization, which the newer groups of nationalized industries do not have. They are run by a member of the Cabinet and are under one of the ministries which is a regular arm of the Government. The newer industries are under public corporations which are only indirectly responsible to a Cabinet minister. For example, the telephone and telegraph are under the Postmaster General, who is a member of the Cabinet. The Royal Ordnance Factories are run by the Minister of Supply, and the Dockyards are operated by the British Admiralty, or what in America would be the Navy Department. The LPTB and the Central Electricity Board have now been absorbed by the second group of nationalized industries. Most of the older activities are seldom thought of as nationalized industries because they are traditional government activities, are run by a Cabinet minister rather than by a public corporation, and were nationalized for a variety of unrelated reasons.

In 1945 the Labor Government came to power. It advocated the nationalization of certain basic industries as a part of its political program. There were several reasons for this, but the distinctive one was that the Labor party felt the need of nationalization to carry out its socialist program, which required a planned economy. In this respect, these nationalized industries differed from the older publicly owned industries. The Labor party believed such a program was necessary to help avoid depressions. The government needed nationalized industries to be able to offset a drop in private investment by increasing the amount of government investment. The Labor party also believed that private ownership of these industries put too much power in the hands of a few people who were not responsible to the public.

There were many practical reasons, too, why these activities were nationalized. A number of them, like coal and the railways, were unprofitable. At the same time, they were essential to the economy of the country. Boards and commissions of all shades of opinion had for a long time advocated reorganizing the coal industry. Electricity, gas, airlines, and railways are forms of public utilities or natural monopolies which are owned or regulated by the governments of many countries because they are "affected with a public interest." Finally, the Bank of England, although privately owned, has long been a quasi-public institution. It served the same purpose as the American Federal Reserve Banks which, although privately owned, served the national welfare almost exclusively.

Yet apart from the ideological reasons for their public ownership, these new nationalized industries do not differ, substantially, from the previous government-owned industries. In fact, most of them were industries for which fact-finding boards dominated by Conservative party members had previously recommended nationalization. This was true of the Bank of England, the coal industry, the electric industry, and the gas industry.

Table 12-3 lists the nationalized industries organized since 1945. How-

Table 12-3. British Industries Nationalized since 1945

Name	Date na- tion- al- ized	Nature of industry
Bank of England...................	1946	Owns the central bank
British European Airways Corpora- tion (BEAC)	1946	Owns and operates domestic and European British airways
National Coal Board	1947	Owns and operates coal mines and ancillary coal industries
British Transportation Commission	1948	Owns and operates the railroads, certain categories of road haulage* (long-distance trucks), and some local means of transportation
British Electricity Authority and the Area Electricity Boards	1948	Generates and distributes electricity
Area Gas Boards and the British Gas Council	1949	Manufactures and distributes gas
Iron and Steel Corporation† of Great Britain	1951	Government owned securities of 80 selected steel companies

* By the act of May 6, 1953, about 40,000 vehicles acquired by the 1948 act are to be offered for sale to private bidders.

† The act of May 14, 1953, "denationalized" steel by transferring the securities from the Iron and Steel Corporation to a Holding and Realization Agency, which was authorized to sell them to private bidders. An Iron and Steel Board is to supervise the industry. The Labor party has pledged to "re-nationalize" steel.

ever, it excludes the National Health Service and the Social Services (Beveridge Plan), for they are not considered, in Britain at least, to be among the nationalized industries.

Each of the new nationalized industries has a different form of organization. Certain general principles about them should be noted, however. First, each is managed by an appointed board, not directly by a Cabinet minister or by an elected board. The members of the boards are appointed by the minister concerned, and he may share in shaping general policy. The day-by-day details are left to the central, area, or divisional boards provided for in the acts or set up by the industries themselves. In this way the individual industries and the Cabinet minister are accountable to the public in the long run and for general policies by the cut and thrust of Parliamentary debate. It avoids, on the other hand, day-by-day interference by politicians in administrative and management decisions.

Second, each board is a corporate entity. It may sue and be sued like any other company. It is taxed in the normal way. Further, it acquires and holds the property of the industry. This includes not only any new property acquired but also certain prewar public corporations, such as the Central Electricity Board and the London Passenger Transport Board. Finally, in most cases each industry is charged with paying its own way, not every year but over a period of years.

Third, each board is charged with long-term planning for the industry concerned. This includes investment policy, marketing procedures, technical changes, foreign and domestic competition, and industrial relations. Little has been achieved in long-term planning thus far. There has not been enough time. Some of the industries had plans under private enterprise which are to be put into effect first. Further, most of the industries have been subject to the limitations of recent economic crises. Parliament has control over these industries' borrowing funds for expansion purposes. Borrowing for postwar rehabilitation, defense, and housing has had higher priority than for expanding the new nationalized industries, with the possible exception of coal. But Parliament does not control the right of these industries to use their own funds. This freedom has made expansion possible in some industries. Much has been done to nationalize the coal industry. Long-term plans are in process of execution. This is also true of the airlines. Coal was given priority because of its decisive place in the economy. The airlines have been nationalized longer than the industries that were nationalized between 1948 and 1951.

It is difficult to know by what yardsticks the success of nationalized industries should be measured, especially at this early date. If the yardstick is profit making, many of them are more successful than they were under private enterprise. Is it fair, however, to use this measure when almost all industries have been more profitable since the war than they were during the prewar depression? Should the goal of nationalized industries be profit making? One of the major arguments for nationalization was that profits, in coal mining for example, could be achieved only at the expense of the public welfare and the workers in the industry. Are the nationalized industries to show a profit at the expense of the public good? It is argued that a public corporation should provide services which would be unprofitable for private industry to render. A case in point is the extension of electrical or railroad services to remote areas where charges could not begin to cover expenses.

Are they to be measured by the yardstick of efficiency? The British steel industry was one of the most profitable and efficient British industries in the postwar years. Yet, compared with steel industries in some other countries, it has been quite inefficient.

Certain things are clear about nationalized industries, however. The results have not been as bad as the prophets of doom predicted. At the same time, the Socialists' hope that nationalized industry would transform society was not realized. It was argued that under nationalization workers would feel a greater sense of pride in their job than under private enterprise. But the worker feels no greater kinship with public absentee owners and managers, in the coal industry, for example, than he did with private absentee owners and managers, despite the fact that conditions in the mines have vastly improved. Finally, the usefulness of nationalized industries for controlling the economy is limited. Does the device of nationalized industries offer the best way for a government to avoid depressions and to maintain full employment? The budget, the allocation of materials, and taxation policy, for example, are probably more effective devices.

CONCLUSION

British industry has made great contributions to world progress. The Industrial Revolution, including many inventions on which it was based, gave Britain a unique place in economic history to begin with. Britain led in supplanting mercantilism with *laissez faire,* and more recently she has led again in turning to a new kind of regulated economy. Two world wars and a world-wide depression brought the British face to face with difficult new problems. Britain had to find ways to produce more at home, to import less and to export more, to pay off her foreign debts, and to maintain her position as a major power. Another problem is how to eliminate inefficiency in some industries without undue resort to monopoly, either private or public. The British have already applied imagination and valiant effort to the solution of these problems. Although they have increased production substantially and bettered their economic position, it is too soon to pronounce the new methods a success, a failure, or another example of Britain's "muddling through."

QUESTIONS FOR STUDY

1. What conditions led up to the Industrial Revolution in Britain? What were some of the important events in this Industrial Revolution?

2. What is the basic distinction between mercantilism and *laissez faire?*

3. What are the three basic ways in which British industry is owned in Britain? What are some of the chief manufacturing industries in Britain? Which industries are growing, relatively, and which ones declining?

4. How did World War II wreck British industry? How rapidly was British industry able to recover from the ravages of war? How much have the British people shared in the fruits of this recovery?

5. How was Britain able to get along without antitrust laws for so long? When monopoly appeared, in what industries did it tend to appear? What did the government do about it? Why did it believe some action was necessary?

6. Different British industries have been "nationalized" under different circumstances. What have been these circumstances? What industries have been nationalized? Which were the last to be nationalized? Have any been denationalized? Why?

7. What seem to be the chief justifications for nationalizing industries?

CHAPTER 13

FINANCE

The term "Financial Revolution" has not yet been adopted to go along with "Industrial Revolution" and "Transportation Revolution," but the changes in finance were just as great. For example, gold coins came into prominence; the gold standard replaced the silver standard and has itself recently been discarded. Paper money was invented. Moneylenders became bankers. A great private bank, the Bank of England, took on more responsibility for keeping other banks from overlending and finally became a government institution. Partnerships proved inadequate for many modern business operations and, first in commerce and later in industry, were replaced by joint-stock companies and then by corporations. Wars became more expensive and total in character. Business cycles appeared, to torment us by their presence or by the fear of their imminence. Finally, government itself saw fit to perform many social services and even to go into some forms of business. Government has devised various new taxes and now handles the expenditure of about a third of the average person's income.

How finances evolved from the relatively simple to the complex is a long story, and only four of the main features can be discussed here. These are capital, money, banking, and taxation. The most basic of these is capital.

CAPITAL GROWTH

Whether the standard of living in a nation will be high or low depends largely on its supply of capital. People with abundant capital make a living easily. Capital is comprised of plants, tools and other equipment, and inventories. It is a means to an end, the end being the goods we consume, such as food and clothing. Capital is not money, although it is valued in terms of money and money is usually essential to buy capital. For that reason money is sometimes called "liquid capital."

Anyone in business needs liquid capital. He must have funds to invest in equipment. Whether he is a manufacturer or a merchant, he must buy raw materials or hold inventories of goods, he must pay his labor, and

188

he must extend credit to some of his customers. When these entrepreneurs are farmers, and for centuries the majority were, they may not be able to pay until their crops are harvested, perhaps many months later. A businessman must get the funds he needs either from his own savings or from other people's. When he must rely on himself, his business cannot grow as rapidly as when he can also draw on the savings of others. But others will not be so inclined to save their money or to invest their savings unless three basic financial conditions are favorable. They will want to be fairly sure that the money is trustworthy and will not be inflated or otherwise debased. They will want the protection of fair laws and just courts to ensure the repayment of loans. They will want a stable government which does not discourage them with unfair or heavy taxes. Given these conditions, the seeds of capital will grow. To be strong, a nation must have lots of capital. Capital is like so many additional hired hands or energy slaves ready to do the bidding of their masters.

Capital had grown slowly down to the sixteenth century when the usury laws were removed. Thenceforth, it increased more rapidly. The "price revolution" was partly responsible. The influx into Spain and then other parts of Europe of American gold and silver caused prices to rise steadily for 150 years. Since prices rose faster than wages, the margin of business profits widened. In the seventeenth century the appearance of Puritanism also increased capital. The Puritans lived simply, worked hard, and so had plenty of profits to invest. Businessmen could always use any idle funds they could attract. Many thousands sought to participate in the activities of the South Sea Company and similar enterprises about 1720. They continued to buy into these common-law companies during the eighteenth century. Company promoting became an important and profitable form of business. Brokers gathered in Exchange Alley and in coffee houses nearby to buy and sell shares of new companies as well as shares of the East India Company and government securities. In 1773 the Stock Exchange was formally founded, and down to World War I securities of any form could be traded on it. About twenty smaller exchanges sprang up in time in other cities. Yet the majority of businesses in England continued to be carried on with the owners' funds, and these businesses grew chiefly by the plowing back of earnings.

As capital became more plentiful in England, the interest rate for loans fell. Many Englishmen realized that greater profit could be made by investing their funds abroad. Promoters from all over the world came to London to market their securities through London investment firms like the "houses" of Baring, Rothschild, and Morgan. Englishmen invested large amounts in American canals and turnpikes in the 1830s and in American and Argentinian railroads later in the century. Just before

World War I England had a national income of £2 billion annually and was investing abroad about £185 million a year. She had already invested some £3.8 billion in foreign railroads, mines, and industries. But wars and depression caused England to use up much of her capital, especially that invested abroad. World War I cost her in the neighborhood of £8 billion. London remained an important moneylending market after World War I—half her investments in new securities were in foreign issues in 1931. Yet London steadily lost ground to New York. Even so, the custom of saving, once formed, is not easy to break. In 1951 the total funds saved and made available for investment in England were estimated at £2.9 billion. Although England has for some years been a debtor nation, her investment houses are still lending large amounts abroad.

MONETARY DEVELOPMENTS

One of the main sinews of a nation's economic strength is its money. Unless money is relatively dependable, people are less willing to save. If they do save, it will be in coin or perhaps jewelry (as in the Orient or pre-seventeenth-century England), which they will be unwilling to entrust to others or to lend out for long. Thus banking has little opportunity to develop. Without adequate savings, capital is slow to accumulate and the whole industrial structure of a nation takes form more gradually. England's monetary unit, the pound, has been remarkably stable over the last thousand years. That has been a source of economic strength to the nation.

The pound began, in the days of Charlemagne (768–814), as a pound of silver. So also did the French livre, predecessor of the franc, and the Italian lira. The pound was divided into 240 silver pennies. Not until the fourteenth century was a gold coin, the florin, introduced and then chiefly for foreign trade and it was not successful. The pound maintained its value fairly well, especially compared with its cousins, the livre and lira, despite several debasements. As gold became more plentiful, England moved from a bimetallic standard toward a gold standard. The basic coin was now the gold guinea of 21 shillings. From 1717, when the gold standard was adopted, until 1797 the price level was fairly stable. The money system still included silver coins, too, and the bank notes of country banks, which circulated locally.

When the French threatened to invade England in 1797, the public got panicky and demanded gold from the banks, and England had to suspend specie payments. Britain did not return to the gold standard until 1821. During the remainder of the nineteenth century and down until 1914, the pound sterling was the symbol of reliability. It was always redeemable in gold and English prices did not fluctuate markedly. One nation after another followed the example of England and modeled its money system on gold, until by 1912 some forty nations were on the gold standard. World War I forced all but a few nations to abandon the gold standard.

World War I probably ruined more currencies than any war in history. The French franc, which had been as dependable as the pound in the nineteenth century, lost four-fifths of its value; the German, Austrian, and Russian units became virtually worthless, and the price level in England tripled. Representatives of many nations met in Genoa in 1922 and passed a resolution urging all countries to go back to the reliable gold standard at the earliest opportunity. The United States had gone back in 1919, Germany and Austria did so in 1924, and England returned in 1925. Making the pound redeemable in gold at the old rate necessitated some deflation. That was politically unpopular, for it is unpleasant to be asked to accept lower prices for your goods or lower wages for your work. Some English labor unions resisted quite strenuously, and economists like John Maynard Keynes agreed with them.

At this point the Government believed that the prestige of the pound and the preservation of billions of savings measured in pounds was more important than the momentary economic comfort of the English workingman and businessman. For a century the government had been more concerned with the welfare of the capitalist than that of the laborer. They did not know what the consequences would be if the immediate welfare of the laborer was placed first, but they were not yet ready to break tradition and make the experiment. Going back to gold at the old rate was a momentous decision.

The return of England to gold in 1925 was the signal for many others to follow her example. Some 23 counties were back on the gold standard in 1925, 43 by 1928, and 47 by mid-1931. Unfortunately, the new gold standards were not as full-scale as the prewar ones had been. Whereas in 1914 there was much gold coin in circulation in England, in 1925 England returned to a gold bullion standard. That has been defined as a gold standard in which the only gold coin that may circulate is a gold bar worth about $8,000. The purpose is to keep gold from circulating and to limit its use to international payments. It is a more economical standard than the gold-coin standard. Many other nations used a still more economical version of the gold standard, called the "gold-exchange standard." This was a parasite gold standard, for a nation using it kept virtually no gold, bar or coin, but made its money payable in pounds or francs or dollars. Usually it was pounds. The Danish central bank, for example, would have an account in the Bank of England and order payments abroad paid out of it. Thus the Bank of England was close to being the Bank of Europe. When in 1931 several of its chief depositors, especially Austria and Germany, drew heavily on it, the pressure became severe on the Bank. On September 21, 1931, England again suspended specie payments. Before the calendar year ended, 24 other nations abandoned the gold standard. This was inevitable because so many nations on the gold-exchange standard had their gold-paying accounts with the Bank of England.

The value of England's pound followed other major currencies down in the 1930s, keeping between $5 and $4. England financed World War II in considerable part through creating bank deposits. Bank clearings doubled between 1938 and 1948, indicating a sizable inflation, although the value of the pound sterling was pegged at $4.03. Rationing and price controls also concealed some of the inflation. Even so, the Board of Trade's index of wholesale prices about doubled between 1938 and 1948. By 1949 the inflation could no longer be concealed and England devalued the pound by 31 per cent. England was refusing to repeat the mistake of bringing the pound back to its prewar level that she had made after World War I. To understand the recent history of the pound, however, one must first understand the English banking system.

BANKING

A commercial bank has three functions: it loans money, it accepts money for safekeeping (receives deposits), and it creates credit (issues bank notes). Some banks began as moneylenders and some began as places for the safekeeping of money. But until an institution performed all three functions, it was not truly a bank. The key function, which marks off mere lending or safekeeping from banking is the third one, the creation of credit. When a goldsmith or a merchant loans more IOUs than he has in customers' money, he has entered on the business of banking.

In the seventeenth century the goldsmiths were the chief moneylenders. Overseas trade was increasing and foreign money was flowing in, especially Spanish coins. Goldsmiths had the melting pots to melt down coins, and they became the money-changers for merchants trading with various parts of the world. They paid merchants interest to leave money on deposit with them so they could melt down the heavier coins. Goldsmiths also began to loan the money they had on deposit. Some goldsmiths now made more profit from moneylending and melting operations than from jewelry making. The goldsmith gave any depositor of gold or silver a receipt, or "cash note." Soon it became the custom to make these notes payable to bearer, and they passed from person to person as money, functioning like bank notes. Also, a depositor would sometimes write an order to his goldsmith to pay a certain amount of his deposit to a third person. These were checks.

Goldsmiths were early aware that all their depositors were unlikely to demand their money at one time. Instead of giving a borrower coin, they began to give him receipts, or IOUs, as if the borrower had deposited gold or silver, even though he really had not. At this point the goldsmiths were creating their own credit; they had become bankers in the modern sense, although they were still known as goldsmiths. Two of the great goldsmith-banking houses of the seventeenth century were Backwell's and Vyner's. Both houses loaned on a large scale to King Charles II.

It is significant that nearby Holland had a bank, the Bank of Amsterdam (1609), almost a century before England established her Bank of England (1694). Amsterdam was the world's foremost financial center until the end of the eighteenth century. England might have had a bank sooner if the Stuart kings had been more circumspect in their financial dealings. The bank had to wait until their dynasty had about ended. When Charles II died in 1685, he was succeeded by his less popular brother, James II, who was driven from the throne in 1688. William and Mary succeeded James II. William was also the Dutch king and knew about Dutch financial institutions and methods. A war with France began in 1689, and the government was soon in great need of funds. It raised tax rates, resorted to all kinds of schemes like lotteries and tontines, and borrowed from merchants and goldsmiths, but it was still short of funds and interest rates were high. Eventually the needy government took advantage of a theory that was growing in popularity at the time.

The theory was that other forms of value besides gold and silver should be equally good as backing for money. Why not mortgages on land, or why not claims on merchandise, or why not government debt, supported as it is by the government's taxing power? All these should be a suitable basis for a "fund of credit," it was argued. Within limits there is merit to this theory, but it is easy for inexperienced bankers or needy government officials to exceed those limits. Either bankruptcy or inflation is then likely. When people ask to have notes redeemed, they want something which has full value right now, like gold, and not something which will be paid off ten years hence and meanwhile must be heavily discounted, like a mortgage or a government bond. At the moment, financial leaders did not foresee this difficulty, and so land-bank schemes and the like were quite popular. One of the more soundly operated of these was the Bank of England. It was the first successful banking institution in England that called itself a bank. It was not, of course, the first bank, for many goldsmiths did a banking business before 1694.

William Patterson, a Scotsman who had lived in Holland for a while, proposed the idea of the Bank of England and the government accepted it. In exchange for its charter the Bank was to raise £1,200,000 through the sale of its stock, and then loan that £1,200,000 at 8 per cent to the government. Now the Bank had an asset of £1,200,000 in the form of government bonds yielding about £100,000 a year. With this as a backing it might issue £1,200,000 in bank notes and loan them to other borrowers. It might also accept money on deposit and loan some of that to borrowers.

The Bank of England was also privileged to be a joint-stock company with limited liability and to be the sole fiscal agent of the government. Soon the Bank had a fine reputation, for those who directed the Bank were cautious in their policies and careful to whom they loaned. About the time that the war with France ended, 1697, Parliament promised that only the Bank of England should have a charter to issue bank notes. By an act of 1708 it forbade partnerships of more than six persons to issue bank notes. Thus for a long time the Bank of England was the only bank of any size in England. Parliament also let the Bank double its capital. In exchange for these favors the Bank cut its interest rate to the government to 6 per cent and made it an additional loan of £400,000. By 1750–1751 the government's credit, thanks to the Bank of England, had so improved that the public debt was placed on a 3 per cent basis and the Bank of England took over administration of it.

All this did not prevent the goldsmith banks from continuing to do a deposit-banking business and using checks. Also, shopkeepers in the country began to carry on a deposit-banking business. When a farmer sold his wool or grain and got a promise to pay from the city buyer, he often left the funds on deposit with his local shopkeeper, who saw to the collecting of the bill. Shopkeepers of all kinds drifted into money-lending and eventually became country banks. Meanwhile, the new industrialists of the Midlands wanted to borrow, and banks appeared in those areas too. The banks in London served as a go-between for the banks in farm areas having funds to loan and those in industrial areas wishing to borrow. Between 1750 and 1793 the number of small banks outside London grew from about a dozen to some four hundred. The bank notes of many of them were unreliable, so that in 1775 Parliament prohibited them from issuing any notes below £1 and in 1777 below £5. Most country banks kept reserves in some London correspondent bank. Few banks kept much gold. They depended on the Bank of England to supply them if they needed it. This gave that institution great power and responsibility.

Yet, officially, England did not have a central bank. The Bank of England was merely the most reputable commercial bank. No other bank was as large, since banks were forbidden to incorporate or to have more than six partners if they wanted to issue bank notes. Failures among country banks were fairly numerous in times of crisis like 1763, 1772, 1783, 1793, and 1797.

The government borrowed heavily from the Bank of England during the Napoleonic Wars. In one four-year period the Bank lent £10 million to the government. That had inflationary consequences. In 1797 the threat of a French invasion led to suspension of specie payments. After that, Bank of England notes, down to £1, became the basic money of the realm, replacing gold. Country banks continued to increase, reaching 721 by 1810. Their growth was especially rapid about 1809 when the war seemed to take a favorable turn and South American trade was opening up. But the Bank of England did not take steps at this time to limit credit expansion. Rather, it took the attitude that as long as it made safe loans there could be nothing improper in its activities. The directors refused to believe for several years that the doubling of the price level that had taken place was partly caused by the Bank's own increased loans and larger note issues. By the time the Bank resumed specie payments in 1821, they had at last accepted this view.

In 1821 there was fear that resumption would diminish the supply of money and cause prices to fall, with consequent hardships to debtors, farmers, and others. Therefore, in 1823 the government permitted 500 country banks to issue £1 notes again. These banks made too many loans. Now there were many more notes than before and all were redeemable in gold. The Bank of England at first refused to give any help, taking the attitude that the country banks had brought the trouble upon themselves and must take the consequences. Later, the Bank directors changed their minds and helped. Suspension of specie payments was narrowly averted, although many banks failed. Parliament promptly took steps to strengthen the country banks and to regulate them somewhat. By the act of 1826, Parliament permitted the formation of banks on a joint-stock basis but with unlimited liability if they were located more than 65 miles outside London. In 1833 joint-stock deposit banking was made legal in London. The Bank of England's monopoly on banking in London was now limited only to the issuing of bank notes. Bank of England notes were also made legal tender in 1833 for sums above £5 (except at the Bank itself). Now other banks could redeem in Bank of England notes or in gold, which lessened the pressure for gold in times of panic. The Bank of England was for the first time required to publish a weekly statement of its condition.

The encouragement given joint-stock banks, plus the current enthusiasm for railways, led to another burst of business expansion and stock-market speculation. A somewhat similar boom was under way in the United States. By 1836 the Northern and Central Bank of England, one of the new big joint-stock banks, was in trouble and went to the Bank of England for help. Then the American boom collapsed in 1837. Over the next two years the Bank's large gold reserve was almost exhausted, and it had to borrow from the Bank of France. Many small joint-stock banks were in distress, too, and when the Bank of England refused to loan to them, they failed. The Bank was not yet accepting full responsibility for regulating the supply of money and credit.

The Bank of England's inadequate policy of controlling bank credit put it in disrepute. Advocates of a new policy called the "currency principle" came forward. They wanted to deprive the country banks of their note-issuing privilege altogether. They believed that only gold or bank notes fully backed by gold should circulate. If money were limited in that way, they felt that the periodic panics resulting from overlending would cease. They refused to recognize that checking accounts were money. Today we recognize these as the most important money there is. Banking principle advocates opposed the currency-principle advocates. Like the Bank of England directors of 1810, they believed that credit could not overexpand as long as banks made only good loans. Both groups were partly right and partly wrong. The currency-principle group won out despite some compromising. The result was the famous Bank Charter Act of 1844.

The Bank Charter Act of 1844 divided the Bank of England into two main departments, the Issue Department and the Banking Department. The Issue Department took over £14 million of securities and as much gold as the Banking Department did not need. For these assets the Issue Department gave the Banking Department £14 million of Bank of England notes plus £5 of notes for every £5 of gold. The Bank of England was thus limited in the notes it might loan to customers. Another important provision of the act was that henceforth the right to issue bank notes was limited to banks that already enjoyed that privilege. If any bank gave up banking or merged with another bank, it had to give up its note-issuing privilege. The note issues of country banks were limited to the £11 million outstanding in 1844 and henceforth declined. The last bank lost its note-issuing privilege in 1921. To make up for the decline in total notes, the Bank of England was allowed to increase its own issues by two-thirds of any lapsed issues.

The sponsors of the Bank Charter Act of 1844 were doomed to disappointment in so far as they hoped that limiting the Bank's note issues would prevent panics. Panics took place about every ten years as usual. On three occasions the government had to suspend the Bank Charter Act and let the Bank of England issue more notes to relieve the money shortage that takes place during a panic. Suspension of the act is not to be confused with suspension of specie payments. The first panic came three years after the Bank Charter Act of 1844 and was in some ways the worst one of the century.

During the next ten years the English joint-stock banks increased their deposits fivefold as large amounts of gold flowed in from Australia and California. France and England fought the Crimean War against Russia in 1854–1856. All this stimulated business expansion and stock speculation. In America railroads were being built too fast, many of them with the help of British capital. When that bubble burst, the panic spread to England. When the Bank of England was besieged with demands for help, it raised its bank rate, but the gold continued to flow out. Finally, the government authorized suspension of the Bank Charter Act of 1844 again. From this crisis the Bank directors learned that it would be a good idea to raise the bank rate as soon as they sensed overexpansion, instead of waiting until the crisis was upon them.

A few years later the Bank had to deal with another menace. This time it was a new kind of "bank," called a finance company. Englishmen were promoting railroads, gas works, docks, and harbors in England and other parts of the world. Instead of getting funds by selling stocks or bonds, these expensive enterprises borrowed from the new finance companies. A financial institution that may have to pay its depositors on short notice should not invest most of its funds in businesses that will not return them for many years. The finance-company experiment came to an unhappy end in 1866 with the shocking collapse of the once-reputable firm of Overend, Gurney and Company.

Henceforth, the officers and directors of the Bank of England became more skillful at anticipating trouble and more expert in handling it. The Bank came to be affectionately known as "The Old Lady of Threadneedle Street." Part of its success was due to the fact that the joint-stock banks of England were now merging into stronger branch systems. In 1864 there were already two big ones with over 100 branches. The number of banking institutions steadily declined, because of mergers, from 600 in 1824 to 55 in 1914. Eventually, the majority of joint-stock banks were to be found in five big systems, namely, Barclay's, Lloyd's, the Midland's, the National Provincial, and the Westminster. Country banks, bill brokers, and others kept deposits in the London banks. These, in turn, kept their reserves in the Bank of England. Thus all deposits rested like an upside-down pyramid on the reserves of the Bank of England. Banks borrowed from the Bank of England only when they needed to do so, much as member banks of the Federal Reserve System borrow from Federal Reserve Banks. The Bank of England was quick to stiffen its bank rate any time it sensed an undue expansion. More than that, its custom of selling securities simultaneously tended to reduce the reserves of other banks and discourage their lending too freely to customers. Yet in times of genuine distress, the Bank of England stood ready to help any worthy institution. It gave the House of Baring prompt assistance in 1890, which kept that crisis from developing into another 1866 disaster.

It was in the 1860s and 1870s that the Bank of England really became a central bank. The writings of Lord Goschen and of Walter Bagehot did much to educate the Bank's directors and the financial world in the functions the Bank of England ought to perform. One consequence was that the Bank of England had to carry larger reserves than other banks and so had to be content with a more modest profit. But so well was the English money market run by the Bank of England that it became the chief money borrowing and lending center of the entire world.

A quotation from Walter Bagehot will reveal how efficient the English banking system had become and what an advantage it gave English businessmen in their competition with businessmen in other parts of the world where credit was less highly developed.

> If a merchant has £50,000 all his own,—to gain 10 per cent on it he must make £5,000 a year and must charge for his goods accordingly; but if another has only £10,000, and borrows £40,000 by discounts (no extreme instance in our modern trade), he has the same capital of £50,000 to use, and can sell much cheaper. If the rate at which he borrows be 5 per cent, he will have to pay £2,000 a year; and if, like the old trader, he makes £5,000 a year, he will still, after paying his interest, obtain £3,000 a year, or 30 per cent, on his own £10,000. As most merchants are content with much less than 30 per cent, he will be able, if he wishes, to forego some of that profit, lower the price of the commodity, and drive the old-fashioned trader—the man who trades on his own capital—out of the market.[1]

The danger in this system of heavy borrowing was that overexpansion of business would easily develop. The Bank of England had to be on constant watch to prevent that and the panics it would engender.

The London money market was very helpful to a nation whose foreign trade was growing. An importer wishing to borrow to finance an order of cotton could do so in London. An exporter wanting to cash a foreign bill of exchange (foreign promise to pay) could get it "accepted" (guaranteed) by a London acceptance house and thus obtain needed funds right away. Acceptance houses, bill brokers, and banks turned any good kind of IOU quickly into cash and enabled exporters and importers to carry on their work more efficiently and economically. The Bank of

---

[1] Walter Bagehot, *Lombard Street* (London: John Murray, 1915), p. 8.

England saw to it that the over-all supply of credit was alway adequate, neither too scarce nor too plentiful.

This nicely balanced financial system was rudely shaken by World War I and has never been the same since. The outbreak of war brought demands for gold from all over England and the world on London and on the Bank of England. Specie payments were suspended. To replace the gold coin that disappeared from circulation, the British government issued £1 and 10 shilling notes. Now, Bank of England notes were backed by these Treasury notes, which, in turn, had little gold back of them and even that was inaccessible. The government borrowed from the banks and that created money just as surely as if the government had printed notes and spent them. It was deposit money instead of paper money. The Bank of England's deposits grew from £59 million in mid-1913 to £192 million in mid-1920. The deposits of joint-stock banks more than doubled in the same period. The price level was triple in 1920 what it had been in 1913. Yet all other nations had inflation also, most of them more than England had. In 1925 England was able to go back to the gold standard by only a partial deflation. Even that was painful. In 1928 the government's £1 and 10-shilling notes were made Bank of England notes, and the Bank's fiduciary limit was raised from about £20 million to £260 million. The limit was later altered several times, reaching £580 million in 1939.

The English blamed many of their financial difficulties on their effort to return too soon to the gold standard. The gold standard now changed from the role of sacred cow to that of scapegoat. Henceforth, England was on a managed currency standard, with the Bank of England doing much of the managing. The views of John Maynard Keynes, more than anyone else, were the basis of British financial policy. Keynes had opposed England's going back to the prewar gold pound in 1925 and had urged the abandonment of gold in 1931. He was primarily concerned with maintaining full employment. To achieve that, he thought it necessary to sacrifice the custom of keeping the pound convertible in gold.

Keynes advocated what amounted to a "low interest rate" standard in place of the gold standard. If interest rates were low, businessmen would borrow readily to expand their activities and this would increase employment opportunities, he said. Low interest rates also reduced interest payments on the large public debt and so kept taxes down. Keynes did not believe low interest rates would discourage people from saving. He said people saved about the same amount regardless of what the interest rate was. If they would not invest it at low rates, he said, the banking system should create the deposit money anyway and loan that. To keep money plentiful at low rates, the Bank of England reduced its basic bank rate to 2 per cent in 1932. This once-important financial weathervane now lost its meaning, for it consistently pointed in the direction of low-cost loans. The Bank of England became an arm of the government for maintaining prosperity. It provided banks with ample reserves for loans, to business in peacetime and to government in wartime.

World War II was financed on a 3 per cent basis, compared with the 5 per cent basis of World War I. How could that be done? If banks were unwilling to loan to the government by buying Treasury bills (a bill is a short-term IOU that is saleable), then Parliament authorized the Treasury to *require* the banks to loan money to the Treasury and at a rate to be determined by the Treasury itself. The bank received a Treasury Deposit Receipt, referred to as a T.D.R., for such a forced loan. These T.D.R.s, which ran for six months and paid about 1 per cent, could not be resold. They could be cashed only at the Bank of England. But the Bank of England, like the American Federal Reserve Banks, stood ready to turn government securities into cash for any bank or discount firm that needed it. Banks had become service institutions for the government and none more so than the Bank of England. The Bank of England no longer told the Treasury what funds it might have and at what interest rate; it provided whatever funds the Treasury wanted and at the Treasury's price.

The decision of the Labor Government in 1946 to nationalize the Bank of England was only recognizing the control over the Bank of England which the Treasury had exercised for some time. Stockholders received Treasury securities in exchange for their Bank stock. These Treasury securities pay the same income that the Bank averaged during the twenty-two years prior to 1946. The Bank of England keeps many of the outward appearances of independent control of the money market. Yet under the nationalization act the directors of the Bank may, "if they think it necessary in the public interest, request information from and make recommendations to banks, and may, if so authorized by the Treasury, issue directions to any banker for the purpose of securing that effect is given to any such request or recommendation." In short, the Bank of England may order banks to do anything. True, the government has not yet exercised this tremendous authority, but it is there, on the statutes.

TAXATION

Taxes are needed to pay the costs of a strong and just government. Such a government is essential to encourage saving and investment and bring about business growth and a rising standard of living. But the power to tax is the power both to create and to destroy; it may be abused. Taxes may be too high, or bear unfairly on certain classes, or the proceeds may be squandered on avoidable wars or to pander to the tastes of an extravagant court, or they may be wasted by a corrupt or inefficient government. Taxes, whether well or ill used, tend to rise with the passage of time; they do not obey the maxim, "What goes up must come down." Over the centuries, especially over the last century, the average man has had to pay an ever-larger proportion of his income to the government in taxes. There are two reasons for this: wars have become more costly; and governments serve and protect the people in many more ways than they formerly did.

In medieval times the king and nobles normally supported themselves from the proceeds of their extensive landholdings. Down to the seventeenth century the rule was that "the king must live of his own." Serfs and other bondsmen paid rentlike dues but free men and nobles generally went tax free. Only in times of emergency, such as a major war, were taxes looked upon as justified. A king or government that abused the taxing privilege sometimes stirred up a serious rebellion. Because of excessive taxes the nobility forced King John to sign the Magna Carta in 1215, and a poll tax caused the Peasants' Rebellion in 1381. Taxes were levied on land, on personal property, and on exemption from military service (scutage). There were some customs duties too.

As England took on the characteristics of a modern nation, it was more difficult for the king to live on his own resources. To supplement their incomes, Henry VIII (1509–1547) debased the currency, and Elizabeth (1558–1603) took shares in Drake's marauding expeditions. Charles I (1625–1649) was less resourceful and quite highhanded. Although the English were coming to regard taxes as a duty of the citizen rather than a burden which those of inferior social status must bear, they insisted that Parliament, not the King, impose the taxes and appropriate the funds. Charles I balked at this. In the Civil War of the 1640s, two taxes came into general use. One was the land tax, which later became a general property tax. The other was the unpopular "excise" or internal-revenue tax, primarily on liquor. The excise tax is not to be confused with an import duty, which is an external-revenue tax. The constant wars with France in the eighteenth century kept the national debt growing. It rose from £1.2 million in 1694 to £227 million in 1784. Taxes rose too. In general, the people preferred that the taxes be on luxury items like windows, but there were taxes on necessities like salt, soap, candles, and coal.

By the time of the Napoleonic Wars the once-unpopular excise taxes were generally accepted but were not sufficient, despite the great variety of them. Sydney Smith complained of "taxes upon everything which it is pleasant to see, hear, feel, taste or smell." Direct taxes were added to the government's tax arsenal. One of them, the income tax, had been talked about in the eighteenth century—Adam Smith disapproved of it—but it had been rejected as too great an invasion of a man's private life. Under stress of emergency the younger Pitt got an income tax law passed in 1798. It was unpopular and was repealed as soon as the war ended. Peel revived it in 1841, and after the 1870s it, too, was accepted as a permanent feature. In 1907 a distinction was made between earned and unearned incomes. In 1909 the graduated income tax appeared. Meanwhile, the indirect taxes declined in importance. Taxes on the poor man's necessities like salt, candles, and soap were removed; only those on liquor remained. Customs duties were also removed or reduced during the nineteenth-century era of free trade. At the end of the Napoleonic Wars, indirect taxes had provided two-thirds of the revenue; at the end of World War I they provided less than one-third. Since 1931, when England abandoned free trade policy, customs duties have grown again in importance as revenue producers.

Although government pried more into each citizen's affairs and took directly more of his personal income, it also undertook to serve and benefit him in a greater number of ways. In 1839 Parliament began appropriating money for public education; in 1908 for old-age pensions, and in 1911 for health insurance. By 1951 the government was spending a third of its income on social services, especially medical service, insurance, and education, and another third on defense and payment for past wars. The portion of national income taken by government expenditures declined during the nineteenth century and rose again after World War I, as may be seen from Table 13-1. Today the English are about the most heavily taxed free people in the world. A childless couple with a $5,000 income would pay the central government $510 in Canada, $760 in the United States, and $1,265 in England (1954). Economists say that,

Table 13-1. Government Expenditure Related to National Income
(Pound figures in millions)

Date	Government expenditure	National income	Percentage G.E. to N.I.
January, 1817	£ 71	£ 400	18.0
March, 1860	69		
March, 1890	86		
August, 1914	212	2,250	9.4
August, 1938	1,019	5,048	20.4
August, 1951	4,249	11,937	35.6
August, 1953	4,512	13,584	33.2

SOURCE: The 1817 and 1914 figures are from *English Public Finance*, (New York: Bankers Trust Co., 1920), p. 148. Others are taken from the *Statistical Abstract for the United Kingdom, 1954*, pp. 220, 247. The national income figures for 1938, 1951, and 1953 are personal income before taxes.

beyond a certain point, high taxes discourage business, stimulate wasteful spending, and lead to inflation. Colin Clark of Oxford University says that the crucial point is 25 per cent. Whatever it is, the English taxpayer, now averaging 33 per cent, is apparently nearer to it than the Canadian or the American, or perhaps has passed it a long time ago.

QUESTIONS FOR STUDY

1. What did the Financial Revolution consist of? Why did it take place when it did? What did it accomplish?

2. How did England get the capital to carry out its Industrial Revolution, its Transportation Revolution, and other economic revolutions?

3. What is the origin of the pound sterling? How stable has it been over the centuries? How do you account for this? How long was Britain on the gold standard? Why did she leave it?

4. What is the origin of Britain's commercial banks? How did the Bank of England get started? Why did the government favor it so?

5. When did the Bank of England become a central bank? Distinguish between the "banking principle" and the "currency principle." How did the Bank of England carry out its responsibility of preventing panics, or at least of moderating them when they developed?

6. Why was Britain so anxious to return to the gold standard after World War I? What mistake did Britain make in returning to gold? What sort of a standard has Britain been on since about 1931? How has this affected the activities of the Bank of England?

7. Show how Britain has proceeded from a nation of virtually no taxes, at least for the wealthy, to one of property taxes, then to one of excise taxes, and finally to one of income taxes, which bear most heavily on the rich. What are some possible dangers of too-heavy taxation?

CHAPTER 14

LABOR

The British Labor movement has both a trade union side and a political side. The relation between the two has never been as close as its critics claim or as its advocates desire. Like so many other British institutions, the Labor movement has assumed forms that are chiefly the results of expedient solutions to specific problems. This is true even of many so-called "socialist" measures, which are more British in design than they are the products of economic or political theory. The Labor movement and its achievements have deep historical roots.

LABOR BEFORE THE INDUSTRIAL REVOLUTION

There were no trade unions as such before the Industrial Revolution, but there was regulation of wages and of the conditions of work by other means. From the fourteenth to the seventeenth centuries a national system of fixing prices and wages developed in which a number of bodies had powers of regulation and enforcement. By the late eighteenth century this national system was becoming less effective. The legal acts of the national system stayed longest in force. Under the common law, combinations of workmen or of masters to regulate prices and wages were acts of conspiracy. This made it difficult for workmen to organize into unions to raise wages or to change their conditions of labor at the time that the Industrial Age began.

LABOR SINCE THE INDUSTRIAL REVOLUTION

At least four periods can be traced in the organization of trade unions from the beginning of the Industrial Age. First, the period until about 1825 was one of embryo organizations and a struggle for existence. Second, the period from 1825 to 1851 was one of utopian movements. Third, craft unions as we know them today began in 1851 with the formation of the Amalgamated Society of Engineers. Unions conducted their affairs conservatively at first and accommodated themselves to capitalism.

Fourth, organizations for the unskilled and semiskilled workmen began with the Great Dock strike of 1889. These brought with them political activity and socialist aims.

Embryo Organizations and the Struggle for Existence, 1776–1825. Early union organizations had their origins in local trade clubs in which craftsmen met together for social purposes in the local "pub," or tavern. They do not date back to medieval guilds, as Sidney and Beatrice Webb showed in their classic work, *The History of Trade Unionism*. Neither do they owe their origins to the new factories. In the factories unskilled workmen, women, and children were the most common types of employees. A trade union usually began as a result of some specific grievance which the craftsmen shared and made plans to remedy. The breakdown of the guild system gave skilled men a bond in common, for they could no longer expect to become owners or master craftsmen. Thus they identified their interests with those of other skilled men rather than with those of their employers. Skilled men who gathered together to drink a pint of ale were more important in the formation of early trade clubs or unions than some later theorists of trade union origins have supposed.

Unions first tried to remedy their members' grievances and then to win the simple right to exist under the law. Before 1799, countless employers had petitioned Parliament for special legislation to prohibit unions and combinations of working people. A maze of prohibitive legislation resulted. Parliament granted the petitions because the fixing of wages and prices was by tradition a matter for the state. But, according to the new economic theory of *laissez faire*, wages and prices should be fixed not by the state but by the free play of market forces. The attempts of working people to combine for purposes of collective bargaining sinned against both the tradition of state control and the principles of *laissez faire*. The employers thus had it both ways.

In 1799 and 1800 the Combination Acts were passed. So many individual industries had petitioned Parliament for legislation against combinations in their own industries that Parliament decided to pass general acts. When the new legislation was not systematically enforced, working people continued to organize. Meanwhile, the courts applied the common-law doctrine of conspiracy. This did not prevent working people from organizing; it simply declared that any action taken by them was a conspiracy. It was quite outside their jurisdiction to change economic conditions.

Parliament attempted to remove the red flag from in front of the bull by repealing the Combination Acts in 1824. It was argued that this would eliminate the motive for forming unions. It did not work that way. A wave of strikes followed. In 1825 Parliament passed another "repeal" act, which was a compromise between the laws of 1800 and 1824. The partial repeal of the Combination Acts, then, was not attributable to the strength of unions but to the fears of their enemies.

Until 1825 the new unions were mostly local, and they persisted, in the main, among such skilled workers as the hatters, coopers, smiths, bricklayers, carpenters, printers, cutlery workers, the skilled workmen in cotton and other textiles, and among brushmakers and basketmakers. Meetings and ceremonies were often held in secret. Owing to the memory of the French Revolution the public feared unions as harbingers of class revolt. The "Philanthropic Hercules," born in 1818, was the first successful national union to organize widespread groups or skills. It and its immediate successors all perished quickly.

Repression of trade union organization by the state and employers on the one hand, and force and violence by working people on the other, distinguish this period. Employers broke a strike of the cotton and woolen weavers in Lancashire in 1808. The government used military force and imprisonment to break the Durham and Northumberland miners' strike in 1810 and a general strike of the Scottish weavers in 1812. All were spontaneous, poorly organized movements.

The workers, too, sometimes used force and violence. The Luddite movement is an example of that. The Luddites were a secret organization of machine breakers who issued statements in the name of a mythical "Ned Ludd" or "King Ludd." After the Luddites had destroyed knitting frames in the Midland hosiery districts, the movement spread to the northern textile areas. People still knitted hosiery there in individual cottages under the putting-out system. The workers systematically broke up the new frames, which produced more goods of poorer quality at cheaper rates.

The Peterloo Massacre was the most important act of violence. Some eighty thousand people gathered at St. Peter's Field, Manchester, in 1819 to demand the reform of Parliament. The yeomanry broke up the demonstration with drawn swords. They killed at least 11 people and injured hundreds more. Although many people were shocked by the affair, the governing group turned the massacre to their advantage by proclaiming it the beginning of revolution. Parliament passed the Six Acts, which were more repressive than the Combination Acts and the conspiracy doctrine.

This was a period of revolt by ineffectively organized working people against the new industrial society, and of a backward look toward the old agrarian society in which their station, if lowly, had been stable and secure.

Idealistic and Utopian Movements, 1825–1851. The period from 1825 to 1851 saw but little strengthening of the trade union movement. Labor was caught up in idealistic and utopian movements. The occurrence of severe economic depressions in 1825, 1836–1837, and in 1847–1848 made successful organization of labor almost impossible. Labor devoted its efforts to chasing after the pot of gold at the end of a rainbow.

Two major movements distinguish this era. The first was the formation of the Grand National Consolidated Trade Union, founded in 1833. Most of the new utopian ideas appeared in it. The leader was Robert Owen, an employer who had gained fame for his experiment in cooperative production at New Lanark. The Grand National Union claimed over half a million members within a few weeks of its birth, but it soon declined. Economic depression and declining wage levels made its success doubtful from the start. Abortive strikes proved that the cleavage between the skilled and unskilled in its ranks was too great an obstacle to unity. A series of prosecutions undermined its legal existence. The radical bent of its leaders, its utopian aims, the public's fears because of the French Revolution, and Owen's earlier espousal of atheism were shaky foundations on which to build. Finally, the strength of the employers made it easy for them to resist the union's efforts. They introduced an instrument called "the document." Individual workmen were required to sign a statement that they were not members of the Grand National Union. It was simply a yellow-dog contract. Men signed for fear of losing their employment and having their names put on a black list, which would keep them from getting a job anywhere.

The most famous trial for organizing a union was that of the Tolpuddle Martyrs who attempted to set up the Friendly Society of Agricultural Laborers in Dorchester in 1834. Six men were prosecuted and ordered "transported" to Australia for taking and administering secret oaths. They were prosecuted under an obscure act of 1797, which had been devised to prevent naval mutiny. The extreme punishment aroused indignation and five of the six were brought back from exile.

The Chartist movement was the second major movement of the period. It grew out of the failure of trade union efforts under the Grand National and was more political. The aim was the extension of political rights to redress economic grievances. The name comes from the workers' Charter, which it hoped to have accepted. The Charter included demands for universal male suffrage, the secret ballot, and a Parliament selected yearly with members paid for their services. Chartism offended where it hoped to do good because of its religious fervor and of its propaganda methods, that is, torchlight parades, machine wrecking, and revolutionary speeches. Its end had come by 1848.

Even though trade union organization was not advanced materially in this period, there was some political reform. Parliament passed the Factory Act in 1833. It provided that certain industries could not employ children under nine. It limited the working day to nine hours and the week to forty-eight hours for children between nine and thirteen years of age. It required three hours of compulsory education a day. And children aged thirteen to eighteen were limited to a twelve-hour day and a sixty-nine-hour week. Inspection, so inadequate in earlier factory acts, was improved.

Ungenerous as these provisions may seem today, they established two principles. The state set a precedent of protecting certain classes of people, such as women and children, who could not fend for themselves. It also established compulsory education for the first time. These were the thin edges of the wedge which soon pried larger openings in the employers' armor and produced further humanitarian legislation.

The New Model Unions and Accommodation to Capitalism, 1851–1889. Several craft unions amalgamated in 1851 to form the Amalgamated Society of Engineers. "The A.S.E. was based, roughly, upon high contributions, high benefits, few strikes, and the protection of the craft against the unskilled."[1] The ASE was termed the "New Model" because other unions carefully copied its structure. The period of the New Model was quite unlike former ones. In previous periods the revolt had been against the discipline of the factory system with its long hours and boredom at the machine, the wage system with its dependence on new and sometimes ruthless employers, and the squalor of the cities. The period that began in 1851 was characterized by an accommodation to capitalism on the part of the skilled workmen. They bent their efforts to gaining a greater share of the increased wealth which the new system provided. The New Model was successful and " . . . the amalgamation and the struggle which followed it made the ASE the leading union in the country."[2] The general upturn in economic activity contributed to this success. It gave a solid foundation on which the new unionism could build.

Five leaders of the craft unions dominated the labor movement and became known as the "Junta." The Junta aimed at making trade unions legal and respectable. They wished to avoid depletion of their funds by strikes and to build membership, in short, to preserve their institutions. They gained these ends but not without conflict with other leaders who preferred more vigorous action. Yet the craft workers, in striving for self-protection, often acted without compassion for their less fortunate unskilled brothers. They were dubbed the "aristocracy of labor."

Labor registered successes in the legal and political fields as well as in the economic field. Parliament enacted a number of important new laws. Two acts of 1871, a second Trade Union Act and the Criminal

---

[1] R. W. Postgate, *The Builders' History* (London: Labour Publishing Company, 1923), p. 183.

[2] G. D. H. Cole, *A Short History of the British Working Class Movement, 1789–1947* (London: George Allen and Unwin, Ltd., 1948), p. 173.

Law Amendment Act, had conflicting effects. The first gave unions legal status: they could now combine freely. Combinations and union agreements were no longer in restraint of trade under the common law. Unions gained the right to hold property, which gave them legal protection for their funds. The second act, however, nullified parts of the first. Violence, threats, intimidation, molestation, and obstruction on the part of unions were made criminal acts. As a result, unions suffered severe penalties for such things as peaceful picketing. The act also codified much of previous laws and thus revived certain restrictions which had been forgotten.

After further agitation, two acts of 1875 and a third in 1876 gained for unions the security that they had hoped for in 1871. The Conspiracy and Protection of Property Act of 1875 repealed the hated Criminal Law Amendment Act of 1871. The Employers and Workmen Act of 1875 replaced the Master and Servant Act of 1867. Contracts between employers and workmen were now civil engagements in which both were equal parties. A breach of contract was no longer punishable by imprisonment. The mere change in name signified a new relationship. A third Trade Union Act in 1876 provided the definition of a trade union which applies, substantially, in Britain today.

Meantime, in the political field, the Reform Acts of 1867 and 1884 made it possible for many more workingmen to vote. An 1862 act gave workingmen a preferential claim for wages against defaulting or bankrupt employers, much as mechanic lien laws did in the United States. In 1867, the Factory Acts were extended to most industries.

The Labor movement continued to strengthen its own organizations throughout this period. Both the Trades Union Congress and the Fabian Society were formed. The former came into being when the Manchester and Salford Trades Council called a national congress of trade unions in 1868. The TUC has met yearly since then, with two exceptions. The Fabian Society began in 1884. It contained a group of highly intelligent pamphleteers such as Sidney and Beatrice Webb, George Bernard Shaw, and H. G. Wells, and aimed at the gradual formation of a socialist society. Its methods were research, education, persuasion, and eventually, direct political action through the Labor party. G. M. Trevelyan once called it a group of "intelligence officers without an army." Yet its success over the years has been great. Another significant event took place in 1874 when two working-class candidates were elected to Parliament as Liberals. Soon, both Conservative and Liberal parties were competing with each other by means of social legislation to win the working-class vote.

In the period of New Model unionism, the foundations of trade unions, although narrowly conceived, became secure. The ground was laid for later action by the formation of bodies like the TUC and the Fabian Society. Political democracy was extended by the Reform Bills, and economic and social gains were made. The results are seen in the scope and character of the British Labor movement today.

The New Unionism, Political Activity, and Socialist Aims. The year 1889 is a landmark in British trade union history. The Gasworkers' and General Laborers' Union was formed in May of that year. By August it had gained an industry-wide eight-hour day in London without a strike. Later in the year a small strike at the West India dock spread through the entire London dock areas. The dockers' demand for a wage of sixpence an hour seemed fair to a public which had been reading about Charles Booth's investigation of the miserable state of the London poor.[3] The strikers received public subscriptions amounting to over £50,000 and at the end of a month they gained their demands.

The cry of "trade unionism for all" began to be heard. Many new organizations were now formed owing to favorable economic conditions and the able leadership of John Burns, Tom Mann, and Ben Tillett. The old unionism, formerly the New Model, also increased in membership. Both grew rapidly.

Even certain white-collar groups began to organize. In 1890 the National Union of Clerks was founded. This was the predecessor of the present Union of Shop, Distributive, and Allied Workers, the sixth largest union in the country today. G. D. H. Cole has estimated that the number of trade union members doubled between 1888 and 1892, increasing from less than 750,000 to over 1,500,000. The unions of less skilled workmen were built on a program of industrial militancy, political action, and working class solidarity.

Although craft unions in the New Model period sought an accommodation to capitalism, unrest was never far below the surface. The old feelings of revolt reasserted themselves in the new form of socialism. The unions hoped to gain socialism in stages by peaceful and democratic means. But the new idealism, unlike the earlier utopian movements, had a practical vehicle in the form of the "New Unionism."

By 1900 the Labor Representation Committee was securing working-class candidates for Parliament, and by 1906 it had become the present Labor party. Two unfavorable judgments by the House of Lords were the immediate spurs of labor's political activity. The first was the Taff Vale judgment of 1901. The Taff Vale Railway Company sued the Amalgamated Society of Railway Servants for damages growing out of a strike. The union had to pay the company a large sum. The House of Lords held that a trade union could be sued despite the 1871–1876 legis-

---

[3] C. Booth, *Labour and Life of the People* (London: Williams & Norgate, Ltd., 1889).

lation by which trade unions had received immunity from such legal action.

When the Liberal party came to power, it passed the Trade Disputes Act of 1906. Section 4 specifically reversed the Taff Vale judgment. The new act sanctioned peaceful picketing, inducement to break a contract, and collective acts not illegal when done by individuals. Meanwhile the Taff Vale decision had spurred trade unionism and political activity by labor groups.

This activity and the formation of the Labor party in 1906, with which some trade unions were affiliated, brought a second adverse judgment by the House of Lords. A member of the same Amalgamated Society of Railway Servants, W. V. Osborne, brought action to prevent his union from using its funds for political-party activity. The House of Lords upheld him. The Lords said that any activity of a trade union was illegal unless it was specifically sanctioned by Parliamentary legislation on trade unions. The power to collect funds for political purposes had not been sanctioned. The Trade Disputes Act of 1913 followed as a result of this decision. It allowed any union to collect and administer funds for political purposes under specified conditions. The most important one was that any union member might "contract out" of such political levies by giving proper notice to his union.[4]

Economic conditions were favorable, and trade union membership rose from two to four million between 1900 and 1914. By 1920 it had doubled again. Labor unions felt strong and aggressive. Then a long period of economic distress in the 1920s and 1930s demonstrated that they could not make economic gains if the government was against them.

A sharp economic decline following World War I and a series of wage reductions put the trade unions in a militant mood. Some leaders advocated direct action and workers' control of industry. Postwar conditions injured the miners most of all. They formed a "triple alliance" with the transport workers and railway men for mutual support. But the triple alliance collapsed on Black Friday, April 14, 1921, when strike notices supporting the miners were issued and then withdrawn.

The miners were also highly instrumental in calling the nine-day General Strike of 1926. Labor learned many lessons from the failure of the General Strike, which was perhaps the most important, yet abortive, action in British trade union history. They learned that they were not sufficiently unified to support a General Strike, that public opinion opposed coercive action against the government, and that peaceful and accepted methods were the only alternatives to direct action. The public reaction to the General Strike was the severe Trade Disputes and Trades

[4] A. Flanders, *Trade Unions* (New York: Longmans, Green & Co., Inc., 1952), p. 18.

Union Act of 1927. It remained the basic labor law until 1946. Strikes or lockouts whose purposes were to coerce the government were declared illegal. Limitations were also put on actions by union members who worked for national or local government authorities.

The period following the General Strike was one of consolidation and retrenchment. Union membership fell off and a period of quiet rebuilding ensued. The Labor movement turned its efforts more and more to political activity.

The Labor party had been reorganized in 1918 and for the first time had officially accepted socialist aims and objectives. Although a Labor Government had come to power in 1924, its discretion was very limited, for it controlled only a minority in the House of Commons. The Labor party came to power again in 1929, thanks to the support of the Liberals, who held the balance of power. That time the depression limited the activity of the Labor party, and it was torn by internal strife as well. The Prime Minister, Ramsey MacDonald, was not in a position to achieve Labor objectives. It was not until the surprising and overwhelming victory of the Labor party in 1945 that Labor was really in a position to carry out its program.

The following Labor party policies were put into effect between 1945 and 1950. First, certain basic industries were placed under public ownership. Second, the Government achieved a redistribution of income. Third, Labor obtained measures to control the economy in order to avoid severe economic fluctuations and to achieve full employment. Fourth, a program of rationing scarce items was instituted to increase production in the vital export industries and to cut expenditure for imports of food, raw materials, and luxury items.

It must be remembered that the trade union movement is only a part of the Labor movement as a whole. It has given enthusiastic support to the aims of the Labor party, but it remained an independent entity even when a Labor Government were in power. The relationship of the trade unions to the Labor party is a close one, but trade union activity remains the unions' fundamental concern. The unions have at times sharply criticized the Labor Government's policies. A Labor Government, for its part, have taken coercive action against trade unions when that was in the public interest. Clement Attlee, on one occasion, called out the army to unload food from ships that had been strikebound by the dockers.

The policies of the trade unions and of the Labor party are made independently of each other and in a democratic atmosphere amidst vigorous discussion and debate. Their views are sometimes at odds, yet each respects the fundamental responsibilities of the other. They generally compromise their differences.

TRADE UNION ORGANIZATION AND INDUSTRIAL RELATIONS

Trade union organization in the United Kingdom is characterized by a wide variety of unions and by a long tradition of free collective bargaining. English unions make collective agreements which are renegotiated yearly but which remain in effect until superseded by new arrangements. Unions and employers ordinarily reach these annual agreements without any third-party or government interference.

Size and Number. Hard and fast definitions of British trade unions must be avoided. The historical movements that shaped them gave them an extremely complex and overlapping structure. It was estimated by the Ministry of Labor in the early 1950s that there were 704 separate and independent unions in the United Kingdom. Their total membership was estimated to be 9,235,000. About one-third of all wageworkers and salaried employees were union members.

Of these 704 unions, 400 had less than 1,000 members. They represented only about 1 per cent of all trade union membership. Most of these unions were old single-craft unions distinguished, apart from their small numbers, by inordinately long names. (The importance of a union in Britain is, generally, in inverse proportion to the length of its name.) About two-thirds of all union members belonged to the 17 large unions of 100,000 members or more. Another 18 per cent were in 33 unions whose size varied from 25,000 to 100,000 members.

In 1900, by comparison, there had been some 1,300 unions. The decline in number is the result of amalgamations and federations. The total membership in 1900 was just over 2 million. It increased to 4 million in 1914 and reached a peak of 8 million in the postwar year of 1920. During the Great Depression membership declined to about half of the wartime figure, then rose to over 6 million in 1939 and was 9.5 million in 1952.

Types and Kinds. The complex and amorphous structure of the British trade unions makes it difficult to classify them. At least three types may be identified. These are the craft or multicraft unions, the industrial unions, and the general workers' unions. The last type is peculiar to Britain.

The British craft unions were the first to form. Craft unions are characterized by their conservatism, strong bargaining power, relatively high wages, limited entry, and the friendly benefits which are paid to their members. These benefits may be for unemployment, sickness, accident, retirement, strike pay, or even burial expenses. In recent years craft workers have suffered a relative decline in their advantage over semiskilled and unskilled workers. This has been true in wage payments because of inflation, taxation, and the unionization of the less skilled, and in security and welfare benefits because of the rise of the welfare state. In addition, technological change has decreased the importance of the craftsmen, for workpeople in the newer mass-production industries have been "de-skilled."

Among the strongest craft unions are the United Patternmakers Association and the London Society of Compositors. Unions like the Amalgamated Engineering Union (the old ASE) and the Electrical Trades Union are examples of multicraft unions which have in recent times broadened their base to include the less skilled and women workers. They are more like the general workers unions but are still thought of as craft unions because of their origins.

The industrial unions rose during the first quarter of the twentieth century. They have had less success in Britain than all the discussion about them would indicate. There are several reasons for this. They arrived on the scene somewhat late. In 1924 a resolution at the annual Trades Union Congress called for a reduction in the number of trade unions to "an absolute minimum" and stated that " . . . the aim should be as far as possible organization by industry." Yet owing to lack of success in organizing industrially, the goal of industrial unionism was amended to the promotion of unity among existing unions. Finally, the rise of new forms of light consumer industries called for a form of trade union organization based neither on craft nor on industry, but wide enough to cover an extensive range of trades.

The Transport and General Workers' Union and the National Union of General and Municipal Workers are the two most important general workers' unions. They make up about one-fourth of the total membership of the Trades Union Congress. The Union of Shop, Distributive and Allied Workers, another general workers' union, is the sixth largest union in the country. They have been highly successful in organizing certain neglected trades and in forcing the older craft unions, like the AEU, to open their ranks to the less skilled and to women workers.

The Transport and General Workers, with over a million and a quarter members, is the largest union in Britain. It dates back to the New Unionism of the dock strike in 1889. The present organization was set up in 1920 when a number of unions amalgamated. It is not a union of unskilled workers but rather an organization made up of workers in various crafts, skills, and industries. These include workers in the automobile and aircraft industries, agriculture, bus and overland transportation, cement, quarrying, rubber, chemicals, food, brickmaking, some textile trades, and even clerical and supervisory work. Its friendly rival, the National Union of General and Municipal Workers, was also formed in 1889.

One of the major features of modern British trade unionism is the federations and amalgamations to which unions increasingly belong. The general workers' unions in the Confederation of Shipbuilding and Engineering Unions, for example, are represented only to the extent that their membership is employed in shipbuilding and the metal trades. The confederation has 37 affiliated member unions. It represents over a million and a quarter workpeople who otherwise would be represented only by their individual unions. This form of organization has brought both unity and flexibility to British labor while simultaneously permitting individualism and separate autonomy to decentralized organizations.

Since 1868 the trade union movement has centered in the Trades Union Congress (TUC), although even in 1950 it represented only 186 unions. Yet some 7.8 million out of the 9.2 million trade union members were affiliated with it. The TUC rarely negotiates agreements with employers. Its purpose is to unite the diverse labor organizations so that trade unions may speak with one voice in their relations with the public, the government, and the Labor party. Most of the influence of the TUC is in the form of moral suasion. It has taken an amazingly responsible view of wartime and postwar problems.

Those who are interested in efficient institutions or tidy organizational charts should not look at the British Labor movement. Yet, what may appear as the paradoxes and anomolies of the TUC are merely the paradoxes and anomolies of the individual unions. It is powerful yet untyrannical, centralized yet highly individualistic, and it represents the conservative, moderate, and progressive views of British trade unions. Even though the TUC is closely allied with the Labor party, it felt able to pledge its sincere cooperation to the Conservative Government in 1951. A measure of its influence is the fact that, while all the members of the House of Lords could not be accommodated in Westminster Abbey for the coronation of Queen Elizabeth II, the principal leaders of the TUC and their wives were invited to attend.

THE CHARACTERISTICS OF BARGAINING AND NEGOTIATING

Collective bargaining in Great Britain is nearly always voluntary. Government authority has been used sparingly. When used, it has most often been for the purpose of promoting responsible negotiating bodies of employers and workers. They arrive at agreements by mutual consent and rely for enforcement on voluntarily established disputes machinery and the force of public opinion. Even during World War II and the early postwar years, when the enforcement of agreements and of arbitration decisions was sanctioned by law, legal methods were seldom used.

Because of the complexity of bargaining organizations, one can speak only in a general way of their methods of negotiating. National groups most often bargain on general questions and minimum terms for various industries. The employers are usually organized on industrial lines, and the unions are represented by their confederations.

The method of bargaining in the engineering industry may be used as an example. The term "engineering industry" includes any industry, like automobile making or metalworking, which fabricates products from iron, steel, nonferrous metals, and even plastics.

The Engineering and Allied Employer's National Federation and the Confederation of Shipbuilding and Engineering Unions agree upon the minimum terms of wages, hours, and other conditions that apply throughout the industry. The confederation would represent those of its 37 member unions who organize workers in engineering. At the bargaining table it would include representatives from (1) craft unions, organized horizontally with members in many industries, (2) industrial unions, organized vertically but none including the entire industry, and (3) the general workers' unions, which represent the portion of their membership within that particular industry.

The agreement would be signed by the national officers of the employer and the union organizations. In addition, each individual union at the bargaining table would become a party to it. The agreement would remain in force until superseded by a later one, but it would not expire a year later and be subject to renegotiation, as generally happens in the United States. Some present-day agreements date back half a century. The major principles of piecework payments in engineering were agreed to in 1907. The application of the general agreement is still subject to local negotiation. The general agreement between the groups is in no sense a legal contract.

Disputes over the interpretation of agreements are handled by long-established disputes machinery. They result, at best, in a recommendation to the individual firm or union. There is no arbitration involved. In 1950, for example, the national disputes machinery in engineering settled only one of 60 cases referred to it. Twenty-three resulted in no agreement. Twenty-one were referred back to the factory, and the others were either retained at the Central Conference for further consideration or were withdrawn.

Certain principles, typical of British bargaining, are exemplified in these arrangements. Bargaining is voluntary and is characterized by the absence of third parties and of arbitration procedures. There are no legal sanctions. Only minimum terms are arrived at nationally with application locally subject to further negotiation. The procedures are slow and deliberate. Many groups are represented at the bargaining table. Enforcement of agreements is by mutual consent. All of these principles are typical of collective bargaining. They enjoy widespread application in Great Britain, the original home of collective bargaining.

The subjects covered in most common agreements are limited, although the application of the agreement is widespread. The agreements generally involve wages, hours, the principles of payment by result, holidays, overtime, and in some cases, provisions for the guaranteed working week. They are usually short. Because of the long tradition of bargaining, fewer items are subjects of negotiation than is generally the case in the United States. In Britain, for example, unions have not sought exclusive bargaining rights through elections on the shop floor, as in the United States under supervision of the National Labor Relations Board. Recognition of but one union is almost unknown in Britain. There has been no internal split between craft and industrial unions, as in the United States. Any union which represents a reasonable number of workpeople in a particular firm or industry is welcomed to the bargaining table, even by its rival union.

There are other differences as well. The closed shop and the union shop are virtually unknown as subjects for collective agreements. In fact, no distinction between the two is made in Britain. The term "closed shop" refers to both. The unions aim for 100 per cent organization and rely on their private strength to attain it. The closed shop exists in practice in a few industries like coal mining or printing, but that is because of social and economic pressures and not because it is an agreed-upon condition.[5] The "checkoff," by which the employer collects dues for the union by a payroll deduction, is also unknown except in certain mining areas where it has existed by tradition. These and other subjects, so important in American trade union "contracts," are seldom found in British collective agreements.

Finally, unions have never relied on employers for such benefits as pensions, sickness and accident insurance, and other security items called "fringe benefits" in the United States. Since few agreements include these, the unions have been forced to rely on their own system of "friendly" benefits and on establishing a welfare state through political action. The major reason for this is the dominant position of employers at the time that collective bargaining developed. Thus the unwillingness of employers to provide security by voluntary and private means is an important reason for the rise of the welfare state.

STATE-SUPPORTED SOCIAL SERVICES

State-supported social services have a long history, but the present program was consolidated by a series of Parliamentary acts in 1946–1948. They are based on the first (or official) Beveridge report, called *Social*

[5] In a "closed shop" a worker must belong to a union to be hired. In a "union shop" he may be hired without belonging to a union, but he must join within a short time afterward.

Insurance and Allied Services (1942). A more famous Beveridge report, *Full Employment in a Free Society* (1944), was unofficial and privately published. William Beveridge, a Liberal in politics, was chairman of a wartime committee appointed by Winston Churchill's Government. When Beveridge's plans went into effect, it was said that the program of a Liberal reformer appointed by a Conservative Prime Minister was carried out by a Labor Government.

The social insurance legislation appeared in four bills. The National Insurance Act (1946) and its supplement, the National Insurance (Industrial Injuries) Act (1946), consolidated much of previous laws and provided the present system of workmen's compensation and benefits for injury. The National Assistance Act of 1948 abolished the old Poor Law. It provided, with the Family Allowances Act (1945), a variety of benefits. Among them are allowances for needy families and allowances, exclusive of need, for families with two or more children. A fifth act, the National Health Service Act (1946), is considered part of the social-service program, but it is not based on an insurance principle of contributions and benefits, as are the other acts.

The social insurance laws provide for a system of weekly contributions from employers, employees, and the self-employed. Benefits are granted for a variety of situations. These include unemployment, old age, sickness, disablement, injury, maternity, widowhood, death, and becoming an orphan. These social services are only partly an insurance plan, for the contributions are inadequate to cover all benefit payments; some of the program is paid for by general taxation. One main principle is that benefit payments are fixed according to predetermined need and not according to the contribution of the individual. The program has been called "security from the cradle to the grave"; it represents one of the most extensive social-service programs in existence.

The National Health Service Act, which went into effect in 1948, superseded the 1911 Health Insurance Act and its amendments. The service is free in that no contribution in the form of weekly payments are made by the recipients. Certain charges for dentures, spectacles, and drugs were added after the program began. Most of it is paid for by general taxation, although National Insurance supplies some funds and so do local rates (taxes). The system provides three types of services: hospital services, medical services by local public-health authorities, and the services of medical practitioners and of auxiliary drug and supply outfits. Costs have exceeded the original estimate by considerable amounts.

There is much misinformation abroad concerning the way the Health Service works, quite apart from its success or failure. Let us take a concrete example to show the operation of both the National Insurance program and the Health Service.

How would the programs affect a worker with a wife and two children employed in a large automobile factory?[6] First, he would make a weekly contribution from his pay packet of 4/11 (four shillings and eleven pence, equivalent to 69 cents), which would be matched by his employer's contribution of 4/2 (58 cents). If he lost his job and was unemployed, he would receive 49/6 ($7) a week until he found a new job or was rehired by his firm. This would be paid for a maximum of 180 days. If he became sick and was unable to work, he would receive the same amount for six months, and a slightly reduced payment beyond that period. If he was injured while at work, he would receive 68/6 ($9.60) per week for the first twenty-six weeks, and after that, if still disabled and unemployable, he would get 88/6 ($12.38) per week. If he died, his heirs would receive a death grant of £20 ($56.00).

His wife would be eligible for certain benefits from her husband's insurance as well. During her last four weeks of pregnancy she could expect £1 ($2.80) a week, and when the baby was born, she would get a lump sum of £4 ($11.20). In addition, if her husband died, she could expect 33/6 ($4.69) a week. In her old age she would receive 16/ ($2.24) per week from her husband's insurance contributions, in addition to any she had earned herself.

If our hypothetical automobile worker was lucky and needed only to see his doctor and dentist for ordinary problems of health, the system would work in the following way. First, when the National Health Insurance Service began, he selected his own doctor. The worker's weekly insurance contributions are not used to pay doctors' bills except very indirectly. In that sense the service is free, that is, free at the time of treatment. But he and almost everyone else helps to pay for it from taxes.

His doctor is paid an annual salary of £300 ($840) and a capitation fee of 15/2 ($2.12) a year for every patient on his list. In addition, the doctor may receive certain "inducement" payments from money which his local doctors' association uses, to compensate able doctors or those located in unattractive areas. Over 90 per cent of the doctors are members of the plan, a decision they made voluntarily. The doctor may see patients privately, or under the health plan, or both, as he desires.

Suppose that stomach cramps overcame our worker one morning at work. He would probably call his doctor or be taken to his office. If there was nothing serious, he would return to the doctor at regular intervals until his problem was solved. He would make no payment for this. If he had appendicitis, his doctor would refer him to the local hospital, where either he or a specialist might operate. If our worker was not satisfied

[6] The amounts of contributions and benefits have been changed and will probably be changed again. The figures cited are those contributed or received at the time the program began.

with his doctor or with the services he received, he could call in another doctor under the health plan or pay for the services of another doctor himself.

If he went to a dentist to have his teeth cleaned, he would do so without having arranged with the dentist to be on a list beforehand. He would make an appointment just as one does anywhere. The dentists are not paid by capitation fees like the doctors; they are paid according to a schedule of fees for the work performed. If our worker needed false teeth, the work would be done free; he would pay only a small fee for the false teeth themselves.

These, then, are the broad outlines of the British program of social services and the way they can be used by an individual. The program provides the minimum security for which the Labor movement strove over many years. It was brought into effect, however, by persons and governments of a variety of political complexions.

QUESTIONS FOR STUDY

1. Under what circumstances did the first trade unions appear in Britain? What difficulties did unions have with English laws at the outset? How did the working people respond?

2. The period from 1825 to 1851 is described as one of idealistic movements. What were some of these movements? What did they accomplish?

3. What were the New Model unions? What did they accomplish? What was some important legislation of their time? What was the general tenor of this legislation?

4. What was the significance of the New Unionism of the period after about 1889? What were its aims and accomplishments?

5. Trace the growth of the Labor party. When did it first share in the government? When did it first control the government? What is its relation with trade unions?

6. How are unions organized in Britain? What portion of workers are in unions? What is a general workers' union? How do British unions negotiate wage contracts? Do unions insist on many fringe benefits?

7. What are some of the benefits that a British worker obtains from his social-security laws? How does the British worker obtain his "free" medical service? Who pays for these benefits?

CHAPTER 15

FOREIGN AND DOMESTIC COMMERCE

Napoleon I contemptuously called England "a nation of shopkeepers." It is true that England became economically great from trade. That trade was mostly local in medieval times, but it grew steadily and by the nineteenth century a large part of it was international. Successful trade or commerce depends on seven factors, namely, resources, location, cheap transportation, good organization, capital, integrity, and salesmanship. The English either had these or developed them.

The products which the English merchants first traded were wool and tin. Later, iron, copper, textiles, leather, and even coal and ships became important. At first, England's location was against her. She was located on the outer edge of European markets until the sixteenth century, and her commerce grew slowly. The discovery of America and its exploitation shifted the center of Europe's trade from the Mediterranean Sea to the Atlantic Ocean. The English now had the inside lane instead of the outside lane in the race for overseas business. England was especially fortunate in her transportation facilities. She is an island and an island in which no town is more than 15 miles from the sea or from a navigable river flowing to the sea. That was important for two reasons. Boats and ships were the least costly form of transportation, for nature provided their highways. And people living in places distant from the sea and having to ship their goods long distances to market usually had to pay large amounts in tariffs and tolls in those days. That was especially true on the Continent, where towns and "robber barons" in castles along the Rhine, Danube, or Seine collected tribute every few miles.

The English have always had a happy faculty for good organization, perhaps because of their part-Norman and part-Teutonic origin. Their joint-stock companies were simple to set up, attracted capital readily, and were operated with considerable efficiency. Capital in England, as in most every nation, came chiefly from the profits of trade. Yet unlike the capital of most nations, England's capital was not periodically reduced by invading foreign armies practicing a scorched-earth policy. That was the fate of southern Germany for centuries. The English Channel, like a medieval moat, gave England a protection which no other European nation enjoyed. The integrity and sense of fair play of the English became a tradition. As for salesmanship, the English sales person is famous for knowing his product and its virtues. It is small wonder that the English have done as well as they have over the centuries, when these attributes are all taken into account. To understand better just how England's commerce grew we must see the story unfold, first on the domestic stage, then on the international stage, and finally back on the domestic stage again.

THE RISE OF TOWNS

In medieval times there were two major institutions of organized trade, the market and the fair. Markets were generally held weekly; food was the chief product sold. There was so little trade that the only efficient way for buyers and sellers to meet was to set a time and place. The normal radius of a market was about 7 miles. Each market had a patron who saw to it that business was carried on in an orderly fashion. For this service he got an income from tolls.

Fairs were large-scale markets, sometimes lasting days or weeks but held less frequently than markets. Many of them were outgrowths of religious festivals and named for some saint. They were usually held in an important town. Among the famous fairs were those of Stourbridge near Cambridge, of St. Ives in Huntingdonshire, and of St. Bartholomew in London. Customers, and especially the merchants, traveled long distances to attend these fairs.

The Crusades so stimulated trade that people demanded more than periodic fairs. Towns, now coming into increasing prominence, met the growing demands of trade. The first towns grew from well-located villages, perhaps at a fording place on some river. Oxford was originally an oxen ford. A few craftsmen and merchants sometimes banded together into a guild and bought greater freedom of action from the lord at a time when he needed funds. A merchant guild was a close-knit organization, something like a modern chamber of commerce, but the members were more loyal to one another. They jealously monopolized all the business and they generally governed the town too. But as the towns grew in size, the merchant guilds, which after all were general organizations, began to lose some of their influence. Their place was taken by various craft guilds, which were specialized organizations. Also, as will be discussed shortly, merchants or companies from overseas got concessions to trade, and in turn, Englishmen got concessions to trade in foreign lands.

The growth of towns, improvements in shipping and navigation, and some betterment of roads began to make the markets, regional or even national, for products like wool or wheat or cloth. People in the towns had to be fed and supplied with raw materials. London was an outstanding example of this. It grew from 6,000 in 1500 to 24,000 in 1600. To feed London, grain was brought from all over the kingdom and even imported. The clothmakers obtained the wool that they needed through specialists called "wool chapmen" or "broggers" who ranged the countryside buying up wool for resale in town. Cloth was marketed at Blackwell Hall in London, where clothmakers gathered and sold their products to London drapers for sale in towns or overseas. Trade was now developing even beyond the town stage; England was beginning to have a national economy by the sixteenth century.

REGULATED COMPANIES

Englishmen began negotiating for privileges in foreign countries, generally in underdeveloped lands. Wool and cloth were the articles of trade. English overseas trade was generally conducted on a large scale in the form of a monopoly. That was because it was dangerous for one or a few merchants to venture far alone in a world full of pirates, privateers, and unscrupulous kings. Therefore, the merchants traveled overseas in sizable fleets to provide one another protection. To maintain the good name of Englishmen, they established rules of business conduct which all in the company must observe. Otherwise the misdeed or sharp practice of one English trader might cost the next one who came along quite dearly. Governments also liked this company system, for it was easier to deal with foreign merchants collectively than individually. And the traders liked it, for they felt that, once they had incurred risks and developed trade with some distant land, they should enjoy all the profits of it and not have to share them with some latecomers. It should be clearly understood, however, that these first companies were simply groups of individual traders, each putting up his own stock of goods.

There was another reason for making foreign trade monopolistic. This was the belief that only a certain amount of business was available. Thus, if many English merchants tried to sell wool abroad, it would not cause more wool to be sold, rather it would depress the price of wool. Similarly, if many English merchants tried to buy goods abroad, they would bid up prices by their competition. It followed from this reasoning that the number of merchants entitled to trade to any region should be limited. Therefore the Crown granted a trade monopoly in each part of the world to a selected group of merchants, once they gained admission to the area.

The trading companies were first of the regulated type and later of the chartered variety. One of the first was the Muscovy or Russian Company, founded in 1553. Later well-known companies were the East India Company, the Virginia Company, and the Hudson Bay Company. It was not long before faults were observed in the regulated-company system. There followed a shift to chartered companies with a joint-stock type of organization. The East India Company began as a regulated type and changed over to the joint-stock type in a few years. But this kind of company also had faults. The best way to see how such companies worked is to examine the famous East India Company.

THE EAST INDIA COMPANY

Parliament gave 218 English merchants a charter in 1600 to form the East India Company. These merchants had a monopoly of trade, as far as Englishmen were concerned, to all the lands lying east of the Cape of Good Hope and west of Cape Horn. The Company opened a trading post in Bengal in 1610. Competition with the merchants of other lands operating under their own East India companies was keen and the English did not gain full control for many years. But they kept planting new trading posts and expanding their operations. The profits became so great that interlopers, including dismissed officials of the Company, were constantly breaking in. The penalty of forfeiture of ship and cargo, if caught, did not seem to discourage them. The interlopers finally formed a rival organization, and in 1694 Parliament said that all Englishmen had an equal right to trade with the East Indies unless forbidden by Parliament. Soon after this, Parliament set up a new East India Company, combining both companies, and again granted it a monopoly.

Meanwhile, both the English and the French were busy expanding their spheres of trading influence. Every time that England and France went to war in Europe, which was half the time, their colonists and friends would come to blows in India, in America, and anywhere else the two nations were in competition. In India each had friends among native princes and aspirants to native thrones. In 1757 Robert Clive decisively defeated the French at Plassey, and henceforth the English built up their administrative as well as their business control of India. Clive proved to be an excellent governor general as well as a brilliant military general. India had become more important to the Crown, and the government was unwilling to let the East India Company have unsupervised control. After 1773 the governor general of Bengal had to be approved by the Crown. In 1784 Parliament set up a board of control over the military, political, and financial aspects of the British administration of India. In 1813 Parliament granted the board of control authority over the Company's commercial transactions. It also abolished the Company's monopoly in the China tea trade. The Company was now little more than an administrative arm of the government. In 1858, following the Indian Mutiny, Parliament abolished even this pretense, and henceforth Britain governed India. India had, in a sense, been fully nationalized.

MERCANTILISM

British merchants and British government officials, we have seen, believed that there was only a definite amount of business to be had in any region. They were thinking much as a shoemaker might who counts the feet in the village and concludes that when he has made that many shoes, he has finished his business for the year. Economists have since explained that under the right advertising and pricing conditions any region may have many more buyers than at first seems possible. At lower prices people will buy more shoes. That was not fully realized then, and each nation wanted to monopolize all the visible trade. It could then draw to itself as much gold and silver as possible.

Precious metals were looked upon as the sinews of trade and war. A merchant with gold and silver could get what he wanted promptly, and a king with gold and silver in his treasury, or even in his realm, could buy military supplies and ships and pay his troops on time. Although Spain was the only nation that had gold and silver mines in quantity, it was apparent that there were other ways of acquiring these metals. Holland had shown how to do it. The Dutch simply sold more goods than they bought and took the difference in gold and silver. The difference was big too. Much of it came directly from Spain, with whom the Dutch carried on a sizable trade. The English secretly admired and copied their prosperous Dutch rivals.

Out of such observations there developed an economic way of doing things that has since been given the name "mercantilism." The basic aim of mercantilism was to make the state strong and self-sufficient. At first the English government was willing to grant regional monopolies to companies of merchants and let them make the rules. Starting in the seventeenth century the government itself made the rules and set the policies. There were basically four policies.

First, the merchants should export more than they imported and take the difference in precious metals. This was called maintaining "a favorable balance of trade." Only rarely was it desirable to permit gold or silver to be sent out to buy goods. The government regarded the East India Company as an exception to the general rule, and the Company was greatly envied. Its charter permitted it to send out as much as £30,000 on one voyage. Since the people of India wanted virtually no English goods, the only way to buy in India was to pay in the silver the Indians demanded. The Company's excuse was that by using some silver to buy spices that could be got no other way, and then reselling them elsewhere, England would get more precious metals in the end than the Company sent out in the beginning.

Second, it was essential to develop a strong merchant marine in order to carry on a lucrative trade with all parts of the world and obtain precious metals. With a strong merchant marine, England would have to buy less from foreign merchants and depend less on foreign shipping. That would mean smaller exports of precious metals and make the country stronger in case of war. A good merchant marine also was a fine training ground for the navy.

Third, it was desirable to be as nearly self-sufficient in agriculture as possible. England lacked adequate forests, produced no sugar, and bought abroad such items as tobacco, indigo, and hemp. Self-sufficiency could be had by subsidizing undeveloped industries in England, or by acquiring colonies that had the desired products, or by persuading the Colonies to produce them. Then gold and silver would not have to be sent out to buy these things. The English encouraged production of masts and naval stores in the American Colonies to avoid having to buy these from the Baltic States. The English treasured their West Indian sugar islands, paid bounties on the raising of hemp and indigo, and insisted that all exports of certain so-called "enumerated" commodities, such as tobacco and sugar, be shipped via England.

Fourth, the first industries, like textiles, to develop were very profitable and of course brought in lots of gold and silver. Therefore, the English sought to keep these occupations for themselves. Inventors and mechanics were forbidden to leave England or take out blueprints of textile and other machinery. England also denied her Colonies the right to manufacture woolen goods, sailcloth, beaver hats, and finished iron products. And she imposed tariffs on imports of manufactures from rival countries.

Mercantilism was a state-dominated policy operated in the interest of the British merchants. These were well represented in Parliament and they got many laws passed to further their interests. The Navigation Acts of the seventeenth century required that all imports come in British ships unless they came in the ships of the country where the goods originated. Colonists might buy European goods only through England. There were also Corn Laws. Likewise there were laws limiting the kinds of money the Colonies might have. In time, England developed a rather highly regulated economy. But England was not the only nation that practiced mercantilism. Spain, France, Holland, and others did also, and most of them to a higher degree.

By the eighteenth century European nations had carried the making of rules and regulations too far. When the great French statesman Jean Colbert once asked a manufacturer named Legendre what the government could do for his industry, Legendre replied, "Laissez-nous faire" (let us alone). A group of writers called the Physiocrats took up the cry in France. Somewhat later, in 1776, a brilliant Scotsman named Adam

Smith published a book that exposed some of the false reasoning behind the web of regulations that constituted mercantilism. The title of this book was *An Inquiry into the Nature and Causes of the Wealth of Nations*. Smith maintained that men worked most effectively when they were free to follow their own interests. Most men knew their own interests better than any regulating board or Parliamentary committee. When many men could work effectively, untrammeled and undiscouraged by detailed or outmoded laws, said Smith, the whole nation would prosper and accumulate wealth. Smith to some extent, and his disciples to a greater extent, implied that men would not underpay their employees or compete unfairly or sell sleazy merchandise. They would realize that such actions would injure them in the long run more than it would help them. That last assumption was optimistic and eventually proved the undoing of *laissez faire* as a state policy. During the century following the publication of Adam Smith's great work, the edifice of mercantilism was steadily dismantled, at first in small pieces and later in large chunks. Another event that contributed to the downfall of mercantilism also took place in 1776—the rebellion of the American Colonies. The colonists rebelled in part from resentment against so many of England's trade rules and customs duties.

How *laissez faire* supplanted mercantilism may be seen in the changes in attitude of Parliament toward business between the 1770s and 1870s. These changes took place in commercial, industrial, labor, and other areas of legislation, but it is commercial legislation that concerns us here. Tariffs were reduced, the Corn Laws and Navigation Acts were repealed, a looser rein was held on the Colonies, and imperialism went out of style.

Adam Smith had admitted that it was absurd to expect the restoration of free trade in England. Yet the trammels of mercantilism were first relaxed in this area. The younger William Pitt negotiated the Eden Treaty with France in 1786, which cut duties on textiles and hardware, and England reciprocated by letting in French wines as cheaply as Portuguese ones. Although this treaty lasted only until the next war (1793), it was a start. The dismantling of mercantilism was suspended during the Napoleonic Wars but was resumed as soon as they were over. By that time the English were more advanced industrially than any other nation and did not fear foreign competition. They thought that by offering reciprocal trade treaties and by buying more foreign goods, they could enlarge the markets for their textiles and other leading exports. That is sound economics. They concluded a new treaty with France in 1826 and one with the United States in 1830. Prime Minister Robert Peel overhauled the tariff twice, in 1842 and 1845. The first time, he reduced duties on 750 out of 1,200 articles and set the maximum rate for raw materials at 5 per cent and that for manufactured goods at 20 per cent. The second time, he abolished all export duties, admitted all but a few raw materials free, and cut the rate for most manufactured goods to 10 per cent. Finally in 1860, by the Cobden-Chevalier Treaty, England prevailed on France to abolish all her prohibitions on imports and to lower her maximum duties on major imported commodities from England to 30 per cent. In return, England lowered her duties on French wines again and removed her duties on all manufactured goods. By now the English tariff consisted of little more than revenue duties on a few articles like wines and liquors, tobacco, coffee, tea, and cocoa. Meanwhile, she had repealed the Corn Laws too (1846). Simultaneously, there was a strong trend toward lower tariffs on the part of other major nations.

Navigation acts, another form of trade restriction, limited the ships that might enter English ports. England's modern Navigation Acts were begun in 1651 to promote the growth of the English merchant marine and to give England's merchants a monopoly of trade with the English Colonies. But as England began to relax her trade restrictions in the nineteenth century, the Navigation Acts seemed out of place. In 1849 Parliament repealed them and threw British ports open to trading vessels of the entire world. Only the coastwise trade was restricted to British ships.

England's attitude toward her Colonies also underwent a change. At the end of the Revolutionary War some forty thousand American Loyalists fled to Canada and became the nucleus for a British province called Ontario, in that former French colony. The English wisely profited from their previous mistakes. In 1791 they gave to the British in Ontario some of the privileges that they had previously denied the American Colonies. Canada got further powers of self-government in 1840 and 1867. Australian provinces also got privileges of self-government during the first half of the century. Although the English continued to acquire some colonies in this period, it was not an era when they tried to enlarge the Empire. Indeed, Benjamin Disraeli remarked in a private letter in 1852, "these wretched colonies will all be independent in a few years and are a millstone around our necks." A few years later, as Prime Minister, Disraeli was the great champion of imperialism and added many tens of thousands of square miles to the British Empire. By then England was moving away from free trade and other forms of *laissez faire* back toward tariffs and a more regulated economy again.

TOWARD A REGULATED ECONOMY AGAIN

With tariffs down and Corn Laws and Navigation Acts abandoned, English manufacturers, farmers, and merchants faced keen competition from all over the world. This competition was made sharper by the rapid improvements that were taking place in railroads and shipping. These improvements brought distant agricultural regions, where land was cheap and taxes were low, such as Canada, Australia, Argentina, and western United States, into competition with high-cost English farms. Two new countries, the United States and Germany, challenged England's industrial supremacy, forcing her to share her markets with them. Other nations maintained higher tariffs than England did. An understandable reaction to all this by England was a desire for areas where English merchants would have special privileges. Between 1870 and 1900 England acquired 4.8 million square miles of territory, mostly in Africa and Asia, 88 million people, and a valuable "sphere of interest" in China's rich Yangtze River valley. About the turn of the century the Conservative party talked of putting a tariff wall around the Empire again, but the English public voted this down in the 1906 election.

England's foreign trade grew steadily during the nineteenth century, for her industry was making rapid strides and her population was quadrupling. By 1913 total trade was over fifteen times what it had been at the close of the Napoleonic Wars. That was the accomplishment of ninety-nine years of relative peace. Before World War I foreign nations accounted for about two-thirds of England's foreign trade and the Empire for the remaining third. But Britain's competitors were making inroads even on the Empire trade; they increased their share from 26 per cent in 1884 to 32 per cent in 1895. According to E. A. J. Johnson, "Seemingly Britain's huge imperial venture before 1914 had only a small effect in changing the direction of her foreign trade."[1] In 1882 England's best customers were the United States (18 per cent), India (10 per cent), France, Germany, and Australasia (8 per cent each) and Holland (6 per cent). A generation later, just before the outbreak of World War I, the situation had not changed markedly. England's main exports were manufactured goods, chiefly textiles and iron products, and her chief imports were foodstuffs and raw materials.

England's imports for over a century have been 55 to 60 per cent of her total foreign trade. That raises the question how she paid for the excess of merchandise imports. The answer is by her shipping services, financial services, and especially out of the returns from her fast-growing overseas investments. For many years before World War II, England enjoyed an annual income of close to £200 million ($1 billion) from her overseas investments and used perhaps half or more of that for new investments. Between 1904 and 1914 new loans abroad increased from £27 million to £226 million a year. England's total investments abroad

---

[1] *An Economic History of Modern England* (New York: Thomas Nelson & Sons, 1939), p. 139.

grew from £1.3 billion in 1885 to almost £4 billion in 1913. Half of this was invested in the British Empire in 1914, 20 per cent in the United States, 20 per cent in South America, and the rest scattered, mostly in Europe, China, Japan, and Turkey.

THE EFFECT OF TWO WORLD WARS

The great financial cost of World War I undermined the strong economic position England had attained during a century of peace. Shipping losses were heavy, the purchasing power of the pound fell, and the prestige of the pound declined. England had to sell most of her American securities, and she went into debt to the United States for over $4.5 billion. Not until 1924 did English overseas investment regain its 1913 size even in terms of depreciated pounds. Surplus real income to rebuild overseas investments was only a quarter of what it had been. Meanwhile, the United States had passed England as the world's chief moneylender.

England fell behind in manufacturing and trade too. The growing demand for oil cut into her coal business, and that for silk and rayon into her cotton-textile business. The United States had gained the lead in new big industries like automobiles, movies, and electrical equipment. Other nations were becoming more industrialized. All had higher tariffs than England. The Balfour Committee on Industry and Trade reported that the 1924 volume of English exports was only 80 per cent of the 1913 volume. Yet England's imports remained as high as before. England had either to increase her exports by reducing costs, which she seemed unable to do, or cut down on her imports. Raising tariffs will reduce imports. For England to impose import duties would mean abandoning the tradition of free trade. The McKenna duties of 1915 had marked the first slight departure. England gave more preference to goods coming from within the Empire after 1919. In 1921 the Safeguarding the Industries Act imposed 33 per cent duties for five years on imports of a few key industries. This was to help the key industries over a period of postwar adjustment. In 1926 the duties were extended for another ten years. Then in 1932 England abandoned all pretense that protection was temporary. Too many nations were dumping their products on England's relatively free market. Parliament imposed a 10 per cent duty on all imports except certain foods, which were left free, and certain luxuries, which paid higher duties. In 1932 some 83 per cent of all goods entering England paid duties, compared with 25 per cent in 1930. England also gave additional preference to goods coming from within the Empire. She also tried to persuade other nations to open their markets by offering to reduce her tariffs if they would reduce theirs. These efforts had some success, for England's share of world trade rose from 12 per cent in 1930 to 14 per cent in 1938. It had been 15 per cent in 1913. Even so, nearly half of England's trade was within her Empire, where she, of course, had a preferred position. Recovery might have progressed further, but at this point World War II broke out.

World War II, like World War I, caused great losses in shipping, led to the sale of overseas assets and investments, put England more deeply into debt, this time to her Dominions rather than to the United States, and caused the pound sterling to depreciate still further. Whereas in 1938 England had had some surplus income from overseas investments to reinvest, in 1946 and 1947 she was going $1.5 billion a year into the red. Not only did merchandise imports exceed merchandise exports, which was usual, but now service and capital imports exceeded service and capital exports. Labor costs were high, and it was impossible to lower the prices of goods for export. In 1949 England accepted the only possible alternative. If she could not cut the prices of her exports, then she would cut the price of the pounds that foreign customers had to buy in order to get those exports. In other words, she devalued the pound from $4.03 to $2.80, or by about 31 per cent.

England took other steps to bring her international payments into balance. Many foods that had to be imported, such as fruits, meats, and dairy products, were strictly rationed to hold down the outgo of funds to pay for them. Certain popular English products, such as chinaware, liquors, and woolens, were largely reserved for the export markets. English people were not permitted to travel abroad except on business. Businessmen in India, Egypt, Scandinavia, and other lands to which English merchants or the government owed money found that the only way they could get paid was by spending their credit in England for English goods or services. This was the so-called "blocked exchange." When American wartime support of English military operations, known as lend-lease, came to an end, something had to be done to replace it. England borrowed $3.75 billion from the United States in 1946 and received sizable amounts under the Marshall Plan after 1950. England also granted India, Pakistan, and Burma self-government to the point of independence. This reduced her military expenditures. Later, she removed her troops from the Suez Canal area in Egypt. With India gone, protecting the "lifeline" of the Empire seemed less imperative. England's economic plight has been reflected in an international policy that seems at times to border on appeasement of Russia and Red China. Yet all these efforts have gradually improved England's balance of payments.

The foreign-trade policies following the two world wars have represented a revival of something akin to mercantilism. These policies have probably been as essential as strict discipline during battle. England's economy has been in dire peril. The question is whether this economic regimentation is temporary, until recovery is made from the effects of war, or whether it is to be more permanent.

DOMESTIC COMMERCE

In England, as in the United States, domestic commerce is larger than foreign commerce even though it is less discussed and less dramatized. The difference is not so great, however, in a small compact nation like England.

For centuries England's population was small and chiefly engaged in agriculture. Families bought most of the goods and services that they needed from neighborhood craftsmen or from itinerant peddlers. Beyond this, a weekly trip to market and one or two a year to a fair sufficed. But specialization in one economic activity stimulates specialization in others. If a farmer produces wheat for market, or if a man becomes a cobbler or works in a clock factory, he needs the food, clothing, and services that other specialists must supply. Most specialists lived in town. England's first towns and cities were concentrated in the south-central and Midlands regions. Before the end of the eighteenth century approximately one-third of the population was urban.

Retail stores were already a highly developed aspect of English life in the early eighteenth century. Daniel Defoe wrote a book about them called *The Compleat English Tradesman*. He estimated that there were about six thousand retail shops in London alone, and some two million tradesmen in all of Britain.[2] He mentions the elaborate shops that some of them had and tells of merchants standing before their shops all day long crying to passers-by, "What do you lack, Sir," and then naming their wares. Because they often criticized one another and one another's wares, merchants did not enjoy a good reputation as a class.

The retailing business was now well organized. Most retailers bought from wholesalers. Pack trains and wagons rumbled across the countryside like modern trucks, bringing goods from city warehouses to country stores. Already there were branded products, standardized credit terms, the one-price system, resale-price maintenance, and some newsprint advertising. Of course these modern practices were not as common as they later became, but they were well established in London and in a few of the larger towns. Thus England had been a nation of shopkeepers for at least a century before Napoleon made his famous remark.

As the Industrial Revolution progressed, output increased, population grew, and the producer, wholesaler, traveling salesman, and retailer performed clearly recognizable functions. It was the wholesaler, rather than the manufacturer, who granted generous credit terms to the retailer. He also performed the valuable function of supplying suitable amounts and

[2] Daniel Defoe, *The Compleat English Tradesman* (London: C. Rivington, 1727), vol. II, pp. 78, 112. This estimate is much too generous.

selections of goods for the retailer, a service which many manufacturers were too busy to undertake. As the number of intermediaries between producer and consumer increased, each having to be recompensed for his services, the margin between factory cost and the price to the consumer got wider. The profits of the middleman seemed large to many consumers. Few of them appreciated the full value of the services performed. Some of these services were new: others were difficult to evaluate anyway.

Endeavors to reduce the costs of getting goods to the consumer have taken two basic forms. On the one hand, the consumers have banded together and organized cooperatives so as to buy directly and in quantity from the factory or the wholesaler. On the other hand, retailers themselves have sometimes integrated their activities so as to buy in large amounts from factories or to sell large quantities of many goods in their stores. The retailers' efforts have given us the chain store or the department store with their economies in overhead. Both cooperatives and department stores and chain stores appeared about the middle of the nineteenth century.

It was in poverty-stricken Rochdale (near Manchester) in 1844 that the first successful cooperative was founded. Some 28 workmen, chiefly weavers, invested £1 of capital apiece in the Rochdale Pioneer Society, a grocery business. The key points of the Rochdale plan were (1) sell at prevailing local prices, (2) sell for cash only, (3) pay a fixed return on the capital invested, and (4) divide the remaining profits among purchasers according to the amount of their purchases. The plan was eminently successful, achieving £45,000 of business by 1854. It is the basis of most consumer cooperatives today. Cooperatives got encouragement from the Industrial and Provident Societies Act of 1852, sometimes called "the charter of cooperators." For retail cooperatives really to succeed, they needed to be able to buy cooperatively wholesale. The first large successful wholesale cooperative was the Cooperative Wholesale Society organized in 1863. Retail cooperatives were especially popular in the Midlands, where they were looked upon as the consumers' most effective retort to the "grasping grocer." By the 1880s the public was buying 6 per cent of its store purchases from retail cooperatives, and these, in turn, made half their purchases from the two largest wholesale cooperatives.[3]

The retail cooperatives, or "coops," have shown a healthy growth since the 1880s, as may be seen from Table 15-1. Total membership has grown twentyfold, total trade over thirtyfold. Their share of the total retail business has about doubled, to 12 per cent. A much larger portion of the

[3] J. H. Clapham, *An Economic History of Modern Britain* (London: Cambridge University Press, 1932), vol. II, pp. 308–310.

Table 15-1. Retail Cooperative Statistics

Year	Membership (000 omitted)	Per cent of population	Trade (000,000 omitted)	Trade per member
1881	547	2	£15.4	£28.2
1911	2,640	6	74.8	28.3
1925	4,911	11	183.6	37.4
1935	7,484	16	220.4	29.5
1951	10,745	21	649.8	60.4

SOURCE: *People's Yearbook*, 1949, p. 114; G. D. H. Cole, *British Co-operative Movement* (London: George Allen & Unwin, Ltd., 1951), pp. 24, 125; *Whitaker's Almanac*, 1954, p. 1123.

population patronizes the coops, but the average annual purchase has only doubled, and if allowance for fall in the value of the pound is made, then it is smaller. Although cooperatives have been more successful in England than in America, they have been less successful than in some parts of the Continent. The English buyer hates to feel tied to one store, and the English cooperative has not vigorously exploited its advantage against the competing private retailer.

Retail-store owners have integrated their operations in several ways in an effort to reduce costs. The two most important of these are the retain chain stores, called "multiple stores" in England, and the department stores. Both have achieved significant development in the last century. In 1928 the chains handled 14 per cent of all retail sales, and the department stores 4 per cent. Consumer cooperatives took care of 8 per cent.[4] Some twenty-two years later the department stores handled 9 per cent and the cooperatives 12 per cent.

The department store appeared in the nineteenth century. As in the United States, some grew out of dry-goods establishments, such as Thomas Wallis, Ltd. (1826), Peter Robinson's (1833), and William Whitely's, all over a century old. Selfridge's, one of the largest English department stores, was founded in 1909 by an American who had been associated with Marshall Field's in Chicago. He brought to the Old World some of the ideas of the New. Other famous English department stores which do a large business are Harrod's, Gamage's, and John Barker and Company. Because England is so urban in character and a department store is so convenient for the city shopper, the department stores have steadily increased their total share of the business.

The chain, or multiple, store also became popular in England. Grocery stores (Lipton's Tea Co.), hat stores, book stores (Smith's), drugstores (Boots, Ltd.), and many others do a thriving business. Grocery chains

[4] *Encyclopaedia of the Social Sciences*, vol. XIII, p. 348.

are less conspicuous than in the United States because of the absence of the supermarkets. Another form of chain store is the variety store. One of the earliest of these, and very prominent still, is Marks and Spencer, which began as a grocery store in the 1870s. Another is Frank Woolworth's, originally called a "three and six penny store." Woolworth, already well established in America, opened his first store in Liverpool in November, 1909. At the time his chief competition was from penny bazaars. The English were amazed and pleased to see how he could improve that type of business. Variety stores grew in popularity more quickly in England than they had in America and were more profitable. By 1910 Woolworth had 6 stores in operation, all of them in or near the industrial Midlands; by 1912, 28; and by 1954, 819.

Mail-order houses never had the popularity in England that they gained in some larger countries. It was the isolated farmer objecting to the profits of the middleman who encouraged the mail-order house in America. In Britain people were less isolated, the margin of profit was smaller, and the cooperative was more highly developed. What mail-order business there is, is carried on by the department stores. Installment selling is another institution that is less conspicuous in England than in America. It is picturesquely and contemptuously known as "the ever-never plan" or "hire purchase." Many Englishmen feel there is something humiliating about having to buy in this way; it is akin to patronizing a pawnbroker.

Notwithstanding these efforts to reduce costs of distribution by integration, between two-thirds and three-fourths of the trade is still carried on by small retail merchants even today. Over 90 per cent of the stores are independents. In 1950 there were at least 580,000 shops, of which half were engaged in selling food.[5] The corner grocer is especially common. Another 13 per cent sold clothing. Other stores found in almost every shopping district were the ironmonger (hardware), the chemist (drugs), furniture, jewelry, books, tobacco, and confectionery stores, and the automobile dealer and the coal dealer. Probably two-thirds of all stores were family-owned. Two-thirds are not found in a main shopping center, but the larger stores, the other third located in main shopping centers, do the bulk of the business. A study of some 86,150 stores selling clothing, textiles, and footwear, about 1943, showed that half the stores were small and did less than 10 per cent of the total business.[6]

How do so many small shops manage to survive? In many lines it is not possible to do so by price cutting. The best items are nationally advertised branded products and the manufacturers have ingenious ways

[5] *Annual Abstract of Statistics*, 1954, p. 192. H. Levy, *Shops of Britain* (New York: Oxford University Press, 1947), cites a figure of 750,000 (p. 32).
[6] Levy, *op. cit.*, quoting *The Board of Trade Journal*, June 3, 1944, p. 40.

of spotting and preventing price cutting. The small merchant competes primarily by the extra service he provides, by his handy location, and simply by working longer hours than he would tolerate if he were an employee. It is the old magic of property. The large-store manager and organized labor often complain that the small storekeeper's family work "for nothing." The extra services consist of carrying many items in addition to the store's specialty, much as the American drugstore does. Under the circumstances, the efforts of department stores and multiple stores to eliminate the small independent has made slight headway in Britain. England is still a nation of shopkeepers. Conservatism is strong in this segment of the economy. Accordingly, there has been less regulation in this economic area than in others, except in time of war or other emergency.

WARTIME AND POSTWAR RATIONING

No discussion of modern England's economy would be complete without some discussion of rationing. Under capitalism, scarce goods go to those who are willing to pay high prices for them. Prices freely obeying the economic law of supply and demand provide the rationing system. We are so used to it that we do not realize that this is our American rationing method. Under socialism, one must still buy goods but their prices are fixed or held down by government edict. To prevent the early birds from getting all the worm, each person is allotted a share. This is usually done on a point system. Thus a housewife who goes shopping must pay in two kinds of "coin"—money and ration coupons to show that she is entitled to make the purchase. The ration system has the virtue of being fairer to people of low and medium incomes, who otherwise would not be able to buy certain necessities. But the rationing and price-fixing system has the disadvantage that it keeps profits low and thus discourages the merchant from handling the very goods that people want most and also discourages the manufacturer or farmer from increasing his production of them. Instead, businessmen seek to produce and sell nonrationed items that will yield them a better return.

The exigencies of war rather than any yearning for socialism led Britain to adopt a rationing system in January, 1940. Even the United States, a land of abundance, rationed a number of items in World War II. The English, especially the conservative small shopkeepers, were not happy about rationing but they realized the necessity for it and acquiesced. At first a straight-line basis was used, that is, each person got so much meat, bacon, sugar, fats, and tea per year. Point rationing began in 1941, each person receiving 66 points, which entitled him to 66 per cent of an average person's prewar consumption. In time, children got priority in receiving certain nourishing foods essential to proper growth, such as milk, eggs, oranges, and the like. Adults got what was left over. Down to 1944 adults got an average of 30 eggs a year, or a fifth of normal consumption. One result of the system was that English children, especially those of the poor, flourished as never before. Adults were often less healthy and energetic than they appeared to be. Yet as long as the war lasted and food was imported with difficulty, rationing seemed the best solution. Incidentally the fact that so much of the food was imported made the job of rationing easier to administer.

Rationing continued until July 4, 1954. The last item, meat, was taken off nine years after the war ended. Bread was rationed after 1946; potatoes were rationed during poor crop years in 1947–1948; meat, milk, oranges, eggs, and other items were rationed during much of this period. People got very weary of rationing, and many resented it. The reasons for continuing it were to enable Britain to pay her war debts and to import the machinery and raw materials so essential to restore the productiveness of her economy. It was a form of forced saving imposed on the people by the government. The Labor Government continued it while they remained in power; the Conservative Government eventually removed it. Rationing divided available food supplies rather fairly but it did little toward increasing them.

QUESTIONS FOR STUDY

1. How did towns arise in the medieval economy? What were regulated companies? What did they do? How did they differ from the chartered companies? What did the East India Company accomplish?

2. What was the nature of mercantilism? Who backed it? What were some of the laws that were enacted in its name? Why did it break down? What took its place?

3. What was the theory of *laissez faire*? Who backed it? What were some of the laws that were repealed because of it? Why did it break down? What took its place?

4. Show how the pressure to abandon free trade and adopt protection grew in Britain from the latter part of the nineteenth century and finally won out about 1932.

5. What have been the effects of two world wars on Britain's foreign investments? On her foreign trade?

6. How early did Britain become a "nation of shopkeepers"? Is that still true of Britain? If so, what is the significance of this?

7. What have the British done in the last century to cut down the costs of distributing goods from factory to consumer?

8. Why did the British resort to rationing in World War II? Why were they so slow to abandon it? What economic problems does rationing solve? What economic problems does it create?

CHAPTER 16

THE BRITISH ECONOMY

Today, we may see in Britain the culmination of trends and forces at work since the beginnings of the industrial age, or even earlier. Those trends necessitate new ways of conducting economic activity, whether it be in field or factory, and new ways of governing the nation. Change goes on all the time, and the secret of survival is sensible adjustment to change. Any nation or class that refuses to adjust to new conditions usually experiences a rude upheaval. That was the fate of the English nobility in the seventeenth century, of the French nobility in the eighteenth century, of the Southern planters of the United States in the nineteenth century, and of the Russian ruling classes in the twentieth century. On the whole, the English, despite their reputation for resisting change, have adjusted rather well, moving neither so fast as to seem unstable nor so slowly as to necessitate revolutionary upheavals. Moreover, the changes over some seven centuries, when viewed broadly, have been very substantial.

DEVELOPMENT OVER SEVEN CENTURIES

The population of Britain has grown from about 2 million to 51 million in an area the size of Illinois and Indiana. From an agricultural economy with much of the population tied to the land in a state of near slavery, Britain has become an industrial economy whose people prize their freedom and enjoy a high standard of living. To obtain the capital to effect this change Britain first developed her overseas commerce. The Industrial Revolution began in the eighteenth century and was accompanied by improvements in transportation, such as turnpikes and canals at first, and railroads and steamships later on. These were necessary to market the commodities being produced by the factories and to bring in needed raw materials and food supplies to factory towns and cities. About a century ago the nation's resources showed signs of inadequacy or exhaustion. That made Britain increasingly dependent on her foreign trade. She practiced a policy of free trade and urged others to do likewise. By the end of the nineteenth century her industries, her overseas investments, and a highly efficient money and banking system had made Britain's economy one of the most efficient and prosperous in the world. Britain was, however, having to face the competition of some large and aggressive rivals, chief of whom then were the United States and Germany.

A GENERATION OF EMERGENCIES

The British were enjoying the fruits of their labors in 1914 when they were suddenly struck down by a succession of three major catastrophes, a world war, a colossal depression, and a second world war. These events had the same effect on Britain that a costly lawsuit, the loss of his job for several years, and then the loss of his house by fire might have on a man who had some savings in the bank, a good job, and a comfortable home. Recovery depended on character, intelligence, and willingness to work hard again to regain a position of economic well-being.

The cost of these three catastrophes was tremendous. World War I cost Britain 2,366,000 casualties (700,000 killed) and £8 billion (including half her merchant marine). Proportionate losses for this nation today would be about 9.5 million casualties, with nearly 3 million killed, and a direct war cost of close to a trillion dollars (about four times our national income). Such a blow would stagger us, and it staggered Britain. During the years 1929 to 1935 there was a devastating depression, with almost three million unemployed between 1931 and 1933, or about 20 per cent of all workers. The depression slowed down Britain's pace of accumulating capital and even ate into it at times. As far as material progress was concerned, Great Britain did little better than mark time during much of the depressed 1930s. Britain's human losses in World War II were only about a third as heavy as in the previous war, but the monetary cost was greater. It has been estimated that a third of all British houses were damaged or destroyed, and a total of $18 billion of capital assets was lost. No longer was Britain able to finance an excess of imports from the proceeds of her investments abroad. She had had to dispose of many of these investments to pay for imports of war materials. Instead she was in debt to her Dominions and to foreign nations to the extent of £4 billion.

When the war ended in 1945, a reappraisal of Britain's economic position was in order. There were not only the questions of continuing to pay off old and new debts and rebuilding the house, so to speak, but also that of whether the British family wanted to rebuild the house as it had been or according to some new plan of architecture. The British were determined to rid themselves of the widespread unemployment and economic inequality of the years of the Great Depression and before. Social barriers had been broken down in World War II as perhaps never before. The evacuation of tens of thousands of people from the East End slums of London gave one half of the British people a view of how the other half lived. The sentiment in 1945 was to improve the lot of the entire people and to rid the economy of the depressions which had plagued the country about every ten years since the industrial age began. If oil could be piped under the sea, if docks and harbors could be towed across the Channel for the invasion of the Continent, and if 50 million people could be organized to defeat Hitler, surely it was possible also to organize the domestic economy to provide food, clothing, housing, and health at a minimum economic level below which they must not fall. Thus the mood of the British people in 1945 was to abolish poverty and eliminate depressions as well as to pay their debts and recover from the war. It was an ambitious program to endeavor to do all of this simultaneously. Yet, in essence, this was the mandate that the British public handed to the Labor party in 1945.

It was appropriate that the Labor party should be put in power to carry out the postwar plans of the British people. Abolition of poverty and of unemployment were policies which the Labor party had been advocating for a long time. It was also important to preserve the wartime willingness to accept regimentation. Without that acceptance, which had been built up over nearly six years of conflict, Britain could not have hoped to carry out such an ambitious program. Accordingly, the military were demobilized after the war, but the civilians were not. They were asked to continue to accept a life of "austerity," which meant continued rationing and regimentation. Let us see what that involved after 1945 in each of the seven segments of the economy. To what degree did the British achieve and to what degree did they fail to achieve their goals?

RECENT PROBLEMS AND THEIR SOLUTIONS

Although Britain is heavily populated, the population is not increasing at a rapid rate, and so the problem was not one of restraining population growth. Rather, the major problem was the exhaustion of British resources. That has been handled in various ways. Certain key industries have been nationalized. Coal mining was nationalized so as to ensure that coal would be sought deeper in the earth and would be obtained with more efficient equipment. Agriculture has been subsidized. Certain foods and basic raw materials are imported duty free or at low rates. It is this kind of import that has precedence on the import side of Britain's closely supervised foreign trade.

Within Britain, strenuous efforts have been made since the war's end, just as they were after World War I, to maintain home production of food at a high level. Farmers have been told that they should grow more grain and other foods eaten directly by humans and raise less forage crops. The government has subsidized the conversion of pasture and woodlands to crop lands and the extensive fertilization of such lands. Support prices for major crops under the Agricultural Act of 1947 have been generous. As a result, agricultural production is higher than in 1945 and much higher than in 1938; however, 1938 was a subnormal year. The food that is raised at home does not have to be imported of course, but it does have to be paid for in other ways. The London *Economist* reported in 1951 that the average farmer was receiving five times his prewar income for one and a half times his prewar output.[1] Thus the taxpayers are paying heavily for the nation's increased self-sufficiency in agriculture.

In transportation the problem was how to revive railways which were run down as a result of a decade of depression and the demands of war. Should they be encouraged to reconstitute themselves and allowed to charge the rates and make the profits that would be essential if they were to do so? It would not have been difficult, for railways are natural monopolies, but the shippers and traveling public would probably have protested. In 1948 the government nationalized the railways. Competing forms of transportation like truck lines were also taken over for a time. The airlines were already in government hands. As a result, Britain has got a somewhat improved transportation system which no longer pays taxes to the government and frequently operates at a loss. Nationalized inland surface transportation produced a net deficit of about £40 millions over four years, and nationalized civil aviation lost £30 millions in three years.[2]

It was in manufacturing that the greatest gains were sought, for Britain, after all, is an industrial nation. British industry would have to carry most of the burden if foreign debts were to be paid, if exports must also pay for imports, if a war-devastated nation must be rebuilt, and if the standard of living was to be raised. What could Britain export? Old industries like coal, iron and steel, and textiles could no longer compete effectively in world markets. The government nationalized coal in 1947 and lost money in 1948, 1949, and 1950.[3] The Labor Government took steps to nationalize steel, but the Conservative Government later reversed them. Increased exports had to come from industries which could compete in world markets, and these were newer industries, such as automobiles, chemicals, machinery, and electric equipment, and, of course, such

[1] *The Economist*, Apr. 7, 1951, p. 782.
[2] Association of American Railroads, *Nationalized Transport in Great Britain*, 1952, p. 6.
[3] Ben W. Lewis, *British Planning and Nationalization* (New York: The Twentieth Century Fund, Inc., 1952), p. 66.

old reliables as whisky, chinaware, and woolens. By dint of great effort the British achieved their goal by 1950 of a 75 per cent increase in exports over the prewar norm. In order to do this the British people had to turn out greatly increased amounts of goods and yet themselves consume only a small fraction of these goods. And when the goal was finally achieved, it proved to be insufficient. Heavy debts remained, imports were inadequate, and rationing had to continue for a while longer.

In the area of finance the government had first of all to encourage investment. In the 1930s that had been necessary to promote recovery and to eliminate unemployment. After World War II it was necessary to rebuild a damaged nation and to modernize its factories and other capital equipment so that Britain might compete more effectively in world markets and raise the standard of living. The device used to effect this goal was low interest rates. For a time the Bank of England kept interest rates low at the behest of the government. Later, the government nationalized the Bank, but this merely publicized a degree of control that had been there for a number of years. The low-interest-rate policy promoted a generous amount of the investment so needed in postwar Britain and was thus partially successful. It also led to, or at least did not discourage, rising prices. Then in 1954 the policy was changed. For the first time in a generation the Bank increased its discount rate substantially, which is to say that it returned to a policy of high interest rates. Whether this is to be a permanent change remains to be seen.

Even increased investment and modern equipment did not lower prices of British commodities enough to increase Britain's export trade sufficiently. Accordingly, the government devalued the pound sterling in 1949. That attracted some bargain hunters to English markets, but it did not increase foreign trade materially in terms of tons, bushels, and dozens. And prices and wages continued to rise to higher levels. Probably the chief benefit of this policy was that it enabled Britain to keep some foreign trade she might have lost.

All this activity by the government in behalf of recovery and reform was bound to be costly. As a result of the war, British taxes were high, and after the war they remained high. They took close to 40 per cent of the national income. Without the social services and without the various nationalized industries operating at admitted or disguised losses, taxes would not have to be so large. Some estimates indicate that 25 per cent might then suffice. Since coming to power, the Conservatives have reduced taxes slightly.

A Labor Government would be expected to try to improve the economic position of the workingman. This the workingman felt was his due, now that his class was politically in control in Britain. The workingman had suffered from the inflationary pinch during and after two world wars, and he had faced unemployment in the depressed 1930s. With a friendly government in office the position of the workingman improved materially. Money wage rates were double in 1952 what they had been in 1939, the working day was significantly shortened, and many workers now enjoyed the five-day week. The government was gentler with its wage controls than with its price controls, and the income tax structure was altered to favor people with low incomes. In addition, there are today all kinds of fringe benefits, such as unemployment insurance benefits for half a year, sickness and accident insurance, old-age pensions, and many free medical services. Altogether, the working classes have never before been so favored.

The problem in commerce since 1945 has been to restrict imports and to expand exports. This has not been easy, for the price of the pound was pegged high in 1945, the prices of British goods have been high, Britain's food, raw-material, and equipment needs for rebuilding have been great, and Britain has had relatively few exports to offer in her war-exhausted condition. When the British talked of the dollar shortage, what they meant was that they had little to sell for dollars and there were many things that dollars would buy which they desperately needed. For a while Britain's annual deficits ran as high as £300 million or £500 million. To remedy this situation Britain borrowed $3.75 billion from the United States in 1946, she devalued the pound in 1949, she was helped by the Marshall Plan in 1950, and she set up an intricate set of controls of her foreign trade. Many foreign debtors could collect their debts only by buying goods in Britain (this was called "blocked sterling"), few Britishers were allowed to travel abroad, for this would use up precious dollars, and the government saw to it that the dollars that Britain did spend were spent to buy needed foods, raw materials, and equipment. Cigarettes were raised to the equivalent of 70 cents a pack to discourage tobacco imports. Britain tried to arrange her buying and selling so that she would sell more goods in the United States and Canada and would buy more in markets where the British could arrange to make payments easily. All in all, the British did rather well with their international trade. They ceased accepting aid under the Marshall Plan a year and a half ahead of schedule, and they increased their exports substantially.

Internally, the government paid relatively little attention to commerce. Most merchants are Conservatives. They had to operate under a program of price controls and rationing until 1954 to hold down imports. They did this fairly efficiently, although in the latter years they allowed themselves to grumble freely.

MERCANTILISM AGAIN?

The British economy has become quite complex as a result of its growth over the centuries and of the three emergencies since 1914. It seems loaded down with government rules and regulations. The government spends a third to a half of the income of most citizens. Has the British economic system traveled a full circle since the eighteenth century? Some two hundred years ago, before the onslaught of then-radical writers like Adam Smith, the state had a large degree of control over the economy. Smith criticized these policies of the mercantile system. With the rise of the industrial age and the factory system, a policy of *laissez faire* and free trade took its place.

The abuses of *laissez faire* in turn led to state policies which attempted at first to make industry compete, somewhat later to regulate certain types of industry in the public interest, and today to give the government the ownership of the means of producing about 20 per cent of the country's goods and services. Although the point can be pushed too far, some see in present-day policies the return to a system like mercantilism.

Many others do not see a return to mercantilism. In the mercantilistic period, governments measured their wealth in large degree by their supplies of precious metals. Domestic industries were subsidized as a part of the nationalism of that era. Self-sufficiency was their economic aim. The Colonies existed to support the mother country. The results of the system were very unequally divided among the citizens of the nation.

The welfare state of the twentieth century serves different ends. It seeks to distribute the benefits of modern inventions and industry more equitably among all the people. It seeks to ensure that a few men of wealth do not dominate society. Wars and depressions have forced on men restrictive actions which many people at first were reluctant to accept but which a majority now welcome. The precious metals as a standard of wealth have given way to regulated or managed paper currencies. Production figures and an abundance of natural resources are now the criteria of prosperity. Britain has made genuine attempts to give colonial peoples their independence and a fair share of the world's goods. The government's role is that of guardian of the whole people rather than of the privileged. For these reasons many people, although not all, conclude that Britain has not returned to another age of mercantilism.

Will this type of philosophy continue when the Labor party is not in power? There is good reason to believe that it will. The history of economic and political trends in Britain indicates that changes in political administration are less significant than might be supposed in altering the basic philosophy of an era.

When the Conservative party under Winston Churchill came to power in 1951, they retained almost all the program initiated by the Labor Government. They introduced only minor changes. They shifted the steel industry from government ownership to government control and "denationalized" the road-haulage section of nationalized transport. Apart from these changes, however, the elections of 1950 and 1951 centered around the questions (1) who could better manage the new nationalized industries and the social services, (2) who was to receive the credit for the introduction of the social services, and (3) who could better manage the problem of the dollar gap abroad and inflation at home.

In the 1920s and 1930s Conservative views dominated the policies of whatever British political party was in power. In the postwar world Labor views have been dominant, no matter which party was in power. The fundamental differences in the foreign and domestic policies of the two parties were sometimes difficult to distinguish. The basic campaign cries of the 1950s were "Me too" and "We'll do it better."

The dominance of the Labor party in the immediate postwar world and the acceptance of its policies by the vast majority of the British people represent yet one more stage in the struggle over the diffusion of power which began as far back as the Cromwellian wars of the 1640s. England had one revolution, and that, apparently, was enough. Since then, power has shifted from group to group by peaceful means. The rural aristocracy first demanded and gained power from the monarchy. Commercial groups gained a share of political and economic power in the seventeenth and eighteenth centuries. In the nineteenth century the new industrialists won their place in the sun. In 1832 the middle classes began to achieve status and position. The twentieth century has seen political power pass from the conservative upper and middle classes to the masses of the people. That this has been achieved peacefully and by democratic methods is no mean accomplishment. It emphasizes, more than any other factor, the distinction between the democracies and totalitarian regimes of the world. In very few countries have the aims of freedom, equality, and security been reconciled by peaceful methods. These countries are mainly in the British Commonwealth, Western Europe, and North America.

QUESTIONS FOR STUDY

1. What are some of the major ways in which the England of the thirteenth century differs from that of today? What have been some of the major changes since the eighteenth century?

2. What were some of the economic effects of the two world wars and of the Great Depression of the 1930s on the British economy?

3. What were some of the aims of the Labor party when it took power in 1945? What did it do to accomplish those aims?

4. How successful has the program of the Labor party been, judged by results in manufacturing? In transportation? In finance? In helping the working man? In commerce?

5. Is the present regulated economy of Britain simply a return to Mercantilism under a new name? Or does it differ in important respects from Mercantilism?

6. To what do you attribute the high degree of government regulation that prevails in Britain? Is it owing to the fact that Britain is crowded? That Britain's resources are nearly exhausted? That she is regimenting her economy to battle the exhaustion from two world wars? That the nation is trying to do too much?

Part Three

SOVIET RUSSIA—TOTALITARIAN SOCIALISM

CHAPTER 17

AREA, POPULATION, AND RESOURCES

The economy of Soviet Russia (Union of Soviet Socialist Republics) must be included in any descriptive study of major modern economic systems. Its tremendous area, its large population and numerous peoples, its great natural resources, and its extremes of climate and topography would make it interesting in any case. And its significance is enhanced because it has been the first large-scale economy to operate under economic planning and socialism.

SOCIALISM AND ECONOMIC PLANNING

Socialistic Institutions. In the socialistic economy of Soviet Russia, land and capital are owned almost completely by society as a whole. Even before World War II some 98.7 per cent of these agents had been brought into socialized or collective ownership. The land of the country (including natural resources) was nationalized as of February, 1918, and is completely owned by society as a whole. Practically all capital goods in manufacturing, and the heavy capital goods in other fields of activity, are similarly owned. On the other hand, individuals are permitted private property in their income from work, in personal savings, dwelling houses, auxiliary husbandry, household articles and utensils, and articles for personal use and comfort.

Most important types of economic activity in Soviet Russia are operated, as well as owned, by the federal, republic, district, local, or other government units. Individuals cannot, as a general rule, found and operate economic enterprises of their own choosing. However, most Soviet agriculture is carried on by some 93,000 collective or cooperative farms, and there are less important cooperatives in merchandising, handicraft production, and the service trades. Freedom of enterprise in the sense of freedom to choose one's own job, occupation, or profession is retained.

Economic motivation, or the desire for rewards of a pecuniary or economic character for accomplishments in production, is relied upon to a considerable extent in Soviet Russia, and there are fair-sized differen-

247

tials in wages and salaries. However, the differences in income are considerably less than those which prevail in a capitalistic country such as the United States. Besides money wages and salaries, individuals receive part of their real income in the form of direct grants of commodities and services. The Soviet Russian economy also relies on such things as altruism, enthusiasm for economic planning and socialism, public honors, prestige, power, and a complicated system of penalties to motivate its people. We shall look into the question of incentives more closely in a later chapter.

A great reduction in the importance of competition in economic life is also one of the features of the socialistic economy of Soviet Russia. Individuals compete to get into the attractive occupations, and consumers compete for the limited supplies of consumers' goods and services. There is some "socialistic competition," or efforts of the workers in socialized enterprises to outdo each other in increasing production and reducing waste, and some unauthorized competition of enterprises and industries to secure materials, fixed capital goods, or labor. In other respects, the governing influence of competition is replaced by the dictates of economic planning, and the economy is intended to be a single great cooperative enterprise.

Economic Planning. One of the most striking features of the socialistic economy of Soviet Russia is economic planning. Decisions concerning the kinds and quantities of economic goods to be produced, the allocation of land and capital among enterprises and industries, and the proportions of the national income which should take the form of capital goods and consumers' goods, respectively, are made on the basis of economic planning rather than on that of price relations. Prices are used to some extent to effect the distribution of workers among occupations and industries and to bring the market demands and supplies of economic goods into balance. Even in these cases, the prices are planned and not freely determined in the market, and their use is always intended to accomplish planned results.

The general objectives to be undertaken by the economic system are selected for several years at a time by the leaders of the Communist party. Within such objectives, Five-Year Plans (and subsidiary plans for various periods of time) must be drawn up in detail for the economy as a whole and for each organization or unit within the system. When a new Five-Year Plan is to be constructed, the State Planning Commission draws up a first draft on the basis of statistical information gathered for the commission by other agencies. The plan is then broken up into parts, which are handed over to various subsidiary planning agencies connected with such functional units as ministries, administrations, trusts, and plants, on the one hand, and such geographical units as republics, provinces, regions, and communities, on the other.

The parts of the plan are examined at each of these functional and geographical levels, and criticisms, suggestions, and counterproposals are offered, ostensibly for the guidance of the State Planning Commission. The parts of the plan, together with the proposed changes, are reassembled in the hands of the commission, which makes the final draft of the Five-Year Plan. After the final draft is approved by the high officials of the Communist party and the legislature, it is again divided up, and appropriate sections are sent back to the various functional and geographical units, so that each may know exactly what is expected of it for the coming period.

Except for the dictates of the leaders of the Communist party, it is probable that the State Planning Commission itself does virtually all the planning under the Russian system. The complicated procedures used in formulating the plans probably exist for the purpose of creating enthusiasm for planning, giving many citizens a feeling that they are participating in the management and direction of the economy, and occasionally getting various factories or trusts to undertake greater productive feats than the commission would have required of them. The plans are bulky documents. The first Five-Year Plan totaled some 1,600 finely printed pages, and the second totaled 1,300 pages.

Under the Soviet Russian planned economy, the activities of every productive unit are closely circumscribed. A plant in industry, for example, is given a specified output to achieve, or to exceed if possible. It is told the amount and kinds of labor it may have and the wages to pay, the amount of working capital which it is granted or may borrow, what is to be done with this capital, the amounts of materials and supplies it may have and at what prices, and the agency to which it is to sell its output and at what prices. The plans are both physical and financial in character. From the physical point of view, they are a matter of so many units of output, so many workers of various kinds, and so much land and capital. From the financial point of view, both selling prices and costs of production are predetermined for the individual productive establishments.

TERRITORIAL EXPANSION AND READJUSTMENT

Soviet Russia has some 8,518,000 square miles of territory, or one-sixth of all the land on earth. It is inhabited by about 210,000,000 people—nearly one-tenth of the world's population. It extends across 160 degrees of longitude, or nearly halfway around the world. Its territory is larger than North America, extending over 6,000 miles from east to west and 1,800 to 2,800 miles from north to south. From Leningrad in the far west to Vladivostok in the far east is a trip requiring 9½ days on the Trans-Siberian Express. If Soviet Russia could be superimposed on the Western Hemisphere, Leningrad would fall just south of Nome, Alaska, and eastern Siberia would touch Norway.[1]

The Kiev State. The great territory of Soviet Russia was built up gradually. The history of Russia goes back to the ninth century, when Varangian princes from Sweden succeeded in unifying a number of independent Slavic principalities in what is now the European section of Russia. The resulting Kiev state eventually extended its borders to the Volga River on the east, the Baltic Sea on the north, and the Black Sea and the northern part of the Caucasus on the south. However, the Kiev state had a stormy career, torn by revolts of the people and by quarrels among the princes of the ruling family.

The Tatar Yoke. The Kiev state had almost disintegrated before Russia was overrun by the Mongolians, or Tatars, from the Far East. Starting with the partial conquest of Siberia in 1207, the Mongolian hordes under Genghis Khan completed the subjugation of Russia by 1240 with the capture and destruction of Kiev itself. It was more than two hundred years later, or in 1480, when Russia escaped from Tatar control. Russia under the Tatars was hemmed in by hostile powers—the Swedes on the north, the Polish-Lithuanian state and the German Knights on the west, and the Turks on the south.

Thus Russia was cut off from Western Europe for a long time and failed to benefit from the progress in the arts and sciences which occurred there. Conditions in Russia remained primitive. The chief economic pursuits were agriculture, hunting, and fishing. Articles for consumption were produced within the household for the most part, trade was extremely limited, and money was little used. The feudal lords owned the land and received payments in kind from the peasants for its use. Since land was more plentiful than labor, it was in the interests of the lords to bind the peasants to the land; the resulting condition of serfdom for the peasantry lasted for many years.

Russia under the Early Czars. Near the end of the thirteenth century, while Russia was still under Tatar control, Moscow became the capital of an independent principality, with the approval of the conquerors. Later, when Tatar control was ended, the principality of Moscow under Ivan III (1462–1505), Ivan the Terrible (1533–1584), and later rulers expanded rapidly. The Tatars were pushed farther east, and progress was made westward into Lithuania and Poland. In 1580 the Cossack

[1] George B. Cressey, *The Basis of Soviet Strength* (New York: McGraw-Hill Book Company, Inc., 1945), pp. 1, 2.

bandit Yermak crossed the Ural Mountains to the east and captured the town of Sibir on the Irtysh River. This marked the beginning of the conquest of Siberia, and the Russians advanced all the way to the Pacific Ocean by 1639. After Alaska was discovered in 1741, Russian colonists advanced southward to within 40 miles of San Francisco by 1812, and Russia retained some control in North America until she sold Alaska in 1867.

The Development of Modern Russia. Under Peter the Great (1689–1725), Russia made great strides in matters of unification, expansion, and westernization. After successful wars with Sweden, Russia gained a foothold on the coast of the Baltic Sea in regions that later became Latvia, Estonia, and Finland, and thus obtained the much-prized "window to Europe." The Russians also reached the western shores of the Caspian Sea and penetrated more widely into Siberia. Russia pushed to the Black Sea during the reign of Catherine II (1762–1796). Under Alexander I (1801–1825), Bessarabia was conquered and Napoleon's fatal march on Moscow occurred.

Russia conquered the Caucasus in 1864 and Turkestan in 1881 during the reign of Alexander II (1855–1881) and moved across Siberia in a new direction to Vladivostok. It was also under Alexander II that a new system of local self-government was introduced, the judiciary was reorganized, court procedure was simplified, trial by jury was introduced, an independent legal profession was established, and municipal administration was reorganized. Most significant of all was the abolition of serfdom in February, 1861, though the peasants were not completely pleased with their new status. Russia emerged from feudalism much later than most of the leading nations of Europe. The period of reforms under Alexander II was followed by a reactionary period under Alexander III and Nicholas II, the last of the czars.

War and Revolution. The expansionist tendency of Russia and her intrigues in Persia, Tibet, Mongolia, Afghanistan, and China proper got her into difficulties with other countries. Examples were the conflict with Great Britain in the Crimean War and along the northern approaches to India, and the Russo-Japanese War of 1904–1905, which followed the completion of the Chinese Eastern Railway to Vladivostok and Port Arthur in Manchuria. Prior to the war with Japan, Russia had been going through a period of economic crisis and unrest. Crops were poor and food shortages recurred. Labor unions had developed, industrial strikes were common, and revolutionary parties of several varieties were active.

When the war with Japan ended in complete defeat for Russia, the general unrest and dissatisfaction boiled over and the result was the Revolution of 1905. Large and bloody but poorly coordinated uprisings occurred in the cities and in rural areas, and even the armed forces were not immune. However, the government was strong and with the aid of loyal troops put down the armed revolts and defeated the revolution. Nevertheless, the revolution was not a complete failure, for the Czar promised the people an elective Duma (Congress) along with other reforms. Unrest continued after the revolution, and the Czar called out the troops to suppress uprisings on 2,559 occasions during 1906.

By 1910 the economic crisis had subsided and prosperity had begun. In the next few years, foreign capital poured in, and large-scale firms and combinations increased greatly in importance in Russian industry and finance. However, the labor movement also revived quickly, undercover revolutionary activities continued, and strikes and demonstrations against unsatisfactory conditions became common. Russia was on the verge of another revolution when World War I broke out.

Participation in the war caused the revolutionary movement to subside temporarily, but when Russia's initial successes were replaced by severe military reverses, unrest reappeared. As the war went on, industrial production became disorganized, prices rose considerably, and agricultural production suffered. Government finances were in bad condition. Strikes increased in number, and revolts had to be suppressed by military force. Food shortages gave trouble in the cities and transportation disintegrated rapidly. The prestige of the Czar dwindled as a result of scandals connected with the disreputable "monk" Rasputin who, as a friend of the Czar's family, had come to have great influence in government matters.

Finally the inefficiency and corruption of the government became unbearable, and revolution brought the czarist government to an end. In March, 1917, there were spontaneous uprisings of great masses of people in the leading cities, and Nicholas II had to abdicate, for he had lost the support of the armed forces and of practically all elements in the population. Groups of workers, known as "soviets," or councils, sprang into action in the chief industrial centers, attempted to maintain order, and administered the food supplies. A provisional government, under the authority of the legislature, was established and operated for a time under the leadership of Alexander Kerensky.

This government, however, did not cope with the situation effectively, economic conditions continued to deteriorate, and in several months' time little progress was made toward establishing a stable government. In the fall of 1917, the Bolshevik party took over the government. This party was a small revolutionary group, but it had control of some local soviets, especially those in Moscow and Petrograd, and believed it could command the support of the masses. Its leaders were Nicolai Lenin and Leon Trotsky, both of whom had just returned from exile. Trotsky reentered Russia with Kerensky's permission, but Lenin and one of his chief lieutenants had been moved from Switzerland across Germany and into Russia in a blacked-out train, with the connivance of the German government.

After a short struggle beginning on November 6, 1917, the government buildings and facilities in Petrograd were taken over, and the Kerensky government fell. An All-Russian Congress of Soviets, welding together the local soviets of workers, was already in session and it undertook the formation of a new government under the guidance of the Bolshevik party (later to become the Communist party of the Soviet Union). Legislative and executive authority was vested in a so-called Council of People's Commissars, with Lenin at its head.

In the next few years, the new government was busy resisting attempts at counterrevolution, fighting civil wars, and staving off the armies which other countries sent into the Soviet Union. When peace had been restored on all fronts, the area of Soviet Russia had been reduced from that formerly held by czarist Russia. Lithuania, Latvia, Estonia, and Finland had become separate nations. Poland had not only broken away from Russia but also had taken a slice of Belorussia. Bessarabia was held by Roumania, and concessions had been made to Turkey in Transcaucasia.

This situation continued until World War II broke out. When Poland fell to Germany late in 1939, the Red Army rushed in and repossessed the western Belorussian and Ukrainian territories which Poland had been holding. Soviet Russia obtained some territory from Finland after a short war in 1939 and 1940. In June, 1940, Roumania gave up northern Bucovina, inhabited largely by Ukrainians, and Bessarabia, which had been taken from Russia at the end of World War I. Finally, Lithuania, Latvia, and Estonia "petitioned" (under considerable Soviet pressure) for admission into the U.S.S.R., and they were admitted in August, 1940.

In June, 1941, Soviet Russia was attacked by Germany. Soviet Russia soon sustained a temporary loss of almost 10 per cent of her territory and severe losses in other respects. In the end, however, Soviet Russia and her allies were victorious, the lost territory was regained, and some additions were made, including the Kuril Islands and southern Sakhalin Island in the Far East, the trans-Carpathian area of Poland, and the Koenigsberg area in what was formerly East Prussia (Germany). Thus Soviet Russia reached her present area.

The Union Republics. Soviet Russia is now organized as a federation of 16 union or constituent republics. As indicated by Figure 3, one of these republics, the Russian Soviet Federated Socialist Republic (R.S.F.S.R.), is larger than all the others combined. It contains more than four-fifths of the area of the country, well over half of the population, and the two largest cities, Moscow and Leningrad. The other union republics con-

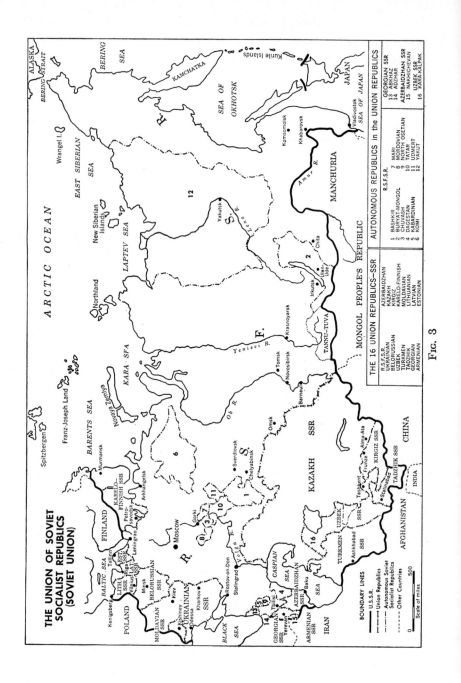

Fig. 3

stitute a kind of fringe around the western and southern outskirts of Soviet Russia. On the west, separating Soviet Russia from Europe, are the Karelo-Finnish, Estonian, Latvian, Lithuanian, Belorussian, Ukrainian, and Moldavian Soviet Socialist Republics. In the Caucasus, the southwestern area between the Black Sea and the Caspian Sea, are found the Georgian, Armenian, and Azerbaidzhan Soviet Socialist Republics. The remaining republics—the Turkmen, Uzbek, Tadzhik, Kirgiz, and Kazakh Soviet Socialist Republics—are on the south side of the country in central Asia.

Other Political Subdivisions. The map also shows the 16 autonomous republics of Soviet Russia, 12 of them being in the R.S.F.S.R. These units have been set up primarily to give some local autonomy to ethnic or racial groups. The same is true of the many autonomous regions and national areas of the country, which are not shown on the map. Other subdivisions, of a more clearly political character, include administrative areas (*okrugs*), districts (*raions*), regions (*oblasts*), and territories (*krais*). All of these divisions are, of course, subsidiary to the union republics.

THE POPULATION AND PEOPLES OF SOVIET RUSSIA

The Growth of Population. During the reign of Catherine the Great (1762–1796), the estimated population of Russia reached 37,000,000.[2] Only three official census enumerations have ever been made in Soviet Russia. In 1897 the population was found to be 129,200,200; it increased to 146,989,460 in 1926 and 170,467,186 in 1939.[3] During the next two years, territories containing some 23,000,000 people were added to the Soviet Union and, allowing for natural increase, the 1940 population was estimated at 198,000,000.[4]

Serious population losses were incurred during World War II. Direct losses amounted to about 7 million persons, but this does not tell the whole story. Under peacetime conditions the population would have increased considerably from 1941 through 1945. It is therefore estimated that the population in 1945 was some 20 million smaller than it would have been had the war not occurred.[5] Since the war the population has been growing again. The birth rate in some parts of the country has sometimes been 50 per thousand of population per year, and has averaged 40 or more for the whole country. In spite of a high death rate, this has

[2] E. J. Simmons (ed.), *U.S.S.R.: A Concise Handbook* (Ithaca, N.Y.: Cornell University Press, 1947), p. 73.
[3] Cressey, *op. cit.*, p. 43.
[4] *Annals of the American Academy of Political and Social Science*, May, 1949, pp. 56–57.
[5] *Ibid.*

meant an annual increase in population of 1 to 1½ per cent. By 1950 the population was estimated at over 200 million[6] and it probably was about 210 million by 1955.

The Peoples of Soviet Russia. Various estimates indicate that there are from 169 to 175 races, nationalities, or tribes of people in Soviet Russia. They speak some 125 languages or dialects and have over 40 different religions. A total of 54 groups, 44 of them mentioned in the Soviet constitution, inhabit their own autonomous territories. Only about 50 of the ethnic groups number more than 20,000 people each, and these groups account for about 99.5 per cent of the population.[7]

The Slavs are the largest ethnic group and make up about three-fourths of the population. The Great Russians are the largest group of Slavs. They inhabit the R.S.F.S.R., make up an overwhelming majority of its population and include over half of the people of the entire country. The Little Russians (or Ukrainians), the Belorussians (or White Russians), the Poles, the Bulgarians, and the Czechoslovaks are also Slavs. The Turco-Tatars, descendants of the Asiatic warriors who once overran Russia, the Japhetic peoples, the Finno-Ugrians, and the Jews are other important ethnic groups. The Russian population also includes Latvians, Lithuanians, Germans, Moldavians, and Iranians; numerous small groups in the Caucasus; some 26 groups in the northern part of Soviet Russia; and as many as 80 groups in the far east.

The Soviet Russian government has been liberal in its treatment of minority groups. The constitution says:

> Equality of rights of citizens of the U.S.S.R., irrespective of their nationality or race, in all spheres of economic, state, cultural, social, and political life, is an indefeasible law. Any direct or indirect restriction of the rights of, or conversely any establishment of direct or indirect privileges for, citizens on account of their race or nationality, as well as any advocacy of racial or national exclusiveness or hatred and contempt, is punishable by law.

As we have seen, many of the ethnic groups have autonomous republics, autonomous regions, and national districts, and these subdivisions are represented in the national legislature. The various ethnic groups develop and maintain their own institutions, customs, languages, and general culture. Laws are printed and judicial proceedings carried on in the local languages. At least 70 languages are in use in the schools, and books are printed in 110 languages. Alphabets and dictionaries have been worked up for about 40 groups which formerly had only oral languages. Such factors have been a great help in reducing illiteracy.[8]

[6] Harry Schwartz, *Russia's Soviet Economy* (New York: Prentice-Hall, Inc., 1950), p. 28.

[7] Simmons, *op. cit.*, p. 4; Cressey, *op. cit.* p. 42; *The Soviet Union Today* (New York: American-Russian Institute, 1946), p. 8.

[8] Simmons, *op. cit.*, p. 11.

Characteristics of the Russian People. Some 80 per cent of the people of Soviet Russia belong to the so-called white race, though intermarriage has been common in the absence of racial antagonism. On the whole, the Russian stock is well developed and virile. In pre-Soviet days, medical care and hygiene had been insufficient, there were frequent droughts and food shortages, and the birth rate was very high. The result was a high death rate among the weaker elements in the population and the survival of the stronger and more resistant people. In general, geographical and political factors, rather than any inherent defects in the people themselves, caused the cultural development of Russia to lag behind that of Western Europe and the United States.

Soviet Russia is primarily a nation of young people. At the beginning of World War II, some 63 per cent of the people were under thirty years of age and 45 per cent were under nineteen.[9] Such people, of course, would have no recollection of life under the czarist regime. The people have become urbanized rapidly under the Soviet regime, whereas formerly the overwhelming majority lived in the country. Cities with a population of over 100,000 increased from 31 in 1926 to 82 in 1939, and practically every city at least doubled its population in the period between the two world wars.[10] Most of the people live in a roughly triangular area based on Leningrad and the Black Sea in the west and tapering off into Siberia in the neighborhood of Lake Baikal. The reasons for this will become clear as we examine conditions of soil, climate, and topography.

PHYSICAL FEATURES

The Cultivated Area. The area of Soviet Russia is great, but much of the land is worthless or almost worthless. It is too wet or too dry, too cold, too infertile, too inaccessible, or too mountainous. The total area underlaid by permanently frozen earth amounts to 3,728,900 square miles, or between 40 and 50 per cent of the land of the country. In a number of regions the frozen earth goes down to depths of 100 feet and its maximum depth is 920 feet. In all Soviet Russia there are no more than 1 million square miles of good agricultural land,[11] or about the same amount as in the United States. This land lies almost entirely within the narrow wedge or triangle based on Leningrad and the Black Sea in the west and tapering off toward Lake Baikal in Siberia. It coincides with the area of greatest population density, and contains most of the farms, cities, railroads, and industries.

Topography. The topography of Soviet Russia presents an almost in-

[9] Cressey, *op. cit.*, p. 45.
[10] *Ibid.*
[11] *Ibid.*, pp. 2, 86.

finite variety. There are low, swampy plains, ordinary plains and prairies, rolling hills and highlands, plateaus and towering mountains. Geographers sometimes divide the country into as many as 18 topographic regions and 82 subregions. There are great plains in the European area of Russia, in western Siberia, and in central Asia around the Caspian Sea. Except for the Ural Mountains, which are old, worn, and relatively low, and the mountain ranges of the far east, the mountains of Soviet Russia lie along the southern boundary and the ranges run east and west. The mountains of the Caucasus rise as high as 18,468 feet, but the Pamir ranges in central Asia have the highest peaks, including Mt. Stalin (24,584 feet) and Mt. Lenin (22,377 feet).

Climate and Precipitation. Soviet Russia has all types of climate except the tropical, but about 80 per cent of the country lies in the temperate zone. Only 16 per cent falls in the Arctic Zone, while 4 per cent is subtropical.[12] Nevertheless, the climate of Russia as a whole, because of its location and topography, is very severe. The country is almost surrounded by oceans and seas but draws very little climatic benefit from them. Only the Atlantic has a moderating influence, and that is many miles away. High mountains and long distances cut off any marine influence from the south. The Pacific Ocean in the far east is on the leeward side of the country and is blocked off by high mountains. On the other hand, the country is open to the north and the Arctic Ocean has an unfavorable influence on the climate.

The climate of Soviet Russia is continental, with long, cold winters and short, relatively warm summers. The winter season dominates the climate. The frost-free part of the year runs less than 60 days in the Siberian arctic, and not over 90 to 120 days in the northern half of the European area and central Siberia. In the central part of European Russia, the Ukraine, and southwestern Siberia, it lasts from 120 to 180 days, but it runs over 200 days only in middle Asia. The ground is covered with snow in Siberia from 160 to 260 days each year, and in the European section, except for the Ukraine, for 100 to 200 days.

Another feature of Soviet Russia's continental climate is light precipitation. Except for a few areas in the west and in the mountains, annual rainfall runs 20 inches per year or less. The western slope of the Ural Mountains receives 24 inches, and the area around Smolensk, not far from Moscow, gets 25.6 inches. Around Batum in the Caucasus the precipitation reaches 98.5 inches on occasion. On the other hand, the rainfall gets as low as 6.3 inches per year in some of the flat country north of the Caspian Sea.[13]

Most of Soviet Russia, including the best agricultural land, is never

---

[12] Simmons, *op. cit.*, p. 22.
[13] *Ibid.*, pp. 22–23.

far removed from the danger of drought. Moreover, the best agricultural land is closely hemmed in on both the north and south. To the north, average annual temperatures are low and there is extreme variation in the length of the frost-free period. To the south, average annual rainfall is low and there are extreme variations in rainfall.

Soil and Vegetation. Soviet Russia can be divided roughly into five zones from the point of view of soil and vegetation, and these zones coincide fairly well with climatic belts. In the far north along the Arctic Ocean is the tundra, which occupies some 887,000 square miles, or about 10 per cent of the total area. It is marked by the absence of forests, for the subsoil is always frozen and only plants with short roots can survive. The soil is made acid by a layer of decaying vegetation, and it is difficult to raise cultivated crops. Low temperatures and short frost-free periods are also obstacles to agriculture.

South of the tundra there is a tremendous belt, stretching east and west, called the forest zone, or taiga. It covers 4,240,000 square miles, or about half the total area, and is the largest forest area in the world. The soil is known as podsol. It has a surface organic layer, derived from the trees, underlaid by a sandy, ash-colored horizon and a dark-brownish, clay-enriched zone. The podsol is acid, but it provides the soil for about a third of the cultivated area of the country.

South of the forest zone is the steppe region. It comprises some 964,000 square miles, or less than 12 per cent of the total area. Much of the soil is the famous chernozem, rich and black with organic matter and well supplied with lime and soluble plant foods. In its natural state, the steppe is grassland and is marked by the absence of trees. The soil is favorable to general agriculture, and a considerable part of the best agricultural land in the country is found in the steppe region.

Farther south, in the southeastern part of European Russia and in huge areas of central Asia, are semidesert and desert lands. The area occupies 1,500,000 square miles, or around 18 per cent of the total area. Average temperatures are higher than in the steppe region and annual precipitation less. Vegetation is sparse. The soil may be suitable for agriculture where adequate water can be supplied through irrigation.

Finally, some areas in the southern part of Soviet Russia fall in the subtropics. These areas, largely in the eastern and western valleys of Transcaucasia, contain a minute fraction of the total area. The soil has little lime but much clay from volcanic ash. Humus has developed in the forest areas, and the soil is similar to the podsol of the northern forest area. Winters are mild, summers are hot, rainfall is plentiful, and the natural vegetation is luxuriant. In addition to the general zones which have been mentioned, the mountainous areas furnish a variety of types of soil and vegetation at different altitudes.

NATURAL RESOURCES

Power Resources. Soviet Russia has a wealth of natural resources and is one of the most richly endowed countries in the world. Coal, the most important source of power, makes up about 70 per cent of all fuels consumed. Out of world reserves of 7 trillion tons, Soviet Russia has about 1⅔ trillion tons. This places her second to the United States, which has 3½ trillion tons. The Russian reserves are scattered among more than 80 fields located all over the country. About 87 per cent of the coal is bituminous.[14]

The actual production of coal amounted to 166 million tons in 1940, 113 million tons in 1945, and 344 million tons in 1954.[15] The largest producing areas are the Donets Coal Basin, lying north of the Black Sea and largely in the Ukrainian Soviet Socialist Republic, and the Kuznets Basin in mid-Siberia. Other producing areas are indicated in Figure 4. Peat is not ordinarily considered an important fuel, but in Soviet Russia it makes up some 6 per cent of all fuel burned. Soviet Russia has the largest reserves of peat in the world—some 151 billion tons, dried weight.[16]

Petroleum furnishes about 12 per cent of all fuels burned in Soviet Russia. Estimates of total petroleum reserves vary from less than 5 to almost 9 billion tons. Soviet Russia's reserves are among the largest in the world. The reserves actually proved and prospected or in sight amount to around a billion tons, and the other reserves are merely a geological estimate.[17] In contrast with the coal reserves, those of petroleum are largely concentrated in the area from the Caucasus and the Caspian Sea north to the central Urals. The actual production of petroleum amounted to 31.0 million tons in 1940, 19.4 million tons in 1945, and 59.5 million tons in 1954.[18]

The rest of the fuel burned for power in Soviet Russia, about 12 per cent of the total, is wood. However, wood is more important as a raw material for industry, and we shall discuss timber reserves in another connection. A final source of power in Soviet Russia is hydroelectric. Most of the rivers flow gently, and in some cases their flow is seasonal, but their size makes the potential of hydroelectric power impressive. Estimates of power based on stream flow available 50 per cent of the time amount to 281 million kilowatts, while power available 90 per cent of the time amounts to 58 million kilowatts.[19] The actual development of

[14] Cressey, *op. cit.*, p. 109.
[15] *The Economist*, Jan. 31, 1953, p. 265, and Jan. 29, 1955, p. 373.
[16] Simmons, *op. cit.*, pp. 28–29.
[17] Cressey, *op. cit.*, p. 114.
[18] *The Economist*, Jan. 31, 1953, p. 265, and Jan. 29, 1955, p. 373.
[19] Cressey, *op. cit.*, p. 116.

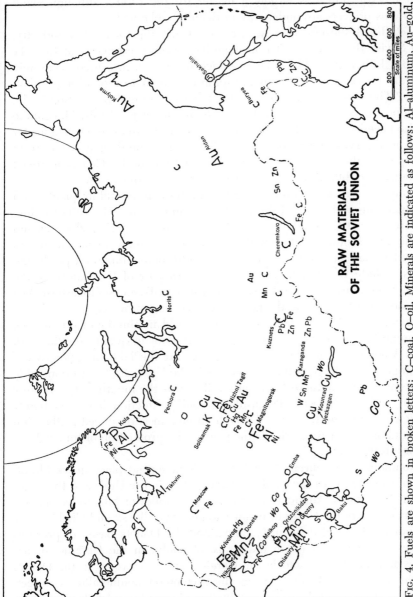

FIG. 4. Fuels are shown in broken letters: C–coal, O–oil. Minerals are indicated as follows: Al–aluminum, Au–gold, Cr–chromium, Cu–copper, Hg–mercury, K–potash, Mn–manganese, Ni–nickel, Pb–lead, S–sulphur, Sn–tin, Zn–zinc. Industrial agricultural products, in italics, include Co–cotton and Wo–wool.

hydroelectric power is largely a matter for the future, although many ambitious projects are under way or definitely planned.

Metallic Resources. Iron is an essential material for modern industry, and Soviet Russia has vast iron deposits variously estimated at from 11 to 16½ billion tons. The reserves which have been measured accurately and are or soon will be available for use amount to around 4½ billion tons.[20] The most important producing areas are around Krivoi Rog in the Ukraine and Magnitogorsk in the southern part of the Urals. Manganese is also necessary to steel production, and Soviet Russia is the world leader both in reserves and in production. The largest producing areas are at Nikopol in the southern Ukraine, at Chiatura in the Georgian Soviet Socialist Republic, and in Sverdlovsk Province in the Urals.

Copper reserves are unsatisfactory both in quantity and in quality, and production is well short of the country's requirements. The chief producing areas are at Kounrad near Lake Balkhash, at nearby Dzhezkazgan, and in the Ural Mountains. Soviet Russia's lead and zinc reserves amount to 11 and 19 per cent, respectively, of the world totals. Important producing areas include Ordzhonikidze in the northern part of the Caucasus, the Altai Mountains in central Asia, the Kuznets Basin, southeastern Asia beyond Lake Baikal, and the far eastern maritime province.

Soviet Russia has ranked third in the world in aluminum production, although her extensive bauxite deposits are poor in quality for the most part. Among the important producing areas are the Tikhvin region east of Leningrad and the Sverdlovsk province in the Urals. Nickel is obtained in the central and southern Urals, at Norilsk near the mouth of the Yenisey River, and on the Kola Peninsula. Actual production has been barely sufficient for domestic needs. Enough chromium is produced in the Ural Mountains so that Russia leads the world. The production of tin has been rather insignificant.

Nonmetallic Resources. Soviet Russia is in second place in world output of asbestos, with the chief producing areas in the Urals and the Altai-Sayan Mountains. Adequate to very large supplies of talc and soapstone are available in the Urals, of magnesite near Sverdlovsk and Chelyabinsk, of industrial salt at Solikamsk, Emba, and the Donets Basin, of precious and semiprecious stones in the Urals, of kaolin in the Ukraine, of fire clays around Moscow and in the Ukraine, and of mercury in the Donets Basin and in the Urals. Besides these common nonmetallic resources, Russia leads the world in the production of apatite and potassium salts. Apatite, important as a source of phosphate, is obtained from deposits in the Khibin Mountains of the Kola Peninsula, while the potash is produced at Solikamsk on the western slope of the northern Urals.

Finally, Soviet Russia has enormous timber resources. Her forest land

[20] Schwartz, *op. cit.*, p. 19.

amounts to 1,527,300,000 acres, or about 21 per cent of the world total. About two-thirds of the Russian forest area is suitable for commercial exploitation. Nine-tenths of the conifers are pine and spruce, while birch and aspen account for four-fifths of the deciduous trees.[21] Although timber production is less than might be expected on the basis of resources, forest products normally constitute the country's second largest export.

Deficiencies in Soviet Russian Resources. The general situation with regard to Soviet Russian resources is one of abundance, but a mere listing of reserves tends to present too optimistic a picture. The discovery of a few million tons of rock containing a valuable mineral does not necessarily mean that an economically workable ore is at hand. Some parts of the natural resources are of inferior grades, so that exploitation probably would not be profitable on a capitalistic basis which required a strict accounting of costs, although it is possible for a socialistic government to develop the resources if it cares to do so.

The natural resources of Soviet Russia are scattered over the country, and materials which need to be used together are sometimes located far apart. To cite a single example, when the large blast furnaces for the production of pig iron were set up at Magnitogorsk in the Ural Mountains, coal had to be brought in from the Kuznets Basin some 1,400 miles to the east. It is also true that some parts of the country are almost entirely without natural resources,

Finally, available resources and actual production are different things, for many Soviet Russian resources are relatively undeveloped. Soviet Russian coal production amounted to 301 million metric tons in 1952, but that of the United States had been 523 million metric tons in 1951. Production of pig iron was 25.2 million metric tons in Soviet Russia and 63.9 million metric tons in the United States in the same years. Soviet Russia produced 47.4 million metric tons of crude petroleum in 1952, but the United States had already produced 309 million metric tons in 1951. Production of electric power in Soviet Russia amounted to 117.0 billion kilowatt-hours in 1952 and that of the United States came to 370.2 billion kilowatt-hours in 1951.[22] Clearly, some care should be exercised in interpreting the natural resources of Soviet Russia.

In the seven chapters that follow we shall see how Soviet Russia uses her population, land, and natural resources to satisfy the needs and wants of her people on the basis of economic planning and socialism. We shall start with the important field of agriculture.

[21] Cressey, *op. cit.*, p. 168.
[22] *The Economist*, Jan. 31, 1953, p. 265.

QUESTIONS FOR STUDY

1. Show how the territories under Russian control grew to their present size. Is it fair to say that Russia has usually shown imperialistic tendencies?

2. Is Soviet Russia or the United States more of a "melting pot" for different nationalities or races? How are minority groups treated in Soviet Russia?

3. How does the rate of population growth in Soviet Russia compare with that of the United States? Where do most of the people live in Soviet Russia? Why?

4. Although Soviet Russia is far larger than the United States, it has only about the same quantity of good land. Why is this true? Where is the good land located? Describe the five zones into which Soviet Russia is divided from the point of view of soil and vegetation.

5. Why is coal currently much more important as a source of power in Soviet Russia than in the United States? Is Soviet Russia well supplied with power resources?

6. Would you agree that Soviet Russia has a wealth of natural resources and is one of the most richly endowed countries in the world? What are some of the weaknesses in her position with respect to resources?

7. The economy of the Soviet Union is generally considered to be socialistic. What does this mean in terms of basic institutions? How are the economic activities of Soviet Russia planned?

CHAPTER 18

AGRICULTURE

Soviet Russia is one of the foremost agricultural countries and is the world's largest producer of several important crops. The country has become increasingly industrialized under Soviet rule, but agriculture is still the backbone of the economy. However, at the time of the Revolution of 1917, Russian agriculture was in an unfavorable situation and was poorly adapted to meet the needs of a modern planned economy. In order to understand the problems of Russian agriculture and the ways in which the economic planners have tried to solve them, it will be necessary to examine briefly the prerevolutionary situation.

AGRICULTURE BEFORE 1917

Peasant Landholdings. Serfdom was abolished in Russia in 1861, or fifty-six years before the Revolution of 1917. After the reform, however, the peasants received for use, but not as private property, only the land which they had formerly been allowed to cultivate for themselves under serfdom. This land had been enough to occupy only about half of their working time, since they had been required to put in the other half of their time working on the estates of the large landowners.

Moreover, in some regions where the land was good, the peasants received 26 to 44 per cent less land than they had farmed before the reform, and only in regions with poor soil were they fortunate enough to receive more land than they had formerly used.[1] Even in 1905 the allotments of land ran less than 8 *desyatin* (20.8 acres) for almost half of all the peasant households.[2] Since the peasants were unable to employ their labor fully on the land allotted to them, they had to seek additional income by renting land from, or working on, estates belonging to the great landlords, the crown, or the monasteries and convents.

[1] A. Baykov, *The Development of the Soviet Economic System* (New York: The Macmillan Company, 1947), p. 9.
[2] *Ibid.*, p. 11.

Community Property in Land. Title to the land allotted to the peasants after the abolition of serfdom was vested in a special organization—the mir, or rural community. This agency assigned land to the individual peasants and also had the right to redistribute it, either periodically or at irregular intervals, on the basis of the number of members (eaters) in the various peasant households. The land received by each household was not a farm in the American sense of the term but consisted of a number of plots or strips scattered over the area owned by the particular commune.

Financial Obligations of the Peasants. Land was assigned to the peasants after the abolition of serfdom only on condition that it be paid for. The payments were often calculated on the basis of higher land values than those actually prevailing at the time, and the peasants were thus required, in effect, to pay ransom for the freeing of their labor as well as for the land. The total compensation was to be paid over a period of forty-nine years and it was viewed as an obligation of the entire community, with all peasants in the community jointly responsible. As a result, the individual peasants were not allowed to leave the community unless they had paid their contributions in full. Since this was unlikely to happen, the peasants were tied firmly to their community and in any case could leave only with its permission. This inferior economic status of the peasants was reflected in an inferior social status and in the limitation of their civil rights.

The small amounts of land allocated to most peasants would not produce sufficient income to meet the redemption payments and the taxes required by the government, besides providing for the subsistence of the peasants. Indeed, the redemption payments required of the peasants were often greater than the total money income from their land. The payments got further and further in arrears as time went on. Falling grain prices and increasing population tended to intensify the distress of the peasants.

The Development of Peasant Classes. However, some Russian peasants were relatively well-to-do. Those with high-grade land, larger allotments, or favorable market situations were able to raise their economic status to a level well above that of most peasants. Moreover, enterprising peasants could get ahead economically by renting or buying more land from the large estates. In 1882 the Peasants' Bank was set up to enable groups of peasants or communities to buy land from the large estates. In time the bank was permitted to buy up estates for resale to peasants.

The renting of land to the more successful peasants became very common. At one time, over half of the large estates were renting all of their land, and 80 per cent of them were renting all or part of their holdings. As time went on, the small and poor peasants began to be sharply differentiated from the large and well-to-do peasants, who cultivated much land acquired from the estates or from less successful and impoverished peasants, in addition to the land assigned to them.

The mir itself, however, tended to obstruct the economic differentiation of the peasants and the formation of peasant classes. The mir stood for equality of landholding by peasant households with equal numbers of members, and it kept this principle in operation to some extent by periodic redistribution of peasant holdings. The only differentiation favored by the mir was that which resulted from the varying sizes of peasant families.

The Mir and Commercial Agriculture. The mir also obstructed the development of commercial farming in Russia. Late in the nineteenth century, the peasants wanted to produce goods for sale on the market rather than for their own consumption or for making payments in kind. They needed considerable sums of money to pay taxes and meet redemption payments. Moreover, the markets for their produce were expanding both at home and abroad.

With the increase in industrial production, the population of urban centers grew and had to be supplied with both food and raw materials. As transportation improved, food and raw materials could be moved more readily from the farms to the cities and to the seaports for export. The situation was favorable in most respects for the development of large-scale agricultural production and for the use of improved methods and equipment. Little could be done along these lines, however, on the mir, with its scattered strips of land assigned to the various peasant households and its redistributions of landholdings.

Attempted Reforms. There was much unrest in Russian agriculture around 1900, and some attempts were made to placate the peasantry. For example, the collective responsibility of all peasants for making redemption payments was ended in 1903, and the redemption payments themselves were canceled in 1905. However, peasant groups participated actively in the Revolution of 1905.

The Stolypin reforms followed in 1906 and were intended to liquidate community property in land and facilitate the transfer to private ownership of community land already used by the peasants. The objective was to develop large groups of prosperous peasants who would own consolidated farms, improve the efficiency of agriculture by using modern methods and equipment, and furnish a politically conservative element in the rural population. In practice, the peasants who were already most successful were able to divert much larger amounts of community land to private ownership than were the poorer peasants, and they had much more land than those peasants who continued to use land belonging to the community.

The result was an increasing differentiation between the more prosperous peasants, or kulaks, and the rest of the peasantry, and the interests of these groups became antagonistic. It was small wonder that the poorer peasants, with their small plots of land, looked with envy at the more prosperous peasants and at the neighboring large estates and felt that they were being deprived of land which should belong to them. After all, some 30 thousand owners of large estates had as much land as 1½ million prosperous peasant households and almost as much as 10½ million poor peasant households.[3]

PROBLEMS OF SOVIET RUSSIAN AGRICULTURE

The Problem of Efficiency. After the Revolution of 1917, the Soviet planners were aware that an efficient agriculture would be indispensable to the creation of a modern industrial economy in the U.S.S.R. and that great changes would have to be made in Russian agriculture before it would come up to specifications. It might have been thought that, with from two-thirds to three-fourths of the people engaged in agriculture, Russia would have been supplied with an abundance of food and raw materials, but such was far from the case. The Russian system of peasant agriculture was notoriously unproductive and inefficient. Before the revolution, there had been thirty-five bad crop years in fifty, and there were to be only three good harvests in the first ten years of Soviet rule.

About half of the peasant households had cultivated 8 *desyatin* of land or less, and it was estimated that a peasant household required from 6 to 12 *desyatin* (depending on the section of the country and the size of the family) before it could be self-sufficient and have any produce available for the market.[4] The fact was that many of the peasant landholdings were too small to permit the use of efficient agricultural methods.

Actually, a third of the peasants had no iron plough and a fourth of them had no horse or ox. Agricultural machinery was practically unknown. Little manure was used and almost no commercial fertilizer. Adequate crop rotation was not practiced in many cases and there was little cultivation of growing crops. Grains were reaped with the hand sickle and threshed with the flail.

Most of the peasants did not own farms, and the community land assigned to a peasant household was likely to consist of several plots or strips often located long distances apart. This in itself was an obstacle to efficient cultivation. Moreover, most peasants had little incentive to improve their land or even maintain it adequately, for they were likely to lose it to someone else when the next redistribution of the land occurred.

[3] *Ibid.*, p. 13.
[4] *Ibid.*, p. 14.

There was also a psychological problem for the economic planners to face. Most of the peasants were not revolutionaries. They had little direct connection with the revolution, and all it meant to most of them was found in a vague notion that they would get more land. On the other hand, the only people in agriculture who were sufficiently intelligent and well trained to serve as the basis for making a system of socialized agriculture operate successfully (the more prosperous peasants) were naturally out of sympathy with the new regime.

It was difficult for the leaders of Soviet Russia to solve the problem of efficiency and productivity in agriculture. Larger-scale farm units, which could make use of machinery, fertilizers, and modern methods in general, were necessary, but it was hard to see how they could be developed. The distribution of the large estates among the rapidly growing peasantry would not have increased greatly the average size of peasant landholdings. If manufacturing and other fields of industry had been developed already, some of the surplus agricultural population could have been siphoned off. But industry had not been developed on a large scale, and its growth seemed to depend upon the creation of a more efficient agriculture.

The combination of the small plots of land used by the peasants into government or cooperative farms would have solved the problem of farm size, but the question of what to do with the surplus rural population would have remained. Moreover, this approach would have involved extensive changes in customary modes of production and consumption in agriculture and in the peasants' general outlook on life. We shall see in the next main section of this chapter how the Soviet leaders actually dealt with the problem of agricultural efficiency and productivity.

The Problem of Coordination. A second important problem was that of coordinating the operation of and results in the field of agriculture with those of the planned economy as a whole. Plans for the economy would have been upset if the farmers could not have been depended upon to produce foods and raw materials of the desired kinds and in something like the desired quantities. The conversion of the system of peasant agriculture into one of state farms under direct government ownership and operation would have solved this problem at once, but this course of action did not seem feasible. On the other hand, if agricultural operations were to be left in the hands of individual peasants or cooperating groups of peasants, there would always have been a chance, in the absence of adequate controls, that these operations would have been suited to the desires of the peasants rather than to the needs and plans of the economy.

The "Scissors Problem." A third problem of Soviet Russian agriculture was found in farm prices and income. Since the prices that the farmers received for their goods were relatively low and the prices that they had to pay for manufactured goods were relatively high, the Russian farmers suffered from the well-known "scissors problem." The farmers were reluctant to furnish large quantities of food and raw materials for the urban and industrial population as long as manufactured goods were scarce and high-priced. On the other hand, Russian industries, faced with a shortage of food and materials, could turn out only a few, high-cost goods for the farmers. This problem was difficult, for the farmers were sure to suffer to some extent during the conversion of a rural system into a modern industrial economy, and the Soviet leaders desired to give favorable treatment to newly recruited workers in manufacturing and other fields.

THE ORGANIZATION AND OPERATION OF SOVIET AGRICULTURE TO 1940

Early Conditions. The Revolution of 1917 was followed by a crude sort of seizure and distribution of the property of the large estates by the peasants of nearby villages. In the process a great deal of property was destroyed and livestock slaughtered. During the next few years, in the period known as War Communism, the peasants were left to do much as they pleased. However, the system of "food collections," under which the government took much of what the peasants produced, caused a great decline in agricultural production. The land under cultivation decreased from 91 to 54 million hectares, the grain crop fell from 65 to 27 million tons, and the yield per hectare slumped from 7.08 centners to 4.8.[5]

Under the New Economic Policy (1921–1927), the government kept its control over large-scale industry, transportation, banking, and foreign trade, but many other sectors of economic activity were reopened for private enterprisers. Markets were restored, and money and prices were used again. In this period there was some revival in Russian agriculture. However, there were restrictions on the right of peasants to sell their produce on the market, on the size of peasant landholdings, and on the right of peasants to rent land or hire help. The government required large compulsory deliveries of farm produce at low prices. With manufactured goods scarce and high-priced, it was difficult to stimulate agricultural production greatly.

The Collectivization of Russian Agriculture. In spite of unfavorable conditions existing at the time, the first Five-Year Plan of the U.S.S.R. (1928–1932) called for the rapid development of agricultural production. On the other hand, it was intended to go slow in the matter of

[5] N. de Basily, *Russia under Soviet Rule* (London: George Allen & Unwin, Ltd., 1938), p. 255. One hectare equals 2.47 acres, and one centner contains 220.46 pounds.

socializing agriculture. The plan called for at least 75 per cent of the marketable farm produce to come from the privately owned sector of agriculture even at the end of the five-year period.

However, agricultural conditions remained unfavorable. The total amount of land under cultivation and the size of the leading food and technical crops remained below the 1913 level. Little progress was made in livestock raising, and there was no grain for export in 1928. The harvest in 1929 was poor again, but the government nevertheless undertook to seize about 14 million tons of grain. Peasant resistance was strong. Crops were left to rot in the fields, or were burned or hidden from the collectors after the harvest. As a result, the Communist leaders decided to bring agriculture under collectivization much more rapidly than had been planned originally.

In 1930 some 25,000 Communists were sent out into the country with absolute powers to bring about collectivization, and the "liquidation of the kulaks" followed. Thousands of resisting peasants were shot, and millions of others (some say four or five million) were evicted from their homes and lands. Their possessions were seized, even their warm clothing was taken away, and they were loaded into unheated cattle cars for transportation to Siberia, where they died like flies from cold, hunger, and exhausting labor. Sometimes only the men were taken, and the women and children were left at home to starve. Nor was the liquidation limited to the really prosperous peasants. Where no kulaks existed, some were invented. Anyone a little better off than his neighbors was likely to become a kulak in the eyes of the Communists.

The remaining peasants were forced to form collective farms and were to pool their productive instruments and livestock. But they regarded this pooling as expropriation, and many peasants killed their livestock or sold it and hid the money. Since they were required to deliver their surplus agricultural produce to the government, the newly created collective farmers decided in many cases to raise only enough produce for themselves. However, the government took its compulsory deliveries anyhow, and the farmers were left to starve on the remainder of the crops. Some estimates indicate that from 5 to 10 million persons perished from starvation during the famine conditions of 1931 and 1932.[6]

Nevertheless, collectivization went forward rapidly. By the end of 1931 some 60 per cent of the peasants' landholdings had been collectivized, and about 78 per cent of the cutivated area was collectivized by the end of the five-year period. As Table 18-1 shows, a complete reorganization of Soviet agriculture had occurred before World War II broke out.

[6] Freda Utley, *The Dream We Lost* (New York: The John Day Company, Inc., 1940), p. 55.

Table 18-1. Distribution of Cultivated Land in Soviet Russia, 1928 and 1939

Type of user	1928		1939	
	Hectares (000,000 omitted)	Percentage of total	Hectares (000,000 omitted)	Percentage of total
State farms.........	1.7	1.5	12.4	9.1
Collective farms....	2.6	2.2	117.2	85.6
Individual peasants.	108.7	96.3	0.9	0.6
Other users*........	.....	.....	6.4	4.7
Total...........	113.0	100.0	136.9	100.0

* Other users were employees in other industries and the individual collective farmers, who were allowed to cultivate small amounts of land for themselves.
SOURCE: U.S. Bureau of Foreign and Domestic Commerce, *Russian Economic Notes*, no. 21, pp. 1–5; A. Baykov, *The Development of the Soviet Economic System* (New York: The Macmillan Company, 1947), p. 327.

The State Farms. In examining the resulting organization of Soviet Russian agriculture, we turn first to the state farms. By the late 1930s there were about 4,000 of these farms. Their average size was about 3,000 hectares, or 7,410 acres. Most of the state farms were specialized agricultural units and produced grain, cattle, pigs, sugar beets, cotton, or other individual products. The state farms raising particular products were combined in trusts, and these were in turn responsible to the Ministry of State Farms, a department of the federal government.

The internal organization of the state farms was simple. All the land, buildings, machinery, and productive equipment was owned by the government, and the farms were managed by government-appointed directors. The employees of the state farms were wageworkers, who had no direct interest in the success of the enterprises and no claim on the products of the farms. The workers and their families had the use of various common facilities on the farms, and they could own small numbers of domestic animals but no draft animals.

The state farms were intended to increase agricultural production by enlarging the land area under cultivation, by using efficient methods, and by serving as experimental stations to set an example for the other agricultural enterprises of the country. The Soviet leaders invested large sums in the state farms, and they became mechanized to a much greater extent than the collective farms. They received the best types of equipment and were the first to be given selected seeds and artificial fertilizers. With these advantages, the state farms achieved considerable increases in total physical output, in value of product, and in output per workday or work-hour.

On the whole, however, the state farms were none too successful as a part of the Soviet program for increasing agricultural efficiency and productivity. They operated at a loss year after year, in the sense that they exceeded budget estimates of cost while actual income fell short of budget figures. They cultivated only a small fraction of their total area of 84.2 million hectares. They were badly managed both because of slackness or dishonesty of the management and because many of the farms were too large to be effectively managed by anyone.

Labor and management turnover was great, personnel costs were high, and livestock mortality was excessive. Far too great a proportion of their produce was consumed on the farms, so that relatively little was available for the market, and there was much theft and waste in production. As a result of these difficulties, some state farms were liquidated by 1937, the size of the individual survivors was reduced, and both the total land at their disposal and the cultivated area declined. After these changes the state farms functioned more satisfactorily, but the collective farms seemed destined to remain for a long time as the mainstay of Soviet Russian agriculture.

The Organization of the Collective Farms. In the late 1930s there were about 250,000 collective farms and their average size was around 469 hectares, or 1,160 acres. They included 93.5 per cent of all the peasant households in the country and averaged about 75 households per farm. Membership in the collective farms was open to all citizens sixteen years of age or over.[7]

The land used by the collective farms was publicly owned, but the collective farmers were granted "perpetual use" of their land. There was cooperative property in the common farm buildings, draft animals, some livestock, tools and implements of production, and stocks of seed. The individual collective farmers were allowed to use small plots of land for their own purposes. They could own homes and small quantities of livestock.

The heavy farm machinery (tractors, trucks, combines, harvesters) were owned and made available by separate government-owned agencies known as Machine Tractor Stations. There were only 158 of these stations in 1930, but their number grew to 6,980 by 1940.[8] The collective farms were required to make use of these stations and their services, if available, and make payments in cash or kind. The collective farmers were real farmers and not government employees. Their incomes depended directly upon the crops which they produced.

The Disposal of Collective Farm Output. However, there was many a slip between the production of a crop and the receipt of income by the individual collective farmers. In the first place, a part of the crop,

[7] M. T. Florinsky, *Toward an Understanding of the U.S.S.R.* (New York: The Macmillan Company, 1939), p. 205.
[8] Baykov, *op. cit.*, p. 331.

known as the "compulsory delivery," had to be sold to the government at a price which was set far below the market value of the product. The compulsory deliveries were large, applied to all sorts of produce raised on the collective farms, and even hit the farm products which the individual farmers raised on their own small plots.

After the compulsory deliveries had been made, it was necessary to pay the Machine Tractor Stations for services rendered and to make payments to the government on account of the interest or principal of loans received in the past from government agencies. In the case of some crops, the government had to be paid for processing a part of the produce for consumption on the farm. After all these deductions had been made, the collective farms were required by law to put aside seeds for the current year, seed reserves, fodder, and funds for mutual aid, relief in emergencies, and insurance. In the end, the amount of the gross harvest available as income to the individual collective farmers was estimated to run not over 35 to 39 per cent.[9]

The net amount of the harvest available to the collective farmers was also sold to the government in the case of the technical crops (cotton, flax, and sugar beets). In the case of other products, the collective farmers had a choice of selling the remainder of the harvest to the government or of selling it on the open market. Sales to the government were called "voluntary deliveries." They brought higher prices than the compulsory deliveries and might also entitle the farmers to purchase scarce consumers' goods which were seldom available in the regular stores.

The alternative to voluntary delivery was the sale of the net produce on collective-farm peasant markets. These were merely open spaces with tables or booths, which were hired by the farmers. The produce sold came only from the immediate local areas, but the farmers sometimes obtained a fourth of their money income from sales in these markets. Only private individuals could buy the goods. The prices received by the farmers approximated those charged in the government stores, but were well above those for compulsory or voluntary deliveries.

Accomplishments under Collective Farming. The collective farms contributed considerably to the solution of the problem of efficiency and productivity in Soviet agriculture. In a few years the former system of peasant farming was replaced by one of collective farming, which furnished the large-scale farms necessary for the use of farm machinery, fertilizers, and modern methods. And Soviet agriculture under collective farming was mechanized at a rapid rate. In 1927 Russia had about 25,000 tractors, all of foreign origin, but the number had grown to 547,000 by 1940, and they had been made in Russia. In 1927 there had been virtually no combines in Russian agriculture, but 182,000 were in

[9] *Ibid.*, p. 311.

use by 1940. The land cultivated by the Machine Tractor Stations increased from 1,200,000 hectares in 1930 to 66,000,000 in 1938.[10]

However, these results were achieved at great cost. The process of collectivization was brutal and costly in terms of human life and suffering. The actual productive results of collectivized agriculture fell far short of expectations for a number of years. Tractors, combines, and other agricultural machines increased in numbers in amazing fashion, but quantity figures tell us nothing about the quality of the machines or their tendency to break down, the cost at which the machines were produced, or the availability of fuel, repair parts, machine operators, mechanics, and repair men. Indeed, it has been stated that the increase in the number of tractors under the first Five-Year Plan, especially in view of great inexperience in their use, did not make up for the losses in draft animals.[11]

In the later years of the period from 1928 through 1940, collective agriculture began to show some of the productive results which had been expected of it, but the results were disastrous under the first Five-Year Plan, as shown by Table 18-2. Grain and flax production were smaller

Table 18.2. Results of Soviet Russian Agricultural Operations in 1932, 1937, and 1940 in Comparison with Planned Estimates for 1932, 1937, and 1942

Commodity	1913	1928	1932 Actual	1932 Planned	1937 Actual	1937 Planned	1940 Actual	1942 Planned
Land under cultivation, million hectares	105.0	113.0	134.4	141.3	135.3	139.7	151.0	157.0
Grains, total production, million metric quintals	801.0	733.0	699.0	1,058.0	1,203.0	1,048.0	1,190.0	1,300.0
Cotton, total production, million metric quintals	6.8	8.2	12.7	19.1	25.8	21.2	25.2	32.9
Flax, total production, million metric quintals	5.1	3.2	5.0	6.2	5.7	8.0	6.7	8.5
Sugar beets, total production, million metric quintals	99.2	101.4	65.6	195.5	218.6	276.0	222.0	282.0
Horses on hand, million head	35.8*	33.5	19.6	36.9	16.7	21.8	20.5	21.9
Cattle on hand, million head	60.6*	70.5	40.7	80.9	57.0	65.5	56.0	79.8
Sheep and goats on hand, million head	121.2*	146.7	52.1	160.9	81.3	96.0	93.0	170.7
Pigs on hand, million head	20.9*	26.0	11.6	34.8	22.8	43.4	28.0	45.6

* 1916 result.

in 1928 than in 1913, while the sugar-beet crop was about the same size as in 1913, and there were considerable declines in grain and sugar-beet production from 1928 to 1932. The total land under cultivation increased

[10] A. Yugow, *Russia's Economic Front for War and Peace* (New York: Harper & Brothers, 1942), pp. 54–55.

[11] Baykov, *op. cit.*, p. 202.

by about 19 per cent from 1928 to 1932, but the production of all the leading crops in 1932 was far short of planned estimates. Actual production as a percentage of planned production was 66 for grains, 66 for cotton, 81 for flax, and 39 for sugar beets.

Production of the leading crops increased considerably during the second Five-Year Plan. Production in 1937 was far above the 1932 level in all cases, and that of cotton and grains exceeded the planned estimates. However, the 1937 results may be discounted in several ways. For one thing, 1937 was one of the most favorable years for agricultural crops in Russian history. It is uncertain how much credit for the large crops should be given to ideal growing conditions and how much to improvement in agricultural organization, methods, and efforts.

Again, statistics for Russian crops since 1933 have been given in terms of "biological yield" rather than actual yield. The biological yield is the estimated amount of a crop standing in the fields minus a small arbitrary deduction for loss in harvesting. If, as is sometimes claimed, the actual loss in harvesting runs far greater than the arbitrary deduction, then the biological yield overstates the actual yield.

Finally, a large part of the increases in crop yields seemed to be due to increases in the quantity of land under cultivation rather than to increases in the yield per hectare of land. Under modern mechanized methods, greatly increased yields per unit of land would be expected, but the actual yields per hectare for some important crops were smaller in 1937 than in 1913. Production of leading crops in 1940 was greater in some cases and smaller in others than in 1937, but in all cases much further progress would have been required, if war had not intervened, in order to reach the planned goals for 1942.

The results of livestock production were most unsatisfactory under the first Five-Year Plan. The total number of livestock considered in Table 18-2 dropped about 55 per cent, although the plans called for an increase of over 13 per cent. The quantity of livestock on hand in 1932 as a percentage of planned estimates was 53 for horses, 50 for cattle, 32 for sheep and goats, and 33 for pigs. After 1932 livestock production made progress, but in 1940 the quantity of livestock on hand was below both the 1928 and 1916 levels for three of the four important categories.

Criticisms of the Collective Farms. The organization and operation of the collective farms were open to several criticisms. After 1934 the individual collective farmers had the right to small homesteads of their own, varying in size from $\frac{1}{4}$ to 1 hectare, on which they could raise crops and livestock. By 1938 the individual homesteads were said to account for almost half of the pigs, cattle, sheep, and goats on hand and for 21.5 per cent of gross agricultural production.[12] Such results seemed incredible in

[12] *Ibid.*, p. 327.

view of the fact that the cultivated land in the individual homesteads amounted officially to only 3.9 per cent of the total cultivated area.

The true explanation was that the managers of the collective farms, under great pressure to fulfill the plans and in despair over the prospect of increasing collective production, had been illegally turning over large quantities of collective land to individual members for private cultivation. The Soviet leaders knew of this development, of course, and by 1939 deemed the position of agriculture strong enough for the rules to be enforced. By a famous decree of May, 1939, new limitations were placed on the size of homesteads held by individual collective farmers, on the amounts of livestock they could own, and on their rights to fodder and pasture. A special corps of inspectors was set up to see that collective land was not improperly turned over to individual collective farmers, and each collective farmer was henceforth required to spend at least eighty days a year working on the collective land, or face expulsion. If the collective farmers formerly spent fewer than eighty days a year on the collective land, they either did not work very hard or were giving a lot of time to private farming.

Administration of the collective farms tended to be high-handed and arbitrary. The leading officials usually turned out to be Communists. Government decrees affecting the collective farms were binding on all the farmers and were placed in effect without any preliminary discussion by the farmers. Collective-farm members were often ejected without adequate reason and without the necessary two-thirds vote of the members. Too much income was sometimes devoted to the construction of community buildings and to the expenses of administration and production. Officials of collective farms were drawing up budgets without consulting members or were disregarding budgets that had been approved.

The system of distributing income on the basis of labor-days was complicated, cumbersome, and difficult to apply in agriculture. Since the farmers were paid on the basis of labor-days worked, some were sorely tempted just to put in their time, for they would get paid as much as those who put forth greater efforts. Moreover, it was alleged that the labor days credited to the individual collective farmers were more likely to depend on the good will or ill will of the farm officials than on anything else.

The Russian leaders had a difficult problem in furnishing the collective farmers with incentives to efficiency. Severe penalties were provided for the recalcitrant farmers. Reprimands, fines, demotions, suspensions, and expulsions were provided for laxity, negligence, or refusal to work. If the farmers' sins involved "counterrevolutionary activities" or "crimes against socialist property," long imprisonment or even death might result. A decree of 1940, which based compulsory deliveries of farm produce on the total areas of collective farms and thus gave the farmers reason to expand output and bring unused land under cultivation, was an attempt to deal with the problem of incentives. The same was true of the 1940 decree, which set up premiums and bonuses for improvements in the quantity or quality of farm production made by individual collective farmers or others.

THE COORDINATION OF SOVIET AGRICULTURE

The Control of State Farms. Mere increases in efficiency and productivity would not have been enough in any case to make agriculture a successful part of the planned economy. It was also necessary for the operations of agriculture to be coordinated with those of the rest of the economy, and in particular for agricultural enterprises to set out to produce the kinds and quantities of food and material called for by the economic plans. This problem was easily handled in the case of the state farms.

State farms were owned and operated directly by the government, and the people who did the work were merely hired employees who had nothing to say about matters of policy. Thus there could be no doubt that the state farms would set out to do the things desired by the government, although their efficiency in carrying out the projects was something else again.

The Control of Collective Farms. The collective farms were not owned and operated by the government, and the problem of coordination and control was more difficult. However, adequate solutions were found. By applying discriminatory compulsory deliveries to various crops or by varying the prices at which the compulsory deliveries were taken, the government could encourage the production of some crops and discourage that of others. The government could refuse the services of Machine Tractor Stations to collective farms that raised the "wrong" crops, or it could make higher charges for the services of these stations.

The government could refuse loans or charge high interest rates to farms which wandered from the path of rectitude. It could alter the prices at which voluntary deliveries would be taken and could control the prices which prevailed on farm products. It could vary the kinds, qualities, quantities, and prices of consumers' goods available for farmers in the retail stores of the rural areas. Surely, if the Russian farmers retained any economic motivation, the government could influence the projects which they would undertake.

The collective farmers were also subject to direct political control. The government issued laws and decrees, supported by heavy penalties, which were binding on all collective farmers. Moreover, each Machine

Tractor Station had two staffs that assisted the director. One was composed of engineers, mechanics, and agronomists, whereas the other was a policy section of the Communist party and was responsible for the political education of the farmers and the liquidation of enemies of the regime. The policy section tried to see that everyone did his duty. It directed grain and other deliveries to the government, summed up accomplishments and failures, analyzed problems, and gave instructions for future production to the farmers.

With this combination of political and economic controls, there was little doubt that the government could control the kinds and quantities of economic goods which the collective farmers would set out to produce. The problem of coordination was handled much more successfully than the other problems of agriculture that the planners faced. However, the efficiency with which the collective farmers would carry out the projects undertaken was another matter.

THE ECONOMIC STATUS OF THE FARMERS

The Unfavorable Price Situation. It is not difficult to find unfavorable factors in the economic situation of the collective farmers. In the matter of prices, it is said that, even during the famine of 1932, the price of grain was only 75 per cent higher than in 1913, although the prices of manufactured goods were about five times higher. In the next few years agricultural prices went up by 25 to 50 per cent, but those of manufactured goods rose several hundred per cent.[13] In 1936 one pood of rye flour (36.11 pounds) would purchase 0.5 kilogram of sugar, 1.3 kilograms of soap, 0.5 meter of cotton print, 4.2 liters of kerosene, or 0.0125 pair of leather boots. In 1913 the same quantity of rye flour would have exchanged for 4.1 kilograms of sugar, 3.3 kilograms of soap, 6.4 meters of cotton print, 27 liters of kerosene, or 0.143 pair of leather boots.[14] Apparently the scissors problem was a serious one for the Soviet farmers.

The Unfavorable Income Situation. The collective farmers received an average money income of not over 350 rubles in 1935, whereas the average wage in industry was 2,270 rubles.[15] By 1939 the average money income of collective farmers had increased to 982 rubles, but the average wage in industry had passed 3,500 rubles.[16] Moreover, there were great variations in income from one collective farm to another. There were 610 collective farms with a money income of more than a million rubles each in 1937, whereas the average farm had a money income of only 60,000

[13] Utley, *op. cit.*, pp. 150–151.
[14] L. E. Hubbard, *Soviet Trade and Distribution* (New York: St. Martin's Press, Inc., 1938), p. 290.
[15] *Ibid.*, p. 298.
[16] Yugow, *op. cit.*, p. 68.

rubles and some of the poorer farms only 1,000 to 5,000 rubles.[17] Since the prosperous farms were only a fraction of 1 per cent of the total and their large incomes raised the average of all collective farms, it follows that most collective farmers were not as well off as the figures for average income indicated.

The manufactured goods allotted to the stores in the rural areas made up only 35 per cent, by value, of all industrial goods distributed through retail trade, although the rural population was between two and three times as large as the rest of the population.[18] Clearly, the farmers received much less than their proportionate share of these products, even though they may have done some purchasing in urban stores. On the other hand, the farmers apparently had smaller quantities of their own produce to enjoy than they had before the revolution. In 1938, for example, 40 per cent of the total grain crop was said to have reached the market, compared with 26 per cent in czarist times, although the crop of 1938 was only slightly larger than that of 1913.[19]

AGRICULTURE DURING WORLD WAR II

Wartime Losses. Soviet Russian agriculture suffered severe losses during World War II. The area occupied by the Germans accounted for over 40 per cent of the sown area of the country and had formerly produced 45 per cent of the wheat, 41 per cent of the rye, 45 per cent of the cattle, and large amounts of sugar beets, flax, hogs, and other farm products. Some 98,000 collective farms, 1,876 state farms, and 2,890 Machine Tractor Stations were ruined.[20] Other losses included 137,000 tractors, 49,000 combines, 4 million plows and harrows, over a million seeders and threshers, 7 million horses, 17 million cattle, 20 million hogs, 27 million sheep and goats, and 110 million poultry.[21]

Wartime Production. In spite of all efforts to overcome the losses, Soviet Russian agricultural production was at low ebb during the war. Most of the able-bodied farm workers were in the armed forces, and the army had taken large numbers of horses and tractors. The remaining machinery deteriorated rapidly, for it was used excessively by relatively unskilled workers who lacked mechanical knowledge and repair parts. Cultivation was poor and the fields became choked with weeds. Another obstacle was the almost complete lack of artificial fertilizers and insecticides. As a result, although it was about the best crop year since be-

[17] *Ibid.*, p. 67.

[18] Hubbard, *op. cit.*, pp. 289–290.

[19] Utley, *op. cit.*, p. 152.

[20] Harry Schwartz, *Russia's Postwar Economy* (Syracuse, N.Y.: Syracuse University Press, 1947), pp. 7, 16; E. Snow, *People on Our Side* (New York: Random House, Inc.), 1944, pp. 69–70; M. Dobb, *Soviet Planning and Labor in Peace and War* (New York: International Publishers Co., Inc., 1943), pp. 101–102.

[21] *International Conciliation*, April, 1948, p. 265.

fore the war, agricultural production in 1945 was only about half that of 1940.[22]

AGRICULTURE IN THE POSTWAR PERIOD

Productive Results. Table 18-3 shows that the results planned for Soviet agriculture in 1950 under the fourth Five-Year Plan (1946–1950) were generally above those actually achieved in 1940 but uniformly below those which had previously been planned for 1942. The actual results in 1950 were in most cases above those of 1940 but in practically all cases fell short of the planned goals for 1950.

Table 18-3. Results of Soviet Russian Agricultural Operations in 1940, 1945, and 1950 in Comparison with Planned Estimates for 1942, 1950, and 1955

Commodity	1940 Actual	1942 Planned	1945 Actual	1950 Actual	1950 Planned	1955 Planned
Grains, total production, million metric tons..........	118.8	130.0	66.5	125.2	127.0	180.0
Cotton, total production, million metric tons..........	2.7	3.3	1.2	3.8	3.1	6.0
Sugar beets, total production, million metric tons........	21.0	28.2	8.9	23.5	26.0	39.5
Sunflower seed, total production, million metric tons...	3.3	4.0	1.8	3.1	3.7	
Horses on hand, million head.	20.5	21.9	10.5	13.7	15.3	15.2
Cattle on hand, million head..	56.0	79.8	46.9	57.2	65.3	68.0
Sheep and goats on hand, million head................	93.0	170.7	69.4	99.0	121.5	159.5
Pigs on hand, million head...	28.0	45.6	10.4	24.1	31.2	35.5

Productive results since 1950 have continued to fall far short of the optimistic goals which were set up for 1955 under the fifth Five-Year Plan. The grain crop in 1954 fell somewhat below 130 million tons. The livestock on hand included 64.9 million cattle, 31.0 million pigs, and 138.4 million sheep and goats.[23] These results were approximately those planned for 1950. Thus, while Soviet Russian agriculture has recovered considerably from the low levels of 1945, its recovery has not nearly reached the expectations of the economic planners. Moreover, increases in output have often been achieved in ways which do not promise well for the future. The increased production of grains, for example, has been almost entirely the result of bringing more land under cultivation. The average yield has remained low and remarkably stable at about 12 hundredweight per hectare.

[22] Schwartz, *op. cit.*, p. 54.
[23] *The Economist*, Feb. 19, 1955, p. 635.

Agricultural Reorganization. The postwar results of agricultural operations have not been pleasing to the Soviet Russian leaders, and drastic
steps have been taken to remedy the situation. For one thing, there have
been changes in agricultural organization. The number of state farms has
been increased to 5,000 and their average cultivated acreage to 6,000.
The number of collective farms has been reduced by amalgamation from
254,000 in early 1950 to 93,000 in 1953, and their average size has been
expanded greatly. The 9,000 Machine Tractor Stations have been
strengthened. Tractor and combine drivers and mechanics are to become
permanent employees with larger salaries and plots of land for their
own use.[24]

Increased Incentives for Farmers. An attempt has been made to stimulate agricultural production by providing increased economic incentives
for farmers. The cultivation of private plots has been encouraged by
lowering taxes, canceling debts, reducing compulsory deliveries, and
raising prices. In collective farming proper, compulsory deliveries have
been reduced and prices raised. The system for remunerating individual
collective farmers has been changed. Farmers who obtain high yields
will receive more income per labor-day than those who are less successful.

The pay of tractor and machine operators has been arranged to vary
according to the success with which planned yields are obtained on the
farms they serve. Technical personnel working directly in the fields with
the farmers have been given a 25 per cent wage differential over technicians functioning in an administrative capacity. Medals and honors
have been provided for farmers who distinguish themselves in acreage
farmed and yields obtained, and socialist competition between farmers
is encouraged. Agricultural planning has been decentralized to some
extent.

Other Measures. New chairmen, recruited from Party cadres and the
ranks of agricultural experts, have been provided for the 93,000 collective
farms. The government has arranged to send 100,000 additional agricultural specialists and mechanics to the rural areas. Formerly only
68,500 out of 350,000 were actually in the country. About a million members of the Communist party are now functioning in rural areas, and the
number of rural centers of the Party has been increased from 12,000
before the war to 76,000 in 1953.[25]

A new official has been installed at each Machine Tractor Station—
Vice-Director of the Political Section—whose duty is to see to it that the
workers at the stations and on the farms do their work properly and according to plan. There has been a great turnover in high administrative
positions relating to agriculture. The government has inaugurated a ten-

[24] *Ibid.*, Sept. 19, 1953, pp. 790–791.
[25] *The Economist*, Sept. 19, 1953, pp. 790–791, and Oct. 17, 1953, p. 167.

year fertilizer plan for increasing agricultural production. It has also undertaken to provide the farmers with 500,000 additional tractors between 1954 and 1957.

Finally, the Council for Collective Farm Affairs has been created. It is headed by a high government official and includes other government representatives and a few chairmen of collective farms. The council is an enforcement agency for legislation and decrees affecting collective farms and will see that penalties are imposed on violators. It hears complaints from members and officials of collective farms and takes action on them. It recommends legislation to improve the operation of collective farms and may have representatives in all major government subdivisions of the country to facilitate the performance of its duties.

These measures may eventually bring the results of Soviet agricultural operations to the desired levels, or they may not. For the present they indicate clearly that large further improvements in agricultural efficiency and productivity are needed and that the Soviet Russian leaders are still greatly concerned about the functioning of the agricultural section of the economy.

QUESTIONS FOR STUDY

1. The abolition of serfdom was not an unmitigated blessing to the former serfs. Why was this true? What reforms were attempted to better their position? What were the results?

2. Why was Russian agriculture so inefficient and unproductive prior to the Revolution of 1917? Why was it difficult for the leaders of Soviet Russia to know what to do about the problem of efficiency and productivity in agriculture? What were the other major agricultural problems with which the planners had to deal?

3. Contrast the state farms and collective farms as types of agricultural organization. Which has accomplished more toward the solution of the problem of efficiency and productivity? Why?

4. Are the collective farms in Soviet Russia really cooperative enterprises? Why? How are they coordinated with the economic plans for the economy as a whole?

5. What were the major accomplishments of Soviet Russian agriculture in the period before World War II? Were they as great as had been expected? Why? What were the leading difficulties in Soviet Russian agriculture?

6. Which problem of agriculture has been handled least successfully in the Soviet Russian planned economy to date? Why? Could it have been handled more satisfactorily under some other regime?

7. To what extent was Soviet Russian agriculture damaged during World War II? How was production affected? Has agriculture operated more or less satisfactorily since the war than before? What has Soviet Russia been doing about the agricultural problem since the war?

CHAPTER 19

TRANSPORTATION

Soviet Russia is a land of magnificent distances. It occupies one-sixth of the world's land surface and has an area roughly three times that of the United States. The development of a well-integrated modern economy in such an area requires a large-scale and efficient system of transportation. The growth of geographical specialization, division of labor, and large-scale production brings many advantages, but it is limited by the size of the market for products. The extent of the market is, in turn, dependent upon the adequacy of the means of transportation. In Russia the fact that natural resources, industrial centers, and principal areas of consumption are often widely separated makes transportation especially important.

In pre-Soviet days the Russian transportation system was backward and primitive. Years ago a writer could say that transportation depended upon dogs and reindeer in a third of the vast expanse of czarist Russia, on camels in a sixth of the country, on horses and oxen in half of the country, and on mules, asses, and buffaloes in some southern areas.[1] Railroad mileage was limited, roads were mere tracks across the country, and the rivers, while used extensively in the warm season, were put out of commission by nature during several months of the year. Progress in the means of transportation was made in czarist Russia, but continued to leave much to be desired.

THE DEVELOPMENT OF TRANSPORTATION TO 1917

Early Railroad Development. Russia got an early start in the construction of railroads. The first railroad, a 16-mile line from St. Petersburg (Leningrad) to Pavlovsk, was finished in 1838. This was only thirteen years after the world's first railroad was built in England, and eleven years after the first railroad was built in the United States. Russia's second railroad, the 200-mile Warsaw-Vienna line, began to

[1] Quoted in E. J. Simmons (ed.), *U.S.S.R.: A Concise Handbook* (Ithaca, N.Y.: Cornell University Press, 1947), p. 276.

284

operate in 1848. The important line between St. Petersburg and Moscow was opened in 1851. In the next few decades the railroad system leading out of Moscow expanded to Gorki, to Kursk, and into the Ukraine. A through line was placed in operation between Odessa, on the Black Sea, and the Baltic Ocean.

Government Ownership and Operation. On the whole, however, railroad construction in Russia did not go forward rapidly, and Russia lagged far behind the United States. The first transcontinental line in the United States, the Union Pacific, began to operate in 1869, but its counterpart in Russia, the Trans-Siberian Railroad, was not finished until more than thirty years later. Once completed, the Trans-Siberian became the longest railroad in the world. Between Leningrad and Vladivostok it covered a distance of 5,435 miles, or about 1.75 times the distance between New York and San Francisco.

The Russo-Turkish War of 1877–1878 revealed the inadequacy of the Russian railroads and means of transportation in general, and the Russian government apparently came to take a dim view of the prospects for an adequate development of the railroads under private auspices. At any rate, the government acquired and operated many railroads after 1880 and was responsible for much of the construction of new lines. From 1881 to 1913 new railroads were built at the rate of 881 miles per year on the average, and the most rapid railroad construction under the czars, 1,787 miles per year on the average, occurred between 1893 and 1902. The government had spent over two billion rubles by 1913 in purchasing old lines and constructing new ones, and two-thirds of the railroads were government-owned.[2]

Thus railroad development in Russia was quite different from that in the United States, where railroads were built and grew large under private ownership and operation, though with considerable assistance from the government. They engaged in destructive competition, formed combinations, and developed abuses which led to their regulation by the Federal government beginning in 1887. Thus the railroads of the United States entered a long period of private ownership and operation under government regulation and control. In Russia, government ownership and operation began at an early date, and a large part of the railroad system was under government ownership even before the Revolution of 1917.

The Railroad System in World War I. The Russian railroad system had a total of 43,798 miles of track in 1913, compared with 240,293 miles owned by railroads in the United States in 1910.[3] The Russian railroads

---

[2] *Ibid.*, p. 270.
[3] *Ibid.; The Economic Almanac for 1949* (New York: National Industrial Conference Board, Inc., 1948), p. 290.

carried about 41 billion ton-miles of freight in 1913, while the railroads of the United States averaged over 277 billion ton-miles from 1911 through 1915.[4] Since Russia was almost three times as large as the United States and had a much larger population, the inadequacy of her railroads is apparent. Moreover, her railroads were described as ribbons of rust, the cars as splintered matchboxes, and the locomotives as battered samovars.[5]

The Russian railroads had important implications in connection with national defense. Few railroads ran east and west across the western boundaries, and those would not have been useful to invading forces, for the Russian railroad tracks were laid 5 feet apart instead of the standard 4 feet 8½ inches. However, the Russian railroad system was also ineffective in supplying the Russian army on and beyond the western boundaries during World War I. The collapse of railroad transportation was a major factor leading to Russia's ignominious exit from the war. The railroads became clogged and swamped with goods and the Russian army was handicapped by lack of materials and supplies. In making peace after World War I, Russia lost territories that deprived her of about 7,500 miles of railroads and reduced her total mileage to around 36,300 miles.[6]

Early Development of Internal Waterways. Russia's major rivers were important as arteries of transportation, trade, and conquest for centuries before the construction of railroads began. The area controlled by the government at Moscow expanded south along the Volga in the sixteenth century, and later expeditions extended it along the Don and Dnepr. The conquest of Asia progressed along the east-west tributaries of the major Siberian rivers, such as the Ob, Yenesey, Lena, and Amur. In view of the difficulties which beset overland travel before the development of the railroads, it was not surprising that the use of the rivers for the transportation of heavy goods followed hard upon their use as avenues of conquest.

Unfortunately, the rivers of Russia were not well suited for transportation. The chief rivers, and especially those in Asia, run north and south, and their use is limited to the warm season. The north-flowing rivers of Siberia are frozen for seven or more months a year. In arid sections of the country, a number of rivers that are usually large become shallow streams in the late summer, and some dry up altogether. Moreover, the Russian rivers are not especially useful as feeders for ocean steamship lines. Most of them flow into the ice-bound Arctic Ocean or into inland

[4] George B. Cressey, *The Basis of Soviet Strength* (New York: McGraw-Hill Book Company, Inc., 1945), p. 134; *Statistical Abstract of the United States, 1948*, p. 530.
[5] *Communism in Action*, 79th Cong., 2d Sess., H. Doc. 754, Washington, Government Printing Office, 1946, p. 79.
[6] Simmons, *op. cit.*, p. 271.

seas, such as the Aral, Caspian, and Black Seas. Russia does not have a single large river which is navigable all through the year and also flows from the interior out into the open ocean.

Nevertheless, the Russian rivers were used extensively for transportation in prerevolutionary days. The rivers were available, and other satisfactory means of transportation were not. Methods of river transportation remained primitive, but about a third of Russia's total freight was carried by her waterways in 1913. A large number of passengers also traveled by river. Some of the more important waterways were connected by the construction of canals in the early 1800s and after. However, the building of canals in Russia in these early times did not develop to the same extent as in the United States.

Ocean Transportation. The boundaries of Russia extend over 40,000 miles, and about 30,000 miles lie on seas or oceans. It might have been expected that Russia would have developed a large volume of ocean traffic and a large merchant marine. Actually, however, a large part of the coastline borders on the icebound Arctic Ocean or on other partly icebound bodies of water. Until recent times, ships could not pass from European Russia to the areas on the Pacific by way of the northern route through the Arctic Ocean and the Bering Strait.

Russia also borders on the Caspian and Black Seas on the southwest. There has long been considerable traffic on these seas, but the Caspian Sea is landlocked, and the only exit from the Black Sea is through the Bosphorus and the Dardanelles to the Mediterranean, and thence to the Indian Ocean by way of the Suez Canal or to the Atlantic by way of Gibraltar. From Odessa on the Black Sea to Vladivostok in the far east, the ocean mileage is 13,264 by way of the Suez Canal and Indian Ocean and 14,177 miles by way of the Atlantic Ocean, Panama Canal, and Pacific Ocean. The distance is only 6,835 miles by using river and canal north to Murmansk and the Arctic Sea the rest of the way, but this route was not available in prerevolutionary days.[7] Under the circumstances, Russia's merchant marine and ocean freight did not develop greatly before 1917.

TRANSPORTATION, 1917–1940

Investment in Railroads. The collapse of the railroads near the end of World War I was intensified during the period of War Communism which followed. Under the New Economic Policy (1921–1927), attention had to be concentrated on the problem of bringing the railroads back to previous levels of operation, although some new construction was undertaken. The railroads came under severe pressure during the first Five-

[7] *Communism in Action*, p. 81.

Year Plan (1928–1932). The economy was being reconstructed, large plants were being built in new regions, new cities sprang up, and tremendous quantities of metal, building materials, and fuel required transportation. Industrialization made many people move from the country to the cities and from one part of the country to another, and millions of peasants moved about as a result of the collectivization program in agriculture.

The plan did not provide adequately for the restoration and expansion of the railroads. The fixed capital of the railroads was only 15 per cent greater in 1931 than in 1913, and the rolling stock had increased only slightly, but the ton-kilometers of freight requiring transportation had increased threefold.[8] Under the first Five-Year Plan, the railroads increased their main tracks only 7 per cent, while the volume of freight traffic increased 82 per cent and the passenger traffic more than tripled.[9] The railroads could not handle the increased traffic, industrial plants became clogged with goods awaiting transportation, and the fulfillment of plans for the economy was impeded.

Soviet Russia made a determined effort to reconstruct the railroad industry under the second Five-Year Plan. Greatly increased amounts of steel, labor, and other productive agents were allocated to the railroads. Some railroads were given heavier rails, more powerful locomotives, freight and passenger cars of increased capacity, and automatic signaling and coupling. Some trackage was electrified, some single-track railroads were double-tracked, and new plants for building cars and locomotives were started. Existing rolling stock was reconditioned, old bridges were strengthened and new ones were built, and tracks, ties, and embankments were repaired. Total new investment in the railroads amounted to 20.7 billion rubles out of 114.7 for the whole economy.[10]

The third Five-Year Plan (1938–1942) called for the speeding up of electrification, a large increase in rolling stock, improved railroad administration, and considerable building of new lines. The new railroads consisted largely of strategic lines leading to the western and far-eastern boundaries, second tracks for important single-track lines which were having difficulty in handling their traffic, and lines leading to new raw-material sources and industries, largely in Asia. The total investment in the railroads over the five-year period was to be 35,800,000,000 rubles.[11]

The Railroad Network. On the whole, there was considerable construction of new railroads under the Soviet regime between 1917 and

[8] A. Yugow, *Russia's Economic Front for War and Peace* (New York: Harper & Brothers, 1942), p. 26.
[9] Harry Schwartz, *Russia's Soviet Economy* (New York: Prentice-Hall, Inc., 1950), p. 337.
[10] Yugow, *op. cit.*, p. 29.
[11] *Ibid.*, pp. 29–30.

1940, and the total railroad mileage increased from 36,300 to 65,900, or by about 80 per cent. However, the concentration of railroads in the European section of Soviet Russia remained striking. Every place south of Leningrad and west of the Volga River was within 35 miles of a railroad. The only other area with many lines was in the central Ural Mountains, and only five railroads (to such areas as Turkey, Iran, Mongolia, and Manchuria) crossed the long southern frontier east of the Black Sea.

Most of the new construction had been in Asia, although a trunk line from Moscow to Rostov by way of the Donets coal fields and one from Kazan on the Volga to Sverdlovsk in the Urals were completed. The original line of the Trans-Siberian went east from Leningrad to Sverdlovsk and thence across Siberia, but the Soviets built a new line through Gorki and Kazan, which provided a shorter route by way of Chelyabinsk. The Trans-Siberian was also double-tracked over a sector of 1,865 miles. Other lines completed included the 896-mile Turkestan-Siberian (Turk-Sib) Railroad connecting the Trans-Siberian with Alma Ata in southern Kazakhstan and a 751-mile line from Petropavlovsk on the Trans-Siberian south to the Karaganda coal basin and the large copper plant at Lake Balkhash.

Two other spectacular lines were partly completed by 1940. One ran from Konosha via Kotlas to Vorkuta in the important Pechora coal fields in the extreme northern part of European Russia. The other was the Baikal-Amur line, which leaves the Trans-Siberian east of Krasnoyarsk and runs north of Lake Baikal and across the upper Lena valley. It was to extend eventually to Komsomolsk on the lower Amur River and thence to the Pacific at Sovetskaya Gavan. These various lines may be seen in Figure 5, which shows the railroad system in 1950.

The Railroad Situation prior to World War II. Soviet Russia's 65,900 miles of railroads in 1940, though only about one-fourth of the total operated in the United States, gave her second place in the world by a considerable margin. Moreover, the Russian railroads were carrying an amount of freight which hardly seemed possible on the basis of their mileage. While the railroad mileage was increasing by 80 per cent, the freight increased from 41 billion ton-miles in 1913 to about 258 billion in 1940, or about 530 per cent.[12] The Class I railroads of the United States carried over 333 billion ton-miles of revenue freight in 1939.[13] Passenger traffic in the U.S.S.R. was less important, but the number of passengers carried increased from 184.8 million in 1913 to 1,343 million in 1940.[14]

[12] Schwartz, *op. cit.*, pp. 332, 335.
[13] *The Economic Almanac for 1949*, p. 293.
[14] Schwartz, *op. cit.*, p. 343.

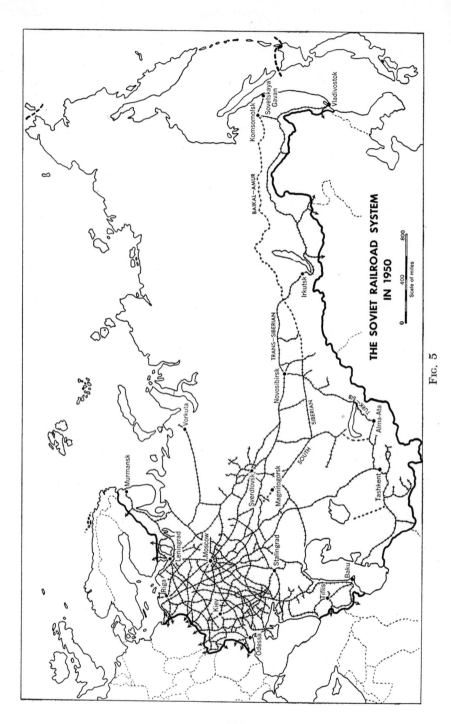

THE SOVIET RAILROAD SYSTEM
IN 1950

Scale of miles
0   400   800

Fig. 5

290

The Soviet Russian railroads were being used very intensively. The annual load per mile of railroad increased from 689,000 ton-miles in 1913 to 2,589,000 in 1937, and the freight being moved per mile of track in 1940 was more than twice the highest figure ever recorded in the United States. Average daily carloadings increased from 27,400 in 1913 to about 98,000 in 1940.[15] Heavy commodities such as coal and coke, oil, ore, and iron and steel made up over 45 per cent of the freight carried. In spite of inferior equipment and heavy loads, railroad freight in Soviet Russia moved only 2 miles per hour more slowly than in the United States. However, there were more than 1½ million persons working on the railroads of Soviet Russia in 1937, as compared with less than a million in the United States.[16]

Transportation on Inland Waterways. Soviet Russia in 1939 had 68,310 miles of inland waterways suitable for regular transportation and another 130,410 miles suitable for rafts and timber only.[17] Actually operating waterways totaled 65,600 miles in 1940.[18] The Volga River, because of its direction, depth, and economic environment, was the leading inland waterway and accounted for about half the freight carried on inland waterways. Baku oil, Donets coal, grain, salt, and fish were carried upstream, whereas much timber moved downstream. Another third of the freight moved on the rivers of the northern and northwestern areas of European Russia. The remainder was divided between the rivers of the southwest (Don, Dnepr, Kuban) and those of Siberia and central Asia (Ob, Irtysh, Lena, Amur).

Soviet Russia improved her system of inland waterways by constructing a number of canals in the period from 1917 to 1940. One of the best known was the Moscow-Volga Canal, which diverts water from the upper Volga River past the city of Moscow and makes it possible for boats drawing 8½ feet of water to pass between the capital city and the Caspian Sea. Another was the Baltic–White Sea Canal, which enables vessels of up to 1,250 tons to proceed from the Gulf of Finland to the White Sea by way of Lake Onega. The Volga-Don Canal was under construction, and its completion was to connect Moscow with the Black Sea.

The river-borne freight of Soviet Russia amounted to 66,600,000 tons in 1938, and an amazing total of 68,000,000 passengers, three times as many as in 1929, were carried on inland waterways.[19] The freight carried amounted to about 23 billion ton-miles.[20] However, traffic on inland

[15] Simmons, *op. cit.*, p. 273; Schwartz, *op. cit.*, p. 339.
[16] Yugow, *op. cit.*, p. 28.
[17] *Communism in Action*, p. 81.
[18] Schwartz, *op. cit.*, p. 334.
[19] Simmons, *op. cit.*, p. 278.
[20] Cressey, *op. cit.*, p. 136.

waterways had undergone a sharp relative decline. The freight carried
in 1938 was only about one-tenth of that carried by the railroads,
whereas in 1913 it had been about one-third.[21] Moreover, the freight
carried on inland waterways expanded only 26 per cent between 1913
and 1940, compared with an increase of 530 per cent for the railroads.[22]
Timber carried on rafts or barges made up over half the freight carried
on inland waterways in 1938. Minerals and construction materials each
accounted for an eighth of the total, while grain and coal were also important.

Ocean Transportation. The ocean transportation of Soviet Russia expanded rapidly between 1917 and 1940. One development in this field
was the opening of the northern sea route from Murmansk and Arch-
angel east to the Pacific area of Russia. In 1932 an icebreaker made the
voyage eastward and in 1934 another covered the same route in the
reverse direction. The route was "officially open" for commercial traffic
in 1939, when 104 vessels sailed over all or part of it, carrying over
100,000 tons of freight. The route was to be kept open by a fleet of 40
icebreakers, ranging in size up to 12,000 tons and assisted by some 50
polar weather stations and a number of airplanes looking for open
water.[23] However, the northern sea route was not actually in regular
operation prior to World War II.

The sea-borne freight carried by Soviet vessels amounted to 30.4 million tons in 1938. This represented an increase of about 350 per cent over
freight carried in 1929. The traffic for 1938 also amounted to about 24
billion ton-miles, or slightly more than the total for inland waterways. Some 3.1 million passengers were carried—an increase of 100 per
cent over 1929.[24] Most of the freight and passengers moved between
ports of the Soviet Union and not between Soviet Russia and other countries. The development of her ocean transportation prior to 1940 did not
make Soviet Russia a leader in this field. In 1939 her merchant fleet included 354 vessels of 1,135,800 gross tons. Some ten other countries exceeded these figures, and the United States had 1,379 vessels of 8,125,800
gross tons.[25]

Highway Transportation. Highway transportation developed slowly in
Soviet Russia before World War II. One reason was that Soviet Russia
did not have the highways. In the United States, surfaced highways increased from 250,000 to 1,596,000 miles between 1914 and 1941. In
Soviet Russia, surfaced highways increased only from 12,500 miles in
1914 to 64,200 in 1938, and only 2,400 miles were really "hard-surfaced."

[21] *Ibid.*
[22] Yugow, *op. cit.*, p. 25.
[23] Simmons, *op. cit.*, pp. 278–279.
[24] *Ibid.*, pp. 279–280.
[25] *The Economic Almanac for 1949*, p. 296.

The rest were surfaced only with gravel or cobblestone.[26] Most of the 840,000 miles of Soviet highways were dirt roads, deep in mud or dust in the summer and in frozen ruts in winter. Even where the attempt was made to build good roads, a shortage of crushed rock made it necessary to use sand or river gravel as foundation material.

There were no paved transcontinental highways in Soviet Russia, although plans were being discussed for building one to parallel the Trans-Siberian Railroad. Motor highways adequate for intercity trucking were developed from Moscow to Minsk, Leningrad, Yaroslavl, Gorki, and Tula, but in the Ural Mountains there were not over 100 miles of paved road outside the cities. In some areas of the country, where railroad service was poor, extensive highways had been built, but the total picture was rather depressing.

A second reason for the backwardness of highway transportation was that the country did not have and could not produce a large number of motor vehicles, as may be seen in Table 19-1. The motor vehicles on

Table 19-1. Motor-vehicle Production and Number on Hand in Soviet Russia and the United States, 1938

(In thousands)

Vehicle	Production		On Hand	
	Soviet Russia	United States	Soviet Russia	United States
Total...............	211.4	2,489	1,060	29,443
Trucks..............	184.4	488	800	4,276
Passenger cars........	27.0	2,001	260	25,167

SOURCE: *Communism in Action*, 79th Cong. 2d Sess. H. Doc. 754, 1946, p. 82; Harry Schwartz, *Russia's Soviet Economy* (New York: Prentice-Hall, Inc., 1950), p. 348; *Statistical Abstract of the United States, 1952*, p. 496.

hand in 1939 represented a great increase over 8,800 in 1913 and 18,700 in 1928, but the number was still small. Motor-vehicle production in 1938 was also far ahead of the 1,390 vehicles produced in 1929 but was a drop in the bucket in comparison with that of the United States. Clearly, Soviet Russia was far behind the pace in regard to production and stocks of motor vehicles. Trucks handled only 2 per cent of the Soviet freight traffic, in terms of ton-miles, just before World War II.

Air Transportation. Air transportation developed rapidly in Soviet Russia in the period before World War II. Civil airlines began to operate in 1922 with scheduled flights on 148 miles of airways. A few years later,

[26] Simmons, *op. cit.*, p. 275.

Soviet Russia set up its own aircraft industry and by 1932 produced its own airplanes and motors without help from other countries. By 1939 the network of airways covered about 87,500 miles.[27] All the major cities of Soviet Russia were connected by airlines, and several international airlines were operated.

Air transportation was very useful in Soviet Russia, for vast distances had to be covered and other forms of transportation were backward. It took about nine days by fastest train to go from Moscow to Vladivostok, but only two or three days by air. From Tiflis in Georgia to Moscow was only one day's flight, but it required three and a half days by rail. Planes required only three hours to fly between Khorog and Stalinabad in central Asia—a trip which used to take thirty days by road. Airplanes were used extensively for fighting farm and forest pests, for emergency ambulance service, for combatting malarial mosquitoes, and for geodetic surveying.

In 1938 Soviet Russian airlines carried over 300,000 passengers and some 19 million ton-miles of freight.[28] Airplane production in Soviet Russia was not disclosed in the prewar period, but during World War II Russia came to produce as many as 40,000 airplanes a year. The United States produced only 5,856 airplanes in 1939 but reached a peak of 96,318 during the war.[29]

TRANSPORTATION IN WORLD WAR II

Wartime Evacuation of Western Russia. If the Germans counted on a collapse of the Soviet Russian railroads in World War II, they were badly disappointed. The Russian railroads did a tremendous job in moving industrial and other machinery and equipment from the western part of the country to new locations in the Ural Mountains or in Siberia. New railroad records were set in the process. Average daily carloadings in the Ukraine increased from 30,000 in 1939 to 80,000 in August and September, 1941. Trainloads of 14,000 tons, the equivalent of a 350-car train, were hauled in some cases. Trainloads of 5,000 tons, or double the normal maximum, were carried rather commonly.[30] The successful evacuation of the west was important to Russia's ability to continue in the war, and much credit was due the railroads for their accomplishment.

Wartime Losses. However, the railroads of Soviet Russia suffered severe losses during the war. The facilities which were wholly or partly put out of commission included 34 railroad lines, over 40,000 miles of track, 13,000 railroad bridges, 4,100 stations, 317 locomotive depots, and

[27] Schwartz, *op. cit.*, p. 353.
[28] *Ibid.*
[29] *The Economic Almanac for 1949*, p. 308.
[30] Simmons, *op. cit.*, p. 273.

129 repair centers, in addition to thousands of locomotives and hundreds of thousands of freight cars.[31] The production of new locomotives declined 87 per cent and that of freight cars 49 per cent.[32] Even in the uninvaded sections of the country, the efficiency of the railroads declined, for shortages of manpower and equipment prevented adequate maintenance of rolling stock and roadbed. At one time, average daily carloadings fell off to less than half the 1940 level.

Railroad Rehabilitation. Soviet Russia did not wait until the end of the war to try to rehabilitate the railroad industry. Almost 7,000 miles of new track were laid during the war. Some lines connected European Russia with new industrial areas in Siberia and the Ural Mountains, while others were constructed in central Asia and other regions. As the western part of the country was reconquered, Soviet engineers and technicians were set to work restoring the railroads. By the end of the war, Soviet Russia had about 70,000 miles of railroad track in use, or somewhat more than at the beginning of the war, and thousands of bridges had been restored.[33]

However, much of the reconstruction was temporary and not adequate for normal peacetime use. The railroads which had continued in operation suffered from prolonged overloading and disrepair, and there was a serious shortage of locomotives and freight cars. Some help was obtained from lend-lease deliveries of 1,500 American locomotives, 540,-000 tons of rails, and numerous freight cars, car wheels, and axles.[34]

Inland Water Transportation. River and canal transportation in western Soviet Russia was disrupted by the advance of the German invaders across many important waterways and up to the Volga itself. Crippling damage was inflicted on canals, rivers, and docks, and many boats, barges, and rafts were destroyed. Water transportation continued in other parts of the country, and in some cases the volume of traffic increased. On the whole, however, transportation on inland waterways in the unoccupied sectors declined in efficiency as it became impossible to secure adequate labor, fuel, repair parts, and new equipment. The total volume of freight carried in 1945 was 11.5 billion ton-miles, or about half the prewar volume.[35]

Other Forms of Transportation. The story was much the same for other forms of transportation. In ocean transportation, many vessels were destroyed or seriously damaged, some important ports were occupied by the enemy and others were damaged by bombing, and docks, warehouses,

[31] Schwartz, *op. cit.*, p. 338.
[32] *Communism in Action*, p. 80.
[33] Schwartz, *op. cit.*, p. 338.
[34] Simmons, *op. cit.*, p. 272.
[35] Harry Schwartz, *Russia's Postwar Economy* (Syracuse, N.Y.: Syracuse University Press, 1947), p. 49.

and other harbor facilities were ruined. The highways were torn up during the war, and many trucks and other vehicles were destroyed. However, the Russians gained much experience in large-scale trucking operations, many drivers were trained, and many vehicles were eventually obtained by capture from the enemy and by lend-lease shipment from the United States. During the war, civil aviation had to take a back seat in favor of military aviation, and it also suffered severe losses from enemy action.

TRANSPORTATION IN THE POSTWAR PERIOD

Railroad Transportation. The fourth Five-Year Plan (1946–1950) proposed great achievements for all forms of transportation. The improvement of railroad transportation was allocated 40 billion rubles of centralized capital investment during the five-year period, or about one-sixth of the total. Some of the important planned results for 1950 are shown in Table 19-2, along with the actual results achieved in 1940 and 1950.

Table 19-2. Planned Results for Soviet Russian Railroads in 1950, and Actual Results for 1940 and 1950

Item	1940 Actual	1950	
		Planned	Actual
Total mileage, thousand miles.....................	65.9	76.6	74.5
Total freight traffic, billion ton-miles..............	257.7	330.4	373.4
Daily carloadings, thousand cars.................	97.9	115.0	118.5
Total passenger traffic, million passengers..........	1,343.5	1,350.0	1,400.0

SOURCE: Harry Schwartz, *Russia's Soviet Economy*, (New York: Prentice-Hall, Inc., 1950), pp. 338–339, 343; *U.S.S.R. Information Bulletin*, May 1, 1951, p.264.

The railroad mileage for 1950 was to result from the construction of 4,495 miles of new lines as well as from the restoration and repair of old lines. Some 3,300 miles were to be electrified. Much of the work of reconstruction was done in the western part of the country and featured the important lines connecting the coal mines of the Donets Basin and the Krivoi Rog iron and steel industry with the rest of the country. New construction was carried on primarily in the Ural Mountains and Siberia. Industrial production had increased greatly in those areas during the war and large further increases were planned for 1950, so that the old railroad lines would have been entirely inadequate.

The largest single project was the completion of the South Siberian Railroad—a 2,400-mile line from Kuibyshev on the Volga River through the southern Urals, northern Kazakhstan, and the Altai territory to Taishet on the Yenesey River. This line serves Magnitogorsk and the important industrial centers of the Kuznets Basin, thus furnishing relief for the old Trans-Siberian Railroad.

As Table 19-2 indicates, most of the plans for the railroads were fulfilled by 1950, even though total mileage fell a bit short. The Five-Year Plan also called for the production of 7,785 locomotives and 472,000 freight cars. As to how this plan came out, the Russians were willing to say only that stocks of locomotives and freight cars were considerably renewed and replenished during the period. The new locomotives were more powerful and the freight cars larger than the old models. The railroads also gained considerably from the seizure of freight cars and locomotives from the defeated enemies after the war.

The increase in locomotives and freight cars in use has been an important factor in the rapid increase in the volume of freight carried by the railroads since World War II. Another factor has been the severe discipline enforced on the railroad employees, who have operated under martial law since 1943. Moreover, all branches of the railroad industry have had special "political departments" for bombarding the workers with Communist propaganda and insisting upon strict labor discipline. Finally, increased loads per freight car and per freight train and an increased daily run per freight car have played a part.

Inland Water Transportation. The fourth Five-Year Plan called for the volume of railroad freight traffic to be about 28 per cent greater in 1950 than in 1940, but the freight carried by all forms of transportation was scheduled to be 36 per cent greater in 1950 than in 1940. This clearly meant that large-scale developments were under way for other forms of transportation. The freight carried on inland waterways was expected to reach 31 billion ton-miles in 1950, or almost three times the 1945 volume and about one-third more than the 1940 volume.

Much heavy cargo was to be shifted from the railroads, with both a saving in cost and a lightening of pressure on the railroads. Before it could be accomplished, however, much work was required to remove mines and other obstacles from rivers and harbors, to replace the boats, barges, and rafts destroyed or worn out during the war, to mechanize the loading and unloading processes, and to rebuild canals and ports. Some 3 billion rubles of centralized capital was assigned for such purposes over the five-year period.

Actual accomplishments were more modest than those planned. The freight traffic on inland waterways increased only to about 29 billion ton-miles, instead of 31 billion, by 1950.[36] Some river ports and ship-repair enterprises were reconstructed. The White Sea–Baltic canal and the

---

[36] *U.S.S.R. Information Bulletin,* May 1, 1951, p. 265.

Dnepr-Bug waterway were restored. The Volga-Don canal was completed and it was expected to add much to the usefulness of the system of inland waterways. Improvements occurred in the utilization of the capacities of towing vessels and barges.

Nevertheless, inland water transportation continues to be criticized for many shortcomings. Goods are handled carelessly. Delivery is slow and irregular. The work of repairing ships lags behind schedule. A high-handed attitude toward customers is maintained, and efforts to attract goods for transport are insufficient. Rates are too high in comparison with those of the railroads. The capacity of the river fleet is poorly utilized, and there are too few transfer points for shifting goods between river boats and railroads.

Ocean Transportation. The fourth Five-Year Plan called for a considerable expansion of ocean transportation and of the merchant marine. The freight carried was to increase by 1950 to 2.2 times the prewar level, or to some 52.8 billion ton-miles. The merchant fleet was to increase by 600,000 tons by 1950 and the tonnage of Russian-built ships was to be double that of 1940. Repair and reconstruction of ships and ports was to go forward on a large scale. Large numbers of people were to be trained as merchant seamen, and increased wages for many jobs were intended to make a sea-going life more attractive than in the past.

The volume of ocean freight actually carried in 1950 exceeded the prewar level by 65 per cent instead of 120 per cent and amounted to about 39.6 billion ton-miles instead of 52.8 billion.[37] The work of restoring seaports and shipyards had been largely completed. The capacity of shipyards and shops was more than double that of 1940, and the number of structures for raising ships had increased by 60 per cent. However, the work of shipbuilding lagged far behind schedule, and the tonnage of sea-going ships in 1949 was only a little above that of 1940.

Highway Transportation. Postwar plans called for a great increase in the relative importance of highway transportation. Trucks were to continue to be used to transport goods to railroad stations and river ports and to carry goods from these places to small towns and villages. In addition, a considerable volume of freight traffic was to be shifted from railroads to highways for short hauls and on routes handling only a small volume of freight. Some 7,000 miles of improved motor roads were to be constructed between 1946 and 1950, and the production of motor vehicles was to increase to 500,000 yearly by 1950, including 428,000 trucks, 65,600 passenger cars, and 6,400 motor busses. The freight transported by highway was to increase to 15.5 billion ton-miles, compared with 5.6 billions in 1940.[38]

[37] *Ibid.*
[38] Schwartz, *Russia's Soviet Economy,* p. 332.

The accomplishments in highway transportation in the postwar period have been considerable. The number of motor vehicles produced increased to over 400,000 in 1950. The freight carried by highway increased to about 12.9 billion ton-miles. Some 9,900 miles of hard-surfaced roads were built in five years, and the network of motor roads with improved surface was 2.5 times larger than before the war.[39] However, Soviet Russia is still not a great power in highway transportation.

Estimates of the number of motor vehicles in operation in Soviet Russia vary from something over a million to more than 3 million. In the United States, more than 48,500,000 motor vehicles were registered in 1950.[40] All the people in the United States could ride in motor vehicles at one time, but the numerous Russians with their small number of vehicles would have to wait a long time before everyone could have a ride, even if they were willing to ride in trucks.

Air Transportation. Aviation received a great stimulus during World War II, and civil aviation was scheduled to develop rapidly in the postwar period. Civil airlines were to cover 108,600 miles in 1950, compared with 87,500 miles in 1939.[41] Important developments were to include connections between Moscow, various regional centers, and the capitals of all the constituent republics, plus new major airlines in the far north, Siberia, and the far east. A large increase in the passengers and freight carried was expected.

In 1950 the Russians claimed that their airlines exceeded those of the United States in length and provided a volume of service eight times that of 1940.[42] This indicated a total volume of some 157 million ton-miles of air freight. In the United States, about 212 million ton-miles of air freight were carried in 1950, not counting about 47 million ton-miles of air mail. Passenger transportation amounted to some 10.5 billion passenger-miles.[43]

Soviet Russia and the United States in Freight Transportation. The freight carried by various agencies of transportation in Soviet Russia and the United States in 1950 is shown in Table 19-3. It will be noted that the freight carried by each type of transportation agency in Soviet Russia in 1950 fell well short of that transported in the United States. It was also clear that Soviet Russia's dependence upon railroad transportation was much greater than that of the United States.

Conclusion. The Soviet Russian transportation system has never been adequate to care for the needs of other sectors of the economy, such as industry and trade. When the Soviet regime began, everything needed

[39] *U.S.S.R. Information Bulletin,* May 1, 1951, p. 265.
[40] *Statistical Abstract of the United States, 1952,* p. 496.
[41] Schwartz, *Russia's Soviet Economy,* p. 353.
[42] *Ibid.,,* p. 354.
[43] *Statistical Abstract of the United States, 1952,* p. 530.

Table 19-3. Amounts of Freight Carried by Various Forms of Transportation in Soviet Russia and the United States, 1950

Type of transportation	Soviet Russia		United States	
	Freight carried, billion ton-miles	Percentage of total	Freight carried, billion ton-miles	Percentage of total
Railroads.............	373.4	89.87	595.9	67.23
Highways............	12.9	3.10	126.0	14.19
Inland waterways.....	29.0	6.98	164.5	18.54
Airways.............	0.2	0.05	0.3	0.04
Total	415.5	100.0	887.8	100.0

to be done at once and on a large scale, and the Soviet leaders tried to maximize the volume of service provided by the various agencies of transportation while holding to a minimum the resources devoted to these agencies. Thus the progress made in transportation under the first three Five-Year Plans hardly kept pace with progress made in production.

In view of the great destruction that afflicted the transportation system during World War II, much of Russia's effort in connection with transportation under the fourth Five-Year Plan had to be devoted to repair and reconstruction. Even the complete fulfillment of the plan would not have given Soviet Russia a really adequate system of transportation, and the available data indicate that the plans for transportation were not completely fulfilled. Soviet Russia lags far behind the United States in regard to available transportation facilities and has to serve a larger population and a much greater area. Transportation will probably continue to be a relatively weak spot in the Soviet Russian economy for some time to come.

QUESTIONS FOR STUDY

1. How was the development of railroad transportation in Soviet Russia different from that in the United States? Why?

2. Have the inland waterways been more or less important as a means of transportation in Soviet Russia than in the United States? Why?

3. How do you account for the backwardness of ocean transportation in the case of Soviet Russia?

4. How does the highway transportation of Soviet Russia compare with that of the United States? Why?

5. Trace the development of transportation in Soviet Russia under the planned economy to 1941. Which phases were emphasized and which were

relatively neglected? What was the general transportation outlook at the beginning of World War II?

6. How well did the transportation system function in World War II? How much damage did it suffer? What was done about it?

7. How and to what extent has the Soviet Russian transportation system been improved since World War II? Is it fair to conclude that transportation will probably continue to be a relatively weak spot in the Soviet Russian economy for some time to come? Why?

Chapter 20

INDUSTRY

Many people seem to think that the Russian economy in the days before the Revolution of 1917 was both backward and stagnant in the matter of industrial development. This opinion would have been correct a few decades earlier but, by the time World War I came along, it was only half right. In other words, the Russian economy was relatively backward but not stagnant. It had enjoyed at least a quarter century of rapid progress in industrial development and was promising still better things to come.

THE EARLY DEVELOPMENT OF RUSSIAN INDUSTRY

Industrial Development before 1861. The beginnings of manufacturing in Russia lie deep in the past. For centuries individuals had used hand methods to turn out manufactured goods from materials which they had produced or purchased. Russia produced cannons as early as the reign of Ivan III (1462–1505) and developed some mining and shipbuilding under Peter I (1682–1725). In fact Russia was an important naval power as long as naval vessels were sailing ships made of wood. Peter I decreed in 1721 that enterprisers could buy or hire serfs from the landed nobility for work in manufacturing. In 1767 about 61 per cent of the workers in Russia's 498 manufacturing establishments were serfs.[1]

During much of the nineteenth century, after the Industrial Revolution had brought machine production and the factory system to the leading industrial nations, Russia lagged far behind in industrial development, although the number of manufacturing establishments increased to 5,261 in 1825 and 15,338 in 1860.[2] The proportion of freemen to serfs among industrial workers increased as time went on, but there could not be a labor supply adequate to the needs of large-scale industrial development until after the emancipation of the serfs in 1861.

Moreover, under serfdom each landed estate and rural community

[1] E. J. Simmons (ed.), *U.S.S.R.: A Concise Handbook* (Ithaca, N.Y.: Cornell University Press, 1947), pp. 214, 217.
[2] *Ibid.,* p. 217.

tended to be an economically self-sufficient unit, so that there was little domestic trade. With trade undeveloped, there was no large class of merchants whose profits could be invested in manufacturing establishments—a development which had provided a great stimulus for industry in other countries. Transportation was backward and there were less than 2,000 miles of railroads in 1861. There was no banking system worthy of the name and only a trifling circulation of money. Under these conditions, it was natural that industry would grow slowly.

Later Industrial Progress. The Industrial Revolution arrived almost a hundred years late in Russia, but it arrived with a bang, and Russian industry made rapid progress. With the freeing of the serfs, a larger labor supply for the factories became available. Many of the former serfs had to supplement their incomes with nonagricultural employment, and some broke away from the land altogether. Foreign capitalists became interested in Russian industrial growth and made large-scale investments in mining and manufacturing establishments. As the government began to build railroads and buy up those which had already been constructed, the situation in transportation became more satisfactory.

Some of the progress made in Russian industry in the twenty-five years from 1888 to 1913 is indicated in Table 20-1. Industrial progress

Table 20-1. The Progress of Russian Industry, 1888–1913

Item	Index numbers	
	1888	1913
Output of large-scale industry	100	400
Number of industrial workers	100	200
Coal production	100	547
Cast-iron production	100	571
Petroleum production	100	281
Spindles in cotton mills	100	264
Cotton consumption in textile mills	100	300
Sugar production	100	400

source: Based on N. S. Timasheff, *The Great Retreat* (New York: E. P. Dutton & Co., Inc., 1946), p. 32.

was accompanied by great gains in national income, which increased from 6,600,000,000 to 11,800,000,000 rubles, or by 79.4 per cent, between 1900 and 1913. The net improvement was 39.4 per cent, after allowing for the price rises which occurred. The net improvement in real income per capita, after allowing for population growth, was 17.1 per cent—a remarkable result for so short a period.[3]

[3] N. S. Timasheff, *The Great Retreat* (New York: E. P. Dutton & Co., Inc., 1946), p. 33.

Many of Russia's new industrial establishments were large. Even in 1866 some 27 per cent of the workers employed in large factories (those with 100 or more workers) worked in factories employing 1,000 or more workers. This percentage increased to 46 by 1890. Large factories in European Russia employed 77 per cent of the workers by 1903, although they made up only 17 per cent of the establishments. The average number of workers per establishment in Russian factories and mines with more than 1,000 employees each in 1890 was greater than the average for Germany in 1895 by more than 600 workers.[4] In 1914, some 2,282,100 workers were employed in large factories which were subject to factory inspection by the government.[5]

Russia's Industrial Status in 1913. Russia's industry in 1913 was still backward in relation to the enormous resources of the country and in comparison with the industrial development of other leading countries. The per capita output of electric power in 1913 was one-seventeenth that of the United States and one-fifth that of Germany. The United States was producing eleven times as much pig iron per capita as Russia, Great Britain and Germany eight times as much, and France four times as much. The situation with regard to steel output per capita was almost the same.[6] Russia's total of 3 million employees in industry in 1913 was dwarfed by the total of more than 10 million workers in manufacturing and mining in the United States.[7]

Russia had a fairly well-developed textile industry, produced wool and leather goods, did some mining and lumbering, produced moderate amounts of iron, steel, and petroleum, and was noted for manganese and platinum production. On the other hand, she had almost no chemical industry, failed to produce automobiles, electrical appliances, and machine tools, and was deficient in the production of machinery in general. Russia's heavy industry was concentrated in the European section of the country, and especially in the Ukraine, while the production of consumers' goods was handled by a large number of scattered firms.

Russian industry in 1913 left much to be desired, but the future looked promising. In total industrial development, Russia was already in fifth place in the world, and additional large-scale developments were in prospect. For example, the government plan for railroad construction called for an additional 30,000 miles of track to be laid by 1925. This would have given Russia about 73,800 miles of track, or more than she was to have under the Soviet regime for many years.[8] When World War I came along, industrial production reached 109.4 in 1916 (1913 = 100).

[4] Simmons, *op. cit.*, p. 215.
[5] *Ibid.*, p. 218.
[6] *Ibid.*, p. 215.
[7] *The Economic Almanac for 1949*, pp. 260, 266.
[8] Timasheff, *op. cit.*, p. 375.

By 1917, however, with the collapse of transportation and shortages of materials and supplies, industrial production slid off to 75.7.[9]

THE ORGANIZATION OF SOVIET RUSSIAN INDUSTRY

The Nationalization of Industry. After the Revolution of 1917, Russian industry was brought into public ownership. A nationalization decree of June, 1918, affected more than 1,100 establishments with a total capital of over 3 billion rubles and brought about three-fourths of large-scale industry under public ownership. Other decrees followed, and by late 1919 the government was operating 2,522 large industrial plants. The number increased to 4,141 by April, 1920. Finally, in November, 1920, all enterprises with over 5 workers (operating with mechanical power) and those with over 10 employees (operating without mechanical power) were taken over.[10]

From midsummer of 1918 to March, 1921, the Russian economy operated under a system known as War Communism. The Supreme Economic Council was to manage industry, and the Labor and Defense Council was to direct the economic system, make economic plans, submit them to the All-Russian Executive Committee for approval, direct the work of government departments, and supervise the carrying out of the plans. Market transactions were suspended, the use of money was discontinued, and wages were received in terms of commodities, with many services provided without charge by the government. All goods were to be turned over to the central authorities and to be distributed by them.

This impromptu system of Communism worked miserably. Industrial production as a whole fell off to 20.4 per cent of the 1913 level, and production by large-scale industries was down to 12.8 per cent. In 1920 only 1.6 per cent of the 1913 output of iron ore was produced. Other percentages were 4.0 for steel, 2.4 for pig iron, 5.0 for cotton manufactures, and 5.8 for sugar. The workers lacked incentives and never knew what kinds and amounts of goods they might receive. Agricultural production was at low ebb and transportation was in a state of collapse. The leaders of the government were greatly concerned over the increasing hostility of the peasants and industrial workers. It was time for a change.

The New Economic Policy. Accordingly, the New Economic Policy was introduced in 1921 in an effort to increase production sharply and overcome the political crisis. The government kept its control over such commanding heights of economic activity as large-scale industry, transportation, the banking system, and foreign trade, but many other sectors

[9] A. Baykov, *The Development of the Soviet Economic System* (New York: The Macmillan Company, 1947), p. 8.
[10] Simmons, *op. cit.*, p. 219.

were reopened to private businessmen. Most of the small-scale industrial enterprises which had been taken over by the government were either leased to private individuals and cooperatives or were returned to their former owners. As a result, the 1923 census showed that 88.5 per cent of all industrial enterprises were in private hands, as against 8.5 per cent owned by the government and 3 per cent by cooperatives. However, the private enterprises employed only 12.4 per cent of all industrial workers, compared with 84.1 per cent employed by government enterprises and 3.5 per cent by cooperatives.[11]

Markets were restored, and money and prices were used again. The private and socialized sectors of the economy were to cooperate and were connected through the market. Under this system, economic activity revived almost at once, private enterprises showed a great deal of life, and domestic trade flourished. Industrial production as a whole regained its 1913 level by 1926–1927, although there was considerable variation from one branch of industry to another. At the same time, national income rose to the 1913 level, and the Soviet leaders decided that it was time to go ahead with the first Five-Year Plan, beginning on October 1, 1928, and to proceed with the struggle for socialism. In the process, the private enterprises which had been tolerated temporarily were once more taken over by the government.

The Ministries. Industrial production in Soviet Russia is controlled at the top by a number of ministries, or government departments. These ministries do not produce anything but are merely administrative agencies. The number of ministries controlling industrial production has changed frequently. A ministry has sometimes controlled a whole group of related industries and sometimes only a single industry or part of an industry.[12]

The Departments. Below the ministries, there are other control agencies called "departments" or "production-territorial sections" in some industries. These agencies are committees heading the lines of production of a given branch of industry and controlling a given territory. They have extensive powers for controlling the lower industrial agencies, furnish guidance on a number of technical and financial matters, and are responsible for getting raw materials and supplies to the lower units and for selling their products. However, there are no departments or sections under some ministries, and in such cases the lower units are responsible directly to the ministries.

The Trusts. Several trusts ordinarily appear in each industry. These units are also control agencies and are comparable to the combinations

[11] Baykov, *op. cit.*, p. 107.

[12] The ministries of Soviet Russia are usually both departments of government and departments of economic activity and are therefore important connecting links between the government and the economic life of the country.

of productive units with which we are familiar in the United States. Some of the trusts are vertical combinations of productive units, while others are horizontal combinations at given levels of production. Some trusts have only plants which are concentrated in a single geographical area, whereas others have scattered plants.

The functions of the trusts are more detailed than those of the departments. Each trust is operated by a board (appointed by its administration), and this board, in turn, appoints the managers of the actual producing plants. Each trust is responsible for the productive equipment furnished to the individual factories by the state. The trusts are to see that their plants interchange technical experience and make use of the results obtained by scientific and technical institutes, laboratories, and research organizations; to furnish their plants with information concerning technical advances in industries abroad and get their plants to adopt similar devices and improvements; to see that the plants make full use of their resources and keep stocks of materials, supplies, and finished products in proper amounts and under satisfactory conditions; to set up an orderly system of accounts within their plants; to see that the plants standardize their products; to supervise the wage contracts which the plants negotiate with labor organizations; and to purchase raw materials and sell finished products for their plants.

The Plants and Factories. Finally, under the trusts there are the actual plants and factories which produce commodities. The manager of each enterprise is appointed by its trust. These managers make the decisions necessary to the day-to-day operation of their plants, but there are not many things for them to decide. Each plant operates under definite assignments derived from the economic plans of the system. Among the factors controlled from above are the kinds and quantities of goods to be produced, the quality of the goods, the prices at which the goods can be sold, the quantities and qualities of productive agents which can be used, and the amounts to be paid for materials, supplies, labor, taxes, and other expenses. About the only things left to the management of the enterprises are routine decisions of everyday operation and the hiring and firing of labor.

Although the powers of the manager are limited, he is held responsible for the successful operation of the enterprise and the fulfillment of its plans. If unsuccessful, he may be punished severely. With prices, costs, and the quantities of productive agents closely controlled, about the only factor which the manager can hope to influence is productivity or efficiency. That is, the manager is supposed to get his costs of production per unit of product down to the planned level by inducing a planned increase in the productivity of his enterprise.

If he can spur his workers on to planned feats of productivity, his enterprise comes out even or makes planned profits. If he induces feats of productivity greater than those planned, he makes unplanned profits and is a very successful manager. In view of the great responsibility, limited power, and meager rewards, it is difficult to see why many people would aspire to be managers in Soviet Russian industry.

Decentralization of Ownership and Control. Most industrial enterprises in Soviet Russia are under government ownership and operation, but not all are owned and operated directly by the federal government. Some ministries, such as those of the Automobile Industry, Aircraft Industry, Chemical Industry, Coal Industry, Electrical Industry, and many others are All-Union Ministries. The various enterprises under their supervision are owned and operated by the federal government through these ministries. Other ministries, such as those of the Fishing Industry, Food Industry, Light Industry, and Timber and Paper Industry are Union-Republic Ministries. The enterprises under their supervision are owned and operated by the republic governments (or lower government units) through these ministries. Finally, some enterprises of local interest, such as some public utilities, are owned and operated by local governments. In addition to government plants, others operated by producers' cooperatives are responsible for a considerable variety of consumers' goods and services. Even private individuals are allowed to produce and sell some kinds of services and certain commodities made from materials which these individuals have produced.

The Location of Industry. We have already noted in earlier chapters the principal areas in Soviet Russia which produce petroleum, coal, timber, metallic and nonmetallic minerals, but we have yet to see where the actual manufacturing of the country is carried on. Some blast furnaces and steel mills are located near the coal mines, some near the sources of iron ore, and some in between. Coal is transported west from the Donets Basin to the iron-ore mines at Krivoi Rog, and iron is moved east to furnaces and steel plants in the Donets Basin, while furnaces and steel plants are also located en route at Zaporozhe and Dniepropetrovsk. In similar fashion, iron and steel are produced near sources of ore at Magnitogorsk and Nizhni Tagil in the Urals, using coal brought west from Karaganda and the Kuznets Basin, but also at Stalinsk in the Kuznets Basin, and at way points. Iron and steel are also produced at many other places scattered over the country.

Railroad equipment is manufactured at a number of places in the Ukraine and in the Ural Mountains. Voroshilovgrad is especially important for locomotive production, while large quantities of rolling stock are produced at Nizhni Tagil and Dnieprodzerzinsk. Moscow, Leningrad, and Kharkov are important centers for general machine production, and mining machinery is turned out at Sverdlovsk in the Urals and at Kramatorsk in the Donets Basin. Large tractor plants are found at Kharkov, Chelyabinsk, and Stalingrad, while harvesters and combines are manufactured at Rostov-on-Don, Saratov, and Kirovo. Kiev on the Dnepr River and Gorki on the Volga are centers for the production of river steamers, and ocean-going ships are built at Leningrad and at Nikolaevsk near Odessa. Electrochemical plants developed on a large scale near the large Dnepr Dam in the Ukraine, and also near less important power sources in the Caucasus and on the Kola Peninsula. Chemical industry is also important on the Kara-Bogaz Gulf east of the Caspian Sea.

Lumber mills are widely scattered over the country, and so are paper mills, though most of them are north of the Volga and Kama and especially near Gorki and Vologda. Mills producing cotton textiles are found for the most part in the area bounded by Moscow, Ivanovo, and Yaroslavl—a long haul from the cotton fields of middle Asia. In recent times, plants have been built near the source of the raw material. The production of linen textiles is also concentrated east of Moscow. Meat packing plants are found in a number of places, but especially at Saratov on the Volga, and in Siberia at Kurgan, Petropavlovsk, Novosibirsk, Barnaul, and Semipalatinsk. Sugar is refined from sugar beets in the Ukraine northwest of Kharkov and southwest of Kiev. Wine and canned fruits are produced in the Caucasus. Flour production is scattered around the wheat-raising area. Centers for fishing are Astrakhan at the mouth of the Volga, Rostov, Murmansk, Vladivostok, and Kamchatka.

Prior to World War II, Soviet Russian industry, and especially heavy industry, was concentrated to a great extent in the western area bounded by Rostov-on-Don, Stalingrad, Gorki, and Leningrad, or, in other words, west of the Volga River. The Donets-Kharkov–Nikolaevsk area was dominant, followed by the Moscow-Gorki region. However, the Ural Mountain region, from Magnitogorsk north through Sverdlovsk to Nizhni Tagil, was rapidly growing in importance, as was the Kuznets Basin and other areas in Siberia and the far east. On the whole, the share of the western area in industrial production was reduced from 90 per cent to 60 per cent before the war had gone on very long.[13]

INDUSTRIAL PROGRESS TO 1940

Difficulties of Evaluation. Industrialization and the achievement of great increases in industrial production were leading goals of the eco-

[13] Much of the material on industrial location is from George B. Cressey, *The Basis of Soviet Strength* (New York: McGraw-Hill Book Company, Inc., 1945), pp. 127–133.

nomic planners of Soviet Russia, and much capital, managerial talent, time, and effort were assigned to them. Considerable progress toward these goals was made in the period from 1928 through 1940, but it is difficult to find out just how much. The government itself was almost the only source of data on the economic system, and this was a biased source. That is, the government, operating in the midst of a skeptical, if not hostile, world, was probably anxious to have its accomplishments appear as great as possible, and like some other governments, it may have touched up its statistics a bit at times. Moreover, there was no way to check the statistics and to measure and correct any inaccuracies.

Statistics stated in rubles were especially open to suspicion, since they were sometimes given in "current rubles" and at other times in "rubles of 1926–1927 value." The Soviet leaders expanded greatly the quantity of money and credit in use and permitted large increases in prices, so that statistics in current rubles represented inaccurately the movements of the underlying physical data. On the other hand, some industries whose output played an important part in the gross value of the output of Russian industry were introduced into the economy only after 1928. It is difficult to see how the figures for the output of industries which did not exist in 1926–1927 could have been calculated in terms of that year's prices for the same goods. In any case, there was no way to determine whether statistics originating in current rubles were deflated accurately into rubles of 1926–1927 value.

The Soviet Russian government also showed a strong liking for percentages as a means of expressing economic developments. The results were sometimes ludicrous, as in the case of an outlying station which reported that in one year 2 per cent of the men married 50 per cent of the women (although only one marriage took place).[14] In similar fashion, it could be stated that automobile production increased by 15,331 per cent in Soviet Russia from 1929 to 1948, compared with an increase of less than 5 per cent in the United States. However, the United States produced about 5,250,000 cars in 1948, and Soviet Russia only 214,000. When the original base is small, industrial progress expressed in terms of percentages seems remarkable.

The statistics of production sometimes reflected only the growing output of large-scale government industries, and an apparent expansion of production meant that the articles in question were being manufactured to an increasing extent in large factories owned by the government instead of, as formerly, in small enterprises, by craftsmen, or at home. In such cases, the increases in official production figures did not represent accurately the changes in the amounts of the goods available for consumption. Finally, data presented by different but equally authoritative

[14] *Ibid.*, p. 125.

government agencies, covering exactly the same economic activities, often differed widely. Attempts were seldom made by these agencies to account for or correct these discrepancies.

Industrialization of the Economy. With such misgivings in mind, we may note that the Soviet economy, prior to World War II, had made considerable progress toward the industrialization of the economy. The share of industry in total industrial and agricultural production amounted to 42.1 per cent in 1913, but it increased to 54.5 per cent in 1928 and 77.4 per cent in 1937.[15] In 1940, the gross value of industrial products was 138.5 billion rubles, while that of agricultural products was 23 billion rubles, giving industrial products 85.7 per cent of the total.[16]

In 1913 Russia accounted for 2.6 per cent and the United States for 38.2 per cent of the industrial production of large nations. In 1928 the comparable figures were 3.1 and 46.3 per cent, but by 1937 they were 13.7 and 41.9 per cent. In 1937 Soviet Russia held second place in the world in industrial production, for her 13.7 per cent exceeded England's 9.3 per cent, Germany's 11.6 per cent, and France's 5.7 per cent.[17] While industrial production in capitalistic countries increased from 97 to 114 (1928 = 100) between 1927 and 1937, industrial production in Soviet Russia increased from 80 to 583.[18]

Increased Production of Industrial Commodities. In Table 20-2 we present statistics of the production of several important industrial commodities in Soviet Russia in the years 1913, 1928, 1932, 1937, and 1940, together with the planned goals for 1932, 1937, and 1942. The production of these commodities increased greatly by 1937 and 1940, and even greater accomplishments were planned for 1942. The increases in industrial production, taken at their face value, would almost cause one to run out of adjectives synonymous with "stupendous" and "colossal." The increases resulted not only from the multiplication of factories and plants but also from intensive utilization of the available facilities.

The Stability of Industrial Production. The Soviet statistics of industrial production suggest the absence of business cycles in the operation of the planned economy. While capitalistic countries were in the throes of a severe depression in 1932 and their industrial outputs had declined greatly, the Russian economy apparently found 1932 a good year, for the output of most commodities was far above the 1928 level. A country which can avoid business cycles does not have to worry about cyclical unemployment for its workers. The Soviet leaders claim that their

[15] Simmons, *op. cit.*, p. 225.
[16] *International Conciliation*, April, 1948, pp. 270–271.
[17] Simmons, *op. cit.*, p. 225.
[18] E. Varga, *Two Systems: Socialist Economy and Capitalist Economy* (New York: International Publishers Co., Inc., 1939), p. 40.

Table 20-2. Production of Important Industrial Commodities in Soviet Russia in 1913, 1928, 1932, 1937, and 1940 in Comparison with Planned Estimates for 1932, 1937, and 1942

Commodity	1913	1928	1932		1937		1940 Actual	1942 Planned
			Actual	Planned	Actual	Planned		
All producers' goods, billion rubles	.....	8.2	18.0	17.4	55.2	45.5	84.0	114.5
Petroleum, million tons..........	9.2	11.6	22.3	21.7	30.5	46.8	31.0	54.0
Coal, million tons...............	29.1	35.4	64.7	75.0	128.0	152.5	165.5	243.0
Electric power, billion kilowatt-hours........................	2.0	5.0	13.0	22.0	36.4	38.0	48.2	75.0
Pig iron, million tons............	4.2	3.3	6.2	10.0	14.5	16.0	14.9	22.0
Steel, million tons...............	4.2	4.2	5.9	10.4	17.7	17.0	18.3	28.0
Rolled steel, million tons........	3.5	3.4	4.2	8.0	13.0	13.0	13.1	21.0
Copper, thousand tons...........	31.1	30.0	46.7	84.7	97.5	155.0	164.7	215.7
Cement, million tons............	1.4	1.9	3.5	6.4	5.4	7.5	5.3	11.0
Sawn lumber and timber, million cubic meters................	11.9	13.6	24.4	42.5	33.8	43.0	33.8	45.0
Autos and trucks, thousands.....	0.1	0.7	23.9	105.0	200.0	200.0	147.1	400.0
Tractors, thousands..............	.....	1.3	50.6	55.0	80.3	88.5	31.1	
Freight cars, thousands..........	11.8	10.6	20.2	12.6	59.1	118.0	51.0	120.0
Locomotives, thousands..........	0.6	0.5	0.8	1.5	1.6	2.8	1.7	2.3
All consumers' goods, billion rubles	.....	10.1	16.3	19.2	40.3	47.2	54.0	69.5
Cotton textiles, billion meters....	2.2	2.7	2.4	4.7	3.4	5.1	4.0	4.9
Woolen textiles, million meters...	95.0	93.2	88.7	270.0	105.1	220.0	124.4	177.0
Leather shoes, million pairs......	8.3	29.6	84.7	80.0	164.2	180.0	230.0	258.0
Sugar, million tons..............	1.3	1.3	1.4	1.4	2.4	2.5	1.6	3.5
Paper, thousand tons............	205.0	284.0	479.0	900.0	833.0	1,000.0	812.0	1,500.0

planned economy can always avoid booms and depressions in economic activity.

The Quality of Industrial Goods. The Soviet Russian accomplishments in industrial production from 1928 to 1940 were open to criticism from several angles. Our statistics are stated for the most part in terms of physical quantities of goods, but the plans for industrial output called for fulfillment in terms of many other factors. In practice, the pressure was heavy on the managers of Soviet industrial enterprises to fulfill plans in terms of physical quantities of goods, and this often resulted in non-fulfillment in terms of other important matters.

Increases in the quantities of commodities produced are of little importance unless the commodities are of good quality, and in this respect Soviet Russian industry was notoriously deficient. One critic said that, under the first Five-Year Plan, unsalable products amounted to 37 to 50 per cent of total output in some whole industries and up to 80 or 90 per cent for individual trusts and factories.[19] The criticisms of outside observers were echoed by the Soviet leaders, who complained bitterly about

[19] B. Brutzkus, *Economic Planning in Soviet Russia* (London: George Routledge & Sons, Ltd., 1935), p. 205.

the wretched quality and variety of manufactured goods and excessive spoilage and wastage of materials. The problem of quality continued to give trouble through 1940, in spite of the imposition of grievous penalties for the production of defective goods.

Labor Efficiency and Productivity. Each of the first three Five-Year Plans called for large increases in labor productivity and reductions in cost of production, but the actual results often left much to be desired. The difficulties experienced in these matters were indicated by other results of Soviet industrial operation. To come even close to plan fulfillment in terms of physical quantities, the number of workers employed in government plants had to be increased from 11.3 to 22.8 million under the first Five-Year Plan, instead of the planned 15.8 million.[20]

Again in 1940, with industrial production lagging, the number of workers in industry had almost reached the planned goal for 1942. The Soviet leaders counted these results as evidences of rapid economic progress, but they undoubtedly should be considered as an indication of low labor productivity in view of the fact that plans for industrial output were less than completely fulfilled. The average productivity of Russian industrial workers improved from 1928 through 1940, but it remained only about two-fifths as high as that of industrial workers in the United States.[21]

Depreciation and Replacement. Statistics for physical quantities of goods do not show what happened to plant, machinery, and equipment in achieving the stated results. Obviously, increasing outputs of commodities need to be discounted if they have been obtained at the cost of an abnormal increase in the wearing out and breaking down of machinery and equipment. And the same is true of increases in new productive facilities of industries if adequate provision has not been made for the maintenance and repair of old productive facilities. If adequate account of the costs of maintenance, repair, and replacement of machinery and equipment is not kept in computing the costs of finished commodities, a further element of unreliability is introduced into claims concerning the results of industrial production. According to both outside observers and Soviet leaders, the Russian planned economy was lax about these matters.

Overfulfillment and Underfulfillment of Plans. According to Soviet authorities, the first Five-Year Plan was fulfilled to the extent of 93.7 per cent, while the second plan was completely fulfilled.[22] However, these estimates were based on the values of products in terms of rubles rather than on physical quantities of products, and fulfillment in terms of rubles may be increased by rises in the prices of products as well as by increases

[20] Freda Utley, *The Dream We Lost* (New York: The John Day Company, Inc., 1940), p. 201.
[21] Simmons, *op. cit.*, p. 226.
[22] Baykov, *op. cit.*, pp. 168, 282.

in their physical output. Simple averages for plan fulfillment in terms of physical quantities of goods, computed from the statistics in Table 20-2, would give around 70 per cent fulfillment for the first Five-Year Plan and 80 per cent for the second plan.

Again, any index of plan fulfillment is necessarily an average, and there is serious doubt about the significance of the average in this case. That is, it is questionable whether overfulfillment in one part of the plan cancels underfulfillment in some other section, as it does in the process of averaging. A fulfillment figure of 150 per cent for automobile chassis and one of 50 per cent for automobile tires would produce an average fulfillment of 100 per cent, and also many a headache for the planners and for the prospective users of the commodities.

In spite of a high average level of fulfillment in the period under discussion, great underfulfillment in important fields led to delays in the development of the more progressive branches of industry, the manufacture of incompletely finished articles, changes in standards, and the incomplete utilization of productive facilities elsewhere in the economy. Overfulfillment and underfulfillment of plans in individual branches of industry resulted from uncontrollable natural factors, unavoidable international influences, military emergencies, interim changes in plans, and mistakes in planning.

Capital Goods and Consumers' Goods. The mere fulfillment of the plans for industrial production would have resulted in a great emphasis on capital goods. The first and second Five-Year Plans called for the production of about as many capital goods as consumers' goods, while the third plan called for the production of 114.5 billion rubles' worth of capital goods in 1942, compared with 69.5 billion rubles' worth of consumer's goods. In actual practice, the output of capital goods regularly exceeded the planned estimates, whereas the production of consumers' goods fell short. Such results were favorable from the point of view of the rapid industrialization of the economy, but they had serious immediate effects on the economic welfare of the people.

INDUSTRY IN WORLD WAR II

Wartime Losses. After the beginning of the war with Germany, the Russians gave ground rapidly before the invaders. The large area lost to the Germans was the home of some 88 million people, or almost half of the total population. It had accounted for 33 per cent of the gross output of industry and a considerably larger proportion of the output of heavy industry. The wartime productive losses, expressed as percentages of 1940 output, were coal 60, petroleum 16, electric power 44, pig iron 73, steel 55, rolled steel 61, freight cars 49, locomotives 87, timber 27, sawmill products 34, plywood 51, paper 37, cement 52, iron ore 63, and matches 40.[23] About 32,000 factories were destroyed or badly damaged. Many people outside Soviet Russia thought that these losses would soon prove crippling.

Industrial Production in Wartime. However, Soviet Russia's war production, although not her total industrial production, was not only maintained but actually increased. Soviet heavy industry produced 14 per cent more goods in 1945 than in 1940, but the production of goods for civilian consumption was at only a little more than half the 1940 level.[24] The secret of Russia's success in war production was the rapid development of the Ural Mountain, Siberian, and central Asian regions. The machines and equipment of many factories, including 1,300 large industrial plants, were transported hurriedly from western Russia to these new regions. They were loaded on cars, sometimes hundreds of cars to a factory, and moved hundreds or thousands of miles. Altogether, more than a million carloads of machines, equipment, and materials were moved eastward in the summer and fall of 1941.[25] In the new regions, sites had been cleared in readiness or were rapidly cleared. Some factory buildings had already been constructed, and others were soon erected. Sometimes large numbers of workers were moved and were housed in hastily constructed barracks.

The Russians had stockpiles of foods and materials, and they were also able to use local materials in the new regions. The Ural Mountain region, for example, contains all but four of the known chemical elements. Reliance was placed on intensification of the workers' efforts, curtailed replacements of machinery in nonessential fields, standardization of products, improvisation, and training on the job. Women and young people of both sexes were brought into employment, given rapid training, and stimulated by honors and socialist competition. Housewives were changed into factory workers in two weeks' time. Technical-training programs were rapidly extended and eventually included about half of all students beyond the seventh grade.

POSTWAR DEVELOPMENTS IN INDUSTRY

The Fourth Five-Year Plan. The Soviet leaders were ready to embark on the fourth Five-Year Plan by April, 1946, about a year after the end of the war with Germany. The new plan, like the previous ones, was ambitious. In terms of capital investment, it expected the wartime losses

[23] *Annals of the American Academy of Political and Social Science*, vol. 263, May, 1949, pp. 54–55.
[24] Harry Schwartz, *Russia's Postwar Economy* (Syracuse, N.Y.: Syracuse University Press, 1947), p. 10.
[25] *Ibid.*, p. 9.

of capital to be made up by 1950 and to have the basic capital of the country increase to 1,130 billion rubles, or 8 per cent above the level of 1940. The total investment in state enterprises was to amount to 250.3 billion rubles over the five-year period, thus providing an annual rate of capital investment 35 per cent higher than that of 1940. This investment was to permit some 5,900 new and rehabilitated state enterprises to go into operation. Only 45 per cent of the investment was to be made in the devastated western areas. For the area from Moscow to the Urals, plus central Asia, 40 per cent was scheduled, while 15 per cent was to go to Siberia and the far east.[26]

Total industrial production was scheduled to reach 205 billion rubles (in 1926–1927 prices) by 1950, an increase of 48 per cent over the 1940 level and of 61 per cent over the 1945 level. The Soviet leaders apparently thought that the needs of the country were about the same under the fourth Five-Year Plan as under the earlier plans, and they called for great emphasis on the development of heavy industry. The products of heavy industry were to make up about two-thirds of total industrial output in 1950 and to reach a level about 60 per cent higher than in 1940. The output of consumers' goods, the remaining third of the total, was to be only 25 per cent higher in 1950 than in 1940. Employment in the national economy (government owned and operated) was to reach 33.5 million workers, an increase of 6.25 million in five years. Wages were to increase to 500 rubles per month on the average. Labor productivity was to increase by 36 per cent over the prewar level, and this was to cause 70 per cent of the growth of industrial production.

Fulfillment of the Fourth Five-Year Plan. Table 20-3 shows the actual production of a number of important industrial commodities in 1940, 1945, and 1950 in comparison with planned goals for 1950. The outputs planned for 1950 were uniformly above those actually achieved in 1940 and were to provide large increases over those of 1945 in most cases. However, although the table does not show it, several of the outputs planned for 1950 were well below those which had already been planned for 1942.

The results of the fourth Five-Year Plan present a familiar picture. In heavy industry the outputs of 1950 left those of 1940 far behind and in many cases reached or exceeded the planned goals. However, the outputs of consumers' goods in 1950 fell far short of the planned objectives and in some cases had not regained the levels of 1940. Thus the results were much more favorable for the continued industrialization of the economy than for the satisfaction of the present wants of consumers. According to the Soviet authorities, the fourth Five-Year Plan was fulfilled in four

[26] *Ibid.*, p. 21.

Table 20-3. Production of Selected Industrial Commodities in Soviet Russia in 1940, 1945, 1950, and 1954 in Comparison with Planned Estimates for 1950 and 1955

Commodity	1940	1945	1950 Actual	1950 Planned	1954 Actual	1955 Planned
Petroleum, million tons.........	31.0	19.4	37.8	35.4	59.5	69.9
Coal, million tons..............	165.5	113.0	260.0	250.0	344.0	372.0
Electric power, billion kilowatt-hours......................	48.2	43.2	90.3	82.0	146.5	162.5
Pig iron, million tons...........	14.9	9.2	19.4	19.5	30.0	34.1
Steel, million tons..............	18.3	11.2	27.3	28.0	40.8	44.2
Rolled steel, million tons........	13.1	.....	20.8	21.0	32.2	34.1
Cement, million tons............	5.3	1.9	9.5	10.5		
Commercial timber, million cubic meters......................	114.0	74.2	155.0	180.0	....	231.8
Window glass, million square meters.......................	44.4	22.2	84.0	80.0		
Tractors, thousands............	31.1	7.3	118.2	112.0		
Autos and trucks, thousands.....	147.1	83.0	405.0	500.0		
Cotton textiles, billion meters....	4.0	1.7	3.8	4.8	5.5	6.1
Woolen textiles, million meters...	124.4	56.9	167.0	168.0	260.0	257.0
Leather shoes, million pairs......	230.0	60.0	205.0	240.0	275.0	318.0
Hosiery, million pairs...........	480.0	83.0	431.6	580.0		
Sugar, thousand tons...........	2,150.0	.....	2,515.0	....	3,200.0	4,477.0
Paper, thousand tons...........	812.0	335.0	1,193.6	1,340.0	....	1,706.8
Watches and clocks, millions.....	2.6	.....	7.2	....	16.8	22.0
Sewing machines, thousands.....	180.0	.....	500.0	....	1,335.0	2,615.0
Bicycles, thousands............	270.0	.....	660.0	....	2,510.0	3,445.0

years and three months, and industrial output for 1950 was 17 per cent in excess of the planned result.[27]

The Fifth Five-Year Plan. The fifth Five-Year Plan called for large further advances by heavy industry, as shown in Table 20-3, but it also provided for sharp increases in the outputs of consumers' goods. On the whole, consumers were promised an improvement of one-third in their standards of living. It was predicted that by 1955 Soviet Russia should be producing 500,000 vacuum cleaners per year, 330,000 refrigerators, 4,400,000 radios, 1,000,000 television sets, and 23,000,000 clocks and watches. During the five years, each family was to get a clock or watch, one family in 10 was to acquire a sewing machine, and one in 30 a bicycle.[28]

[27] *U.S.S.R. Information Bulletin,* May 1, 1951, p. 259.
[28] *The Economist,* Oct. 10, 1953, pp. 105–107.

Soviet Russia and the United States. Even after the fourth Five-Year Plan, Soviet Russia lagged far behind the United States in industrial production. Complete fulfillment of the fifth plan could not change the situation. Table 20-4 shows the expansion in Soviet Russian industrial

Table 20-4. Soviet Russian Production Necessary in 1970 to Equal the United State Per Capita Outputs of Selected Commodities in 1948

Commodity	United States per capita output, 1948	Total Soviet Russian output required, 1970	Actual Soviet Russian output, 1950
Steel............	549 kilograms	134.0 million metric tons	27.3 million metric tons
Pig iron.........	372 kilograms	90.8 million metric tons	19.4 million metric tons
Petroleum.......	1,888 kilograms	460.7 million metric tons	37.8 million metric tons
Electric power....	2,298 kilowatt-hours	560.7 billion kilowatt-hours	90.3 billion kilowatt-hours
Cotton textiles...	59 meters	14.4 billion meters	3.8 billion meters
Woolen textiles .	3 meters	732.0 million meters	167.0 million meters
Leather shoes....	3.15 pairs	768.6 million pairs	205.0 million pairs
Hosiery.........	12 pairs	2.9 billion pairs	0.43 billion pairs

SOURCE: Harry Schwartz, *Russia's Soviet Economy* (New York: Prentice-Hall, Inc., 1950), p. 559; *The Economist*, Jan. 31, 1953, p. 265, and Oct. 11, 1952, p. 103.

production which will be necessary by 1970 if production per capita is then to equal that of the United States in 1948. The necessary increases would range from about four to roughly twelve times the 1950 outputs and, even if these miraculous results were achieved, Soviet Russia would still be running over twenty years behind the United States.

QUESTIONS FOR STUDY

1. How can one say that Russian industry was backward but not stagnant in the years before World War I? Why did the Industrial Revolution arrive about a hundred years late in Russia?

2. How much progress was made in Russian industry from 1888 to 1913? If the same rate of progress had continued to 1938, how would the status of Russian industry in that year have compared with its actual status?

3. How is Soviet Russian industry controlled and managed under the planned economy? How would you evaluate the existing organizations and arrangements for controlling industrial production?

4. Why is it often said that extreme difficulties are involved in trying to ascertain just how much progress Soviet Russia has made in the field of industrial production?

5. What were the most important accomplishments of Soviet Russian industry under the planned economy to 1940? In what respects was the operation of industry defective? On net balance, what is your opinion of Soviet Russian industry in this period? Why?

6. How did Soviet Russian industry fare during World War II? Would you consider the wartime performance of industry commendable? Why?

7. How does the capacity of Soviet Russian industry compare with that of industry in the United States? Is the same thing true of actual production? How much progress has Soviet Russian industry made since the war?

Chapter 21

MONEY, CREDIT, AND BANKING

The development of money, credit, and banking in any economy ordinarily runs parallel with the development of agriculture, industry, transportation, and commerce. As long as production remains on a small scale, economic units are largely independent, transportation is deficient, and exchanges of goods seldom occur, large amounts of money and credit are not needed and banks remain unimportant. On the other hand, the growth of large-scale production means that a tremendous volume of exchanges must take place, large amounts of goods must be transported, and the need for money and credit will increase. Moreover, some way must be found to get the savings of the people into the hands of persons who want to make investments and to furnish enterprises with funds to take care of their day-to-day operating expenses when their own funds are inadequate to permit smooth and efficient operation. The result is the development of banks and of commercial and investment credit.

MONEY, CREDIT, AND BANKING BEFORE 1917

Russian Money in Early Times. The ruble was the Russian monetary unit under the czars. Coins of silver and copper had been in use for many years before the first paper money, the assignats, were issued by the government in 1769. The assignats were supposed to be redeemable in copper coins, and their issue was to be limited. In practice, however, they were grossly overissued, and their value declined steadily. By 1810, just before Napoleon's invasion of Russia, 1 silver ruble would command about 4 rubles in assignats.[1] Early attempts at monetary reform proved unavailing, and it was not until 1839 that the silver ruble was proclaimed the standard monetary unit of the country. A fixed relation of 3.5 assignat rubles for 1 silver ruble was established, and the assignats were withdrawn from circulation.

A new type of paper money, the so-called credit notes, began to be is-

[1] A. Z. Arnold, *Banks, Credit, and Money in Soviet Russia* (New York: Columbia University Press), 1937, p. 4.

sued in 1841, but before long they suffered the same fate as the assignats. During the Crimean War, 1853–1856, the government issued the credit notes in large quantities as a means of paying its expenses, and their value depreciated. It became necessary to stop redeeming the notes with coin, and the cycle of inflation was repeated.

The Monetary Reform of 1897. Russia's monetary system reached a stable basis only when a series of measures, known as the monetary reform of 1897, were adopted in the 1890s. The free coinage of silver was stopped in 1893. In 1895 it was provided that all lawful transactions could be stated in terms of gold coin and that payments arising therefrom might be made in gold or credit notes at the current rate of exchange. The State Bank was authorized to buy and sell gold at a fixed price. In 1897 the monetary unit was devalued by one-third, and the redemption of paper money in specie was resumed. In the same year, the State Bank was given the right to issue paper money. The volume of paper money was to be limited to the needs of circulation, and amounts up to 600 million rubles were to be backed by a gold reserve of 50 per cent. Additional paper money was to be covered ruble for ruble by gold.

This series of acts placed Russia on the gold standard for all practical purposes. The adoption of the gold standard occurred under unfavorable conditions, for the government was operating at a deficit and Russia's balance of trade was none too favorable. However, the results were rather satisfactory up to the beginning of World War I. The paper money in circulation increased by over 60 per cent from 1897 to 1914, but the policy with regard to the issuance of paper money was conservative, gold reserves were adequate, and the redemption of paper money in gold was maintained. The gold standard also tended to inspire confidence in the Russian monetary unit and enabled Russia to attract the foreign capital so necessary to her economic development.

Money during World War I. With the outbreak of World War I, Russia found herself in monetary difficulties once more. It became necessary to suspend specie payments, and the State Bank was authorized to increase that part of its paper money which was not secured by gold from 300 million rubles to $1\frac{1}{2}$ billion rubles. Later, the limit was raised until it reached $6\frac{1}{2}$ billion rubles. The State Bank was also authorized to discount short-term obligations of the government known as treasury bills. Gold coins disappeared from circulation soon after specie payments were suspended. A few months later, silver coins began to vanish, and toward the end of 1915, all metallic money disappeared.

Under her backward tax system, Russia could not finance much of her war expenditure by means of revenue from ordinary sources. Expenditures to the extent of 19.5 billion rubles were financed through the sale of long-term government bonds. Other expenditures were financed through the issue of 18.7 billion rubles worth of treasury bills, which were converted into purchasing power by borrowing on them at the banks. Finally, some expenditures were financed simply by issuing large additional amounts of paper money, and the total currency in circulation rose from 1.6 billion rubles on July 1, 1914, to 18.9 billion rubles on October 23, 1917.[2]

The Russian government's methods of financing the war were non-inflationary to the extent that the government derived increased revenue from taxation and sold government bonds to citizens who paid for them out of savings or current income. In these cases, spendable funds were taken away from the citizens as the government received increased purchasing power. On the other hand, the methods of finance were inflationary when the government sold bonds to the banks, discounted treasury bills, or printed paper money to cover its expenditures. By these methods the government acquired spendable funds, in the form of bank deposits or cash, without taking similar amounts from the individual citizens. Thus there was a large increase in the funds at the disposal of government and citizens, which was not matched by an increase in the quantities of goods available for purchase, and prices tended to be pushed up.

In the early part of the war period, prices did not rise nearly so fast as the volume of money in circulation increased. Large quantities of goods which would ordinarily have been exported were sold in the domestic market, and the disappearance of metallic money partly offset the increase in paper money. Moreover, the people had faith in the money and in the government. Later, as production became converted to war purposes and civilian goods became scarcer, as the Russian army suffered crushing defeats, and as people lost confidence in the currency, prices rose more rapidly than the quantity of money in circulation increased. People who received money hastened to spend it for almost anything obtainable, and the rapidity with which money turned over added to the inflationary effect. By November, 1917, the quantity of money in circulation reached 1,201 (July, 1914 = 100), and the price level was 1,020 (1913 = 100).[3] Thus the Bolsheviki faced an inflationary situation when they took over and, as we shall see later, they proceeded to pour gasoline on the fires of inflation.

Banking in Early Times. As long as Russia operated an economy based on serfdom, and industry, trade, and transportation had not developed, the Russian banks were primitive in character. In 1754 the state set up two banks under government ownership and operation. The State Loan

[2] *Ibid.*, p. 35.
[3] *Ibid.*, p. 49.

Bank for the Nobility made long-term loans to the landed aristocracy on the basis of their estates, and the State Commercial Bank was to make loans to merchants on the basis of merchandise. Both banks were badly managed, loans were made largely to a few influential individuals, many loans were unsecured, and adequate accounts were not kept. The Commercial Bank was finally closed in 1782 and the Loan Bank for the Nobility folded up in 1786.

The State Loan Bank, established in 1786, also was to make loans to the nobility based on their estates, as were savings institutions known as "charitable boards" and "widows' banks." Too often, however, loans were made without security by imperial order, favoritism was practiced, and loans proved difficult to collect. In 1817 another State Commercial Bank was established to aid industry and trade. Besides accepting funds for deposit or transfer, it could discount bills and make loans against merchandise. Actually it never developed a high level of activity. Serious runs on the banks occurred in the late 1850s after the Crimean War. The State Loan Bank was closed on May 31, 1860, and its affairs were turned over to a government savings institution. At the same time, the affairs of the State Commercial Bank were transferred to a new State Bank.

Russian Banking, 1860–1914. The new State Bank, operating as a government institution under the Ministry of Finance, was established to promote trade and stabilize the currency. It could accept time and demand deposits, discount commercial paper, make loans on various types of security, and buy and sell securities, bills of exchange, and precious metals. It did not receive the right to issue bank notes until 1897. The bank made few loans in its first three decades of operation, for it was involved in such projects as caring for the obligations of former credit institutions, handling financial matters for the government, accumulating a stock of gold, and stabilizing the currency. After 1890 its loans and discounts expanded rapidly.

As time went on, the State Bank became something of a central bank, and it made an increasing proportion of its loans to other banks rather than to individual borrowers. By 1913 almost 75 per cent of its loans were made to other banks.[4] In times of depression it went to the aid of other bankers, extended them additional credits, and organized groups of bankers to stabilize security prices. Its conservative policy in issuing paper money was also an important factor in stabilizing the value of the ruble.

With the State Bank functioning as a central bank, most of the loans to businessmen and other borrowers were made by other banks. Among the commercial banks, the privately owned joint-stock banks were most important. The first of these was established at St. Petersburg in 1864.

[4] *Ibid.*, p. 19.

By 1914 there were 47 of them, with 743 branches. Besides carrying on a normal commercial banking business, the joint-stock banks invested heavily in the securities of industrial and commercial enterprises and made a large volume of loans based on such securities. Many of their short-term loans were also made to firms in which the banks were financially interested. Thus the banks combined commercial and investment banking under one roof—a practice which could be dangerous if the banks tied up in nonliquid assets large funds which demand depositors could call for at any time. A considerable part of the stock of these banks was owned by foreign bankers, and they were also instrumental in securing funds abroad for the development of Russian industry.

Besides the joint-stock banks, there were municipal banks which received deposits, made short-term loans against real estate and securities, and granted funds to municipalities, and also mutual credit societies organized on a cooperative basis for making short-term loans to small tradesmen and artisans. By 1914 Russia had 319 municipal banks and 1,108 mutual credit societies. Out of a total of 5,279 million rubles of loans and discounts outstanding at the time, the State Bank was responsible for 1,072 million rubles, the joint-stock banks for 3,162 million rubles, the mutual credit societies for 813 million rubles, and the municipal banks for 232 million rubles.[5]

Banking in World War I. The outbreak of World War I was followed by a banking crisis. Frightened depositors withdrew large sums from the banks, the inflow of foreign funds was cut off, and the banks could not recover large parts of the balances which they were carrying with banks in England, France, and Germany. The banks became unable to dispose of their security holdings, for a sharp fall in security prices led the government to close the security exchanges. The banks' clients were saved from bankruptcy by a moratorium which the government declared on all commercial paper drawn in the southern and western parts of the country before the war. The banks themselves were saved by large credits from the State Bank.

As the war went on, the State Bank became more and more an agency of the Treasury, and its volume of ordinary loans and advances to other banks declined. The regular commercial banks did a considerable volume of business during the war, but the business was largely of an investment character. They made loans to enable firms to expand their plants or construct new ones, to purchase machinery and equipment, and to store commodities. The banks even did a bit of speculating in commodities. They bought securities, made loans on the basis of securities, opened current accounts against them, and accepted them as the basis for commercial loans to firms in which they had invested.

[5] *Ibid.*, p. 19.

On the whole, the Russian banking system was not well developed in the period before the Revolution of 1917, although the banks' capital, deposits, and loans and discounts had been increasing. The banks had not developed to the point where they could care for the needs of the country for fixed capital and short-term funds without recourse to foreign sources of funds. The Russian capital market was especially weak. Even in the period from 1908 to 1912 some 30 per cent of all new issues of Russian securities were marketed in other countries.[6]

On the other hand, we must not lose perspective in matters of banking. The National Banking System of the United States was not established until 1863, and central banking did not come along until after the passage of the Federal Reserve Act in 1913. However, the United States did have 25,510 commercial banks in mid-1914, and these banks had over 13 billion dollars' worth of loans outstanding. The latter figure may be compared with the Russian figure of 5¼ billion rubles, if we note that the Russian gold ruble contained something over half as much fine gold as the dollar.[7]

FROM THE REVOLUTION TO THE FIVE-YEAR PLANS

Money under War Communism. The overissue of paper money and inflation of prices, which had developed during World War I, got entirely out of hand during the period of War Communism (1918–1921). The Russian government collected rapidly increasing sums in taxes, but the buying power of the money was so slight that the amounts collected fell far short of covering necessary government expenses, and the government had to resort increasingly to the printing of paper money. At the same time, the government was trying to develop a moneyless type of economy. Agricultural products were requisitioned. Industries were to turn their products over to the government, and rationed goods were to be passed out to consumers without charge. Factories were supplied with raw materials in similar fashion. Wages were paid in part in terms of commodities, and a number of services were distributed freely by the government. Production fell off to a small fraction of the 1913 level.

With the need for money declining and the supply of it increasing rapidly, the monetary unit depreciated in value and prices went up to astronomical levels. In November, 1917, the amount of money in circulation had been over 12 times as great as before the war and the price level over 10 times as high as in 1913. By July, 1921, which marks the approximate end of the period of War Communism, the amount of money in

[6] *Ibid.*, p. 26.
[7] Board of Governors of the Federal Reserve System, *Banking and Monetary Statistics,* 1943, p. 19.

circulation was 1,440 times as great as before the war and the price level was 80,700 times as high.[8]

Money under the New Economic Policy. The great inflation did not end with the period of War Communism. For a time the government had to continue to finance its deficits by printing paper money even under the New Economic Policy (1921–1927), and prices continued to rise rapidly. The progress of the inflation over the entire period from 1918 to 1924 is shown in Table 21-1. In March, 1924, the quantity of money in circulation was almost 497 million times as great as on July 1, 1914, and the price level was almost 62 billion times as high as in 1913.

Table 21-1. Increases in Money in Circulation and in the Price Level in Soviet Russia, 1918–1924

Date	Money in circulation, million rubles	Index of money in circulation (July 1, 1914 = 1.0)	Index of prices (1913 = 1.0)
January, 1918.....	27,650	17.0	21
January, 1919.....	61,326	37.6	164
January, 1920.....	225,015	138.0	2,420
January, 1921.....	1,168,597	716.7	16,800
January, 1922.....	17,539,232	10,757.6	288,000
January, 1923.....	1,994,464,454	1,223,597.8	21,242,000
January, 1924.....	225,637,374,014	138,427,836.8	5,457,000,000
March, 1924......	809,625,216,667	496,702,886.9	61,920,000,000

SOURCE: Harry Schwartz, *Russia's Soviet Economy*, (New York: Prentice-Hall, Inc., 1950), p. 398.

Even before the inflation had run its course, the government began to issue limited quantities of a new and stable currency in October, 1922. The monetary unit of the new currency was called a "chervonets," and it had the value of 10 prerevolutionary gold rubles. It had a 100 per cent reserve behind it, including 25 per cent in gold and 75 per cent in various kinds of short-term notes and in readily marketable goods owned by the State Bank.

Its issue was carefully restricted, but within a year the chervontsi accounted for 25 per cent of the value of all money in circulation, for the old paper money depreciated all the more rapidly in the presence of the new, more stable currency. There remained little profit for the government in printing more of the old currency, and the need for a single stable currency was felt ever more keenly as agricultural and industrial production revived and the volume of trade and credit transactions increased.

In 1924 the government undertook a thorough monetary reform. A

[8] Arnold, *op. cit.*, pp. 76, 91.

new paper currency, called State Treasury notes, was established. Its issue was to be limited by the needs of trade and was never to exceed 50 per cent of the amount of chervontsi in circulation. The issue of paper money to cover government deficits was to cease after July 1, 1924. There were to be no more issues of the old depreciated paper currency, and the amounts already in circulation were to be redeemed. One new ruble was given for 50 million rubles of the pre-1921 type and one for 50 thousand of the 1923 variety.

The monetary reform was successful. The amount of the new money in circulation increased from 332 million in 1924 to 2,773 million in 1930, but this increase was accompanied by a great expansion of the economic activities of the system. The new currency was not used for balancing the government's budget. The index of prices (1913 = 100) increased only from 182.3 on January 1, 1924, in terms of the new currency, to 220.6 on January 1, 1930. Such a change in the value of money was scarcely noticeable after what had gone before.

Banking under War Communism. After a short-lived and unsuccessful attempt at collaboration with the old State Bank and the joint-stock banks, the Soviet government took them over late in 1917. The State Bank continued to function under government ownership and operation, but all private joint-stock banks were merged in the State Bank. Mutual credit societies and city public banks were not liquidated until late in 1918, while municipal and regional credit societies were abolished in May, 1919.

Thus all private credit institutions were either liquidated or nationalized, and all credit transactions were concentrated in the State Bank. However, an effort was being made at the same time to develop a moneyless economy, and the rapid depreciation of the ruble was undermining the basis of all credit transactions. The State Bank lost its credit functions and became little more than a government office. For this reason it was liquidated in January, 1920. Its assets and liabilities were taken over by the Ministry of Finance.

Banking under the New Economic Policy. Under the New Economic Policy, the money economy was restored and this called for the reestablishment of banking. A new State Bank began to operate under government ownership in 1921. The bank was authorized to extend both short-term (commercial) and long-term (investment) credit to government, cooperative, and private enterprises. Gold and foreign exchange were concentrated in the bank, and before long it was given the right to issue paper money. The bank operated with great difficulty during the inflation, and it stopped losing capital only after a stable currency had been established.

The new State Bank was intended to be the only credit institution of the economy. In practice, however, it became necessary to permit other types of credit institutions to be set up to provide specialized credit services for various branches of economic activity. On the eve of the monetary reform of 1924, there were over 150 main banks and credit institutions with 750 branches, and more than 2,500 savings banks.[9] The number of banks continued to grow until 1927. All through the period, however, the loans and discounts of the State Bank were more than double those of all other banks, and its deposits were two to four times as great.[10]

In the latter part of the 1920s, a movement got under way to concentrate the banking and credit of the economy in the State Bank. It culminated in the credit reform of 1930–1931, when the State Bank was given a complete monopoly of short-term credit operations. Investment banking was concentrated in a small number of government institutions under the supervision of the State Bank. The various enterprises of the economy were forbidden to extend credit to each other and were required to settle all obligations to each other through the State Bank.

MONEY, CREDIT, AND BANKING IN THE PLANNED ECONOMY

Functions of Soviet Money. Actual cash plays a relatively unimportant role in the planned economy of Soviet Russia. The quantity of paper money and coins in circulation, as issued through the Ministry of Finance and the State Bank, depends on the planned turnover of commodities and services within the country. The money furnishes a medium of exchange for the citizens in dealing with each other or with the stores, but it is not used in interenterprise transactions. It is a common denominator in terms of which the values of commodities and services can be expressed. It furnishes a unit for keeping accounts, for making plans, for checking the fulfillment of plans, and for the extension of credit. It is also a device which may be used for storing up values through time. Nevertheless, it is far less important than bank credit for the economy as a whole.

Money as Internal Currency. The money of Soviet Russia is a purely internal currency. All importing and exporting is done through a government monopoly, and individual citizens have no need for foreign exchange. The rubles used inside Russia cannot be exported or imported. The trading monopoly acquires foreign currencies through exporting goods and uses foreign currencies to pay for imports. The rates of exchange between rubles and foreign currencies are nominal. They are set

[9] A. Baykov, *The Development of the Soviet Economy* (New York: The Macmillan Company, 1947), p. 88.
[10] *Ibid.*, pp. 97, 98.

by the Soviet government and are seldom changed. The rate of exchange between rubles and dollars was 5.3 rubles to the dollar for many years. By keeping its money as domestic currency Soviet Russia insulates its economy as far as possible from international influences which might disrupt the operation of the planned economy.

The Value of Money. The money of Soviet Russia is backed by large reserves of gold and other precious metals, but it is inconvertible and cannot be redeemed in specie. As far as is known, the quantity of money in circulation in Soviet Russia has increased considerably under the planned economy. It rose from a little over 2 billion rubles in 1928 to more than 11 billion in 1936.[11] Further large increases have undoubtedly occurred since then, but statistics on money in circulation have been unavailable.

Prices are under government control and increases in the volume of money in circulation cannot result in the bidding up of prices by any automatic process. However, the planners may see fit to increase prices as the quantity of money in circulation expands, and this has often happened in practice. One writer estimated that the cost of the "Moscow weekly food basket," which had been 2.50 rubles in 1928, increased to 19.20 rubles in 1935, 20.80 rubles in 1937, and 24.25 rubles in 1939—an increase of almost ten times in twelve years.[12] Prices of other consumers' goods were also raised sharply in the period from 1928 through 1940.

Inflationary pressures were increased during World War II as the production of consumers' goods fell off to about one half of the 1940 level while large amounts were paid out to the citizens in wages and salaries. Moreover, the government resumed the printing of paper money to cover budgetary deficits, and the money in circulation increased by 2.4 times in a three-year period during the war. The prices of rationed goods were held steady, but the prices of goods in the farmers' markets often soared to levels 100 or more times as high as those of the same goods at the ration stores.

The Revaluation of the Ruble. The situation during World War II, in which large amounts of money income were paid out to the citizens while the goods available for purchase by civilians were extremely scarce, resulted in a continuing problem. Large hoards of cash, bank deposits, and government bonds were built up by the citizens, and they continued to hang over the market for goods in the postwar period. The Soviet authorities felt that the rationing of consumer's goods could not be ended until at least a part of this surplus purchasing power had been

[11] A. Yugow, *Russia's Economic Front for War and Peace* (New York: Harper & Brothers, 1942), p. 144.
[12] *Ibid.*, pp. 207, 209.

destroyed. Out of the several methods available for this purpose, the revaluation of the ruble was chosen.

On December 16, 1947, the Soviet government began to issue the new ruble currency and to convert outstanding assets into it at varying rates. Actual holdings of cash had to be brought to the banks, where they were converted at the rate of 1 new ruble for each 10 of the old rubles. The citizens who had deposited their money at the savings banks received 1 new ruble for each old one on the first 3,000 rubles of deposits, 2 new rubles for each 3 old ones on the next 7,000, and 1 new ruble for each 2 old ones on all deposits above 10,000 rubles. Citizens who had invested their hard-earned cash in government bonds were given new bonds with a face value of 1 new ruble for each 3 rubles of face value of the old bonds. At the same time, the rationing of consumers' goods was eliminated, all enterprises were directed to pay wages at the same rates in the new rubles as they had in the old, and the prices of some consumers' goods were reduced below the previous levels.

As the production of goods for civilian consumption increased after 1947, the government proceeded to lower the official prices for such goods. The sixth (and second-largest) reduction in prices since the monetary reform of 1947 occurred in April, 1953. The prices of potatoes, vegetables, and fruits were slashed to half their previous levels. Reductions of 10 to 20 per cent occurred in the prices of other foods, while the prices of clothing, shoes, household furnishings, and other consumers' goods were cut by 5 to 25 per cent.

The State Bank. Both commercial credit and commercial banking continue to be used in Soviet Russia. Commercial banking is a government monopoly operated by the State Bank, or Gosbank, which has several thousand branches scattered over the country. In addition to granting commercial credit to all types of economic enterprises, the Gosbank has charge of the emission of currency, the receipt, holding, and disbursement of all government funds, and the flotation of state loans.

Several million enterprises have accounts at the State Bank. All transactions between economic units or enterprises pass through the State Bank and are paid and received by a simple debiting and crediting of accounts. Enterprises are still not allowed to extend commercial credit to each other by means of book accounts, promissory notes, or any other device. This interenterprise credit had been permitted before 1930, but it made the total amount of credit difficult to control and interfered with planning.

When one enterprise buys goods from another, its account at the State Bank is debited when it notifies the bank of its approval of the invoice for the goods or authorizes the bank by letter of credit to pay the account. The account of the selling enterprise is then credited. In earlier years, the State Bank used to credit the seller's account before debiting that of the buyer. This practice resulted in many abuses on the part of sellers, such as filling orders with substandard goods, charging excessive prices, and disregarding delivery dates. Individual citizens, unlike economic enterprises, carry on their dealings in cash and are not allowed to have accounts at the State Bank.

Grants and Loans. Every new enterprise which is to have an account at the State Bank receives its original working capital as a grant from the Bank out of budget funds. That is, the enterprise's account at the State Bank is credited with an amount which is supposed to be sufficient to enable it to carry on all its "normal" operations without any need for borrowing. If the enterprise operates with expected efficiency, its bank account will be replenished by income from sales before it is entirely used up in paying ordinary operating expenses. These original grants of commercial credit do not have to be repaid and bear no interest.

In addition to these grants, the State Bank makes both planned and unplanned loans to meet the anticipated and unanticipated temporary needs of economic enterprises for additional working capital. These commercial loans are always made for specific purposes, vary in length from thirty days to six months, and are repayable with interest which varies from 2 to 4 per cent depending on the type of loan.

Russian and American Commercial Banking. The methods of the State Bank in extending credit may seem peculiar at first glance, but they are not very different from those used in the United States. We think of American enterprises as getting their commercial credit from commercial banks by means of short-term loans which are repayable with interest. Actually, a new enterprise which is just being formed and which is not yet in operation or producing anything might experience great difficulty in obtaining its original fund of working capital by means of a short-term loan at a commercial bank in the United States. Its original funds, both for fixed and working capital, are likely to be obtained through the sale of securities if it is a corporation.

To the extent that funds are obtained by the sale of stocks, they amount to a grant rather than a loan which is repayable with interest. A return does not have to be paid to preferred stockholders unless it is actually earned, and even the presence of available earnings does not necessitate a payment to common stockholders. Moreover, stocks do not obligate the corporation to repay at any time the amounts which the stockholders have invested. The difference between the Russian and American systems is that the Russian enterprises receive their original grants of working capital from the people as a whole through the government and on the basis of the economic plans, while American corporations receive such grants from limited groups of security purchasers and on the basis of the prospective profitability of the enterprises. Operating enterprises in both systems, when they need additional funds for temporary purposes, go to a commercial bank and obtain loans which are repayable at definite times with interest.

Economic Control through the State Bank. The State Bank is much more than an agency for issuing commercial credit and for clearing obligations between enterprises. The administration of the bank is divided into numerous departments for the supervision of credit activities and for planning in connection with specific branches of economic activity. In fact, the State Bank plays an important part in connection with economic planning, for it draws up a financial counterpart of the economic plans of the country in addition to keeping individual enterprises within their financial plans.

The State Bank keeps a constant check on the efficiency with which the individual enterprises operate, and its vigilance extends to almost all phases of the operation of the enterprises. It has insisted on standard "turnover" periods, accurate credit allowances, and prompt repayment of loans. It attempts to control the quality of manufactured goods and to obtain reductions in the quantities of defective goods produced and in the number of "mistakes" such as those involved in shipping machines with important parts missing. If a plant is irregular in its manufacturing processes, falls short of its planned quotas of finished goods, or runs its proportion of "seconds" or "rejects" too high, it can be brought back into line by having its supply of funds cut off or reduced. In the case of purchasing and supply agencies, checkups by the bank every week or ten days are expected to reveal any irregularities in purchasing or distribution, and a curtailment of bank funds will force the agencies to use their own funds to restore their required balances.

Evaluation of Soviet Russian Commercial Banking. The Soviet Russian system of commercial banking experienced some difficulties and growing pains in the early years of the planned economy. It was a trying task to establish a large-scale system of commercial banking using new personnel and to make it operate. New enterprises in business and industry had to become accustomed gradually to keeping books and using their accounts at the State Bank, and to coordinating the bookkeeping with the bank accounts. The opening of hundreds of bank branches and the starting of hundreds of thousands of accounts by enterprises led to endless confusion in the absence of a large, trained banking personnel. In many cases the banks could not even determine the status of their clients' accounts when claims came in for debiting and crediting. Frequent changes in the main economic plans of the country were a disruptive influence in connection with financial plans constructed and operated through the State Bank.

On the whole, however, the State Bank and its subsidiary organizations have operated successfully, as is evidenced by the fact that there have been no important changes in the State Bank or its methods of operation in many years. Moreover, the total short-term credit extended by the bank has increased steadily over the years. Although the commercial banking system sustained losses of facilities and personnel during World War II, it was probably less disrupted by the war than any other phase of Soviet Russia's economic activity, and it was ready to continue operating in its usual fashion in the postwar period.

The system of commercial credit centered around the State Bank seems well suited to the planned economy. Both the total volume of commercial credit and its distribution among enterprises and industries are in the control of the government and the economic planners, and it should be possible to coordinate them closely with the economic plans of the system. In other words, commercial credit serves as a lubricant of the economic machine. It is not able to interfere with planned economic development or influence the content of the planners' decisions.

The results which are planned may or may not suit the wishes of the individual citizens and may or may not furnish consumers with high standards of living, but any such faults will not be chargeable to the system of commercial credit. Since commercial banking in Soviet Russia is only a device for facilitating the making and carrying out of the economic decisions of the planners, there is no point in comparing the deposits or loans and discounts of the State Bank with those of commercial banks in the United States.

Sources of Investment Funds. The government of Soviet Russia pays out to the citizens a total annual sum which is much more than enough to permit them to buy all available consumers' goods and services, and then proceeds to recapture a part of it. Some of the funds thus regained are used for investment in fixed capital.

The devices used to separate the citizens from their surplus income include the turnover tax, the profits tax, income taxes and other direct taxes on individuals, customs duties, social insurance levies, and state loans, or the sale of government bonds.[13] The bonds are sold in part to the individual citizens, who are allowed to receive interest on them, and in part to savings banks, which must invest all their available funds in these bonds.

Investment Banks. The funds which the government devotes to new investments are turned over to enterprises and industries by four investment banks—the Bank for Financing the Capital Construction of Trade and Cooperatives, the Bank for Financing the Capital Structure of Industry and Electrification, the Bank for Financing Socialist Agriculture, and

[13] These taxes will be analyzed in some detail in Chap. 24.

the All-Union Bank for Financing Municipal and Housing Construction. These banks extend grants of funds to government enterprises and loans to cooperative enterprises. They handle both government funds and those which may be accumulated by the enterprises in their respective fields. Besides distributing investment funds, they must supervise the construction of productive facilities, try to eliminate waste, extravagance, and unbusinesslike practices, and work for increased efficiency in capital construction.

The Extent of Capital Investments. The capital investments of the planned economy have been most impressive in terms of rubles and have been responsible for the rapid industrialization of the economy and the mechanization of agriculture. Up to 1928, the socialized economy had made capital investments of only 26.5 billion rubles. Under the first Five-Year Plan, total capital investments amounted to 60 billion rubles and investment in the socialized sector of the economy came to 50.5 billion rubles. The latter investments exceeded the planned estimate of 46.9 billion rubles.

The second Five-Year Plan called for capital investments of 133.4 billion rubles, whereas the actual investments came to 114.7 billion rubles. Capital investments under the third Five-Year Plan were to amount to 188.2 billion rubles, and the economy was well along toward the realization of this goal by the end of 1940.[14] The fourth Five-Year Plan called for total investments of 250.3 billion rubles in the socialized sector of the economy. It is claimed that this goal was exceeded by 22 per cent by the end of 1950, so the actual investments must have reached some 305 billion rubles.[15]

Evaluation of Soviet Russian Capital Investments. We have no criticisms to make of the mechanism by means of which capital investments are made, for this mechanism seems both suitable and inevitable in a socialized economy. Decisions concerning the total quantity of saving and investment and concerning the distribution of capital funds and capital goods among industries and enterprises are made by the planners at the head of the system and not on the basis of the market mechanism. There is no way to determine in advance whether the results of these decisions will be better suited to the needs and desires of the individual citizens than are the results achieved under capitalism. All we know is that the results achieved in Soviet Russia are based on a consideration of social need, in so far as the planners are able to determine it, and are not those which come rather automatically from the pursuit of profits by private investment bankers.

The program of capital investments may be criticized from several

[14] Baykov, *op. cit.*, p. 421.
[15] *U.S.S.R. Information Bulletin,* May 1, 1951, p. 265.

angles. In the first place, the investments have been very costly. Inefficiency and low labor productivity have been just as common in the construction of new production facilities as in other phases of productive activity, and the new capital goods have often cost much more than had been planned. Thus the physical quantities of productive facilities and capital goods obtained have usually been well under the planned estimates. Much of the capital construction has been of low quality in spite of high cost, and large amounts of unfinished production facilities have sometimes been included in official reports of accomplishments.

Soviet Russian capital construction has been afflicted by the delusion that, if an ordinary large-scale plant is efficient, a plant many times as large must be still more efficient. For example, in setting up an electric power station for the Moscow area, the plans called for an enormous plant with a capacity of 200,000 kilowatts. Construction began in 1932, but the station was still unfinished at the end of the second Five-Year Plan in 1937. If the plans had provided for 8 or 10 stations of 20,000 or 25,000 kilowatts each, some of the stations at least could have been completed and in operation by 1937.

In similar fashion, it is claimed that other gigantic enterprises, such as the Magnitogorsk and Kuznets metallurgical works and the Molotov motor works at Gorki, were too large to be managed efficiently. Their early difficulties may have been due to inexperienced management, but even after years of experience the plants were not able to improve their efficiency greatly or increase the rates of output to anything like theoretical capacity. The extremely large plants were also sometimes located far from the necessary raw materials and markets, so that their operations placed an immense burden on the transportation system. However, the planners have learned by experience and in recent years have provided for more plants of moderate size.

The investment program has been weighted heavily in favor of the capital-goods industries. This does not mean merely that the Russians have been receiving a large amount of national income in the form of capital goods instead of consumers' goods, for that result is inevitable under any investment program. It means that the Russians have been concentrating on the construction of capital goods which will produce more capital goods rather than on capital goods which will produce consumers' goods. For example, the third Five-Year Plan called for investments of 87.2 billion rubles in heavy (capital-goods) industries, 16.4 billion rubles in light (consumers' goods) industries, 18.0 billion rubles in agriculture, and 35.8 billion rubles in transportation.[16]

Such investment programs imposed great hardships on the Soviet Russian consumers, for consumers' goods have always been scarce, and in

[16] Baykov, *op. cit.*, p. 421.

some cases (cotton textiles, for example), the machinery in use has been inadequate for processing even the available supplies of raw materials. Moreover, when low efficiency and high cost have made it necessary to fall short of planned goals in connection with the investment program or to impose further sacrifices on the consumers, the Soviet leaders have never hesitated to choose the latter alternative. Under the second Five-Year Plan, for example, investments in heavy industries amounted to 49.8 billion rubles, or over 93 per cent of the planned amount, while investments in consumers' goods industries were only 8.8 billion rubles, or less than 55 per cent of the planned amount.[17]

It is clear that the Russians, under the planned economy, have been, and to a large extent still are, trying to "starve through to future greatness." In view of the plight of the consumers and the fact that Soviet production facilities still fall far short of those of the United States, it is clear that much of this future greatness is still to be attained. Every economy should have a healthy regard for future as well as present productivity and welfare, but unbalanced emphasis on the future may be just as unfortunate as unbalanced emphasis on the present. Too-great neglect of consumers' present wants may endanger future productivity and welfare.

These criticisms should be considered as qualifying but not negating the gains received from the investment program. Certainly, Soviet Russia has experienced a very rapid capital development. It is sometimes estimated that Soviet Russia under the planned economy has been taking about a third of her national income, on the average, in the form of new production facilities. This is a rate of capital development which would be difficult to match in any other country. In the United States, for example, gross private domestic investment in 1952 amounted to about 52.5 billion dollars, or somewhat over one-sixth of the national income of 291.6 billion dollars.[18] In some years during the 1930s, the comparison would have been still less favorable to the United States.

The large investment program may not have been (and still may not be) well suited to the collective wishes of the Russian people, but it has given the planners a large part of what they have wanted and of what they thought the people and the country needed. As a matter of fact, Soviet Russia needed every scrap of her newly developed production facilities in the struggle with Germany. If the planners had decided to give the people more consumers' goods and fewer capital goods for heavy industries in the past, the people might have regretted this decision bitterly long before now.

[17] *Ibid.*
[18] *Survey of Current Business*, July, 1953, pp. 10–11.

QUESTIONS FOR STUDY

1. Why was Russia's monetary situation unsettled down to the 1890s? How was the monetary system placed on a stable basis during the 1890s?

2. Why did Russia experience considerable inflation during World War I? Why did the situation get worse after the war? What was finally done about it?

3. Why did the Russian banking system remain rather primitive down to the Revolution of 1917?

4. What is the role of money in the Soviet Russian planned economy? Of banking? Why?

5. How does the operation of commercial banks in Soviet Russia compare with that of commercial banks in the United States? Are the similarities or the differences more important? Why?

6. Was the value of the ruble stable during the 1930s? During World War II? How and why was the ruble revalued after World War II?

7. Has the Soviet Russian system of commercial and investment banking been a relatively successful part of the planned economy? Why? How would you evaluate the Soviet Russian activities in the field of capital investment?

CHAPTER 22

LABOR

In all economic systems most people, except the very young and the very old, have to be workers. However, there may or may not be a separate economic class known as "labor," whose members do not own the land and capital necessary to their employment and must work for other people for wages and salaries. Such a group tends to come into being with the development of modern industry, transportation, and exchange, and in any economy it brings with it a host of problems which clamor for solution.

LABOR BEFORE THE REVOLUTION OF 1917

The Development of the Working Class. Modern industry developed in Russia only after the serfs were freed in 1861, and it did not advance rapidly until the last quarter of the nineteenth century. In earlier years, therefore, the Russian working class was a small group. There were 210,600 workers in some 5,261 establishments in 1825, and the number increased only to 565,100 in 15,338 establishments by 1860, the year before the abolition of serfdom.[1] Manufacturing plants in these early days were not large-scale modern factories with large amounts of machinery and equipment, but were usually small workshops in which products were made almost literally by hand.

The labor group grew more rapidly in the decades that followed. By 1897 there were 2,098,200 workers employed in 39,109 establishments.[2] The labor group grew to 11,200,000 in 1913, when the population was 139,700,000 and the population of working age (sixteen to fifty-nine) numbered 81,500,000.[3] Thus labor as such made up 14 per cent of all persons of working age. The rest were self-employed in various branches

---

[1] E. J. Simmons (ed.), *U.S.S.R.: A Concise Handbook* (Ithaca, N.Y.: Cornell University Press, 1947), p. 217.
[2] *Ibid.*
[3] A. Yugow, *Russia's Economic Front for War and Peace* (New York: Harper & Brothers, 1942), p. 159.

of production, largely in agriculture. Table 22-1 shows the distribution of the wageworkers among several branches of economic activity.

Table 22-1. Distribution of Russian Wageworkers among Fields of Economic Activity, 1913

Field of activity	Number of wageworkers
Manufacturing and mining	2,776,000
Agriculture	3,000,000
Transportation	1,047,000
Commerce and banking	510,000
Building trades	500,000
All others	3,367,000

SOURCE: A. Yugow, *Russia's Economic Front for War and Peace* (New York: Harper & Brothers, 1942), p. 160.

Characteristics of Russian Labor. The nonagricultural branches of production in Russia drew most of their workers from agriculture down through the years. Early in the eighteenth century, enterprisers could buy or rent serfs from the landed nobility for work in industrial establishments. In 1767, when Russia had only 498 such establishments, about 61 per cent of all the workmen were serfs. By 1825 this proportion had declined to 45.6.[4] Even after the abolition of serfdom, the workers did not sever all connections with agriculture, and many were seasonal workers who returned to the farms in the summer. In fact, 20.9 per cent of the factory workers in European Russia still took some part in agricultural production just before the Revolution of 1917, and another 31.3 per cent had some property interest in the land.[5]

The labor group in Russia did not expand fast enough to absorb the increases in the general population and in the number of persons of working age. For many years, as people became of working age, they found employment in agriculture, and the nonagricultural branches of production merely drew off from agriculture such numbers of workers as they needed. On the other hand, membership in the working class gradually became hereditary. In 1908, 52.4 per cent of the male and 38.8 per cent of the female workers between the ages of twenty and twenty-five in the Moscow province were sons and daughters of workers.[6]

Wages, Hours, and Working Conditions. Even after modern industry had secured a foothold in Russia, the working class labored long hours for low wages under miserable working conditions. This situation was perhaps a carry-over from the time when many workers were serfs, who did not have to be given favorable treatment. At any rate, a working day of twelve hours was considered favorable during the 1880s. Most of the workers put in thirteen or more hours per day and some worked sixteen

[4] Simmons, *op. cit.*, p. 217.
[5] *Ibid.*, p. 218.
[6] *Ibid.*

or seventeen hours. Their wages were a mere pittance, and they were paid only two to four times a year. Wages averaged 187 rubles a year in industry for men and half that for women (a ruble was worth about 50 cents). The employers were free to levy fines against the workers' wages, and this power was used to reduce the wage bill considerably. Working conditions were both unsafe and unsanitary.

These conditions persisted even though labor regulations, dealing with most phases of factory life, had been decreed as early as 1741. The first labor ordinance of practical significance was that of June 1, 1882. It prohibited the employment of children under twelve years of age. It also outlawed night work for older children and limited their hours of work. In 1885 night work was prohibited for employees under seventeen years of age. A law of 1886 required employers to give workers an accurate accounting of their wages and fines, to pay regular workers twice a month, to limit fines against the workers, and to use the proceeds from fines only for welfare purposes.[7]

After a period of considerable labor unrest, further advances were made in 1897. The labor laws of that year restricted the working day to 11½ hours and to 10 hours on Saturday. Work on Sundays and 17 holidays was prohibited, and hours of overtime were limited to 120 per year. Additional progress came gradually. The railroad workers won a 9-hour working day in 1905, and the 11½ hour day disappeared rapidly in other industries after that. Just before World War I, the average working day was 9 hours and 36 minutes, and this was more favorable than it sounded. The workers were given a large number of holidays, including days of church festivals, as well as Sundays. They did not work more than 270 days in the year, and this made their annual hours of work lower than those of any other country at the time.[8]

The wages of Russian workers improved only slowly for two decades after 1880; the average pay in 1900 was not much higher than in 1880. However, the average annual wage rose from 194 rubles in 1900 to 300 rubles in 1913, or by about 54 per cent. The increase in real wages was much smaller and has been estimated at about 15 per cent, for inflation canceled much of the increase in money wages. While the average money wage in 1913 was 25 rubles per month, the range was from 17 rubles for workers in the textile industry to 35 rubles for metallurgical workers.[9]

Wages improved in the years before World War I, but they remained well below those prevailing in leading industrial countries. A study of the period from 1905 to 1908 indicated that the average annual wage in Russia was about one-half that of Germany, one-third that of England,

---

[7] M. Gordon, *Workers before and after Lenin* (New York: E. P. Dutton & Co., Inc., 1941), pp. 18–19.

[8] *Ibid.*, pp. 65–66.

[9] *Ibid.*, pp. 67–68.

and one-fourth that of the United States.[10] As a result, the scale of living of the Russian workers was low. Their food was coarse and lacked variety, and they lagged far behind the workers of other countries in dress, housing, and transportation. However, the Russian workers were not so badly off as their wages would indicate. Many of them derived some income from agriculture or had friends or relatives in the country from whom they could obtain extra provisions, and their working conditions, as well as their hours of work and wages, had been improving.

Labor Unrest. Labor unrest was almost continuous in Russia after 1880. There were 48 strikes between 1881 and 1886, and they represented a protest against the undesirable conditions which labor faced. Strikes became more numerous in the 1890s, averaging 143 per year from 1895 to 1900, and they began to have a political complexion. The workers became associated with radical political movements and parties, and they began to desire the overthrow of the existing regime and its replacement with a better society, as well as an immediate improvement in their own wages, hours of work, and working conditions. Labor demands increased after 1900, and there were 550 large strikes in 1903.[11]

The workers took an active part in the Revolution of 1905. Uprisings, general strikes, and insurrections were common. These were ruthlessly put down by the armed forces, and numerous workers were slaughtered. The year 1905 also set a record for ordinary strikes, for Russia had five times as many strikes as the United States and Germany. The number of strikers in Russia in 1905 was 2,863,000, compared with 1,164,000 in the United States, England, France, Germany, Austria, Italy, and Belgium combined. The Russian workers were successful in almost 25 per cent of their strikes, and another 55 per cent were settled by compromise.[12] In later years, depressed conditions of business, stern repressive measures on the part of government, and inflexible opposition by employers reduced the number of strikes. However, labor unrest increased, and the workers became convinced that the existing government of Russia needed to be replaced.

Trade Unions. There were no trade unions in Russia prior to 1905. Certain types of workingmen's societies had existed previously, but they were not unions. The Revolution of 1905 led the Czar to make some concessions to the people, and under their new liberties the workers rapidly grouped themselves in unions. The first one was formed in St. Petersburg early in 1905, and the number in that city grew to 62 by March, 1907. Some 31 unions sprang up in Moscow. Estimates of the number of unions formed in the whole country vary from 652 to 861.[13]

[10] *Ibid.*, p. 71.
[11] *Ibid.*, pp. 16, 22, 26.
[12] *Ibid.*, p. 45.
[13] *Ibid.*, p. 56.

A law to regulate unions was enacted in March, 1906. It was declared illegal to fine participants in peaceful strikes, but every union was required to have a constitution which conformed to the law and was registered with the government. By 1908 the government was convinced that the unions inspired strikes and extravagant demands by the workers, and that they were being used as a tool by radical organizations bent on overthrowing the monarchy. So the word went out to dissolve the unions for the slightest violation of the regulations of 1906. After 1908 the unions almost disappeared and new ones were put out of business about as fast as they were set up, though efforts to establish them persisted down to World War I.

Social Security. In regard to social security, a law of 1903 made the employers responsible for all accidents which resulted in an employee's losing more than three days' work. Employers were required to pay medical and hospital expenses, immediate aid in the form of a part of the employees' wages, pensions to the permanently disabled, and burial expenses and survivors' pensions in the case of fatal accidents. However, the law also provided that the employee must try to reach an agreement with his employer concerning the amount of his compensation and that employer and employee could agree on a lump-sum settlement amounting to ten times the annual payment.[14]

Another social insurance law became effective in July, 1912. It made workmen's compensation in case of accidents a collective responsibility of the employers, so that voluntary liquidation or bankruptcy of a firm would not terminate the obligation. The law also provided for the establishment of funds to pay benefits to sick workers. The workers contributed three-fifths and the employers two-fifths of such funds. Payments to workers were from one-fourth to one-half of wages for unmarried workers without dependents, and from one-half to two-thirds of wages for workers with dependents incapable of self-support. Benefit payments began with the fourth day of illness, but continued for no more than a month. The benefit funds also paid maternity benefits and made contributions toward the burial expenses of deceased workers.[15] This legislation was rather advanced for its day.

LABOR IN SOVIET RUSSIA, 1917–1940

Labor under War Communism. In the period of War Communism, 1918–1921, elected councils of workers were to participate in the work of managing productive enterprises. In this way, the worker-managers of the future were to receive valuable training. In most cases, however, the workers' councils could not be restrained, and they took over the man-

[14] *Ibid.*, pp. 26–28.
[15] *Ibid.*, pp. 58–60.

agement of the enterprises. Their inexperience and lack of adequate staff, the opposition of former managers and administrative personnel, and the antagonism of workers to surviving members of the former managerial class, all operated to reduce output.

The productivity of labor declined sharply in this period. By 1919 hourly productivity had fallen to about 47 per cent of the 1913 level, and annual productivity to about 28 per cent.[16] Many factors in addition to defective management were responsible. Supplies of tools, raw materials, and fuel were scarce. The workers' money wages would buy little because of the inflation, and their scale of living declined. Intelligent and active workers were absorbed into the administrative apparatus of the economy. Absenteeism and other defects in labor discipline were common. In 1919 absenteeism in industry amounted to an average of 191 days per year, or 65 per cent of the total working days.[17] Many industrial workers went back to the country. Wages no longer depended on qualifications, skills, or kinds of work performed, but became approximately equal for all workers. Eventually conscription was applied to workers of all grades, and labor, like industry, was nationalized. As time went on, the workers received more and more of their wages in kind. Wages of all sorts, including money, rationed goods, and communal services, declined to a small fraction of their 1913 level.

The Soviet Labor Force and Its Distribution. With the introduction of the New Economic Policy in 1921, compulsory labor service and relatively equal pay in kind were abolished, and the labor situation began

Table 22-2. The Growth of the Soviet Russian Labor Force, 1921–1939

Year	Number of wageworkers (000,000 omitted)	Percentage of all persons of working age
1921	6.6	8.2
1932	22.9	25.2
1939	28.7	29.5

SOURCE: A. Yugow, *Russia's Economic Front for War and Peace* (New York: Harper & Brothers, 1942), p. 159.

to settle down and assume permanent form. Table 22-2 shows how the labor force grew, both in absolute numbers and as a proportion of all persons of working age, between 1921 and 1939. Table 22-3 indicates the changing distribution of the labor force among the various fields of production between 1924 and 1937.

[16] A. Baykov, *The Development of the Soviet Economic System* (New York: The Macmillan Company, 1947), p. 41.
[17] *Ibid.*

Table 22-3. Distribution of Soviet Russian Wageworkers among Branches of Production, 1924 and 1937

Branch of production	Number of wageworkers	
	1924	1937
Manufacturing and mining...........	2,107,000	10,112,000
Agriculture........................	1,785,000	2,483,000
Transportation.....................	1,058,000	2,783,000
Government administration...........	965,000	1,743,000
Education.........................	551,000	2,303,000
Commerce.........................	374,000	1,994,000
Construction......................	287,000	2,023,000

SOURCE: A. Yugow, *Russia's Economic Front for War and Peace* (New York: Harper & Brothers, 1942), p. 160.

Hours and Working Conditions. The workers found the basic specifications concerning their hours of work and working conditions in the Labor Code of 1922, as amended. The standard workday for industrial workers and office employees eventually became seven hours. A six-hour day was prescribed for difficult and dangerous occupations and for young workers between the ages of sixteen and eighteen. Except for purposes of training, no employment was permitted for persons under sixteen years of age. The work week was continuous, but the individual workers enjoyed a day off after every five days of work. The workers were entitled to an annual vacation of from two weeks to a month with full pay. These provisions compared favorably with those which prevailed in the leading capitalistic countries.

However, hours of work were increased even before Soviet Russia became involved in World War II. In June, 1940, the standard workday was increased to eight hours for ordinary workers and to seven hours for very heavy work. The six-hour day was retained for dangerous or harmful work. Eight hours also became the standard day for office workers and for young workers. The common six-day week was instituted, and the seventh day became the day of rest for workers in general.

Money Wages. The general conditions with respect to money wages were established by the Labor Code, and the total funds to be used for wage payments annually in individual industries and in the whole economy were determined by the economic planners. In the end, each enterprise and industry knew in advance how much money it could pay out for wages during each year. The government also set up minimum wage rates for various classes of workers and established piece rates for different occupations. Exact levels of wages were supposed to be settled by collective bargaining between management and unions of workers. In practice, however, collective bargaining was widely abandoned after 1934.

Wages were placed on a piecework basis wherever possible. About three-fourths of all wages were based on piece rates before World War II began, and in about a third of the cases additional bonuses or premiums were provided for output beyond established norms or for improved quality of output. Wages had the usual functional aspects. They were a reward for accomplishment in production and an incentive to continued productive activity. They also were a device for evoking a distribution of labor among occupations and industries which was appropriate for carrying out the economic plans. Conscription of labor was reserved for emergencies.

Wage Differentials. The average money wage for workers in the labor force increased from 703 rubles in 1928 to over 4,000 rubles in 1940, but there was considerable inequality in wages between workers. The original scale adopted in 1921 and 1922 provided a differential of only 3.5 to 1 between highly skilled workers and unskilled workers. The ratio between the highest and lowest wages became 10 to 1, 12 to 1, 18 to 1, and even 20 to 1 before World War II. Inequality of 20 to 1 was, of course, extremely small in comparison with that which prevailed in capitalistic countries, where the ratio between the highest and lowest incomes before taxation was several thousand to one (some Socialists say 40,000 to 1 in the United States).

Socialized Wages. In addition to money wages, the workers received benefits in the form of "free social services." They received the use of parks and playgrounds, rest homes and sanatoria, resort hotels and vacation facilities. They also received, or their families did, educational, health, hygiene, and medical services. Even expenditures on cultural activities through the trade unions and on the training of apprentices in the factories were counted. Some of these items appeared to be genuine additions to wages, but others looked fictitious.

Public Honors and Awards. Economic rewards were often combined with public honors and prestige values. Exceptionally productive workers were sometimes made "Heroes of Socialist Toil," a title which carried with it a great amount of honor and prestige and also such advantages as additional pay, free streetcar service and passes for travel, and preferential housing. Other valiant workers were given the medals "For Prowess in Labor" or "For Distinguished Labor." Outstanding material and cultural achievements were rewarded with "Stalin Prizes" to the value of 100,000, 50,000, and 20,000 rubles.

The Stakhanovite Movement. Another combination of public honors and economic advantages was used by the Soviet leaders in their sponsorship of the famous Stakhanovite movement. It was on August 31, 1935, that the coal miner Alexei Stakhanov produced 102 tons of coal in a six-hour shift, instead of the usual quota of 6 to 7 tons. As a result of this prodigious feat, he earned 225 rubles in one day and also became a sort of social lion. His accomplishment was widely publicized, countless honors were bestowed on him, and other workers were urged to go and do likewise. And they did. The amount of coal knocked down in one day by one man, assisted by mechanical equipment and a squad of helpers, advanced eventually to 981 tons. A shoemaker produced 1,860 pairs of shoes in a season, a woman tended 208 automatic looms in a textile mill, instead of the usual 50 to 80, and a bricklayer laid 6,554 bricks in a 7½ hour day.[18] All received greatly increased earnings as well as fame and public acclaim.

Other Noneconomic Incentives. The Soviet leaders tried to get the workers to engage in friendly contests in connection with maximizing output and minimizing breakage, waste, and scrap. Again, the Soviet system appealed to idealism, altruism, and devotion to the cause. Workers were supposed to devote a part of their free time to voluntary labor. The workers might be stimulated by pride in their work, by the realization that they were part owners and part managers, and by their opportunities to suggest improvements and changes in methods. On the other side of the picture were various negative incentives, or penalties and punishments for unsatisfactory performance.

Criticisms of Hours, Wages, and Working Conditions. Soviet Russia used the piecework system of wage payment to a much greater extent than other countries. In fact, the system was applied to some types of work, such as watch repairing and the barber trade, which might be considered poorly adapted to it. In some cases, the piecework system led to large quantities of low-quality product, to an unduly large amount of overtime work, and to a failure to use safeguards for workers.

The Stakhanovite movement indicated that old work quotas (norms for the incentive wage system) were out of date. Increases of 15 to 50 per cent in these quotas were decreed in 1936, and further changes were made in 1940. It was then decreed that work quotas should be increased and piece rates decreased in proportion to the increase in the working day which occurred at that time, and that existing rates of pay for workers paid by the day be retained in spite of increases in hours. The net results were both increased hours of work and reduced hourly rates of pay. Thus the Soviet government eventually came to treat the workers much as it had often accused capitalistic employers of treating them.

The Stakhanovite movement led to great increases in productivity and made possible a revision of obsolete production norms, but it also had

[18] Gordon, *op. cit.*, p. 171.

many bad effects. It led to a craze for record breaking, and many a spurious record was made by selected workers under artificially favorable conditions. Elementary rules for the safety of the workers were forgotten, the number of accidents increased, and the health of the workers suffered. Machinery and equipment were carelessly used, and large quantities of spoiled and incomplete products were turned out. The raising of production norms aroused discontent on the part of ordinary workers who were not capable of achieving records, and the high earnings of the Stakhanovists tended to put them in a social class by themselves.

The efficiency and productivity of workers of all grades remained low in spite of all incentives and inducements. At the end of the second Five-Year Plan it was not some carping outside critic but a special committee of the State Planning Commission that estimated average labor productivity throughout all Soviet industries to be only 40.5 per cent of that of the United States, although average labor productivity in Russia had increased by 82 per cent during the second Five-Year Plan.[19] The average production of coal per worker was 370 tons in Russia, compared with 844 tons per worker in the United States. The amount of cast iron per blast-furnace worker was 756 tons in Russia and 1,260 tons in the United States. Soviet plants often required two or three times as many workers as did American plants of similar size and output.

It is difficult to know the extent to which low labor productivity should be charged to the inexperience and lack of training of the workers, ineffective management, and shortages or low quality of machinery and equipment, instead of to inadequate incentives. However, it is certain that the Soviet workers found it difficult to adjust themselves to the strict discipline of urban industrial life. They were inclined to be late for work, to miss work altogether if they wanted to do something else on a given day, to take it easy on the job, to disregard safety rules, and to be careless in the use of materials and equipment.

Conscious of a general shortage of labor in industry and certain that they could get a job almost anywhere, the workers changed jobs frequently and moved about in search of greener pastures. Labor turnover was amazing. In some individual plants there was a complete change of personnel, office employees as well as production workers, as often as two or three times a year. In one year, over the whole economy, 176.4 per cent of the average number of workers on the payrolls were hired, and 152.4 per cent quit work.[20] Rapid labor turnover was costly and had a destructive effect on labor productivity.

Some critics regarded the Soviet system as a dictatorship over the

[19] Baykov, *op. cit.*, p. 345.
[20] Yugow, *op. cit.*, p. 184.

workers and contended that the wages, hours, and working conditions specified by the laws and collective agreements were meaningless. The managers of enterprises were under great pressure to fulfill the plans and were subject to severe punishment if they failed to do so. As the lesser of two evils, they violated the conditions of the Labor Code. Workers were compelled to put in fourteen or sixteen hours per day rather than eight; and nine or ten hours, instead of seven, in the heavy or dangerous occupations. They were compelled to work on their rest days. The workers "volunteered" for such work, but it was proposed to them by Party men, and workers who did not volunteer might be turned over to the secret police as counterrevolutionaries.[21]

Regimentation of the Workers. In the last years before Russia's entrance into World War II, the government imposed severe controls on the individual workers. Starting in 1938, each worker had to carry a labor book, which contained a full record of his career, including social origin, history, training, types of employment, past sins and fines, and reasons for dismissal from past jobs, or for changing jobs without being dismissed. A worker could not be legally hired unless he had his labor book.

Beginning in 1938 a worker had to give one month's notice in order to leave his job. Later on he was allowed to change jobs only if the manager of his plant would release him. Severe penalties were provided for absenteeism, lateness, soldiering on the job, quitting work early, and other breaches of labor discipline. Penalties included dismissal from the job, eviction from living quarters, correctional labor at the usual place of employment at a 25 per cent reduction in wages, fines, and imprisonment.

The effect of the restrictions and penalties was not very great up to 1940, perhaps because their enforcement would have deprived many enterprises of an important part of their labor supply. In June, 1940, however, plant managers and heads of government bureaus who failed to prosecute workers guilty of breaches of labor discipline were themselves made liable to prosecution and imprisonment up to three years for abuse or nonexercise of power. Some plant managers were removed from their positions and sent to prison under this decree, and so were doctors who showed a "lack of class consciousness in the issuance of hospital certificates," and public prosecutors and judges who failed to prosecute or punish workers or managers under the various decrees.

Real Wages. Increases in money wages over the period from 1928 to 1940 were actually of little benefit to the workers. Where labor productivity is low, real wages and scales of living must also be low, whatever may happen to money wages. Just how low real wages were in Soviet

[21] Freda Utley, *The Dream We Lost* (New York: The John Day Company, Inc., 1940), pp. 172–178.

Russia is difficult to determine because of a lack of statistics relating to price levels, the value of money, and other matters.

According to one source, nominal minimum wages went up by about eleven times from 1911 to 1937, while the cost of food became eighteen times as great. From 1929 to 1937 the food expenditures of a worker's family increased 5.4 times, while the family's income in rubles increased only 3.3 times.[22]

In 1937 the average annual per capita consumption of meat in Soviet Russia was 21.1 kilograms, compared with 62 kilograms in the United States and England and 48 kilograms in Germany. Per capita milk consumption was 170 kilograms per year, compared with 400 kilograms in England and 355 in Germany. Sugar consumption was only half that of the United States, one-third that of England,[23] and two-fifths that of Germany.

Studies of consumption among the workers in large-scale industries in Moscow, Leningrad, Kharkov, and other large cities indicated that in 1937 the average worker had 0.9 of a suit of clothes and 1.5 pairs of shoes. Some 20 per cent of the workers' families had radios, 3 per cent had phonographs, 2.8 per cent had bicycles, and 0.8 per cent had cameras.[24] Housing was scarce and crowded, though the rents charged by the government were relatively low. Clothing and shoes were in very short supply. These conditions were to be expected in view of the heavy rate of capital accumulation and investment, the underfulfillment of plans for the production of consumers' goods, and the need for rationing many products. It is sometimes claimed that the real wages of Soviet workers were lower in the late 1930s than they had been in 1928 or at the end of the first Five-Year Plan.[25]

Labor Unions. The workers were practically compelled to belong to labor unions, and virtually all of them joined. The unions were organized on an industrial basis for the most part, and a union was likely to include all workers throughout the country who worked in enterprises turning out the same kind of products. The union members paid dues which amounted to about 1 per cent of their wages.

The unions were supposed to have many functions. They were to bargain collectively with management concerning the exact wages, hours, and working conditions which were to prevail. Second, they were to participate in management. This involved discussing, and advising management with respect to, the economic plans for particular plants and industries, and helping to make managerial decisions. Again, the unions

[22] Gordon, *op. cit.*, pp. 159, 162.
[23] Yugow, *op. cit.*, p. 203.
[24] *Ibid.*, p. 212.
[25] Harry Schwartz, *Russia's Soviet Economy* (New York: Prentice-Hall, Inc., 1950), pp. 461–463.

"cooperated" with management in several respects. They promoted labor discipline (by discouraging absenteeism, lateness, and labor turnover), encouraged socialist competition, tried to improve the workers' productivity, took some responsibility for the maintenance of machinery and equipment, handled the minor delinquencies of union members, engaged in labor recruiting, and worked for the fulfillment of the plans. Finally, the unions performed several functions for their members. They protected workers against accidents by promoting and enforcing safety measures, saw to it that pleasant and healthful conditions of work were maintained, carried on factory inspection, administered the social insurance and relief systems, protected the workers against arbitrary treatment by management, and carried on activities in connection with vacations, education, recreation, and culture.

Critics of the system, while they could not deny the widespread membership of the unions, contended that their alleged functions were a sham. Collective bargaining amounted to nothing at all because wages, hours, and working conditions were determined by government agencies and the unions never questioned them. Union participation in management was nominal. The union representatives would content themselves with recommending the installation of drinking fountains or shower baths and would avoid questions of great importance to the workers.

The unions were said to be completely unable to protect the workers against summary dismissal, eviction, or imprisonment; against violations of the wages, hours, and working conditions provided by law; or against the violation of safety codes and other protective measures. Their "cooperation" with management meant merely that they functioned as slave drivers, employment bureaus, and collectors of forced loans. They represented the ruling bureaucracy and not the workers. According to this opinion, real labor unions did not exist in Soviet Russia any more than they did in Nazi Germany.[26]

Social Insurance. Soviet Russia seemed to have a comprehensive system of social insurance. There was supposed to be no unemployment, and no unemployment insurance was furnished, but apparently generous benefits were provided in connection with childbirth, illness, accidents, old age, death, and other eventualities. The funds for social insurance were contributed by the various enterprises of the system on the basis of payrolls. Admission to benefits and the actual distribution of funds were in the hands of the labor unions, which functioned on the basis of government standards and plans.

Criticisms of the social insurance system were numerous. Even though the enterprises of the system contributed the funds, the workers were in effect taking a part of their wages in the form of pensions and benefits.

[26] Utley, *op. cit.*, p. 178.

In a system in which all income available for consumption was to be divided among the workers anyhow, there was only one place where the burden of cost could rest in the end, and that was on the workers. Several classes of persons were excluded from the system, and comparatively few people actually received benefits. Total and individual pension and benefit payments ran far under the scheduled amounts. Finally, the social insurance system was used to try to prevent labor turnover, and it was reported that maximum benefits were paid only to workers who had spent six years or more in one job.

Unemployment. The leaders of the economy proudly referred to Soviet Russia as the land without unemployment. The federal constitution guaranteed employment as one of the rights of the citizens, and the planned economy had apparently gone far toward making good on this guarantee. Unemployment benefits and the labor exchanges were eliminated after 1930, and the official story was that Soviet Russia was struggling with a labor shortage rather than an unemployment problem.

However, critics doubted whether Soviet Russia should be considered an economy of full employment. They claimed that many persons who would otherwise have been unemployed had been put to work at forced labor on a variety of government projects (such as the White Sea Canal, the Baikal-Amur Railroad, and the Turksib Railroad). In ordinary industries, large numbers of workers were employed at very low wages and a subsistence standard of living. These workers might well have been unemployed if decent wages had had to be paid, for their actual low wages indicated that their products were of slight value.

Workers, when they were no longer needed in industry and business, were not allowed to hang around and clutter up the streets of the industrial cities. Instead, they were sent back to the farms, and it was in agriculture that unemployment showed itself—not in the form of completely idle workers, for it is easy to appear to have something to do on the farm, but in the form of an excessive labor supply. Thus it was contended that unemployment was merely concealed, and not eliminated, in the Soviet system.

LABOR DURING WORLD WAR II

The Size of the Labor Force. Soviet Russia could not maintain her labor force at prewar size during World War II, and the number of persons employed at wages and salaries in the national economy fell from 31.2 million in 1940 to 27.2 million in 1945.[27] The labor force also came to consist to an increasing extent of women and young and old persons

[27] *Annals of the American Academy of Political and Social Science*, May, 1949, p. 75.

of both sexes. There was full employment for all available labor during the war.

Wages, Hours, and Working Conditions. Work norms, or the quantities of output which workers had to achieve to earn standard wages, had already been raised considerably on two occasions shortly before the war. The length of the standard working day had also been increased. However, as soon as Soviet Russia entered the war, a new decree made it possible for enterprises to require two or three hours of overtime work per day from their employees, with pay at the rate of time and a half. All vacations were discontinued, but additional pay was provided for work during what would normally have been vacation periods.

The Soviet economy was generous in paying for work accomplished beyond the standard tasks. The average annual earnings of workers in the national economy increased from 4,100 rubles in 1940 to 6,000 rubles just after the war.[28] It is probable that the degree of inequality between the highest-paid and lowest-paid workers increased considerably during the war.

Other Factors. The incentive of patriotism was added to those ordinarily in use in Soviet Russia, and workers put forth strenuous efforts during the war. Regulations and controls affecting individual workers were already about as severe as they could be and did not have to be extended during the war period. In fact, the need to maintain an adequate labor force was so great that it led to some relaxation in the enforcement of the regulations already in existence. Thus, for example, many new workers did not have the famous labor books during the war, and the managers of plants were allowed to disregard this matter in hiring workers.

Labor productivity was well maintained during the war, especially in view of the fact that large numbers of workers were lost to the armed forces or to the enemy and had to be replaced with youths, housewives, and old men. On the whole, labor productivity probably did not decline over 15 per cent. The real wages of the workers declined sharply, however. Production was increased somewhat in the heavy industries, but in the industries producing consumers' goods it fell off by close to 50 per cent. Real wages had to change for the worse even though money wages increased. The workers and their families could not purchase and consume more goods than were produced for them.

LABOR IN THE POSTWAR PERIOD

The Labor Force. The number of workers in the Soviet Russian labor force was scheduled to increase from 27.2 to 33.5 million between 1946

[28] *Ibid.,* p. 80.

and 1950 under the fourth Five-Year Plan, and the Soviet leaders did everything possible to increase the size of the labor force. In two years after the war, some ten million veterans were absorbed in the civilian economy, although by no means all of them joined the ranks of those who work for wages and salaries. An effort was also made to retain in the labor force the women, young people, and old people who had accepted temporary employment during the war.

Even the revaluation of the ruble in December, 1947, was intended in part to draw into the labor force people who would otherwise have been inclined to live off their savings for a while, for the reform wiped out liquid savings or reduced them substantially, while improving the relative value of current income from work. The number of workers in the national economy actually reached 39,200,000 in 1950.[29] This was an increase of 12 million over the 1945 figure and 8 million over the 1940 figure. Under the fifth Five-Year Plan, the number was to grow to 43,700,000.

Wages, Hours, and Working Conditions. Average money wages, which had reached 6,000 rubles per year just after the war, increased to 7,400 rubles by 1948.[30] Further increases have occurred since that time. Inequality in the distribution of income has increased rapidly. Some skilled workers have been reported as earning 5,000 to 10,000 or more rubles per month, whereas some workers receive as little as 150 or 200 rubles per month. Thus the ratio between the earnings of the highest-paid and lowest-paid workers may well be 50 to 1 or even higher. Stalin Prize winners have received as much as 200,000 rubles in a year's time, or at least one hundred times as much as the earnings of the lowest-paid workers.[31]

The wartime practice of requiring overtime work was eliminated, but the eight-hour day was officially substituted for the seven-hour day as the basic workday. In 1953 the 8-hour day and the 48-hour week were still in effect for ordinary workers. In the United States, the average actual work week of the employees in all manufacturing industries was 40.5 hours in 1950, while in nonmanufacturing fields (excluding agriculture) it varied from 32.1 hours in anthracite coal mining to 45.7 hours for employees of automotive and accessories dealers.[32] The annual vacation of two weeks or more with pay was reinstated in Soviet Russia after the war.

Real Wages. The real wages of Russian workers have remained at low levels. Such prices as 360 rubles for the cheapest suit, 227 rubles for a

[29] *U.S.S.R. Information Bulletin,* February 23, 1951, p. 110.
[30] Schwartz, *op. cit.,* p. 460.
[31] *Ibid.,* pp. 466–567.
[32] *Statistical Abstract of the United States, 1952,* pp. 189–190.

low-grade pair of leather shoes, 400 rubles for a deal table, and 110 rubles for an aluminum kettle, as reported from Moscow in 1953, were very high from the point of view of a low-paid worker making 200 rubles per month.[33] And such prices would have made large dents in the wages of the average worker.

At the same time, the minimum diet for a family of five in Moscow required 255 rubles per week. This was about 94 per cent of the wages of an ordinary worker in the Moskvich automobile factory and was about half of the net earnings from a large monthly wage of 2,500 rubles.[34] It was estimated that only the highest-paid Russian worker could live as well as the average British worker. Per capita consumption of common consumers' goods in Soviet Russia in 1950 had little more than regained the levels of 1940.

Labor Productivity. Labor productivity was at a low level in 1946—probably 20 or 25 per cent below the wartime level. This was due to the disruption of production caused by rapid and large-scale reconversion from wartime to peacetime production; the bad condition of factories, machines, and equipment in the western area, which had been occupied by the Germans; the wearing out of much machinery and equipment in other parts of the country; and the weariness of the workers after the strenuous efforts and privations necessitated by the war.

The leaders of Soviet Russia made determined efforts to increase labor productivity in the next few years. Many things were tried besides increasing wages in general and enlarging the differentials in income. In September, 1946, the government raised the prices of rationed foods substantially, whereas wages were raised to a much smaller extent. This made it necessary for workers to work harder in order to maintain their usual scales of living. It may also have induced some idle people to go to work and may have led some wartime workers to retain their jobs.

In March and April, 1947, work quotas were raised again for workers on the piecework basis. This resulted in wage cuts for workers who did not increase their outputs, for workers were often paid both bonuses and higher piece rates for production in excess of their work quotas. Higher norms, therefore, meant that the workers had to produce more before they could cash in on the higher piece rates or bonuses.

The revaluation of the ruble and the general currency reform of December, 1947, tended to make workers more dependent than formerly on their current incomes and thus gave them an incentive to increase productivity. The concurrent abandonment of rationing acted in the same direction, since it meant that thereafter the workers could spend their incomes as they pleased. An effort was also made to eliminate

[33] *The Economist,* Jan. 3, 1953, pp. 13–14.
[34] *Ibid.*

clerical and administrative jobs, while increasing the number of workers employed directly on products.

The trade unions were also adapted to the task of increasing labor productivity. Collective bargaining resulting in collective agreements between workers and management was revived in 1947. The subjects to be covered by the new collective agreements were means of increasing the productivity of the workers, substitution of piece rates for time rates, improvement of production norms, programs for training workers and technical personnel, devices for improving labor discipline, measures to improve the safety of working conditions, improvement of the workers' housing, living conditions, and food, and improvement of recreational facilities for the workers.[35] The implications of these subjects are most obvious.

The Stakhanovite movement was continued and extended in the postwar period, and socialist competition was more vigorous than ever before. Public honors were also used to stimulate the workers. Between 1945 and 1949, orders and medals were conferred on 510,000 workers and others. Some 4,800 workers had been made Heroes of Socialist Toil and there had been 2,450 winners of Stalin Prizes.[36]

According to the authorities, the efforts to increase labor productivity were strikingly successful. It was reported that by the end of 1950 the productivity of the workers surpassed the prewar level by 37 per cent.[37] This was slightly more than the 36 per cent improvement called for by the fourth Five-Year Plan. However, it left much further improvement to be desired, for the productivity of Russian labor had been low in the last years before World War II.

Control of the Individual Workers. The Soviet leaders wanted some redistribution of workers among industries in the postwar period in order that the economic plans might be carried out. However, they got more redistribution than they needed. Workers were anxious to move from one enterprise to another and from one area to another in search of better opportunities. In particular, workers who had been employed in the Ural Mountain region, Siberia, or central Asia wanted to return to the west.

Employers were anxious to acquire an adequate labor force and to fulfill the plans for production, so they were willing to employ almost anyone who applied, without asking too many questions. Labor turnover rose to high levels once more, and the old problems of absenteeism, lateness, and soldiering on the job again reared their ugly heads. The reaction of the government was to enforce again the regulations and con-

[35] Harry Schwartz, *Russia's Postwar Economy* (Syracuse, N.Y.: Syracuse University Press, 1947), p. 76.
[36] *U.S.S.R. Information Bulletin,* Nov. 18, 1949, p. 691.
[37] *U.S.S.R. Information Bulletin,* May 18, 1951, p. 289.

trols affecting the individual workers, which had sometimes been disregarded but never officially repealed. The workers were required to have and carry labor books in order to obtain employment. They were not allowed to leave their jobs without their employers' permission. Penalties for lateness, absenteeism, and loafing were invoked.

Social insurance benefits and pensions, as well as earnings, began to depend heavily on the number of years a worker had remained an employee of the same enterprise. Attempts to reduce labor turnover and to solve the other problems of labor discipline also had important implications for the improvement of labor productivity. On the whole, it seems necessary to conclude, on the basis of evidence available, that Soviet Russia still falls far short of being that "workers' paradise" which some extreme "friends of the Soviet Union" have always professed it to be.

QUESTIONS FOR STUDY

1. Why was Russia slow to develop a working class? How were the workers treated with regard to wages, hours, and working conditions in the 1880s? How much had their status improved by 1913?

2. Why was labor unrest almost continuous in Russia after 1880? Did the workers have unions? Social security?

3. Why is it said that the nominal situation of Soviet Russian labor was very favorable under the planned economy before World War II? In what respects and to what extent did the actual situation differ from the nominal?

4. Are the Soviet Russian workers well paid in terms of money? Real wages? What other devices besides payment are used to stimulate the workers? Have the workers been strictly controlled by the government?

5. What are the functions of unions supposed to be in the Soviet Russian planned economy? How do the Russian unions compare with those of the United States? What do you think is the actual significance of unions in Soviet Russia?

6. How has Soviet Russia been trying to increase the productivity of its workers in the period since World War II? Have the efforts been successful?

7. All things considered, how do you think the economic status of the average worker in Soviet Russia compares with that of the average worker in the United States?

CHAPTER 23

COMMERCE

Modern economies are known as exchange economies. Production occurs on a large scale and in anticipation of demand. It uses tremendous amounts of plant and equipment and depends on an extensive labor force composed of specialized individuals who work for wages and salaries. A large volume of exchanges is necessary to the successful functioning of such economic systems. The growth of commercial activities is, in turn, dependent upon the development of transportation and the evolution of money, credit, and banking.

COMMERCE BEFORE THE REVOLUTION OF 1917

Internal Commerce in Early Times. Internal commerce was slow to develop in Russia and was unimportant until after 1861, the year in which the serfs were freed. In earlier times, manufacturing amounted to little, and the labor force was small. Most of the people were employed in agriculture, and the large estates operated by landowners and serfs were relatively self-sufficient units. Only a few railroads were in operation, and the period of rapid construction was still to come. Roads were practically nonexistent. Banks and credit facilities were primitive, and the money of the country was unstable in value. Under these conditions, it was not surprising that internal commerce remained at a low level and that no records of its volume were kept.

Internal Commerce, 1861–1890. Russia's internal commerce expanded somewhat after 1861. The emancipated serfs had to pay money to the landowners each year and so had to sell part of their produce for cash. Much of the commerce was in grains originally, but it gradually spread out to take in other things. The freeing of the serfs provided a growing labor supply for industry, and the number of persons working for wages increased. In a country of such vast distances, the development of the railroads was of tremendous importance to the growth of internal commerce, as was the expansion of traffic on inland waterways.

According to a report of the Russian government, data on the volume

of goods traded in 1890 were available for only a few items. The internal
trade that year included manufacturing and mining goods to the value
of 1,656 million rubles, breadstuffs worth 1,400 million rubles, foreign
imports valued at 416 million rubles, and a transport turnover amounting to 523 million rubles.[1] However, it was estimated that there were
383,740 commercial enterprises in Russia, including 740 joint-stock companies. The total turnover of these enterprises was estimated at 14,055
million rubles, of which the joint-stock companies accounted for almost
one-half.[2]

Marketing methods remained primitive in this period. Only the centers
of population had retail stores. Many sections of the country were
reached only by itinerant peddlers and hawkers. A large part of the
total volume of exchanges was made at fairs. These were held where
rivers or other avenues of travel came together, and they were attended
by many people, who came from near and far to buy and sell or barter
goods. According to an estimate of the Russian government, there were
2,825 fairs held in 1880, and they were attended by 194,000 tradesmen.[3]

Internal Commerce, 1890–1917. After 1890 internal commerce expanded rapidly in Russia, for all conditions were favorable. The volume
of manufacturing increased sharply. The railroads went through a period
of active construction, though they did not expand as fast as the volume
of trade. With the improvement of railroad service, commercial travelers
began to appear, purchases of goods could be made directly from producing and distributing centers, such as Moscow, and agencies furnishing information about the financial standing of commercial enterprises
began to spring up.

During the 1890s Russia went on the gold standard, and the ruble acquired a stability of value which was encouraging to commercial activities. Banks and credit facilities multiplied, and Russia came to have
a real banking system for the first time. A large force of workers sprang
up, who received their pay in cash and had to translate it into commodities and services. The total number of trading enterprises reached
854,024 in 1900 and 1,123,683 in 1910. The latter total included 8,462
large-scale concerns and 29,707 peddlers and hawkers. The rest of the
firms were medium-sized, small, and very small.[4]

This growth did not give Russia an adequate marketing system. Even
in 1913, Russia's retail network was small and widely scattered. The
country's many peasants were served for the most part only by village

[1] Russian Ministry of Finance, *The Industries of Russia* (St. Petersburg: Trenke
and Fusnot, 1893), vol. II, p. 479.
[2] *Ibid.*, p. 480.
[3] *Ibid.*, p. 482.
[4] A. Raffalovich (ed.), *Russia: Its Trade and Commerce* (London: P. S. King &
Staples, Ltd., 1918), p. 275.

(farmers') markets, small country stores, and pack peddlers, who could carry only small stocks of goods but who penetrated far into the depths of the country. Distances were enormous, roads were impassable during much of the year, postal and telegraph services were inadequate, and the railroad network was still not extensive. The cities were better off with respect to trade facilities, but not very much.

Commercial activities were primitive. The Russian stores did not furnish delivery service, and it was up to the customers to haul their goods home. Moreover, the Russian stores had not gone over to the one-price system. The price to be paid was determined by higgling and bargaining with the storekeeper, and the customer who paid the first price asked was sure to be robbed. There were about 16,000 fairs in operation, and they had a total turnover of about 5 billion rubles. The largest fair, that held at Nizhni-Novgorod, had about 2,500 shops and 10,000 booths.[5] However, the relative importance of fairs was declining.

Russia's International Trade in Early Times. Even a country with little internal commerce is likely to have some trade with other countries, and that was the case with Russia in early times. Even before 1861 surplus grains and other raw produce were exported at times, and the Russian nobility and royalty desired to import luxury goods which could not be secured readily at home. Better statistics are usually available for international trade than for domestic, for imports and exports have to pass through the government customs houses and stand and be counted. Thus we know that, from 1841 to 1851, Russia had average exports worth 97.8 million rubles per year and average imports worth 85.9 million rubles. From 1851 to 1860, the average annual figures were 129.3 million rubles for exports and 119.2 million rubles for imports.[6]

International Trade, 1861–1890. The volume of Russia's international trade, as measured in rubles, increased several times over from 1860 to 1890. Average annual exports amounted to 622.2 million rubles from 1880 to 1890, and average annual imports came to 471.8 million rubles.[7] Toward the end of the period, grain was the leading export by a wide margin, followed in order by flax and tow, forest products, oilseeds, hemp and tow, and wool. The leading imports in order of importance were cotton, drugs and chemicals, wool, tea, and machinery. Thus Russia's leading exports were raw or partly processed products, while her leading imports were either manufactured goods or raw products which were not produced at home in any large quantity.[8]

In the period from 1886 through 1890, Germany was the leading

---

[5] W. H. Beadle, *Commercial Russia* (London: Constable & Co., Ltd., 1918), p. 203.
[6] Raffalovich, *op. cit.*, p. 301.
[7] *Ibid.*
[8] Russian Ministry of Finance, *op. cit.*, pp. 444–445.

source of Russian imports, furnishing 34.1 per cent of the total. Great Britain, the United States, Austria-Hungary, and France followed in that order. The leading market for Russian exports was Great Britain, which received 34.7 per cent of the total. Other leaders were Germany, the Netherlands, France, and Italy. Thus Russia's trade was primarily with the various countries of Europe.[9]

International Trade, 1890–1917. Russia's international trade continued to grow until World War I broke out. In 1913 Russian exports were valued at 1,520.1 million rubles and her imports at 1,374.0 million rubles.[10] Russia had come to have a considerable excess of merchandise exports over merchandise imports and enjoyed what is sometimes called a favorable balance of trade. However, the amount that other countries owed Russia in each year was used for the payment of interest on foreign capital invested in Russia and of freight charges on Russian goods carried in foreign vessels.

Russia's chief articles of export were about the same in 1909–1913 as they had been in 1886–1890. Grain was the leading export by a tremendous margin, followed in order by forest products, flax, butter, sugar, and hides and leather. The leading imports were cotton, tea, wool, iron and steel, agricultural machinery, and nonferrous metals.[11] Russia's exports were still primarily raw and partly processed goods, and her imports were primarily manufactured goods or raw products which could not be produced at all, or could not be turned out in adequate quantities, in Russia.

For the period 1908–1912, food products made up 60.8 per cent of Russian exports; raw and partly processed materials, 33.1 per cent; animals, 1.7 per cent; and finished manufactures, only 4.4 per cent. Total Russian imports were made up of food, 19.1 per cent; raw and partly processed materials, 48.5 per cent; finished manufactures, 31.4 per cent; and animals, 0.9 per cent.[12] Germany was the leading market for Russian exports in 1913, followed by Great Britain, the Netherlands, France, and Italy. Germany was the leading source of Russian imports by a wide margin, followed by Great Britain, the United States, China, and France.[13] Except for a considerable increase in total volume, Russia's international trade showed great stability for several decades before World War I.

After the war broke out, Russia's trade with other countries changed sharply. She required many imports but could not maintain her exports,

[9] *Ibid.*, p. 451.
[10] Raffalovich, *op. cit.*, p. 301.
[11] A. Yugow, *Russia's Economic Front for War and Peace* (New York: Harper & Brothers, 1942), pp. 101, 105.
[12] Raffalovich, *op. cit.*, p. 303.
[13] Yugow, *op. cit.*, p. 107.

both because she had fewer goods to spare than usual and because she faced grave difficulties in getting her exports to their destinations. Thus Russian imports amounted to 1,098.0 million rubles in 1914 and 1,114.0 million rubles in 1915, while her exports fell off to 956.1 million rubles in 1914 and 397.2 million rubles in 1915.[14]

INTERNAL COMMERCE, 1918–1940

Early Experience in Internal Commerce. All private trade in Russia was abolished by decree in 1918, and the distribution of commodities was carried on through consumer cooperatives and government distribution centers. With the introduction of the New Economic Policy in 1921, private trade and markets came into existence once more and flourished. In 1922–1923, private trade accounted for 75.3 per cent of total retail business, compared with 14.4 per cent for state trade and 10.3 per cent for cooperative trade.[15] About two-thirds of the private stores were one-man stalls or shops, and only about 4 per cent employed more than four sellers.[16]

Private enterprisers were treated badly even under the New Economic Policy. Private traders were barred from other occupations and from trade union membership, and their position in a socialized economy was risky. Their business was hampered by discriminatory railroad rates and by government interference in deciding which districts should get industrial products and in what quantities. And the government was encouraging the development of cooperative stores and laying the foundations for a large-scale system of state stores.

The Growth of State Marketing. By 1928 private retailers made up 77.8 per cent of the total number, but handled only 22.4 per cent of the total business. Government stores had only 15.9 per cent of the total trade, and cooperative stores did the lion's share of the business, 61.7 per cent.[17] In 1929 private trading was again abolished. By 1933 government stores made up 28 per cent of the total number and did 44 per cent of the business, the rest being handled by cooperative stores.[18] In 1934 the right of the collective farms (and of individual peasants and collective farmers) to sell surplus produce on the collective-farm peasant markets was established. Competition between cooperative stores and government stores continued until late 1935, when a decree excluded co-

[14] Raffalovich, *op. cit.*, p. 301.
[15] A. Baykov, *The Development of the Soviet Economic System* (New York: The Macmillan Company, 1947), p. 55.
[16] L. E. Hubbard, *Soviet Trade and Distribution* (New York: St. Martin's Press, Inc., 1938), p. 14.
[17] Baykov, *op. cit.*, p. 65.
[18] Hubbard, *op. cit.*, p. 254.

operative stores from the 654 leading cities and towns, although they
continued to function in rural areas. In 1938 there were 327,000 retail
stores, compared with over a million in 1912. Government stores handled
60 per cent of the retail trade in 1940, cooperative stores a little more
than 20 per cent, and farm markets something under 20 per cent.[19]

Cooperative Stores. Cooperative stores continued to be important in
rural retailing, handling about 75 per cent of that business, with local
cooperative associations running from one to five or more stores. The
stores were both general and specialized. Some of the large stores had
their own dairies, bakeries, and manufacturing plants to supply them
with goods. Large cooperative stores had their own accounts with the
State Bank and dealt directly with the commercial departments of industries in obtaining goods for sale to their members.

Government Stores. Government stores were operated by the governments of republics and provinces, the federal government, and even by
the commercial departments of industries which were under the ministries in charge of food and manufactured consumers' goods. The stores
themselves included simple specialty stores, chain stores, department
stores, all-union provision shops, and other types. Besides government
stores, cooperative stores, and farm markets, private individuals and
producers' cooperatives were allowed to sell their own products, but
they were not allowed to operate trading enterprises which bought and
sold finished goods.

Centralized Control of Marketing. The Ministry of Internal Trade
became the chief planning and administrative agency in connection
with the marketing of goods. The internal organization of the ministry
was similar to that of the ministries in other fields, such as industrial
production. Like all other departments of economic activity, internal
trade operated on the basis of plans drawn up by the State Planning
Commission.

Such matters as the supplying of goods to individual stores and the
selection of goods which individual stores should carry were difficult
to plan at national headquarters. Many stores were given some freedom
in ordering their goods. How much freedom an individual store was
allowed to have depended on the size of its turnover, its importance,
and the class of customers it served. Stores were required to post official
price lists for their goods, and there were inspectors to see that they
abided by official price and quality standards. On the other hand, the
plans set no limits on the amount of business which the individual
stores might do and they were encouraged to expand their volume.

Price Control. It goes without saying that prices were controlled in
the Soviet Russian planned economy. All the really important economic

[19] Harry Schwartz, *Russia's Soviet Economy*, rev. ed. (New York: Prentice-Hall,
Inc., 1954), pp. 430, 436.

decisions were made by economic planning and not on the basis of prices. Under these conditions, price control was an integral part of economic planning and not something superimposed upon an economy which would ordinarily have operated in some other fashion. Subject to the directives of the Communist party, the power of price control resided in the Council of Ministers and the State Planning Commission, although the detailed work of price fixing was done at various levels. Retail prices, as finally set up, included wholesale prices, turnover taxes, expenses (and planned profits) of the retail enterprises, and transport expenses.

Under the influence of extreme scarcity, consumers' goods were distributed largely on the basis of rationing, under the first Five-Year Plan and part of the second Plan. The prices placed on rationed goods were kept low in comparison with those which would have prevailed in a free market. However, it was not always easy to adjust prices to compensate for changes which occurred in the production of consumers' goods, and on the whole there were not enough goods available to use up the money incomes of the people at the low fixed prices for rationed goods. The output of consumers' goods in terms of physical units increased only slightly, if at all, under the first Five-Year Plan, but the wages and salaries of workers more than quadrupled. The workers often found that there was nothing on which to spend the rest of their money incomes after the rationed goods were purchased. This situation led some wag to remark that the Russian workers were the richest in the world, since they had more money than they knew what to do with.

At any rate, the "commercial" stores which the government developed under the first Five-Year Plan furnished an outlet for the surplus money incomes of the workers, since they would sell any quantities of goods to any purchasers at very high prices. They handled only 3 per cent of all retail trade in 1932, but 15 per cent in 1933 and 25 per cent in 1934.[20] The differences in the prices of the same goods from the ration stores to the commercial stores were extremely large. In Leningrad and Moscow in 1931, the ration price of bread in workers' ration stores was 1 ruble per kilogram, but it was 2 rubles in the commercial stores. Sugar was four times as high in commercial stores as in ration stores, tea three times, fish four times, soap two to five times, meat five to eight times, butter five to six times, and eggs five times.[21]

This relation between prices in the ration and commercial stores tended to make differences in real incomes among workers smaller than the differences in their money incomes. If a worker who received 1,000 rubles a year could spend all his income for rationed goods, while one who received 5,000 rubles per year could spend only 1,000 rubles for

[20] Hubbard, *op. cit.*, pp. 55–58.
[21] Yugow, *op. cit.*, p. 206.

rationed goods and had to spend the remainder in the commercial stores, the difference in real income between the two workers would have been nearer 2 to 1 than 5 to 1.

With the abandonment of rationing in 1935, both government and co-operative retail stores began to operate on a commercial basis. They would sell any quantity of any good to any purchaser at prices which were originally in between those that had formerly prevailed in ration and commercial stores. Consumers' goods were supposed to sell at single prices, but this did not mean that the prices of the same goods were uniform all over the country. Instead, they were uniform within zones. Eight zones were established for bread and cereal foods, five for meat and fish, four for sugar and confectionery, four for vegetable oils, and five for butter.

Individual retail stores had no pricing problem. Wholesale and retail prices were fixed from above, and the difference was the gross margin of the retail enterprise, from which overhead and operating costs had to be paid. The gross margin was so contrived that the retail store which operated with normal efficiency would be able to make a small net profit. Sometimes the gross margin was more favorable for some goods than for others, and the managers of stores, with some freedom to determine their assortments of goods, naturally emphasized the goods which afforded the larger margins.

Rationing. The first Five-Year Plan provided for a high rate of capital investment and a great increase in the number of industrial workers. The total money income distributed to the people increased sharply, but the quantity of goods available for consumption could not be increased to the same extent because of the heavy capital investments, the exportation of commodities to acquire foreign exchange with which to buy machinery and hire technical experts, and the many difficulties encountered in carrying out the plan. Rationing was introduced to share scarce consumers' goods and provide the urban industrial workers with as high a standard of living as possible. Rationing began in Leningrad in November, 1928, and was extended to the whole country in 1929. By 1934 about 70 million persons were receiving rations.[22]

The rationing system led to very inefficient retailing. The stores were dirty and unkempt. Store employees were too few in number and seemed quite indifferent to the wishes of the customers. The buyers were required to pay for their purchases before selecting them, commodities which required wrapping were left unwrapped, people had to bring their own cans or containers, and there was no delivery service. There were too few stores and too little room in each one, goods were not marked with price tags, commodities were poorly displayed, and

[22] Hubbard, *op. cit.*, p. 209.

conditions of storage were frightful. Goods were just thrown into the stores, and scarce consumers' goods sometimes spoiled before anyone was able to purchase them. These conditions were possible because store employees and officials had little personal interest in the business and because, under the rationing system, they were sure of their customers' business. It was difficult to improve efficiency in retailing as long as rationing continued.

The rationing of bread and flour ended on January 1, 1935, and the rest of the rationing system was eliminated by January, 1936. All the stores then operated on the "commercial" basis. The rationing system was liquidated for several reasons. Foods and other consumers' goods were being produced in larger amounts, and it was less necessary to use rationing to ensure ordinary people the bare necessities of life. It no longer seemed necessary to use rationing to favor certain classes of people. With rationing ended, differences in money wages would represent differences in real wages more accurately than before, and this seemed desirable in the light of the Soviet principle of payment according to the work done. It was easier to distribute workers among industries on the basis of differences in money wages than by manipulating rations. Finally, an increase in the efficiency of retailing was desired. With all stores selling the same goods at the same prices in any quantities desired or available, the managers and employees had to attend to business and attract patronage in competition with other stores.

Accomplishments of Soviet Marketing through 1940. The total volume of internal trade increased by leaps and bounds from 1928 through 1940. Exclusive of sales on the farm markets, it increased from 15.2 billion rubles in 1928 to 25.5 billion rubles in 1932, 125.9 billion rubles in 1937, and 174.5 billion rubles in 1940.[23] The change in the physical volume of trade was much less, for prices increased sharply during the period. In the second place, the efficiency of retailing improved. This was an almost automatic accomplishment because, if the quality of Russian retailing changed, it had to change for the better. Nevertheless, it was a far cry from the miserable stores of ration days to some of the modern establishments in the large cities, which had large varieties of goods, numerous and attentive sales people, tearooms, restaurants, and nurseries. These stores were well decorated, displayed their goods in modern fashion, engaged in some advertising, and wrapped and delivered purchases.[24]

Weaknesses of the Marketing System through 1940. The Soviet Russian marketing system was far from a complete success in the period under discussion. This was due in part to peculiarities of the Soviet

[23] Baykov, *op. cit.*, pp. 235, 260.
[24] Hubbard, *op. cit.*, pp. 241–242.

Russian situation and in part to difficulties in the operation of any system of large-scale state marketing. First, it was unfortunate that the new marketing system had to be started practically from scratch, with new principles, new facilities, and new personnel. Scarcely any of the facilities, owners, or managerial personnel of the former system of private trading were suitable for the new state marketing system, and the development of the new meant the liquidation of the old.

Again, it was unfortunate that the new marketing system had to be set up in a period when conditions elsewhere in the economy required the rationing of consumers' goods. Under rationing the new personnel developed the habit of merely distributing goods to depersonalized ration-card holders instead of selling them to customers who could buy goods freely in any store on the basis of prices, quality, and service. This difficulty went all the way back to the central headquarters of the marketing system, where distribution plans were made on the basis of an abstract average consumer. The real consumer was often forced to behave like the average consumer and accept goods that he did not want in order to acquire those that he did want. And the store managers, since they did not have to worry about the tastes of the real consumers, carelessly accepted defective and substandard goods for the stores.

Marketing suffered also because the planners did not see fit to devote large quantities of effort, funds, and managerial ability to its development. The large investments of funds and managerial talent were made in other phases of economic activity, such as heavy industry. It was probably inevitable, with a shortage of capital and managerial ability, that some fields of activity should be slighted, but the result was unfortunate for retail trade. Stores continued to be few and they were often inadequately staffed and poorly managed. Moreover, it was at the retail level that the problems created by the government's economic policies came to a head. Large investments in heavy industry and rapidly expanding production of capital goods in a backward economy were bound to create shortages of consumers' goods, and the resulting dissatisfaction of the people was exposed in their attitudes toward the stores and their struggles to get a share of the limited goods.

Finally, it may be questioned whether marketing (and especially the retailing phase) is as well suited to large-scale management by the government as is, for example, heavy industry. If retailing requires quick decisions, flexibility, and ingenuity on the part of store managers, the operation of retail stores on a tremendous scale by the government is almost certain to be awkward, cumbersome, and inefficient. Thus in the Soviet system, small errors at headquarters would deprive whole areas of certain types of goods, or create shortages in some stores although others in the same region were well supplied. Seasonal goods would arrive after the season was over, or would be sent to the wrong places. Supplies sent to the stores were sometimes poorly adapted to local tastes and customs, and goods would pile up on the shelves in some areas while unsatisfied demands for the same products existed elsewhere.

If the government set the price of a product too low, the Russian consumers would rush in and buy up the entire stock before the government got around to change its price. If the price of a product was inadvertently set too high, large stocks of it would be frozen in the stores until the appropriate government agency got around to reducing the price. Lastly, store managers, with little chance for personal gain from the operation of their stores and under pressure to achieve the planned volume of turnover, were sometimes reluctant to stock new types of goods because these products might move slowly. The problem of developing individual initiative and responsibility in management in a government-owned marketing system proved difficult.

The Mechanism for International Trade. After early 1918, international trade was monopolized by the government in Soviet Russia. A special Ministry of Foreign Trade had general responsibility for all import and export transactions. Neither private individuals nor government enterprises could enter into international transactions except through this Ministry. The Ministry formulated the plans for international trade, which had to be correlated closely with the general economic plans of the country, and saw that they were carried out, through its branches, its trade missions to various countries, and its export and import corporations, which specialized in particular types of goods.

Through the monopoly of foreign trade, the government maintained strict control over imports and exports, obtained protection against the competition of other countries and against the upsetting influence of world prices on the Russian domestic market, and could use its trade with other countries to pursue political and social ends as well as economic ones. The ruble used in domestic trade was not officially quoted in foreign markets, and fluctuations in the internal purchasing power of the ruble were not represented accurately by the official rate of exchange. The government prohibited the import and export of the rubles used within the country and the exchange of such rubles for foreign currency.

The Development of Foreign Trade. Soviet Russia's trade, which had been declining, virtually collapsed after the Revolution of 1917. In 1919–1920 it was running at about one-eightieth of prewar levels. Foreign trade began to revive with the introduction of the New Economic Policy in 1921, and continued to grow for a time under the planned economy. In 1930, in the middle of the first Five-Year Plan, foreign trade attained the highest level it was to reach under the planned economy up to 1940. Exports amounted to 4,500,000,000 rubles and imports to 4,600,000,000 rubles. The total volume of trade was at 73 per cent of that which had prevailed before World War I.[25]

Foreign trade reached this fairly large volume because of the great program of industrialization at home. Soviet Russia's needs for machinery, precision instruments, other industrial equipment, and certain raw materials were great, and she satisfied them by any means which lay ready to hand. Exports were based on the desire to acquire foreign purchasing power, and any goods were exported which promised to have a ready sale in foreign markets, regardless of whether domestic supplies were adequate or inadequate. Grain production was low in these years and near famine conditions prevailed at times, but Russian grain exports averaged 453 million rubles annually from 1929 to 1932. The production of cotton textiles even by 1932 amounted to only a little over half the planned output, but exports of cotton textiles averaged 204 million rubles annually from 1929 to 1932.[26]

Large exports were needed in order to pay for imports, but the exporters of other countries were entrenched in world markets. Many Soviet goods could not yet compete on the basis of quality, and there seemed to be no way to obtain foreign markets except by charging extremely low prices for exports. The prices charged were frequently below cost of production in Soviet Russia. In fact, one critic alleged that it was considered a brilliant feat to obtain prices for exports of cotton textiles which would cover 20 to 25 per cent of the costs of the enterprises which produced the goods and that more commonly the prices would only cover about 15 per cent of the costs.[27] This dumping of Soviet products in foreign markets caused a great deal of irritation abroad. The foreign exchange acquired was used to purchase the various items needed for rapid industrialization. In spite of great domestic shortages of consumers' goods of all kinds, imports of these goods made up only 10.2 per cent of all imports from 1929 to 1932, while 89.8 per cent consisted of capital goods for use in industry.[28]

During the second Five-Year Plan (1933–1937), Soviet Russia became able to satisfy more of her own needs for industrial materials and equipment, and she greatly reduced her imports of automobiles, tractors, electrical equipment, agricultural machinery, machine tools, iron and steel, cotton, wool, and paper. With pressure to import lessened, Soviet Russia followed a policy of holding down foreign trade. The

[25] Yugow, *op. cit.*, p. 100. These rubles are not the same as the prerevolutionary rubles.

[26] *Ibid.*, p. 101.

[27] Freda Utley, *The Dream We Lost* (New York: The John Day Company, Inc., 1940), p. 234.

[28] Yugow, *op. cit.*, p. 104.

announced policy was to limit exports to "surplus products of the domestic economy," and to restrict imports to whatever level was reached by exports. In 1938 the total volume of foreign trade amounted to only 23.9 per cent of foreign trade before World War I.[29] However, trade picked up considerably in 1939 and 1940 as Soviet Russia began to stockpile materials which would be indispensable if she became involved in World War II.

The composition of Soviet Russian imports had not changed greatly by 1938. They still consisted largely (87.9 per cent) of goods for use in industry rather than of consumers' goods. On the other hand, the composition of Soviet Russian exports had changed greatly. In the period 1909–1913, agricultural exports made up 70.6 per cent of Russian exports, and industrial products only 29.4 per cent. Industrial goods exported in relation to total exports increased to 41.3 per cent from 1922 to 1927, 61.3 per cent from 1929 to 1933, and 72.8 per cent from 1933 to 1937, while agricultural exports declined correspondingly.[30]

COMMERCE IN THE WAR AND POSTWAR PERIODS

Wartime and Postwar Rationing. The internal marketing system of Soviet Russia suffered severe losses during World War II. It was reported, for example, that 216,700 shops and stores, or well over half the prewar total, were destroyed during the war.[31] However, the most striking feature of the war period was the overwhelming shortage of things to sell. In July, 1941, soon after the beginning of the war with Germany, it became necessary to reintroduce rationing of bread, butter, meat, tobacco, shoes, clothing, and other goods in Moscow, Leningrad, and other centers of population. Rationing was soon extended to the rest of the country. Some of the early wartime rations, such as those of meat, fish, and macaroni, were considerably more generous than those which had prevailed in the earlier rationing period. Other rations, such as those of sugar and bread, were of almost identical quantity as those of the earlier period.

As time went on, some of the rations had to be tightened. In 1947 it was reported that the top Soviet rations, for heavy workers, amounted to only 2340 calories per day. Growing children received 1114 calories, and other dependents, 892. The average for the entire population was about 1500.[32] In the war period and after, as in the earlier rationing period, consumers were divided into several classes for rationing.

[29] *Ibid.*, p. 100.
[30] *Ibid.*, p. 102.
[31] *Soviet Russia Today*, May, 1948, p. 15.
[32] *Time*, Nov. 17, 1947, p. 34.

Wartime and Postwar Prices. The prices of all sorts of goods sold in the stores were still under government control during the war, but prices nevertheless increased rapidly. After the end of the war, the prices of many goods were ten or fifteen times as high as in the prewar period. An American correspondent in Moscow reported that in 1946, at the official rate of exchange between rubles and dollars, half soles for a pair of shoes cost $19; an ice cream bar, $1.20; a bottle of beer, $2.25; eggs, 90 cents each; milk, 80 cents a quart; an ordinary nickel chocolate bar, $2.50; and sugar, $12 a pound.[33]

Another report stated that, in 1946, a pair of men's leather shoes sold in the commercial stores for from 810 to 1,600 rubles, and an ordinary dress brought 1,500 to 2,200 rubles, while the average worker's monthly wage ran less than 500 rubles. These prices reflected production of about one-quarter of a pair of shoes and 9.5 meters of cotton cloth per citizen in 1946.[34] Apparently the government decided to use higher prices as a means of bringing the large total of money wages paid out to workers into adjustment with the limited supplies of consumers' goods available.

Currency Revaluation and the End of Rationing. Although prices were decreased earlier, including cuts in food prices ranging from 63 per cent for white flour to 10 to 15 per cent for meats at the commercial stores in 1946, it was not until December, 1947, that anything could be done about rationing in Soviet Russia. At that time, coincident with a revaluation of the ruble and the issue of new rubles for old in such a fashion as to relieve the citizens of practically all their hoarded cash and a large part of their bank deposits, the rationing of all foods and industrial products was ended.

A unified system of prices was reestablished, instead of the practice of setting separate and widely varying prices at ration and commercial stores. At the same time, some changes in prices were announced. The price of bread was cut 12 per cent under the former ration price. Prices of cereals and macaroni were slashed 10 per cent. Meats, fish, fats, sugar, confectionery, salt, potatoes, and vegetables remained at their old ration prices, while the prices of tea, milk, and some other items were increased.[35] Several other reductions in prices occurred between 1947 and 1953, the largest being in 1950 and 1953. However, the prices of goods sold to consumers have remained high. Prices of food in state stores in Moscow in 1950 were more than 20 times as high as in 1928.[36]

The Recent Status of Marketing. According to official reports, signifi-

[33] *Champaign-Urbana News-Gazette,* Oct. 8, 1946.

[34] Harry Schwartz, *Russia's Postwar Economy* (Syracuse, N.Y.: Syracuse University Press, 1947), p. 42.

[35] *Champaign-Urbana News-Gazette,* Dec. 16, 1947.

[36] Harry Schwartz, *Russia's Soviet Economy,* (New York: Prentice-Hall, Inc., 1950), p. 378.

cant achievements were registered in internal trade under the fourth Five-Year Plan. By 1950 sales of state and cooperative stores, not counting sales of goods available from local resources, had increased over those of 1940 by 33 to 67 per cent. Total retail turnover in 1953 was about 80 per cent higher than in 1940.

On the other hand, there were only 85 per cent as many food stores and 83.3 per cent as many stores selling manufactured goods as there had been in 1940, when the number was a quite inadequate 327,000.[37] In the United States there were 1,769,540 retail stores in 1948, serving a much smaller area and population.[38] The number of stores in Soviet Russia in 1953 was about 14 per cent greater than before the war. Some Russian stores are high-grade establishments, but many others are still dirty and unkempt, carry small assortments of goods, and frequently do not have the most common types of consumers' goods for sale. Employees are few and are often untrained, impolite, and lacking in information concerning goods on hand. Some stores do not have certain goods even though the warehouses are groaning with them. Goods arrive out of season and are sent to the wrong parts of the country.

The shortcomings of the marketing system are clearly recognized by leading Soviet officials. Witness, for example, a statement of A. I. Mikoyan, member of the Politburo, in March, 1950: "It is necessary to organize scientific planning in trade organizations. Trade planning has its peculiarities, its specific features. This planning must take into account the relation of supply and demand, the needs of consumers, national and local peculiarities, climatic conditions."[39] That this could still be said when the economy was completing its fourth Five-Year Plan is a sad commentary on the operation of the Soviet Russian marketing system.

International Trade during World War II. Soviet Russia's foreign trade changed radically after she became engaged in World War II. Between 1940 and 1943 exports fell off about 75 per cent, whereas imports increased about sixfold.[40] Exports declined because Russia needed at home about all the goods that she could produce and because it was difficult to get exports delivered to other countries. Imports were large primarily because almost 13 billion dollars' worth of goods were received without charge from Russia's wartime allies. She received over 11 billion dollars' worth of goods from the United States under the lend-lease program.

Postwar Developments. Since the end of World War II, Soviet Russia has apparently been trying to get as much economic assistance as possible from other countries while exporting the minimum possible amount of her domestic resources. The surplus of imports was necessary to repair

[37] *Ibid.*, p. 369.
[38] *Statistical Abstract of the United States, 1952*, p. 894.
[39] Schwartz, *Russia's Soviet Economy*, p. 371.
[40] *Ibid.*, p. 511.

war damage and permit the completion of ambitious plans for economic expansion.

Soviet Russia has acquired large amounts of goods from other countries by means of "noncommercial" methods. The Red Army in occupied lands has lived off the country, seizing the commodities it has needed. In addition, Soviet Russia has stripped occupied territories of industrial and agricultural machinery, railroad locomotives and cars, livestock, and other items. Especially large quantities of such goods were taken from East Germany and Manchuria. The total value of the goods acquired had run to something like $4 to $5 billion by the end of 1950.[41]

In trading with other countries since the war, Soviet Russia has favored the development of bilateral agreements, which commonly provide that her exports to and imports from the other countries shall be equal in value in each year or other specified period of time. Bilateral agreements have been concluded with all her European and Asiatic satellites, and with several other countries, such as England, Norway, Sweden, Denmark, and even Argentina and India. The satellite countries, such as East Germany, Poland, Roumania, Hungary, Bulgaria, Czechoslovakia, China, and North Korea, are other countries with Communist governments and are usually referred to as "people's democracies" by the Soviet leaders.

The reasons for the preference for such bilateral agreements are easy to understand. Their terms can be kept relatively secret, and each country can be treated only as well as it needs to be. In dealing with one country at a time, the full weight of Soviet Russian strength can be brought to bear to obtain price and other concessions. The agreements eliminate or minimize the need for currency transactions, and this may be an advantage when the values of many countries' currencies are unstable. Finally, the imports and exports of Soviet Russia can be meshed into the economic plans more readily when the trade with each country is determined once and for all for each year.

The satellite countries have come to play an increasing part in the foreign trade of Soviet Russia. In 1953 Russia's foreign trade amounted to about 23 billion rubles, or almost four times the prewar volume. About 90 per cent of this trade was with the various people's democracies, which had accounted for 10 per cent or less of Soviet Russia's foreign trade before World War II.[42] In 1953 it was also reported that from 58 to 100 per cent of the foreign trade of the satellite countries occurred within the Soviet bloc.[43] These countries have long-term trading agreements with each other as well as with Soviet Russia. One-year agree-

[41] *Ibid.*, p. 517.
[42] Schwartz, *Russia's Soviet Economy*, rev. ed., pp. 598, 601–602.
[43] *The Economist*, May 30, 1953, p. 609.

ments were negotiated within the long-term agreements. The trade of the satellite countries is geared to Russia's needs, and the extent to which these countries may trade with the West is spelled out.

Conclusions on Foreign Trade. Soviet Russia has never been, and shows little promise of becoming, a great trading country. If the goods which were taken from her or which she received by noncommercial methods during World War II and those secured by similar methods in the postwar period are disregarded, her foreign trade shows subordination to the objectives of the national economic plans. It has been merely a tool for attaining the general goals of the economy. In recent years, however, foreign trade has been directed in part to political objectives and has been used as a weapon in Russia's determined struggle with the West and especially with the United States.

Soviet Russia has not attempted to import all goods that could be produced more cheaply in other countries than at home or to export only those goods that could be produced more cheaply in Soviet Russia than in the other countries. Adherence to this policy might have caused Soviet Russia to remain a backward agricultural country, exporting largely raw materials and partly processed commodities while importing large quantities of finished manufactured goods. In order to attain industrialization and economic development, she has exported at considerable sacrifice goods that were both inefficiently produced and badly needed at home. She has also attempted to produce at home many types of goods that could have been purchased more cheaply in foreign markets. The results have been, in addition to a low volume of trade, the attainment of a considerable degree of economic self-sufficiency and the placing of additional burdens on the Russian consumers and their scales of living.

QUESTIONS FOR STUDY

1. Why did internal commerce develop slowly and remain rather unimportant in Russia prior to 1861? Why did it develop more rapidly from 1861 to 1890? From 1890 to 1917? Did Russia have an adequate marketing system at the time of World War I?

2. Why is international trade likely to develop more rapidly than domestic trade in the case of a country such as Russia was before 1861? Indicate the development of Russia's international trade from 1861 to 1913.

3. Trace the changing organization of the Soviet Russian marketing system under the planned economy. How is marketing controlled? How are prices determined?

4. Why was it unfortunate that Soviet Russia had to ration goods by physical quantities during the years in which her new marketing system was being developed? Is such rationing a regular part of the socialist scheme of things or peculiar to Soviet Russia? Why?

5. How did the Soviet Russian policy with respect to international trade change from the first to the second Five-Year Plan? Why? What has Soviet Russia's policy been in the years since World War II? Why?

6. Does the Soviet Russian experience indicate that marketing is or is not a phase of economic activity well suited to large-scale government ownership and operation? Why?

7. Do you think that Soviet Russia is likely ever to become a large-scale trading country? Why, or why not?

CHAPTER 24

THE SOVIET RUSSIAN ECONOMY

We have seen that the government of Soviet Russia dominates the economic life of the country. This domination usually results from government ownership and operation of enterprises, but sometimes it involves strict regulation of activities carried on by nongovernmental agencies. When the government plays such an important part in economic life, some understanding of the government is essential to an understanding of the economic system. Moreover, the identity and objectives of those who control the government become matters of supreme importance.

THE PREREVOLUTIONARY GOVERNMENT

The Absolute Monarchy. The government of Russia under the czars was an absolute divine-right monarchy. The czar was a despot, and the government functioned without constitution, without legislature, and without public participation. There were no limits on the powers of the czar. He ruled the many provinces of the country through governors whom he appointed. The leading agencies of the central government included the Council of Ministers, made up of the heads of various government departments; the Imperial Council, composed of 100 appointed members; a Senate composed of privy councilors and operating as the highest administrative and judicial agency; and the Holy Synod of the Orthodox Church. All these officials were appointed by and responsible to the czar. The Imperial Council prepared laws, which the czar could either accept or reject.

Much wealth and some power were enjoyed by a landed nobility. Some members had held their land and position from early times, but a growing part was composed of nobles who had been given estates more recently for service to the czar. The nobility lacked independence and was subservient to the ruler. Most of the citizens were illiterate serfs, working on the landed estates and being allowed to work some land for themselves. Serfdom was on the wane in Western Europe as early

375

as the seventeenth century, but in Russia it was consolidated and extended. The common people of Russia had nothing to say about the government of their country.

The Development of Opposition. Serious opposition to the czarist government developed only after the freeing of the serfs in 1861. Then, with the expansion of industry, transportation, and commerce and the growth of large cities, two new social classes sprang up—the working class and the owners of enterprises. Both groups became enemies of the czarist regime and the nobility. The enterprisers desired more widespread participation in the government and constitutional limitations on the power of the czar. Many of them became affiliated with moderate groups, such as the Conservative Democrats and the Octobrists. Most of the workers, on the other hand, fell in with radical groups, such as the Social Revolutionaries and the Social Democrats.

The Communist party of Soviet Russia is descended from the Social Democrats. The Social Democrats split into two factions at the second congress of the party in 1903. The minority group, or Mensheviki, was moderate and reformist in character, but the majority group, or Bolsheviki, stood for the achievement of socialism through revolution and the dictatorship of the proletariat. The Bolsheviki took over the reins of govenment late in 1917 and later decided to be called the Communist Party of Soviet Russia.

Minor Government Reforms. After the Revolution of 1905, which was sternly repressed by government forces, the czar issued a manifesto which promised the people civil liberties and the right to elect a legislature which would have lawmaking powers and control over the government ministry. These changes amounted to little. Before long, the right to vote was restricted to ensure that the legislature would be filled with conservatives and reactionaries. In any event, the legislature had no power over the ministers and little over legislation. The czar could adjourn or dissolve the legislature at will, had veto power over all laws, and could himself issue decrees having the force of law.

Successful Revolution. In the years after 1905, radical movements were treated roughly and driven underground, but large-scale unrest continued up to the outbreak of World War I. After subsiding for a time in the early years of the war, unrest again became serious in 1916 and 1917 as the war resulted in bitter defeats for the Russian armed forces and in increasing misery, confusion, and corruption on the home front. Strikes, riots, and mutinies brought about a situation in which Czar Nicholas II was forced to abdicate on March 15, 1917. For a few months Russia operated under a provisional government, but the Bolsheviki seized power in early November, 1917, and the checkered career of Soviet Russia began.

THE GOVERNMENT OF SOVIET RUSSIA

The 1936 Constitution. The first constitution of Soviet Russia was adopted in 1923, but it was not until 1936 that the present constitution was adopted. This latter document declares the U.S.S.R. to be a socialist state of workers and peasants, with political power residing in the working people. It provides for social ownership of the means of production, but it allows private property in income from work, in personal savings, dwelling houses, auxiliary husbandry, household articles and utensils, and articles for personal use and comfort. The economy is to operate on the basis of economic planning. All citizens who are able to work must do so if they expect to eat. The principle of income distribution is that each person is to produce according to his ability and to receive income according to his accomplishment.

The Supreme Soviet. The highest agency of government is nominally the Supreme Soviet of the U.S.S.R., or the national legislature. It is made up of two houses, whose members serve four-year terms. The members of one house, the Soviet of the Union, are chosen from electoral districts on the basis of one representative for each 300,000 population. The other house, the Soviet of Nationalities, contains 25 representatives from each constituent republic, 11 from each autonomous republic, 5 from each autonomous region, and 1 from each national region. Prior to the elections of 1951, the Soviet of the Union had 682 members, and the Soviet of Nationalities, 657. The houses have equal rights, and bills pass by a simple majority in each house. The Supreme Soviet has the right to amend the constitution by a two-thirds vote.

The Presidium of the Supreme Soviet, a body of 33 members chosen by the Supreme Soviet, is an executive committee of the legislature. It convenes and dissolves the Supreme Soviet, calls new elections, holds referendums, interprets the laws, carries on administrative functions, and exercises most legislative powers when the legislature is not in session. Most of the Presidium's actions require the approval of the Supreme Soviet, but that approval is sure to be given.

The Council of Ministers. The U.S.S.R. has a cabinet type of executive. The highest executive and administrative agency is the Council of Ministers, whose members are elected by the Supreme Soviet. The Council is subsidiary to the legislature and responsible to it. It includes all the government ministers and some other high officials. The Council has a five-man inner cabinet, or Presidium, and functions by issuing decrees based on existing laws. It has no veto powers over acts of the legislature.

The individual ministers have charge of the work of their ministries or departments in much the same fashion as do the cabinet officers of other countries. These ministries have an important place in the Soviet Russian scheme of things, for they are usually both government departments and departments controlling specific phases of economic life. They form one of the main connecting links between government and economic activities. The State Planning Commission is a sort of sub-committee of the Council of Ministers. It is the most important single economic agency of the country, for it has charge of making national economic plans and supervising their fulfillment.

The Judiciary. The judiciary, like the executive, is subsidiary to the legislature. The Supreme Court of the U.S.S.R. is composed of 45 judges and 20 assessors, who are elected by the Supreme Soviet. The republics, territories, provinces, and regions also have courts whose judges are elected by the legislatures of these units of government. Only the judges of the lowest courts, called People's Courts, are elected by the voters of local areas by direct secret ballot. No court has the power to pass on the constitutionality of legislative acts.

The Rights of Citizens. The constitution guarantees the citizens freedom of speech, of the press, and of assembly, but with the proviso that these rights must be used in the interests of the working people and for the strengthening of the socialist state. Cultural, scientific, and technical groups, youth organizations, trade unions, cooperative associations, and (for especially worthy citizens) the Communist party, are among the approved organizations. The constitution promises freedom from arbitrary arrests, inviolability of homes, secrecy of personal correspondence, equality of all citizens, freedom of conscience, separation of church and state, freedom of religious worship and of antireligious propaganda, the right to work, the right to leisure, the right to education, and the right to material security. The right to vote is extended to all citizens aged eighteen or over who are not insane and have not been convicted of crimes. Elections are direct and by secret ballot.

The Communist Party. The government of Soviet Russia cannot be understood merely by examining the various agencies and the functions given them by the constitution. Regardless of these things, political and governmental power is concentrated in the hands of the Communist party. In other words, the Party completely dominates the government and has its members in practically all important offices and positions.

Applicants for membership in the Communist party must be at least eighteen years of age and must agree to live up to certain requirements, which include unity of doctrine and practice, implicit and complete obedience to Party authority, and the famous "vow of poverty," by which the applicant agrees to be content with a salary not substantially greater than that of a skilled and zealous manual worker. Applicants must be endorsed by three Party members of at least three years' standing who have known the applicants as fellow workmen for at least one year. The applicants may be admitted to full membership after spending one year as "candidates." The qualifications of Party members are frequently reexamined from the point of view of individual character and behavior, ideological orthodoxy, and general devotion to the cause of the Party, and those members who are found wanting are cast into the outer darkness.

Membership in the Communist party is considered a privilege, for it brings the individual prestige and possibly power, as well as economic advantages with respect to travel, rations, and (at times) shopping rights, and the securing of desirable living quarters. Nevertheless, membership in the Party has been severely restricted. In 1941 for example, the Party included only 2,515,481 members and 1,361,404 candidates.[1] The Party grew rapidly during World War II, when requirements for admission were temporarily relaxed, and the membership reached 6,300,000 by the end of the war.[2] This number, however, was only about 3 per cent of the population, and the tendency toward increased membership has not continued.

The Party has usually refused to admit new adult members and it intends to rely largely on its youth organizations for new members. In this way it secures young and enthusiastic members who have been brought up along Party lines and have been educated in Party principles. The youth organizations include the All-Union Leninist Communist League of Youth (Comsomols), which has some 15 million members ranging in age from fourteen to twenty-three, of whom half were acquired during World War II; the Children's Communist Organization of Young Pioneers in the Name of Comrade Lenin (Young Pioneers), whose members are from ten to sixteen years of age; and the Little Octobrists, aged 8 to 11.

The Communist party is highly organized. It progresses from factory, farm, village, and city units, through district and regional congresses, to the All-Union Congress of the Communist Party, which has had as many as 1,657 voting delegates. This group is too large to serve as the head of the Party, so it elects a Central Executive Committee to function in its place. It is in this latter group and in the committees which it appoints (the Organization Bureau, the Central Control Commission, and, above all, the Political Bureau or Politburo) that the control of the Party actually lies. The importance which the Politburo has had can be seen from its membership of a few years ago, which included Stalin, Molotov, Malenkov, Beria, Voroshilov, Mikoyan, Bulganin, Kaganovich,

[1] *The Soviet Union Today*, (New York: The American Russian Institute, 1946), p. 30.
[2] *Annals of the American Academy of Political and Social Science*, May, 1949, p. 22.

Andreyev, and Kosygin. More recently a Party Presidium of 10 members has taken the place and functions of the Politburo.

Democracy or Dictatorship? What sort of government is produced in the end by this combination of democratic constitution and all-powerful single political party? There is little difference of opinion on this point. Despite the democratic front provided by the constitution, the government of Soviet Russia is a dictatorship of the most absolute and complete variety, with the Communist party in full control. The methods through which control is maintained are comprehensive and effective.

The Party dominates the electoral process. In theory, any citizen can run for office and be elected. In actual elections, although several candidates (for the legislature, say) may be nominated in each electoral district, all the candidates except one withdraw before the election is held, and only one candidate is actually presented to the voters. The surviving candidates are those fortunate individuals who have the approval of the Party, although they may not all be Party members.

The candidates are likely to run for office on the basis of a platform sponsored by the "election bloc of Party and non-Party people," which would make any independent candidate a counterrevolutionary. In the 1951 elections more than 113 million people, or 99.98 per cent of all registered voters, went to the polls, and 99.82 per cent of the votes cast favored the single candidates sponsored by the Party.[3] Over 80 per cent of the members elected to the legislature are members of the Communist party. Such results would not be expected in a real democracy.

Again, the Communist party maintains Party officers and agencies to match the various officers and agencies of the government. The legislative bodies of localities, districts, regions, provinces, and republics are paralleled by Party organizations in all of these geographical subdivisions. The All-Union Congress of the Communist Party is the counterpart of the national legislature, the Central Executive Committee of the Party is similar to the Council of Ministers in the government, and so on through the list of government officers and agencies. There is great duplication of personnel between the Party and government officers and agencies.

The results are not at all difficult to understand. The Supreme Soviet is a mere figurehead. Its members approve the proposals and accomplishments of the Party leaders unanimously and almost without discussion. Laws desired by the leaders are passed automatically, and the persons appointed by the Supreme Soviet to be judges, prosecutors, or members of the Council of Ministers are those who are approved by the Party leaders. The Party itself has considerable legislative powers, for its leadership issues directives with the force of law to government de-

[3] *U.S.S.R. Information Bulletin,* Mar. 23, 1951, pp. 182–183.

partments, and many laws come into effect under the joint signature of the Party Secretary and the Chairman of the Council of Ministers. The various government officers pursue objectives chosen by Party leaders, and the State Planning Commission makes its economic plans on the basis of general objectives provided by the Party leaders. There is no overt opposition to the will of the Party as expressed by its leaders.

The Party has at its disposal an elaborate organization for the "protection of the regime." It maintains a large and well-trained secret police, which has almost unlimited power over the individual and which operates largely outside the courts and established judicial procedures. The secret police is charged with discovering and destroying all counter-revolutionary and antistate activities, and these activities are defined so broadly that almost any individual regarded as undesirable can be liquidated or placed in durance vile. Constitutional guarantees concerning individual rights mean little if anything. Add Party control through the government over the religious, educational, and leisure-time activities of the citizens and the result is a complete dictatorship in action.

PUBLIC FINANCE PRIOR TO 1917

Government Expenditures. It is also important to know how a government finances its activities. The fiscal system of Russia dates from the budget reforms of 1862, which were a part of the general reform movement that included the liberation of the serfs. During the following fifty years, 1863–1913, the expenditures of the national government increased from 432 to 3,382 million rubles, or by 681.9 per cent.[4] A leading factor in this growth was the expansion of state enterprises, such as the railroads and the liquor monopoly, although such expansion, of course, increased both expenditures and revenues. Higher military expenditures, extensions of the political frontiers, the growth of population and of national prosperity and income, and the increasing need for cultural developments were other factors which played a part in increasing government expenditures.

The operation of state enterprises required 27.0 per cent of total ordinary expenditures in 1913. National defense took 26.6 per cent; productive and general development projects, 16.9 per cent; general administration, 16.4 per cent; and service of the national debt, 13.1 per cent.[5] Extraordinary expenditures, according to Russian government accounting, included those for the construction of new railroads, for wars and national disasters, for the redemption of government obligations

[4] A. Raffalovich (ed.), *Russia: Its Industry and Commerce* (London: P. S. King & Staples, Ltd., 1918), p. 329.
[5] *Ibid.*, pp. 331–332.

before their due date, and for the expropriation of private undertakings. Extraordinary expenditures amounted to 4,476 million rubles between 1903 and 1913, and over half of this total resulted from the Russo-Japanese War.

Government Revenues. In the period from 1863 to 1913 the revenues of the Russian government were usually enough to cover ordinary expenditures and yield a margin which could be applied to extraordinary expenditures. However, the revenue system was primitive. In 1913 the government derived 30.4 per cent of its revenues from royalties, which included income from mining, from the operation of the mint, post office, and telephone and telegraph lines, and from the liquor monopoly. Another 30.2 per cent came from other property and funds belonging to the government (rents and leases, forests, state railroads, mills and works, interest on funds and banking operations, annuities from railroad companies, profits of private railroad companies shared with the state, and the reimbursement of loans and advances).[6]

Indirect taxes yielded 20.9 per cent of revenues. These taxes were excises on matches, petroleum products, sugar, tobacco and cigarettes, and spirits, beer, mead, and yeast. Direct taxes, including taxes on pecuniary capital, commerce and industries, land and other real estate, and rents and other receipts from real estate, provided only 7.8 per cent. Another 6.4 per cent was yielded by "duties," which included revenue-stamp duties, legal fees, registration fees, death duties, duties on the transfer of property, port dues on ships and cargoes, and duties on fire insurance.[7] Taxes produced a little over one-third of government revenues, and there were no personal income taxes or other progressive taxes. Persons with small incomes undoubtedly bore a relatively greater proportion of the cost of financing the government than did persons with large incomes.

The National Debt. A part of extraordinary expenditures had to be financed by borrowing from time to time. From the beginning of the nineteenth century to 1914, the Russian government borrowed about 15 billion rubles at home and abroad. However, a part of the debt had been paid off at various times, so that the total debt outstanding amounted to a little less than 9 billion rubles in 1914.[8] About two-thirds of this debt was held within the country. In the financial emergency created by World War I, the national debt increased several times over.

[6] *Ibid.*, pp. 338–342.
[7] *Ibid.*, p. 343.
[8] *Ibid.*, p. 345.

PUBLIC FINANCE SINCE 1917

The overissue of paper money which began during the war got entirely out of control in the period of War Communism and in the early years of the New Economic Policy. As money lost value rapidly, the Soviet government found that the amounts collected through taxation, although they increased greatly, fell far short of covering necessary government expenses. The government's deficit, which had been 31.1 billion rubles in 1918, increased to 21,937 billion rubles in 1921.[9] The government derived only 2.7 per cent of its revenues from taxation in 1922, with 10.6 per cent coming from state undertakings and properties, and 86.7 per cent from new currency issues.[10] The public finances of the Soviet government were in a state of collapse prior to the monetary reforms of 1924.

Government Expenditures. After the value of money was stabilized, government finances settled down and began to take permanent shape. Both government expenditures and revenues have grown rapidly under the planned economy. If the expenditures and revenues of 1928 are taken as 100, those of 1933 amounted to 546, those of 1938 to 1,574, those of 1941 to 2,672, and those of 1952 to 6,176.

Two factors have been responsible for most of the increase. First, the economic activities of the country have been brought more and more under government control, so that account must be taken of them in the government's budget. This is suggested by the fact that the rate of increase shown by the budget has been greater than that of national income or retail sales. Second, the productivity of Russian industries and the general scope of economic activity have increased greatly over the years. Since the operation of the economy is largely in the hands of the government, this increase has been reflected in the revenues and expenditures of the government.

In 1955, expenditures for financing the national economy were to be 39.5 per cent of the total. Industry, agriculture, transportation, trade, and other branches of economic activity are financed largely by appropriations from the national budget. These grants are made for a considerable number of purposes, but most of the money goes for (1) capital investment and (2) the endowment of new enterprises with working capital and the allocation of supplementary funds to operating enterprises. Expenditures for national defense were to be 19.9 per cent of the total, while expenditures for social and cultural services (education and train-

[9] A. Baykov, *The Development of the Soviet Economic System* (New York: The Macmillan Company, 1947), p. 36.
[10] *Ibid.*, p. 82.

ing, public health, physical culture, social insurance benefits, and other items) were to amount to 26.1 per cent. Finally, expenditures for general administration and other purposes, including interest on the national debt, were to be 14.5 per cent of the total.[11]

Government Revenues. Most of the income of the government is derived from the operation of the national economy rather than from direct taxes on the incomes of the individual citizens. However, some of the methods of deriving income from the national economy are also dignified by the name of taxes. A leading example is the turnover tax, which was to produce 39.5 per cent of total revenues in 1955.

The turnover tax is applied in simple fashion. The final prices which the government sets on goods include the costs of production, transportation, and distribution; the planned profits, if any, of the producing and distributing enterprises; special taxes in some cases; and last but not least, the turnover tax. The tax represents the difference between the total cost of production of a commodity and the price which it brings on the market. The tax is paid but once on each product, either at the production or the wholesaling level, and the burden falls eventually on the final consumer. The turnover tax is levied on practically all commodities but at widely varying rates. It makes up from 1 to 90 per cent of the final selling prices of goods to consumers.

Another part of the revenues derived from the national economy is produced by the profits tax, which was to yield 19.9 per cent of total revenues in 1955. The part of the final selling prices of commodities which is received by the producing enterprises is often intended to cover not only planned costs of production but also planned profits. Each enterprise has the right to retain a small part of its planned profits, but the government takes from 95 to 99 per cent. The enterprise keeps from 25 to 90 per cent of any unplanned profits.

Direct taxes were to yield only 8.2 per cent of total revenues in 1955. Part of the revenue from direct taxes comes from income taxes, which are mildly progressive with respect to the amounts of income received by individuals and also with respect to the sources of the income. A given amount of income derived from private activities is taxed more heavily than the same amount obtained from employment in state or cooperative enterprises. Another part of revenue from direct taxes comes from the so-called cultural and housing welfare tax.

Sales of government bonds are regarded as a regular source of income and not as a means of covering deficits. They were to bring in 5.2 per cent of total revenues in 1955. Finally, 19.9 per cent of total revenues in 1955 were to come from other sources, including social insurance

[11] *The Economist,* Feb. 12, 1955, p. 547.

levies, customs duties, and compulsory deliveries in kind and other items paid by agricultural enterprises.[12]

The National Debt. The Soviet Russian government repudiated the national debt of the czarist regime, but it has piled up a fairly large national debt of its own. Its borrowings amounted to 50 billion rubles prior to World War II, another 76 billion during the war, and perhaps 175 or 200 billion rubles from the end of the war through 1952. According to the Soviet authorities, each issue of government bonds is snapped up eagerly by the people, although the interest-bearing bonds pay only 4 per cent interest and other issues pay no interest but rather entitle the owners to participate in a semiannual lottery in which cash prizes are awarded to the owners of bonds bearing the lucky numbers. Such interest and prizes are exempt from taxation.

The eagerness of the people to buy government bonds is somewhat overstated. The bonds are sold on a supposedly voluntary basis, but the citizens are virtually required to buy them. In some cases, deductions of certain percentages of the workers' pay are made for this purpose, and in other cases the workers pass resolutions, at the suggestion of representatives of the Communist party, agreeing to buy the bonds. Thus subscriptions to the bonds may almost be regarded as taxes on which the government sees fit to pay interest or award prizes.

THE SOVIET RUSSIAN ECONOMY AS A WHOLE

After the Revolution of 1917 the Soviet Russian regime inherited a land of tremendous size, population, and resources, although many of the resources were undeveloped. The economy was predominantly agricultural, and yet the agricultural system, although it produced large amounts of certain crops, was unproductive and inefficient. Manufacturing, transportation, banking, trade, and the labor force had developed largely after 1861, and the period of most rapid development had been from 1890 on in most cases. However, the prerevolutionary economic system, while backward, was not stagnant. It had begun to advance rapidly and was showing considerable promise for the future. In this concluding section, we shall evaluate the stewardship of the Soviet Russian leaders and attempt to decide how well they have done with the resources at their disposal.

Continued Operation of a Planned Economy. One accomplishment with which we may credit Soviet Russia and its leaders is found in the fact that it has been possible to keep a planned economy operating and to make considerable progress under it. Before the Russian experiment

[12] *Ibid.*

began, there were many people who denied that a planned economy could be operated at all or who contended that, if by chance it did succeed in avoiding complete collapse, such an economy must necessarily be stagnant and unprogressive.

Methods of Planning. The Russian methods of economic planning seem appropriate. The State Planning Commission has the assistance of its council, its large staff of planning workers, various statistical, accounting, research, and training agencies, and a large number of subsidiary planning bodies, both functional and regional. The method of making out tentative plans, submitting them to a variety of subsidiary planning agencies in order to obtain suggestions, criticisms, and counterplans, and then constructing the final plans seems logical. The final plans are detailed, comprehensive, and have reasonable internal consistency, and yet they are flexible and subject to constant revision.

The State Planning Commission receives too much advice and control from the leaders of the Communist party, and it pays too little attention to the criticisms, suggestions and counterplans received from below. As a result, there is no way of knowing whether the planned results are well or poorly suited to the needs and desires of the citizens, or even whether the planned results provide more total satisfaction than would some other set of results which could be accomplished with the use of the same resources. These drawbacks, however, may be attributed largely to the dictatorial government under which the economy operates. Under conditions of democracy the planning mechanism would merit approval.

The Elimination of Capitalistic Wastes. The planned economy has been successful in eliminating several types of waste that plague capitalistic productive systems. There is no abuse of the profit motive, or restriction of production in order to make more money than could be made by maximizing production. Since Soviet industries do not operate under competition, there is no competitive tendency to overshoot the mark with regard to the quantities of productive facilities which are set up in individual industries. The planners make mistakes in estimating human needs or demands for goods, but once they have reached decisions about desirable outputs, they do not set up unduly large quantities of productive facilities and then allow many of the facilities to stand idle.

The Soviet productive system has not gone in for excessive varieties of goods. In fact, any error in this connection has probably been in the other direction. The Soviet economy has not devoted large quantities of productive agents to the advertising of competitive brands of essentially the same economic goods, nor has it turned its natural resources over to private individuals for wasteful competitive exploitation. The

Soviet economy has not entirely lived up to the principle of "necessities for all before luxuries for any," but its record has been relatively good.

National Income. Some idea of how well an economy operates through time can be obtained by observing what happens to national income. In the case of Soviet Russia the record looks good. National income, after some decline from the level of 21 billion rubles in 1913, rose again to 25 billion in 1928, 45.5 billion in 1932, 96.3 billion in 1937, and 125.5 billion in 1940. After receiving some setback during the war, it soared to 205.8 billion rubles in 1950. This level was almost ten times that of 1913.

Of course, we must remember that these are ruble figures. They are supposedly stated in rubles of comparable purchasing power, but there is no way to be sure that corrections for the changing value of the ruble have been made accurately. Again, the increase in national income looks large because the base was small. The national income of the United States, after adjustment for changing price levels, may have been only four times as great in 1950 as in 1913, but an increase of 150 billion dollars over the years meant much more than an increase of over 180 billion rubles in Soviet Russian national income.

Industrial Production. The organization for industrial production in Soviet Russia is complicated and it has been subject to extensive revision, but the results in the field of industry deserve some favorable comment. Considerable progress has been made toward the planned goal of industrialization. This industrialization and the relatively full use of productive facilities have caused the production of many manufactured goods not only to increase but to increase several times over. Industrial output has increased in absolute terms and in relation to the industrial output of the world as a whole. Finally, the progress in industrial production has been fairly steady in peacetime and has been free from cyclical booms and depressions.

On the other hand, large quantities of defective and low-quality products have been produced, and there has been excessive wastage and spoilage of materials. Labor productivity and efficiency have been low and costs of production high. Machinery and equipment have worn out and broken down at unduly high rates, and maintenance and repairs have been neglected. Progress in industrial production has been uneven from one industry to another, and there has been much overfulfillment and underfulfillment of plans. Greater success has been enjoyed in fulfilling the plans for the production of capital goods than in carrying out those for the production of consumers' goods. Finally, it is claimed that the large increases in production which have occurred are no greater than would have been expected by now, on the basis of trends in the twenty-five years before 1913, even if the Russian economy had continued to operate under its old management after 1917.

Agriculture. The goals of collectivizing and mechanizing agriculture have been largely attained, and these results were undoubtedly desirable in view of the needs of the planned economy and the status of Russian agriculture. It has been wise to leave the agricultural activities of the country largely in the hands of collective or cooperative farms instead of transferring them to enterprises owned and operated by the government. Effective devices have been developed for controlling collective agriculture and for keeping agricultural production in line with plans for the whole economy. Additional quantities of land have been brought under cultivation. Actual outputs of farm crops have had their ups and downs, but in many cases improvements in outputs have occurred.

On the other hand, the mechanization of agriculture has been slow to show the expected results. Collectivization occurred too rapidly and by means of a brutal and costly process. The accompanying slaughter of livestock resulted in a setback from which the agricultural economy has never recovered. The state farms have been a costly experiment. The collective farms have been said to be cooperative in name only, both because they have been controlled by the government and Party and because they have relied to a considerable extent on private farming by individual collective farmers.

The distribution of income on the collective farms has been complicated, cumbersome, and difficult to work out, and it has been unsatisfactory from the point of view of incentives. It has been necessary to supplement the income incentives with fines and punishments. The economic status of the collective farmers has remained unsatisfactory. Increases in income have been small and slow in coming. Increases in crop production have occurred, but they have been far smaller than those hoped for originally. Results in livestock production have been especially disappointing.

Transportation. Soviet Russia has extended her railroads fairly rapidly and has increased the freight carried much more rapidly than the lines themselves. Inland water transportation has been improved and has come to carry an increased volume of traffic. In recent times, air transportation has developed at an unprecedented rate and promises to have a brilliant future. On the other hand, the railroad mileage is only a small fraction of that of the United States even though the country to be served is almost three times as large. Russia's ocean-going merchant marine has remained small and unimportant, and her highway transportation has developed at all only in recent times. On the whole, transportation has been neglected relative to industry, and the transportation system has remained rather backward.

Money, Credit, and Banking. Commercial credit is in widespread use on the basis of methods which are fundamentally not very different from those used in the United States, except that commercial banking is a government monopoly in Soviet Russia and the volume of commercial credit to be extended is under planned control. It was a difficult task to establish a large-scale system of commercial banking and make it operate after the old banks had been liquidated, but the system of state banking has functioned more and more successfully with the passage of time, in spite of a steadily increasing volume of business. The banking system is well adapted to the needs of a planned economy, and since the volume of commercial credit is under control, the commercial banking system should play no part in causing economic instability.

The situation in regard to money in Soviet Russia has been something else again. The wild inflation of the early years was halted, but the monetary unit has been far from completely stable in value. The quantity of money in circulation has increased greatly, and although prices have been controlled, they have been allowed to rise considerably. A large amount of purchasing power accumulated in the hands of the people during World War II, and a revaluation of the ruble was necessary before rationing could be abandoned in the postwar period.

The mechanism for handling saving and investment has been what one would expect in a planned economy. With planners controlling both the total amount of saving and investment and the distribution of capital funds and capital goods among industries, many of the problems which are commonly associated with investment credit and banking in capitalistic countries do not arise in Soviet Russia. Saving and capital formation have gone on rapidly, and it is often estimated that Soviet Russia has been taking about a third of her national income in the form of new production facilities. She seems to have disproved the notion that a great volume of saving and capital formation can occur only under capitalism, only when national income is adequate to start with, and only when national income is divided very unequally among the individual citizens.

On the other hand, inefficiency and low labor productivity have been common in the construction of new productive facilities, and these facilities have often cost more than had been planned. Much of the capital construction has been of low quality. Some of the plants constructed have been too large to be operated and managed efficiently. The location of new production facilities in relation to raw materials and markets has sometimes been unsatisfactory. The investment program in general and the heavy emphasis on capital goods to produce more capital goods rather than capital goods to produce consumers' goods have been criticized as placing undue burdens on Soviet consumers. That is, it was criticized for placing excessive emphasis on the future to the neglect of the present, although Soviet Russia's new production facilities served her well in the war with Germany.

Internal Commerce. The system of marketing goods has made considerable progress over the years. The total volume of internal trade has increased enormously since 1917, as we should expect on the basis of increased outputs of most kinds of goods, and efficiency in marketing has improved noticeably. The marketing system has also gone far toward achieving the goal of having a single set of state and cooperative stores selling all types of available goods to all purchasers in any desired quantities and at a uniform scale of prices.

However, the marketing system has been one of the less successful parts of the Soviet economy. It has been relatively difficult to transplant modern merchandising methods into the backward Soviet economy, for improved marketing methods ordinarily develop gradually. Moreover, it seems unlikely that merchandising, and especially the retailing phase, is as well adapted to large-scale management by the government as is, for example, heavy industry. The marketing mechanism has also suffered because the planners did not or could not see fit to devote large quantities of funds and managerial ability to it. Even at the end of the fourth Five-Year Plan and later, the leaders of Party and government were still dissatisfied with the operation of the marketing system and were still deciding to take energetic measures which would result in the satisfaction of the legitimate demands of the people for the common necessities of life.

International Trade. The policy with respect to international trade has been favorable only in that it has shielded the country from disruptive international influences and in that it has been well coordinated with the goals of the planned economy. In importing only what the national economy needed and exporting only what the planners thought the national economy could spare, Soviet Russia's international trade has not developed greatly, and a high degree of economic self-sufficiency has been achieved. This has been possible only at the cost of furnishing her citizens with scales of living lower than those which could have been attained on the basis of geographical specialization and international trade.

The Distribution of Income. The distribution of income has been handled experimentally. Following a brief attempt to distribute income on the basis of needs under War Communism, Soviet Russia soon returned to paying wages and salaries in cash. Since then, inequality in wages and salaries has been constantly increasing and has become comparable to that which exists in the United States after taxes. Total inequality in income distribution is much smaller in Soviet Russia than in the United States because property incomes have been largely eliminated in the former economy.

Inequality in the distribution of income in Soviet Russia has been criticized as being too great to be consistent with the ideals of modern socialism. However, the distribution of income has been criticized more often over the years for having too little inequality between persons than for having too much. The major weaknesses of the planned economy have included, among other things, low efficiency and productivity on the part of workers of all grades, including managerial, and the failure to develop loyalty, disinterestedness, and devotion to duty as rapidly as expected. These results are what we should expect if the combination of economic rewards and other motivating factors were inadequate to provide incentives for all the people.

The Status of Labor. Differentials in wages between workers exist in Soviet Russia, and these differentials were intended to be adequate to provide incentives. Wages are on a piecework basis wherever possible, and the payment of additional bonuses for increased quantity or improved quality of output is common. The Labor Code promises the workers short working days in most occupations and especially short ones for young workers and workers in difficult and dangerous occupations. Rest days have been frequent, the workers have enjoyed annual vacations with pay, and the use of child labor has been prohibited. Many public honors are available for exceptional workers.

Most workers belong to unions, which perform a variety of functions. The workers have been relatively sure of employment. Soviet Russia has a comprehensive system of social insurance which promises liberal benefits. Finally, while the real wages of the workers and the people in general have remained low in comparison with those enjoyed by the citizens of leading capitalistic countries, real wages and scales of living have been slowly and gradually improving.

The favorable wage rates, hours of work, and other working conditions which apparently existed for Soviet workers prior to World War II were changed for the worse during the war period, and it appears that some of the less satisfactory wartime standards are to be continued. Production norms in connection with the piece-rate wage system have been raised considerably. Some critics contend that the laws, decrees, and collective agreements specifying wage rates, hours of work, and working conditions have been meaningless except as devices for deceiving outside observers. In other words, wages have been substandard, hours of work long, and working conditions miserable.

Severe problems of labor turnover, absenteeism, lateness, and loafing have cropped up, and the Soviet leaders have imposed restrictions and regulations on the workers which, according to the critics, amount to enslavement. The labor unions have no real bargaining function, are unable to help or protect the workers, and serve primarily as tools of manage- ment and the government. The social insurance system excludes many people, rather few people actually receive benefits, and the benefits paid are less than those promised. Moreover, the benefits are manipulated in an effort to prevent or reduce labor turnover. And the real wages and scales of living of the workers remain low in spite of some improvement.

Economic Stability. Soviet Russia has received much publicity as the land without depressions and unemployment. In over twenty-five years of operation under economic planning, the economy has not experienced a depression in business and economic activity, nor has there been any troublesome volume of unemployment. Mistakes in planning have oc- curred, and productive results have often fallen far short of those planned, but these things have not been allowed to cumulate into de- pressions nor result in mass unemployment for the workers. If the results which were planned could not be accomplished, men and resources were merely put to work at something else.

A planned economy such as that of Soviet Russia does and should have an advantage over capitalistic economies in the matter of prevent- ing depressions, but the advantage has not been so great as it appears. Economic maladjustments have thrown many people out of work at least temporarily. To be sure, these workers have not been allowed to remain unemployed, and jobs have been found for them, but what kinds of jobs have they been? Many persons who might otherwise have been unem- ployed have been put to work at forced labor on a variety of govern- ment construction projects. Others have been employed in ordinary in- dustries at low wages and on a subsistence scale of living. Still others have been literally "farmed out"—that is, sent back to the country, where they could appear to have something to do. Thus it is claimed that un- employment is disguised rather than eliminated and that depressions are avoided by carrying on some types of production that are not very im- portant or carrying on other types with more men and resources than would be necessary.

Conclusion. Only the hardened Russophile or Russophobe could con- clude that the Soviet Russian economy is either perfect or worthless. Some of its methods and results seem desirable, others undesirable. Soviet Russia has shown that it is possible to keep a planned economy operating, to eliminate or reduce some types of waste and inefficiency which prevail under capitalism, and to make considerable economic progress. On the other hand, Soviet Russia has encountered many serious economic problems in operating her planned economy and has demon- strated clearly that not all types of waste and inefficiency are peculiar to capitalistic systems.

The supporters of Soviet Russia attribute these wastes and inefficiencies to the youth and inexperience of the planned economy and expect that they will gradually disappear. The critics believe that many types of waste and inefficiency are inherent in the nature of the planned economy and will prove as troublesome in the future as in the past. For the present, it seems clear that the Soviet Russian planned economy, although it provides some kind of alternative to capitalism, is not the kind of system which most Americans would prefer to their own on economic grounds. And most Americans would probably require that a planned economy should operate much more satisfactorily than the capitalistic system if they had to accept along with it a dictatorial government of the kind which exists and functions in Soviet Russia.

QUESTIONS FOR STUDY

1. Do you agree that the government of Soviet Russia would be democratic if it operated strictly on the basis of its present constitution? Why? How does the actual government differ from that which the constitution provides? What kind of a government results in practice?

2. How does the Communist party of Soviet Russia differ from one of the major political parties in the United States? Indicate as many differences as you can. Are there any similarities?

3. Would you describe the revenue system of the Russian government before World War I as advanced or backward? Why? How has it been changed under the planned economy?

4. Does a socialistic country such as Soviet Russia need to levy taxes? Must it have a public debt? Why? If it does levy taxes, do you think it makes much difference what kinds of taxes are used? Why?

5. Indicate the major accomplishments of the Soviet Russian planned economy to date. Which do you regard as most significant? Why?

6. List the failures and difficulties of the Soviet Russian planned economy to date. Which do you regard as most important? Why?

7. On net balance, how well do you think the Soviet Russian planned economy operates in comparison with that of the United States?

Part Four

GERMANY—FASCISM AND RETURN
TO CAPITALISM

CHAPTER 25

AREA, POPULATION, AND RESOURCES

We conclude our study of several types of modern economic systems with the economy of Germany. Our chief emphasis will be on the economic system that existed in Germany in the years just before and during World War II. Economic activity in Germany was then largely under private ownership and operation, and yet it was almost completely under government control through regulation and interference. The German economy differed considerably from that of Soviet Russia, although each was a government-controlled system.

NATIONAL SOCIALISM AND ECONOMIC PLANNING

Economic Institutions. The economy of Germany before World War II and during that conflict was known as National Socialism, although it was essentially similar to that of Fascist Italy. According to the leaders of National Socialism, the goals of their system were found in the objectives of the nation as an entity separate from the many individuals who composed it at any particular time. Economic policies were followed or abandoned according to whether they appeared to be consistent with the general goals of the system. Such a system did not need to make any change in the character of economic institutions. It needed merely, by intervention and restriction, to control the operation of these institutions to further the aims of the system.

Under National Socialism there was no such concentration of productive wealth in public hands as is presupposed by socialism or Communism. The various government units owned and operated some production facilities, but most were left in private hands. However, the private owners were not supposed to think that they had any sacred property rights; they held their wealth only on the sufferance of the "leader," Herr Hitler. The uses which could be made of productive wealth were controlled, and private wealth was expropriated on occasion. When the ruling party or government found itself short of funds, examiners could be sent out to go over the books of private firms for many years past. Fines of millions of marks might be levied for any false entries or even trivial mistakes in bookkeeping. There were no courts capable of preventing such arbitrary actions.

National Socialism made much of such things as individual initiative, economic motivation, and freedom of enterprise as devices for securing the efficient operation of the economy. Seemingly, the individual was free to be a business enterpriser, produce any commodity or service which he liked in any quantity which seemed appropriate, hire and fire labor, obtain supplies on as good terms as he could get, make money, and spend or save his income as he desired. It seemed that the economic system would be highly competitive, and private businessmen appeared able to make their decisions on the basis of price movements and relationships.

Actually, interference with the private operation of business and industry existed to an almost unbelievable extent. The government could and did restrict, or prohibit altogether, the entry of individuals into certain businesses. The government at times controlled the prices at which commodities and services could sell or at which labor could be obtained; it regulated the marketing of economic goods; it set up production quotas or hours of operation for plants and enterprises; it rationed supplies; it compelled employers to hire and fire labor along party lines; and it controlled the use of foreign exchange and the importation and exportation of goods.

Business enterprisers could seek profits, but the government decided whether they could be paid out to the owners and to what extent, and it could require them to invest their earnings in the securities of new plants that were being set up for purposes of economic self-sufficiency, or in government bonds. Differentials in wages existed between various occupations and industries, and the workers sometimes had a choice of occupations, but as time went on there appeared a tendency to freeze the workers in their jobs and to mold the class structure into semi-permanent castes. In view of the levies which the government made on wages, it is questionable whether much economic motivation remained for workers.

National Socialism, then, was different from capitalism in that an all-powerful central government, unrestrained by constitutional limitations, interfered with economic and other activities to an enormous degree to direct them toward whatever goals seemed desirable to the leaders of the government. National Socialism accepted the institutions of capitalism in name only, for it refused to let them operate in capitalistic fashion lest they enhance the welfare of the citizens as individuals instead of contributing to the achievement of those different and often conflicting goals of the semimystical nation.

Economic Planning. When the National Socialist party came into power in Germany early in 1933, it had a severe business depression to cope with. It did not wait long before starting to interfere with the economic life of the country. On May 1, 1933, the first Four-Year Plan was announced. It was not a plan covering the general functioning of the economy, but was supposed to deal with unemployment. Among the measures included were public works; subsidies to building operations; rebates of taxes on renewals of industrial equipment; work spreading; the absorption of workers by means of the labor service, labor subsidies for agriculture, and tax remissions for the employment of female domestic servants; restrictions on dismissals; subsidies for the employment of older workers, and especially those with families; the prohibition of "multiple earnings" within the family; the reintroduction of universal compulsory military service; the payment of bonuses to newly married couples if the wife agreed not to resume employment; and eventually the great rearmament program.

Unemployment had virtually disappeared by the fall of 1936, and Germany embarked on a second Four-Year Plan. This plan also dealt with a specific problem and did not cover all details of economic activity. Its purpose was to further war preparations by making Germany self-sufficient with respect to necessary foods and materials. The plan was organized under six divisions, each headed by a staff of army officers and big businessmen. The specific aims were to increase the output of raw materials; to distribute them, especially iron and steel, so that the armaments industries and other key industries could attain their objectives; to distribute labor with especial regard for the needs of armaments industries; to increase agricultural production, especially in lines which produced raw materials for industry; to keep prices and wages stable; and to control foreign exchange.

During the Four-Year Plans, many phases of German economic life were brought under government control. The Labor Front was organized, and many agencies to control employer-employee relations were established. The so-called Estates of Industry and Trade, Handicrafts, Transportation, and Agriculture were created for purposes of government control in these fields. The government organized controls over prices and wages, international trade, credit, and investment operations.

Until the second Four-Year Plan, the most important economic decisions were entrusted to the Minister of Economic Affairs (a Cabinet officer) under the general supervision of the party leaders. Later there developed a considerable duplication of functions between the Ministry of Economic Affairs and the authorities of the second Four-Year Plan, and the Ministry of Economic Affairs was reorganized. In 1940, General Hermann Göring and an advisory council were placed in charge of German economic activities, and the Ministry of Economic Affairs took a subordinate position. The advisory council was composed of secretaries from the Ministries of Economic Affairs, Labor, Transportation, and Interior, the Reich Forest Office, and the Four-Year Plan; a delegate from the Nazi party; and the chief of the war economy office of the High Command.

Thereafter, this General Council for the War Economy made economic decisions for the whole economy, even though the group may not have been called the state planning commission. The ultimate power of decision making, in the economic sphere as in others, lay in the hands of Hitler. Some important businessmen also had a great deal of influence and may have been able to affect the economic decisions which were ultimately reached.

The German economy under National Socialism, at least in its later years, operated on the basis of economic planning. The most important economic decisions—those involving the goods to be produced, the allocation of productive agents, the distribution of consumers' goods, and the balance between spending and saving—were made by the government and not by private individuals on the basis of price relationships. On the other hand, there seems to have been no definite and continuously functioning body, known as a state planning commission, which was charged with making economic plans. There is little indication that detailed plans were drawn up for several years at a time, with supplementary estimates of proposed achievements in individual years. There seemed to be no public participation in planning. The identity of those who did the planning was not always clear. The ownership of productive wealth and the detailed operation of economic activities seemed to be left in the hands of private individuals.

There is little indication that any attempt was made to adapt the operation of the economy to the wishes of the citizens as private individuals. The leaders realized that the citizens would have to have certain minimum necessities and comforts in order to function efficiently in serving the state, but that was all. Apart from this consideration, the leaders did not care what the desires of the citizens might be. Only the interests of the nation were deemed worthy of consideration.

THE ECONOMIC SYSTEM OF THE FEDERAL REPUBLIC

In recent years, the economic system of the Federal Republic of Western Germany has been quite different from that of Germany in the National Socialist era. In 1948 a currency reform was carried out which allowed people to claim 1 new mark for each 10 old ones that they possessed. This wiped out the savings of many people, but it ended the currency inflation and gave the people money in which they could have faith. Rationing was abolished and nearly all price controls were removed. The price system became once more the mechanism for the operation of the economic system.

In Western Germany individuals and firms are free to carry on production activities in most fields. Since the prices of most goods have been free to find their own level, business firms have been able to make money. The tax system has been adjusted to induce firms to invest their earnings in new capital goods. Capital investment has been high. Relatively high prices for final commodities have restricted consumption, but the workers have had maximum incentives to work hard to increase their money wages.

Western Germany has returned toward the capitalistic operation of her economy. The economic system again operates on the basis of freedom of enterprise, economic motivation, private property, and the price system. The government still plays a more important part in guiding the economy than it would under theoretical capitalism, but most of the things which it does are also done by government in the United States or other ostensibly capitalistic nations. We shall comment later on the remarkable economic recovery which has occurred in Western Germany under these conditions.

TERRITORIAL EXPANSION AND READJUSTMENT

The Development of Prussia to 1796. The area and population of Germany developed through a long and complicated process. The German Empire dates only from 1871, but the development of the country occurred over several centuries. The rise of the Electorate of Brandenburg and its expansion into modern Prussia began with Frederick William, the Great Elector, who came to the throne in 1640. He engaged in many military adventures and once received East Prussia for helping out in a war between Sweden and Poland. He was also responsible for the reform of the system of land tenure, the introduction of improved methods in agriculture, the encouragement of industry and trade, the building of roads and canals and the development of the post office, the encouragement of education, the founding of trading companies, and the establishment of the first German colony on the west coast of Africa. The Electorate was converted into the Kingdom of Prussia in 1701.

King Frederick William I of Prussia (1713–1740) was an ambitious ruler, so he tried to create a larger and more efficient army, a stronger national feeling and consciousness, and a more purposeful national policy. Prussia acquired the territory of western Pomerania in 1720 after a series of wars with Poland, Russia, and Denmark. Frederick William I also did much for commerce and agriculture and worked for the protection of domestic industries. He is sometimes credited with creating the qualities of the "typical" Prussian—energy, order, application, discipline, and frugality, but also belligerence, self-assertiveness, and inability to see more than one side of a question.

Prussia made noteworthy territorial gains under Frederick the Great (1740–1786), who inherited a large army and a well-stocked treasury. Prussia gained Upper and Lower Silesia in 1742 and the northern coastal region of East Friesland in 1744. Prussia participated in the partition of Poland in 1772, gaining West Prussia, land along the lower reaches of the Vistula River, and the Netze district. At home, Frederick the Great worked for the development of Prussia's resources, agriculture, trade, and industry, the stabilization of her administration and finance, and the development of her intellectual life. He was responsible for a code of common laws which has endured to modern times.

Prussia in the Napoleonic Wars. As a result of later partitions of Poland, Prussia came into the possession of Thorn and Danzig, the Posen, Gnesen, and Warsaw districts, and other areas which formerly belonged to Poland. However, Prussia suffered great losses during the Napoleonic Wars, and by 1807 had lost half of her territory. From 1807 to 1813 a vigorous recovery effort was made. Serfdom was abolished, the people were accorded freedom of choice of trades and occupations, the towns gained powers of self-government, and the educational system was reformed and extended. The army was also reformed so that the nobility would no longer hold all high positions, and universal military service was instituted.

Napoleon's invasion of Russia in 1812 resulted in ghastly failure, and Prussia joined forces with Austria, Russia, Sweden, and Great Britain to put Napoleon entirely out of business. In the final re-forming of the European map, Prussia received northern Saxony, some territory east of the Elbe River, part of Westphalia, Swedish Pomerania, and some districts along the Rhine River, but ceded East Friesland, Goslar, and Hildesheim to Hanover, and Ausbach and Bayreuth to Bavaria.

The Founding of the German Empire. With Bismarck as Chancellor, Prussia acquired the duchies of Schleswig and Holstein from Denmark by military force in 1864. After the Bohemian War against Austria, which ended in 1866, Prussia got four formerly independent German areas—Hanover, Electoral Hesse, Nassau, and Frankfurt. The Franco-Prussian War of 1870–1871 ended in the total defeat of France. Besides paying a considerable indemnity, France gave up Alsace, with the city of Strasbourg, and the German-speaking part of Lorraine, with the city of Metz.

The German Empire was proclaimed on January 18, 1871, and was made up of 25 sovereign states and the imperial province of Alsace-Lorraine. The King of Prussia was to be the German Emperor, and the Minister-President of Prussia was to function as Imperial Chancellor, so Prussia controlled the new empire. Germany was a late entrant in the international race to obtain overseas colonies. However, she acquired the African colonies of Cameroons, Togoland, West Africa, and East Africa between 1884 and 1889, as well as part of New Guinea, and the Caroline, Palau, Marianas, and other islands in the Pacific. In 1890 Germany received Heligoland from Great Britain in exchange for some land in East Africa and German approval of the British protectorate in Zanzibar.

The Results of World War I. No further important changes in German territories occurred until after World War I, which began in August, 1914. During the greater part of the war, it seemed likely that Germany would win or at least be able to achieve a stalemate, but eventually the tide turned against her. Revolution broke out on October 30, 1918, with a mutiny in the fleet at Wilhelmshaven. The war came to an end by armistice in November, the German Emperor abdicated, and the Socialists took over.

When the peace settlement was made, Germany lost some 27,250 square miles in Europe. Parts of the Rhine Province (Eupen and Malmédy) went to Belgium, Alsace-Lorraine to France, and part of Silesia to Czechoslovakia. Posen, much of West Prussia, and part of Upper Silesia were transferred to Poland. This created the Polish Corridor, which gave Poland access to the sea and isolated East Prussia from the rest of Germany. Another slice of West Prussia was given to the Danzig area, with Danzig itself becoming a free city under the League of Nations. Memel was given to Lithuania. The fate of northern Schleswig and the Saar industrial area in southeastern Germany was to be settled by plebiscites later. The East Rhineland was to be demilitarized, and the West Rhineland was to be occupied for a time. In addition, Germany lost all her colonies. France and Great Britain took most of them.

The Interwar Period and World War II. The territory of Germany remained constant until after Adolph Hitler came to power in 1933, at which time the area of the country was 181,662 square miles. The Saar area was returned to Germany by plebiscite in 1935, and Germany secured full control of her territory east and west of the Rhine. Austria, with its 32,369 square miles, was brought into the German Reich in 1938, and in the same year the Sudetenland, a mountainous area in northern

**GERMAN TERRITORY
1919-38 & 1938-41**

1919-1938
1938-1941
Annexed by Germany
Occupied by Germany
German Protectorate

Fig. 6

Czechoslovakia, was annexed. This gave Germany a total area of 218,258 square miles and a population of about 79,000,000 in 1939. Germany's area at the time made her the second largest country in Europe, although her size was small compared with that of Soviet Russia or the United States.

Fig. 7. Present Germany, as divided between the Russian zone and the Federal Republic, with some surrounding territory.

World War II began when Germany tried to acquire territory from Poland in 1939. The German armed forces met with amazing success, and German territories expanded rapidly. Germany added Norway, Denmark, Belgium, the Netherlands, Hungary, Roumania, Bulgaria, Yugoslavia, Greece, Poland, France, a large part of European Russia, and other areas to the territory under her control. Figure 6 indicates the extent to which the map of Europe was changed prior to the German invasion of Russia in 1941.

In the end, World War II resulted in disastrous defeat for Germany, and she was deprived of much of her prewar territory. For example, East Prussia was divided between Poland and Soviet Russia; West Prussia and most of Silesia and Pomerania went to Poland; and the Sudetenland was returned to Czechoslovakia. Germany was immediately reduced to an area of 139,975 square miles. This was divided into four zones for supposedly temporary administration by the United States, Soviet Russia, Great Britain, and France. The zones varied from 16,491 square miles administered by the French to 42,235 square miles administered by the Soviet Russians.

The Federal Republic. The American, British, and French zones were later united to form the Federal Republic of Western Germany. In area, the Federal Republic makes up only 52 per cent of the German Reich of 1937, but it has about 75 per cent of the total German population. Figure 7 shows the small present size of Germany and the division of the country between the Soviet Zone to the east and the Federal Republic to the West.

THE POPULATION AND PEOPLES OF GERMANY

The Growth of Population. Over much of the past century and a half, Germany has had a rapidly expanding population, as shown in Table 25-1. However, this growth received a sharp setback in both world wars.

Table 25-1. The Growth of Population in Germany

Year	Total population
1816	25,000,000
1871	35,000,000
1882	39,834,000
1895	45,925,000
1907	54,991,000
1913	66,978,000
1925	62,410,000
1933	65,218,000
1938	68,000,000
1939	79,000,000*
1946	65,000,000

* Including Austria and the Sudetenland.

Many people were lost in the wars, and others were transferred to other countries afterwards. The area which is now the Federal Republic of Western Germany had a population of only 39,300,000 people in 1939. In the 1950 census, it had a population of 47,700,000, of whom 25,300,000 were women and 7,800,000 were Germans who had come from other formerly German territories since the war.[1] The population of the Federal Republic was estimated at 50,000,000 in 1954, compared with 17,-000,000 in East Germany.[2]

The German birth rates and death rates per thousand inhabitants have had their ups and downs over the years, but both have shown a long-run tendency to decline. The greatest excess of births over deaths since 1850 was reached in 1888 and again in 1902. During World War I, deaths exceeded births. Births exceeded deaths by 11.4 in 1921, but by only 3.5 in 1933. From 1934 to the outbreak of World War II, the figure was stable at 7 or 7.1.[3] In 1951 it was 5.2 for the Federal Republic of Western Germany.

The People of Germany. The Germans are a mixture of ethnic groups. Even the Nazis, despite their ravings on the subject of racial purity, conceded that the Germans included nine different races—Nordic, Ostic, Dinaric, East Baltic, Falic, Westic, Sudetic, Inner Asiatic, and Negro. The first six of these account for the bulk of the population. Jews and gypsies were not officially regarded as German. The Jewish people, so despised and mistreated under the Nazi regime, were a small element in the population. In the middle 1930s, they numbered about 500,000, or 0.8 per cent of the total population. Four-fifths of them were German Jews, and the rest were alien. About one-third of them lived in Berlin.

Although there has been considerable intermixture, the German people continue to differ from one part of the country to another. However, the German people as a whole are sturdy, industrious, highly literate, and rather well educated, although the educational system was corrupted under the Nazi regime. The Germans have needed to be both hard-working and ingenious to achieve a fairly high standard of living for a large population on the basis of limited total area and resources.

The German population has become increasingly urban. Persons employed in agriculture and forestry and their dependents amounted to 42 per cent of the total population in 1882, but this proportion declined to 35.6 in 1895 and 25.8 in 1907. The number of people who lived in cities of more than 20,000 inhabitants was 8,600,000 in 1885, or 18.4 per cent of the total population. In 1910 the number was 22,400,000 or 34.5 per cent of the total. In 1936 the population was about half urban, and there were 26 cities of 200,000 inhabitants or over. The first five cities were Berlin, the capital, with 4,250,000, Hamburg with 1,131,000, Cologne with 765,000, Munich with 735,388, and Leipzig with 713,740.

---

[1] *The Economist*, Oct. 18, 1952, p. 206.
[2] *Time*, Feb. 15, 1954, p. 91.
[3] V. Trivanovitch, *Economic Development of Germany under National Socialism* New York: National Industrial Conference Board, Inc., 1937), p. 53.

PHYSICAL FEATURES

Surface Features. Germany before World War II was a land of plains and mountains—Lower Germany and Upper Germany. More accurately, Germany, on the basis of topography, was divided into three parallel belts running east and west. In the far south were the Alps and their tableland. In the middle was a region of lesser mountains and hills, while to the north there was the great German plain, which really extended from the North Sea to the Ural Mountains of Russia, or far beyond the boundary of Germany.

In the western part of the northern plain, there is a rim of marshland along the coast. Farther inland is an area of sandy Geest, or dry heath interspersed with boggy moors, and then a stretch of rather good agricultural land at the foot of the hills of the central region. Farther east, along the Baltic Sea, there is a region of sand dunes along the coast, and then an area of low hills and lakes. South of the hills is a depression reaching from the Elbe River eastward beyond the German boundary. This is the location of the Prussian province of Brandenburg and also of Berlin.

Below Brandenburg the northern plain stretches southeast, forming the Silesian depression along the Oder River. On the south, Silesia is separated from Czechoslovakia by the Sudetic Mountains, which are the highest in Germany, except for the Alps. West of Silesia are Saxony and Thuringia. Saxony is flat in the north but mountainous in the south, while Thuringia is sometimes called the "green heart" of Germany.

South of Thuringia is Bavaria, with its largest city, Munich, lying between the Danube River and the Alps. Bavaria is largely a plateau, which rises from Munich to the Bavarian Alps in the south, with the Alps including such peaks as the Zugspitze (9,719 feet) and the Watzmann (8,902 feet). West of Bavaria are the mountainous regions of Württemberg and Baden, and also Hesse-Darmstadt, Pfalz, and the Saar Basin. Finally, west of Thuringia are the Prussian province of Hesse-Nassau and the Prussian Rhine Province, the latter being perhaps the best-known area of Germany.

Germany has about 7,000 miles of waterways, including a well-developed system of canals. The six main rivers, including the Rhine, Elbe, Oder, and Danube, flow a total of some 2,100 miles through Germany, mostly toward the north or northwest. There are 1,550 miles of tributary rivers, many of them flowing east and west, and 1,937 miles of smaller watercourses. The coastal areas of Germany, both on the North Sea and the Baltic, are low and flat, and poor in natural harbors. The tides are almost imperceptible. The mouths of the leading rivers tend to become choked with sand unless they are kept open by dredging.

The chief ports of Germany are river ports, some distance removed from the ocean.

Climate and Precipitation. Germany has a wide range of latitude, but its climate is uniform. It is of the continental type. The ocean has its greatest influence in the northwestern section; there the winters are mild, the summers are cool, and there is an extended growing season. The warmest climate in Germany is found in the Rhine valley, which is the northernmost area in Europe for vine culture.

The German climate differs more from east to west than from north to south. The southern parts are cool because of their altitude, while the northern areas receive some warmth from the Gulf Stream. Thus Bavaria and other southern regions are cooler than the province of Holstein and the Frisian Islands in the far north. The average July temperature is 65 degrees in Berlin, compared with 63 degrees in Munich some 300 miles south. As one moves from west to east in Germany, the climate becomes more severe and the seasonal range of temperatures increases.

In general, adequate rainfall is brought in by the prevailing west and southward winds. The precipitation averages 20 to 30 inches per year on the German plains, and somewhat less on the southern plateau. There is also a decrease in precipitation from the west to the east and southeast, with Silesia receiving the smallest amount. On the plains, the rainfall is well distributed seasonally. There is no really dry season.

Soil and Vegetation. Germany's area prior to World War II furnished 1.7 acres per inhabitant, but only about half the land was suitable for cultivation, and even that half required meticulous care, the use of large quantities of commercial fertilizer, and scientific methods of agriculture. Many years ago, glaciers scoured much of Germany flat and left a deposit of light, sandy, and rather infertile soil. In combination with the cool, moist climate with relatively little sunshine, this land is poor for general agriculture and has to be used largely for such crops as rye and potatoes. Occasional areas of clay are interspersed with the sandy soil, and these areas are more fertile. Most of the wheat and sugar beets are grown on them. In the south and southwest the soils are better than those of the plains, but the rough topography limits their usefulness.

In about one-fourth of Germany, the soil and other conditions are more favorable for the growth of trees than for cultivation. In the first half of the eighteenth century, the forests were being cut down rapidly and a shortage of fuel impended, but the situation was saved by the introduction of scientific forestry. Forests have come to be treated as crops. The removal of mature timber and the replacement of trees are regulated by law, with the harvest limited to the annual growth. About half the forests belong to various governmental units; the balance is divided between the wood lots of the peasants and the landed estates.

NATURAL RESOURCES

Power Resources. For a great industrial nation and a world power, Germany before World War II was not liberally supplied with natural resources. Coal was the most important source of power. Germany had about 40 per cent of all the coal deposits in Europe at the time of World War I but lost much of it by the peace settlement. In 1936, after the recovery of the Saar, her coal output amounted to 158 million tons, compared with 448 million tons for the United States and 1,252 million tons for the world as a whole.

The most important source of coal in Germany was the Westphalian field lying in the lower Rhine valley. It had an area of about 1,500 square miles, only one-fourth of which had actually been developed. The coal was high grade, suitable for making coke, and could be extracted cheaply. The Saar area in southwestern Germany was a second source of coal. Finally, some coal was produced in Upper Silesia and much more in Lower Silesia.

Germany had reserves of lignite or brown coal amounting to 13 billion tons, or about the same as those of Soviet Russia and Czechoslovakia. The output of lignite in 1936 came to about 161 million tons, or somewhat more than that of coal. However, since the heat value of lignite is only about two-ninths that of coal, lignite was a much less important source of power. Much of the lignite is produced in central Germany, although the Cologne area in western Germany is also important. In the former area lignite is used in the chemical industry, giving off oil, tar, gas, and wax as by-products. It is also used as a fuel in the sugar, potash, glass, porcelain, textile, and chemical industries. In the Cologne area, lignite is used in the generation of electric power. A large amount of lignite is made into briquettes for use as an industrial and household fuel.

Petroleum was an important fuel in Germany, but domestic production was negligible. Domestic production was adequate to meet only one-tenth of the total demand in 1936.[4] Consumption of motor fuels and oils amounted to 5.15 million tons in 1937, and close to half of this was imported. Synthetic petroleum products manufactured in Germany accounted for another 35 to 40 per cent.[5] The synthetics were made from coal by a process of hydrogenation. In 1939 Germany was about 50 per cent self-sufficient in the production of petroleum products.

Finally, electric power was important to German industry prior to

[4] *Ibid.*, p. 126.
[5] W. R. Deuel, *People under Hitler* (New York: Harcourt, Brace and Company, Inc., 1942), p. 302.

World War II, but this was additional power only to the extent that it was hydroelectric. All the rest had to be produced by burning coal, lignite, or other fuels. Less than one-sixth of the German total was hydroelectric. The main rivers of Germany meander slowly across the plains and are not prolific sources of power. A river's power is most readily tapped near its source, where it tumbles from mountains or hills, and Germany's large rivers rise outside the country. The output of electric power was 42.5 billion kilowatt-hours in 1936, compared with 114 billion in the United States and 387 billion in the world.[6]

Metallic Resources. Iron is indispensable for modern industry, and Germany had about one-third of all the iron ore in Europe prior to World War I. However, the loss of Lorraine to France after the war took away 69 per cent of the iron-ore reserves, and those that remained were low in quality and inconveniently located for exploitation. The most important remaining reserves were those at Siegerland, east of Cologne in western Germany. The production of iron ore amounted to 9.6 million tons in 1937, compared with 73.3 million tons in the United States. In 1938 German production amounted to 10.9 million tons.[7] The German output was inadequate for domestic needs, and Germany imported almost four-fifths of her iron ore in 1936. Germany also had very little manganese, which is essential to steel production.

Germany led the world in aluminum production prior to World War II (28.6 per cent). Germany was supposed to be self-sufficient during the war, with the aid of the occupied countries.[8] However, Germany was almost completely dependent upon other countries for bauxite, the ore from which aluminum is made. Germany produced 53,000 tons of copper in 1934 out of a world production of 1,323,000 tons, and she was the world's leading importer of copper in 1938.[9] Domestic production was from low-grade ore in northwestern Germany. The world output of lead in 1940 was 1.7 million tons, with Germany producing 181,000 tons, of which 40 per cent came from Silesia.[10] However, Germany was a large importer of lead as well.

Germany was almost completely dependent upon outside sources for both nickel and tin in the days before World War II. She required from 12,000 to 15,000 tons of tungsten each year, all of it imported. She produced zinc from mines in Silesia but had to import about as much as she produced. Germany was eighth in the world in the production of

[6] U.S. Office of Military Government for Germany, *Economic Data on Potsdam Germany*, 1947, p. 4.
[7] J. B. DeMille, *Strategic Minerals* (New York: McGraw-Hill Book Company, Inc., 1947), p. 242.
[8] *Ibid.*, p. 45.
[9] *Ibid.*, pp. 153.
[10] *Ibid.*, pp. 274–275.

mercury in 1938. Vanadium was not actually produced in Germany but it was recovered from blast-furnace slag and as a by-product in the reduction of bauxite.

Other Minerals. Germany's position before World War II was favorable with respect to some minerals. In 1938 she produced 58.9 per cent of the world's total output of potash.[11] The leading deposits are found around Stassfurt in central Germany. They contain an estimated 20 billion metric tons—a quantity which would last the world for many hundreds of years. Until after World War I, Germany also controlled important potash deposits in Alsace, containing 300 million metric tons.[12] These deposits were of somewhat higher quality.

Until she lost Alsace, Germany had a virtual monopoly in the production of potash, and even afterward had 80 per cent of world reserves. Potash is an ingredient of almost all commercial fertilizers, and about 90 per cent of total production was used for this purpose. Potash is also used in the manufacture of soap, glass, matches, explosives, chemical reagents, and for dyeing and photographic work. Potash was an important export for Germany and strengthened her hand considerably in bargaining with other nations. The importance of potash to German agriculture can scarcely be overestimated, for it has been in great measure responsible for the large yields from soils which are low in fertility.

Germany was the world's largest producer of fluorspar, with 32.5 per cent of world output in 1938.[13] This mineral is used as a flux in smelting metals and for the production of hydrofluoric acid. On the basis of high-grade deposits and nearness to large markets, Germany was the world's leading producer of barite (barium sulphate) before the war, with 50 per cent of world output. Germany was self-sufficient in the production of nitrogen, useful in the making of fertilizers, explosives, and dyes. Finally, Germany led the world in producing magnesite (magnesium carbonate) until 1943.

Nonmineral Raw Materials. With respect to nonmineral raw materials, the picture in Germany was in general one of shortage. She was especially short of raw materials for textiles, since she produced no cotton or silk and only 9 per cent of the wool she consumed. According to one estimate covering cotton, wool, flax, rayon, silk, and textile fiber, Germany produced about 34 per cent of her requirements just prior to World War II.[14]

Germany developed a method of producing rubber synthetically which

[11] *Ibid.*, pp. 406–407.

[12] W. O. Blanchard and S. S. Visher, *Economic Geography of Europe* (New York: McGraw-Hill Book Company, Inc., 1931), pp. 248–250.

[13] DeMille, *op. cit.,* p. 160.

[14] O. Nathan, *The Nazi Economic System* (Durham, N.C.: Duke University Press, 1944), p. 860.

enabled her to provide at home for one-fourth of her needs in 1938 and one-third in 1939. However, she was still greatly dependent upon outside sources.[15] Germany's forests served her well in the prewar period but provided only two-thirds to three-fourths of her requirements of wood. She was able to produce at home only 6 to 8 per cent of her required supplies of oil cakes and vegetable oils. She was dependent upon outside sources for resin, shellac, and turpentine. She imported more than half of all hides and skins and about 90 per cent of her tanning materials. Over 70 per cent of her tobacco was imported.[16]

On the basis of her resources as outlined above, it seems hardly credible that Germany would allow herself to become involved in a war against most of the rest of the world, as she did in 1939. However, she had a tremendous war machine, was much better prepared than her adversaries, had accumulated stockpiles of materials that normally had to be imported, had developed artificial substitutes for scarce materials, and was confident that she could win the war. For a time her conquests added to her current supplies and basic reserves, but in the end her efforts were unavailing.

The Resources of the Federal Republic. The situation of the Federal Republic of Western Germany with regard to natural resources is moderately favorable. Its coal deposits are only about three-fourths as great as those of prewar Germany, for the Saar district and Upper Silesia have been lost. Important lead and zinc resources were also lost with Upper Silesia. Still, the Federal Republic is fairly well off with respect to power resources and metallic and nonmetallic minerals.

On the other hand, important areas in the eastern part of prewar Germany, which once had the largest surpluses of grain, sugar, and potatoes, have been lost to Soviet Russia and Poland. There has been a considerable deficiency in the Federal Republic's supplies of home-grown food, and this has resulted in pressure on the country's balance of international payments. On the whole, however, the Federal Republic has become adjusted to the partition of Germany. A sudden reunion of the Federal Republic and Eastern Germany might actually precipitate an economic crisis.

QUESTIONS FOR STUDY

1. Indicate the increases and decreases in German territory from the founding of the German Empire to the establishment of the Federal Republic of Western Germany.

[15] G. Reimann, *The Vampire Economy* (New York: Vanguard Press, Inc., 1939), p. 209.
[16] Trivanovitch, *op. cit.,* p. 122.

2. Has the population of Germany usually grown slowly or rapidly? What was the effect of World Wars I and II? Of the Great Depression after 1929? What are some of the characteristics of the German people?

3. Show how, from the point of view of topography, Germany prior to World War II was divided into three parallel belts running east and west. In view of this, why was its climate relatively uniform and why did it vary more from east to west than from north to south?

4. Did prewar Germany have a large amount of land well suited to agriculture? How did it manage to feed its people?

5. Was prewar Germany well supplied with power resources? What was the relative importance of coal and other power resources?

6. What was the position of prewar Germany with regard to metallic minerals? Other minerals? Nonmineral raw materials? Was the general resource position of Germany suitable for undertaking a program of national economic self-sufficiency?

7. How did the National Socialist economic system of Germany differ from a capitalistic system, such as that of the United States? From the planned economy of Soviet Russia?

CHAPTER 26

AGRICULTURE

Since Germany had a large and growing population to support on the basis of limited land and resources, agriculture was a matter of extreme importance. Germany had changed from a country with an agricultural surplus to one with an agricultural deficit long before the National Socialists came to power in 1933. We shall better appreciate the agricultural problems faced by the Nazis if we glance at the development of German agriculture over the preceding century.

AGRICULTURE BEFORE 1871

Agricultural Organization. In the early years of the nineteenth century, the typical organization of German rural life was the compact village surrounded by open fields cultivated by the village inhabitants. Agriculture was carried on by means of a communal routine that featured the three-crop rotation, the common pasture, the rights of grazing on the stubble, and the distribution of the landholdings of individual peasants over the open fields belonging to the village. There were exceptions, of course. In some areas, the compact villages gave way to small hamlets and scattered farmsteads. In other areas, villages were strung out in a long line along streams or dykes, with each family's land consisting of a single strip with the dwelling at one end. In still other areas, the peasant's landholdings, whether scattered or compact, were free of communal control and were his to cultivate as he pleased. However, the most common situation was the compact village surrounded by open fields.

A peculiarity of the eastern sections of Germany was the extent to which the land was owned by a small group of lords of the manor, called Junkers. Originally, the Junkers, as a result of conquest, had been lords over various grades of peasants and had held some land to support their families. However, as the result of the decimation of the rural population in wartime, the Junkers were able to increase their landholdings enormously. Most of the Junkers cultivated their land and did not let it

413

out to others. In other parts of the country, large landed estates were less numerous, and much of their land was turned over to outside people to cultivate.

The Status of the Peasants. The legal and economic position of the German peasants was subject to great variation. Some peasants were almost independent, owing their lords only ceremonial duties, dues when land passed from father to son, and a quitrent payable in money or kind. At the other end of the scale were peasants who had no rights in their land but held it only because of the charity of their lords. These peasants were obliged to render personal services to their lords, and sometimes to give the services of their families and draft animals. They had to bake in the lords' ovens, grind their grain in the lords' mills, and put their grapes through the lords' wine presses. In general, the peasants of the eastern part of the country were more servile and of lower estate than those of other parts of the country.

There was no completely landless class in Germany in the early nineteenth century, but in most parts of the country there was a class of peasants whose lands were too small to support them. Such people performed various types of agricultural labor for the landlords or the larger peasants. In many cases they had to earn what they could through handicraft production or, later on, by working in factories.

The Emancipation of the Peasants. The freeing of the German peasants was a tedious process. It began in the late 1700s in some of the smaller states. At about the same time, Frederick the Great of Prussia took steps to lighten the peasants' services, give them some rights of inheritance, and improve their legal status. These changes applied at first only to peasants on the land belonging to the ruler, which then amounted to about a third of the kingdom. Later, the emancipation edicts of 1807 and 1808 made the Prussian peasants freemen, able to acquire property and relieved of heritable subjection.

Under still later laws and regulations (1811, 1816, 1821), it was provided that peasants whose land was heritable could become full proprietors by turning over a third of their land to the lords in return for the rights which the lords were giving up. Peasants whose land had not previously been heritable had to give up one-half of it. Those whose holdings were so small that they could not live on a fraction of their land might keep it all and pay a rent. No peasant could become a full proprietor until all matters between him and his landlord had been settled.

These changes were not to the advantage of all the peasants. Many of the more favorable provisions applied only to the full peasants—those who owned plow oxen and had lands in the regular village fields. Freemen could acquire property, but they could also sell their rights to it. The peasants, as freemen, were on their own. They had to keep their houses in repair, take care of their families and themselves in periods of adversity, and so on. Lesser peasants often sold out or were evicted by the landlords. Some of them were lucky enough to hold on to small amounts of land as tenants at will, while others simply became laborers.

The work of freeing the peasants went on slowly. There were some states in which no serious attempt was made to revise traditional relationships until after 1848. The early laws in Prussia in many cases went into effect only on the application of the peasants. It was 1850 before Prussian law assisted the lesser peasants who were not eligible to take advantage of the provisions of earlier laws. By then, many of the peasants had lost their land altogether or had become tenants at will. Legal emancipation in Prussia was completed by 1870, but traces of the old customs lingered until the end of the century. In other German states, financial aftermaths of emancipation remained down to the beginning of World War I in 1914.

Agricultural Efficiency. The old system of agriculture, under which individual peasants held scattered strips of land and were bound by communal routine in the crops which they could raise, was inefficient, but changes in it came slowly. The emancipation of the peasants gave many landlords an opportunity to acquire more land and to rearrange their holdings. The same reshuffling of land gave surviving peasants a chance to acquire more compact holdings, and some of the more prosperous peasants moved out of the villages and erected dwellings on their land. However, many of the peasants were highly conservative, found the use of common pasture and woodland congenial, and were interested in supporting their families rather than in the sale of products on the market. Such people were not likely to change their practices quickly.

There was not much interest in the rearrangement of peasant landholdings until the decade from 1840 to 1850. The matter was touched for the first time in Hanover only in 1842 and it was not pushed until 1856. Baden did not wrestle with the problem until 1856. Bavaria did not make a beginning until 1861. Prussian law did not attack the problem directly until 1872, and effective action came even later in other states. Remnants of the problem lasted well into the early part of the next century.

In the period before 1871, improvements in agricultural efficiency came most rapidly on the large estates in the eastern part of the country, where production for the market was more important. Among the important developments were deep ploughing and improved implements, stall feeding of cattle, raising of merino sheep, widespread cultivation of oilseeds (rapeseed, linseed, hempseed), improved rotation of crops, the use of clover and grasses on fallow land, the use of guano, the use of earthenware drainpipe, better knowledge of agricultural chemistry, and improved methods of record keeping.[1] In such matters the peasants followed slowly and at a respectful distance.

Sugar beets and potatoes were the most important root crops developed. The first expansion in the growing of sugar beets and in the construction of sugar factories came in the 1830s in Silesia and Saxony. Sugar beets require deep cultivation and drilling and so led to the use of better machinery. Potatoes were not new but their cultivation increased sharply in this period. They were important as a source of food and as a raw material in the distilling of spirits.

AGRICULTURE, 1871–1933

Agricultural Organization. The German Empire, as founded in 1871, was primarily a country of free landowning peasants and great landlords who actually cultivated their estates. There was almost no tenant farming. A fair amount of land was rented, but it was held in small scraps or garden plots by people who were not farmers, or it was rented by people who also cultivated farms of their own. Farming on shares was practically nonexistent.

Throughout the life of the Empire, there were few important changes in the distribution of the various classes of landowners, though there was a tendency for the largest and smallest types of holdings to decline at the end of the century. Landholdings of more than 250 acres declined from 24.1 to 22.2 per cent of the total agricultural area between 1895 and 1907, while those of less than 5 acres fell from 5.6 to 5.4 per cent.[2] In 1895 big peasant holdings of 50 to 250 acres numbered about 280,000 and covered a larger area than any other type of holding. The middle peasants holding 12½ to 50 acres overtook the larger peasants by 1907 and had almost a third of the agricultural area of the Empire in their million holdings.

In 1907 there were about a million small peasants holding from 5 to 12½ acres but covering only about 10 per cent of the cultivated area. The people who held less than 5 acres, and were considered "scrap holders" rather than peasants, numbered 3¼ millions but held only 5 per cent of the cultivated area. At the other extreme, the large landlords held about a quarter of the agricultural area. The typical Junker managed an estate of some 2,000 acres of cultivated land including meadows, along with some forest and waste land.[3] Table 26-1 indicates that these

[1] J. H. Clapham, *The Economic Development of France and Germany, 1815–1914* (London: Cambridge University Press, 1923), pp. 51–52.
[2] *Ibid.*, p. 198.
[3] *Ibid.*, p. 200.

conditions had not changed significantly by the time Hitler came into power.

Table 26-1. The Size, Number, and Acreage of Farms in Germany, 1935

Size, acres	Number	Acreage	Percentage of total acreage
Under 5..........	3,378,509	4,276,338	5.4
5–12.5...........	1,006,277	8,163,049	10.4
12.5–100.........	1,065,539	25,741,263	32.7
100–250.........	262,191	23,025,549	29.3
Over 250.........	23,566	17,425,845	22.2
Total..........	5,736,082	78,632,044	100.0

SOURCE: M. E. Tracy, *Our People, Our Country, and Theirs* (New York: The Macmillan Company, 1939), pp. 23–24.

Increased Agricultural Production. One of the striking features of the period from 1871 to 1914 in Germany was the rapid expansion of agricultural production. The change resulted largely from increased yields on the old land rather than from the cultivation of additional land. According to one source, all the land suitable for cultivation had come into use by 1900, with 95 per cent of the area productive in some fashion and 44 per cent of it arable.[4] Agricultural output not only increased up to the beginning of World War I but increased faster than population. After the war, considerable areas were turned back into meadows and pastures as a result of depression, the absence of tariff protection, and high prices for machinery and labor.

In view of the cool and moist climate and the light, sandy soil, it would not have been expected that large yields per acre would be obtained, but they were. Table 26-2 shows the increase in the yields per hectare

Table 26-2. Increases in the Yield per Hectare of Selected Farm Crops in Germany, 1883–1887 and 1908–1912
(In tons)

Crop	1883–1887	1908–1912
Rye.................	1.00	1.78
Wheat...............	1.34	2.07
Potatoes.............	8.74	13.34
Oats.................	1.13	1.90
Meadow hay..........	2.85	4.21

SOURCE: K. Helfferich, *Germany's Economic Progress and National Wealth, 1888–1913* (New York: Germanistic Society of America, 1914), pp. 53–54.

[4] W. O. Blanchard and S. S. Visher, *Economic Geography of Europe* (New York: McGraw-Hill Book Company, Inc., 1931), p. 245.

(2.47 acres) of certain crops between 1883–1887 and 1908–1912. In the period from 1909 to 1913 the average yield of rye per acre was 29 bushels in Germany and 17 in France. For potatoes, it was 202.7 bushels in Germany and 129.6 in France. Germany outscored France in wheat production by 32.6 to 29.7 bushels to the acre on the average.[5] It was also true in 1912 that the German yields per acre of land exceeded by far those of Russia, the United States, Argentina, Canada, and other agricultural countries in wheat, rye, barley, oats, and potatoes.

Extensive Use of Fertilizers. Several factors accounted for the upsurge in German agricultural production between 1871 and 1914. One was the use of artificial fertilizers to give the German soil elements in which it was deficient. Between 1890 and 1910 the consumption of commercial fertilizers in German agriculture increased from 1.6 million metric tons to 6 million. The consumption of potash increased from 220,000 tons to 2,220,000, and that of nitrate of soda from 250,000 to 540,000 tons.[6] From 1910 to 1925 the consumption of potash per acre doubled, while that of nitrogen tripled.[7] Fertilizers were plentiful in Germany, and they were put to profitable use.

Increased Use of Machinery. The use of machinery also showed a phenomenal increase. Between 1882 and 1907 the number of agricultural establishments using ordinary threshing machines increased from 268,000 to 947,000, the number using steam threshing machines from 76,000 to 489,000, the number using drilling and seeding machines from 64,000 to 290,000, and the number using mowing machines from 20,000 to 301,000.[8] Mechanization played a significant part in increasing yields.

Scientific Methods and Agricultural Education. Before 1871 progress in agricultural methods had been chiefly limited to the large estates, but now these methods became more widely used. The emancipation of the peasants had been largely completed, and progress was being made in the consolidation of scattered peasant landholdings. Gradually the operation of farms came to be characterized by deep ploughing, seed drilling, careful seed selection, scientific livestock breeding, intelligent rotation of crops, surface and subsoil drainage where necessary, irrigation where necessary, and the ploughing under of clover and similar green crops.

Progress in scientific agriculture was dependent on the education of the farmers. Agricultural colleges, which had been scattered, were concentrated at the universities and fitted out with experimental stations. The first agricultural school had been founded only in 1858, but there

[5] *Ibid.*, p. 247.
[6] K. Helfferich, *Germany's Economic Progress and National Wealth, 1888–1913* (New York: Germanistic Society of America, 1914), p. 52.
[7] Blanchard and Visher, *op. cit.*, p. 245.
[8] Helfferich, *op. cit.*, p. 53.

were 28 such schools by 1900. Winter schools, which agricultural students and farmers could attend, increased from 12 in 1870 to more than 240 in 1906. By 1910 there were over 2,000 continuation schools, which the children of peasants and laborers could attend on winter evenings.[9] Thus agricultural knowledge was available to all levels of the rural population.

The Use of Large Quantities of Labor. Heavy crop yields were obtained in part by the use of large amounts of labor on the farms. There may have been a shortage of wage laborers, as we shall see later, but there was no scarcity of labor as furnished by the peasants and their families. Before World War I, England was using 5.8 persons per 100 acres of land, including 1.2 women, but Germany was using 18.3 persons, including 10 women.[10] Cultivation in Germany was very intensive.

Cooperation in Agriculture. Large numbers of German peasants were assisted by various agricultural cooperative societies. Some 1,400,000 peasants, or around one-fourth of the total, belonged to various cooperative credit societies by 1907. There were almost 2,000 cooperative procuring societies, with over 200,000 members, which helped the peasants to acquire cattle feed, fertilizers, plough oxen and other livestock, and machinery, on reasonable terms. Cooperative dairies had about 250,000 members, and cooperative retail stores had a total membership of over 1,100,000.[11]

The Tariff on Agricultural Products. The tariff for the protection of agricultural commodities became effective in 1880. The rates of duty applied by Germany to agricultural commodities fluctuated considerably, but it was noticeable that German agriculture turned to the production of the more highly taxed commodities. The tariff policy was undoubtedly a costly one for the workers and consumers, but it probably helped to maintain agricultural production and may have been useful from the point of view of preparedness for war.

Unfavorable Developments. Although agricultural production increased rapidly in Germany, it did not suffice to meet her needs. In the 1850s Germany was a net exporter of agricultural produce, but she had an import balance by the 1880s. The change occurred chiefly between 1865 and 1875. Later increases in agricultural production did not reverse the situation, and Germany was only 70 per cent self-supporting just before World War I.[12] The situation was much the same after the war and at the time Hitler came to power.

Agriculture in Germany was also troubled by a shortage of wagelabor. Most of the peasants could get along with their own labor and that of

[9] Clapham, *op. cit.*, p. 216.
[10] Blanchard and Visher, *op. cit.*, p. 247.
[11] Clapham, *op. cit.*, pp. 224–226.
[12] Blanchard and Visher, *op. cit.*, p. 242.

their families, but the larger peasants and the owners of large estates required considerable numbers of wageworkers, at least at certain seasons. In former times enough labor had been furnished by scrap holders and dispossessed former peasants, but these people began to move to the cities. The movement of people was facilitated by the development of railroads, the weakening of customary social ties, liberal legislation, and the greater freedom which resulted when the many German states formed the empire. The shortage of wageworkers began to be felt by 1875, and foreign workers had to be used on a seasonal basis. This problem continued down to Hitler's time.

The decline in the number of agricultural wageworkers was a symptom of the general decline in the rural population of Germany. Rapid urbanization of the population began in the 1860s, and from 1850 to 1890 there was also heavy emigration, especially to the United States. Between 1871 and 1890 the population living in communes of less than 2,000 inhabitants remained almost constant while the total population increased rapidly. Between 1895 and 1907 the total number of people connected with agriculture and forestry declined from 35.8 per cent of the total population to 28.6 per cent.[13] This tendency was still a matter of great concern to the National Socialists in 1933 and after.

The Production of Leading Crops. Potatoes were a very important crop in Germany between 1871 and 1933, and the German lowlands were ideally suited to their cultivation. Much of the soil was too sandy for other crops. The increase in the production of potatoes between 1883–1887 and 1908–1912, as shown in Table 26-3, was accomplished with an increase of only about one-fourth in acreage. Just before World War I, less than one-third of the crop was used directly in human consumption, though the per capita consumption was about two pounds daily. The rest went into alcohol, starch, potato flour, and stock forage. Hogs were fed on potatoes in Germany much as they were fed on corn in the United States. In 1921–1925 the German potato acreage was about twice that of the United States, and the crop was four times as large.[14]

Rye was the potato's chief competitor for the use of the light soils and the cool climate of the German plains. The per capita consumption of rye was twice that of wheat just before World War I, whereas in France the per capita consumption of wheat was seven times that of rye. The rye crop, after increasing sharply, fell off considerably by 1933, as shown in Table 26-3.

The cultivation of wheat and sugar beets was complementary to that of potatoes and rye. Wheat was grown on the occasional areas of fertile clay soil in the north and in the valleys which marked the southern

<hr>

[13] Clapham, *op. cit.,* pp. 208–209.
[14] Blanchard and Visher, *op. cit.,* p. 244.

Table 26-3. Results of German Agricultural Operation in Selected Years

Item	1883–1887	1908–1912	1933
Potatoes, million tons	25.5	44.2	44.1
Rye, million tons	5.9	11.0	8.7
Wheat, million tons	2.6	4.0	5.8
Sugar beets,* million tons	8.7	13.4	8.6
Horses,† million head	3.3	4.5	3.4
Cattle, million head	15.8	20.2	18.9
Hogs, million head	7.1	21.9	22.8
Sheep, million head	25.0	5.8	3.9
Goats, million head	2.3	3.4	2.5

* Data for sugar beets are for 1886–1890, 1906–1910, and 1933.
† Data for livestock are for 1873, 1912, and 1935.
SOURCE: K. Helfferich, *Germany's Economic Progress and National Wealth, 1888–1913* (New York: Germanistic Society of America, 1914), pp. 53–54: J. H. Clapham, *The Economic Development of France and Germany, 1815–1914* (London: Cambridge University Press, 1923), pp. 217, 220; C. W. Guillebaud, *The Economic Recovery of Germany* (New York: The Macmillan Company, 1939), p. 142.

plateau. The wheat crop, unlike the other major crops discussed here, was greater in 1933 than in 1908–1912. Germany was the world's leading producer of sugar beets. The most productive area was around Magdeburg on the Elbe River. Beets were usually rotated with cereals and helped to increase their yield. The beet tops and the pulp left over after the extraction of the sugar made excellent feed for livestock.

Besides the important crops already mentioned, barley, oats, and hay were raised in various parts of the country, while hardy fruits tended to do well everywhere. Flax and hemp were raised in the central region, quantities of hops in the south, and large amounts of grapes in the sheltered valleys of the Rhine, Moselle, Main, and Saar Rivers. Peas and beans, like potatoes, fared better in the northern part of the country. A little corn was grown in the south.

Livestock Production. The raising of livestock was another important phase of German agriculture. As shown in Table 26-3, all important varieties of livestock except sheep increased in number between 1873 and 1912. It was difficult to raise sheep on small, uninclosed landholdings, mutton was not popular among the Germans, and there was no tariff on wool. Germany was not self-sufficient in regard to livestock and livestock products in 1912. She imported 200,000 cattle, beef worth £2 million, bacon worth £1 million, milk and cream worth £1 million, and over £16 million worth of butter, lard, suet, margarine, and animal fats of all kinds.[15] Twenty years later, livestock numbers were somewhat

[15] Clapham, *op. cit.*, p. 221.

smaller than they had been in 1912. In 1935 only hogs were more numerous than before World War I.

AGRICULTURE UNDER NATIONAL SOCIALISM

The leaders of Germany under National Socialism professed to regard the farmers as unusually worthy people deserving of special treatment. The agricultural population had never succumbed to the lures of socialism, Communism, and other radical movements, as many industrial workers had. Indeed, the farmers had been a mainstay of the National Socialist movement. The birth rate among the agricultural population was above that for other groups, and a large population seemed indispensable for a great and warlike nation. Finally, an expansion of agricultural production was essential to Nazi dreams of an economically independent country. For all these reasons the leaders emphasized the significance of the "man on the land" to the progress of the nation, and they lost no time in setting out a program supposedly designed for agricultural improvement.

The Settlements Program. If the National Socialist leaders had really wanted to help the farmers, it would have been easy to do. Several million German farmers had less than $12\frac{1}{2}$ acres or even less than 5 acres of land, and they found the lack of an adequate amount of land an important obstacle to their welfare. On the other hand, some of the large estates were not being utilized effectively and were heavily burdened with debt. It would have seemed logical to break up some of the large estates and distribute the land among the poor peasants.

This the Nazi leaders proposed to do, and there was a great fanfare about returning the people to the land and finding them some land to which to return. The proposed program called for large estates to be liquidated. The land was to be made into peasant farms of various sizes, as well as into villages and communities. The new farms were to be cultivated without hired labor. All the work was to be done by the farmers and their families or through the various free labor services which the government furnished. The projects were to be financed with government credit. In actual practice, the program did not amount to much. It barely got beyond the proposal stage. Only a few estates were broken up, and the owners of these were bankrupt or wanted to sell out.

Labor Service. The Nazi leaders attempted to supply almost free labor to agriculture through the land-help system. The employment offices placed young men and women on the farms for limited periods of time, with food and shelter furnished by the farmers and a little pin money furnished by the employment offices. Men and women were required to spend a year on the land after finishing their formal education.

A series of decrees in 1934 and 1935 deprived unmarried men under twenty-five years of age of their jobs in the cities and required them to go to farms as agricultural helpers; it also prohibited industries and businesses from employing workers who had worked in agriculture during the preceding three years and required such workers to return to the country or face criminal prosecution.[16] German agriculture still suffered from a shortage of workers.

The Agricultural (Food) Estate. Agriculture was controlled by the government under National Socialism. The main agency was the Reich Agricultural Estate, set up in July, 1933, as a self-administrative statutory corporation. Membership was compulsory and included all individuals, associations, and agencies working in the field of agriculture (or in forestry, hunting, fishing, market gardening, and viticulture). They were divided into five classes: (1) persons engaged in these fields of production or directly related to them, (2) agricultural unions, including their head organizations, such as leagues of control and central unions, (3) all companies and persons who traded in these products or used them in manufacturing, (4) related organizations, such as the Council of German Agriculture, the Prussian Central Chamber of Agriculture, the Working Union of Rural-Supply Companies, and the National League of Rural Sick Funds, and (5) marketing organizations.

Dealers in products which came under the Reich Agricultural Estate had to belong to this estate as well as to one of their own (the Estate of Industry and Trade). In similar fashion, manufacturers and other processors of the products (millers, brewers, butchers, bakers, and candymakers) had to belong to the Agricultural Estate as well as to the Estate of Industry and Trade.

The head of the Agricultural Estate was the national peasant (farm) leader, who was appointed by Hitler and was responsible to him. The national peasant leader appointed lower officials of the estate and assigned duties and functions to them. He was in fact, though not of necessity, the Reich Minister for Food and Agriculture as well. His term of office was indefinite, and his control over the estate was complete. The division of functions between the Reich Minister of Food and Agriculture and the same individual as national peasant leader was not altogether clear. The Agricultural Estate functioned through 3 main divisions, 20 regional associations, 520 district associations, and numerous local associations.

The Functions of the Agricultural Estate. One of the main divisions of the Agricultural Estate dealt with "man," or personal questions relating to agriculture. It had to do with social relations in agriculture, legal

---

[16] M. Y. Sweezy, *The Structure of the Nazi Economy* (Cambridge, Mass.: Harvard University Press, 1941), pp. 191–192.

matters, the attainment and maintenance of the proper attitude on the part of farmers, farm problems involving persons, the selection and settlement of new peasants, and land-reclamation projects. The administration of the Hereditary Farm Act (to be described later) was carried on through this main division, but labor problems were handled in other ways, since the Agricultural Estate "belonged" to the Labor Front.

The second main division dealt with "the estate" or with questions of agricultural production. It controlled all activities having to do with the farm as a productive enterprise. It controlled professional education, farm schools, agricultural science and experimental stations, the functions of agricultural chambers and societies, and the agricultural portion of the national program for attaining economic self-sufficiency.

The third main division of the estate had to do with "the market" and controlled the marketing associations which had been set up for specific farm products. The marketing associations were organized along regional lines, and the regional divisions were combined into central associations. These associations supervised and controlled distributive activities all the way from actual production to sale to the final consumer, including financial and credit matters. They saw to it that trading and marketing went on in accordance with rules of fair competition, standards of quality, and labels of quality identification. They had power to license new enterprises or extensions of old ones. They had some control over production areas, conditions and terms of deliveries, costs of production, prices, advertising allowances, and profit margins.

In addition, government boards were set up which also had powers in connection with the control of prices and were responsible for the importation and exportation of farm products. The boards also bought and sold both domestic and imported farm products. Anyone who wished to buy imported food to sell in Germany had to obtain a permit from the government and had to turn over to it the difference between the cost of the imported food and the higher price which prevailed in Germany. Domestic producers also needed permits to sell farm products and could be compelled to sell specified quantities of foodstuffs to the boards at fixed prices. In 1942 a new decree provided fines up to 10,000 marks, imprisonment, or even the death penalty, for farm producers who failed to turn over their marketable surpluses to the government. Since they controlled the quantities and prices of imported farm goods, the domestic surpluses of such products, and the exportation of goods not needed at home, the government boards were able to influence the domestic prices of these goods. To add to the confusion, however, the activities of the marketing associations and of government boards in controlling the prices of farm products had to be brought into adjustment with those of the national price commissioner, who was in general charge of price control.

The Hereditary Farm Act. Under National Socialism, a Hereditary Farm Act was passed which bound many of the "racially pure" Germans to their land and their occupations. Farms which were large enough to support a peasant and his family automatically became hereditary farms if they were owned by persons who could claim the status of peasant. To be a peasant within the meaning of the act, the farmer had to be a German citizen, had to possess an honorable character, and had to show that his stock had been racially pure since January 1, 1800. The proof of racial purity had to be validated by court action.

The size of the hereditary farms could vary from 20 to over 300 acres. The farms could not be divided and distributed among several heirs but had to be passed on intact, with all buildings and equipment, to the eldest son or the youngest son, according to local custom. They could not be sold to anyone and could not be mortgaged. They could not be taken by foreclosure under previously existing mortgages. The owners could obtain only short-term loans, based on their personal credit and not in excess of sums which could be repaid out of current crop receipts. Thus the owner could lose his farm only through government action, which might be taken if he were inefficient, became incapacitated, or failed to live up to the "peasant honor code." Disputes concerning inheritance were settled by Estate Courts, which were under the control of the national peasant leader. Some 650,000 to 700,000 farms were accepted as hereditary farms, compared with a goal of 1 million.[17]

German agriculture, like other phases of economic activity under National Socialism, appeared to be greatly overorganized. In the face of so many divisions, associations, and boards, it is difficult to get any clear picture of the functioning of the Agricultural Estate. In practice, however, its operation was simpler than it seemed. The national peasant leader was in full control, and duties, instructions, and orders passed directly down the line through inferior officers to the individual peasants.

Agricultural Self-sufficiency. The National Socialist plans for general economic self-sufficiency assigned an important role to agriculture, for Germany was dependent upon other countries for about 20 per cent of her food supply as well as large quantities of agricultural raw materials. The plans for agricultural self-sufficiency involved attempts to increase agricultural production. Thus, for example, farmers were asked to double the quantity of land used for raising fibrous and oil-bearing plants and to double the number of sheep raised for wool.

[17] *Fascism in Action*, 80th Cong., 1st Sess., H. Doc. 401, 1947, p. 140.

Serious obstacles stood in the way of a sharp increase in agricultural production. When the Nazis came into power, about 63 per cent of the land was cultivated or was meadowland, 27 per cent was in forests, 6 per cent was used for site purposes, and 4 per cent was moor and waste land. While it would have been possible to reclaim some of the moor and waste land, the costs seemed prohibitive. Clearing some of the forest land would have helped with farm production but would have impaired the limited timber supply and would have raised other problems. Increasing the number of sheep from 4 to 50 million might have made Germany self-sufficient in wool, but it would have diverted much farm land to pasture use.

Increased production in one sector seemed likely to decrease production in some other sector. About the only method for increasing agricultural production as a whole seemed to be more intensive cultivation of the land already in use. However, cultivated land had been inadequate for many years past and it was already intensively worked. Improved methods of cultivation, on the other hand, would have involved larger quantities of expensive machinery, and it was difficult to see how the German farmers were going to get it.

In spite of all obstacles, German agriculture made some progress toward self-sufficiency. A small amount of waste land was reclaimed, but simple hard work on the part of the farmers, coupled with some government assistance, was chiefly responsible for increased production. The government assistance took the form of cash subsidies and other types of grants. Typical of the latter was the program of hog raising in 1940. Early in the year, the government contracted with the farmers to raise an additional 1½ million hogs to weigh at least 110 kilograms each. The government was to furnish 200 kilograms of barley or corn and 175 kilograms of sugar-beet flakes for each hog. In December, contracts were drawn up for an additional 900,000 hogs.[18]

Some pressure was taken off agricultural production in the fight for self-sufficiency by the development of artificial substitutes which would take the place of farm products in whole or in part. Large quantities of "acorn meal" were used in making chocolate, low-quality vegetable fats in making edible fat compounds, mineral oils in making soaps, and artificial textile fibers in making cloth. The progress toward self-sufficiency had the results which would have been expected in terms of higher prices, lowered qualities of goods, and decreased standards of living.

Changes in Agricultural Output. In the years before World War II, the outputs of some agricultural products increased considerably, while those of others changed but little. On the whole, if the physical volume of agricultural production in 1928 is taken as 100, that for 1932 was 106

[18] *Foreign Commerce Weekly*, Dec. 14, 1940, and Jan. 4, 1941.

and that for 1938 was 115.[19] The value of agricultural production in 1939 was 1 billion marks (7 per cent) greater than in 1938 and 5.5 billion marks greater than in 1933.[20]

In the early years of the war, when the tide was in Germany's favor, she was well supplied with agricultural products. Levies on the crops of conquered territories were added to Germany's own crops and, in some cases, stockpiles. In the later stages of the war, this help from outside dwindled and stopped. Germany was hard pressed to maintain her own production, for many farmers and workers were in the armed forces rather than on the farms, new machinery and supplies were hard to get, and the old equipment was wearing out. However, German agriculture came through the war in better condition than most parts of the economy.

The Status of the Farmers under National Socialism. A small number of farmers may have had their hunger for more land partly satisfied. Some farmers obtained a measure of debt relief and dignity at the cost of being bound to their occupation and residence. There were higher prices for those farmers who had produce to sell. But, on the whole, the National Socialist agricultural policies did little to improve the lot of the small and average farmers.

Even the increases in the prices of farm products did not give the farmers a larger share of the national income. Agriculture and forestry received 8.3 per cent of the national income in 1933 but only 7.3 per cent in 1938.[21] On the other hand, outside of increased regimentation and control, National Socialist policies did little damage to the farmers. They suffered less than most groups.

If any class of farmers gained under National Socialist agricultural policies, it was the large farmers. The Nazi leaders left them undisturbed on their large estates. The Hereditary Farm Act was supposed to apply only to farms of 125 hectares or less, but in practice large estates could be made into hereditary farms if the public interest required it. Some owners of large estates, harrassed by creditors, obtained the preferred status provided by the act. Also, small peasants were sometimes deprived of their lands so that large-scale hereditary farms could be created.

Most of the cash subsidies were received by the large landowners and prosperous farmers, and the same was true of other subsidies under the self-sufficiency program. The policy of raising the prices of agricultural products was not applied uniformly. The government raised prices most for grains and other commodities that were popular on the large estates,

[19] Sweezy, *op. cit.*, p. 206.
[20] *Facts in Review,* June 3, 1940, p. 236.
[21] Sweezy, *op. cit.*, p. 208.

which could make use of mechanized farming methods. High prices for farm products in any case would not benefit small peasants who consumed all that they produced or had to buy additional supplies.

Much of the virtually free agricultural labor service furnished by the government went to the owners of large or medium-sized farms. By contrast, the status of rural workers and small peasants under National Socialism is indicated by the severe measures which the government imposed to keep these people on the land. Fascist agricultural policies were successful only in the sense that they produced many of the results desired by the government. However, the program of agricultural self-sufficiency was far from successful, and the people had to go on short rations once they were dependent on domestic production.

AGRICULTURE AFTER WORLD WAR II

When the German territory east of the Oder-Neisse line was divided between Poland and Soviet Russia after World War II, Germany lost about one-fourth of her arable land. Eastern Germany, occupied by Soviet Russia and cut off from Western Germany, contains another large amount of Germany's former agricultural resources. The Federal Republic of Western Germany has an area 52 per cent as great as that of the 1937 Reich and it has about 75 per cent of the German population, but it contains less than half of the arable land of prewar Germany. Western Germany was left with a large part of the manufacturing, mining, and other industry, but it has a considerable deficiency in food production. The situation in the Soviet zone is, of course, just the reverse.

Agricultural Production in Western Germany. Western Germany was in need of greatly increased agricultural production after the war, but production declined for a time. In 1946–1947, for example, agricultural production was 30 per cent lower than in 1939.[22] Transportation and communication were disorganized. The number of livestock decreased, for the government requisitioned many, and feed shortages were severe. It was impossible to obtain adequate supplies of fertilizers and of farm equipment. Farmers' incentives were inadequate because regulations inherited from the National Socialist regime were continued, and the currency was unstable. Vegetable production increased, but this furnished little help in view of the decline in the number of livestock and the low level of grain production.

In recent years, Western Germany has staged a remarkable economic recovery, and agriculture has participated in the upswing. If 1950 is taken as the base year, agricultural production in Western Germany in-

[22] *Annals of the American Academy of Political and Social Science,* November, 1948, p. 205.

creased from 65 in 1946 to 107 in 1952.[23] This increase seems truly remarkable in this period of time and under existing conditions.

However, agricultural production has remained inadequate for the needs of Western Germany, and it is estimated that the country is dependent upon outside sources for 30 to 35 per cent of its food.[24] Germany imported some 1.6 million tons of wheat alone in 1952.[25] The difficulties involved in importing farm products from other countries are greater than those connected with obtaining them from another part of the same country. But the foreign trade of Western Germany has increased spectacularly, and she has recently been able to pay for her imports.

QUESTIONS FOR STUDY

1. What was the organization of German agriculture in the nineteenth century down to the founding of the German Empire? What were the implications of this organization for efficiency in production? Why?

2. How did the situation of the various classes of German peasants differ? Show that the emancipation of the peasants was a long and tedious process.

3. Why did agricultural production increase so rapidly in Germany from 1871 to 1914? What were some unfavorable elements in the agricultural situation during this period?

4. Most German farmers found the lack of an adequate amount of land an important obstacle to their economic welfare. Did the National Socialists do anything significant about this problem? Why?

5. How was German agriculture controlled under National Socialism? Indicate the organization, divisions, and functions of the Agricultural Estate. What happened to agricultural output under National Socialism?

6. What problems were involved in a program of self-sufficiency for German agriculture? How and to what extent were they met?

7. Enumerate the agricultural policies of National Socialism. Were these policies of greatest assistance to small farmers? Medium-sized farmers? Large farmers? Why?

[23] *International Financial Statistics* (Washington, D.C.: International Monetary Fund, August, 1954), pp. 96, 97.
[24] *Time,* Feb. 15, 1954, p. 90.
[25] *The Economist*, Oct. 18, 1952, p. 209.

CHAPTER 27

TRANSPORTATION

All phases of economic life are interdependent, but transportation occupies an especially strategic position in the functioning of any economy as a whole. Without adequate markets, modern industrial production, with its large-scale operations, division of labor, and geographical specialization, cannot develop to any great extent. Without effective transportation, people tend to live and die at or near the places where they were born, and an adequate labor force does not develop.

Agriculture was an important phase of economic activity even in early times, but there was no future for Germany as a purely agricultural nation. Thus the development of transportation was of greater importance to Germany than to some other nations. It was difficult for an efficient system of transportation to come into being as long as the area which was to become the German Empire remained divided into a number of independent states, though impressive beginnings were made before 1871.

TRANSPORTATION BEFORE 1871

Railroad Transportation. Interest in railroads sprang up in Germany as early as 1825, and by 1833 the German economist Friedrich List had a plan for a German railroad system. The first railroad to operate in Germany, a 5-mile line from Nürnberg to Fürth in Bavaria, was opened in December, 1835, ten years after the world's first railroad in England. A second line, government-owned in this case, was opened in Brunswick in 1838. The line from Leipzig to Dresden in Saxony began to operate in April, 1839, and carried 412,000 people in its first year.[1]

The government of Prussia doubted the wisdom of large-scale railroad construction in these early years. The kingdom was inadequately supplied with roads, traffic prospects along the railroad routes did not seem promising, and there was some thought that rapid travel was unhealthy. The first Prussian law concerning railroads, issued in 1838, was not en-

[1] J. H. Clapham, *The Economic Development of France and Germany, 1815–1914* (London: Cambridge University Press, 1923), p. 151.

430

couraging to private enterprise nor did it provide for a program of government construction. However, it tended to prevent the construction of wasteful competing lines and the founding of companies which had little chance of success.

The Magdeburg-Leipzig line was opened by 1840, and a number of other lines (Düsseldorf-Elberfeld, Berlin-Köthen, and Berlin-Stettin) were in prospect under the law of 1838. After 1840 the Prussian government began to feel more optimistic, granted concessions freely, and began to invest in private railroad companies or guarantee interest on their securities. Still later the government, with a full treasury, planned railroad lines for private companies to construct and offered to guarantee interest on the securities of railroad-construction companies. The lines contemplated included the Rhine-Weser, the Thuringian line to connect Prussia with the south, the line between Frankfurt an der Oder and Breslau, a Posen line for Prussian Poland, and an eastern line running through the Prussias. Railroad construction went on apace, and the lines open in Prussia increased from about 500 miles in 1844 to about 1,500 miles in 1848 and about 3,500 miles in 1860.[2]

In the western and southern German states, the railroads were constructed, owned, and operated by the governments. The first state railroad in Germany was the short line opened in Brunswick in 1838. The government of Hanover had constructed 150 miles by 1848, and all Hanoverian lines were built by the government down to 1866, when Hanover was annexed by Prussia. Railroad construction in Bavaria began under private auspices, but the government did all the building for a number of years after 1844. Würtemberg decided to have a government system and opened its first line in 1850. Baden operated its first section of government-owned railroad in 1843.

In Germany as a whole, there were about 3,000 miles of railroad lines in operation by 1850, compared with 2,000 miles in France. Germany was ahead of France in the construction of through routes. Between 1850 and 1875 the density of the German railroad network increased rapidly. In 1870 the total mileage in the area which was to become Germany amounted to over 12,000 miles.[3]

Railroad construction in Germany was relatively inexpensive. Land was cheap, and the railroads followed the natural level of the country instead of seeking straight and level routes through the construction of expensive bridges, tunnels, and viaducts. As might have been expected in a country whose towns and cities had been small and whose road system had been incompletely developed, railroads had an almost revolutionary influence.

[2] *Ibid.*, p. 153.
[3] *Ibid.*, p. 339.

The German Roads. At the beginning of the nineteenth century, the roads of Germany were bad. Even people traveling long distances often found it wiser to walk than to venture out in wheeled conveyances. The first "made road" in Germany, as distinguished from wheel tracks across the country, was constructed between Nördlingen and Oettingen by the Bavarian government in 1753. Similar road construction in Prussia began in 1788; it progressed slowly because of political troubles, shortages of funds, and lack of essential materials.

In 1816 there were only 420 miles of first-class roads in Prussia, and 239 miles of them were in the newly acquired Rhenish and Westphalian provinces. Even by 1841 Prussia had only 1,280 miles of first-class highways.[4] At this time, the mileage of first-class highways in France was about 3½ times as great.[5] In the early 1850s it took over eleven hours for a wagon of goods to cover the 25 or 26 miles from Posen to Gnesen in Prussian Poland.[6] The period of most rapid construction of the Prussian road system began in 1845 and extended to 1870. By comparison, France's system of first-class roads was almost complete by 1840 and required few additions during the remainder of the century.

Internal Water Transportation. Transportation on inland waterways was of great importance in Germany before the construction of the railroad network. The German states were well supplied with navigable rivers and some work was done in the construction of canals. However, river transportation was interfered with by the tolls exacted by the states through which the rivers passed. In 1800 a cargo passing along the Elbe River between Hamburg and Magdeburg had to pay toll fourteen times, and tolls were collected at 33 points on the Main River between Bamberg and Mainz.[7] It was not until after the Zollverein, or customs union, was set up in 1834 that river tolls were abolished. Improvement of the Rhine above Mannheim was neglected until after 1900.

On the other hand, the development of the steamboat was a stimulus to river transportation. The steamboat revolutionized river traffic early, for it could make its way up river in any weather and take on fuel as needed. While the German railroad network was being actively developed, the construction of canals and the improvement of rivers was neglected. However, canals connected many important river basins by 1870, and many river improvements had been made.

Ocean Transportation. The development of ocean transportation came after the founding of the German Empire in 1871. The important seaboard states of Germany, including Prussia, Mecklenburg, the Hanse towns, and Hanover, had only 24 sea-going steamboats with a total ton-

[4] *Ibid.*, p. 108.
[5] *Ibid.*, p. 349.
[6] *Ibid.*, 350.
[7] *Ibid.*, p. 109.

nage of less than 5,500 around 1850.[8] At the same time, Great Britain had 168,000 tons of ocean-going steamers, and 3,565,000 tons of ocean vessels of all types. The German merchant marine was unimpressive, and the leading seafaring nations did not fear German competition.

TRANSPORTATION, 1871–1933

The Railroad System, 1871–1914. The main lines of the German railroad system were completed during the decade 1865–1875. After that, railroad development was a matter of increasing density and efficiency in relation to the country's area, population, and resources. The railroads of the country increased from around 12,000 miles in 1870 to 26,700 in 1890 and almost 38,000 in 1910.[9] Over the period of twenty-six years from

Table 27-1. Growth of Railroad Transportation in Germany, 1886–1911

Item	1886	1911	Percentage increase
Total length (standard gauge), 1,000 kilometers..	37.2	59.8	60.7
Capital invested, billion marks.................	9.7	17.8	83.5
Railroad employees, thousands.................	333.4	713.2	113.9
Locomotives in use, thousands.................	12.5	28.1	125.6
Passenger cars in use, thousands...............	22.7	59.9	163.3
Freight cars in use, thousands.................	250.6	596.8	138.1
Goods carried, billion ton-kilometers...........	16.6	61.9	272.7
Passengers carried, billion passenger-kilometers...	7.9	37.9	377.1

SOURCE: K. Helfferich, *Germany's Economic Progress and National Wealth, 1888–1913* (New York: Germanistic Society of America, 1914), p. 70.

1886 to 1911, other phases of railroad operation expanded more rapidly than railroad mileage, as Table 27-1 indicates.

A part of the funds for constructing the main railroad lines came from the indemnity paid by the French after the Franco-Prussian War of 1870, but most of the lines had been financed with the savings of the German people. By the 1870s, however, the ownership and operation of the railroads had become rather complicated. The Prussian government had acquired the railroad systems of Hanover, Hesse-Cassel, and Nassau when these territories were absorbed, and the government of the German Empire received the railroads of Alsace-Lorraine in 1871. Thus there were private railroads, state railroads, and imperial railroads, and in addition there were privately owned lines operated by states and state-owned lines operated by private companies.

[8] *Ibid.,* p. 111.
[9] *Ibid.,* p. 339.

Partly for strategic reasons, the Prussian government began a large-scale program of railroad buying in 1879. By 1909 the lines owned by the Prussian government had increased from 5,300 to 37,400 kilometers, no private lines were operated by the government, and the private lines in Prussia had decreased from 9,400 to 2,900 kilometers. At the same time, Bavaria and other large states owned 17,000 kilometers of line, and there were only 3,600 kilometers of standard-gauge line under private ownership in the whole Empire.[10]

While the German railroads belonged to the states, such as Prussia and Bavaria, rather than to the Empire, there was coordination between the Prussian railroad department and the Imperial Railway Office. The resulting management was highly successful. The financial position of the railroads was sound, and provisions were made to take care of the debts created when railroads were acquired. Freight rates were systematized all over the Empire, although the rate structure became increasingly complex and discriminatory rates came to be charged for similar services. The railroads, though government owned and operated, tried to make profits and, when successful, did not lower rates or increase services but kept on making money. The government liked this revenue, which was not dependent on acts of the legislature, and the public did not mind, since railroad profits meant a lower burden of taxation.

The ownership and operation of the railroads by the government was important from the military point of view, and the railroads came near being a department of the German army. Railroad directors, in Prussia at least, were sometimes high army officers, and the railroad employees were subject to military discipline. This helped to account for the efficiency and punctuality of the railroad service, and also probably for the fact that a railroad labor movement was completely lacking in Germany.

The Railroad System, 1914–1933. The railroad system entered World War I in good condition and functioned efficiently during that struggle. The wartime volume of traffic placed a heavy burden on the railroads, but the war was not lost because of any failure of railroad transportation. After the war, the railroad system suffered considerable losses. Under the terms of the Versailles Treaty, Germany was deprived of 13 per cent of her territories in Europe. These ceded territories took their railroads along with them when they passed into the possession of other countries. In addition, Germany had to give up 5,000 locomotives, 40,000 freight cars, and other facilities.

During the 1920s the German railroads gradually recovered from these losses, and their recovery was nearly complete by 1927. However,

[10] *Ibid.*, p. 348.

they deteriorated again during the Great Depression which began in 1929. Locomotives, coaches, and freight cars which suffered damage or became too old to use were not always replaced, and maintenance and repairs were often neglected. Table 27-2 shows the status of the German railroads in 1927 and 1932 in comparison with 1911.

Table 27-2. Status of the German Railroads, 1911, 1927, 1932

Item	1911	1927	1932
Total length, thousand kilometers............	59.8	56.3	58.2
Locomotives in use, thousands...............	28.1	26.0	24.0
Passenger cars in use, thousands.............	59.9	90.0	85.0
Freight cars in use, thousands...............	596.8	660.0	639.0
Passengers carried, millions.................	.....	2,057.0*	1,352.0
Freight carried, million tons.................	.....	531.0*	307.0

* 1929 figure.
SOURCE: M. Y. Sweezy, *The Structure of the Nazi Economy* (Cambridge, Mass.: Harvard University Press, 1941), pp. 54, 57.

Inland Water Transportation, 1871–1914. The construction of canals and the improvement of rivers were neglected during the period of most rapid railroad building, but they received attention again after the formation of the Empire. Numerous canals were built, including the famous Kaiser Wilhelm (Kiel) Canal, connecting the North Sea with the Baltic, and the Dortmund-Emden Canal, which permitted ships to carry the coal and iron of Westphalia to the seaports of the north without crossing Dutch territory. By World War I, Germany had over 1,600 miles of canals, while France had over 3,100 miles.[11]

Germany's navigable rivers afforded almost twice as much mileage as France's. Since most of them rose in other countries or flowed from Germany into other countries, they tended to serve as international highways. The main problem in connection with the rivers was to increase their useful length and to improve their efficiency by making it possible for larger boats to use them. Much progress was made between 1870 and 1914, and so much work was done on the rivers that it became difficult to distinguish between a natural waterway and an artificial one.

In spite of improvements in inland water transportation, the waterways did not make serious inroads on railroad freight traffic, nor did they come to carry a greatly increased proportion of freight between 1870 and 1914. The waterways carried 21 per cent of all the traffic in Germany in 1875 and 22 per cent in 1895. In 1910 the waterways probably did not carry over 20 per cent of the traffic.[12]

[11] *Ibid.*, p. 353.
[12] *Ibid.*, p. 354.

Inland Water Transportation, 1914–1933. The canals and rivers of Germany were an important aid to the railroad system during World War I, and after the war, work on canals and other waterways was resumed on a large scale. By the middle 1920s the inland waterways included 6,252 miles of navigable rivers and 1,383 miles of canals in a smaller Germany.[13] Under construction were the Weser-Elbe Canal, a continuous water route from the Rhine to the Oder and on to the Vistula; the Mittelland Canal to complete water connections between the Rhine and the Berlin canal area; and a project for deepening the Neckar for 71 miles to permit the passage of boats of up to 1,200 tons.

Among the rivers of Germany, the Rhine was by far the most important. In an ordinary year its traffic was five times as great as that of its nearest competitor, the Danube, and half again as great as that of all other German rivers combined.[14] Five countries depended on it for transportation. Factors contributing to its importance included its location in an industrial region with dense population and producing heavy goods which required cheap transportation, the fact that it drained into the busy North Sea, its even flow, its freedom from ice during most of the year, and the extensive improvements which had been made on it.

Inland water transportation in Germany was somewhat more important in 1929 than it had been in 1910. The volume of freight carried was about one-fourth as much as that carried by the railroads. The facilities for inland water transportation were well maintained in the Great Depression after 1929, as shown by Table 27-3, but the volume of freight was cut almost in half.

Table 27-3. Inland Water Transportation in Germany, 1929 and 1932

Item	1929	1932
Boats with motor power, thousands..............	4.9	4.8
Boats without motor power, thousands...........	14.6	12.9
Freight carried on waterways, million tons........	140.7	73.7
Freight carried by railroads, million tons.........	531.0	307.0

SOURCE: M. Y. Sweezy, *The Structure of the Nazi Economy* (Cambridge, Mass.: Harvard University Press, 1941), p. 57.

Ocean Transportation, 1871–1914. Germany's ocean fleet had been considered negligible up to 1850. However, she made rapid progress in this field after 1870, as shown in Table 27-4. The development of a mer-

[13] W. O. Blanchard and S. S. Visher, *Economic Geography of Europe* (New York: McGraw-Hill Book Company, Inc., 1931), p. 261.
[14] M. Y. Sweezy, *The Structure of the Nazi Economy* (Cambridge, Mass.: Harvard University Press, 1941), p. 57.

Table 27-4. Development of the German Merchant Fleet, 1870, 1900, 1912

Item	1870	1900	1912
Total tonnage, thousands of tons..............	982	1,942	3,000
Steam-driven tonnage, thousands of tons..........	82	1,348	2,500
German steam-driven tonnage as a percentage of the French..	50+	250	300

SOURCE: J. H. Clapham, *The Economic Development of France and Germany, 1815–1914* (London: Cambridge University Press, 1923), p. 356.

chant fleet was handicapped until the early 1880s by the fact that Hamburg and Bremen were not completely absorbed in the Empire. Both cities came to terms with the Empire between 1882 and 1885, and their ports and merchant fleets expanded rapidly thereafter. Germany had a steam fleet of 158,000 tons in 1880. By 1900 the fleet amounted to 1,121,-000 tons, and this was doubled by 1914.[15] Especially noteworthy was the increase in power of the two largest lines, the Hamburg-America and the North German Lloyd.

Ocean Transportation, 1914–1933. Germany lost a part of her merchant marine during World War I, and under the Versailles Treaty she had to surrender most of the rest to her victorious opponents to replace shipping sunk by German submarines during the war. Starting all over with a merchant fleet of 50,000 tons, Germany built her ocean shipping up to almost 3,500,000 tons by 1927 and had risen to sixth place among the countries of the world. Most of her new fleet consisted of modern oil-burning ships.[16] In 1929 her merchant shipping amounted to 4,093,000 tons, and by 1932, in spite of the depression, it came to 4,164,000 tons.[17]

Highway Transportation. The states which later formed the German Empire were backward in constructing first-class highways prior to 1845. The network of main highways was built between 1845 and 1870. Standards of construction, grading, and surfacing did not improve much between 1870 and the time when the automobile came into general use.

In the United States the 1920s was a period of rapid expansion in the production and use of automobiles and trucks. In Germany the lower and medium middle classes had been impoverished as a result of the war and the inflation that followed, and most people were simply too poor to own motor vehicles. The figures for various types of motor vehicles in use, as presented in Table 27-5, show that motor transportation in Germany was relatively undeveloped in 1929 and 1932.

[15] Clapham, *op. cit.*, p. 359.
[16] Blanchard and Visher, *op. cit.*, p. 267.
[17] J. Kuczynski, *Germany: Economic and Labour Conditions under Fascism* (New York: International Publishers Co., Inc., 1945), p. 70.

Table 27-5. Motor Vehicles in Use in Germany and the United States

Type of vehicle	Germany, 1929	Germany, 1932	United States, 1932
Passenger cars............	423,000	549,000	20,832,000
Motorcycles..............	608,000	866,000	
Trucks and busses........	155,000	186,000	3,300,000

SOURCE: J. Kuczynski, *Germany: Economic and Labour Conditions under Fascism* (New York: International Publishers Co., Inc., 1945), p. 356; *Statistical Abstract of the United States, 1953*, p. 533.

Air Transportation. It was not until after World War I that air transportation began to be important, but in the 1920s Germany was the scene of rapid expansion. She was limited in producing military airplanes, but this was a stimulus to the production and operation of commercial airplanes, since she wanted to have large numbers of pilots, mechanics, navigators, and so on. Germany soon became the leading European country in commercial aviation. German airlines carried 97,000 passengers and 2,456 tons of freight and mail in 1929. By 1932, in spite of the depression, the figures had increased to 99,000 passengers and 2,503 tons of freight and mail.

TRANSPORTATION UNDER NATIONAL SOCIALISM

The Estate of Transportation. After 1933 government controls were imposed on virtually all economic activity in Germany. When the Estate of Industry and Trade was set up in 1934, it was intended that transportation should be included under it. In 1935, however, it was considered better to set up a separate organization, the Estate of Transportation. Since 80 per cent or more of all enterprises in transportation were government-owned, the problem of control differed from that in other areas of the economy.

The Estate of Transportation included all transportation enterprises, public and private. At the head was the Reich Minister of Transport, assisted by a National Transport Council. The estate was divided into seven functional groups—ocean shipping, inland shipping, motor transport, railroads, carrier services, forwarding agencies, and auxiliary transport services. Freight and passenger rates, schedules, additions of facilities, and the hiring of personnel were left to the Minister of Transport and his advisory council, but the estate also dealt with the division and interchange of traffic among various types of transportation agencies and with the unification of transportation services generally.

The Nazi Plans for Transportation. The Nazi regime stressed the development of air and highway transportation, apparently in preparation for war on a blitzkrieg basis, which would require the armed forces to cover long distances in a hurry. Large numbers of airplanes, automobiles, and trucks were to be produced, a great new highway system was to be constructed, and millions of people were to be trained to use mechanized transportation equipment. The railroads, inland waterways, and ocean shipping were to be neglected, for the most part. This decision may have been influenced in part by the fact that the Russian railroads were of a different gauge than the German railroads.

Railroad Transportation. The railroad lines in Germany had about the same mileage in 1937 as in 1932—a little over 36,000 miles. The addition of the Austrian railroads in 1938 brought the total to 40,706 miles, or about 17 per cent of the mileage in the United States. Each mile of railroad track in Germany served an average of 1,955 persons, compared with 552 in the United States.[18] Such new railroad construction as did occur between 1932 and 1938 was largely for military and strategic purposes. The German railroads carried many more passengers and tons of freight in 1937 than in 1932, as shown in Table 27-6.

Table 27-6. German Railroad Transportation, 1932 and 1937

Item	1932	1937
Total mileage, thousands........	36.0	36.0
Locomotives in use, thousands...	24.0	24.0
Passenger cars in use, thousands.	91.0	87.0
Freight cars in use, thousands....	639.0	587.0
Passengers carried, millions......	1,352.0	1,824.0
Freight carried, million tons.....	307.0	547.0

SOURCE: J. Kuczynski, *Germany: Economic and Labour Conditions under Fascism* (New York: International Publishers Co., Inc., 1945), p. 70.

Besides being rigidly limited in the matter of equipment and being required to construct some lines for war-economy purposes, the German railroads were sometimes required to use their funds and technical experts for the construction of superhighways. Noneconomic factors were important in connection with the rate making by the Minister of Transport. In 1938 almost three-fourths of all the railroad passengers paid less than full fares, and over 70 per cent of the freight was carried at reduced rates. It was an advantage to the railroads, however, to have common-carrier trucks compelled to adopt the same rate schedules as the railroads.

With railroad expansion neglected and freight and passenger traffic

[18] *Fascism in Action*, 80th Cong., 1st Sess., H. Doc. 401, 1947, p. 142.

rapidly growing, a crisis in railroad transportation developed even before the outbreak of World War II. Indeed, there was a shortage of freight cars in 1937. An attempt to increase railroad facilities came too late to do much good. After the war began, the number of passenger trains was severely reduced, it was required that freight cars be unloaded at once, and commissioners were appointed to establish priorities for freight movement and thus to ration railroad freight service.

Later, German conquests provided additional rolling stock. French passenger cars, Belgian locomotives, and Roumanian tank cars filled part of the gap left by the neglect of earlier years. The relief was temporary, however, for the burdens resulting from the war in Russia almost broke down the German transportation system, especially the railroads. The situation became even worse toward the end of the war as enemy airplanes bombed transportation facilities unmercifully.

Inland Water Transportation. Improvement in inland waterways continued under National Socialism. The Mittelland Canal connecting the Rhine and Elbe Rivers, begun during the 1920s, was completed under the Nazi regime. The location of the Hermann Göring Iron Works and the People's Car Works was influenced by the availability of this canal. A second important feat was the Adolph Hitler Canal, connecting industrial Upper Silesia with the Oder River and indirectly with the center of the country. When World War II began, plans were under way for a Rhine-Main-Danube canal and a Rhine-Neckar-Danube canal.

The shipping situation on inland waterways was similar to that on the railroads. The number of boats in 1937 was 17,881, or almost the same as in 1932. But a greater proportion of the boats were motor-driven, so the carrying capacity of the river fleet was greater than in 1932. The freight carried on inland waterways in 1937 amounted to 133,080,000 tons, compared with 73,744,000 tons in 1932—an increase of over 80 per cent.[19]

When the war broke out in September, 1939, efforts were made to increase the volume of shipping on inland waterways. By 1941 there were 2.3 times as many tugs in operation as in 1939 and a large construction program was under way. The German conquests meant less to the waterways than to the railroads, and the waterways were hard pressed to carry the traffic available for them before the war was over.

Ocean Transportation. Ocean shipping was less important than inland shipping to the Nazi regime. The program of national economic self-sufficiency meant less reliance on international trade than in the past. However, the Nazis were interested in ocean shipping both for reasons of prestige, preparedness, and appearance and as a source of foreign currency. A combination of the North German Lloyd and Hamburg-

[19] Kuczynski, *op. cit.*, p. 70.

America lines was sponsored, government loans previously granted were extended, operating subsidies were given, and a shipbuilding fund was set aside for creating employment.

The Nazis did not make large new additions to the merchant fleet. Gross tonnage of the fleet increased only from 4,164,000 tons in 1932 to 4,493,000 tons in 1939. The fleet was fifth largest in the world in 1939, when the merchant fleet of the United States amounted to 8,126,000 tons and that of Great Britain to 17,771,000 tons. While the size of the German merchant fleet did not change greatly, the volume of freight carried increased from 33,137,000 tons in 1932 to 56,695,000 in 1937.[20] During the war, large amounts of shipping were lost and the merchant fleet had declined to an estimated 1,068,000 tons by June 30, 1945.[21]

Highway Transportation. Transportation by motor vehicles was important in the Nazi scheme of things. One development which was intended to stimulate highway transportation was the construction of superhighways, or Autobahnen. These were also intended to enhance German prestige, constitute a monument to Hitler, and aid the movement of the armed forces in time of war. Contributions to their financing were made by the railroads, by cities and states, and by the central government. After the outbreak of World War II, work was continued only on sections of great strategic importance. By the end of 1940 the completed superhighways totaled 2,323 miles and those under construction amounted to 1,465 miles.[22]

The Nazis also devoted themselves to stimulating the production and use of motor vehicles. Taxes on new automobiles were reduced, and numerous subsidies were given to the automobile industry. Increases in the production of motor vehicles and in the number in use from 1932 to 1938 are shown in Table 27-7. Data for the United States in 1938 are presented for comparison.

There was only one automobile for every 50 persons in Germany, compared with one for every 5 persons in the United States, and the Nazi leaders were far from satisfied. So they came forward with the Volkswagen, or people's car, in 1938 and 1939. This was to be a car cheap enough for Germany to become a nation of motorists. Its cost was to be 950 marks ($380). A large plant for its manufacture was constructed at Fallersleben, near Brunswick. When the war began, however, the new plant was converted to war production, and few cars were ever delivered to private customers.

The beginning of the war brought forth strenuous efforts to increase automobile production, but the cars were for official use only. Some help

[20] Sweezy, *op. cit.*, p. 60.
[21] *Fascism in Action*, p. 147.
[22] *Ibid.*, p. 147.

Table 27-7. Motor Vehicles in Germany and the United States

Vehicle	Germany		United States 1938
	1932	1938	
Automobiles in use, thousands...............	549	1,272	29,434
Trucks in use, thousands....................	174	366	4,224
Passenger cars produced, thousands..........	60*	277	2,001
Trucks produced, thousands.................	14*	65	488

* 1930 figure.

SOURCE: J. Kuczynski, *Germany: Economic and Labour Conditions under Fascism* (New York: International Publishers Co., Inc., 1945), p. 70; *The Economic Almanac for 1949*, pp. 305, 369; *Fascism in Action*, 80th Cong., 1st Sess., H. Doc. 401, p. 146.

was obtained by taking over the well-developed French automobile industry, along with its skilled workers, methods, and inventions. Nevertheless, motor traffic in Germany had to be limited to save gasoline. The use of motorcars for private purposes was banned, and only small cars could be used for official purposes. Even long-distance trucking was forbidden unless it was in the interest of the war effort.

Air Transportation. Air transportation was a second form of transportation greatly stressed by the Nazi leaders. As early as May, 1933, all aviation, civilian and military, was placed under the Ministry of Aviation, with General Göring in charge. Passengers carried by airlines increased from 99,000 in 1932 to 323,000 in 1937, while the freight and mail carried increased from 2,503 tons to 8,721 tons.[23] The airlines of the United States carried 985,000 passengers in 1937. At the same time, Germany built up a force of military airplanes such as she did not have in 1932. Airplane production increased rapidly after World War II began, and additional help was obtained by taking over the airplane industry in Holland and other countries.

TRANSPORTATION SINCE WORLD WAR II

In the field of transportation the Nazi leaders had everything their own way. For several years during World War II it appeared that they had planned wisely in emphasizing the development of highway and air transportation at the expense of the railroads, inland water transportation, and ocean shipping. In the end, however, the transportation system contrived by the Nazis proved inadequate.

The Railroads. At the end of the war, the German transportation system was in a state of virtual collapse. It has been estimated that scarcely

[23] Kuczynski, *op. cit.*, p. 70.

10 per cent of the railroad-track mileage in Western Germany remained in full operation.[24] In the American and British zones alone, more than 2,300 bridges had been destroyed, along with 3,000 kilometers of track, 12,800 switches, 1,600 signal booths, and nearly 5,000 main signals.[25] Most of the rolling stock had been destroyed or lost. Many of the remaining freight cars lacked roofs, and the passenger cars had no windows or upholstery.

Building new locomotives was forbidden by the occupying powers, and new freight and passenger cars could be constructed only over a long period of time. Railroads had to rely largely on repairs of existing facilities. Repairs, however, were handicapped by shortages of fuel, materials, and spare parts, a lack of protective clothing and work shoes for the workers in the shops, and insufficient food for workers. By 1948 Western Germany had about 235,000 usable freight cars, compared with about 700,000 at the beginning of the war. However, 70 per cent of the damages to roadbed and track had been repaired, and 90 per cent of the bridges and signal booths had been restored on a temporary or permanent basis.[26]

Despite the reconstruction, the railroads operated ineffectively in the early postwar period. Roundabout routing to avoid zonal boundaries was sometimes necessary. Trains had to travel slowly over temporary bridges, and the coal for the locomotives was often of poor quality. Inadequate maintenance of tracks and cars slowed up movements, and breakdowns were frequent. Financial incentives to speed up traffic were often lacking. The freight requiring transportation in early 1948 was only half as great as the 1936 volume. However, passenger traffic was running at about double the 1936 level, and was using about half as many trains.

Railroad transportation in Western Germany was hard hit in the severe winter of 1947–1948, but reconstruction went forward rapidly after that. Contributions received under the Marshall Plan were of considerable help. Soon, railroad transportation was no longer an obstacle to economic recovery. In 1951 the passenger traffic amounted to 18.6 billion passenger-miles and the freight traffic to 37.7 billion ton-miles. The situation in Eastern Germany has developed less favorably. Reconstruction has been slower, it has been necessary to run the locomotives on the lignite coal found there, and practically all second and third tracks have been removed as reparations.

Inland Water Transportation. The Federal Republic of Western Germany contains about 4,500 of the 7,700 kilometers of navigable water-

[24] G. A. Almond (ed.), *The Struggle for Democracy in Germany* (Chapel Hill, N. C.: University of North Carolina Press, 1949), p. 136.
[25] *Annals of the American Academy of Political and Social Science,* November, 1948, p. 82.
[26] *Ibid.*

ways within the 1937 boundaries of Germany, but practically none of the waterways could be used for any great distance after the war. Navigation was obstructed by blasted bridges and by the wrecks of thousands of vessels. Along the Rhine, 194 out of 197 bridges had been destroyed, along with 355 out of 395 bridges over the canals. By the end of 1947, 320 out of 900 destroyed bridges had been temporarily or permanently repaired, and 2,400 out of 3,000 sunk vessels had been salvaged.[27]

Shipping on the inland waterways had also suffered during the war. In 1947 tug capacity was half the prewar total, barge tonnage less than half, and freighter capacity about two-thirds. Moreover, 10 to 15 per cent of the barges and 25 to 30 per cent of the tugs and freighters were out of commission. In 1947 total freight traffic on the inland waterways was about one-eighth the amount carried by the railroads. Before the war the proportion had been more nearly one-fourth.[28] Western Germany has had its hands full in restoring inland water transportation to its former position.

Highway Transportation. In Western Germany the war destroyed 1,775 highway bridges of over 10 meters in length and about 16,000 kilometers of roads. By the end of 1947 only 423 bridges had been repaired completely; about 1,000 had been repaired temporarily, and some 2,000 kilometers of roads had been reconstructed. Production of motor vehicles was far below prewar output and was only 10 per cent of the amount permitted by the occupying powers. Ninety per cent of the passenger cars in use, 70 per cent of the trucks, and 75 per cent of the busses, were more than ten years old.[29] Highway transportation was handicapped by a shortage of spare parts, tires and fuel, as well as by the lack of vehicles.

Much progress has been made in highway transportation since 1947. The roads have been repaired and the bridges rebuilt. The production of motorcars has increased tremendously. The entire automotive industry had produced 245,000 passenger cars in 1936. One company (Volkswagen) turned out 180,000 in 1953. In February, 1948, only 1,100 passenger cars were produced in all Western Germany, but in mid-1954 the Volkswagen output alone was running 1,000 per day.[30] By 1951 passenger cars and trucks in use numbered 1,501,000, compared with 1,638,000 in 1938.[31]

Ocean and Air Transportation. By the end of the war, the German merchant fleet had been reduced from over 4,000,000 tons to about 1,100,000 tons. Germany was then deprived of the remains of her mer-

[27] *Ibid.*, pp. 85–86.
[28] *Ibid.*
[29] *Ibid.*, p. 87.
[30] *Ibid.*, *Time*, Feb. 15, 1954, p. 85.
[31] *Statistical Abstract of the United States, 1953*, p. 956.

chant fleet and was prohibited from building new vessels. It was left 200,000 tons of shipping for coastwise traffic. Early in 1948 only 165,000 tons were actually available. The ships had an average age of more than thirty years, and 60 per cent of them were badly in need of repairs.[32] The ownership and construction of commercial airplanes was also forbidden under the Potsdam Agreement. For some years the airlines in Germany were operated by foreign companies, mostly American.

Restrictions on ocean and air transportation have been relaxed. In February, 1954, the luxury liner *Gripsholm*, leased from Sweden, set sail for the United States on the first trans-Atlantic voyage of a passenger ship under the German flag since the war. Western Germany wants to have her own passenger ships, but she has not yet been able to finance them. She also wants to operate airlines, and one company for the purpose had been formed by 1954. Outside of the fields of ocean and air transportation, the German transportation system has recovered from the war to a remarkable extent.

QUESTIONS FOR STUDY

1. How did Germany come to have a railroad system composed of private railroads, state railroads, imperial railroads, privately owned lines operated by states, and state-owned lines operated by private companies?

2. Why did the German railroads operate so efficiently through the cooperation of the Prussian Railway Department and the Imperial Railway Office?

3. What was the German policy with respect to inland waterways after the founding of the Empire? Did the waterways make serious inroads on railroad freight traffic? Why?

4. How did the development of German highway and ocean transportation to 1933 compare with that of the United States.

5. How did the National Socialists control German transportation? Which forms of transportation were most emphasized and favored by the National Socialists? Which were relatively neglected? Why?

6. What were the obstacles to efficient transportation in Germany after World War II? What was done about them?

7. To what extent has the transportation system of Western Germany recovered since World War II? Which forms have lagged behind? Why?

[32] *Annals of the American Academy of Political and Social Science,* November, 1948, p. 88.

CHAPTER 28

INDUSTRY

Germany in modern times has been one of the greatest industrial nations, but this was not the result of a long process of development. Industry in Germany, as in Soviet Russia, remained backward for many years after it had been thriving in England and other countries, and then it came on with a rush over a relatively short period of time. The period of most rapid industrial development in Germany, as in Russia, included the last few decades before World War I, but German industry reached much the higher levels.

INDUSTRY BEFORE 1871

One good index of industrialization is the size and growth of the towns and cities of a country. On this basis, Germany advanced but little in the first half of the nineteenth century. In 1815 the 12 largest towns in Germany had altogether about 50 per cent more people than Paris. In the next thirty-five years Paris gained on the 12 German towns, for in 1850 Paris had over 1,000,000 people and the German towns only 1,340,-000. On a percentage basis, some 73.5 per cent of the Prussian population was classed as rural in 1816. All persons living in towns of 2,000 or more were considered urban population. The rural percentage was still 72.0 in 1846 and 71.5 in 1852.[1]

Survivals of the Guild System. Features of the guild system survived in Germany down to 1850 or even longer. Included were such practices as apprenticeship, the exclusion from production of irregularly trained workmen, and rigorous tests before individuals could become master workmen. In some places there were laws that each village could have only one tailor, shoemaker, carpenter, butcher, baker, and so on.

Business was none too thriving for the master workmen even so, for the stagnant towns did not demand many industrial products. Many

[1] J. H. Clapham, *The Economic Development of France and Germany, 1815–1914* (London: Cambridge University Press, 1923), p. 82.

446

masters, in some places 80 or 90 per cent, had neither a journeyman nor an apprentice. In Prussia in 1816 there were only 56 workpeople (journeymen or apprentices) for each 100 masters. By 1843, the beginning of the real railroad age in Germany, there were 76 workpeople for each 100 masters, and almost a fourth of the masters worked alone.[2]

The Scale of Production. There were only a few large enterprises of the factory type in 1840. Many years earlier the Grand Duke of Baden had induced the establishment of a plant for printing calico, which was intended to employ 200 workers. Frederick the Great had set up a medium-sized iron foundry at Berlin. There were good-sized sugar refineries at Bremen and Hamburg. A machine-making plant employing 50 men was established at Berlin in 1837. There was a large engineering works at Ruhrort, and large ironworks at Sterkrade and Oberhausen; the plant at Oberhausen employed over 1,000 men. And the Krupp steel works at Essen was already of substantial size. However, these plants were quite exceptional in Germany at the time.

Apart from the few factories, about the only form of capitalistic industrial organization was the loose associations of workers, common in the textile trades. In many cases, the workers were not really wage earners. Rather, they owned their own equipment, bought their own materials, and sold their finished products to the enterpriser. In other cases, the workers were wage earners, for they were dependent upon the enterpriser for materials and worked them up for a piece-rate wage. This system of production was common in other countries in the early days of manufacturing.

A large part of manufacturing production was carried on in or around homes by hand methods. The number of people engaged in manufacturing to the exclusion of everything else was small. Much of the manufacturing was done by individuals primarily engaged in agriculture but working in manufacturing to supplement their incomes. On the other hand, many industrial workers engaged in agricultural operations as a sideline.

The Use of Mechanical Power. The prevalence of hand methods is indicated by the slow development of power. In Berlin there were only 30 steam engines in 1837 with an average of 13 horsepower. Berlin was already a community of over 250,000 inhabitants. In the same year, in all of Prussia, including the future great industrial districts along the Rhine, in the Saar Basin, and in Upper Silesia, only 7,500 horsepower were employed in mining, manufacturing, and all other branches of production. The horsepower in use rose rapidly to 22,000 in 1846, with 14,000 of it in mining and metallurgy.[3]

[2] *Ibid.*, pp. 84–85.
[3] *Ibid.*, pp. 88–89.

The Backwardness of Mining. Mining, like manufacturing, was slow to grow into large-scale production. The Ruhr coal field was worked to an important extent only after 1815, and the great eastern coal field in Silesia was not worked seriously until nearly 1840. The Prussian output from the three leading fields amounted to only about 3,200,000 tons even in 1846; Prussia was not producing as much coal in each year as the city of London burned.[4] The situation was much the same in other areas of mining. In 1837, a working force of only 30 or 40 men was ordinary in copper, lead, and silver mines.

The Influence of the Zollverein. German industry began to stir as early as 1835, and by 1845 signs of industrial awakening became apparent. Many people have attempted to trace these events to the creation of the Zollverein in 1834. The Zollverein was a customs union formed by German states which were eventually to make up three-fourths of the country. Duties were especially low on raw materials, with many admitted free of duty, while moderate duties were applied to manufactured goods. The states within the Zollverein traded freely with each other.

Coming after a long period in which the movement of goods between states had been restricted, the Zollverein was of course stimulating to industry and trade within and between the member states. Other factors which were of importance in stimulating industry were better roads, the first railroads, the gradual spread of knowledge, and the increased mobility of people.

Beginnings of Modern Industry. The 1850s and 1860s were a period of preparation for a great industrial boom. One symptom was a rapid movement of people toward towns and cities. The rural population of Prussia had been 71.5 per cent of the total in 1852, but it declined to 67.5 per cent in 1871.[5] Coal production, which had been 3,200,000 tons in 1846, advanced to 12,300,000 metric tons of coal and 4,400,000 of lignite in 1860 and put Germany ahead of France and Belgium. A further advance to about 38,000,000 tons of coal and lignite was registered by 1871.[6] Significant gains were also made in iron ore, pig iron, and other important commodities.

INDUSTRY, 1871–1933

The Urbanization of the Population. In the period from 1871 to 1914, or from the founding of the German Empire to the beginning of World War I, German industry expanded rapidly. The rural population, which

---

[4] *Ibid.*, pp. 90–91.
[5] *Ibid.*, p. 278.
[6] *Ibid.*, pp. 280–281.

had been 63.9 per cent in the Empire in 1871, declined to 57.5 per cent in 1890 and 40 per cent in 1910.[7] Between 1849 and 1910 German industry and commerce absorbed most of the increase in the population. While the total population increased from 35 million to 65 million, the rural population increased by a million persons at most. Thus an urban population of 10 million was replaced by one of almost 40 million in about sixty years. The movement of the population was toward the cities, and especially toward the largest cities. The cities of 100,000 inhabitants or over contained 11.4 per cent of the population in 1890 and 21.3 per cent in 1910.[8]

Progress in Coal Mining. In 1871 Germany produced about 38 million tons of coal and lignite. France and Belgium each had a coal output about one-third as large as Germany's, while Great Britain's output was more than three times as large. Thereafter, German production of coal and lignite increased sharply. It was almost equal to Great Britain's by 1913. This result, of course, was accompanied by a great increase in the number of workers in coal and lignite mining.

The steam power used in mining and smelting increased from 995,069 horsepower in 1895 to 2,332,968 horsepower in 1907. Much electrical power was also used in 1907.[9] In the latter years of the nineteenth century Germany had a net export balance of coal. She still imported some coal from England, but it was coal of a quality which could not be obtained in Germany or coal which could be transported to certain parts of Germany very cheaply.

Iron and Steel Production. The territory which was to become the German Empire produced 838,000 tons of iron ore in 1850. This was no more than one-sixth of the British output. This proportion had not changed significantly by 1860.[10] Thereafter, Germany's output increased to 10,664,000 tons in 1887 and 29,879,000 tons in 1911. However, this was inadequate to fill the needs of domestic production, and she imported 9,810,500 tons in 1912.[11]

In the production of pig iron and steel, Germany started far behind Great Britain, later caught up, and finally went far into the lead, as Table 28-1 shows. Between 1887 and 1911, the number of blast furnaces increased by one-half, and the value of the output increased over fivefold. Just before World War I, Germany held second place behind the United States in the production of both pig iron and steel.[12] Germany

---

[7] *Ibid.*, p. 278.
[8] *Ibid.*, p. 279.
[9] K. Helfferich, *Germany's Economic Progress and National Wealth, 1888–1914* (New York: Germanistic Society of America, 1914), p. 65.
[10] Clapham, *op. cit.*, p. 283.
[11] Helfferich, *op. cit.*, p. 62.
[12] Clapham, *op. cit.*, p. 285.

Table 28-1. Pig-iron and Steel Production in Germany and Great Britain, 1860–1912

(In millions of tons)

Year	Pig-iron production		Steel production	
	Germany	Great Britain	Germany	Great Britain
1860	0.5	3.9		
1880	2.7	. . . .	1.5	3.7
1890	4.7	. . . .	3.2	5.3
1900	8.5	9.1	7.4	6.0
1910	14.8	10.2	13.1	7.6
1912	17.9			

SOURCE: J. H. Clapham, *The Economic Development of France and Germany, 1815–1914* (London: Cambridge University Press, 1923), p. 285; K. Helfferich, *Germany's Economic Progress and National Wealth, 1888–1914* (New York: Germanistic Society of America, 1914), p. 62.

produced many kinds of machinery, was a leader in cutlery, and developed an important shipbuilding industry. The number of employees in the production of machinery increased from 356,000 in 1882 to 1,172,-000 in 1907. Steam power in the production of machinery increased from 185,000 to 1,126,000 horsepower between 1895 and 1907. In addition, machine building used 225 million kilowatts of electric power in 1907.[13] Just before World War I, Germany's exports of iron, steel, iron and steel goods, and machinery were running around £100 million per year.[14] Coal, iron, and steel were the basis of Germany's industrial progress between 1871 and 1914.

The Textile Industries. Great advances were made in the textile industries too. Germany collapsed as a producer of wool between 1871 and 1914, but wool spinning and weaving went steadily forward. The same was true of cotton and silk textiles, although the German manufacturers had to operate on the basis of imported raw materials. On the other hand, the linen industry had fallen far behind in previous decades while other countries were adopting the factory system, and it was never able to make up the lost ground. The period after 1871 was one of rapid adjustment in the textile industries. Formerly, there had been a tremendous number of producers using hand methods and in many cases producing textiles only as a side line. Now, there came into being modern factories employing large numbers of full-time wage earners. The steam power used by the textile industries increased by 72 per cent in the

[13] Helfferich, *op. cit.*, p. 65.
[14] Clapham, *op. cit.*, p. 285.

twelve-year period between 1895 and 1907. The textile industries also used 75,126,000 kilowatts of electric power in 1907.[15]

The Chemical Industry. Another industry which made great progress between 1871 and 1914 was the chemical industry. The potash beds in Prussian Saxony were discovered in 1852 and came to be worked regularly by 1860. The potassium salts obtained there, plus Germany's sodium chloride, sulphur, coal, and coal tar, provided the basis for about all the "heavy" chemicals and most of the "light" chemicals. The chemical industry was not a large employer of labor. The steam power used in the industry increased from 84,000 to 192,000 horsepower between 1895 and 1907, and the industry also used 42,288,000 kilowatts of electrical power in 1907.[16] Increases in chemical production were spectacular. The output of sulphuric acid increased twelvefold between 1878 and 1907. The production of sodium chloride expanded tenfold between 1871 and 1911, and the production of the vital potassium salts was some twenty-five times greater at the end than at the beginning of the same period.[17]

The Electrical Industry. The electrical industry provides a final example of Germany's industrial progress. In 1860 Germany scarcely had an electrical industry. Then came the invention and practical adoption of the telephone, the dynamo which permitted electrical energy to be generated in any amount desired, and advances in transmitting electricity over distances. Germany produced lighting and power equipment and appliances on a large scale, and the cities quickly obtained electric lights and streetcar systems.

In the early years of the present century Germany was a leader in specialized applications of electricity. She made electrical furnaces for steel production and other fields of metallurgy, developed the electrical method for securing nitrogen from the air, began to electrify railroads, and learned to drive agricultural machinery, including even ploughs, by electricity. Germany also developed an important export trade in electrical products. By 1913 electrical exports had reached the neighborhood of £11 million.[18]

All the forces making for industrialization and urbanization hit Germany almost at the same time. As late as 1840 Germany had experienced no industrial revolution.

Then, crowding fast on one another in two generations, came the railways; the abolition of the last remains of medieval economic restriction after 1848; the expansion of the Zollverein; the creation of a modern financial and banking

[15] Helfferich, *op. cit.*, p. 65.
[16] *Ibid.*
[17] Clapham, *op. cit.*, p. 305.
[18] *Ibid.*, p. 308.

system; the great steel inventions; the swift, cheap, glorious and exhilarating achievement of national union; and the period of electricity, overseas expansion and world policy.[19]

The Kartell Movement. The period from 1871 to 1914 was also noteworthy for the Kartell movement. The Kartells were combinations of firms in various industries and were designed to restrain the destructive forces of competition. Kartells usually tried to maintain prices at levels which would be remunerative for the firms in an industry and to stabilize these prices. The devices used by the Kartells were many and varied. Some early Kartells were little more than price-fixing agreements among producers of rather uniform products. Other Kartells went into the regulation of output, assigning production quotas to members, dividing market areas among members, selling products for them, and helping them acquire supplies on reasonable terms. For the most part, the Kartells were not agencies for dealing with labor.

Only half a dozen Kartells have been traced to a date prior to 1870. Of the Kartells still active at the end of the century, 76 had been set up between 1879 and 1885 and 120 between 1885 and 1890.[20] Since there had been a prolonged period of falling prices and business depression in the 1880s, many people concluded that the Kartells were a product of economic distress. There was an element of truth in this, but many German industries in their youthful exuberance had overexpanded, and many Kartells were formed in periods of good business. The higher tariff policy followed after 1880 was also a factor in their formation.

At any rate, more than 350 Kartells had been formed in Germany by 1900 and, although some of them had collapsed, about 275 remained active.[21] There was hardly a branch of production from antimacassars to zithers which did not have a Kartell of some sort by 1900. The Kartell movement resembled the trust movement in the United States, except that the German government did not get excited about the matter, and there was no Kartell-busting or policy of enforced competition on the part of the government.

World War I and After. From 1914 to 1918 German industry was struggling to meet the needs of a war economy and, on the whole, it did a very good job of it, although production declined in the late stages of the war. When the war was over Germany suffered industrial losses under the Versailles Treaty. She was deprived of 19 per cent of her coke, 74.5 per cent of her iron ore, 26.6 per cent of her blast furnaces, 19.2 per cent of her raw iron and steel, 15.8 per cent of her rolling mills, and 68.5 per cent of her zinc foundries. Two of the three most important

[19] *Ibid.*, pp. 279–280.
[20] *Ibid.*, p. 311.
[21] *Ibid.*

industrial districts of Germany, the Lorraine-Rhine-Westphalian and the Upper Silesian areas, were broken up. Coal mines were separated from cokeries, cokeries from blast furnaces and steel mills, and steel mills from mills making fabricated steel products.[22] However, what was left of German industries came through the war in relatively good condition, and recovery was not long in coming.

German Industry in the 1920s. The great inflation which reached its peak late in 1923 occasioned a temporary setback, but German industry attained high levels later in the decade, as Table 28-2 indicates. The in-

Table 28-2. Increases in German Industrial Production in the 1920s

Type of production	1923	1924	1925	1926	1927	1928	1929
Pig iron, thousand tons	4,941	.....	.....	9,636	...	.....	13,239
Steel ingots, thousand tons	6,208	.....	.....	12,226	...	.....	16,023
Coal, million tons	.....	118.8	.....	......	...		164
Automobiles, thousands	.....	.....	39.0	......	...	101.6	
Trucks, thousands	.....	.....	9.4	......	...	20.0	
Nitrogen, thousand tons	.....	.....	450.0	......	...	700.0	

SOURCE: F. K. Bieliegk, *Statistical Truth* (London: Hutchinson & Co., Ltd., 1942), pp. 39–44.

dex number of industrial production, with 1925 as 100, advanced to 122 in 1929. Industrial production in Great Britain and the United States increased by 13 and 14 points, respectively, between 1925 and 1929. Some 40 to 45 million marks of new capital were invested in German industry between 1924 and 1930.[23]

The Great Depression. German industry suffered severely in the Great Depression after 1929. Industrial production fell off between 30 and 35 points from predepression levels, the number of unemployed tripled between 1929 and 1932, and German exports stood at 42.4 in 1932 on the basis of 1929 as 100.[24] Sources of foreign credit, which had played a part in supporting the boom of the 1920s, dried up all at once. Before Germany was able to recover from the depression, Hitler became Chancellor, and the National Socialist regime was in power.

INDUSTRY UNDER NATIONAL SOCIALISM

The Estate of Industry and Trade. The Nazis set up their official organizations for controlling production (including industrial production)

[22] R. A. Brady, *The Spirit and Structure of German Fascism* (New York: The Viking Press, Inc., 1937), p. 9.
[23] F. K. Bieliegk, *Statistical Truth* (London: Hutchinson & Co., Ltd., 1942), pp. 39–44.
[24] *Ibid.*, pp. 56–57.

early in 1934. The control organizations in the field of industry and trade were placed under the Estate of Industry and Trade. One of the top agencies in the estate was the National Economic Chamber, which was composed of the seven National Groups into which the field of industry and trade was divided, the Provincial Economic Chambers, the local Chambers of Industry and Commerce, and the local Chambers of Handicrafts. The Minister of Economic Affairs appointed the leader of the National Economic Chamber and his deputies. The leader of the chamber was assisted by an advisory council of officials from control organizations both inside and outside the Estate of Industry and Trade. Alongside the National Economic Chamber was the Cooperative Council of Chambers of Industry and Commerce, which was made up of the local Chambers of Industry and Commerce.

The Group Organizations. Under the National Economic Chamber, the general field of industry and trade was divided into a number of types of group organizations. In the first place, there were seven National Groups of industry and trade—Industry, Trade, Banking, Insurance, Power, Tourist Industry, and Handicrafts. The National Group of Industry was subdivided into seven Main Groups. The other six National Groups were not so subdivided, but all seven National Groups had other subsidiary organizations. The National Group of Handicrafts was divided into 50 National Guild Associations, while the other 6 National Groups were divided into some 46 Economic Groups, 328 Branch Groups, and 327 Sub-Branch Groups.[25]

There were also provincial economic chambers and provincial guild associations. At the bottom of the heap there were 100 local Chambers of Industry and Commerce, 70 Chambers of Handicrafts, and guilds and local organizations of the higher groups. The German industrialists, businessmen, and handicraft producers belonged directly to the appropriate local organizations and indirectly to the appropriate higher organizations. Ordinary workers were not represented in these groups, but the employer groups in general were represented in the Labor Front.

The Functioning of the Control Organizations. Outside observers differed in their views of how these control organizations actually functioned. According to one school of thought, the entire setup was under the control of German businessmen, with the government merely underwriting the program. Other writers reached the opposite conclusion that German businessmen did not control the economic situation and were mere pawns of the state. Still others reached the perhaps more reasonable conclusion, to which we subscribe, that much control was exercised by both businessmen on the one hand and by government on

---

[25] F. L. Neumann, *Behemoth: The Structure and Practice of National Socialism* (New York: Oxford University Press, 1942), pp. 242–245.

the other. At the top, of course, the leaders of the government were supreme, for no businessmen were big enough to prevail against Hitler and his immediate associates.

With regard to the specific functioning of the individual organizations, the actual policies and programs were formulated by the Minister of Economic Affairs and his advisers. The powers of the Minister extended through the leader of the National Economic Chamber down through the functional and regional agencies. He controlled all nominations for office, the deputy officers, the council members, and the leaders of all the various groups. He removed officers at his discretion, made investigations, obtained reports, called meetings, and supervised the control agencies. He had the power to approve or disapprove Kartell agreements or decisions, to compel outside firms to join a Kartell, and to forbid new enterprises and the expansion of existing establishments.

The policies and regulations were enforced by the Cooperative Council of Chambers of Industry and Commerce and the local chambers. These organizations had the task of keeping the businessmen in line. The local Chambers of Industry and Commerce were set up as public corporations. They were representatives of the state and could levy taxes on their members. The various groups and economic chambers would discuss programs and policies, and give advice to the higher authorities, but they seemed to have no power of their own. The individual businessmen wielded influence primarily by their ability to "reach" the high leaders and officials.

Later Additions to the Agencies for Production Control. As time went on, government control over productive activities operated through new agencies, as we noted in Chapter 25. The Office of the Second Four-Year Plan began functioning in 1937. Two years later, Hitler appointed a Council of National Defense, headed by Göring, with wide powers to control economic activities. This group was superseded early in 1940 by the General Council of the War Economy, also headed by Göring. The new Council had control over all economic activities, including those of the war department, the civil government, and private business. The formerly powerful Minister of Economic Affairs was subordinate to the Council. The chief administrative agencies seemed to be the Office of the Second Four-Year Plan and the General Commissioner for Economics, who was also chief over the Ministers of Economic Affairs, Labor, Finance, Food, and Forestry. The General Commissioner for Economics and the Office of the Second Four-Year Plan worked through various national, provincial, and local agencies.

Merits of Fascist Controls over Production. From the point of view of efficiency, there are some things to be said for the controls over production used in Germany. They gave the government the power to direct production, without taking away from businessmen the customary capitalistic incentives. Private individuals continued to own and operate their businesses and to be motivated by considerations of profit and loss. This situation may be better, in relation to efficiency, than one in which businessmen are reduced to the status of government employees on a salary.

The businessmen of Germany, or at least those connected with the larger enterprises and combinations of firms, fared rather well under National Socialism. The fascist objectives of conquest, glory, and the stabilization of the regime appeared consistent with the desires of big business for full and profitable operations. Under a government-sponsored concentration movement, thousands of small firms were eliminated, and many new combinations and Kartells were formed. Large firms were assigned the task of founding and operating new industries needed for the self-sufficiency program. The payment of dividends was limited, but this affected only the distribution of profits, not corporate profits as such. Even under strict price control, the enterprises with the lowest costs could make plenty of money. Finally, the policies with respect to labor were favorable for the employers.

The results, in terms of profits, were clear. Statistics for the largest 46 per cent of German corporations, which owned 92 per cent of corporate capital, showed that the average profit ratio (net earnings as a percentage of net worth) increased from −10.59 per cent in 1931 to 5.66 per cent in 1938.[26] Production did not become unprofitable for large German businesses after the beginning of World War II, for 833 large corporations had increased their capital from 4.9 to 7.8 billion marks by reinvestment of profits by the middle of 1942. However, these figures do not show what happened to the smaller German enterprises.[27]

The concentration and combination movement was another factor with implications for efficiency. The number of corporations declined from 11,690 before the depression to 5,518 in 1938, but corporations with a capital of 5 million marks or over decreased only from 750 to 616. These giant corporations, which had controlled about 56 per cent of the capital of all corporations in 1928, controlled 77 per cent in 1938.[28]

There was also a considerable development of Kartells in Germany under National Socialism. In 1933 the powers of the Kartell court were transferred to the Minister of Economic Affairs, who could decide whether Kartell arrangements and decisions were unfair. He could also make outside firms join Kartells and could prohibit the establishment of new firms and the expansion of existing firms. These powers were used

[26] *Ibid.*, p. 73.
[27] *In Fact*, Jan. 5, 1943, p. 3.
[28] *Foreign Commerce Weekly*, Jan. 4, 1941, pp. 13–14.

on a number of occasions. Since many of his controls were capable of benefiting the Kartells, the number of Kartells increased from 2,000 in 1925 to 2,500 in 1936.[29]

Thousands of small businessmen were forced out of business because they could not continue operating under officially set prices, because they could not obtain funds to modernize their plants, because they could not obtain raw materials from the rationing boards, or because their workers were shifted to other plants. The elimination of inefficient producers or their absorption by larger and more efficient concerns may have contributed to the efficiency of production in fascist Germany. Moreover, the government could deal more effectively with a few large firms than with many small ones.

The German economy under National Socialism could also move toward the elimination of competitive wastes in production. The government could cut down idle capacity and duplication of facilities. It could reduce the varieties of goods and concentrate on a few standardized products. It could limit advertising and discourage waste in the competitive exploitation of natural resources. Finally, it could keep the productive system operating at high levels and avoid the depressions which occur in uncontrolled economies.

Disadvantages of Fascist Controls over Production. On the other hand, there were a number of factors in the National Socialist system which were less favorable from the point of view of efficiency. One was the overwhelming complexity of the controls. For example, the government issued 24 pages of orders printed in fine type to regulate chimney sweeping. One can only imagine what the regulations for the chemical industry must have been like!

The complexity of these control organizations must have confused the German businessmen on many occasions. However, as W. R. Deuel said:

There is only one formula the nazis seem to know for dealing with this confusion: whenever the situation threatens to get completely out of hand, they set up a new office to coordinate and rationalize the ones already in existence. In time, even the coordinators and rationalizers become so numerous and confusing—and confused—that coordinators of the coordinators have to be appointed to rationalize the rationalizers.[30]

Deuel also said, after a leading Nazi was reported to have lost his mind: "It is not surprising that a man in a position of responsibility in the

[29] M. Y. Sweezy, *The Structure of the Nazi Economy* (Cambridge, Mass.: Harvard University Press, 1941), p. 94.
[30] W. R. Deuel, *People under Hitler* (New York: Harcourt, Brace and Company, Inc., 1942), pp. 337–338.

458 Germany—Fascism and Return to Capitalism

nazi economic and financial system should go mad—the surprising thing about it was that anyone should have noticed that he was mad."[31]

Amid such a welter of control agencies, and especially when the power to regulate a particular phase of economic life (for example, prices) was divided among four or five different agencies of the government, businessmen in Germany had difficulty in deciding just who their bosses were or where they should look for guidance or orders. Delays in getting decisions or in securing permits were troublesome in the extreme. Businessmen were expected to comply with fat sheaves of regulations which the ordinary individual would find it impossible even to understand. And frequently the various regulations conflicted with each other.

The government also issued an almost endless succession of forms, reports, and questionnaires, all to be filled out posthaste and usually with many copies. The National Socialist policy seemed to be to tie the businessman hand and foot and then tell him to go ahead, operate his business, and make profits. Either the businessman became so hopelessly enmeshed in regulations and red tape that he could not operate efficiently, or else evasion of regulations, black marketing, and bribery of government officials flourished so that businesses might continue to operate. In either case, the results desired by the fascist leaders would not be completely obtained.

German Industrial Production. Industrial production in Germany increased by leaps and bounds in the first several years under National Socialism. The index numbers of industrial production presented in Table 28-3 show that industrial production in 1938 was more than double that of the depression year of 1932. However, the production of capital goods in 1938 was about three times as great as in 1932, while the pro-

Table 28-3. Index Numbers of Industrial Production, Capital Goods Production, and Consumers' Goods Production in Germany, 1932–1939

Year	Index of industrial production, 1928 = 100	Index of capital goods production, 1928 = 100	Index of consumers' goods production, 1928 = 100
1932	58.7	45.7	78.1
1933	65.5	53.7	82.9
1934	83.3	77.2	87.6
1935	95.8	99.4	91.0
1936	106.7	112.9	97.5
1937	116.7	126.0	102.8
1938	124.7	135.9	107.8
1939 (May)*	130.1	148.9	116.1

* Levels attained by the indexes in the month of May, 1939.

[31] Ibid., p. 336.

duction of consumers' goods was less than 50 per cent greater. Since these index numbers use 1928 as the base year, it is also obvious that the production of capital goods in 1938 was about 36 per cent greater than in 1928, and the production of consumers' goods was only about 8 per cent greater.

Even these figures should be used cautiously. One estimate of German national income claims that per capita income, as deflated for changes in the value of money, increased only 23 per cent from 1932 to 1938 and only 13 per cent from 1929 to 1938. Moreover, most of the increase went into the armaments program. It is estimated that, if we eliminate the goods produced for the armaments program, then per capita income, including both civilian consumption and ordinary civilian investment, increased only about 8 per cent from the depths of the depression.[32]

The Location of German Manufacturing Industries. Manufacturing proper was scattered all over the country, though there was some concentration in the southern two-thirds of the country. One important manufacturing region was located in the south-central part between the Erz Gebirge on the south and Hanover and Berlin on the north. Saxony, in the southern part of this area, had long been noted for its industry, based in part on minerals from the Erz Gebirge, plus coal and water power. Saxony was a textile center too, specializing in cottons and woolens. It was also a center of the chemical industry. Dresden was noted for its china, made from kaolin deposits nearby, and Leipzig was a fur center and a famous publishing city. Berlin, at the northern edge of this area, was well known for its electrical manufacturing.

A second important manufacturing region was found in the western part of the country in Rhenish Prussia, Westphalia, and the Saar Basin. This area was noted for its iron and steel production, but important chemical works were also located in Rhenish Prussia, while Westphalia produced cotton and linen textiles.

A third and less important manufacturing region was on the upper Rhine and the Bavarian Plateau. It had some textile mills, was a world center for toy production, turned out large amounts of jewelry, and was noted for its breweries. The new plants for the production of war goods were well scattered over the whole country, in part to make them less vulnerable to enemy attack.

German Industrial Production in Wartime. When World War II broke out, the German economy was operating with substantially full employment of men and resources, and it was difficult to get increases in industrial production. Increased production of war goods could be obtained domestically only by shifting men and resources from other fields of production to industry or from less essential to more essential

[32] Sweezy, *op. cit.*, pp. 204–205.

industries. Germany's military successes in the early years of the war provided her with additional amounts of supplies and machinery and gave her control over foreign industries. However, as the war went on, and especially as Allied air attacks became increasingly severe, German industry had difficulty in maintaining production.

The iron and steel industry is an example of an industry important for war purposes. German output of steel stood at about 22 million tons in 1938. Through strenuous efforts at home and with the help of conquered territories, some 34 million to 35 million tons of crude steel were produced at the peak of production in 1943.[33] By January, 1945, steel production had fallen off by about two-thirds to an annual rate of about 10 million tons. By contrast, consider the motorcar industry. In 1939 it turned out almost 600,000 vehicles and their sales value was second only to that of coal. When the war began, the production of passenger automobiles virtually ceased, truck production was cut 40 per cent, and the industry seemed to have been put in moth balls to await the end of a short war. Later on, truck production was emphasized once more and output passed the prewar peak, but it was virtually wiped out by 1945.[34]

Government controls over industrial production became more and more direct, specific, and severe during the war. Industries producing consumers' goods were permitted to run only a few hours per week or were even closed down altogether. Scarce materials were severely rationed. Thus firms producing consumers' goods, even though they had permission to operate, were sometimes unable to do so because they lacked necessary materials. Firms were required to report their stocks of scarce materials, the consumption of these stocks, and their prospective needs. Intensive drives were carried on to collect and re-use scrap and waste materials. Industries producing consumers' goods were required to limit themselves to one or two standard types of goods and were made to use considerable amounts of ersatz, or substitute materials. Finally, manufacturers were often required to report their stocks of finished products and reserve portions for government use. Heavy penalties were provided for violations of these controls.

INDUSTRIAL PRODUCTION SINCE WORLD WAR II

The partition of Germany after World War II left the greatest concentration of industry, and especially heavy industry, in the zones which were later to become the Federal Republic of Western Germany. How-

[33] British Intelligence Objectives Subcommittee, *The Ferrous Metals Industry in Germany, 1939–1945*, Overall Report 15 (London: HMSO, 1949), p. 11.
[34] British Intelligence Objectives Subcommittee, *The Motor Car Industry in Germany, 1939–1945*, Overall Report 21 (London: HMSO, 1950), p. 7.

ever, the industrial cities of Berlin, Dresden, and Leipzig, and much of the great industrial area in the south-central part of prewar Germany fell in the Soviet zone. Many industrial firms in the west had plants in the east which were lost to the Communists. The textile industry was especially hard hit because spinning and weaving had been divided between the eastern and western parts of prewar Germany.

Postwar Productive Capacity of Western Germany. The production capacity of industry in Western Germany a year or two after the war probably did not exceed 75 per cent of the prewar level. Industrial facilities had been badly damaged. In the Ruhr some 30 per cent of industrial production facilities had been bombed out and another 20 per cent damaged.[35] Other production facilities were dismantled by order of the victorious powers.

The machinery of industry in Western Germany was obsolete. The situation was worse in consumers' goods industries than in heavy industry, because the former industries had been neglected during the late 1930s and the war period. The problem of obsolescence had been accentuated by the fact that the most modern enterprises were commonly selected for dismantling. At that, the situation was better in Western Germany than in the Soviet zone, where industrial production capacity in 1947 was from one-third to two-fifths of the prewar capacity.[36]

Industrial Production in the Early Postwar Period. The production capacity of industry in Western Germany in 1947 may have been roughly 75 per cent of prewar capacity, but this did not mean that actual production ran at 75 per cent of the prewar level. The production index, based on 1936 as 100, was 33.7 in 1946, and it moved up only to 43 in 1947.[37] Many factors were responsible for this situation. Raw materials were not available in adequate quantities. The same was true of mechanical power. Transportation difficulties restrained production. Worker productivity was low because of malnutrition, lack of clothing and housing, and miserable living conditions. Industry still operated under government controls. The currency had not been stabilized. Black and gray markets had a disorganizing influence. Businessmen were often hesitant to undertake needed projects.

Industrial Production in Western Germany since 1948. Industrial production in Western Germany staged a remarkable recovery starting in 1948. The index of production in general jumped from 43 in 1947 to 76 in 1948. Before the middle of 1950, production in Western Germany passed the 1936 level for the whole of prewar Germany, and in 1953 it

[35] *Life,* May 10, 1954, p. 135.
[36] *Annals of the American Academy of Political and Social Science,* November, 1948, p. 55.
[37] *Time,* Feb. 15, 1954, p. 88.

reached 154 per cent of prewar production.[38] Industrial production proper has almost tripled since 1948, moving from an index number of 100 in 1948 to one of 280 in 1954.[39]

In 1953 the output of chemicals was 102 per cent greater than in 1936, while that of electrical equipment was 238 per cent greater. Coal production lagged behind prewar levels as late as 1952, but the 1953 output was 20 per cent above that of 1936. Early in 1954 the shipyards of Western Germany were building 633,904 gross tons of shipping—a total second only to that of Great Britain.[40]

How were these feats accomplished? The currency reform of 1948 was one important factor. Providing 1 new mark for every 10 old ones wiped out most of the savings of many people, but it ended the currency inflation which was threatening the country and it gave the people a currency which they could trust. The currency reform was followed by the removal of price controls, rationing, and most other government controls. This gave German businessmen a chance to operate their enterprises in their own way.

Prices were allowed to find their own level, and the level that they found was higher than the official prices which had nominally been in effect. Business firms were able to operate profitably, and they were encouraged to reinvest their earnings in new production facilities. The government granted tax concessions to industry to permit rebuilding and expansion, and tax rebates were given in connection with goods sold directly abroad. In the first half of 1952 gross domestic investment in Western Germany amounted to 25 per cent of gross national product, compared with 16 per cent in Great Britain.[41]

In the early years of the great recovery, wage rates did not advance as fast as prices. It was not until recovery was well advanced that the trade unions were able to obtain higher wage rates. In the meantime, the worker had to fill his pay envelope by working overtime, and hours of work were not closely restricted by the unions. The workers worked both hard and long, and there was a considerable improvement in labor productivity.

Foreign aid also played an important part in Western Germany's industrial recovery. In 1948 Germany started receiving assistance under the Marshall Plan, and this assistance eventually reached a total of $3 billion. American aid made available a flow of raw materials for industry and food for the hungry population. The currency reform could hardly have succeeded without these flows of goods, for inflation would

[38] *Ibid.*
[39] *The Economist,* May 7, 1955, p. 509.
[40] *Time,* Feb. 15, 1954, p. 90.
[41] *The Economist,* Oct. 18, 1952, p. 206.

have started again if goods had remained scarce. Moreover, the workers were stimulated by the thought that, if they worked hard and made more money, they could translate the money into enjoyable goods.

QUESTIONS FOR STUDY

1. Why was German industry rather slow to develop in the years before 1871?

2. Give some evidence of the progress made by German industry in the fifty years after 1871. Why did German industry develop so rapidly in this period?

3. How did the National Socialist government of Germany control industry? What were the advantages and disadvantages of this system of controls?

4. What was the nature of the Kartells in German industry? When did most of them develop, and why? How did the attitude of the German government toward them differ from that of the United States government toward the trusts?

5. Would you argue that industry is more likely to operate efficiently under government ownership and operation as in Soviet Russia or under private ownership with severe government controls as in Germany? Why?

6. How did German industry fare under National Socialism from 1933 to 1939? During World War II?

7. How was industry handicapped in Western Germany after World War II? Why did actual production fall well below capacity? How and to what extent has industrial recovery occurred? How do you account for this recovery?

CHAPTER 29

MONEY, CREDIT, AND BANKING

The development of money, credit, and banking in Germany paralleled the development of agriculture, industry, transportation, and commerce. Germany had no banking system and no unified monetary system, and she needed none as long as production remained on a small-scale basis, economic localities were self-contained for the most part, roads and railroads had not yet been constructed, and exchanges of goods had not yet become important. Later on, money, credit, and banking institutions made rapid progress and rivaled those of leading nations.

MONEY, CREDIT, AND BANKING BEFORE 1871

Monetary Conditions before 1871. In the states which were later to become the German Empire, silver was the standard money and some gold coins circulated, too. Otherwise there was much confusion. Many states used silver thalers for their large coins, but there were various kinds of thalers; the relations between gold and silver coins varied from state to state; and there was indescribable complexity in the systems of small coins. The few bankers functioned chiefly in the safekeeping of money and in exchanging the coins of different states.

The situation improved under the Zollverein when, in 1838, a 2-thaler piece was adopted as the standard unit within the customs union. This unit was equal to 7 of the gulden used in a number of the southern states. However, at the time of the founding of the Empire, there were seven distinct currency areas and 33 banks which issued currency. These banks put out their paper money under different rules and regulations and were unconnected with each other. The states did have agreements specifying the relative values of their currencies, and in Prussia the ratio between gold and silver coins was fixed by law.

Banking before 1871. The German banking system developed very slowly in the first half of the nineteenth century. The Knights Bank of Stettin issued currency from 1824 to 1834, when the privilege was withdrawn. Bavaria in 1834 and Saxony in 1838 approved banks of issue privately owned but under government supervision. No truly private banks with the right to issue bank notes existed before 1840.

The Royal Bank in Berlin functioned until 1846, but it was a state bank, had no stockholders, issued no banknotes, and had no checking accounts. It discounted bills, made loans against goods, and did some mortgage lending. The Prussian Bank replaced it in 1847. This institution was a joint-stock company, privately owned for the most part, and had the right to issue banknotes up to 21 million thalers. However, it had no real independence and was directed by the government. It was set up in part to silence a growing demand for privately owned and managed banks with the right of note issue.

Many banks were founded after 1847, and many important banks were established between then and the early 1870s. This bank expansion accompanied the industrial expansion which followed the discovery of gold in California and elsewhere. The Schaafhausensche Bankverein of Cologne was founded in 1848. It had the privilege of issuing bank notes and received its charter from Prussia. It was followed by the Disconto-Gesellschaft in 1851, the Darmstadter Bank in 1853, and the Berliner Handelsgesellschaft in 1856. Considerably later, the Deutsche Bank was founded in 1870 and the Dresdner Bank in 1872.

Investment banking scarcely existed in Germany in the first half of the century, for there were almost no corporations to finance. Prussia's law of 1838 covering railroad companies permitted corporations or joint-stock companies in that field, and it was followed by a more general company law in 1843. No other German state had a general company law before 1850, although some Hanse towns, operating under the French Commercial Code, permitted joint-stock companies. In most states, joint-stock companies could come into existence only by special acts of the government. This situation slowed up the development of companies, but it also tended to prevent fraud and speculation. Most of the states passed company laws in the 1850s, which, like the Prussian law of 1843, required joint-stock companies to receive authorization from the state.

MONEY, CREDIT, AND BANKING, 1871–1933

Monetary Conditions, 1871–1914. Soon after the Empire was formed, Germany established a unified monetary system for the whole country. She adopted the gold standard and was the second major country to do so (England had been first). Thus Germany was a leader of the movement toward international monetary stabilization on a gold basis. The new monetary system was effected in three steps. In 1871 a law was passed governing the minting of gold coins. The mark became the new official unit, its ratio to the value of existing silver coins was determined, and the latter were withdrawn. In 1873 the gold standard was provided for by law, and the use of silver was limited to small coins. Finally, in 1875 the Prussian Bank was made into a central bank, known thereafter as the Reichsbank, and steps were taken toward giving it a monopoly of bank-note issue.

The German mark was not completely stable in the years that followed. Like some other countries, Germany experienced a trend toward lower prices down to 1896. After that, the trend in prices was reversed by large gold discoveries and production in various parts of the world. On the whole, however, the mark remained relatively stable down to the beginning of World War I.

The Reichsbank. As the central bank of the new Empire, the Reichsbank came into a position of great power. In the first place, it came into control of bank-note issue. The 32 other banks which had the right of note issue could not be deprived of it immediately. However, provision was made for them to transfer their right to the Reichsbank if they cared to, and in the meantime they were subjected to onerous regulations and excluded from some lucrative phases of banking. Fourteen of these note-issuing banks surrendered in 1876, and by 1907 only four banks retained the right of note issue. These were seminational banks in Bavaria, Würtemberg, Baden, and Saxony. By 1912 Reichsbank notes amounted to nearly 2,700,000,000 marks, and the centralization of currency issues had been achieved for all practical purposes.[1]

A second function of the Reichsbank was to hold the Empire's main cash reserves. These increased from about 500,000,000 marks in the late 1870s to around 1,200,000,000 before World War I. Originally, a large part of the reserve was in silver, but the gold component gradually increased to around 75 per cent of the total.[2]

The third main function of the Reichsbank was to furnish banking facilities for the whole Empire, without discrimination between persons and places. In its first thirty years, the Reichsbank set up nearly 100 main branches and about 4,000 subbranches.[3] It transferred cash at low cost from one place to another for all who asked and thus largely forestalled the custom of paying by check. While it stood ready to discount commercial paper for the public, more than half of its discounting business was with other banks. It was ready to consider applications for loans or discounts from anyone, whether or not he carried an account at the bank.

---

[1] J. H. Clapham, *The Economic Development of France and Germany, 1815–1914* (London: Cambridge University Press, 1923), pp. 391–392.
[2] *Ibid.*, p. 392.
[3] *Ibid.*, pp. 392–393.

Growth of the Large Banks. Meantime the large, joint-stock banks of Germany kept growing. By 1911 the total capital (share capital plus reserves) of commercial banks having at least 1,000,000 marks of share capital amounted to 3,731,000,000 marks. Out of this, about three-quarters was owned by the Schaafhausensche Bankverein and the four D-banks (Deutsche Bank, Dresdner Bank, Disconto-Gesellschaft, and Darmstadter Bank). At about the same time, 48.3 per cent of the deposits of all commercial banks were held by the great Berlin banks, and of these the four D-banks alone held 40.2 per cent.[4]

The large commercial banks, unlike those of England, maintained branches only in the large centers of population. They reached the smaller places by controlling the stock of local banks, and in some cases they absorbed the local banks, but they were not especially interested in local deposit banking. Control and absorption went forward rapidly after 1900, but the number of nominally independent banks went on increasing, at least down to 1907. There had been 71 banks in 1883, and there were 144, or about twice as many, in 1907.[5] In addition to these joint-stock banks, there were many private banks and savings banks.

Combinations of Commercial and Investment Banking. The German banking system differed from that of other countries, such as the United States, in that there was virtually no separation of commercial and investment banking. The large German banks engaged in what might be called department-store banking. They did a commercial banking business and also cared for the long-term financial needs of German corporations. They made short-term loans to corporations, which sometimes ripened into long-term loans through regular renewals; they invested in corporate securities with their own funds; and, acting alone or in groups, they bought large security issues from corporations and resold them.

Being allowed to vote their customers' holdings of corporate securities as well as their own, and with their influence as financial sponsors of the corporations, the large banks came to be represented on the boards of industrial corporations and to take part in their management. Frequently, also, the large industrial corporations had representatives on the boards of the banks which financed them. By the twentieth century, the large banks had their recognized industrial spheres of influence. For example, the Dresdner Bank was allied with the great Krupp concern and expected to take an important part in any Krupp financial project.

The close relation between banking and industry helped to promote the concentration movement in both fields. As time went on, the emphasis in industry shifted to fields in which firms required large initial

[4] G. Stolper, *German Economy, 1870–1940* (New York: Reynal & Hitchcock, Inc., 1940), pp. 50–51.
[5] Clapham, *op. cit.*, p. 395.

investments, as the heavy industries, shipbuilding, and the electrical industry. Such firms required powerful banks to bear the burden of their financing, and concentration in banking was promoted. Eventually, the large banks themselves began to take over some other good-sized banks. In 1895 the Disconto-Gesellschaft took over the Norddeutsche Bank, and the Deutsche Bank acquired the Hannoversche Bank in 1897 and the Essener Creditanstalt in 1903.

The large banks were also sponsors of the Kartell movement. They were interested in seeing their concerns acquire some protection from competition. Moreover, the large banks often became interested in several firms operating in the same field of industry or in firms operating in interrelated fields. In such cases, the banks would frequently encourage them to enter into horizontal or vertical combinations and Kartells.

The Growth of Corporations. At the time of the founding of the Empire, laws were passed freeing joint-stock companies from the need for government authorization and setting up general rules governing their organization and operation. In view of the favorable situation for financing corporations, it is not surprising that the formation of corporations went forward rapidly. However, abuses in their promotion and management led to some restrictive laws, of which the most important were those of 1884 and 1887. In the end, Germany came to have a more strict and in many respects a better company law than other great countries.

The procedure involved in founding a company was complex and exposed to public scrutiny. It was not well suited for small and confidential enterprises. There was also objection to the rapid growth of speculation in the securities of joint-stock companies. In 1892 a law was passed providing for companies of a new type, which were to have limited liability but would be organized simply, enjoy privacy, have fewer owners, and not provide a mass of securities to be sold to the public. The new companies were called "companies with limited liability" as distinguished from the "joint-stock companies."

The new type of company proved popular. Almost 200 of them were set up in 1893. There were over 9,000 of them in operation in 1907 and 16,500 by 1909. Their average capital ran just over 220,000 marks. They were widely used in wholesale and retail trade and in branches of manufacturing in which large size was not essential. The regular joint-stock companies also increased from 2,100 in 1886–1887 to 5,400 in 1912. These companies had an average capital of about 3,200,000 marks in 1912 and were large-scale concerns. They included many banks and other credit institutions, engineering concerns, transportation companies, coal and iron businesses, and breweries. Germany had only about half as many companies in 1909 as Great Britain but was catching up rapidly.[6]

[6] *Ibid.*, pp. 399–400.

Wartime Financial Policy. When World War I broke out, Germany's monetary system was in excellent condition. Although the quantity of money in circulation had increased from 4.022 billion marks in 1898 to 5.553 billion marks in 1913, Germany's gold holdings had increased proportionately and the mark was as "sound as a dollar."[7] However, Germany's methods of financing the war were most unfortunate. Some 97 billion marks, or 60 per cent of total expenditures, were derived from sales of government bonds. The bonds carried interest at 5 per cent.[8] They could be called by the government at any time but had no due dates on which the government would be compelled to repay them.

The situation would not have been so bad if the other 40 per cent of total expenditures had been raised through taxation, but taxes were increased reluctantly and inefficiently. Meanwhile, the government raised large sums by disposing of Treasury bills to the banks, which were willing to invest in safe, short-term, and rediscountable assets bearing interest at $4\frac{1}{2}$ to 5 per cent. This was highly inflationary, since it furnished the government with money to spend without taking the money away from anyone else. The banks merely created deposits for the government when they took over the Treasury bills.

Wartime Inflation. The total amount of money in circulation in Germany increased from 7 billion marks to 44 billion, or sixfold, during the war. The increase in demand deposits from 4 billion marks to 19 billion was more moderate, but the total of the two items was five times as great at the end of the war as at the beginning. The effect on security prices and foreign-exchange quotations could not be seen clearly during the war, since the German stock exchanges remained closed and quotations of foreign currencies were not published. However, by the end of the war the German mark had fallen to about half its prewar value on the exchanges of neutral countries. German wholesale prices increased by about 130 per cent, according to official estimates, but this took account only of legal maximum prices and not the prices paid on black markets, which indicated more nearly what was happening to the mark.[9]

The Great Postwar Inflation. The relatively mild inflation of the war period became runaway inflation after the war. By the terms of the peace treaty, Germany lost a considerable amount of territory and population, large amounts of resources, important parts of industries, almost all her merchant marine, her colonies and investments abroad, and large amounts of railroad equipment. All this left Germany in an unbalanced position with respect to international trade and payments. Larger imports of food became necessary, minerals formerly produced at home had to be imported, and exports of other minerals had to be smaller. She

[7] J. Bithell (ed.), *Germany*, (London: Methuen & Co., Ltd., 1932), p. 148.
[8] Stolper, *op. cit.*, p. 104.
[9] *Ibid.*, pp. 107–108.

no longer received income from foreign investments or from her merchant fleet. She had to pay others to carry her goods. In addition, she had to pay heavy reparations to her erstwhile enemies to make up for war damage suffered by their civilians. Also, the important Ruhr industrial district was occupied by French and Belgian troops to enforce deliveries in kind.

In the years from 1919 through 1923, the German government could not begin to make ends meet. There was a large excess of expenditures over revenue from taxation, and the deficits were met by increasing the supply of currency. Besides making advances to the government, the Reichsbank, and other banks, made large inflationary loans to business firms. As Germany struggled with her difficulties, the value of the mark depreciated faster and faster and prices rose to unheard of levels. The German mark, which was quoted at 14 to the dollar in July, 1919, was at 493.2 to the dollar in July, 1922, and at 4,200,000,000,000 to the dollar in November, 1923.[10]

Effects of the Inflation. Early in the period of inflation, the value of the mark at home did not depreciate as rapidly as its value in terms of foreign currencies. This made German goods appear relatively cheap to the people of other countries, and Germany exported freely. Industrial production boomed and employment was high. However, the replacement costs of the goods sold always exceeded the prices received for them, since prices in Germany were going up rapidly, and in the end the great boom turned out to have been a liquidation sale at sacrifice prices. Many individuals made large gains during the inflation by borrowing at the banks and investing in physical properties or foreign assets. Later on, when the mark had depreciated, they could pay their debts to the banks with a fraction of the value of the assets they had acquired.

On the other hand, many middle-class persons were ruined by the inflation. All property claims having a value expressed in a fixed number of marks, such as government bonds, mortgages, mortgage bonds, and deposits in savings banks, became virtually valueless. Their owners were wiped out financially. For example, near the end of the inflation, a farmer could come into town and sell a dozen eggs for enough to pay off a mortgage of many thousand marks on his farm.

In time, the value of the mark in Germany became as depreciated as it was in terms of foreign currencies. Then it depreciated so rapidly that the printing presses could not keep pace, and the total real purchasing power of all German money declined sharply. But the velocity of circulation of the money was amazing, for money was the last thing that people wanted to hold for any length of time. Workers, on receiving

[10] *Ibid.*, p. 151.

their basket of paper money as their daily wage, would rush out to spend it for any goods available before returning home from work. Bachelors would even buy diapers and baby shoes. Businessmen would close their shops at noon so as to calculate new prices before making any more sales. Patrons of restaurants would be quoted a price on their meals after they finished eating rather than before they began.

Money reached the point where it could no longer perform its normal function. People resorted to direct exchange or barter. All sorts of economic calculations and relations became confused, and the economic machine was so thoroughly disrupted that industrial production fell off and unemployment increased in spite of the rising prices.

Stabilization of German Money. The inflationary period came to an end in November, 1923, when a new currency system was introduced. The Reichsbank was forbidden to make further advances on certificates or bills of the Reich Treasury. A second bank having the right to issue bank notes, the Deutsche Rentenbank, was established. It had a nominal capital of 3 billion Rentenmarks. None of the capital was paid in, for it consisted of "real estate debts" of the agricultural population and similar debt titles of industrial enterprises. The Rentenbank's claims on agriculture and industry furnished the "collateral" for the issue of 2 billion Rentenmarks in paper money. The Rentenmarks were exchangeable for the old paper marks at the ratio of 1 to 1,000,000,000,000.[11] Taxes were increased and put on the basis of the new currency, and the government balanced its budget once more. The German people accepted the new monetary system with enthusiasm, and the stabilization went off smoothly.

After 1924 Germany was back on a gold basis once more. Gold coins worth 10 and 20 new marks were legal tender. Bank notes were also legal tender and had a 40 per cent reserve composed of gold and foreign exchange. The currency system also included silver coins worth 2 and 5 marks, nickel coins of 1 mark and 50 pfennigs, and other coins with values of 1, 2, 5, and 10 pfennigs. Though the new currency system was satisfactory, the memory of the great inflation was etched deeply in the minds of the German people. Even in the Great Depression after 1929, when prices fell very low, the leaders of the government were unwilling to devalue the mark, although they used several kinds of cheap marks to stimulate international trade.

Further Concentration in Banking. In the period from 1914 to 1933, further concentration took place in German banking. Besides absorbing and controlling the smaller banks, the large banks began to amalgamate among themselves. Before the war began, the Schaafhausensche Bankverein, which dates back to 1848, was absorbed by the Disconto-Gesell-

[11] *Ibid.*, pp. 166–167.

schaft. After the war, the Mitteldeutsche Privatbank and the Commerz-
and Discontbank joined forces to form the Commerz and Privatbank.
The Darmstadter Bank amalgamated with the Nationalbank fur Deutsch-
land to form the Darmstadter and Nationalbank in 1921. Two of the
large D-banks, the Deutsche Bank and the Disconto-Gesellschaft, combined in 1929, and the Dresdner Bank took over the Darmstadter Bank
in 1931. The result was a virtual banking monopoly in the hands of a
few banks.

Dangers in the Banking Situation. After doing a lively business during
World War I, the German banks lost most of their invested capital during the great inflation. The prosperity after 1923 brought a large increase
in the business of the banks. They continued as co-partners in industry
and financed the long-term capital needs of industrial concerns, but now
their position was less secure than before. Having lost much of their
own capital, they were now risking the depositors' money in financing
risky ventures. The ratios of capital to deposits were low, and small
losses would wipe out the banks' capital and make it impossible to pay
off depositors.

Large foreign loans were received by Germany during the 1920s and
almost half of them took the form of short-term credits. While these
funds could be demanded on short notice by foreign creditors, the German banks proceeded to invest them in industry like any other funds.
The Reichsbank could do little to control the other German banks and
reduce these dangers. There were almost no legal regulations for banks
in Germany. They could do almost any kind of banking business, and
amounts of paid-in capital and ratios of reserves to deposits were not
specified.

The Banking Crisis. In the depression after 1929, the German banks
were hit hard. The banking crisis of 1931 was precipitated by the success
of the National Socialist Party in the elections of September, 1930, which
frightened foreign creditors, and by the failure of the Austrian Creditanstalt, a large and old international bank. Foreign governments tried
to help out with direct credits to the Reichsbank and with a one-year
moratorium on reparations payments, but the crisis arrived anyhow. The
Darmstadter Bank suspended payments on July 13, 1931. Fatal runs on
other banks threatened, and the government proclaimed a "bank holiday" which lasted for several weeks.

The government decided to guarantee the deposits of the Darmstadter
Bank and to invest in a reorganization of the large banks. Their paid-up
capital was reduced sharply, and new capital was furnished either directly by the government or through the Reichsbank. All the banks except the old Berliner Handelsgesellschaft, which survived the crisis on
its own power, became government institutions, although they remained

nominally private. The government sponsored the amalgamation of the Darmstadter Bank and the Dresdner Bank and declared a moratorium on the payment of foreign short-term credits. This moratorium had to be renewed several times.

MONEY, CREDIT, AND BANKING UNDER NATIONAL SOCIALISM

When the National Socialists took over in 1933, the German government had large investments in the major banks. Either directly or through the Gold Discount Bank (a government institution set up originally to help finance foreign trade) the government owned large amounts of bank stock and controlled about 70 per cent of all German corporate banks. However, the National Socialist government decided against nationalizing the banks and subsequently returned most of its bank stock to private ownership.

Control Agencies for Banking. While the German banks became privately owned and operated once more, they were subject to strict government supervision. In the first place, the Reichsbank became a tool of the government under National Socialism. A revised law stated that the Reichsbank must act for the attainment of the objectives of the National Socialist government. Ownership of shares in the bank was limited to German citizens and legal persons or concerns within the country. Before the end of World War II, about 96 per cent of its assets consisted of government obligations.

A Credit Supervisory Board, set up late in 1934, was later transformed into an independent Reich Board for Credit Control, with power to act as an executive agency under the Minister of Economic Affairs. The authority of the board extended to all banks and credit institutions, including the Reichsbank and the Gold Discount Bank. It had the power to control combinations of banks and the number of new banks and branches. It could refuse to license banks which seemed unnecessary under local economic conditions or whose managers and owners lacked necessary training, experience, character, or other qualifications. The board also had extensive powers of audit and examination and could require banks to furnish any needed information.

Banking was one of the National Groups under the Estate of Industry and Trade, the National Economic Chamber, the Ministry of Economic Affairs, and the General Council for the War Economy. Like the other National Groups, that for banking was divided into a number of Economic Groups and Branch Groups. Bankers were also represented in Provincial Economic Chambers, local Chambers of Industry and Commerce, and the Cooperative Council of Chambers of Industry and Commerce.

The Control of Bank Loans. The banking law of 1934 provided detailed regulations concerning the extension of bank credit and severely limited the loans which banks could make to individual firms. Ostensibly, these regulations were to prevent banks from getting too tied up with individual firms, to keep several banks from making large loans to the same firms, and to compel banks to distribute small credits among a large number of firms. Actually, "exceptions" to most of the regulations enabled large firms to get their credit needs cared for, and the regulations did not apply to credits extended to the government or guaranteed by the government. The regulations made it difficult for new firms to establish themselves or expand on the basis of bank credit. As a result, such firms would want to sell securities, but to do so they would have to secure the government's permission. The regulations had the effect of directing bank credit toward the ends desired by the state.

The Control of Bank Reserves. The banking law gave the Board for Credit Control the power to determine bank reserves. The cash reserves of commercial banks were set at rather low levels, while secondary reserves were set relatively high. The banks were expected to keep their secondary reserves largely in the form of bonds issued by the national, state, and local governments. The reserves of savings banks had to be kept at the banks and consisted largely of government bonds. The banks, under these regulations, furnished a large and ready market for government bonds, and they were also active in promoting the sale of bonds to other investors.

The Banker as Agent of the Nazi State. Although the government gave the appearance of not interfering in the daily operations of the banks, the actual position of the banker was not enviable. Each banker was practically a state official as well as a private enterpriser, and he was likely to have a party man watching over him at all times. When instructed by the government, the banker had to advise his customers to buy government bonds or the securities of new firms which were being set up to produce ersatz materials under the national self-sufficiency program. He was required to hold the official optimistic view of state finances. He had to try to restrain individuals who wanted to withdraw their deposits for private uses, report individuals who made large-scale withdrawals, and inform the government concerning customers who had large liquid balances.

Control of Long-Term Interest Rates. The National Socialist government interfered with investment credit and banking activities in many ways. For one thing, it carried on a successful campaign to lower the rates of interest on long-term funds. Many security issues were converted into other issues bearing lower rates of interest. High rates of interest had operated against the borrowing of funds for long-term purposes by private firms, had placed a burden on debtors and government units, and had made it difficult for the government to convert short-term borrowing into long-term.

The government also limited severely the dividends which companies could pay on their securities. Dividends declared in excess of government limitations usually had to be invested, directly or indirectly, in government bonds. These surplus dividends were supposed to be returned to the companies at a later time in the form of cash or non-interest-bearing tax certificates which could be used in the payment of taxes after a certain date.

The limitations on corporate dividends were intended to facilitate government financing and to make firms finance long-term capital investment out of their own earnings. Low dividend rates on corporate securities increased the relative attractiveness of government bonds bearing moderate rates of interest. The program also permitted control of the distribution of long-term funds among industries. Plants producing goods for civilian uses were not allowed to float new security issues and could not make earnings large enough to finance expansion. Plants producing armaments could avoid investment in government bonds by ploughing all earnings in excess of 6 per cent back into the business. If such plants tried to pay out a larger part of earnings as dividends, the dividends over 6 per cent of earnings went to the government, which could use the funds to finance extensions of production facilities. Finally, the securities of firms which could not earn the dividends permitted by law tended to drop in price, and this made it difficult for them to obtain new funds.

Complete Governmental Control of Investment Credit. The German government was in complete control of investment credit operations, and there was no danger that it would lack funds as long as business firms or private individuals had cash or other liquid assets. Regardless of the attitude of the government toward the payment of its own obligations, it could continue to take over private funds. It could forbid the payment of private debts or decrease the interest rates on them and take for its own purposes the funds which would have been devoted to them. Savings banks, insurance companies, and municipalities were required to invest portions of their liquid funds in government bonds or treasury bills. The proportion was sometimes as high as 75 per cent for municipalities. Before 1938 insurance companies needed government permission to make private loans even though the loans were secured by first mortgages, and after 1938 private loans by insurance companies were forbidden.

The national government planned to use directly some 80 to 90 per cent of available long-term funds, and the remainder had to go into

projects approved by the government. The development of the government monopoly of investment funds is indicated by the fact that, whereas
government bonds made up about 28 per cent of new issues of securities
in 1928, they amounted to over 89 per cent in 1938.[12] The investment
funds obtained by the government were used to develop only those activities which were in line with the general aims of the government. Any
industries which were not essential to those aims had to finance themselves or go without funds.

Under these circumstances, the activities of German stock exchanges
fell to a low level under National Socialism. On the basis of tax receipts
from sales on the stock exchanges, transactions on the exchanges in 1937
were only about 20 per cent of what they had been ten years before.[13]
This was due in large part to the drying up of security issues by private
companies, but direct government regulation also played a part. The
stock exchanges were regulated by a decree of March, 1934. Each exchange had to obtain a charter from the national government, and the
president and other members of exchange boards were appointed by
the appropriate chambers of commerce.

Quotations on the exchanges were made by official brokers who were
appointed and recalled by state governments. All stock transactions had
to be made on a cash basis, and "blocked balances" in financial institutions could be used to purchase stocks only if they arose out of the sale
of stocks. The number of stock exchanges was reduced from 21 to 9,
and only the larger issues of stock were listed on the exchanges. An issue
had to have a nominal value of 1,500,000 marks to be listed on the Berlin
exchange. Since stock issues had to come out in units of 1,000 marks,
individuals of small means found it impossible to buy and sell them
on the required cash basis.

There was a considerable investment of long-term funds in Germany
which involved no issues of securities either by private firms or by the
government. The government insisted frequently that industrial firms
expand their facilities by reinvesting a part of their earnings. In other
cases, firms were ordered to construct dugouts and bomb shelters, put
in lunchroom or toilet facilities for their workers, or install new types of
machinery necessary to the processing of ersatz raw materials.

Firms were often reluctant to increase their production facilities to
meet needs of a temporary character, but government plants were likely
to be established if they failed to follow orders. Moreover, if they accumulated financial reserves and failed to keep them hidden, the gov-

[12] G. Reimann, *The Vampire Economy* (New York: Vanguard Press, Inc., 1939),
p. 165.
[13] M. Y. Sweezy, *The Structure of the Nazi Economy* (Cambridge, Mass.: Harvard
University Press, 1941), p. 144.

ernment was likely to send out inspectors to look over their accounts. If any errors or false statements were found, the firms were likely to be penalized by fines which approximated the size of their financial reserves.

Firms were reluctant to operate beyond normal capacity because of increased costs and wear and tear on production facilities. They never knew when they would be allowed to replace or even repair their equipment. In 1938 capital construction ran about 45 per cent beyond the 1929 level, but replacements were actually less than in 1929.[14] Production equipment was allowed to decline considerably; witness the decline in numbers of locomotives, freight cars, and passenger cars which took place in the 1930s in spite of a general increase in transportation needs.

Besides being required to make investments in expanding their own production facilities, German firms with large earnings were often compelled to invest funds in new plants for quite different purposes, such as the production of ersatz materials. The Krupp firm was required to underwrite an artificial rubber factory and to furnish financial assistance to the Krupp firm in Austria, which was in the machine-tool business. The I. G. Farbenindustrie, a chemical concern, which was already helping the government by operating one plant producing synthetic gasoline, was once required to finance two other large plants.[15]

When the Hermann Göring Iron Works was set up, the government furnished 270 million marks out of a capitalization of 400 million marks. The remainder of the stock, without voting rights, was assigned compulsorily to other iron and steel firms, and to firms in other industries. Even the workers in some enterprises were required to buy 50 marks' worth of stock each.[16] This new iron and steel enterprise furnished a type of investment which established firms and private individuals would ordinarily have avoided. It had to make use of ore of low quality and with too high a content of silicic acid, so that new types of blast furnaces, more coke, and other expensive changes were required. Finally, the government itself sometimes underwrote the construction of desired plants in fields which were too risky for private investment. One such case was the cheap "people's automobile"—a project which was interrupted by the war.

In addition to these positive requirements as to what German firms should do with their earnings, there were many types of negative interference. We have already noted the limitations on dividends. Firms in some industries were also forbidden to reinvest their earnings or to expand their productive facilities. In many industries the construction of

[14] Reimann, *op. cit.*, p. 139.
[15] *Ibid.*, pp. 125–129.
[16] *Ibid.*, pp. 129–131.

new plants and the establishment of new firms could not be undertaken without permission from the government.

The Changed Position of German Banks. As the government increased its influence in the field of long-term financing, the importance of the banks as financiers of industry declined steadily. In 1941 the five leading German banks held less than half as much cash as in 1929 and their advances to business enterprises amounted to less than two-fifths the 1929 total. The amounts of bills and securities other than Reich securities were small and not very different from the 1929 levels, but the holdings of Reich securities had increased by almost 2,000 per cent over 1929.[17] These banks were turning into depositories for government securities. They not only helped to market government bonds but had to take an increasing amount themselves.

On the whole, government control of commercial and investment credit and banking probably eliminated some waste of funds and kept funds from being used for purposes which seemed undesirable to the state. And the Nazis did not do much tinkering with the monetary system. On the other hand, no definite agency, such as a national investment board, existed to plan Germany's investments. The uses into which the government directed funds probably were not at all suited to the desires of the German citizens as individuals.

Wartime Finances. During World War II, the German government operated at a deficit. In the period from 1940 through 1942, total expenditures of 278 billion marks were covered by taxation only to the extent of 109 billion marks. Some funds were borrowed outside the country, and conquered territories were required to pay occupation costs. About 113 billion marks were borrowed inside the country, most of it from the banks.[18]

It was characteristic of German methods of war finance that the public was never asked to subscribe to a war loan during the war. Government control of production and investment, rigid rationing, and heavy taxes ensured that individuals and corporations would not have much surplus income. When surplus income did exist, it would find its way to the various credit institutions where the government could reach it.

In the later years of the war the government depended more on borrowing, and an increasing part was on a short-term basis. In the second half of 1944 about four-fifths of all borrowing was short-term and large sums were obtained from the Reichsbank and the commercial banks. Such methods result in large net additions to the supply of bank money in use. The inflation of the currency and the decline in the value of the

---

[17] J. Kuczynski, *Germany: Economic and Labour Conditions under Fascism* (New York: International Publishers Co., Inc., 1945), p. 84.

[18] *Fascism in Action*, 80th Cong., 1st Sess., H. Doc. 401, 1947, p. 65.

mark were largely concealed because prices were officially held in check by the price freeze of 1936, but there is no doubt that the value of the mark fell considerably.

THE POSTWAR PERIOD

In the early postwar years the mark continued to decline in value. Official prices of goods were stable, but there were very few goods for sale in the stores. The prices paid in black-market transactions were terrific. A pair of shoes might sell for 50 times the official price, while a pound of butter might bring 120 to 150 times the official price. German money largely lost its function as a medium of exchange, and barter transactions were common.

Trade by barter was forbidden by law, so the barter transactions did not appear on the books of the sellers and did not produce any taxes for the government. In any case, the tax rates were so high that the sellers would have found it ruinous to hand in honest returns. The barter trade also made it difficult to determine the total volume of exchange transactions, and information on this was necessary for economic planning. The money situation was an obstacle to economic recovery in the postwar period. Something needed to be done about it.

The Currency Reform of 1948. Currency reform was finally accomplished as of June 20, 1948. According to the terms of the reform, for every 100 Reichsmarks the holder was to receive 5 Deutsche marks for free circulation and 5 Deutsche marks credited to a blocked account. These blocked accounts were freed as of October 4, 1948. In the end, then, 1 new Deutsche mark was received for every 10 old Reichsmarks.

The currency reform had favorable and unfavorable results. The savings of the people were reduced to 10 per cent of their former nominal amounts, and this was serious for people who were unable to work and were living off their savings. For the country as a whole, some 450 billion marks' worth of government debts and other obligations were wiped out. This was hard on the German banks, for they were loaded with government obligations.

However, the people were given a new and presumably reliable monetary unit. With 90 per cent of the money supply destroyed, price controls could be removed and prices allowed to find their own levels. Rationing could also be discontinued. Goods reappeared in the stores as if by magic, and shopkeepers, farmers, and others became willing to swap goods for money once more.

The prices of goods in terms of the new marks became higher than the official prices in terms of the old Reichsmarks, while wage rates were held down rigorously. This made it difficult for the workers to buy the goods in the stores, but it gave the workers a strong incentive to work hard and increase their incomes. Business firms were also stimulated to increase their outputs. These developments were depended upon to keep prices from rising too far.

Recent Developments. The results of the currency reform seem to have been generally good. The money supply of Western Germany in 1953 was approximately double what it had been in 1948, but production had increased by leaps and bounds and prices have remained stable or have even moderated somewhat. Wholesale prices, for example, increased from an index number of 100 in 1948 to 165 in 1952, but fell off to 160 in 1953 and 158 in April, 1954.[19] Meanwhile, wages have increased from an index of 100 in 1950 to one of 130 in 1953.

With the monetary situation stabilized, the various taxes have yielded something like the revenue to be expected of them. The financial position of the Western German government has improved considerably. After operating at small deficits in 1950 and 1951, it enjoyed a surplus of 739,-000,000 marks in 1952 and one of 1,490,000,000 in 1953. Western Germany has a national debt once more, but it amounted to only 1,200,000,-000 marks in 1953. Such a debt was insignificant, since national income was running at 103,000,000,000 marks.[20]

When the currency reform first became effective, the extension of bank credit to business enterprises was forbidden. The purpose was to force every businessman to sell his goods, but it created immediate problems in primary industries, in capital-goods industries, and in the construction industry. Later, the restriction had to be removed, for credits were necessary if production was to be expanded in some lines and restricted in others. As time went on, the banks issued lavish short-term credits but at high interest rates. Many firms so needed capital funds that they used such short-term credits for investment in fixed capital assets. This was risky, but it seems to have paid off and there have been few bankruptcies.

On the whole, capital investment has been high. In 1952, when the national income of Western Germany amounted to only 90 billion marks, investment was at the rate of 23 billion marks annually.[21] Much of the investment has been financed in recent years out of the large earnings of business enterprises. Savings by private individuals have also started to rise. By 1952 private savings had reached 4 billion marks.[22] This amount was not large, but it was a remarkable sign of confidence on the part of a people who had lost most of their savings twice in a generation.

[19] *The Economist*, July 24, 1954, p. 317.
[20] *International Financial Statistics*, August, 1954, pp. 96, 97.
[21] *The Economist*, Oct. 18, 1952, p. 212.
[22] *Ibid.*

QUESTIONS FOR STUDY

1. Why did Germany have no unified monetary system before 1871? Why did the banking system develop for the most part only in the second half of the nineteenth century?

2. How did the Reichsbank come into existence? What were its main functions as a central bank? How did its nature and functions compare with those of the Bank of England?

3. What favorable or unfavorable implications do you see in the fact that the large German banks did a combined commercial and investment banking business?

4. How did the German government finance its expenditures in World War I? What were the results? Why did inflation become ruinous after the war? What were the effects of the great inflation?

5. How was the National Socialist government of Germany able to control commercial banking completely while leaving it under private ownership and operation? How and to what extent were investment-credit activities controlled?

6. How did the German government finance its expenditures during World War II? How did the results differ from those that occurred during World War I?

7. What was the currency reform of 1948? Was it successful or unsuccessful? What have been the results?

CHAPTER 30

LABOR

The rapid growth of industry, increases in agricultural production, an extensive network of transportation, and an elaborate system of money, credit, and banking are all desirable developments. They are signs of economic progress. However, an economic system is not operating satisfactorily unless the gains from these developments are widely shared among the citizens. The workers and their families make up a large part of the population in any modern economy, and the question of how these people fare is important in analyzing such an economy. The workers are vitally interested in wages, hours, and working conditions, but they are also concerned with social security measures, the availability of employment, labor organizations, and real wages and standards of living.

LABOR BEFORE 1871

Slow Development of the Labor Class. A wage-earning class was slow to develop in Germany. Most workers in the first half of the nineteenth century worked for themselves or worked under a loose arrangement with a capitalistic employer. Many persons whose main occupation was agriculture did some manufacturing work on the side, and persons who worked for wages in manufacturing were part-time farmers in many cases. Labor was far from being a class-conscious group.

The rapid construction of roads and railroads did not get under way until after 1840, the first large wave of company promotions came along in the 1850s, the main banks were established between 1847 and the early 1870s, and Germany did not really come into her own as an industrial power until the founding of the Empire in 1871. It was probably to be expected that development of a German labor movement would wait upon these events. The growth of labor unions, the use of collective bargaining and collective agreements, the beginnings of social insurance, and even freedom of entry into various occupations did not appear until after 1871.

Guild Survivals and the Labor Class. The survival of the guilds in Germany was an obstacle to the development of the labor movement as well as to the development of modern industry. In the early 1800s freedom of entry to occupations was limited to a small number of trades and a few places. When the Prussian government got around to dealing with the question in 1835, a commission considered it for ten years and then recommended that much of the system should be retained. Under the Ordinance of 1845, some forty trades were specified in which no one except a full-fledged member of a guild could take on an apprentice. Most of the German states retained the guild system for most branches of handicraft production, conceded freedom of entry only for a few industries, and had the system supervised by the police. In some places, no business could be operated without the approval of local authorities, and approval was normally extended only to master workmen.

Another Prussian law of 1849 made membership in a recognized guild or proof of competence before a commission a condition for founding a business in some seventy fields, including most handicrafts. Storekeepers could sell goods only if they were masters of the trades that produced them, and factory owners were restricted as to the number of guild-trained workmen they could employ. However, freedom of entry into occupations gradually developed in spite of the law, and many businesses were carried on that nobody was legally qualified to run. The legal movement toward freedom of entry was not resumed until the 1860s, and it culminated successfully only with the founding of the Empire.

LABOR, 1871–1933

The Changing Distribution of the Labor Force. As German industry expanded after 1871, the labor class began to take definite shape and increased rapidly in numbers. The number of gainfully employed reached 16,885,000 in 1882. Agriculture and forestry employed the greatest number of workers and the largest proportion of the total, as shown in Table 30-1, but industry and crafts was not far behind. Twenty-five years later, in 1907, some striking changes had occurred. The number of workers in agriculture and forestry had increased by almost 1,500,000, but the proportion had declined from 42.3 to 34.0 per cent. On the other hand, there had been an increase of about 4,000,000 in industry and crafts, and the proportion had increased from 35.5 to 39.7 per cent. There was also a large increase in the number employed in commerce and communications, and a sizeable decline in the number in domestic service. The total number of the gainfully employed increased by almost 50 per cent from 1882 to 1907.

Table 30-1. Number of Gainfully Employed, by Occupations, 1882 and 1907

Occupations	1882		1907	
	Number	Per cent	Number	Per cent
Agriculture and forestry..........	7,135,000	42.3	8,557,000	34.0
Industry and crafts..............	5,988,000	35.5	9,981,000	39.7
Commerce and communications...	1,420,000	8.4	3,441,000	13.7
Public and private services.......	984,000	5.8	1,712,000	6.8
Domestic service................	1,358,000	8.0	1,465,000	5.8
Total......................	16,885,000	100.0	25,156,000	100.0

SOURCE: G. Stolper, *German Economy, 1870–1940* (New York: Reynal & Hitchcock, Inc., 1940), p. 41.

The Growth of Labor Unions. The first important development of labor unions among the German workers also occurred in the period after 1871. The formation of labor unions in Germany had been prevented by legislation for many years. Saxony in 1861 was the first state to repeal the antiorganization laws. In 1869 the North German Federation adopted a Trades Code which permitted workers to organize, and this code was made the law of the Empire in 1871.

Unlike the labor unions of England and the United States, those of Germany had a strong political flavor. The so-called Free Unions, the most important group, were affiliated with the Social Democratic (moderate socialist) party. They were organized by Socialists for the most part, and their programs had a socialist tone. The Christian Unions, which had been founded with the idea of enabling the church to maintain its hold on the workers, were assoicated with the Center party. A third group, the Hirsch-Duncker Unions, were allied with liberal or progressive parties.

The government looked upon the Socialists with disfavor and in 1878 directed strong legislation against them. The party was driven underground for a number of years, although it gained rather than lost in strength, and the development of the closely associated labor unions was retarded. It was not until 1890, when the legislation was withdrawn, that most of the unions were free to grow as fast as they could. Even in 1895 there were only about 269,000 union members, although the male industrial population was approaching 8 million. The number of members reached 1 million in 1902 and 2 million in 1906.[1] In 1913, just before World War I, the German unions had 3,293,000 members, including

[1] J. H. Clapham, *The Economic Development of France and Germany, 1815–1914* (London: Cambridge University Press, 1923), p. 329.

2,525,000 in Free Unions, 342,000 in the Christian Unions, 107,000 in the Hirsch-Duncker Unions, and 319,000 in independent groups.[2]

The German unions went in for propaganda, programs, congresses, union statistics, and a labor press, but collective bargaining lagged. The rapidity of German industrial development had brought a social cleavage between workers and employers, and the unions were suspect because of their association with radical political groups. The employers wanted to remain complete bosses in their own establishments, and the workers were none too anxious to negotiate with employers who, according to socialist teaching, were on their way out. Consequently, collective bargaining and collective agreements were of little significance before 1900, and it was not until the period 1906–1914 that they came to have a place in labor-management relations in Germany similar to the place they had in England a whole generation earlier.

Labor relations between the unions and the parallel organizations of employers were carried on with practically no intervention by the government in the period before World War I. German industry was expanding rapidly, and cycles in economic activity were mild. Relations between labor and management were peaceful on the whole.

Social Insurance. Imperial Germany was a pioneer in the field of social insurance. In 1883, only five years after the enactment of the antisocialist legislation, the first social insurance law in Germany provided for compulsory health insurance for workers and their families. In the next year, accident insurance was organized. The addition of old-age and sickness insurance in 1889 completed the social insurance picture in Imperial Germany. Unemployment, in view of the expansion of the economy, was not regarded as particularly dangerous, and unemployment insurance did not come into effect until 1926.

In case the worker or his wife or child became sick, medical attention, hospital service, medicine, and financial aid became available. When he had an accident, all medical costs were cared for by the insurance system. In the event of partial or total disablement, and after reaching age seventy, he received a pension. If he died prematurely, his wife and children were eligible for an annuity. Accident insurance was paid for by the employer. The cost of health insurance was shared by employers and employees. The government, as well as workers and employers, contributed to the fund for old age and sickness.

The spirit of the social insurance system was more paternal than anything else in the early days. The government was conferring favors instead of giving the workers their just due. In fact, Chancellor Bismarck was as much interested in deflating the Socialists and stealing their

[2] G. Stolper, *German Economy, 1870–1940* (New York: Reynal & Hitchcock, Inc., 1940), p. 90.

thunder as he was in benefiting the workers themselves. The Socialists were not highly enthusiastic about the social insurance system at first, but they came to accept it.

Other Protective Legislation. Long before 1914 the German workers had the benefit of other protective legislation. The first important law in 1891 limited the working day to eleven hours for women and ten hours for children. It prohibited night work for women and children, and any kind of work in industry and trade for children under fourteen years of age. It made Sunday free and the observance of various hygiene rules obligatory. Other protective legislation followed.

Wages, Hours, and Working Conditions. Legislation to protect the workers was needed. Of course, the workers made some gains in wages and standards of living in a period of unprecedented expansion such as that between 1871 and 1914, but their share was meager. As in other countries at the time, working hours tended to be very long, wages were often low if not actually exploitative, and the conditions under which the employees worked could be almost anything that the employers made them.

Labor during World War I. The position of labor unions in Germany improved during World War I. Although unions had been legal for many years, they had been regarded as revolutionary because of their association with the Social Democratic party, which still pretended to be a revolutionary party. During the war, the Social Democratic party cooperated with the government to a considerable extent, and labor organizations were better regarded. Their influence was also increased by the wartime labor shortage, though they did not take unreasonable advantage of the situation. The unions entered into an agreement with the employers to end all labor strife during the war. In the last days of the war, however, strikes became fairly common.

The war period also saw the beginning of unemployment relief in Germany. When the war broke out it was thought that a serious volume of unemployment might result. A number of cities began to dole out relief early in the war, and after December, 1914, the German government began to furnish the cities with funds. Relief was given only when genuine need could be shown. This system was retained until 1926.

Most industries in Germany maintained a high level of output and employment during the war, but there were some exceptions, especially among the consumer-goods industries. The textile industry was badly handicapped by a shortage of raw materials. Though many employees had been lost to the armed forces, there was much unemployment in the industry, and wages failed to keep pace with the cost of living. The government tried to secure employment for the workers and divide the employment opportunities equitably among them. Workers could be discharged in the textile industry only in exceptional cases, and working hours were reduced. Finally, relief payments were made available to needy textile workers, including the employed.

Although Germany had maximum-price legislation and a great degree of government control of the economy, prices rose considerably during the war. Wages lagged well behind the rising prices. Unrest developed, and the government not only approved but also instigated negotiations between the employers and the unions. Minimum wages were sometimes required of employers who obtained government contracts, and the government on occasion set up conciliation committees in the factories.

In December, 1916, when the government sought complete control over the economy of Germany under the Hindenburg program, the Social Democrats were willing to agree to the militarization of factory workers only if the workers' interests would be protected by workers' councils. Workers' committees were elected by secret ballot in every plant with 50 or more workers. Conciliation committees with equal representation for workers and employers under the chairmanship of official conciliators were also set up to pass on wage questions and hand down binding decisions.

The Great Inflation. In the early days of the great inflation following World War I, the German workers did not suffer greatly. Production was booming, employment was plentiful, and wages did not lag much behind rising prices. However, in the later stages of the inflation, the workers discovered that they could remain employed only at sharply decreasing real wages. They devised many ingenious schemes for wage payment to keep their wages abreast of soaring prices, but in spite of everything, wages lagged further and further behind. By the fall of 1923, the real value of hourly wages in Berlin had fallen as much as 80 per cent by comparison with July, 1914, for some classes of workers.[3] And in the end, falling production and increasing unemployment were added to the woes of the workers.

Labor in the 1920s. The remaining years of the 1920s, after the great inflation came to an end in November, 1923, were relatively good ones for German labor. The period was prosperous and production increased once more. Wage and salary incomes increased from 34.9 to 43 billion marks between 1925 and 1929, or from 1,617 to 2,036 marks per capita. Real wages stood at 110 in 1929 and 116 in 1930 on the basis of the prewar level as 100. Labor unions had about double their prewar membership and bargained actively with employers. Almost the only disturbing factor was the continued high level of unemployment, which seldom fell much below 1,000,000 and amounted to 1,915,025 in 1929.[4]

The German workers were well protected for the most part. Maximum

[3] F. K. Bieliegk, *Statistical Truth* (London: Hutchinson & Co., Ltd., 1942), p. 28.
[4] *Ibid.*, pp. 52, 56.

hours and minimum wages had been set up. Women and children were thoroughly protected. The eight-hour day had been proclaimed as the legal maximum. The social insurance system had long been complete except for unemployment insurance, and it had been extended to cover more classes of workers. A scheme for unemployment insurance, based on taxes on wages to be paid by employers and employees, was introduced in 1926.

Before the war, collective agreements between labor and management had been regarded as private affairs, but this was no longer true. The government had become interested in seeing that labor and management reached collective agreements. Government mediation authorities had the duty of intervening in difficult cases to see whether the parties could be induced to reach a compromise. This much was desirable, but the powers of the government went much further. It could make a collective agreement binding on employers and employees in a given industry and district even though they had taken no part in drawing up the agreement. Moreover, when a collective agreement could not be reached, the government mediator could hand down a decision. If it was accepted by either party, it became binding for both labor and management as if it were a voluntary collective agreement.

This was originally intended to be an exceptional procedure, but it became the standard practice. The political wages set by the government came in for severe criticism. In the prosperous years of the late 1920s, the government was attacked by employers and economic journalists for raising wages too high, while, on the other hand, union leaders sometimes blamed the government for their inability to get higher pay for the workers. As the depression came on, workers blamed the government for letting wages decline, while others criticized the government because of a wage policy that prolonged and intensified the depression.

Some 32,009,000 persons were gainfully employed in Germany in 1925. This was a fair increase over the 25,156,000 employed in 1907. The distribution of the workers had changed somewhat, as shown in Table 30-2. The workers in agriculture and forestry increased by over a million persons, but their proportion declined from 34.0 to 30.5. The workers in industry and crafts, and those in commerce and communications, gained both absolutely and relatively. Those in public and private service just held their own as a proportion of the total. Workers in domestic service declined.

The Great Depression. After 1929 the position of German labor deteriorated for several years. Unemployment increased from an average of 1,915,025 in 1929 to one of 5,579,858 in 1932. The number gainfully employed was slightly larger in 1933 than in 1925, but in a growing population, this did not keep unemployment from mounting swiftly.

Table 30-2. Number of Gainfully Employed, by Occupations, 1907 and 1925

Occupations	1907		1925	
	Number	Per cent	Number	Per cent
Agriculture and forestry..........	8,557,000	34.0	9,763,000	30.5
Industry and crafts..............	9,981,000	39.7	13,479,000	42.1
Commerce and communications...	3,441,000	13.7	5,185,000	16.2
Public and private services.......	1,712,000	6.8	2,188,000	6.8
Domestic service................	1,465,000	5.8	1,394,000	4.4
Total.......................	25,156,000	100.0	32,009,000	100.0

SOURCE: G. Stolper, *German Economy, 1870–1940* (New York; Reynal & Hitchcock, Inc., 1940), p. 41.

The decline in wages was less spectacular than the increase in unemployment. With 1928 as 100, wages declined from 107 in 1930 to 86 in 1932. The decline in real wages was more drastic, however, for the cost of living fell less rapidly than wages.[5]

LABOR UNDER NATIONAL SOCIALISM

All matters pertaining to labor were brought under strict government control under National Socialism. The first step was the liquidation of labor organizations. This was accomplished by simple and direct methods. In many cases, union leaders were jailed as enemies of the people, union offices and facilities were broken up, and union buildings, funds, enterprises, and activities were taken over by the government. The Nazis eliminated trade unions, collective bargaining, strikes and lockouts, and class warfare in general.

The Labor Front. The next step was an official government organization for workers and employers. A Labor Front was set up almost as soon as the Nazis came into power, though the decree providing for it was not issued until October, 1934. The Labor Front was anything but a true labor organization. It was more nearly a section of the National Socialist party. Its leader, Robert Ley, was a high party man, and his appointees were party members. The territorial organization of the Labor Front was the same as that of the party. Membership in the Labor Front was voluntary in theory but compulsory in practice. In normal times it had about 30 million members—five times the former membership of the labor unions.

The nonunion character of the Labor Front was indicated by two

[5] *Ibid.*, pp. 56, 61.

other factors. First, employers and professional men, as well as workers, belonged to it. The National Economic Chamber, the National Agricultural Estate, the National Transportation Council, and the National Chamber of Culture all "belonged" to the Labor Front. The organization was a gigantic national "company union." Second, it made no attempt to improve the economic position of its employee members by collective bargaining. It did not seem to be greatly concerned with employer-employee relations. It operated business enterprises which had formerly been operated by German labor unions. It furnished vocational training and cultural education for the workers, provided assistance for members in times of emergency, assisted in settling labor disputes, attempted to promote "understanding and solidarity" between workers and employers, sponsored the "people's car" and the "people's tractor," and propagated the Strength through Joy and Beauty of Work movements.

The Determination of Wages, Hours, and Working Conditions. There was no fuss about collective bargaining and collective agreements under National Socialism. The National Labor Law said that in each plant the enterpriser, as "leader" of the establishment, and the salaried employees and wage earners, as "followers," must work together for the commonweal of the people and the state. The leader had authority in the conduct of all affairs of his enterprise as long as he did not break any laws. The leader might make decisions over against the followers in the fixing of all labor conditions.

By himself, or after conferring with his Confidential Council in plants employing 20 or more workers, the employer laid down ordinances binding on all members of the enterprise. These ordinances covered such matters as the beginning and end of the working day, times for the payment of wages, principles for calculating piece rates, the collection of fines, the grounds for discharge without notice (where permitted), and the utilization of forfeited pay. Except as he was limited by general laws or decrees or was directly interfered with by government officials, the employer was a law unto himself.

The Settlement of Disputes and Protection of Employees. Several agencies were available for protecting the workers and settling labor disputes, for the Nazi leaders insisted on industrial peace. The Confidential Councils were supposed to protect the workers' interests in establishments employing 20 or more workers. According to the original method of selection, the employer, after consultation with the local party leader, would select a panel of "reliable" workers to be candidates for the Confidential Council. These were voted on by the workers and had to be accepted or rejected as a group. If the group was rejected, the Labor Trustee of that district would appoint the Confidential Council for the plant. In practice, the employers' candidates were so frequently rejected that the electoral feature of the system was eliminated after 1935.

The Confidential Council was supposed to act as a buffer between the employer and the employees. It was expected to discuss measures to increase efficiency, to assist in the making and enforcement of the works regulations provided by the employer, to discuss the fixing of fines (such as those for lateness, uncleanliness, or smoking in the plant), and to assist in settling disputes. The Confidential Councils had no power except that of appealing to the Labor Trustees, and since the members were hand-picked, they probably had little influence on the employers' actions.

A more important limitation on the employers was that their regulations concerning hours, wages, and working conditions had to conform to the general rules laid down by the Labor Trustees. There was one Labor Trustee in each of the 14 industrial districts of the country. The Labor Trustees were not workers or workers' representatives but were political appointees. They were supposed to maintain industrial peace in their districts and to settle labor questions which could not be settled within the individual firms.

The Labor Trustees appointed, removed, and supervised the constitution and activities of the Confidential Councils, settling any disputes that arose; decided appeals from the Confidential Councils; quashed employers' rulings and issued substitute ordinances; gave or withheld approval of mass dismissals by employers; laid down general rules and supervised their observance; issued wage schedules; cooperated with the Courts of Social Honor; and kept the government and party supplied with detailed information.

The highest agencies set up to pass upon relations between employers and employees and to protect each group from the other were the Courts of Social Honor. There was one court in each of the 14 industrial districts of the country. Each court was composed of a member of the judiciary as chairman, a leader of a business (employer), and a member of a Confidential Council. The courts could punish offenses against social honor by warnings, reprimands, and fines not to exceed 10,000 marks, and by depriving an owner or manager of the right to do business, depriving a member of a Confidential Council of office, and dismissing a workman or employee.

According to the Act for the Organization of National Labor, social honor was offended (1) when the owner of an undertaking, the leader of an enterprise, or any person in a position of supervision abused his authority by maliciously exploiting the labor of his followers or wounding their sense of honor; (2) when a follower endangered industrial peace by maliciously provoking other followers, and in particular when a member of the Confidential Council interfered unduly in the conduct of the establishment or maliciously disturbed the community spirit within the enterprise; (3) when a member of the plant community repeatedly made frivolous and unjustified complaints to the Labor Trustee or disobeyed instructions given him in writing; (4) when a member of a Confidential Council revealed confidential information or technical or business secrets.[6]

Malicious exploitation of labor included unlawful overtime work, paying wages below the prevailing scales, undue speeding up of labor, providing unsanitary working conditions, and denying vacation rights. Wounding the workers' sense of honor involved arbitrary dismissal and insulting language.

Evaluation of Labor Organizations and Policies. The German workers under National Socialism were deprived of all rights which they once had. They had no labor organization worthy of the name. They had no right to bargain collectively with their employers in the usual way. They were allowed none of the weapons of industrial conflict to bring their desires to the attention of their employers. And the wages, hours, and working conditions were determined, for the most part, by the fiat of the employers and at their pleasure. Of course, the employers were also deprived of their organizations, lost their weapons of industrial conflict, and were compelled to live in peace with the workers. However, equal treatment for employers and workers left the employers with a decided upper hand.

German workers may have been well treated at times, but this was due to the benevolence and good will of the employers and not to the rights and activities of the workers. And if the employers treated their workers badly, there was virtually nothing that the workers could do about it as long as the employers did not break general laws or decrees or go against the will of government officials. The Confidential Councils were powerless to check the employers, and the Labor Trustees, as political appointees, were not much concerned with justice for workers. Their job was to maintain industrial peace so that production might continue efficiently and to see to it that the employers did not treat the workers so badly that national interests would be endangered.

The Courts of Social Honor did not hold forth much hope for the workers either. Cases were decided by a judge, an employer, and a "reliable worker" (Confidential Council member) appointed by a Labor Trustee. Such a board could hardly be biased in favor of labor. In specifying the offenses with which the courts could deal, the emphasis was clearly on offenses against employers, rather than on offenses against

[6] Act for the Organization of National Labor, art. 36, p. 14.

workers. Moreover, if the workers brought cases against the employers and could not prove their points, the workers could be punished for bringing frivolous and unfounded complaints.

It is not surprising that most of the cases handled by the Courts of Social Honor were decided in favor of labor. The employers brought few cases to the courts because they could impose almost any conditions which they desired on the workers anyway, without court procedures. Most cases were decided in favor of the workers because the workers would not bring their cases to the courts unless they were so strong that even biased judges would have to decide in their favor. This meant, of course, that most of the time the workers swallowed their grievances and did not bring complaints to the courts. From the workers' point of view, the Nazi organizations and policies were exceedingly poor substitutes for labor unions, collective bargaining, collective agreements, and strikes.

Wages, Hours, and Working Conditions. At the bottom of the post-1929 depression, wages in Germany were 36 per cent below the 1928 level, and more than 6 million workers were unemployed.[7] From 1932 to the outbreak of World War II, there was a revival of economic activity, but the workers did not prosper greatly. The average money wage rate per hour for skilled male workers, which had been 81.6 pfennigs in 1932, was only 79.1 pfennigs in 1939. For unskilled male workers the rate was 64.4 pfennigs in 1932 and 62.8 pfennigs in 1939.[8]

Average weekly money wages increased from 22.88 marks to 27.84 marks between 1932 and 1938 because of the greater number of hours worked.[9] However, weekly wages were still very low. In 1936, for example, the earnings of full-time employed workers of the Labor Front averaged $6.95 per week, and even in Berlin the average earnings of insured workmen amounted to only $8.16 per week.[10] The total wage bill almost doubled between 1932 and 1938 because of the increase in employment and in hours worked.

When the war broke out, wages were supposedly blocked at the levels then prevailing, and they were rather well stabilized. The average money wage rate per hour for skilled male workers rose only from 79.1 pfennigs in 1939 to 80.8 pfennigs at the end of 1942, while the rate for unskilled male workers increased only from 62.8 to 64.1 pfennigs. Average weekly and hourly earnings continued to increase in the war period

[7] *Facts in Review,* May 27, 1940, p. 212.
[8] J. Kuczynski, *Germany: Economic and Labour Conditions under Fascism* (New York: International Publishers Co., Inc., 1945), pp. 102, 173.
[9] *Ibid.*
[10] W. R. Deuel, *People under Hitler* (New York: Harcourt, Brace and Company, Inc., 1942), pp. 308, 313.

because of the increasing length of the work week and the shifting of workers from low-paid jobs in consumption-goods industries to jobs with higher wage rates in war industries.[11]

The hours worked per week increased greatly under National Socialism. Even before the war, the average weekly working hours of all workers increased from 41.46 in 1932 to 46.79 in June, 1939. During the war, the average number of hours worked per week rose as high as 52.2 for male workers and 50.4 for all workers in 1942.[12] Since these are average figures, the hours worked in some occupations rose to phenomenal heights.

It would be supposed that working conditions at least would have been more favorable for the workers, for the employers had to comply with the rules of the Labor Trustees and were subject to penalties by the Courts of Social Honor if they treated their workers too badly. Moreover, the Beauty of Work movement, sponsored by the Labor Front, sought to secure "happy, beautiful work places." With funds furnished by the Labor Front and the employers, the movement undertook such projects as redecoration and painting, ventilating and lighting systems, washrooms, dressing rooms, toilets, public rooms, dining rooms, reading rooms and libraries, auditoriums, gymnasiums, community houses, kindergartens for workers' children, swimming pools, athletic fields, playgrounds, gardens, and flower beds.

On the other hand, it is reported that many German workers, especially after war production began in earnest, had to work in overcrowded work places, that workrooms were unheated or overheated, that lighting and ventilating systems were poor, and that some factories lacked decent toilet facilities and drinking water. Even before the war, workers receiving less than 1,000 marks per month had to have work books as a condition of employment. These contained histories of the workers, including apprenticeships, training, past positions held, present employment, and their familiarity with driving, flying, and agricultural work. Workbooks were a means of increasing the effectiveness of government control over the workers.

Conscription of labor began in June, 1938. The head of the Employment Offices was given the power to conscript all workers and put them to work for six months or less in any industries where they were needed or require them to undergo vocational training. Early in 1939, conscription was extended to aliens, and the period of service was extended indefinitely. After the war began, workers were forbidden to change jobs unless they obtained official permits and gave three months' notice.

[11] Kuczynski, *op. cit.*, p. 217.
[12] *Ibid.*, pp. 177, 216.

Former restrictions on hours of work for men, on night work for women, and on the employment of children under eighteen years of age and women were suspended. Some of these latter developments were abandoned later when they failed to have the desired effect on production.

Real Wages and Standards of Living. The real wages of German workers, and their standards of living, were unsatisfactory under National Socialism. For one thing, money earnings were subject to many taxes and other deductions. Moreover, the net wages would not buy much. The prices of goods were high in relation to wages. Net real wages per hour worked averaged 13 per cent lower in 1937 than in 1932, and net weekly real earnings of employed workers were only 5 per cent higher in 1937 than in 1932.[13] Whatever the trend in real wages, they could not have been high when average money earnings ran between 6 and 8 dollars per week and the prices of many things were almost as high as in the United States.

After World War II began, great sacrifices were required of workers and their families, and real wages declined significantly. The average adult male consumed 1,200 grams of bread, 1,060 grams of meat, and 585 grams of fat per week in 1937. By 1942 rations had been cut to 300 grams of meat and 206 grams of fat per week for the normal consumer, while the bread ration amounted to 2,000 grams per week.[14] And the quality of many foods deteriorated as substitute products were used in their preparation. Shoes, clothing, and many other things were rationed.

Social Insurance. The system of social security which Germany had had for many years was continued under National Socialism, but it became badly corrupted. In spite of a great increase in the number of people eligible to receive benefits, relatively few people were able to obtain them, and the size of the individual benefits decreased considerably. The revenues of the social insurance system, excluding unemployment insurance, increased by more than 40 per cent between 1932 and 1937, but the expenditures increased by only 15 per cent. The social insurance fund grew by about 60 per cent.[15] Social insurance became an auxiliary tax system. The money found its way into armaments by way of government bonds. The social insurance situation became even worse during the war.

However, many millions of German workers belonged to a welfare organization known as the Strength through Joy movement, which carried on various activities for the benefit of the workers. The best-

[13] *Ibid.,* p. 106.
[14] *Ibid.,* pp. 205, 215.
[15] *Ibid.,* pp. 126–129.

known activity was vacation trips at very low cost, but the organization also sponsored athletic programs, concerts, plays, opera, vaudeville, moving-picture performances, art exhibits, tours of museums and art galleries, and other cultural and recreational events, and operated a program of adult education. Some of these activities were greatly enjoyed by the workers, for they helped to make up for the workers' strictly controlled existence and the flatness of their purses. But the workers had almost no freedom of choice in the activities, and they were the "beneficiaries" of a strong program of political education.

Unemployment. The number of the unemployed reached 6 million at the worst of the post-1929 depression, and the National Socialist government made a spirited attack on the unemployment problem after 1933. The devices used for this purpose were noted in Chapter 25. As time went on, active preparation for war and finally war itself eliminated the unemployment problem and created a severe labor shortage. In 1935 the Employment Office was given a monopoly over employment service, vocational guidance, and the placing of apprentices. By a series of steps, workers were tied to their job. Wives of soldiers were denied social insurance benefits if they were available for work but refused employment. By 1937, when unemployment fell below 1 million, women who had received marriage loans or grants were allowed to return to work.

In 1938 every young woman was required to spend a year in the compulsory labor service before entering any ordinary occupation. Even the prisons were opened in a drive to find workers. In 1939, when unemployment fell to 38,379, all German women of working age were required to fill out work questionnaires, giving details concerning their experience and capabilities. The information was used to force women into employment. Workers who reached retirement age after January, 1939, were not permitted to retire on old-age pensions, and many workers who had retired were compelled to return to active employment. After February, 1939, enterprises employing Jews were no longer penalized.

Workers were forced from handicraft trades into industrial and business employments. Itinerant workers, such as peddlers, were heavily taxed and deprived of their businesses whenever their labor would be more useful in industry. Extensive programs for training new workers and for retraining all workers were carried out. When the war began, the number of workers employed in the old Reich was about 30 per cent above the 1933 level, but even this was inadequate. By October, 1943, the number of women employed had increased further, some 5,500,000 foreign workers had found employment in Germany, and about 1,700,000 war prisoners had been set to work. The German economy under National Socialism became as near to a full-employment economy as any country can be. However, we may well wonder what increases in employment are worth if they do not bring improvement in standards of living.

Conclusion. National Socialist labor policies produced many of the results desired by the leaders, but there is not much else to be said for them. The workers were pawns in the great game which the Nazi leaders were playing. The workers lost most of the rights and privileges which they had won over the years. They were overworked, underpaid, and subjected to regimentation and control. Their living standards declined, and they met with increasing accidents and illnesses. They had employment, but to no gain for themselves. The Nazi leaders treated the workers just well enough so that they could continue functioning as desired. The welfare of the workers was scarcely an issue.

LABOR IN THE POSTWAR PERIOD

Wages, Hours, and Working Conditions. The status of labor in Western Germany has improved in the postwar period, but it could not improve nearly so much as the workers desired. The workers emerged from the war with their wages frozen at relatively low levels, and it was some time before they could be raised appreciably. The simple fact was that the productivity of the workers was low too.

The workers suffered from malnutrition, lack of clothing, and miserable living conditions. Many of them were incapable of sustained physical or mental effort. Large quantities of machinery and other production facilities had been destroyed or damaged during the war, and many workers had to be employed under makeshift conditions. Shortages of supplies were an obstacle to productivity. Money wages did not provide adequate incentives because many goods were almost unobtainable at official prices and through regular marketing channels. The workers' wages would not go far in the "black" and "gray" markets, and these markets probably affected the workers' morale. Unions were returning, but they had little power as yet. A final major item was that the workers had to do a great deal of work apart from their jobs in order to live.

When the currency was reformed in 1948 and price controls were ended, prices went up rapidly but wage rates were held down. In order to fill their pay envelopes and acquire the goods which were reappearing in the stores, the workers had to put in long hours at their jobs. Later, as production expanded, the wage situation improved. Wages paid per hour in industry reached an index number of 168 in July, 1952 (1938 = 100) as compared with only 93 in 1949.[16] In spite of all increases, how-

[16] *The Economist*, Oct. 18, 1952, p. 207.

ever, money wages in Western Germany remain low. In 1953 the average industrial wage was 38.8 cents per hour, compared with 47 cents in Great Britain and $1.78 in the United States.[17] The average work week has been one of many hours. In 1952, for example, the average work week for men in industry was reported as 48.2 hours.[18] And many of the workers had to spend these hours under working conditions which were far from satisfactory.

Real Wages and Standards of Living. Real wages and standards of living in Western Germany have improved since the war, but they remain unsatisfactory. German workers cannot afford to buy and use many of the goods which they produce. For example, early in 1954 only 412 of the 20,000 employees of the Volkswagen company owned the kind of automobile which they made. Per capita meat consumption in 1953 was 88 pounds, compared with 134 pounds in France and 90 in Great Britain (under rationing).[19]

Private consumption has reached the prewar level only recently. Late in 1953 the average German consumed only two-thirds as much meat and butter as before the war. To buy as much food as the average English worker, the average German worker would have had to work two to three times as long. Some 2 million family dwelling units had been constructed since the war, but 4 million to 5 million more were needed. Ten million out of 50 million persons had less than the minimum necessary income in 1953, and more than 2 million got less than 40 marks ($10) per month. On the other hand, 10,000 people in Western Germany had incomes of 65,000 marks after taxes, compared with only 60 persons in Great Britain.[20]

Labor Unions. When World War II ended, Hitler's Labor Front was dissolved and its property confiscated. Thus the hopes of former labor-union officials to take over the Labor Front with the well-equipped administrative machinery, and particularly its press and propaganda service, were dashed. The regular labor unions had to start on their own power. They did a remarkably good job of it. By the middle of 1948 they had a membership in all the zones of roughly 9 million, or 2 million more than in 1933.[21]

On the other hand, the labor unions seemed to be much less powerful than they were in the old days. The workers have needed to work long hours. No amount of union pressure could have brought about satisfac-

[17] *Time*, Feb. 15, 1954, p. 91.
[18] *The Economist*, Oct. 18, 1952, p. 207.
[19] *Time*, Feb. 15, 1954, p. 91.
[20] *News from Germany*, August, 1953. Published by the Socialist Democratic Party of Germany.
[21] *Annals of the American Academy of Political and Social Science*, November, 1948, p. 93.

tory working conditions in a great many industries. The ever-present danger of unemployment served to limit the demands of the workers and their unions. Some observers suggest that real collective bargaining has scarcely existed in Western Germany in the postwar period, and the workers are said to look to workers' councils rather than to labor unions in case of grievances.

In many plants and industries a new principle of codetermination has been adopted to settle labor-management controversies. Disputes are referred to boards of 11 men, composed of workers, company directors, and one neutral observer. The labor unions are sometimes charged with being as rich as banks, about as militant, and not much closer to the workers. As a result of all factors there has been a decade of labor peace in Western Germany.

Employment and Unemployment. After the war there was much unemployment in the zones which were to become the Federal Republic of Western Germany. The number of persons employed later increased, but this did not remedy the unemployment, for it did not decrease, but rather increased, at the same time. The explanation is that many people migrated to Western Germany from other areas.

In recent years unemployment has been dwindling in importance. Total employment increased from 13.5 to 16 million between 1948 and 1953. Unemployed persons, as a percentage of the labor force, declined from 10.2 in 1950 to 7.5 in 1953.[22] And the official figures may have greatly overstated the actual magnitude of the unemployment problem. Some of the people who register at the employment exchanges are practically unemployable, some do not intend to take jobs, and others have part-time employment which they do not disclose.

The status of labor in Western Germany immediately after the war was anything but a bed of roses, and the workers were slow to gain from the economic revival of the country. On the other hand, great gains for the workers right after the war would almost certainly have impeded recovery. The status of labor has improved considerably in the last few years and the future outlook seems relatively bright.

QUESTIONS FOR STUDY

1. When did labor unions develop in Germany? Why not earlier? How did the German unions differ from those of the United States?

2. Is it correct to say that Germany was a leader in the development of social security programs for labor? Why?

3. How did German labor fare during World War I? During the great inflation? In the late 1920s?

[22] *International Financial Statistics*, August, 1954, pp. 96, 97.

4. Evaluate the German Labor Front as a labor organization.

5. How were wages, hours, and working conditions determined under National Socialism? How were the workers supposed to be protected from rapacious employers?

6. Do you agree that, from the workers' point of view, the Nazi organizations and policies were poor substitutes for labor unions, collective bargaining, collective agreements, and strikes? Why?

7. How has German labor fared in the years since World War II? Could the results have been different? Why?

CHAPTER 31

COMMERCE

Any country, regardless of its stage of economic development, is likely to do some importing and exporting. Internal trade, on the other hand, develops more slowly and becomes important as the country progresses economically. As a network of roads and railroads is constructed, as manufacturing comes to compete strongly with agriculture, as a system of credit and banking is established, and as a labor force springs up having to buy most articles of consumption, internal trade begins to flourish.

COMMERCE BEFORE 1871

Internal Trade in 1840. The internal trade of Germany was still unimportant in 1840. The states which were later to become the German Empire were largely agricultural, and local areas were self-sufficient for the most part. The era of road building and railroad building lay ahead. The first banks of permanent importance were yet to be established. Manufacturing was on a small scale and relatively insignificant; the first period of joint-stock companies was to come in the 1850s; and the development of a labor force was in its earliest stages. Under these conditions, internal trade could not amount to very much.

There were some specialized shops in the largest centers of population, but in most places shops were uncommon. About the only shops available were the workshops of handicraft producers, such as tailors, carpenters, and cobblers. Here and there the general store, carrying all types of merchandise from A to Z, was beginning to appear. The farmers and town dwellers would get together once a week at the local market for the purchase of foods, and most areas lived largely off local produce.

In many places, if the consumer wanted anything that he could not himself produce or purchase from peasants or handicraft producers, he had to buy from a peddler or wait for the local yearly market to roll around. Some peddlers were specialists, dealing in metalware, glassware, foreign textiles, or clocks, but more often they carried a heterogeneous stock of goods. They filled a real need and were not easily dis-

501

placed by other marketing agencies. The yearly markets were outstanding events. Traders, from small peddlers to merchants, brought in a wide variety of goods. Entertainment was also provided, and many peasants and town dwellers attended to make purchases and perhaps dispose of some local produce as well.

In addition to the yearly markets, there were the great fairs. The most important were held at Frankfurt an der Oder for the east, Leipzig for the central part of the country, and Frankfurt am Main for the west. The fairs had already begun to show signs of decline by 1840, although the one at Frankfurt an der Oder continued to grow until 1855. The fairs were tending to become places where traders met with traders, rather than places where traders dealt with consumers.

Later Developments. After about 1840, specialized shops became more numerous in the larger centers of population, and in the face of trading throughout the year, the old yearly markets gradually faded into insignificance. They were still held, but they were no longer an indispensable source of merchandise not produced locally. They became a holiday for peasants who poured into town to have a good time and acquire cheap luxuries and "fairings." The yearly markets remained important, however, in some of the smaller towns and especially in the eastern and northern provinces, where they served as local centers for the wares of handicraft producers.

The great fairs, which had begun to decline in importance and to serve primarily as meeting places for traders even by 1840, continued to lose importance thereafter. The merchants began to deal directly with each other through the year instead of waiting to meet and trade at the fairs. In the 1850s the nature of the business done at the fairs began to change. The traders met not to deal in goods which they brought with them, but rather did their business on the basis of samples. It was far more convenient to fill orders for goods directly instead of dragging the goods to the fairs. This trading on the basis of samples made the fairs the forerunners of modern commodity exchanges.

International Trade before 1871. Germany, of course, did not have any international trade as a separate country before 1871, although the German states did some importing and exporting. Grain was the leading export, and the grain quotations at Danzig set the standard for all markets of Western Europe for a long time. Other exports included oilseeds, vegetable oils, wine, spirits, merino wool, and some meat and dairy products. German manufactures were also exported in considerable absolute amounts, but they were insignificant in world trade and other countries were not dependent on them. Imports consisted of manufactured goods, tropical produce, and some raw materials.

Commercial Policy. Prior to 1834, each German state had its own system of tariffs and duties, which applied to goods coming from other

German states as well as to those coming from outside areas. This situation changed after January 1, 1834, when the Zollverein, or customs union, went into operation. Thereafter, the German states within the customs union traded freely with each other while presenting to the outside world a barrier which was substantially the Prussian tariff of 1818. This was a moderate tariff. Duties on raw materials were low and many materials were admitted free of duty. Specific duties, consisting of flat amounts per gallon, pound, or yard, were applied to manufactures, but their average level was not much over 10 per cent when calculated on the value of the merchandise.

Between 1834 and 1848 the duties on manufactures became more burdensome. The specific duties became heavier on an ad valorem basis as foreign manufacturing industries improved in efficiency and offered their wares at lower prices. Moreover, German manufacturing interests obtained increases in some duties, especially in those on pig iron and cotton yarn. Protectionist sentiment, on the basis of the arguments advanced by Friedrich List, was strong in Germany during this period.

After 1848, the trend in Germany was toward free trade. In the 1850s the desire to keep Austria, which was accustomed to a high tariff, out of the Zollverein led Prussia to keep the tariff of the customs union at a low level. The new states that came into the customs union increased the free trade element, there was a growing belief in free trade on the part of statesmen and students of commercial policy, and Bismarck left commercial matters to his colleague, Delbruck, who was a confirmed free trader. The duties on grain were eliminated in 1865, and further progress was made by 1871. When the Empire was founded, the free trade movement was still gaining rapidly.

COMMERCE, 1871–1933

Internal Trade, 1871–1914. Almost all towns still had markets in 1871, where peasants and consumers met to buy and sell food. However, buying at the markets by consumers was on the decline, and with a widening gap between producers and consumers, the quality of the produce deteriorated. As a result, a number of cities erected central market halls to narrow the gap between producers and consumers, assure a steady supply of foodstuffs, and eliminate some of the abuses of the retail shops. Frankfurt led the way in 1879, and many other cities followed. When Berlin organized its food markets in 1886, it established a central market for wholesale transactions and a dozen regional halls for retail trade. Up to 1914 the Germans did not depend on retail shops for perishable foodstuffs to the extent that the people of some other countries did.

In general, retail shops came steadily to the fore. The yearly markets sank into oblivion, and the fairs continued their trend toward buying and selling on a sample basis. Eventually the fairs became largely local events. The total volume of internal trade expanded steadily as Germany's national income grew. One evidence is the increase in the number of persons regularly employed in trade. The number directly employed in trade and transportation increased from 1,420,000 in 1882 to 3,441,000 in 1907.[1] About half of the employees in trade and transportation were in trade.

Price Control and Rationing during World War I. Germany had her first experiences with price control and rationing during World War I. At the beginning of the war, tariff duties on agricultural products were lifted, embargoes were imposed on the exportation of foodstuffs, and a general law was passed empowering the states to fix maximum prices on foods. It was not intended originally that maximum prices should be applied to many foods, but as time went on almost every foodstuff was brought under a maximum price. Many manufactured articles and other products were also brought under price control. However, the cost of living increased rather sharply under the influence of the financial policies of the government.

Rationing also appeared during the war. At first, the government tried to get by with such expedients as meatless days and requiring various ersatz materials to be mixed with flour in the making of bread. Card rationing began in 1915. Bread cards fixed the maximum amounts of bread to be purchased for each household. This was followed by cards for other necessary foodstuffs, such as meat, fats, milk, and butter. In the end, a very complicated system of rationing was built up, and the rationing was extended to other articles besides food. Before the war was over, rations were not only small but people also had difficulty in finding the amounts to which they were entitled.

From World War I to the Great Depression. The German system of marketing and internal trade was upset during the inflation which followed the war, but it revived quickly. By 1925 there were 5,185,000 persons employed in trade and transportation, compared with 3,441,000 in 1907. Although internal trade was hard hit by the Great Depression after 1929, the number of people employed in trade and transportation increased to 5,939,000 in 1933.[2] By this time, the German marketing system was similar to those of other leading industrial countries.

Germany's International Trade, 1871–1914. Germany's international trade, which had been unimportant before 1871, increased rapidly between the founding of the Empire and the beginning of World War I. The volume of German exports doubled from 1872 to 1900 and more

---

[1] G. Stolper, *German Economy, 1870–1940* (New York: Reynal & Hitchcock, Inc., 1940), p. 41.

[2] *Ibid.*

than doubled again in the next thirteen years. Finished and semifinished products of German industry made up an increasingly important part of her exports, advancing from 38 per cent of the total in 1873 to 63 per cent in 1913.[3] The situation was different with regard to imports. Manufactured goods as a proportion of total imports were almost halved between 1887 and 1912, while raw materials and foods increased in importance.

Once a wool-exporting country, Germany became almost completely dependent upon other countries for wool. She also came to import large amounts of cotton, rubber, jute, rice, petroleum, tin, copper, and other materials. In the 1880s Germany spent from 800,000,000 to 1,000,000,000 marks per year on imported food, including live animals. By 1910 the figure reached 2,600,000,000 marks.[4] In 1913 imports of foods and raw materials amounted to over 8,000,000,000 marks out of total imports of 10,770,000,000 marks.[5]

Foreign Investments. German banks facilitated the growth of Germany's trade by setting up branches and establishing financial connections all over the world, and Germany developed foreign investments on a large scale. German companies set up industrial plants and trading enterprises in foreign countries. German capital helped to finance foreign companies and purchased foreign securities, and German banks underwrote and sold foreign securities issued in Germany. By World War I, German foreign investments amounted to some thirty billion marks, of which two-thirds were invested in foreign securities.[6]

German Colonies in Relation to Trade. Germany became an important colonial power in the period from 1871 to 1914. Large colonies in Africa were acquired in 1884 and 1885. The ninety-nine-year "lease" of Kiaochow was obtained from China in 1897, and in 1899 and 1900 the Caroline Islands and a part of Samoa were acquired in the Pacific. In 1914 the colonies had an area of 1,135,000 square miles and a population of over 13,000,000. However, the colonies were a disappointment and amounted to little as a stimulus to trade. There were only about 24,000 white persons in all the colonies in 1914, and about one-fourth of these were in police or military service. German capital investment in the colonies amounted to about one-sixtieth of total German foreign investments.[7] Germany's trade with them in 1912 and 1913 amounted to only $\frac{9}{10}$ of 1 per cent of her exports and $\frac{1}{2}$ of 1 per cent of her imports.[8]

[3] *Ibid.,* pp. 52–53.
[4] J. H. Clapham, *The Economic Development of France and Germany, 1815–1914* (London: Cambridge University Press, 1923), p. 361.
[5] Stolper, *op. cit.,* p. 53.
[6] *Ibid.,* p. 57.
[7] *Ibid.,* pp. 68–69.
[8] *The Economist,* Apr. 18, 1936.

The Balance of Trade. In the early years of the Empire and through the 1880s, Germany's balance of trade was generally favorable. That is, her merchandise exports exceeded her merchandise imports. She had begun to invest abroad but was not yet receiving large amounts of goods as interest and profits on her investments. Also, foreign countries still carried more goods for Germany than she did for them. In the 1890s Germany's balance of trade turned "unfavorable" and remained that way up to 1914. Her large receipts from foreign investments, the proceeds of her shipping, the profits of German foreign banks, and the income from the sale of German patents abroad enabled her to import more merchandise, by value, than she exported. It was difficult for the German people to get accustomed to a surplus of imports, but they finally understood that this meant that Germany was reaping the fruits of her industry and thrift and was not living beyond her means.

Commercial Policy. The German Empire in 1871 continued the movement toward free trade. Liberal trade treaties were made with other countries. Duties on pig iron, scrap iron, shipbuilding materials, and other articles were abolished in 1873, while those on iron manufactures were reduced and scheduled to disappear by 1877. The trend, however, was soon reversed. A deep depression settled on Germany, as well as on other countries, in 1873, and it stayed for several years. German farm products were relatively costly, and the German market was flooded with cheap farm produce from undeveloped areas overseas. Large amounts of iron and its manufactures flowed into Germany from Britain.

Delbruck, the Minister in charge of commercial affairs, resigned "for reasons of health" in 1876, and Bismarck worked for the reinstitution of a protective tariff. The duties on iron manufactures were dropped on schedule in 1877, but only three years later, in 1880, Germany got a protective tariff once more. Most of the new duties were moderate. Raw materials, except for oil, tallow, and timber, could enter duty free, and the only part of the tariff which caused many objections was the duty on foreign grain.

Not many increases in duties came in the 1880s. Bismarck was finally dismissed as Chancellor in 1890, but his successor, Leo von Caprivi, also followed a moderate commercial policy. The agricultural and some industrial duties were lowered in the hope of getting other countries to reduce rates on German manufactures. However, this movement toward freer trade was short-lived. The German tariff was raised again in 1902 under Chancellor Heinrich Von Bulow, but duties were still moderate. They continued so down to World War I. In 1904 the ad valorem equivalent of the German duties on Britain's principal manufactured exports was 25 per cent. Comparable figures were 27 per cent for Italy, 34 per cent for France, 35 for Austria, 73 for the United States, and 131 for Russia.[9]

Foreign Trade from 1914 to 1933. During World War I, Germany was blockaded by the Allied Powers. She could trade with her own allies and with neutral countries, such as Holland, Denmark, and Switzerland, which she could reach by land, but that was all. Additional supplies of some commodities were gained by conquest in Southern and Eastern Europe, but they did not amount to much. Germany was cut off from supplies of indispensable materials, such as rubber, petroleum, and certain metals, while in other cases she had to rely on her own limited resources. Her foreign trade fell to a low level.

Germany's export trade boomed in the early part of the postwar inflation, for the purchasing power of her money at home did not decline so rapidly as it did abroad, and German goods appeared cheap. Later in the inflation this difference between the foreign and domestic value of the mark disappeared and her trade suffered.

Germany's foreign trade increased sharply as soon as the inflation was over. Despite the fact that she had been reduced in area, population, and resources, and had lost colonies, merchant marine, and foreign investments, her exports amounted to 9.281 billion marks in 1925 and her imports to 12.324 billion marks. By 1929 her exports had grown to 13.483 billion marks. Her imports stayed about the same.[10] Thus the outlook for Germany's foreign trade appeared bright when the Great Depression struck.

In the depression, the German government did not dare to tamper with the monetary system or attempt devaluation, so the deflation was allowed to run its course. German prices fell so much that her exports declined only moderately to 9.6 billion marks in 1931.[11] However, this was not the whole of the story, for Germany's receipts from tourist expenditures, shipping, insurance, and banking services declined greatly. Meanwhile, she was supposed to make reparations payments and to pay interest and principal on her private debts to other countries. Moreover, her sources of foreign credit had dried up. Her total situation with regard to international payments was unfavorable. The Reichsbank's holdings of gold and foreign currencies, which had amounted to 2.284 billion marks at the beginning of 1929, declined to 449 million marks in May, 1933.[12]

[9] Clapham, *op. cit.*, p. 322.
[10] J. Bithell (ed.), *Germany* (London: Methuen & Co., Ltd., 1932), p. 160.
[11] *Ibid.*
[12] M. T. Florinsky, *Fascism and National Socialism* (New York: The Macmillan Company, 1936), pp. 211–212.

INTERNAL COMMERCE UNDER NATIONAL SOCIALISM

Control Organizations. The basic forms of organization of internal trade under National Socialism were similar to those of any modern capitalistic economy. There were all the general types of middlemen, and retail stores of all kinds existed. Enterprises in domestic trade could be single proprietorships, partnerships, corporations, or cooperative associations, and combinations of marketing enterprises were permitted. Under National Socialism, enterprises in domestic trade were under the supervision of the Estate of Industry and Trade and the National Group for Trade. This was one of six such National Groups. The National Group for Trade was in turn divided into several Economic Groups, such as Wholesale Trade and Retail Trade; and the Economic Groups were subdivided into Branch Groups, each of which was composed of the dealers in specific products or classes of products.

Price Control. Price control under National Socialism began in earnest in 1936, when Hitler appointed a Price Commissioner and placed him under the Four-Year Plan. The first major action of the Commissioner was to issue the drastic decree of November 26, 1936, which set the prices of all commodities and services at the levels that had prevailed on October 18, 1936. All price increases henceforth were illegal unless approved by the Commissioner. Business enterprises could fix, agree upon, or change prices (to the disadvantage of purchasers) only with the approval of the Commissioner. Similarly, producers and dealers could fix or change retail prices to the disadvantage of consumers only with the approval of the Commissioner. Changes in credit or delivery conditions to the disadvantage of purchasers were prohibited as hidden price increases. Finally, no price-fixing agreement on the part of Kartells or other associations could remain in effect more than three years unless the Commissioner approved an extension.

The price-stop decree was extended by the War Emergency Act of 1939. In addition to some important provisions affecting wages, hours, and working conditions, the act declared that all price calculations should be reexamined. Prices could not be adjusted on the basis of war risks, although they could be changed on the basis of actual increases in costs, and certain war taxes could be included in prices. To secure efficiency, the principle of uniform prices for each industry was set up, with prices generally at the level of the average costs of all the firms except those subsidized by the government. Government subsidies went to firms producing important commodities under especially disadvantageous conditions.

Evaluation of Price Control. In spite of these efforts, general price control was not a great success in Germany. It was intended in 1936 that increases in prices should be very limited in number. Actually, the Price Commissioner's office was swamped with requests for price adjustments. Many were granted. The Commissioner stated that he had permitted adjustments freely when they had seemed to be justified. The price level continued to move upward slowly. Over the period from 1933 to April, 1941, the index of general wholesale prices rose from 90.7 (1913 = 100) to 111.9, whereas that for the wholesale prices of consumers' goods rose from 109.2 to 147.3.[13] In the later years of the war, prices were not kept stable, but they were controlled to such an extent that inflation was not a major difficulty of the period, at least according to the official indexes of prices.

The chief indication that price control was unsuccessful was the difference between official indexes of prices or cost of living and the real cost of living as experienced by consumers. Apart from permitted increases in prices, there were innumerable violations of the maximum prices, and black-market dealings flourished. They continued despite the use of secret fiscal police, who made purchases in the shops, and severe penalties, ranging up to life imprisonment or death, for violations. The penalties and attempts at enforcement merely made black-market prices higher. Wartime reports told of shoelaces selling at $4 a pair, coffee at $18 a pound, eggs at $2.16 a dozen, butter and chickens at $1 a pound, chocolate at $6.80 a pound, and a pound of tea or a whole ham at $25.[14] Such prices paid in black markets are never taken into account, of course, in figuring official indexes of prices or cost of living.

There were other devices which German businessmen used to combat the price-control scheme. One was the combination sale. It is illustrated by the tale of the German farmer and his dog. The farmer raised and sold hogs. When anyone approached him to buy a hog, he would charge only the legal maximum price, but would make no sale unless the customer also purchased his dog. Shortly afterward the dog would escape from his purchaser, return to his former owner, and hold himself in readiness for the next sale. Combination sales were not regarded as fair, but it was difficult to prevent them, especially when the buyers were willing.

Prices could not be fixed as of a given date for commodities which did not exist at the time. As a result, manufacturers were tempted to alter their products so that they would become "new" products which

---

[13] F. L. Neumann, *Behemoth: The Structure and Practice of National Socialism* (New York: Oxford University Press, 1942), p. 311.
[14] *The Chicago Tribune*, May 18, 1942.

were not subject to the old maximum prices. When the price-control agency got around to set a maximum price on the "new" product, the producer would make another alteration and create another "new" product, and so on. Each new product was sold at highly profitable prices until it, too, came under control. This practice was also condemned by government authorities, but it was not always possible to prevent it.

Again, the producers found that high-priced goods, often of a luxury character, could be produced with a greater margin of profit than low-priced staple articles. As the staple goods at low prices disappeared from the market, consumers either had to buy better goods at high prices or go without the goods altogether. Clearly, it is no boon to the consumer to have the price of low-grade shoes fixed at $5 if he finds that he must buy a higher-grade shoe at $10 or go without new shoes.

Even under controlled prices, price increases could be obtained in effect by lowering the quality of the merchandise. A producer might profit as much by selling an article of lower quality for the stable price of a good of better quality as by selling a good of the old quality for a higher price. When goods were sold by the package, rather than by definite units of weight and measure, producers could sometimes obtain a price increase by reducing the contents of the package without changing the price or the quality of the product. And, if all other measures failed, it was difficult to keep a purchaser from paying the legal maximum price for a good and then wagering 100 marks that the seller could not jump over his own wastebasket.

These practices and resulting difficulties of enforcement are likely to appear whenever a system of government price control is superimposed on an economic system in which productive wealth is privately owned and the operation of business is in the hands of profit-seeking private individuals. All the practices described above tended to increase the cost of maintaining a scale of living composed of commodities and services of given quantity and quality. Yet none of the practices caused even a flurry in the official indexes of prices or cost of living. Whenever such practices are widespread, the success of price control cannot be measured accurately by the official price or cost-of-living indexes.

Rationing. Supplies of food were adequate under National Socialism in peacetime, but severe rationing was the order of the day during World War II. The meat ration fell off to a pound per week and then to less. Coffee was rationed at 2 ounces per month and later replaced by substitutes. The egg ration came down to 2 per month and the butter ration to 2 ounces per week. Conditions were the same for other consumers' goods. Clothing was rationed by means of cards and a "point" system, and quality deteriorated rapidly. Overcoats could be purchased only if worn-out overcoats were turned in. The shoe situation was desperate. People were urged to lay aside their leather shoes in the late spring and summer and use wooden shoes until fall. There were no ration cards for shoes, but an individual was allowed to buy new shoes only if he showed that his old shoes were worn beyond repair. Shoes were resoled with artificial rubber, for there was no leather available. To the great dismay of a part of the population, the sale of women's hats was discontinued.

Each man was allowed one 3-ounce stick of poor shaving soap every four months—a ration which produced a temporary boom in other shaving devices. Tobacco rations were extremely limited. Men with ration cards could obtain only two or three cigarettes or one small cigar daily, and women over twenty-five were put on half rations. Restaurants were compelled to serve a *feldkueche*, or one-dish field-kitchen meal, two days a week. The fuel situation was so bad that only one heated room per family could be maintained during the winter. Hotels in the large cities were forbidden to rent rooms for office purposes or to keep guests for more than three weeks, for some people had been trying to get around the restrictions on house heating by living in warm hotel rooms.

Even short rations did not tell the entire story. As the self-sufficiency program substituted ersatz products more and more for natural products, the quality of many consumers' goods declined. Moreover, it was often impossible to obtain certain goods at all, whether the goods were rationed or not, whether the customer for rationed goods had an unused card or coupons, or whether the goods were produced by natural or artificial means. Before the end of the war, some 80 per cent of all production for civilian consumption had been stopped. It was difficult to find in the stores such common articles as toothpaste, shoelaces, buttons, thread, envelopes, paper, paper clips, dust cloths, suspenders, floor wax, light cords, typewriter ribbons, or photographic films.

FOREIGN COMMERCE UNDER NATIONAL SOCIALISM

Control Devices. German payments of principal and interest on foreign debts were suspended almost as soon as the Nazis came into power. Instead of being transferred to the creditor countries, these payments were deposited in Germany in the form of "blocked marks," which could be used for various purposes within the country, and especially for financing exports, but could not be moved in cash to other countries. All exporters were soon required to register all sales abroad with the Reich Foreign Exchange Board and the Administration of Self-Help of German Industry (or Export Subsidy Fund). Prices of exported goods were strictly controlled, and all foreign exchange received from exports had to be sold to the government, which would then ration it to permit necessary imports. Several schemes were tried from time to time for rationing limited supplies of foreign exchange among the numerous claimants. Goods could not be imported without licenses or permits.

Although the various devices used were successful in stabilizing the foreign trade and balance of payments of Germany, they gave a great deal of difficulty in other respects. Many officials were required to administer them. Also, the devices tended to favor the larger firms, which were better known, had more influence with the controlling agencies, and could finance the necessary time-consuming negotiations. The controls involved German importers and industrial firms in much expense and inconvenience. Since enterprises always wanted greater quantities of imported and other materials than were available, a system of priorities was developed to make sure that the limited quantities of materials would satisfy the most urgent needs. However, upon occasion, urgency certificates were issued for greater amounts of materials than were available. The problem of allocating limited quantities of imported and other materials among industries, and among firms within industries, was a trying one.

Government Trading Agreements. The government of Germany negotiated trading agreements with the governments of a number of other countries. Sometimes the agreements were "payments agreements," under which the total amounts of foreign exchange received from exports and used to pay for imports were balanced. In other cases they were "clearing agreements," under which the total value of goods imported and exported were balanced. Under clearing agreements trade was conducted on a barter basis and supplies of foreign exchange were not required. The German government was a master in the use of these barter agreements.

The German government would induce other countries to send foods or raw materials to Germany and would offer to pay prices well above the world level for these goods. The prices were paid in blocked marks, which were deposited to the credit of the foreign countries. Germany was then supposed to export manufactured goods to the other countries to complete the transactions. In the early stages, Germany would accept almost any available surpluses of foods and raw materials and would give the other countries manufactured goods, which they needed. Later, after the other countries had piled up large balances of blocked marks in Germany, these countries were made to furnish exactly the foods and raw materials which Germany wanted and to take almost any goods which Germany could spare in exchange.

Germany would not furnish goods which could be sold directly in other countries to obtain foreign exchange, goods which were scarce in Germany, or goods made largely of foreign materials. She would give the other countries a choice between receiving nothing at all and taking any products of which Germany had a surplus. In this way, Germany developed a host of dissatisfied customers. Thousands of typewriters were sent to Roumania; machinery-needing Turkey was given a bumper supply of coffee mills, gramaphones, and radios; the peasants of Bulgaria and Yugoslavia were regaled with field glasses and optical instruments; and the warehouses of Mexico were made to groan with their load of barber chairs.

Even the Standard Oil Company of New Jersey sent some oil to Germany and received in return enough mouth organs (harmonicas) to give each boy in the United States at least two. While some South American countries, which sent food or raw materials to Germany, were undoubtedly surprised to receive shiploads of aspirin in return, they must at least have found this import useful, as would any other country which engaged in barter trade with Germany. The unpopularity of the barter deals was increased upon occasion by Germany's practice of reselling certain barter imports (such as coffee) on the world markets—a practice which often worked to the disadvantage of the countries which had furnished the barter imports.

Results of National Socialist Trade Policy. From 1933 to World War II, the objective of National Socialist trade policy was to satisfy part of the domestic demand for imports as a supplement to home production and an aid to preparation for war, not to achieve the maximum volume of exports or to exploit every opportunity for foreign trade which might bring profits. Under the various control measures, Germany stabilized her trade and kept her exports and imports well balanced, but her total trade remained on a rather low level.

German exports had fallen from 12.3 billion marks in 1928 to 4.17 billion marks in 1934, and her imports had declined from 14 billion marks to 4.45 billion marks.[15] In the years 1934 through 1938 German exports varied between 4.1 billion and 5.8 billion marks, imports varied between 4.1 billion and 5.4 billion marks, and the net balance of trade ranged only from an export surplus of 500 million marks to an import surplus of 300 million marks.[16] German exports in relation to industrial production declined from 22.5 per cent in 1933 to 13.1 per cent in 1938. In many cases, it was more profitable for German industries to produce armaments and other goods for the government than to turn out goods for export. To have enough foreign exchange to obtain necessary raw materials, Germany had to curtail imports of food, since foreign loans

---

[15] Florinsky, *op. cit.*, p. 208.
[16] Reichskreditgesellschaft, *Economic Conditions in Germany in the Middle of the Year 1939*, pp. 32–33.

could not be obtained and since only about 20 per cent of German exports were producing foreign exchange.

German trade slumped after the outbreak of World War II, for overseas trade was largely eliminated. In late 1940 the Nazi leaders claimed that foreign trade had reached prewar levels. Losses due to the war had been offset by "trade" with the occupied countries and with Soviet Russia. However, trade with the occupied countries was on a noncommercial basis and meant that the Germans helped themselves to whatever they could lay their hands on. Such expropriations, while immediately profitable, could not go on indefinitely, and their continuation depended upon additional conquests.

The Self-sufficiency Program. It was clear long before World War II that the foreign trade of Germany, under National Socialist policies, was not likely to return to the levels of 1928 and 1929. Thorough preparation for war seemed to require her to be as independent as possible of foreign sources of raw materials and foods which might be cut off in time of war. As a result, Germany embarked on a comprehensive program to attain economic self-sufficiency. This program included three related parts.

In the first place, efforts were made to increase the production of articles which were not being turned out in adequate amounts. Farmers were asked to double the number of sheep raised for wool, to double the quantity of land used for raising fibrous and oil-bearing plants, and to increase the production of flax. Efforts were made to increase farming land by draining swamps and reclaiming meadowland. The program also aimed at increased production of metals such as aluminum and magnesium and at establishing plants which could use low-grade domestic deposits of iron ore, zinc, lead, and copper.

A second phase of the self-sufficiency program involved attempts to substitute articles of which Germany had adequate supplies for others which were more scarce. More concrete and less steel was used in building; alloys and plastics were substituted for scarce metals in making some kinds of machinery; glass was used for pipes, insulation, and food containers in the place of metals. Door handles, hinges, curtain rods, and other door and window hardware were made from wood instead of metal. Gasoline was saved by running automobiles and busses on illuminating gas or generator wood gas. Aluminum was substituted for tin, zinc for brass and bronze, and copper for lead.

The final phase of the self-sufficiency program was the development of synthetic materials to replace natural products which could not be produced at home. Textiles made of "cell wool," developed from wood fiber, partly supplanted wool and cotton materials. Synthetic rubber and synthetic gasoline were also produced in substantial quantities. Fish skins were made into imitation leather, and potato peelings into "linoleum" and "cork." An "excellent" butter was made from coal tar. It was discovered that 32 pounds of cheap fish would yield 1 pound of extract which was said to equal 160 eggs in food value. The Germans claimed that a saving of 400 million dozen eggs a year was possible through the use of these "Viking eggs."[17]

The Results of the Self-sufficiency Program. The economic consequences of the self-sufficiency program were far from satisfactory. Farmers and others were led to carry production beyond the point at which they would normally have stopped producing. They got into the field of higher cost, with the result that prices were high and individual consumption was restricted. The natural substitutes were less satisfactory than the goods which they replaced. If, for example, better buildings could be constructed by using more concrete and less steel, builders would have discovered this fact, and acted upon it, long before the self-sufficiency program.

There is evidence that many of the artificial substitutes were mere makeshifts and did not come into popular favor. These substitutes were usually costly. Synthetic gasoline cost 3½ times as much as imported gasoline would have cost, synthetic rubber about 4 times as much as natural rubber, and the lowest-priced textiles of artificial wool some 30 to 40 per cent more than natural textiles. The substitutes were often of poor quality. Clothing made of artificial wool was stiff, heavy, and retained moisture, and some of the synthetic gasoline was too poor to use in aviation, according to some experts.

The manufacture of substitutes gave rise to fresh problems elsewhere. If textiles were made of wood, there tended to be a shortage of wood. The use of synthetic rubber in manufacturing required different types of machinery from that used in processing natural rubber. Funds had to be found for financing the factories required in producing the synthetics, and these funds were often taken from established industries. The result was that plant and equipment in these older industries were allowed to run down, and their products became higher in price, or poorer in quality, or both.

Conclusion. The control of internal commerce under National Socialism was consistent with other government economic policies and tended to give the leaders what they wanted, but that was all. The rationing of foods and other consumers' goods may have served to distribute the burdens and hardships, caused by Nazi economic policies, fairly equitably among the citizens. However, the rations available to the people resulted in low standards of consumption. These burdens

[17] P. T. Ellsworth, *International Economics* (New York: The Macmillan Company, 1938), p. 506.

and hardships would not have been necessary if the economy had not been geared to the objectives of national economic independence and war. The attempts at price control were necessary and desirable under the circumstances, but the mechanism for controlling prices left much to be desired in spite of severe penalties.

The rigid control over foreign commerce under National Socialism served only to stabilize trade and to balance imports and exports, for the total level of trade was never high. The self-sufficiency program was fairly successful from the point of view of the Nazi leaders, but it had an unfortunate effect on the real incomes of the German citizens. Of course, the Nazi leaders did not claim that they were going to improve the real incomes of their people, to improve the quality of goods available for immediate consumption, or to cause industries producing consumers' goods to prosper. We criticize the Nazi leaders not for failing to get what they wanted but for paying so little attention to the fundamental needs and desires of the people.

COMMERCE SINCE WORLD WAR II

Internal Trade. In the first few years after World War II, internal trade was at low ebb in the zones which were to become the Federal Republic of Western Germany. The official prices for goods in the stores were still those set by the price-stop decree of late 1936. These prices were unrealistic in the postwar situation. The scarcest goods after the war had the lowest official prices.

The money in the hands of the people was more than adequate to take off the market, at official prices, all the goods which were produced. In this potentially inflationary situation the German people had little confidence in the Reichsmark. The small quantities of goods produced were not usually for sale for money. They were hoarded or traded directly for other goods. It is sometimes said that Germany was on a cigarette monetary standard, with the American PX stores and camps for displaced persons as the banks of issue. When goods exchanged for money, the prices charged were usually many times as high as the official prices. Sales of shoes at fifty times the official price and of butter at 150 times the official price were reported.

This situation cleared up rapidly after the currency reform of 1948. Small quantities of the new Deutsche marks were exchanged for large quantities of the old Reichsmarks, rationing was ended, and prices were set free to find their own level. The prices which resulted were higher than the meaningless official prices which had been in effect, but they were real prices and they remained in bounds. Issuance of the new currency was restricted, and the production of goods began to increase sharply on the basis of the sound monetary unit. Goods reappeared in the stores after the currency reform, and the mechanism of internal trade began to function once more. The shops in Western Germany are loaded with consumers' goods and are crowded with prosperous-appearing buyers.

International Trade. International trade has also improved greatly in the last few years. Immediately after the war it was critical. The zones which were to become Western Germany needed large quantities of goods from other countries but encountered extreme difficulty in getting the exports to pay for them. Goods normally produced in adequate amounts, such as coal, had to be imported in considerable volume. Food supplies, which had once come from Eastern Germany, now had to be obtained elsewhere. Large quantities of capital goods were needed, and raw materials for consumers' goods also had to be imported. It seemed impossible to obtain these things unless Germany had goods for export, and also impossible to produce goods for export unless Germany could obtain capital goods and materials.

Several factors were important in extricating Western Germany from this situation. The currency reform helped by providing a stimulus to domestic production and by giving the German monetary unit a stable relation to those of other countries. Relief funds and Marshall Plan aid from the United States also played an important part. These two types of assistance had amounted to $3.4 billion by 1952. They furnished needed goods directly and helped Western Germany increase production.

Finally, certain policies of the Western German government have helped to increase exports and hence to revive international trade. Firms endeavoring to produce for export have been granted credits, subsidies, and tax concessions. These firms have been enabled to grant long-term credits to foreign customers who were willing to buy German goods.

The exports of Western Germany, as measured in money, were much smaller in 1948 than in 1938, but exports in 1954 were over three times as great as those of 1938. The total volume of trade (imports and exports) averaged 2,876 million Deutsche marks per month in 1954, as compared with 973 million per month in 1938. Increases in the physical volume of trade since 1948 have been spectacular. Exports were at 970 in 1954, with 1948 as 100, compared with 530 in 1938. Imports were at 341, compared with 249 in 1938.[18]

In 1950 Western German imports exceeded exports by about 3 billion Deutsche marks, but in 1954 exports exceeded imports by more than 2.7 billion Deutsche marks.[19] This shift in the balance of trade brought

[18] *The Economist,* May 7, 1954, p. 509.
[19] *Ibid.*

about a great change in Western Germany's position in the European Payments Union. Western Germany was once the largest debtor to the Union, but it later became the biggest creditor of the Union, with a balance of $800 million early in 1954. Moreover, Western Germany's holdings of gold and foreign exchange, which had been practically non-existent in 1948, amounted to $2,682 million on the average in 1954.[20] The growth of international trade has been a representative part of the miracle of Western Germany's postwar economic recovery.

QUESTIONS FOR STUDY

1. How did the Zollverein affect the international trade of the German states? Why?

2. Indicate the changes which occurred in German commercial policy during the second half of the nineteenth century. How do you account for these changes?

3. Trace the development of Germany's internal trade from the middle of the nineteenth century to 1920.

4. Why did Germany have a surplus of merchandise exports in the 1870s and 1880s, a surplus of imports from the 1890s to 1914, and a surplus of imports again during the 1920s?

5. How did the National Socialist government of Germany attempt to control prices? How could the cost of living of the German citizens increase rapidly even though the official indexes of prices remained relatively stable?

6. Under National Socialism, Germany aimed to control her international trade and still have a large volume of trade. Were her efforts successful? Why? How did the government try to stimulate trade?

7. What were the various parts or phases of the National Socialist program for attaining national economic self-sufficiency? Was the program successful? Which phase do you think was most costly? Why?

8. How do you account for Western Germany's amazing progress in internal trade in recent years? In international trade?

[20] *The Economist*, Apr. 16, 1954, p. 239.

CHAPTER 32

THE GERMAN ECONOMY

It has become clear that the government regimented all phases of economic life under National Socialism and ruled with an iron hand. Now we must see what that government was like, how it came into being, what it inherited from previous governments, what it added on its own account, and how it financed itself. Later we shall examine the government of Western Germany and try to evaluate the whole economy.

THE GOVERNMENT

The Government of the Empire. There was no government for Germany as a whole until after the founding of the German Empire in 1871. The German states, and especially Prussia, had had autocratic governments, and there were no significant democratic traditions in any of them. The new Imperial government made some concessions to democracy, but the Kaiser had almost complete control over foreign affairs and over the armed forces. The German Chancellor (Prime Minister) was an appointee of the Kaiser and was responsible to him rather than to the legislature. The upper house of the legislature, the Bundesrat, was made up of representatives of the German states, and its members were not elected by popular vote. The lower house of the legislature, the Reichstag, was popularly elected, but it could be dissolved by the Kaiser, had no control over the Chancellor or the Cabinet, and was the underdog in legislative matters.

The Imperial government had no administrative organs other than the army, the navy, the foreign service, the customs administration, the post office, and the colonial administration. Education, justice, fiscal administration, and the police remained under the control of the individual states. Considered as a whole, however, government was master of all it surveyed. There was a lack of creative forces other than the government, and the people were content with a government which would tell them what to do under all circumstances. The Junkers, or large-estate owners of the eastern and northern parts of the country, supplied a large number of officers for the army and of civil servants for the government.

The Weimar Republic. The Imperial government collapsed in the latter days of World War I. The new government that replaced it, known as the Weimar Republic, was an approximation to democracy. The people were granted civil liberties, and those twenty years of age or over were entitled to vote. The chief executive was the President, elected by popular vote, and he was given powers similar to those of the President of the United States. However, he could be impeached and was also subject to recall by popular vote.

The Chancellor held office at the pleasure of the President who appointed him, although he was theoretically responsible to the Reichstag. He gave direction to government policy. The upper house of the legislature, now called the Reichsrat, still represented the German states rather than the people at large. The lower house, or Reichstag, was elected by popular vote on the basis of proportional representation. When the policies of the Chancellor did not meet with favor in the Reichstag, the President could either dissolve it and call an election or appoint a new Chancellor. In an emergency, he could practically suspend the constitution and rule by decree. The civil liberties of the people could be taken away temporarily in such a situation.

The government of the Weimar Republic had some noteworthy accomplishments. It carried the country through the greatest inflation and the most severe depression in modern history, perfected a system of social insurance, and developed vast programs of housing, public works, and relief. By meriting the respect of foreign countries, it obtained large loans abroad, which were used to stabilize the currency and make reparations payments. It organized effective resistance to French occupation of the Rhineland, had foreign troops removed from the Rhine long before the time provided by the peace treaty, and in 1932 got a virtual cancelation of reparations.

The government of the Weimar Republic was never able to get rid of the stigma which was attached to it for yielding originally, however unwillingly, to the demands of the Allies. Moreover, the new democratic government functioned none too well in the hands of a German people who were accustomed to autocracy. They could apparently derive a feeling of strength and security only from a government which gave them orders and not from one whose rulers were chosen by the people and whose policies were determined by the electorate.

Germany had many political parties under the Weimar Republic, with no fewer than 38 participating in the 1932 elections to the Reichstag. In this situation and with proportional representation, no one party could obtain an outright majority in the legislature. The results were coalition governments, frequent stalemates, lack of parliamentary action, and too-frequent elections. Between 1919 and 1933, 21 cabinets under 12 Chancellors came and departed.

The Weimar Republic, although liberal in its treatment of labor, left much power in the hands of large industrialists and landowners. The Junkers continued to furnish most of the leaders of the army, as under the old regime, but their loyalty to the Republic, many of whose leaders were Socialists, was never more than skin deep. Moreover, the government did not rate well with its own civil servants, many of whom held over from the former government. The Republic did not produce leaders who could fire the imagination of the people. Finally, the government suffered by being too gentle to its enemies, who were relatively free to agitate against it and to execute treasonable acts.

The Rise of National Socialism. The National Socialist party, which eventually captured the German government, got its start after World War I. Adolph Hitler, soon to be its leader, was unknown in 1919. He was an Austrian, had migrated to Germany in 1912, had served in the war as a corporal in the army, and had been wounded and gassed. In 1919 he attended a meeting of the German Workers party, an organization of only 28 members, which had been founded in the same year by Anton Drexler, a locksmith.

Hitler joined the party, becoming its leader in 1921, and its name was changed to the National Socialist German Workers party. The party adopted an official platform written by an engineer named Gottfried Feder. The platform contained a great deal of nationalism and some ideas which might be construed as socialistic, but little to indicate that the party represented the interests of the workers. It also contained a strong flavor of racialism, or anti-Semitism, which the name of the party did not imply. On the whole, the platform indicated a desire to appeal to a large number of people and to be all things to all men.

The National Socialist party did not grow so rapidly as its leaders had hoped. Nevertheless, Adolf Hitler, in collaboration with General Erich Ludendorff, led the organization into a revolt against the republican government of Bavaria in November, 1923. The revolt failed and Hitler was arrested, tried, and convicted, along with many of his henchmen. Hitler received only a short prison term for his treasonable activities. During his stay in prison, he is supposed to have written his book, *Mein Kampf*, which was to become the party bible. At this time, the National Socialist movement was at low ebb.

In the years from 1924 to 1929, Germany was at peace and enjoyed considerable prosperity, so the party made little progress. In the elections of May, 1928, the party received only some 800,000 votes and captured only 12 seats in the Reichstag. The period of the Great Depression was another story. The depression arrived early in Germany and the economy suffered greatly. International trade declined, foreign credit dried up, industrial production and prices fell, and the number of unemployed grew to six million. It appeared that the system could not continue as it was. Either the conservative groups, such as industrialists and landowners, would have to take strong action to retain their dominant position, or some radical group would come into power and alter the system.

The German labor organizations had grown in power since 1924, and many of their members belonged also to various radical parties. Strikes, picketing, and mass demonstrations were disturbing to the conservative groups. It is a disputed question whether the radical groups could have taken over the government, since these groups were so numerous and so unable to get along with each other, but there is little doubt that many industrialists and landowners were desperately afraid that Communism was in prospect.

In this situation, these conservative groups turned to the National Socialist party as a bulwark against Communism. The party had some following among the lower middle-class group, whose support was needed, and the party itself seemed as confused as the people it was trying to attract. The party program contained some elements calculated to please almost all groups in the population and it seemed (at the time) that it could be used for almost any purpose. Leaders of the conservative group conferred with Hitler, and the party received support from the industrialists and landowners, both openly and secretly.

The power of the National Socialist party grew rapidly in the depression. Its votes increased from 800,000 in the 1928 election to 6,409,000 in September, 1930, and 13,779,000 in November, 1932. In 1932 Hitler was defeated for the Presidency by Von Hindenburg, but he received 11,300,000 votes on the first ballot and 13,400,000 in the run-off election. In November, 1932, Hitler was offered a position in the cabinet, but he refused to serve. Finally, in January, 1933, after another cabinet crisis, President Paul Von Hindenburg made him Chancellor of the German Reich. National Socialism had come into power.

Factors in the Growth of the National Socialist Party. Many factors played a part in the rapid growth of the National Socialist party after 1928, in addition to the support given by industrialists and landowners. One was unemployment, for large numbers of recruits to the party came from the unemployed. Again, the children of the war years had just come of age. Many of them had experienced only unemployment, hardship, and poverty, had lost all faith in the existing system, and were ready to follow any leader who promised a way out.

Members were attracted to the party by its militant character, the thrills and novelty, the uniforms, the fights, and the heroic trappings and phraseology. It offered a strange mixture of brutality, racial pride, anti-Semitism, vague radicalism, romanticism, and sentimentality which seemed to suit the confused young citizens of Germany.[1] Other factors were the magnetic personality and effective oratory of Hitler, the skillfully staged mass meetings, the improved party organization, the constant propaganda and agitation, and the clever lies and distortions of the truth which the party placed before the people.[2]

Consolidation of Power. The first Cabinet under National Socialism contained only three Nazis (Adolf Hitler, Wilhelm Frick, and Hermann Göring) among its eleven members. However, Hitler was Chancellor, Frick was Minister of the Interior, and Göring was Minister without Portfolio, Commissioner of Air Communication, and Commissioner of the Interior for Prussia. Thus the police organizations were under the control of Nazi ministers, and the party was free to subdue opposition groups. The new government dissolved the Reichstag and called a new election for March 5, 1933.

In spite of intensive preparation for a controlled election, prospects of victory were apparently not developing well and the famous Reichstag fire was staged a week before the election. While a weak-witted Dutch Communist named Marinus van der Lubbe was executed as a scapegoat, there is little doubt that the conflagration was started by the National Socialists themselves. It was an excuse for dealing harshly with the various radical groups and for using violence and intimidation in the election period.

On the day after the fire, President Von Hindenburg suspended the constitutional provisions relating to freedom of speech, freedom of the press, freedom of assembly, and other civil rights. In the election the Iron Front, composed of Socialists, Communists, and the radical and democratic parties in general, competed against the National Front, which included the National Socialist party and the German National party. The National Socialists received 17,300,000 votes and 288 seats in the Reichstag, while the German National party received 3,100,000 votes and 52 seats. This gave the National Socialists and their allies a clear majority of the 608 seats in the Reichstag, a majority which was increased by barring some radical members from their seats. From this point on, the National Socialist Party made rapid progress toward dictatorship.

The Executive Department. The government under National Socialism operated without any constitution, although the Weimar constitution was never formally repealed or amended. The government, in effect,

[1] M. T. Florinsky, *Fascism and National Socialism* (New York: The Macmillan Company, 1936), pp. 43–45.

[2] K. Loewenstein, *Hitler's Germany* (New York: The Macmillan Company, 1939), pp. 5–7.

had the power to change the constitution at will, and the constitution and the courts were unable to restrict the activities of the government. The famous Enabling Act of March 24, 1933, gave the executive the power to make laws by decree and specified that such laws could deviate from the constitution if they did not affect the Reichsrat or Reichstag or the powers of the President. Even these limitations were soon removed.

After the death of President Von Hindenburg in August, 1934, Hitler took over the Presidency by decree and added it to his offices as Chancellor and party leader. Government power was concentrated in Hitler's hands. He appointed and dismissed Cabinet ministers and other officials, summoned and dissolved the legislature, commanded the armed forces, controlled the passage of all laws or made laws by decree, ruled the court system, dominated the lower units of government, and was supreme in the field of foreign relations. The Cabinet ministers were subordinates and trusted henchmen of the dictator but not colleagues. Each minister had power in his own department, but Cabinet meetings were infrequent and differences between ministers were resolved by the dictator rather than through debate. The Cabinet changed very little through time.

The Legislature. The legislative power was exercised primarily by the executive and especially by the dictator himself. The Enabling Act of 1933 gave him almost unlimited powers for four years and the right to make laws by decree. This law was renewed periodically. The Reichsrat was abolished in 1934, but the Reichstag continued to exist. Its membership was increased to more than 800 deputies, all selected by party leaders from the National Socialist party.

The function of the legislature was supposedly the formation of laws. Actually, it initiated no legislation and approved enthusiastically any proposals of the executive. The Reichstag met briefly eleven times in the first six years of National Socialism and passed only five laws. The legislature was probably kept to give an appearance of legality, to rubber-stamp government policies, and to serve as a cheering section for the speeches of the dictator.

The Court System. Germany retained the court system which had existed previously, although courts, judges, and officials were brought under the national Ministry of Justice. Moreover, the court system was "purified" through the removal of politically unreliable and Jewish judges and officials. Law ceased to exist as an objective concept. The law of the land depended on the changing will of the dictator, and the judges were loyal party men who were willing to follow the whims of the leader.

The Nazis added some courts to the old system. They set up a special

court for the defense of the state against treasonable activities and political crimes. The Nazis also maintained a secret police force, the Gestapo,
which operated in part outside the formal government. It was charged
with ferreting out individuals engaging in treasonable activities and
political crimes, or who might be thinking of doing so, and bringing
them to "justice." The methods of the secret police included the inspection of private correspondence, the tapping of telephone lines, the use
of spies, informers, and dictaphones, the control of passports and border
traffic, espionage and counterespionage, and a constant checkup on party
members.

The laws dealing with political crimes and treasonable activities were
stated in general terms so that almost any activity could be interpreted
as an offense. Indeed, the special courts punished acts deemed in conflict with the healthy sentiment of the people, even though the acts were
not covered by any formal laws. Individuals were punished for acts
which were not crimes at the time they were committed, since laws
dealing with such matters were sometimes made retroactive. Individuals
who could not be accused successfully of any crimes were often placed
under "protective arrest." The secret police apparently disposed of many
cases, and many individuals languished in Nazi concentration camps.

Individual Rights. The individual citizens had virtually no rights.
Since any criticism of the policies of the government or ruling party
could be interpreted as treason, freedom of speech did not exist. In a
one-party dictatorship, with other parties strictly forbidden and with
any nonparty gathering of citizens likely to be regarded as subversive,
there could be no freedom of assembly. Freedom of the press also disappeared. Each newspaper had to have a "responsible" editor and could
not employ journalists who were not approved by the government. The
propaganda agency of the government rewrote the "news" and gave out
elaborate instructions concerning the manner in which important news
items must be handled. The newspapers were reduced to a phonographic
level, and the citizens had little reason to prefer one paper to another,
since they all dealt with the same topics in the same ways. Education and
religious activities were also rigidly controlled.

The only individual right which survived long was the right to vote.
German citizens twenty years of age or older enjoyed universal, equal,
secret, and direct suffrage. However, Jews or part Jews were not regarded as German citizens, whereas, by contrast, Germans who lived
abroad were still regarded as German citizens. Since the elections were
controlled and since very few offices were filled by election, the question
of who had the right to vote was of slight importance. However, everyone who was eligible turned out and voted as the party leaders desired.
To do otherwise might be considered opposition to the Nazi regime.

Anti-Semitism. The ordinary citizens may have been badly treated under National Socialism, but their status was heavenly compared with that of the unfortunate Jews. The Jews were deprived of citizenship, the right to hold public office, and the right to vote. They were cast out of the professions. They could not belong to a labor organization or work in retail or mercantile fields. Their property was confiscated in many cases and they were subjected to close espionage. The rights of their children to education were curtailed, as was their right to make a living through the use of land. They suffered personal indignities and physical violence, and severe injury or death was the portion of many. Some of the more fortunate were able to flee the country, but those who remained lived in a constant state of terror and abject misery, if they lived at all.

No one outside Germany took much stock in the National Socialist doctrine of racial superiority. While many Germans were decorated with blue eyes and blond hair, most people who understood such matters regarded the Nordic or Aryan race as a pure myth, and anyone could be greatly amused when the National Socialists began to rave on about Italian Nordics and Japanese Nordics. There seem to have been two real reasons behind the anti-Jewish campaign.

The Jews furnished the National Socialists with a scapegoat on which all misfortunes, domestic or international, could be blamed. The Jews were blamed for the loss of World War I and for the bad features of capitalism, such as profiteering or unemployment. They were charged with responsibility for Communism, Bolshevism, class war, trade union activities, and internationalism. Even World War II was blamed on the "intrigues of Jewish international bankers." Obviously, the chastisement of such a scapegoat distracted the attention of the people from their immediate woes and frustrations.

The second reason was even more practical. It was thought that the elimination of the Jews would give jobs to deserving Germans in general and party men in particular, and that Jewish wealth could be expropriated with the transactions disguised as a righteous crusade. During World War II, the campaign against the Jews knew no bounds. Millions of these unfortunate people, both in Germany and in countries overrun by the Germans, were killed by devices whose fiendish ingenuity almost baffles the imagination. Those who were lucky enough to escape with their lives usually salvaged little else.

The National Socialist Party. The National Socialist party controlled the government completely, and its control rested upon an official basis. Many people belonged to organizations affiliated with the party, but membership in the party proper was limited to about four million persons. Except by special permission from above and in exceptional cases, the party did not accept new adult members. It relied upon the development of new members from junior fascist organizations. Both boys and girls were members of youth organizations, which included groups of various ages from five or six up to twenty-one. Several million budding National Socialists were in these youth organizations.

The requirements for party membership were severe and included blind devotion, loyalty, and obedience to the leader, and a willingness to devote one's time, labor, money, or other resources to the objectives of the leader and the party. The members were reexamined periodically to see if they were exhibiting the prescribed virtues. If found wanting, they were at least expelled from the party, and were sometimes jailed or even liquidated. Nevertheless, party membership was eagerly sought, for it carried with it prestige and economic advantages. And the National Socialist party not only controlled the government but was the government.

The Government of Western Germany. The National Socialist government came to an end with the unconditional surrender of Germany in 1945, and the party was promptly outlawed. For about four years there was no government of Germany as such. The country was divided into four zones, to be governed by the United States, Great Britain, France, and Soviet Russia. The Berlin area was to be administered jointly by these four powers. During this period, great differences existed from one zone to another in the form of government and the extent of participation by the Germans themselves in matters of government.

In 1949 the three zones occupied and governed by the United States, Great Britain, and France were combined to form the Federal Republic of Western Germany. A Parliamentary Council of 65 members, elected by the parliaments of the states in the three zones, had been working on a constitution for the new government since October, 1948. This constitution was agreed upon in May, 1949.

The legislative system of Western Germany consists of two houses. One, the Diet or Bundestag, is directly elected from all over the country every four years. The other, known as the Bundesrat, or Federal Council, consists of representatives of the various state governments. The states have from three to five representatives each in the Bundesrat, but each state has only one vote. Practically all the legislative power resides in the popularly elected Bundestag.

The President of Western Germany is elected by a body consisting of the Bundestag and 40 delegates from the parliaments of the states. Once elected, the President nominates the Chancellor, and he in turn selects his Cabinet. Technically, the Allied High Commissioners (one each representing the United States, Great Britain, and France) have also participated in the governing of Western Germany. However, the Commissioners actually turned most government powers over to the new government of Western Germany.

The first elections were held on August 14, 1949, the first President was chosen on September 12, and the first Chancellor, Konrad Adenauer, was selected on September 20. No political party won a majority of the seats in the Bundestag in the elections, and the first Cabinet was based on a coalition of three parties. However, Chancellor Adenauer led his Christian Democratic party to a sweeping victory in the elections of 1953, and his coalition government captured 334 out of 487 seats in the Bundestag.

Western Germany now appears to have the most stable parliamentary government in Western Europe. The parties of the extreme Right and Left were badly beaten in the elections of 1953. The powerful conservative elements in the German population have for the first time become strongly committed to a republican form of government. The present government is the first which has not been at the mercy of the country's military establishment. The center of gravity of government has been transferred from Prussia and Berlin to the West.

The government of Western Germany is also protected by two items in the constitution which were not in the constitution of the Weimar Republic. The constitution forbids the existence of political parties which are dedicated to overthrowing the existing form of government. Second, the Bundestag is allowed to pass a vote of no confidence in the Chancellor only if it chooses a successor by majority vote and asks the President to dismiss the present Chancellor. Stability of the present government of Western Germany seems highly desirable, for this government is overwhelmingly superior to the one which it succeeded.

PUBLIC FINANCE

Public Finance under the Empire. When the German Empire was formed in 1871, practically the whole internal administration of the country was reserved for the states. About all the Empire had as sources of revenue were the customs duties, some excise taxes, some contributions from the states, and the operation of the post office, the telegraph, and the railroads of Alsace-Lorraine.

The whole field of direct taxation belonged to the states, which also derived much income from the operation of the state-owned railroads. However, the Imperial government in 1906 was granted a share of the revenue from estate taxes, as collected by the states, and in 1913 it imposed a capital levy to finance armaments. Nevertheless, the revenue of the Imperial government in 1913 was less than that of Prussia alone, while the public debt of the Empire was less than half that of Prussia and well under a third of that of all the German states taken together.[3]

Public Finance during World War I. In the last fiscal year before World War I, the expenditures of the Imperial government amounted to 3.848 billion marks. In the war period, expenditures increased rapidly to over 66 billion marks in 1918. The total spent on the war came to over 164.3 billion marks.[4] The German government intended to finance these huge expenditures by public borrowing and it was able to do so.

Some new taxes were levied during the war, and the rates of old taxes were increased, but the total revenue of the Imperial government increased only from 2.357 billion marks in 1914 to 7.83 billion marks in 1917. This increase did not even suffice to cover the ordinary expenses of the German government. From 1914 to 1918, total Reich expenditures, exclusive of those directly for war, amounted to 26.449 billion marks, while total revenues, exclusive of income from borrowing, came to only 20.74 billion marks.[5]

Public Finance under the Weimar Republic. The government had to abandon any thought of financing itself through taxation in the great inflation which culminated late in 1923, and it resorted increasingly to the printing press. However, it ended the period with the slate wiped clean as far as the public debt was concerned. After things settled down, it had a revenue system like those of other leading countries.

The government got along well enough during the rest of the 1920s, but taxes were raised during the depression and were high when National Socialism came into power. Taxes on personal incomes, corporate net incomes, and sales of goods were leading sources of revenue in 1933. Other sources included inheritance taxes, property taxes, excise taxes, and customs duties. The Weimar Republic succeeded in paying its expenses out of income from taxation, and it bequeathed a national debt of only 12 billion marks to the National Socialist regime.

Public Expenditures under National Socialism. The total expenditures of the German government increased from 9.7 billion marks to 25 billion marks between 1933 and 1938. In the fiscal years from 1939 to 1945, the government spent an average of 114.5 billion marks per year. About 75 per cent of total expenditures on the average were for war during this period.[6]

Government Revenues under National Socialism. Ordinary revenues increased from 6.6 billion marks in 1933 to 17.7 billion marks in 1939. The increases resulted from increases in national income rather than

[3] G. Stolper, *Germany Economy, 1870–1940* (New York: Reynal & Hitchcock, Inc., 1940), p. 30.
[4] *Ibid.*, p. 101.
[5] *Ibid.*, p. 106.
[6] *Fascism in Action*, 80th Cong. 1st Sess., H. Doc. 401, 1947, p. 66.

from new taxes or higher rates of taxation. Ordinary revenues reached a peak of 44.1 billion marks in 1943, before declining moderately in 1944 and 1945. Other receipts, including war contributions from states and communities and occupation costs assessed on occupied territories, increased rapidly during the war period, but total revenues fell short of expenditures in every year.[7]

In the early years of National Socialism, income taxes produced about one-fifth of all tax revenues. This proportion grew to more than one-third at the end of World War II. Taxes on corporate incomes grew from an insignificant amount to nearly one-fourth of total tax revenues. The turnover tax produced one-sixth or more of the total, and customs duties and excise taxes, which produced more than one-third in 1933, declined to a point where they yielded about one-fifth of the total.[8] The rates of many of these taxes were substantially lower than those which prevailed in the United States and Great Britain during the war.

The Public Debt under National Socialism. Germany's national debt increased from 12 billion marks in 1934 to 34 billion in 1939 and 473 billion at the end of World War II. Both long-term and short-term obligations were issued by the government, but about four-fifths of all borrowing was short-term toward the end of the war.[9] The government borrowed from the central bank and from the commercial and savings banks of the country. The general public was not asked to subscribe to a war loan. However, the government borrowed from productive enterprises by using tax-credit certificates and delivery bills in paying for purchases, and from the wage earners through semicompulsory savings from wages.

Public Finance in Western Germany. The government of Western Germany has had a difficult course to steer in the field of public finance. Mindful of the past, it has not dared to maintain a large and inflationary excess of expenditures over revenues. On the other hand, it could not follow a deflationary policy which would restrain increases in production, investment, and exports.

On the whole, the government has done a remarkable job of maintaining expenditures and revenues on an even keel. Deficits of 606 million and 633 million Deutsche marks were incurred in 1950 and 1951, but these gave way to surpluses of 739 million and 1,490 million in 1952 and 1953. Since total expenditures were running from about 17 billion to more than 20 billion Deutsche marks per year, these deficits and surpluses seem relatively small.[10] The public debt of Western Germany is negligible. It ran a little over one billion Deutsche marks in 1953.

[7] *Ibid.*, pp. 64–65.
[8] *Ibid.*, p. 64.
[9] *Ibid.*, p. 73.
[10] *International Financial Statistics*, August, 1954, pp. 96, 97.

The government has derived a considerable part of its revenues from excise taxes, customs duties, and a turnover tax, which has been levied at the rate of 4 per cent on all sales of goods. In the field of corporate income taxation, the tendency has been to keep the tax rates high but to grant concessions when the firms do things regarded as desirable by the government, such as exporting goods or investing earnings in plant, machinery, and equipment. Personal income tax rates have been less progressive than those of some other leading countries.

Government finances were in such good condition that tax cuts were made in fiscal 1953–1954. There was an average reduction of 15 per cent in personal income taxes, and the tax-free income limits were set fairly liberally. The tax on corporate profits distributed as dividends was also reduced from 60 per cent to 40. At the same time, the administration of the corporate income tax was tightened with respect to investment and the necessary expenses of doing business. Formerly, corporations had been allowed to decide for themselves what their expenses of doing business were, but these expenses were now to be determined by local inspectors. In the past, investment had been guided by the desire to avoid taxation. The result was wasteful investment by firms of minor importance while basic industries could not get capital funds. Now, the tax concessions for investment of earnings were to be granted with greater discrimination.

THE NATIONAL SOCIALIST ECONOMY AS A WHOLE

In evaluating the National Socialist economy of Germany as a whole, it might perhaps be regarded as an accomplishment that the Nazis were able to keep the economy operating in view of the peculiar compromise between capitalism and a planned economy. Its operation was successful primarily from the point of view of attaining the ends desired by the Nazi leaders, but even that was something.

Industrial Production. Highly complex government organizations were set up to control production activities under National Socialism. It was sometimes difficult to ascertain what functions were performed by various parts of the control mechanism, and there was some controversy about the results which the mechanism produced. A considerable amount of power and control over production was enjoyed by both businessmen and the government.

The regulation of production activities by the government probably minimized many of the wastes which are likely to be found in the capitalistic operation of industry. German industries were able to avoid to some extent such things as the overexpansion of plant and the duplication of production facilities, undue numbers of styles, shapes, sizes, and colors of goods, and the wasteful advertising of competing brands of the same products. The Nazi economy may have had an advantage in that it permitted private individuals to own and operate businesses, bear the risks, and make the profits or losses. This may have furnished more effective incentives to efficiency than those available under government ownership and operation. Finally, the elimination of small and weak producers and the concentration of production in large-scale concerns probably contributed to both efficiency of production and ease and effectiveness of government control.

However, any such advantages were offset by the bureaucracy and red tape, countless forms and regulations, bribery, "wangling," and the necessity of worming into the good graces of Nazi officials. Businessmen were deprived of most of the economic freedom under which business may be expected to be successful and satisfying. They faced unfair competition from party men, some of whom went into business and used the powers of the one-party state for their own economic advancement. And, regardless of questions of efficiency, virtually all increases in total production were directed toward economic independence, armaments, and war, rather than toward increasing the real incomes of the citizens.

National Income. National income increased from 45.2 billion marks in 1932 to 130 billion marks in 1942, while the expenditures for armaments and war increased from 1 billion to 91 billion marks. Thus the national income available for other purposes actually declined from 44.2 billion to 39 billion marks between 1932 and 1942. Since there was a considerable increase in prices, the real goods at the disposal of the citizens must have declined even more.

Agriculture. The government under National Socialism was prompt in recognizing the existence of an agricultural problem. A number of steps were taken to assist the hard-pressed farmers. Some of the Nazi agricultural policies may have benefited individual farmers or groups of farmers, but the farmers' lot as a whole did not improve significantly. If any one group gained more than others, it was the large and well-to-do farmers.

No really determined attack was made on such fundamental farm problems as the concentration in the ownership of farm land or the great disparities in income and economic welfare between the poor and prosperous farmers. The extension of the racial program to agriculture and the attempt to force the farmers into a definite caste tied to the land seemed particularly deplorable. The Nazi agricultural policies may have contributed to the attainment of the national goals desired by the government leaders, but that is all they did.

Transportation. The Nazi policy was to neglect certain forms of transportation. Thus the numbers of locomotives, freight cars, and passenger cars on the railroads were allowed to decline as economic activity picked up during the 1930s, while every effort was made to speed the development of motor and air transportation. It was thought that the latter forms of transportation would be more useful in wars of rapid conquest. When Germany became embroiled in a long war, it was too late to rectify the mistake.

Credit and Banking. The activities of the commercial banks were brought more closely under government control. Changes in the field of investment credit and banking were even more revolutionary. Interest rates were driven down, corporate dividends were strictly limited, the uses to which retained earnings might be put were controlled, new security issues were severely curtailed, and private firms had to look to the government for investment funds. The entire investment credit mechanism was brought under the thumb of the government.

In theory, there might be something to be said for government control over commercial and investment banking, if not for actual government ownership and operation. Either device might eliminate the various economic problems which are found in these financial fields under purely private operation. Under National Socialism, however, government control of commercial and investment credit and banking was directed toward national economic self-sufficiency and readiness for war, and not toward the economic welfare of the people.

Internal Trade. Activities in internal trade were brought under government control by means of the same general mechanisms used for controlling other production activities, and with similar results. In addition, the economic policies which Germany was following made necessary strict rationing of consumers' goods and control of prices. There is little to be said for either policy on economic grounds, although both may have produced a more equitable sharing of burdens and sacrifices than would otherwise have existed, and both may have made the lot of the consumer better than it would otherwise have been. These policies, at best, were merely consistent with the other economic policies of National Socialism.

International Trade. Germany experienced severe difficulties in her international trade after 1929. As a result, the Nazis applied all manner of controls to imports, exports, and the use of foreign exchange. The devices included tariffs, import and export licenses and quotas, export subsidies, private trading agreements, clearing agreements, payments agreements, and direct barter deals. The results were a stabilized total volume of international trade and a good balancing of imports and exports, but a low volume of trade.

Germany also turned to a comprehensive program for achieving economic self-sufficiency under National Socialism. The program included increasing the production of articles being produced in Germany in amounts inadequate for domestic needs, attempting to substitute articles which were less scarce for those which were more scarce, and producing artificial substitutes for articles which could not be produced by natural methods. There are no direct economic gains in terms of maximizing production and standards of living to be obtained from curtailing international trade and from developing economic self-sufficiency. In fact, the program reduced the real incomes of the German citizens.

However, the results of the economic self-sufficiency program should not be considered as evidence of inefficiency on the part of National Socialism. The objectives were independence and preparation for war, and Germany was successful in reaching them. The Nazi leaders never claimed that they were going to improve the real incomes of their people. We criticize the Nazi leaders not for failing to get what they wanted but for failing to pay attention to the basic needs and desires of the citizens.

The Distribution of Income. Any notion that there was anything socialistic about National Socialism is quickly dispelled when we observe the distribution of income. With productive wealth privately owned and most industries privately operated, individuals were allowed to receive rent, interest, and profits, as well as wages and salaries. There was no tendency for the proportion of national income going into wages, salaries, and other earned compensations to increase in relation to the proportions going into profits, interest and dividends, and rent. The tendency was fairly strong in the other direction; inequality in the distribution of income among persons increased significantly. There was no feature of the distribution of income under National Socialism which could be regarded favorably except that inequality in the distribution of income among persons was not allowed to accomplish its usual undesirable results, since large portions of all incomes were taken by the government.

The Status of Labor. There is not much to be said in favor of the status and treatment of labor. To be sure, industrial peace was maintained, and this was one feature of Nazi economic operation which commended itself to businessmen in other countries. The workers were permitted to have an organization of a sort; a system of social insurance was maintained; the paternalistic government nominally protected the workers against the more rapacious employers; the "dignity" of the workers was said to have increased; and the Strength through Joy movement provided activities to occupy the workers in their spare time.

On the other hand, money wage rates were kept low and were subject to many taxes and deductions. Real wages were unsatisfactory before World War II and got worse during the war. The workers had no real right to bargain collectively with their employers, and they were allowed to use none of the weapons of industrial conflict to bring their demands forcefully to the attention of their employers. The wages, hours, and working conditions which were so important to them were determined, except for the supervision of the government, by the fiat of the employers. The interests of the workers were not adequately protected by the Labor Trustees, Confidential Councils, and Courts of Social Honor that were set up for this purpose.

The situation of the workers with respect to hours of work and working conditions was not favorable even before World War II, and in later years it became worse. The famous (or infamous) work books or labor passports, the conscription of workers of almost all kinds, the freezing of workers in their jobs, the application of semimilitary regulations to the workers, and the suspension of former limitations on hours of work and other working conditions were all part of National Socialism.

Economic Stability. In the process of preparing actively for total war and carrying on war itself, Germany under National Socialism was able to achieve a steadily rising level of economic activity and relatively full employment of labor and other resources. However, it is no feat of magic to bring about expanding economic activity in wartime or even in a period of preparation for war. The same results can occur in capitalistic systems under similar circumstances. On the other hand, operating on the basis of economic planning of a sort, National Socialist Germany should have had an advantage even in peacetime in avoiding business depressions and unemployment. On the whole, there seems to be little about National Socialism which should lead us to regard it as a desirable alternative to capitalism.

THE ECONOMY OF WESTERN GERMANY

The economic system of Western Germany has been dedicated wholeheartedly to the task of economic recovery, and the degree of economic recovery it has attained has bordered on the miraculous. Practically all phases of economic activity have come to life again and have made rapid progress. Perhaps the best over-all measure of economic recovery is national income. That has increased from 29.5 billion Deutsche marks in 1948 to 103 billion in 1953.[11]

It is true that consumption has had to be restrained, that real wages have remained unsatisfactory, and that there has been a great degree of inequality in the distribution of income. However, the rise in real wages and the decrease in unemployment indicate that the people have not had to wait indefinitely to share the gains of economic recovery.

[11] *International Financial Statistics*, August, 1954, pp. 96, 97.

The monetary reform of 1948 was basic to the economic recovery of Western Germany. Without it, rationing and price control could not have been abandoned, and many other developments would have been impossible. Another important element was the assistance received in the form of relief funds, Marshall Plan aid, grants under the Mutual Security program, and occupation expenditures. Recovery might have been achieved without this assistance, but it would have been achieved more slowly.

Finally, the wise policies of the German government have contributed much to economic recovery. The government has helped to increase production and restore balance in international transactions by giving individuals and companies the strongest possible incentives. By setting the price system free, it has restrained consumption and at the same time stimulated the workers to strenuous activity. It has spurred enterprises on by furnishing extensive but costly credits and by rearranging the taxation of industry so as to encourage the rebuilding of the capital of the economy.

People elsewhere should feel indebted to Western Germany for showing once more the truth of the simple but often forgotten principle that, apart from windfalls, a country can increase its national income and improve its standards of living by working and saving alone. It has been refreshing to have Western Germany show that the economic forces of capitalism, once set free, can still produce remarkable results.

QUESTIONS FOR STUDY

1. How did the Weimar Republic differ from the German government which it replaced? What were the failures and weaknesses of the Weimar Republic?

2. What were the chief factors in the rise of the National Socialist party in Germany? Could such a party come to power in the United States?

3. Why was the government of Germany under National Socialism considered to be a complete dictatorship? Is the same true of the government of the Federal Republic of Western Germany? Why?

4. What, through the years, have been the leading differences between the public-finance system of Germany and that of the United States?

5. What were the strong points and leading accomplishments of the German economy under National Socialism? What were its chief failures and weaknesses?

6. How does the economic system of the Federal Republic of Western Germany differ from that of Germany under National Socialism?

7. What is your final evaluation of the Nazi type of economic system? Of the type of economy now operating in Western Germany?

Part Five

CONCLUSION

CHAPTER 33

COMPARISON OF FOUR ECONOMIC SYSTEMS

In this final chapter we shall summarize the nature of each of the economic systems which we have studied. We shall also describe the difficulties involved in evaluating any economic system as a whole. Finally, we shall present a summary evaluation of each of the four economic systems studied.

THE NATURE OF THE ECONOMIC SYSTEMS

The United States. The economic system of the United States is capitalistic. The economic institutions or customs of the system furnish individuals with both motive and opportunity for the carrying on of economic activity. People find incentives to economic activity in the desire to make a living and to advance the economic interests of themselves and their families. The institution of freedom of enterprise gives individuals the right to engage in occupations and businesses of their own choosing, and the institution of private property extends to them control over the necessary means of production and the right to use and enjoy the fruits of their efforts. However, in pursuing their economic self-interest, they find themselves subject to the influence of various kinds of competition with other people who have much the same objectives in mind.

In the United States, as elsewhere, the means of production are scarce relative to the uses which people would like to make of them or the wants which they would like to satisfy. It is therefore necessary to make decisions about (1) the kinds and quantities of goods which will be produced, (2) the allocation of the productive agents (land, labor, and capital) among industries and businesses, (3) the extent to which new capital should be created instead of making more goods for immediate consumption, and (4) the allocation of final products among the consumers.

It is characteristic of our capitalistic system that these decisions are made, for the most part, on the basis of prices and price relationships.

537

Goods get produced if they can probably be sold for more than they cost. If cost of production exceeds price, a product is not likely to be produced for long. Agents of production and final products tend to go to individuals and firms who will pay the highest prices for them or for their use. Individuals save money and devote it to capital formation when it appears that the interest rate is adequate to make up for the loss of some consumer good they would have bought.

As our previous discussion has suggested, the economic system of the United States is not one of pure capitalism, for its various economic institutions do not operate in unrestricted fashion. Various units of government, with the public welfare in mind, step in with regulations, restrictions, and prohibitions, and the result is a modification of the operation of our basic institutions. However, the individual is still left relatively free in economic matters in this country.

The basic economic decisions are not made entirely through the price system and on the basis of price relationships in the United States. The government may restrict the production of some goods, prohibit the production of others, and require the production of still others. At times it has allocated raw materials, capital funds and goods, and even labor. It has set rent ceilings, held interest rates down, and controlled the prices of finished goods and the wages of labor, as it did in the 1940s. However, most economic decisions are made by individuals and firms on the basis of price relationships, and our economic system is more nearly capitalistic than anything else.

Great Britain. The British economic system is rather difficult to characterize, although it is sometimes described as democratic socialism. That the British system is democratically controlled is scarcely open to question, but there is considerable doubt whether it should be called socialism. Socialism, for example, stands for the public or collective ownership of the material means of production, land and capital. In Great Britain, however, only a few industries have been nationalized; most industries and businesses are still privately owned and operated.

Socialism stands for the elimination of property incomes (rent, interest, profits) and the distribution of income to the people through the medium of wages and salaries. In Great Britain all the customary capitalistic types of income exist and in about the usual proportions. Under socialism, economic planning is detailed and comprehensive, and agencies of the government are to have the power not only to make plans but also to enforce them. Economic planning replaces the price system as the mechanism for making economic decisions and controlling the operation of the economy. In Great Britain economic plans have been somewhat vague and general, their enforcement has not been vigorous, and the price system retains a considerable part of its capitalistic significance.

On the other hand, there is no doubt that the British have been trying, in their own way, to achieve some of the objectives of socialism. For example, they have been trying to attain economic stability and to eliminate booms and depressions, to reduce inequality in the distribution of income (after taxation), and to provide increased economic security for the people. Thus the situation is somewhat confused. It may be best to characterize the British economy merely as a welfare state instead of trying to fit it into any of the standard categories.

Soviet Russia. From the strictly economic point of view, the Soviet Russian economy is definitely socialistic. All the land of the country is owned by the people as a whole through the government, and practically all the capital is in some form of collective ownership. Rent, interest, and profits have been virtually eliminated as private incomes, and that part of the national income which is paid to the individual citizens takes the form of wages and salaries. Detailed and comprehensive plans, covering the economic activities of the country and many other phases of human life as well, are made and enforced by the government.

In spite of these considerations, some people refuse to admit that the Soviet Russian system is socialistic or insist on giving it some such title as totalitarian socialism. The reason is found in the government of the country, which is a strong dictatorship. It is more nearly correct to say that the government controls the people than it is to say that the people control the government. The citizens have few rights and almost no power. They have little to say about the manner in which the economy is operated, and the economic plans are largely made over their heads. Socialism, by contrast, stands for democracy in government and in economic planning.

Germany. The economic system of Germany under National Socialism was fascist in character. Its economic institutions were nominally those of capitalism. The great bulk of productive wealth was left in private hands. On paper, the system made much of such institutions as individual initiative, economic motivation, and freedom of enterprise as devices for securing the efficient operation of the economy. Unless and until he was interfered with, the individual was free to be a business enterpriser, produce any commodity or service which he liked in any quantity which seemed most appropriate, hire and fire labor, obtain supplies of other production agents on as good terms as he could get, make as much money as he could, and spend or save his income as he desired.

Actually, as we have seen, government interfered with the private operation of business and industry to an almost unbelievable extent in Germany under National Socialism. The government could and did restrict, or even prohibit altogether, the entry of individuals into businesses and industries. It controlled the prices at which commodities and services could sell and at which labor or other production agents could be obtained, it regulated the marketing of economic goods, it set up production quotas or hours of operation for plants and enterprises, and it rationed raw materials and supplies. It controlled commercial and investment credit, compelled employers to hire and fire workers along party lines without regard for ability, and regulated the use of foreign exchange, the importation of raw materials and supplies, and the exportation of finished goods.

National Socialism, then, was different from capitalism in that an all-powerful central government, unrestrained by constitutional or other limitations, interfered with and controlled economic and other activities to an enormous extent for the purpose of directing them toward the achievement of whatever goals seemed desirable to the leaders of the National Socialist party and government. Germany had the institutions of capitalism in name only, for it refused to let them operate in the ordinary capitalistic fashion lest they enhance the welfare of the citizens as individuals instead of working toward those different and often conflicting goals which the leaders attributed to the state or nation. On the other hand, in recent years the economic system of the Federal Republic of Western Germany has been becoming more and more like the capitalistic system of the United States.

PROBLEMS OF EVALUATION

In evaluating an economic system, it is difficult to concentrate attention entirely on economic processes and results, and yet the consideration of noneconomic matters would further complicate the task of evaluation. If a country had greatly increased production and the standards of living of its people and at the same time had acquired a strong dictatorial government which strictly regimented the activities of the people, how and to what extent should we balance one of these factors against the other? If a country had greatly enlarged its educational facilities, increased the literacy of its people, and improved the position of women, but at the same time severely limited the religious activities of the people and weakened the family as a social institution, how should we balance these results against each other and how should we relate them to economic accomplishments and failures? Some people would regard the strictly economic accomplishments of a country as virtually worthless if they were accompanied by the destruction of religious liberty or the establishment of a nondemocratic government.

The process of evaluation is made still more difficult by the fact that some economic systems which we are studying are relatively young or have had only short careers. The Soviet Russian economy has been operating only about forty years, and it has been functioning under economic planning only about thirty years. The German economy operated under National Socialism only about twelve years. On the other hand, the capitalistic system of the United States has been operating under its present form of government for 165 years. It is often difficult, in the early years of an economy, to see exactly what it will be like after many years of development. There is no completely satisfactory method of comparing what one economic system has accomplished in a few years with what another has accomplished over a much longer period of time.

It is a trying task to separate the influence of the type of economic system from the influence of other factors which may affect a country's economic successes or failures. If the American economy has operated successfully, what part of its success has been due to the existence of the capitalistic system in the country and what part to the large quantities of fertile land, abundant natural resources, and relatively sparse population, which might have ensured that almost any type of economic system would have been able to operate with at least fair success? What part of the results achieved by the Soviet Russian economy can we attribute to socialism itself, and what part has been the product of various peculiarities of the Russian situation? Perhaps complete socialism would have a much better (or much worse) chance to succeed in Great Britain or the United States.

It is far from completely satisfactory to try to compare and evaluate economic systems only in general terms; and yet it is sometimes true that important types of statistical data are either unavailable or of questionable value. The governments of some countries either have not had or have not cared to publish statistical data on certain vital economic matters. Even when they have issued statistics on certain points, they may have put out only the favorable data and suppressed the rest, or they may have exaggerated or altered the figures in order to give a favorable impression of the economic results which they have achieved.

A final difficulty in evaluating economic systems is found in the fact that we lack generally acceptable standards of evaluation. We cannot know whether the results produced by various economies are good or bad unless we have decided what results should be considered good or bad for an economic system. Many persons attempt to evaluate other economic systems by attributing to them the same goals or objectives which are deemed appropriate for the United States, and by considering other economies successful if they achieve these objectives, or unsuccessful if they fail to achieve them.

This method is not entirely valid, for different economies may have somewhat different objectives. Clearly, it is not altogether fair to criticize a person for not winning a contest in which he is not even entered, or to criticize an economy for not achieving a result which was no part of its intention. We should not condemn an economy as inefficient because it produces a low standard of living for its people, unless we have reason to believe that it is trying to produce a high standard of living in the period in question. In other words, we should try to relate the methods and results of each economy to its own goals and objectives. However, there may be no harm in pointing out, where it is true, that the objectives sought by some economies are repugnant from the point of view of our own ethical standards.

THE EVALUATION OF ECONOMIC SYSTEMS

The United States. The operation of the economy of the United States has produced many desirable results. All the various conditions affecting economic growth have been favorable in varying degrees in the past. As a result, this country has achieved a phenomenal rate of economic growth and development in the past century or more. Total physical production and total real output per capita and per man-hour have increased greatly, although it is difficult to measure exactly how much. Total production has increased in part because we have used larger quantities of labor and other production agents, but also in part because we have been able to devise improved methods and facilities of production.

Increases in total and per capita physical production have meant increases in total and per capita real income. In matters of production and real income, whether total or per capita, the United States is the undisputed champion of the world. Our increases in real income have included more goods of the same kinds, more kinds of goods, and goods of improved quality. In general, production has been well suited to the needs and wants of the people.

Hours of work over the whole economy have been decreased sharply as real incomes have increased. We have come to have both more goods and more leisure. Increases in total real income have been widely shared, and all major groups in the population have participated in the gains. Labor productivity has been stimulated by a simple and effective system of pecuniary rewards. And, along with everything else, the people of this country have enjoyed a large measure of economic and political freedom. This is important because many people would prefer to make their own decisions, choose their own occupations, and select their own goods even though a somewhat superior total group of decisions could be made for them by someone else.

On the other hand, the American economy has been beset by many problems. Increasing production has been accompanied by a great deal of waste and inefficiency. The trend toward greater production and income has been interrupted and delayed at relatively frequent intervals by the onset of business depressions. These have resulted in much human misery and suffering besides being costly in terms of production and income. Increases in production and income have been divided unequally among individuals and families. Some few individuals and families receive tremendous incomes, whereas many millions of others must get along with relatively little.

The development of modern production has resulted in increased economic insecurity for millions of people, and especially for wage earners and their families, in connection with such risks as unemployment, illness, accidents, and lack of income in old age. In many industries, economic power has become concentrated in a few firms, or even in one firm. The resulting complete or partial monopolies have often tried to maximize income by restricting output and charging high prices. This has placed burdens on the consumers and may be unfavorable to continued economic growth.

These and other economic problems have not gone unrecognized. Various units of government, and especially the Federal government, have tried to do something about them. However, we may well wonder today whether the government can regulate and control the economic system to the extent necessary to solve these problems without converting the system into something very different from what it was originally.

Great Britain. For many years the development of the British economy paralled roughly that of the American economy. However, the results achieved by the welfare state in recent years have tended to set Britain somewhat apart. A comprehensive program for the maintenance of full employment and the avoidance of depressions has been placed in operation. Workers have been favored with higher wages, shorter hours, and tax concessions. The workers and other citizens have been provided with a complete and comprehensive system of social insurance and social-welfare activities in general.

The British tax system goes far toward equalizing the disposable incomes of the citizens. The standards of living of large numbers of people have been raised to the highest levels which have been enjoyed in Great Britain. Real poverty has been almost abolished, and the erstwhile poor have better food, housing, and general health than ever before. Thus considerable progress has been made toward the goals of security, stability, and equality.

On the other hand, increases in industrial and agricultural production have been less impressive in Britain than elsewhere since World War II. The nationalized industries have found it difficult to operate efficiently and make ends meet financially. Labor troubles have been frequent and costly. Great Britain has had great difficulty in holding up her end in the field of international trade and payments.

The welfare state in Britain seems to have proved conclusively that the problem of production has not yet been solved completely and that the distribution of income on a fair basis is not yet the only issue standing between us and the economic millennium. The means for building the welfare state have been found to be limited, while the needs of the people are not. The incomes of the wealthy, even if taken by the government, do not suffice to finance the welfare state. Long before the working people get everything they want, they find themselves paying for their own benefits. And it seems to many people that the welfare state has important indirect costs in terms of impaired incentives, interference with capital plans, and effects on workers.

Soviet Russia. Soviet Russia has been able to keep her planned socialistic economy operating and to make considerable progress. Industrialization has been rapid, and increases in industrial output have been great. Some competitive wastes have been avoided or eliminated. Russian agriculture has been thoroughly collectivized, mechanized, and coordinated with the plans for the economy as a whole. The operation of the system has not been marked by booms and depressions or widespread unemployment. The status of labor has been nominally favorable, and an attempt has been made to provide adequate incentives and security for the workers.

On the other hand, the fulfillment of plans for industrial production in terms of physical quantities of goods has apparently been associated with neglect of quality, low labor productivity, high cost of production, excessive wear of machinery and equipment, and other unfavorable results. Plan fulfillment has been rather uneven from one field of industry to another. Agricultural production has been slow to increase, and the livestock situation has been particularly unfortunate.

Some critics claim that economic instability and unemployment have been concealed rather than eliminated in the Soviet Russian system. The real incomes and standards of living of the workers and their families have remained very low in comparison with those enjoyed in other leading industrial countries. The workers have been closely controlled and not infrequently mistreated. Political and economic freedom have been lacking for all the people. In general, it seems clear that the Soviet Russian system, although it furnishes some kind of alternative to capitalism, is not the kind of economic system which most Americans would prefer to their own.

Germany. Apart from its political and racial aspects, National Socialism in Germany involved the imposition of numerous, complex, and rigid government controls on what was otherwise a capitalistic economic system. These controls were intended to ensure that the results produced by the economic system would be those considered appropriate by the leaders of party and government from the point of view of national goals and objectives.

The National Socialist system of economic control compared favorably with other systems of complete government control from the point of view of the technical efficiency of production and management. It left the risks and responsibilities of operating economic enterprises to private individuals and stimulated them by means of competition and the prospect of private profit, while making sure that the results were those desired by the National Socialist leaders. This tended to produce better results, in terms of efficiency, than the Russian system of outright government ownership and operation. Indeed, the National Socialist methods of control differed only in degree rather than in kind from government controls which are sometimes employed under capitalism.

Apart from a dislike of the completeness of government control over economic activity under National Socialism, our chief criticism concerns the nature of the national objectives of the system. The general goal of attaining national power by means of economic independence and aggressive warfare seems both monstrous and inhuman. It is doubtful that the most persuasive of leaders could have kept the German people full of devotion and enthusiasm for such an objective if the government had been democratic and responsible to the people. This seems especially true in view of the unfortunate effects which the policies adopted in pursuit of this objective had on the standards of living and general economic welfare of the people as individuals. As a matter of fact, the objective in question was forced on the people by a strong dictatorial government which controlled almost every phase of the lives of the individual citizens and deprived them of virtually all their liberties.

In recent years the German economy has returned a long way toward capitalistic operation. It has produced many of the favorable results which would be expected of a capitalistic system and has experienced some of the attendant difficulties. However, neither this economy nor any other actually operating economy is likely to produce a higher level of general economic welfare for its people than does the economy of the United States. In the foreseeable future, better economic systems than ours are likely to be found only on paper.

INDEX

Letters in parentheses following entries indicate the countries Germany, Great Britain, Russia, and the United States.